D1601204

Processes of
International Negotiations

THE INTERNATIONAL INSTITUTE FOR APPLIED SYSTEMS ANALYSIS

is a nongovernmental research institution bringing together scientists from around the world to work on problems of common concern. Situated in Laxenburg, Austria, IIASA was founded in October 1972 by the academies of science and equivalent organizations of twelve countries. Its founders gave IIASA a unique position outside national, disciplinary, and institutional boundaries so that it might take the broadest possible view in pursuing its objectives:

To promote international cooperation in solving problems from social, economic, technological, and environmental change

To create a network of institutions in the national member organization countries and elsewhere for joint scientific research

To develop and formalize systems analysis and the sciences contributing to it, and promote the use of analytical techniques needed to evaluate and address complex problems

To inform policy advisors and decision makers about the potential application of the Institute's work to such problems

The Institute now has national member organizations in the following countries:

Austria
The Austrian Academy of Sciences

Bulgaria
The National Committee for Applied Systems Analysis and Management

Canada
The Canadian Committee for IIASA

Czechoslovakia
The Committee for IIASA of the Czechoslovak Socialist Republic

Finland
The Finnish Committee for IIASA

France
The French Association for the Development of Systems Analysis

German Democratic Republic
The Academy of Sciences of the German Democratic Republic

Federal Republic of Germany
Association for the Advancement of IIASA

Hungary
The Hungarian Committee for Applied Systems Analysis

Italy
The National Research Council

Japan
The Japan Committee for IIASA

Netherlands
The Foundation IIASA–Netherlands

Poland
The Polish Academy of Sciences

Sweden
The Swedish Council for Planning and Coordination of Research

Union of Soviet Socialist Republics
The Academy of Sciences of the Union of Soviet Socialist Republics

United States of America
The American Academy of Arts and Sciences

Published in Cooperation with the

INTERNATIONAL INSTITUTE FOR
APPLIED SYSTEMS ANALYSIS

IIASA

Laxenburg, Austria

Processes of
International Negotiations

EDITED BY

Frances Mautner-Markhof

Westview Press
BOULDER, SAN FRANCISCO, & LONDON

Published in 1989 in the United States of America by Westview Press, Inc., 5500 Central Avenue, Boulder, Colorado 80301, and in the United Kingdom by Westview Press, Inc., 13 Brunswick Centre, London WC1N 1AF, England

Library of Congress Cataloging-in-Publication Data
Processes of international negotiations.
  1. Pacific settlement of international disputes.
2. Diplomatic negotiations in international disputes.
I. Mautner-Markhof, Frances.
JX4473.P33 1989   341.5′2   88-33890
ISBN 0-8133-7721-8

Printed and bound in the United States of America

10   9   8   7   6   5   4   3   2

Preface

Negotiations are essential mechanisms for the peaceful resolution of disputes and for maintaining stability in international relations. Negotiations can and should contribute to predictability, equity, and security among states. In achieving these goals, negotiations become important confidence-building measures.

The increasing role of negotiations and of international organizations for managing the system of international order and for pursuing/achieving states' interests/policies through peaceful means has produced a fundamental evolution in the agenda, functions, and intensity of international negotiations.

In the view of both researchers and negotiators over the recent past, the negotiations process that is organized along traditional lines is becoming more complex, difficult, and less effective. The processes of negotiations are in general taking more and more time and lagging behind the evolution of the international environment. Not only are the issues themselves more complex, but also, in the implementation of any agreements reached, the resolution of the issues involved will need to take place over a longer time and therefore to be managed jointly or multilaterally.

Because of the increasing complexity of issues and the fast pace of changes affecting both national and international interests, it has become essential for international agreements to contain sufficient flexibility in certain of their provisions to permit dealing with uncertainty and the needs of the parties to adapt to new and changing circumstances. In this sense, international negotiations and agreements must be not only reactive but also anticipatory.

These considerations indicate that a much-needed approach is one which is concerned specifically with bringing about a multinational, multicultural, and multidisciplinary understanding of and perspective on international negotiations and which also bridges the gap between practitioners and researchers.

A specific objective and unique aspect of the IIASA Project on the Processes of International Negotiations (PIN Project), which started in April 1986 and was funded by the Carnegie Corporation, is the international, multidisciplinary approach brought to bear on all of the Project's activities. This was especially evident at the IIASA Conference on the Processes of International Negotiations, held in May 1987. The PIN networks in IIASA's member countries played an essential role in this Conference. To keep the focus of the work on substantive issues and on relevant applications-oriented results, while taking into account the importance and impact of different cultural and political systems in the various national approaches to negotiations, both practitioners and researchers involved in the processes of negotiations made presentations at the PIN Conference and took part in the panel discussions. These presentations form the basis for the chapters of this book.

The goals of the Conference were to foster increased communication and understanding between practitioners and researchers and among various research disciplines, to present and discuss research results, and to identify possible future research activities. The participation and interaction of both high-level negotiations practitioners and researchers were considered especially valuable and unique aspects of the Conference.

All of the subjects dealt with at the Conference have direct and obvious relevance to improving negotiations outcomes on, and the ability to deal effectively with, such issues as the transboundary effects (environmental, economic, etc.) of technological risk, security and confidence-building measures, and international economic cooperation — all of which are high on the negotiations agenda of many countries.

Laxenburg, Austria   *Frances Mautner-Markhof*
November 1988

Contents

II. International Trade Negotiations

III. Cultural, Psychological, and Political Factors in International Negotiations

Introduction

Efforts to understand and improve international negotiations will increasingly have to take into account the complexity and unpredictability of such negotiations and of the systems in which they are embedded. The reasons for this are the impact of interdependence and globalization, and the fact that real systems are becoming more complex.

It is no longer sufficient to treat dynamic complex systems by disaggregation into components which are more accessible for analysis, with subsequent linear superposition. This approach may no longer suffice for the adequate and coherent comprehension, representation, and management of complex systems. Not only is the whole greater than the sum of its parts, but it is usually different — and in critical ways.

Complexity is associated with information which we need but do not have — thus the role of information is essential for dealing with complex processes and for discerning underlying patterns.

It is necessary to consider the processes associated with international negotiations in the context of their cultural and political environments. Negotiations are dependent not only on the system in which they are embedded but also on the various perceptions of those involved. Thus, it is important to identify and deal with the impacts of cultural, political, and psychological factors on international negotiations.

The viability and dynamic stability of a complex social system depends on its capability for innovation and adaptation. The mechanisms for achieving innovation and adaptability will depend increasingly on effective international cooperation and negotiations, based on reliability, sufficiency, and confidence in communication.

Negotiations are essential mechanisms for maintaining dynamic stability, which depends on achieving an optimal balance between the options and constraints available to the system and its parts. Cooperation will be necessary for identification of and agreement on changes in options and constraints. When these are not arrived at cooperatively, crises and instabilities may result.

Negotiations enhance the capability of a system to deal with uncertainty, unpredictability, uncontrollability, and disputes. International negotiations provide the means for developing innovative approaches for political, legal, institutional, technological, environmental, and economic issues and disputes.

International negotiations have become an integral factor in international relations, and in some cases have achieved an ongoing or longer-term character which reflects their increasing role in maintaining international stability and in resolving trans-boundary problems and disputes. The rapid pace of technological change has had and will continue to have a critical impact on the development and stability of international and national systems. Therefore, negotiations processes and the resultant agreements should contain sufficient flexibility to deal not only with actual and imminent disputes, but also with technological and other changes and surprise, and must therefore be not only reactive but also anticipatory.

In the analysis and understanding of the processes of international negotiations, a distinction can be made between approaches based on assumed strictly rational behavior, on the one hand, and the problem-solving adaptive approaches which recognize the limits to rationality, on the other. Knowledge of the successes and limitations of the various analytical methods and models is necessary to understand and structure problems more effectively and to evaluate more efficiently complex alternatives. When dealing with systems and processes which are highly complex and interdependent, and where there are limits on the capacity to acquire, process, and disseminate the necessary information, there are many aspects which are more amenable to the problem-solving approach. In the real world, the actual situation may not permit the attainment of preferred goals, but rather the objective may have to be a sufficient outcome — or even sheer survival.

The need to deal with the totality, diversity, and unpredictability of international negotiations requires a multidisciplinary, international, and cross-cultural approach. The Proceedings of the Conference on the Processes of International Negotiations, organized by the IIASA Project on the Processes of International Negotiations, which was funded by the Carnegie Corporation, represent a cross section of papers from practitioners and researchers from various disciplines, countries, cultures, and backgrounds. These papers deal with the role of international organizations and other multilateral mechanisms, theoretical approaches and analytical methods, cultural and political factors, and actual experiences on international security, nuclear safety, international economic cooperation, and environmental issues. In their breadth and depth they offer various approaches for dealing with complexity and unpredictability in order better to understand and improve the processes of international negotiations.

International organizations and other multilateral mechanisms have become increasingly important for resolving disputes, for dealing with actual or potential crises and risks, and for creating and maintaining international systems and regimes. The processes of international negotiations in international organizations and other multilateral fora are characterized structurally by the increasing interdependence of states and negotiating fora and by the shift from a bipolar to a diversified or multipolar world order. They are characterized functionally by the increasing importance of economic as opposed to military power, and of technological and other innovation as opposed to the sheer production of goods and commodities.

Thus, the role of international organizations and other multilateral mechanisms is studied to see if their capabilities match, or could be made to match, the complexity and scope of the actual and emerging issues and the needs of the potential sides involved, and to assess the nature and characteristics which international problem-solving mechanisms should have.

International economic cooperation, and in particular East–West joint ventures, are increasingly important areas for international negotiations. They provide new dimensions and mechanisms for improving peaceful relations among states by enhancing their capability to deal with the needs and problems of international trade and economic development and the increased interdependence which characterizes the global economy. Joint ventures may thus represent the forward edge of an enhanced international modality not only of East–West and North–South economic cooperation, but also of international financing.

East–West joint ventures have emerged not only as a form of international economic cooperation but also as an expression of new market-oriented economic mechanisms. Such modes of cooperation can play an important role, but only when key issues have been studied, problems resolved, and mutual understandings achieved on critical aspects of joint ventures, such as the purposes of a joint venture, legal issues, ownership and control, management and operation, labor policy, financial issues, and dispute settlement mechanisms.

International negotiations are, by definition, intercultural, and many of the problems in such negotiations arise from fundamental cultural, political, and psychological differences. The environment and culture of negotiators are reflected in certain "negotiating styles" and perceptions whose importance has led to an increasingly intensive study of sociopolitical and other culture-based and observer-dependent factors. These factors include political culture; attitudes toward cooperation, conflict, compromise and the use of third-parties; and the concepts and role of sovereignty.

Theoretical foundations and methods of analysis span a wide spectrum. Negotiations can be treated as part of a larger system, or as an object and process in itself, to achieve specific political, economic, or other aims. A negotiation as such can be studied from various points of view, e.g., as an exercise in communication, decision making, conflict management, or dispute resolution. As part of a system, negotiations can be studied and understood in terms of the characteristics and functioning of a complex system. These and other approaches are best considered as complementary rather than contradictory, as elucidating different and important aspects, which yields a more coherent and accurate representation of international negotiations.

The extensive work and accomplishments in the methodological aspects and mathematical approaches to negotiations are well represented in these Proceedings. Diverse mathematical approaches can be used in the search for cooperative agreements and in conflict analysis. The general trend is to find sufficiently realistic mathematical examples to make abstract tools more useful for computerized analysis of negotiations problems. In the work on methodological issues, the common thread is the stress on complexity and attempts to find ways to deal with it.

The issues and disputes that constitute the substance of present and future international negotiations, e.g., environmental issues such as ozone and CO_2, international economic cooperation in the form of trade and joint ventures, nuclear safety, and international security reflect the effects of increasing interdependence and the growing importance of technology and in particular information technology — as contributing both to the issues and to their solutions.

An increasingly important task is to investigate and develop more effective negotiations support systems, including the use of computer systems and models, to enhance the efficiency and effectiveness of the processes and outcomes of international negotiations. Knowledge bases, expert systems, and simulations are some of the key aims of these research activities.

The training of negotiators and others involved in negotiations processes can be enhanced by the use of computer aids and negotiations support systems, e.g., for dynamic simulations and for knowledge bases and databases in connection with the storage, management, and retrieval of information. Research and researchers, as well as practitioners and the experience they bring, should be integral parts of the training process.

If useful models of negotiations processes are to be developed, it is essential that such efforts be based on a conceptual understanding of the possibilities and limitations of different modeling systems within the realm of systems theory. One of the key aspects of this problem is the concept of complexity — and the characteristics, limitations, and possibilities it brings to the reality of structuring international negotiations.

Frances Mautner-Markhof

PART I

The Role of International Organizations
and
Other Multilateral Mechanisms

CHAPTER 1

Toward an Integral Analysis of International Negotiations

Johan Kaufmann

Netherlands Institute for Advanced Studies in the
Humanities and Social Sciences
Wassenaar
The Netherlands

All theories of the decision-making process encounter conceptual difficulties (Dougherty and Pfaltzgraff, 1980).

1.1. Preliminary Observations

Decision-making and negotiations are, of course, not identical, but there is a considerable overlap. Negotiators are constantly making decisions during the course of their negotiations, and presumably aim at a result, which can be called a "decision", acceptable to all participants in the negotiation. Decision makers in any social context negotiate with others involved in the preparatory process prior to the decision.

In the international arena, many decisions have undergone elements of negotiation prior to the decision. Indeed, many negotiations are "precooked" in some prior process (e.g., the press communiqué of the seven heads of government after their annual meeting, which is largely pre-negotiated by the so-called "sherpas", or the press release after the annual OECD ministerial meeting, which is prepared by the permanent representatives to OECD). Unilateral decisions to interrupt diplomatic relations are wholly unnegotiated internationally. The US decision to send armed forces to Korea (later endorsed by the UN Security Council) was essentially unilateral.

International negotiations have a number of elements which are either absent or normally far less prominent than those inherent in domestic negotiations. These elements concern the cultural, anthropological, linguistic, and other differences reflected in national or group negotiating characteristics that have repercussions in negotiations — sometimes visible, sometimes below the surface or perhaps surfacing much later. We can delineate international negotiations as negotiations between governments or private entities (the latter including corporations and nonprofit organizations) involving persons of different nationalities. Contrary to the case where an individual is negotiating on a private matter (e.g., the purchase of a house), the "delegated negotiator" will combine in his negotiating behavior his own individual characteristics and elements deriving from (specific or general) instructions and the general cultural or psychological attitude of the entity (government, corporation, or other) he or she represents. Of course, we are comparing apples and peanuts: and individual bargaining over the purchase of a car or a house is under different constraints and influences than the government of a superpower negotiating on nuclear arms control, to take two extremes. To the extent that the delegated negotiator is operating under detailed instructions from his principals, his individual characteristics are of less importance.

1.2. Theories and Practice

One of the aims of the PIN Project is to bring practitioners and theorists closer together, "to bridge the gap". At this time the gap remains large, and writings on the subject have a labyrinthian character. Roughly, these writings can be divided as follows (cf. Mastenbroek, 1984; Dupont, 1986):

Advice to negotiators. A great many books concentrate on how to negotiate successfully. (Fisher and Ury, 1981; Nierenberg, 1968; Raiffa, 1982; Zartman and Berman, 1982; Mastenbroek, 1984; Dupont, 1986). These books are based, on the one hand, on common sense; on the other hand, on insights derived from numerous case studies and (apparently less) the personal experiences of the writers.

Theoretical analysis. Following Dupont (1986, p. 129) one can roughly distinguish these theoretical approaches: psychological, sociological analysis (and combinations) (Kelman, 1965; Jones, 1974); economic and game theory analysis (Schelling, 1960; Raiffa, 1982); process theories (Iklé, 1964; Burton, 1968; Cox and Jacobson, 1974; Kremenyuk *et al.*, 1985; Dupont, 1986); descriptive and historical works (including "case studies") (Hadwen and Kaufmann, 1958; Blaker, 1977; Kaufmann, 1987; Weiss and Stripp, 1985; and many others) In addition, it is justified to list, as a separate category, cultural-comparative analysis (Hofstede, 1984).

Undoubtedly, each of these approaches has considerable significance. Negotiations, and certainly international negotiations, are an elastic concept where all elements of human behavior, and of interpersonal and interorganizational contacts are in some way amalgamated according to patterns which differ from situation to situation.

Functionalism and the newer neo-functionalism as put forward by Ernest Haas (1964) would ideally have implied a facilitating approach to international negotiations: national self-interest is supposed to become submerged under the common ground of the objective truth to be found by experts. Yet we all know that national self-interest continues to dominate the international negotiating scene. The attitudes of experts involved in international negotiations, certainly in the initial stages of negotiation, tend to reflect perceived national interests and national traditions.

As Cox (1965) has shown, the neo-functionalist approach à la Haas does not explain the "political processes ... whereby inputs are transmuted into outputs". The essence of what I have called an "integral analysis of international negotiations" is that not only the political processes, but all relevant variables and constants, including especially cultural, psychological and linguistic factors, ought to be taken into account in the analysis of and training for international negotiations.

1.3. Toward an Integral Analysis of International Negotiations

It can be argued that, to gain deeper insights into the nature of international negotiations, all elements should be investigated. The need for a more comprehensive, here called integral, approach is apparent in several of the writings referred to above. Kremenyuk *et al.* (1985) refer to the need to develop a "global" formalized framework of what they call "the negotiation situation".

It is far from easy to integrate all relevant variables into a single model. An effort in that direction has been made in *Figure 1.1*. While this figure is intended to be self-explanatory, a few comments are nevertheless given below.

(Column) Inputs: For most negotiations, points 1, 2, and 3 (substantive aspects and positions of the various negotiators) attract most attention. Yet the success or failure of a negotiation can only be fully understood if cultural and psychological aspects and negotiating styles are taken into account. In a more refined model, cultural and psychological elements become quasi-independent constants or variables affecting positions of governments or other negotiators.

(Intermediate column) Rules and Instructions: In most multilateral negotiations there are usually agreed rules of procedures. These are, by their nature, explicit, although interpretation may vary according to cultural differences. In multilateral negotiations the influence of the secretariat of the international organization under whose auspices the negotiation takes place may be considerable. This influence can be short-term, expressed as the secretariat position on the subject at hand, and long-term, reflected in traditions of the organization of which the secretariat is the custodian and to which negotiating delegations will normally conform.

OUTPUT

(15) Binding instruments: agreements, treaties
(16) Nonbinding instruments: UN-type resolutions, declarations, agreed press communiques, etc.

NEGOTIATING TOOLS: FROM NEGOTIATING TO DRAFTING
FACTOR X: UNDERSTANDING/MISUNDERSTANDING/TRUST

PROCESS

(8) Interaction of actors/negotiators (governments, secretariats, chairmen, others)
(9) Headquarters-negotiator intercommunication (intracommunication)

Atmospherics/Tactics
(10) Public or private negotiation (audience effect)
(11) Atmosphere:
    - positive (–sum)
    - negative (zero-sum)
    - intermediate
(12) Negotiating tactics
    - accelerating
    - decelerating

Fact-finding/Communication
(13) Style: easy, intermediate, difficult
(14) Time horizon

RULES   (EXPLICIT, IMPLICIT)   INSTRUCTIONS

INPUTS

Negotiation Aspects
(1) Substantive aspects (short-term)
(2) Substantive aspects (long-term)
(3) Positions of governments or other negotiators, as related to external or internal political or economic influences including binding or nonbinding international agreements
(4) Negotiating style (national, group, corporate)

Cultural/Psychological Aspects
(5) Cultural traits (including variables)
(6) Collective psychological characteristics
(7) Individual psychological characteristics

Figure 1.1. Integral analysis of international negotiations.

In the case of bilateral negotiations, the absence of explicit rules can provoke strange situations (e.g., at the Reykjavik summit, where the US and the Soviet sides obviously had different conceptions of the significance of what was or was not agreed).

(Column) Process: Here again elements which are often neglected, both in the preparation and the execution of a negotiation, call for special attention. The factors grouped together under "Atmospherics" and "Time Horizon" belong to this category. When Henry Kissinger had secret encounters with the Vietnamese in 1970, the "neutral" Paris environment became an important "atmospheric" element (Kissinger, 1979, Chapter XII).

In multilateral organizations and conferences, an atmosphere of confidence/optimism (as in most World Bank/IMF meetings) versus an atmosphere of lack of confidence/pessimism (as prevailing often in certain UN, e.g., UNCTAD, meetings) can have an important influence on the results of negotiations.

Transition from "Process" to "Output": This transition can be helped by certain negotiating tools. One of these is the device of a "single negotiating text" incorporating both what is agreed and what is not yet agreed. Another is a scientific, computer-aided model. Such a model, prepared at MIT, was helpful in negotiating (in 1979) draft provisions on deep-seabed mining during the Third Law of the Sea Conference (1973–1982) (Raiffa, 1982, pp. 275–287). The same Conference also made extensive use of the technique of a single negotiating text.

With factor X, the intangible factor of "increasing understanding and trust" or "increasing misunderstanding and lack of trust" is meant. This factor may decide at the last moment whether a negotiation is going to have tangible results.

(Column) Output: The dividing line between binding instruments is not clear-cut. Some UN resolutions, after having been adopted unanimously and after having been accepted by most or all governments in their domestic laws and regulations, assume the character of a binding instrument. Moreover, some decisions may be binding for one party in the negotiation, e.g., an international secretariat, and nonbinding for governments.

Often the significance of the results of negotiations is differently assessed. An example: when the European Economic Community or the United States has negotiated trade matters with Japan, the results achieved, while initially welcomed, may be in dispute later, because no precise interpretation had been agreed upon at the conclusion of the negotiations.

1.4. Interaction between Practice and Research

Simulated negotiation excercises have occasionally served to produce research results. A more ambitious effort would be to observe actual negotiations in as many places in the world as possible. The paper by Poortinga and Hendriks (Chapter 17 in this volume) outlines a methodology which combines video- and/or audiotaping of real negotiations with an interview/questionnaire method.

According to the latter, negotiators are asked to reply to a series of questions before and after the negotiation. The results are reviewed by an independent team of experts.

Ideally, an exercise of this kind should be undertaken at several main centers of negotiation, including the UN at New York and Geneva. Obviously it is far from easy to obtain permission to video- or even audiotape a negotiating session, especially if its relates to a sensitive matter. A second-best approach would be to aim at observing relatively innocuous sessions, e.g., a meeting on cultural exchanges between two countries. The cooperation of a research mechanism with a global network, such as UN University or UNITAR, is desirable.

An investigation of this kind is especially justified in the light of the paucity of "objectively correct" material on international negotiations. Memoirs are bound to be subjectively biased. Official archives open up only after a long time.

The PIN project, by bringing together a great many experiences and insights, offers real hope for advancing the understanding of international negotiations.

References

Blaker, Michael (1977), *Japanese Negotiating Style*, Columbia University Press, New York.

Boulding, Kenneth E. (1962), *Conflict and Defense*, Harper and Row, New York.

Burton, J.W. (1968), *Systems, States, Diplomacy and Rules*, Cambridge University Press, Cambridge, UK.

Cox, Robert W. (1965), Towards a General Theory of International Organization, *Industrial and Labor Relations Review*, October.

Cox, Robert W. and Jacobson, Harold K. (1974), *The Anatomy of Influence*, Yale University Press, New Haven, CT.

Dougherty, J.E. and Pfaltzgraff, R.L. Jr. (1980), *Contending Theories of International Relations: A Comprehensive Survey*, second edition, Harper and Row, New York, p. 481.

Dupont, Christophe (1986), *La Négociation Conduite, Théorie, Applications*, second edition, Dalloz, Paris.

Fisher, R. and Ury, W. (1981), *Getting to Yes*, Houghton Mifflin, Boston.

Haas, E.B. (1964), *Beyond the Nation-State, Functionalism and International Organization*, Stanford University Press, Stanford, CA.

Hadwen, John G. and Kaufmann, Johan (1958), *How United Nations Decisions are Made*, Sijthoff, Leiden.

Hofstede, Geert (1984), *Culture's Consequences: International Differences in Work-Related Values*, Sage Publications, Beverly Hills, CA.

Iklé, Fred Charles (1964), *How Nations Negotiate*, Praeger, New York.

Jones, E. (1974), *Pscho-Myth, Psycho-History*, Hillstone, New York.

Kaufmann, Johan (1987), *Conference Diplomacy*, revised edition, Nijhoff International Publishers, Dordrecht.

Kelman, Herbert C. (ed.) (1965), *International Behavior*, Holt Rinehart and Winston.

Kissinger, Henry (1979), *White House Years*, Little, Brown and Company, Boston.

Kremenyuk, Victor A. *et al.* (1985), *Towards Systematic Research of Negotiations*, Background Paper, PIN Task Force Meeting, December.

Mastenbroek, W.F.G. (1984), *Onderhandelen*, Marka-spectrum, Utrecht.

Nierenberg, Gerard I. (1968), *The Art of Negotiating*, Cornerstone Library, New York.

Raiffa, Howard (1982), *The Art and Science of Negotiations*, Harvard University Press, Cambridge, MA.

Schelling, T. (1960), *The Strategy of Conflict*, Harvard University Press, Cambridge, MA.

Weiss, Stephen E. and Stripp, William (1985), *Negotiating with Foreign Business Persons: An Introduction for Americans with Propositions on Six Cultures*, New York University, Faculty of Business Administration, Business Negotiations across Cultures, Working Paper No. 1, February.

Zartman, I. W. and Berman, M. (1982), *The Practical Negotiator*, Yale University Press, New Haven, CT.

CHAPTER 2

Increasing the Role of International Negotiations and International Organizations

Artem V. Serguiev

USSR Ministry of Foreign Affairs
Moscow
USSR

A new evaluation of the role of international negotiations and their active utilization for the resolution of disputes and conflicts between states is a part of the new political thinking in the USSR, which is a characteristic of a new approach to international problems. Because of this, we should like to stress the profound interest on the Soviet side in research on how to achieve the increasing effectiveness of international negotiation mechanisms, and in the IIASA Project on Processes of International Negotiations in particular.

2.1. Introduction

When we speak about a New Political Thinking, we mean, first of all, an understanding and realistic evaluation of the present international situation, which is characterized by the growing economic, political and cultural interdependence of countries and by the development of modern technology.

Indeed, the present international situation with regard to all these parameters differs markedly from the situation of a few decades ago. This demands quite a different approach on the part of all states toward the questions of development, cooperation and security, and toward the settlement of contradictions and conflicts.

Not long ago, states sought guarantees of their security and solutions of international problems of concern to them by military means. This led to the increasing danger of military conflicts between countries and groups of states on a regional and global scale. As the strengthening of the military potential of a state (even significant superiority over other states) could not guarantee its own security, such a way of providing security is ineffective. So the security of a country could not be built on the basis of military technical means alone and at the expense of the security of other states. Under these conditions the security of any country becomes an organic part of universal international security acceptable for all countries concerned.

At present we see an entirely different situation. During the last decades most states have seen the need for eliminating military force to serve national interests or resolve disputes. Such a situation presents the opportunity to create a system of international security that would guarantee the peaceful settlement of international disputes and conflicts. The establishment of such a system of international security has become a condition for the survival of humanity.

Above all, security for all states becomes possible and necessary no longer on the basis of military force and superiority, but on the basis of observing certain standards of international law and rules of conduct of states, particularly on the basis of the peaceful settlement of international disputes and conflicts.

Under these conditions bilateral and multilateral negotiations become the main and even the only rational means for solving disputes between states and settling international problems and conflicts. In this respect, the future focus of the international activities of states will move toward working out bilateral and multilateral solutions and agreements. All of this creates the necessity of developing effective procedures and mechanisms on which states can agree.

The system(s) of international order and security can be maintained and enhanced by qualitative strengthening of the effectiveness of international organizations and institutions, the whole mechanism of international contacts, international negotiations, the system of international law, and the observance of standards and rules of conduct of states.

In the past, when states faced any international dispute or crisis, mechanisms for negotiations as a rule were established after the problem appeared, often even after a "test of forces" (military, economic, etc.). Now the problem is how to create or to make more effective and permanent a whole system of negotiations mechanisms on a global scale and how to deal with the mutual interrelations of ongoing negotiations mechanisms. The United Nations and its specialized agencies may become a basis of such a global system of negotiating mechanisms.

Of course, such a system of international order can be built only on the basis of confidence among the states concerned, which requires *inter alia* predictable conduct of states in international relations. Negotiations and the resulting agreements can become confidence-building measures. The implementation of and compliance with agreements may require that the agreement contain verification and control provisions (e.g., in the areas of nuclear nonproliferation, disarmament).

2.2. Negotiations as an Art or Science?

The quality as well as the skill or art of preparation, organization and conduct of international negotiations are factors of great importance. For a long time such a skill or art depended upon the personality of the diplomats conducting negotiations. Of course, the personal, subjective aspects and capabilities of participants of negotiations do play an important role. But this skill should be complemented by a solid scientific foundation.

There is a large gap between scientific thought and theoretical generalization, on the one hand, and the practice of international negotiations, on the other. This practice has been studied mainly in its concrete historical aspects, as a description or history of different cases and processes of international negotiations in the past.

International negotiations are both an art and a science. It is important to develop the science aspect — i.e., to create a scientific basis for the analysis and management of such a complicated process of relations between states, to discern whether there are structure and laws of functioning of negotiating mechanisms and what these are, and to equip the diplomats and practitioners with this knowledge.

Information technology also opens new possibilities for improving the processes of international negotiations. Nowadays, diplomatic institutions in some countries use "computerized files" of information or data banks on the questions and issues under discussion in the various negotiations stages. So far, the use of computers has been mostly for data banks. The computer has not yet begun to be deeply involved in the functions of analysis, evaluation and forecasting of international systems and processes, which are necessary in the course of any international negotiations. The (most sophisticated) functions are still performed by the participants of the negotiations via traditional methods and intuition.

So there is a need for the enhanced utilization of the achievements of cybernetics and computer technology to create the scientific prerequisites for the transition from traditional empirical methods of preparing, organizing and conducting negotiations to new, more effective methods and mechanisms of negotiations, which would achieve more rational and faster resolutions of international problems taking better into account the national interests of various countries.

2.3. Modeling Negotiations: Stages of Development

In our view, the main path to the fulfillment of these tasks could be a methodology of scientific modeling and the use of models of negotiating mechanisms reflecting the practice of negotiations, on the basis of computerized systems of information.

Science has so far not succeeded in creating a generalized model of the negotiating mechanism for either bilateral or multilateral negotiations. Here we mean not only a formal (mathematical) model which could be used in a computer system, but also a simple abstract, verbal, descriptive model of the negotiating mechanism. The constructing of this type of model is a task for the general theory of international relations and foreign policy.

To "build a bridge" between theory and practice by the use of modern scientific and technical means, especially computer systems for aiding and improving the mechanism and process of international negotiations and increasing their effectiveness, involves research in the sphere of very complicated methodological, theoretical and mathematical problems.

We believe that the whole process of creating the preconditions for using computers to improve the information flow and feedback for the participants of negotiations — to help them in analyzing and evaluating a situation, forecasting changes in the object of negotiations, and working out an optimum set of decisions — could be divided into several main stages, from the simple to the more complicated:

1.   The first stage would involve finding ways to use computers in the process of providing information for and among the participants of negotiations — in other words, the accumulation, quick search and delivery in a convenient form of primary information, including textual, statistical, graphical and bibliographical information.

      This category of task seems to be the least complicated to realize, because many countries have already accumulated significant experience in the research, construction and use of such data banks, or computerized files on various subjects. In this case the problem is how to generalize and untilize that part of this experience applicable to tasks of information service on international negotiations. Here, we think data banks or computerized files could be planned and designed on the following subjects:

      -    The net-graphic of preparations for the beginning of negotiations.

      -    Data bank (file) of general information on the object of negotiations; its status; estimation of the situation.

      -    Data bank (file) on the regulations of international law, international agreements, UN documents and other information concerning the object of negotiations.

      -    Data bank (file) on the official positions of the participants on questions concerning the object of negotiations (e.g., official statements and declarations, positions of various segments of the public).

      -    Data bank (file) of unofficial statements of government leaders and diplomats of states or participants in negotiations on their second or fallback positions, or on possibilities of a compromise.

- Data bank (file) of texts of statements of participants on different questions arising in the course of negotiations.

Certainly, the subjects of data banks or computerized files on problems of negotiations could be supplemented and significantly widened by taking into the account the opinions and experience of diplomats and specialists on international matters.

2. Developing the use of computers for analyzing, estimating and forecasting changes of international systems and processes is much more complicated and difficult. This group of tasks is connected with the analysis of the object of negotiations, the real interests of various states, and the accurate definition of their positions — in other words, with the qualitative examination of substantive issues, which is a basis and precondition for the beginning of any international negotiation.

As experience shows, attempts to use various complicated systems of expert estimations for these purposes (e.g., game methods, development of scenarios) have not had as yet a significant positive effect, and usually are not accepted by diplomats, often being dismissed as an unknown and unproven innovation. In this context we believe that the most rational and promising way to use computers in the practice of international negotiations is the method of scientific modeling of the system and processes of international negotiations to analyze, estimate and forecast the international situation and to work out variants of solutions of international problems. This calls for constructing an adequate scientific model of the mechanisms and processes of international negotiations on the basis of complex qualitative (verbal) and quantitative (mathematical) descriptions. We feel that the right way would be to begin with creating a descriptive or verbal model, and then realize its formalization.

Naturally, in doing this we shall face the necessity of the preliminary examination and solution of many problems of methodology, theory and methods of scientific modeling of international relations, and of constructing appropriate algorithms and programs. This involves a whole set of scientific problems, which could be effectively solved only through a significant input of and cooperation between researchers and negotiators.

Without the knowledge and assessment of the broad framework of international relations, the concrete international situation or problem under discussion cannot be realistically and correctly understood and estimated. Because of that, a preliminary condition for effective modeling of the international negotiations mechanisms is research on the general problems of creating an overall model of international relations. The results of such research could be the creation of the theory and methodology as well as programming foundations of a model of the system of international relations, together with its ecological, economic, political, military and ideological subsystems. We believe that this could represent the second stage of our research on international negotiations.

3. The third stage of our work, we think, should be research on the theoretical, methodological and mathematical problems of creating operative models for concrete international situations — in other words, models that would reflect various regional and bilateral conflicts and disputes as objects of negotiations among countries. We believe that such models of concrete international situations and problems should be built on the basis of a single methodology and would be a continuation and concretization of a common global macro-model of the world system of international relations. This would help the participants of negotiations to arrive more quickly at mutual understandings of estimating situations and of the consequences of changes resulting from certain solutions and provisions that would be incorporated in international agreements. The complexity of such a range of problems undoubtedly will demand participation of significant scientific forces.

4. The fourth stage could involve the exploration and formulation, on the basis of scientific modeling, of a theory and practical methods of forecasting changes in the system of international relations and concrete political situations. The creation of such forecasting models, which could provide a possibility to see trends and prospects in the development of concrete situations, would create a good foundation for a state to identify its policy aims in any international conflict or dispute.

5. The fifth stage or set of problems involves research on the formulation of practical methods for the construction of operative models of a "system of aims" of any state and its representatives at negotiations. Such a "system of aims" usually finds its expression in a set of proposals and demands put forward by this state at negotiations. This research is needed, because a task of great importance in the preparation of negotiations would be an accurate and rational definition of the policy aims of a state with regard to a given international problem or dispute.

6. All of the above-mentioned tasks belong to the sphere of improving information and consultative services for those involved in the various stages of preparations of negotiations. The following set of tasks deals with problems of analytical services during the process of negotiations.

The most complicated group of problems in our opinion revolve around the use of a complex model of a concrete political situation to examine which positive or negative results for each side of a negotiation are implied by the realization of a state's proposals, positions or demands. We think that such a use — if possible — of a computerized model for examining the consequences of the realization of various proposals could take the form of a "What would happen if ...?" principle.

We consider that the possibility of examining, with the help of a computer model, all variants and implications of the proposals and positions of states or participants in the processes of international negotiations to be the most important task of scientific modeling of the mechanisms and processes of international negotiations. International negotiations in their essence are an exchange of information about positions and demands of states or participants — that is, a process of comparing demands and of achieving compromise solutions through concession-making, for the benefit of all sides.

In the process of such a comparison of positions and consideration of variants of solutions, it could be possible to define more efficiently or effectively common, mutually acceptable positions, as a basis for working out agreements.

The creation of such complex models would demand the solution of many new methodological and theoretical interdisciplinary problems, which require the participation and advice of specialists in many areas, such as philosophy, political science, sociology, international relations, systems analysis, programming and diplomacy. The creative unification of their efforts in solving this complicated task is necessary to achieve useful results.

If it turns out to be possible to develop such a set of models for the mechanisms and processes of negotiations, this could become a "soul" of computer consultative systems in various institutions involved in the processes of international negotiations, and a means for increasing the effectiveness of international negotiations, through aiding in the search for quicker and better solutions of international disputes.

We believe the development of such models is a worthwhile task and aim, because it represents the development of a possible means for developing and strengthening peaceful cooperation of peoples, directed to the acceleration of social, economic, scientific, technical and cultural progress of all countries and people.

Our group of Soviet researchers is ready to participate actively in this work and hopes that the cooperation of scientists from IIASA and from various countries will be possible in the solution of these large and complicated tasks.

CHAPTER 3

Multilateral Negotiations: The Role of Presiding Officers

Winfried Lang

Ministry of Foreign Affairs
Vienna
Austria

3.1. Introduction

Multilateral negotiations, which take place mainly in the framework of, or under the auspices of, an international organization, play an increasingly important role in international relations. They not only determine the evolution of international law, but also have an impact on the development of the North–South dialogue. Decision-making at regional or global levels takes care *inter alia* of the environmental consequences of nuclear energy. Such negotiations also exert some influence, albeit limited, on the defense posture and security perceptions of a number of countries or on the debt situation of developing countries.

To the external observer, multilateral negotiations present themselves as an intricate network of *relations, a complex system of interactions*, which vary considerably as to their visibility. Some key delegations or the respective chairpersons brief the media on their expectations or the outcome of a conference. Press releases drafted by the secretariats try to catch the attention of the public; interest groups address themselves to the press to convey to a broader circle their positions and evaluations. To the extent that records are available to researchers, a relatively accurate account of what has really happened can be given, although records do reflect reality only in a very limited way; they constitute the small tip of the iceberg that can be seen above the waterline. A full account of reality would require knowing the content of the reports submitted by delegations, at least the most important ones, to their respective governments, because only these reports give concrete information on the informal, private part of the negotiation. *Since such knowledge is unlikely to be obtained, any research on negotiations has to rely also on personal accounts of negotiators, who have participated in a conference;* from this insight stems the practice of interviewing negotiators, of collecting their written accounts, of screening official records and documents against the background of these personal accounts.

This study is an effort to match academic analysis and negotiating experience by focusing on an actor who stands usually in the limelight of multilateral negotiations — the presiding officer. To evaluate properly the role and performance of presiding officers, it is proposed to scrutinize at first the general set-up of multilateral negotiations, which includes factors determining the behavior of actors, factors determining the negotiation situation as a whole and finally those mechanisms through which the process is channeled toward its final objective.

3.2. Multilateral Negotiations

3.2.1. Factors determining the behavior of actors

To study the factors determining the behavior of actors, one has to address at the outset the question: who participates in the negotiating process? As the nation-state, far from being obsolete, still constitutes the main moving force of international relations, delegations, which represent nation-states and their governments, continue to be the key actors of multilateral negotiations. One caveat, however, has to be inserted with respect to negotiations at which delegations of regional economic integration organizations participate, delegations that either themselves substitute for national delegations or act in parallel with the representatives of the member states of these organizations. For the purposes of this study such collective actors can, however, be aggregated with national delegations.

Another actor in his or her own right is the presiding officer of a meeting. Although he is usually the head of a national delegation, his non-national role imposes upon him the duty of impartiality and obliges him to orient his endeavors toward an objective shared by the greatest number of delegations. Any partisan posture would be incompatible with his function and could seriously jeopardize the prospects of a successful outcome.

Secretariats, in particular their respective heads and other leading officials, have also to be considered as actors. They may even be at the origin of negotiations; their performance can accelerate or delay the negotiating process; the value of their input into negotiations, such as studies, reports, synoptic surveys etc., may affect to some extent the actual outcome of interstate negotiations. The role of the secretariat could be a catalyzing one, merging and matching national positions; it should not lose sight of the common weal of the participating states, sharing in that respect the duties of the presiding officer. This commonality of outlook imposes on both the necessity of close cooperation and of mutually reinforcing activities.

A fourth category of participant should not be neglected, and is gaining full recognition as actors to the same extent as international negotiations affect areas traditionally within the internal purview of states, such as human rights, the regulation of economic activities, the protection of the environment, etc. These private interest groups, labeled non-governmental organizations, represent business, labor, human rights activists, ecologically concerned movements and others. Some international bodies, in particular those in the human rights field, rely heavily on these groups, the information they furnish etc. As this fourth category of actor usually has only observer status in interstate negotiations, they exert their influence indirectly and informally, either at home by approaching their respective governments or on the conference premises by lobbying the individual delegations.

Turning now to the question as to which factors determine the behavior of these actors, answers will have to be given separately for each type of actor.

National delegations act in the first instance along the lines drawn by their instructions. This guidance itself reflects the general position of the sending state as regards traditional indicators of power (gross national product, degree of socioeconomic development, population, military strength, etc.); its allegiance toward alliances, political or economic groupings; its dependence on economic assistance, imports of raw materials or energy, etc. Another factor determining the content and general direction of the brief addressed to the delegation is the interest the government has in that particular organization and conference and its status in this framework. A main financial contributor will harbor views different from a country contributing only marginally to the organization or to the particular endeavor under consideration. A government represented in the more restricted bodies of an international organization, or a government acting on behalf of regional or political interest groups may act and react in ways at variance with governments not considered as part of the core groups.

Of special importance is the interest the sending state has in the issue at stake or in a particular outcome of the negotiation process. Its position in certain negotiations can be prejudiced by declarations made earlier in the same or some other forum. Since instructions have to be carried out by delegates, the human factor in a delegation's behavior should not be underestimated; personal reactions toward stress and the speed of negotiations are of significance similar to the rank of a negotiator, the latter determining to a certain extent his freedom of maneuver with respect to instructions received. Being thoroughly familiar with the subject matter is as important as a good knowledge of the conference languages. National cultural backgrounds, in particular those related to decision-making styles (contradictory versus consensual) influence negotiating behavior as well as the individual facility of a delegate to make contacts with other delegates, and to approach other participants with a more or less open mind.

Most of the factors determining the behavior of national delegations have also to be taken into account when examining the performance of presiding officers. They are, however, not supposed to abide by any instructions addressed to them by national authorities; their ultimate goal should be the early and successful conclusion of the process to the helm of which they have been called. Presiding officers should be committed to the overall interest common to most, if not all, delegations. The human factor, their sense of equity and fairness, their knowledge of the rules of procedure and their empathy with respect to conflicting positions can play a decisive role.

A mediating function can also be assumed by the secretariat, provided that national delegations are willing to accept such a task for an actor whose main interest should be the smooth running of the negotiation process. Members of the secretariat are to a certain extent affected by their respective national backgrounds, which should however not lead them to espouse one or the other national viewpoint. Their loyalty should be directed exclusively to the organization, its object and purpose, although one has to admit that not all concerned comply fully with that obligation. If the international organization servicing a particular negotiation has a more or less official "ideology", e.g., some progressive attitude regarding North–South relations, this can be an important factor determining the concrete action of the officials of that organization. If this amounts, however, to some kind of partisan position not shared by the entire membership, such behavior most certainly will weaken the credibility of the respective officials as honest brokers or neutral mediators facilitating the interactions of delegations. Technical expertise, full knowledge of legal and financial implications of decisions to be adopted, awareness of previous decisions and other relevant precedents that may have a bearing on the ongoing negotiation are the qualities a secretariat is supposed to have. To this should be added the availability of the secretariat for devising compromise formulae and for proposing innovative solutions, which turn a zero-sum game into a positive-sum game and results all actors can live with.

Non-governmental organizations are mainly influenced by the interests for whose pursuit they were established — interests of an economic, social or humanitarian nature, etc. Events such as concrete cases of human rights violations can have an immediate impact on interstate relations, if activist groups assume responsibility for their presentation at those international fora in which they enjoy consulative status. The behavior of these organizations is most closely linked to partisan interests and concrete events. Whereas governments attempt to strike a balance between the various interests they are supposed to defend at the international level, these groups exist for the very purpose of defending particular views and interests; they are not expected to mediate between conflicting interests. Although these groups play only a secondary role in interstate negotiations, their impact on the media and public opinion should not be underrated; being frequently well versed in public relations, their comments on a particular negotiation may very well mould the public perception of a particular intergovernmental process.

3.2.2. Factors determining the negotiation situation

Factors that exert their influence beyond individual actors determine the overall situation within which a negotiation takes place and constitute the second set of elements to be considered in this context.

Most important among these factors is the type of decision that should be the result of negotiations. This decision may be a legally binding instrument, a political commitment, the establishment of a new international organization, an election, etc. Actors will adjust their activities to the particular nature of the decision to be taken. If the result is supposed to be a convention or treaty, lawyers will be included in most delegations as the so-called "legal niceties", frequently neglected by negotiators, will acquire special importance. If a new organization is to be created, experts on financial matters will be called in, to give advice to the generalists normally in charge of these negotiations. If, however, a certain meeting is only a preliminary or intermediate step on the long road of decision-making, technical experts are likely to dominate the process. Their influence tends to decrease as the end of a negotiation is approached; this does not necessarily imply that their impact on the ultimate outcome is lost; quite to the contrary, it happens frequently that texts elaborated during painstaking sessions at expert levels acquire a life of their own, so that little freedom of choice is left for the final round at which negotiators of a political rank approve a text already finalized at a lower level.

Elections constitute another type of decision: eminent persons to be selected for some special task, well-known lawyers required to fill the vacancies at international tribunals, or countries competing for a seat in a limited membership body. These elections are preceded by full-fledged campaigns; incumbents compete with newcomers. The principle of rotation is invoked against the advantages of continuity. Special merits are weighed against specific qualities and important national interests. Regional groups strive to present to the plenary body a "clean slate", i.e., not more candidates than seats allotted to that group. Governments sometimes declare themselves willing to vote for a particular candidate, on the condition that their candidate for some other function is supported by the government of the former candidate. Considerations of prestige are not alien to this kind of contest.

Decisions to be taken as the result of a negotiation are also viewed in their overall context: does this decision constitute a major element, an asset or a liability within the framework of the East–West confrontation, or is it rather a milestone in the North–South dialogue? The type of decision not only affects individual behavior, but also determines to a certain extent the mechanisms selected for the negotiation process.

Another factor determining the overall situation is the degree to which the decision is linked to precedents or related to decisions to be taken in other fora. If the subject matter under consideration allows it to be split into different elements, which can enter into a broader scheme of compensation, then the process of mutual accommodation may be greatly facilitated, as benefits in one area may be tradeable against losses in another field. In cases, where negotiations take place in several subcommittees, cross-cutting deals may allow for the balancing

of advantages and disadvantages. Such efforts aimed at equalizing the results
and leaving no participant with a net loss are the special responsibility of presiding officers or middle-of-the-road delegations that assume mediating roles. No
delegation can be expected to leave the conference table without at least the semblance of some positive result; if this were to happen, the government concerned
would probably not comply with that decision and would challenge its logic and
legality. It would spare no effort to reverse such a decision or to invalidate it by
an opposite decision adopted in another body more conducive to its interests.
These considerations confirm the view that a balanced result approved by consensus guarantees most effectively the compliance with that decision. To conclude negotiations with a consensus decision means that patience and skill, perseverance and flexibility — and not haste and brinkmanship — are required.

The time and duration of a conference as well as its venue may have a
bearing on the negotiation and its outcome. If a meeting is convened at the
headquarters of an international organization, the "diplomatic milieu" present at
that place is likely to be familiar with the issues and may benefit from existing
informal channels of communication. The same applies to the role of the secretariat, which is likely to function more efficiently on home ground than anywhere
else. Organizing a conference at another place than the seat of the competent
administrative unit may be justified on grounds of political convenience — the
opening session of a new trade negotiation may be held in a developing country
to stress the importance of this negotiation for developing countries — or
because the majority of states wishes to achieve results they do not consider to
be attainable if that meeting were held at the traditional location. Governments
may wish to host a conference at their capital for reasons of prestige, or because
they wish to identify themselves with a particular cause.

The size of a meeting room can be important for the progress of negotiations; chairpersons tend to call informal consultations in their offices, the size of
which allows only for one or two persons per interest group to be present and to
participate in the core negotiation.

The duration of a conference is usually fixed in advance. If, for financial
reasons, a very short time is allotted to a particular meeting, not at all commensurate with its task, delegates may show themselves reluctant to be fully engaged
in that negotiation, because they believe that nothing meaningful can be
achieved during the short time available. They will press either for an extension
or for a new meeting at a later date.

Climatic conditions prevailing at the place of a conference should not be
neglected; if a great number of delegates feel uncomfortable, their eagerness to
work hard and to participate at sessions going from the early morning until late
in the night may be muted.

This list of factors determining the general situation at the negotiating
table is certainly not exhaustive. Some reference is frequently made to the general political climate. This implies that the overall state of affairs between the
superpowers is likely to influence multilateral negotiations in certain fields, in
particular the area of disarmament and arms control. The North–South dialogue
was for a considerable time affected by the developing countries' striving for the
establishment of a New International Economic Order. Almost any negotiation

between developing and developed countries was influenced by this posture. The results of many negotiations were assessed in terms of this comprehensive strategy — to what extent could a particular result be considered as an achievement or as progress toward the overall goal? The general political climate constitutes, however, a rather vague indicator for forecasting the outcome of multilateral negotiations. Positive results have been achieved even during periods of increasing tension between East and West. Nevertheless, an easing of tensions and progress realized in a particular context may generate spill-over effects for other fora, particularly in cases where the subjects are interdependent or at least interrelated, e.g., confidence-building measures and the review of a treaty prohibiting the production of certain weapons.

3.2.3. Mechanisms of the negotiation process

The multilateral negotiation process may be viewed as a two-track exercise; although these tracks — the public debate and the informal private negotiations — run for some time in parallel, they are expected to join toward the end and to produce a single and final result. Events occurring on one track influence developments that take place on the other track. Delegations showing a high profile in the public process may play a marginal role in the informal negotiations, whereas delegations almost silent during the debate can dominate the process of negotiations proper, if for instance they are able to benefit from a well-established bipartisan posture and are ready to submit compromise formulae, to be innovative in the search for solutions or to induce new flexibility in opposing parties.

Several types of mechanisms are at the disposal of actors in order to make progress:

The so-called *formal structural* mechanism comprises all those organs and institutions that constitute the official structure of a conference. These include the plenary of a conference, its committees, its bureau and the regional groups. The plenary serves as the main forum for delivering formal statements, electing officers, establishing working bodies, and approving the final document. The bureau, composed of the president, the vice presidents and the chairpersons of the various suborgans, is supposed to function as the steering body of the conference, to prepare the procedural decisions of the plenary and to assist the president in the conduct of business. Formally established committees and commissions can be open-ended or may be restricted to a smaller number of delegations, which raises the problem of balanced regional participation and representation. These bodies work usually under a specific mandate, decided by the plenary; they may deal with the first or second reading of a proposed treaty, resolve detailed questions of a legal or drafting nature, or look into technical or financial matters. All these bodies share one common task: preparation of the final text (treaty, declaration, resolution), which is approved in the plenary by the greatest possible number of delegations. Regional groups (Africa, Asia, Latin America, Eastern Europe, Western Europe and others) perform mainly electoral functions related to the nomination of officers and the membership of subsidiary organs (drafting committee, credentials committee, etc.). Such groups, almost indispensable for the proper take-off of a conference, can acquire long-lasting political significance, if they convert themselves into interest groups the membership of which may coincide with that of military alliances or other political or economic groupings.

The *formal procedural* mechanism covers important elements, such as the rules of procedure that stipulate the formal requirements of decision-making and the majorities necessary to approve amendments and to adopt the final text. These rules also indicate the powers of the president, define the linkages between the various main and subsidiary organs, etc. A delegation that is well versed in the use of these rules (points of order, right of reply, etc.) may well be able to dominate or to manipulate the formal decision-making process. Another element, the agenda of a conference, is frequently considered a routine matter; although this might be true in most cases, there are always instances when the structure of the agenda may be politically significant. This applies in particular to meetings dealing with a large number of different and competing issues. The order in which these agenda items are arranged indicates an order of priorities; items at the very bottom of an agenda are likely to be postponed for consideration at a later meeting due to lack of time. Opposing interest groups that assign priority to two different items may insist that one single debate be conducted on both items at the same time, because they wish to preclude their favorite issue receiving somewhat lesser treatment than the primary issue of the other group. Decision-making on such preliminary matters may take precious time away from substantive work. It has therefore become frequent practice to settle these matters (rules of procedure, agenda, allocation of officers to regional groups) before the conference is formally opened, either by means of informal consultations or through some preparatory committee.

A main element of this formal procedural mechanism is also the public debate (general and special) and the decision-making itself, the voting of amendments, the handling of procedural motions, the final vote and the concluding statements of delegations, which may contain reservations or interpretations with respect to the text adopted. Whether the final document is approved by consensus or by formal vote depends mainly on its content; a clear-cut majority vote is sometimes preferred to a vaguely drafted consensus text that gives too much leeway to differing and even contradicting interpretations. Consensus texts are, however, believed to carry more weight than documents approved by a majority. The relative merits of each approach will have to be judged on a case-by-case basis.

Turning to the *informal structural* mechanism, one is immediately faced with those informal groups that act as the main moving force of multilateral negotiations. These groups exist in the first instance as gatherings of like-minded delegations, of representatives sharing the same political background or defending identical or similar political interests; they are primarily interest groups. But groups have also a second function — they may serve as a device for consultations and informal negotiations, if they are composed of representatives of various interest groups. Teams of negotiators instructed by their respective interest groups meet in a framework that has received several labels: "contact group", "negotiating group", "working group", "friends of the president". Actors resort to this kind of negotiating device wherever the likelihood of agreement is rather low as regards proceedings in the formal committees of a conference. Such informal negotiating groups are usually convened by the presiding officer, and they are chaired either by himself or by another leading officer of the conference. Selecting participants for such an exercise may reveal itself as a very delicate task; on the one hand, the number of participants has to be kept as low as possible to allow for a meaningful person-to-person dialogue; on the other hand, nobody having a primary interest in the matter under consideration should be left out. Quite frequently several negotiating groups are established; they are devoted to different items and their membership varies in accordance with the concerns expressed by delegations during public debate or informal contacts with the chair. If delegations or interest groups join forces in some kind of coalition, this has also to be considered under the heading of the informal structural mechanism, although one may expect that most of these common endeavors are limited and short-lived.

A fourth mechanism contributing to progress in multilateral negotiations may be qualified as *informal procedural*. In this context all interactions may be considered that take place among delegations belonging to the same interest group, as well as interactions that link various interest groups by means of negotiating devices, such as contact groups. In this most informal environment coordinators or spokesmen of interest groups receive detailed negotiating mandates from their like-minded fellow delegates. After having carried out their instructions in the framework of a contact group, and having negotiated with the opposite side in the most traditional manner, these emissaries return to their interest groups and will try to "sell" the result achieved to its members or ask for new instructions, in order to pursue the dialogue. At this juncture the intervention of the presiding officer, a middle-of-the-road delegation or a prominent member of the secretariat may be helpful. Innovative proposals, to which nobody is formally committed, may provide a way out of a deadlocked situation; seemingly vague suggestions may contain a face-saving solution acceptable to all parties concerned.

When texts agreed most informally among a small number of delegations arrive before the official organs of a conference, the most delicate moment of a multilateral negotiation is at hand. One can practically never be fully assured that all delegations, in particular those that had no part in these private dealings, will graciously approve these informal agreements. The risk of failure at this point can be reduced, however, if each and every delegation having a major interest in a particular question was continuously consulted and briefed on these informal developments. Time constraints as well as social pressures contribute their part to the final formal approval of agreements informally arrived at. Most delegations show themselves reluctant to insist at the very end on minor points, even if they are of some importance to them, because they are afraid that such insistence might wreck the fragile compromise. Many breathe a sigh of relief or even applaud, when the chair announces that the text has been adopted. Such emotional reactions reflect the stress most negotiators have been under during long days and sometimes even weeks of arduous proceedings. After a brief moment of euphoria, the average delegate will return to business, to brief his own government and to assess the results against the background of competing interests and sometimes adverse circumstances.

3.3. Role of Presiding Officers

3.3.1. Selection

The rules of procedure usually provide for the formal election of a president or chairperson. This kind of democratic decision is supposed to convey to the officer the support of all delegations, to confer upon him the authority that is required to direct without challenge the meeting and to control the proceedings of the conference. This mode of selection also has the advantage of giving delegations, which represent sovereign states, at least the semblance of control over the officer, his performance and his actions. Owing to the great number of participating countries and to the fact that delegations belong to competing or even opposing political groups, the nomination of the presiding officer has developed in many cases into a highly political matter. In complex bodies, such as the General Assembly of the United Nations, detailed arrangements have been devised to assure the rotation of presidential functions (plenary and committees) among the various political and regional groups. But even in *ad hoc* meetings, such as review conferences in the disarmament field, questions of balance and equal distribution of functions can play a certain role; it may happen that the number of functions (vice presidents, vice chairpersons, etc.) must be increased in order to accommodate the wishes of all regional groups. Except for expert bodies of the most technical kind, considerations of national prestige, political equilibrium, and general acceptability of a country and person dominate the selection process. If a certain regional group is entitled to the presidency in a given context, no other group will as a rule challenge the candidate proposed by that group, although the semblance of a democratic election is maintained. Elections as the mode of selection have in fact been replaced by consultations. These private dealings may precede the official election date, which usually coincides with the opening of the conference, by weeks or months.

As regards the participants in this selection process, various actors have to be considered: The secretariat in charge of a particular conference has a primary interest to assure a smooth start. The formal opening of a meeting will have to be postponed and time necessary for substantive work is lost, if there are competing candidacies and if no preliminary understanding on the distribution of the different functions (president, vice presidents, rapporteur, chairpersons of subcommittees, etc.) has been reached. In cases where a series of meetings takes place or where a permanent organ holds periodic sessions, the outgoing chairperson can exert some influence on the nomination of the successor. If the conference is more technical than political — a distinction not easily made — the professional qualifications of a candidate might prevail over considerations of a more political nature. In expert bodies, chairpersons are frequently elected from among those who have a longer period of service in that particular committee, who have already gained a profile as mediators and/or who have developed ample experience in submitting gap-bridging proposals, thus facilitating the work of that committee. As far as conferences of a political character are concerned, these preliminary consultations will be dominated by some key countries, such as the superpowers, the coordinators of the various regional and political groups, and/or governments, which have a special interest in the subject matter being considered at the conference.

The question as to where the initiative comes from for the nomination of a person for a specific presidential function has no clear answer. Personal ambition or considerations of national prestige may be at the origin of a candidacy; a country that hosts a conference at its own expense in its capital is inclined to consider its chief delegate to that conference as a natural candidate for the presidency. Some governments that appreciated the performance of a presiding officer in the past may wish to see him again in the chair of a meeting covering the same or some related subjects. These countries are likely to do the canvassing for that candidate, even if he or she does not belong to their own group. In some instances, this selection process amounts to a delicate search for an alternative solution, when a deadlock has developed between two or three equally strong primary candidates. Although those instances are rare, they may occur in particular in areas of a very sensitive nature. A device to prevent such situations has been agreed upon in the Conference on Disarmament, in which the presidency is assumed every month by another delegation.

Since most multilateral negotiations take place in the realm of diplomacy, questions of protocol and problems of precedence and rank cannot totally be ignored. In cases where most delegations to a conference are headed by a cabinet minister, the president of that conference is supposed to be of ministerial rank. The same applies to meetings at which delegations are led by ambassadors or heads of mission; a government presenting its candidate for the presidency of that meeting will have to assure that this person holds the title of ambassador or is of some equivalent rank in its national administration; and prominent professors and experts may sometimes be considered equivalent to such high-ranking officials.

Expectations of various kinds are focused on the person thus elected; some delegations expect the presiding officer to stay aloof from the ordinary give-and-take of a negotiation and to perform a mainly ceremonial function, whereas others have supported a candidate because they consider him an efficient negotiator, able to push matters ahead. Still other delegations believe that they may able to manipulate the presiding officer, either because he owes them his function or because he belongs to their political grouping. The only expectation a presiding officer should always strive to fulfill is that of impartiality and fairness. To what extent he really can contribute to the positive outcome of a negotiation depends on many factors, most of which are well beyond his control.

3.3.2. Factors determining the actions of the presiding officer

Some of the factors that determine the behavior of a presiding officer have
already been mentioned. Important among these are his national and professional background, his previous experience as a negotiator, and the support he
receives during the negotiation from his own delegation and from the regional
group or political group to which he belongs. To a certain extent his performance will also depend on the secretariat and the other members of the bureau
(the vice presidents, rapporteurs, chairpersons of committees, etc). Another
important factor, which has already been identified as crucial for the entire negotiation situation, but which also has its impact on the role of the presiding
officer, is the subject matter or the objective of the conference. Negotiating a
treaty or resolution places considerably more stress on the president than the
chairing of a meeting devoted only to the presentation of national viewpoints,
which are reflected more or less accurately in a concluding report.

Comparing various conferences reveals that the most important factor for
the performance of a presiding officer is the structure of a conference — the distance that separates him from the mainstream of negotiations. A conference of
plenipotentiaries, which is entrusted with the elaboration and adoption of a convention, possibly has its center of gravity in the drafting committee or the committee of the whole. The president of the conference may, therefore, have less
bearing on the final text than the chairpersons in charge of either committee,
provided all outstanding issues can be settled at the level of these bodies. If,
however, certain questions remain unresolved in these subsidiary organs, it will
be the task of the president to schedule informal consultations, contact groups,
etc., to which he invites only those delegations and group coordinators he considers indispensable for the settlement of problems left open at the committee level.
Although not formally participating in the work of the official committees, the
president will follow most closely, either in person or by means of somebody
reporting to him, negotiations taking place at this lower level. Keeping abreast
with the proceedings at whatever level can sometimes be more important than
the actual direction of formal meetings. A conference that is much less structured than a plenipotentiaries conference, however, at which the presiding officer
is acting close to the mainstream of negotiations, may require from him some
direct involvement in the drafting exercise. This type of conference, frequently
called a meeting of experts, allows for the full participation of the presiding
officer in substantive work. In this context he might himself try his hand at
preparing compromise papers that chart some medium course between the
differing or opposing positions of national delegations or interest groups. The
structure of the conference and the more or less controversial nature of issues
determine quite frequently the nature of the presiding officer's activity: whether
it is a ceremonial or a steering function or a substantive negotiating role.

A factor not entirely to be neglected is the membership of the conference.
The task of the presiding officer will sometimes be less difficult if only governments sharing the same ideology, for instance, developed countries with a market
economy, participate in a negotiation. Meetings with delegations from all parts
of the globe are occasionally burdened by issues not directly related to the

subject matter under consideration — issues, however, that may be of considerable importance to one or two delegations. The full powers of a delegation, whose sending government is recognized only by a small number of states, may give rise to a dispute. Another question that may arise is the status of regional integration organizations with respect to their adherence to the treaty adopted by the conference. Such side issues may delay the conclusion of a negotiation. A presiding officer, mindful of a smooth conclusion of a conference, will use his best endeavors to dispose of these problems at the earliest possible moment.

Ideological homogeneity does not, however, guarantee the success of a conference. Countries that share common values to a considerable extent tend to strive for rules and regulations that touch matters hitherto exclusively within their domestic jurisdiction. The further these agreements advance into the traditional, internal sovereignty domain of states, the more national administrations try to resist efforts aimed at a harmonized or uniform system of law, economic affairs, trade regulations, environmental protection, etc. This means that even negotiations in a relatively closed circle, such as the OECD, can be arduous and lengthy. National interests are defended with vigor at whatever level, be it regional or universal.

3.3.3. The powers of a presiding officer

The formal powers of a presiding officer are traditionally laid down in the rules of procedure; these powers include the following:

- Opening and closing the meeting
- Directing discussions and ensuring the observance of the rules of procedure
- According the right to speak
- Putting proposals to a vote
- (With the agreement of the conference) limiting the speaking time, closing the list of speakers, closing the debate, suspending or adjourning a meeting, adjourning the debate on an item, etc.

A particularly crucial moment occurs for every presiding officer when the conference proceeds to formal voting, in particular if separate voting on amendments to the basic proposal is required. If several competing amendments have been moved to a proposal, it is up to him to decide which amendment is furthest removed from the original proposal and should therefore be voted upon first. He will also be well advised to dispose quickly of points of order, even at the risk that his ruling is challenged and overruled by a majority. Although procedural debates tend to become rather rare events, any presiding officer has to be prepared to deal with such situations and should be fully acquainted with all the intricacies of these rules. Formal voting has been replaced in many instances by an adoption of texts by consensus. This mode of decision-making puts less strain on the procedural abilities of the presiding officer. It imposes upon him, however, at least in some instances, a much stronger involvement in substantive negotiations and an active engagement in numerous behind-the-scene dealings, if the delegations concerned fail to agree in their direct contacts.

The informal powers of a presiding officer are neither codified nor really limited — whatever serves the purpose of the conference and is accepted by the participants may be undertaken by him in order to proceed to a final document that is approved or at least not objected to by the greatest possible number of delegations. In this context he is entitled to take any initiative he considers advisable: he may submit procedural or substantive proposals to break a deadlock; convene whatever informal body he deems appropriate; circulate working papers; and put pressure on some key delegations to conclude their bilateral or trilateral dealings, on whose results hinges the outcome of the overall negotiation. As the chief officer of the conference he will also keep the media informed of the progress of negotiations, without, however, revealing points whose public knowledge could damage the proceedings. A full account of the negotiation will be reserved for a final briefing at the end of the conference. The extent to which a presiding officer may use most of his informal powers depends on the permissive consensus of the participants, and in particular the key delegations among them. If, for instance, these key delegates prefer to settle some outstanding issues among themselves without interference from the chair, the presiding officer will abstain from any kind of separate and intrusive activity. Faced, however, with the likelihood of other delegations growing impatient, he will press those key delegations to finalize their negotiations as early as possible and not to abuse any *de facto* privileged position they may enjoy as a consequence of their political power.

The powers of a presiding officer are extensive and fragile at the same time; to what extent he avails himself of these powers depends also on his personality, on the human factor.

3.3.4. The characteristics of a "good" presiding officer

Whoever undertakes to sketch the profile of an "ideal" presiding officer will do so in the light of personal experience, either by judging the actual performance of chairpersons he has become acquainted with, or by scrutinizing his own actions in the past, if he has had the privilege to serve as presiding officer. Considerations submitted hereinafter draw on both sources of information; these reflections have, therefore, to be considered as rather subjective and personal ones. As lessons learned by the author in specific circumstances, they are not necessarily applicable to all instances and every type of international negotiation. Any recommendation given on the basis of concrete experience may reveal itself as totally erroneous in other cases, as the circumstances prevailing in the different negotiation situations are rarely identical. Bearing in mind these caveats, one may summarize the qualities of a "good" presiding officer as follows:

- As regards questions of procedure, he should develop a certain degree of firmness in order not to be manipulated by other actors; this requires that his procedural decisions should be based on a comprehensive knowledge of the respective rules.
- As far as questions of substance are concerned, he should display some flexibility, because he is supposed not to have a vested interest in a particular outcome of the negotiations he is directing, except for the overall objective to obtain for the final document the broadest possible support. To divest himself of his specific views and to exchange his own national perspective for some vague type of open-mindedness is less easy than expected.
- It goes without saying that he should be well versed in the intricacies of the subject matter, although he should not lose sight of the broader perspectives.
- A person gifted with creativity and innovativeness can be an ideal president, provided his ideas do not go too far beyond what has been called the permissive consensus of the participants; proposals departing too radically from well-established models of thinking may be perceived as troublesome and disturbing.
- To be constantly aware of the mood prevailing among key actors, he should seek the advice of the most important delegations, in particular before taking decisions related to the structure and procedure of the conference; at the same time the mere semblance of being dependent on these delegations will have to be avoided.
- He should exercise some kind of "preventive guidance". This means that he should be aware of delegations that may create problems and include them, if necessary, in the inner circle of decision-making. He should foresee most obstacles that may arise during the course of a negotiation and should try to dispose of them even before they appear on the negotiating table. Such obstacles may include political side issues, such as the representation of certain governments or other questions of status (national liberation movements, etc.); problem delegations are sometimes satisfied if the presiding officer deals personally with their particular problem.
- If the presiding officer is about to submit his own gap-bridging proposals to the conference, he should do it at the latest possible moment, after the exhaustion of all other remedies. The importance of the time factor in such circumstances must not be neglected. If his presentation occurs too early, these proposals risk being attacked from various quarters, thus losing their value as a common meeting ground. Another tactic consists of presenting various and successive drafts to informal groups, these drafts being modified step by step in the light of comments received from delegations participating in these groups.
- An important quality of the presiding officer is his "availability", his readiness to be at the disposal of all participants and his ability to listen carefully to all concerns expressed to him either in public or in private.

-   A presiding officer who is fully involved in substantive negotiations should not only be gifted in the art of splitting up issues and of devising alternative or parallel courses of action, but should also be able to merge the results of separate proceedings into one single outcome.

Corresponding to this catalogue of positive requirements, which is certainly not exhaustive, is a series of recommendations of a more negative nature. To be efficient the presiding officer should *not*

-   Be a loner, which implies that he should seek private contacts with as many delegations as possible and at a minimum the most important ones, although certain decisions he will have to take alone. Keeping the appropriate balance between too much reliance on the general sentiment and too strong an impulse toward solitary action remains one of the most crucial elements of a good chairmanship.
-   Hesitate to exert pressure on delegations that, deliberately or not, delay the overall progress of the negotiation. To this end he may propose time limits or target dates. He may even convey to those concerned the idea that he is going to present his own proposal, if the opposing parties are unable to come up with an agreed solution after the lapse of time allotted to them for informal proceedings; this idea may be perceived by those concerned as a threat and could facilitate agreement among them.
-   Impose himself as long as some movement in private dealings among key delegations and interest groups is visible, because he should always keep in mind that any kind of pressure is resented by delegations, unless it is justified by the objective lack of progress in these consultations. This amounts again to a delicate balancing act between patience and activism, between respect for particular (minority) interests and the general commitment to the early achievement of common goals.

It is sometimes a demanding task to direct a conference at which hundreds of delegates pursuing differing, if not opposing, interests and objectives participate. The means at the disposal of a presiding officer are quite limited; as his most important assets one should consider his reputation, authority, record of fairness and impartiality. Drawing sparsely and carefully on this capital, he may succeed and avoid the numerous pitfalls just enumerated. His action cannot, however, compensate for the lack of political will on the part of the other actors. If the great number of delegations, and in particular the most important ones, are not ready to compromise, to accommodate their respective interests, if a minimum amount of confidence is absent from a multilateral negotiation, no agreement will be achieved, whatever efforts are undertaken by the presiding officer.

3.3.5. The consequences of a presiding officer's actions

The structure of a conference, the distance that separates a presiding officer from the mainstream of negotiations in a conference, will be a decisive condition for the impact of his actions on concrete events. The influence a president performing mainly ceremonial functions can exert on the final outcome of a meeting will be almost nil. A "steering president", who, although acting mainly in the back chambers of a conference, directs the overall process and coordinates several subsidiary proceedings, may affect the final result to a slightly more significant extent. If the structure of the conference allows for a "negotiating president", a chairperson directly involved in the elaboration of the final document, his action may be considered as important, if he makes full use of his formal and informal powers. Such a statement should, however, be qualified to the effect that without his active participation either the result might not have been achieved at that very moment or a result of much lower quality and less substantive content might have been obtained. Whatever type of presidency delegations are faced with, they will have to assume the main responsibility for the success or failure of a negotiation. If one were to compute the relative influence of the various actors on the outcome of a conference, one should realistically admit that even a "working" and "negotiating" chairperson, with the maximum of negotiating skills at his or her disposal, will see his or her contribution to the final result limited to not more than ten percent of the total impact of all negotiators. In some instances, however, this ten percent makes the difference between success or failure.

Some aspects of a multilateral negotiation may be more strongly affected by a chairperson's activity than others. The general mood prevailing among delegates (controversy versus consensus) can probably be influenced by the presiding officer; the same applies to the timely closure of a conference. In a much more restricted manner the presiding officer may help to improve the quality of the final document, provided the structure of the conference and most other factors favor such concrete action. If the chairperson deems himself responsible for protecting minority interests and acts with some success in that direction, he could also contribute to a broader acceptability of the final document.

To put it into a nutshell, one could sum up the preceding reflections as follows: a bad chairperson cannot easily prevent the positive conclusion of a multilateral negotiation, if most other factors and actors are geared toward that objective; a good presiding officer can, however, facilitate the task of delegations having the necessary political will by accelerating the process of inching toward the final result and assisting delegations to remove minor and medium obstacles from the road to success.

3.4. Conclusions

The foregoing analysis has been devoted to two distinct tasks. In the first instance, when scrutinizing the forces at work in a multilateral negotiation, the main objective was to convey a more transparent picture of reality. Concepts such as factors and mechanisms were used as tools to throw more light on an intricate network of complex interactions among actors, such as national delegations, international organizations, etc. The group as a mechanism with two different functions — namely, to defend partisan interests and to merge differing or opposing interests — was recognized as one of the main elements of the negotiation process. A second lesson to be drawn from this more general study would be that informal proceedings have a much stronger impact on the final outcome of negotiations than more or less public debates. In this respect it was also recognized that traditional negotiating methods or tactics have not disappeared from the realm of diplomacy, even in a context in which more than two actors meet in order to arrive at a result satisfactory to all or at least most participants.

Whereas the first part of this study could draw on a broad body of research on conference diplomacy, etc., as well as the personal experience of the author, the second part turned out to be a somewhat subjective reflection of numerous negotiations in which the author took part. This chapter, focusing on the role of the presiding officer in multilateral negotiations, should be considered an invitation extended to negotiators with a similar experience to embark on a thorough dialogue aimed at an objective evaluation of this role. Such common investigation may help improve the performance of chairpersons in the future by assessing the respective value of certain types of action under different circumstances. This personal account was concluded by what is hoped was a realistic appraisal of the contribution that presiding officers can make to the final outcomes of various multilateral negotiations.

Realism being the hallmark of international relations, a study on multilateral negotiations should not be closed without admitting that this type of joint decision-making is far from having met all expectations. In a world of more than 150 states faced with a variety of most urgent universal and regional problems, multilateral diplomacy has become an important instrument to mould our common future. However, in view of its many flaws, its frequent disconnection from reality, its tendency to be manipulated either by big powers or interested organizations, this instrument requires improvement.

Bibliography

Alger, Chadwick F. (1965), Personal Contact in Intergovernmental Organizations, in: Kelman, Herbert (ed.), *International Behavior, A Social-psychological Analysis*, New York, pp. 523-547.

Alger, Chadwick F. (1968), Interaction in a Committee of the United Nations General Assembly, in: Singer, J. David (ed.), *Quantitative International Politics: Insights and Evidence*, New York, pp. 51-84.

Alger, Chadwick F. (1972), Negotiation, Regional Groups, Interaction and Public Debate in the Development of Consensus in the United Nations General Assembly, in: Rosenau, J.D. *et al.* (eds.), *The Analysis of International Politics*, New York and London.

Alker, Hayward and Russett, Bruce (1965), *World Politics in the General Assembly*, New Haven and London.

Bailey, (1984), *The General Assembly of the United Nations*, London.

Bellenger, Lionel (1984), *La négociation*, Paris.

Best, (1960), Diplomacy in the United Nations, Ph.D. dissertation, Northwestern University, Evanston, IL. (Available from University Microfilms, Ann Arbor, MI.)

Bretton, Philippe and Folliot, Michel (1984), *Négociations internationales*, Paris.

Buzan, Barry (1981), Negotiating by Consensus: Developments in Technique at the United Nations Conference on the Law of the Sea, *American Journal of International Law*, April, pp. 324-348.

Charney, Jonathan (1982), Technology and International Negotiations, *American Journal of International Law*, January, pp. 78-118.

Codding, George (1981), Influence in International Conferences, *International Organization*, Autumn, pp. 715-724.

Commonwealth Group of Experts (1982), *The North-South Dialogue, Making it Work*, London.

Cox-Jacobson, (1973), *The Anatomy of Influence: Decision-Making in International Organization*, New Haven and London.

Crott, Helmut, Kutschker, Michael, and Lamm, Helmut (1977), *Verhandlungen II, Organisationen und Nationen als Konfliktparteien*, Stuttgart.

Dean, Jonathan (1986), East–West Arms Control Negotiations, The Multilateral Dimension, in: Sloss-David (ed.), *A Game for High Stakes: Lessons Learned in Negotiating with the Soviet Union*, Cambridge, MA, pp. 79-106.

Dubey, Muckund (1985), The Main Forces at Work (North–South Negotiations), in: Lall, A. (ed.), *Multilateral Negotiation and Mediation*, New York, pp. 154-176.

Dupont, Christophe (1986), *La négociation: conduite-theorie-applications*, Paris (second ed.).

Fisher, Glen (1979), The Cross-Cultural Dimension in International Negotiations, Foreign Service Institute (mimeographed).

Fisher, Roger and Ury, William (1981), *Getting to Yes*, Boston.

Graham, Norman and Haggard, Stephan (1979), Diplomacy in Global Conferences, in: *UNITAR News*, vol. XI, pp. 14-21.

Hovet, (1960), *Bloc Politics in the U.N.*, Cambridge, MA.

Iklé, F. (1964), *How Nations Negotiate*, New York.

Jessup, Philip (1956), Parliamentary Diplomacy, in: *Recueil des Cours* 1956/I, Académie de Droit International, La Haye.

Kaufmann, Johan (1968), Conference Diplomacy.

Kaufmann, Johan (1980), United Nations Decision-Making.

Kaufmann, Johan (1985), A Methodological Summary (North–South Negotiations), in: Lall, A. (ed.), *Multilateral Negotiation and Mediation*, New York, pp. 133-153.

Keohane, Robert (1973), The Study of Political Influence in the General Assembly, in: Goodrich-Kay, *International Organization, Politics and Process*, Madison, WI.

Kielland, (1972), The Role of Limited Membership Committees in the United Nations General Assembly, Ph.D. dissertation, University of Oslo.

Lall, A. (1966), *Modern International Negotiation*, New York and London.

Lang, Winfried (1977), Multilaterale Entscheidungsprozesse, in: *Österreichische Zeitschrift für Aussenpolitik*, No. 6/77, pp. 263-274.

Lang, Winfried (1983), Multilateral Disarmament Diplomacy, in: *Österreichische Zeitschrift für Öffentliches Recht und Völkerrecht*, pp. 25-45.

Lennkh, Georg (1978), Willensbildung im Sicherheitsrat der Vereinten Nationen, in: *Österreichische Zeitschrift für Aussenpolitik*, 1/78, pp. 5-26.

Luterbacher, Urs and Caflisch, Dee Ann (1982), *Negotiating Disarmament*, United Nations Institute for Disarmament Research, Research Paper No. 2, Geneva.

Merle, Marcel (1980), De la négociation, in: *Pouvoirs* (15), pp. 5-29.

Miles, Edward (1977), The Structure and Effects of the Decision Process in the Seabed Committee and the Third United Nations Conference on the Law of the Sea, in: *International Organization*, Spring, pp. 159-234.

Mitchell, C.R. (1981), *The Structure of International Conflict*, New York, 218-250 (The Structure of Negotiations).

Peck, Richard (1979), Socialization of Permanent Representative in the United Nations: Some Evidence, in: *International Organization*, Summer, pp. 365-390.

Plantey, Alain (1980), *La négociation internationale, principes et méthodes*, Paris.

Putnam, Robert and Bayne, Nicholas (1984), *Hanging Together: The Seven Power Summits*, London.

Raiffa, Howard (1982), *The Art and Science of Negotiation*, Cambridge, MA.

Rittberger, Volker (1980), Globale Konferenzdiplomatie im Dienste der Entwicklung, in: *Österreichische Zeitschrift für Aussenpolitik*, 1/80, pp. 1-23.

Sawyer, Jack and Guetzkow, Harold (1965), Bargaining and Negotiation in International Relations, in: Kelman, Herbert (ed.), *International Behavior, A Social-Psychological Analysis*, New York, pp. 466-520.

Schwartz, (1965), A Description and Analysis of the Role of Public Speaking and its Relation to Parliamentary Diplomacy in the UN, 1965, Ph.D. dissertation, Purdue University, West Lafayette, IN. (Available from University Microfilms, Ann Arbor, MI.)

Sizoo, Jan and Jurrjens, Rudolf Th. (1984), *CSCE Decision-Making: The Madrid Experience*, The Hague.

Unger, (1973), The General Assembly and its Main Committees: A Study in Voting Alignments, Ph.D. dissertation, Tulane University, New Orleans, LA. (Available from University Microfims, Ann Arbor, MI.)

Vincent, Jack E. (1972), An Application of Attribute Theory to General Assembly Voting Patterns, Some Implications, in: *International Organization*, Summer, pp. 551-582.

Volgy, Thomas J. and Quistgard, Jan E. (1974), Correlates of Organizational Rewards in the United Nations, in: *International Organization*, Spring, pp. 179-205.

Walbek, (1972), Public Debate in International Organizations, Ph.D. dissertation, Northwestern University, Evanston, IL. (Available from University Microfilms, Ann Arbor, MI.)

Zartman, William (ed.) (1978), *The Negotiation Process*, Beverly Hills, CA.

Zartman, William and Berman, Maureen (1982), *The Practical Negotiator*, New Haven, CT.

Zemanek, Karl, Majority Rule and Consensus Technique in Law-Making Diplomacy, in: McDonald-Johnson (ed.), *The Structure and Process of International Law*, pp. 857-887.

CHAPTER 4

The CSCE as a Collaborative Order

Esko Antola

Department of Political Science
University of Turku
Turku
Finland

4.1. Two Orders of the CSCE

The multidimensionality of the CSCE is a self-evident fact to every student of the subject. It expresses itself throughout the process. Even the concept itself, Conference on Security and Cooperation in Europe, speaks for it. Among the most visible dimensions of the process are those between great powers and lesser powers, between the aligned and non-aligned states, between socialist and capitalist states and so on. Multidimensionality runs through the system and also very much determines the nature of the whole process. One could also argue, with good reason, that if some of the basic propositions of bargaining theories were true, the CSCE should never have taken place (Holsti, 1982).

This paper focuses on one of the most fundamental dimensions of the CSCE, i.e., the coexistence between the *security or competitive order* and the *collaborative order*. [For more detailed analyses, see Antola (1985 and 1986).] These dimensions not only describe an aspect of tension in conceptual terms but, even more, they reflect the confrontation between the basic philosophical interpretations concerning the nature of international relations. That is, they reflect the contrast between competitive theories, which see international relations in a constant state of conflict, and cooperative approaches, which stress the harmony of interests as the basis of international relations.

The matters of military security and state sovereignty in the CSCE reflect the competitive interpretaton of international relations. This argument claims that in a world of sovereign states the only way to maintain one's sovereignty is to be ready to defend it. International relations are in a state of competition where no country can feel secure without relying on the eventual use of military power: basically international relations are in a state of anarchy. This has led to the so-called security dilemma: fear of the hostile intentions of other states provides justifications for an arms race and provokes countermeasures (Hertz, 1950).

The collaborative order of the CSCE reflects the philosophical ideas that are often called Grotian visions of world order. They stress the common interests of nation-states in preserving the given international order. They start from the sovereignty of states as the basis of international orders, but assume that this is best guaranteed by establishing institutions of collaboration whereby the common interests of states can be maintained.

The coexistence of the two orders in the CSCE is demonstrated in the Final Act itself. The Principles, while constituting the basic norms and rules of the European order, recognize state sovereignty as an untouchable principle. This is strengthened by the postulates of anti-expansionism (inviolability of frontiers, refraining from the use of violence). But at the same time basic preconditions of collaboration have been included in the document and are expressed throughout the baskets of the Final Act.

I have developed here an argument asserting that the CSCE indeed reflects the philosophical argumentation on how interstate relations should be conducted. Primacy should be given either to the recognition of the legitimate interests of sovereigns by emphasizing the need to put constraints on the use of force, to strengthen norms and settlements that could permit nations to restrain their hostile or provocative behavior in the belief that others will reciprocate (Jervis, 1982), or the main emphasis should be on enhancing collaboration between the signatories in the widest possible areas as a means to strengthen security. These interpretations coexist both in the letter and in practice.

The two interpretations are seen also in the ways of organizing the work of the CSCE process. The so-called forums where special issues have been discussed have emphasized the collaborative side of the process. Forums such as the Cooperation in the Mediterranean (1979 and 1984), the Scientific Forum (1980), Cultural Forum (1985), Forum on Human Contacts (1986) and Forum on Human Rights and Fundamental Freedom (1985) are all based more on the cooperative elements in the Final Act than on the immediate security dimensions.

On the other hand, Forums on the Peaceful Settlement of Disputes (1978 and 1984) and the Conference on Disarmament in Europe are examples of efforts to deal with the problems of direct military security between the signatories. The follow-up conferences as well as the Final Act and the Tenth Anniversary Meeting have aimed at reviewing the process and add a third dimension to the complexity of the CSCE: how to accommodate the two competing orders of needs and interests in order to keep the process integrated. The task is to maintain an optimal balance between the security aspects and cooperation aspects of the whole endeavor.

4.2. How to Create Cooperation?

Cooperation is not only a matter of the collaborative part of the CSCE, although one could expect better results in a shorter period of time, e.g., in matters of economic cooperation and trade than in matters of military security. The two-dimensionality of the process is seen in the methods of creating cooperation as well. I shall employ the distinction between the *cooperation-under-anarchy approach* and the *functionalist approach*.

4.2.1. Cooperation-under-anarchy approach

Much of the theoretical research on cooperation in this approach is conducted within the framework of the Prisoners' Dilemma (PD). In particular, in the US international relations studies community, the problem of how to create cooperation under anarchy has been a widely debated matter. Robert Axelrod has defined the problem by asking, "Under what conditions will cooperation emerge in a world of egoists without central authority?" (Axelrod, 1984).

It is both fair and important to note that scholars interested in this type of reasoning do not necessarily argue that international relations are in a state of prisoners' dilemma. In fact Axelrod and Robert Keohane argue that the similarities lie in the basic assumption: that both in the PD-situation and in international relations the "myopic pursuit of self-interest can be disastrous", and that both sides can benefit from cooperation (Axelrod and Keohane, 1986). They further argue that political-economic and military-security issues can be analyzed within the same analytical framework of the PD type.

Promoting cooperation under anarchy does not mean that international relations necessarily have to be in an actual state of anarchy. In fact, the notion of international society, or a society of states, is accepted by scholars subscribing to the cooperation-under-anarchy school. But the direction of international relations is not structured effectively, and there are great differences between sectors of international life. It is quite obvious that the conduct of international relations depends very much on the issue area, which should be kept in mind when seeking to enhance collaboration in the CSCE.

The cooperation-under-anarchy school argues that cooperation is indeed possible under two conditions: that there is a guarantee of reciprocity and that actors can base their individual calculations on the projections of future expectations. States shall engage in cooperation expecting a continuation of reciprocal reactions and the durability of the relationship. The message of this analysis is obvious: cooperation is a viable alternative also in the conditions of a security dilemma, where trust as such is often not present and where the problem of defection is always a real alternative.

From the point of view of the CSCE, the major implication of this approach is seen in the notion of trust. The traditional view has been that trust actually is the major factor contributing to the progress of détente and the CSCE. Therefore, one should not expect any progress in cooperation unless there is minimum of trust. In the balanced and keen military security environment of the CSCE the trust between the Great Powers is seen as the key to the process. But the history of the CSCE, in particular in the 1980s, shows that the signatories have been able to keep the process alive in spite of unfavorable Great Power relations. The problem of the approach is that collaboration is not easily created in the security order, since possible areas of cooperation are in the realm of the hard core of national security interests of states.

The issue of reciprocity is important here. Cooperation in security matters is normally of a type of specific reciprocity, where "specific partners exchange items of equivalent value in a strictly delimited scope" (Keohane, 1986) — i.e., situations where cooperation and common understanding are limited to very precise matters and values. Cooperation is intended to cover only those areas upon which an agreement is reached and is limited to negotiations for such agreements. The spill-over effect of such actions is limited.

It is fairly obvious, and well demonstrated by the problems of the Stockholm conference, as well as the difficulties in its follow-up, that the concept of diffuse reciprocity would be more suitable for the CSCE. In such a case "the definition of equivalence is less precise, one's partners may be viewed as a group rather than as a particular actor and the sequence of events is less narrowly bounded" (Keohane, 1986). In a system of 35 nations, vastly different in their power bases and interests, with a number of cross-cutting alignments, the concept of reciprocity must be seen in a rather loose, larger and more flexible framework. This would enable a balancing of interests and the linkage of different issues.

4.2.2. Functionalist approach

The contrasting method of initiating collaboration rests on the functionalist doctrine: meaningful and permanent international collaboration cannot be enforced through institutionalizing international relations by principles and conventions, but rather by organizing international activities according to needs. This is a concept of cooperation reflecting the ideas of David A. Mitrany (1946). The logic of the doctrine is, in brief: first identify the areas of collaboration, then furnish them with appropriate procedures so that favorable results are secured and spill-over promoted. Finally, the whole complex arrangement must be made permanent through institutionalization.

In initiating collaboration, priority must be given to areas and sectors where progress is most likely to be achieved and where the "take-off" threshold is lowest. The likelihood of progress is determined by needs: cooperation is likely where the need is greatest. The precondition is that the area selected must be sufficiently comprehensive and far-reaching so that reinforcing results may be obtained. The criterion of comprehensiveness implies that functional cooperation must be able to deal with the subject matter in a comprehensive manner. Issues where cooperation is promoted do not necessarily have to be of the greatest relevance and importance from the point of view of state interests, but collaboration must be effective in bringing about meaningful results which would not have been achieved otherwise. This leads through a demonstration effect to the proliferation of functional collaborative efforts.

The functionalist strategy faces three critical problems. The first is the question of *institutionalization*. Institionalization is often seen as a necessary precondition for functional cooperation: only the institutionalization of cooperation makes it stable and secure. In many ways, institutions in the functionalist approach have tasks equivalent to what future expectations have in the cooperation-under-anarchy approach. But institutionalization is also thought to be necessary for spill-over and learning, which are important elements of this strategy.

In the framework of the CSCE, institutionalization means that there should be a proliferation of permanent methods of cooperation instead of *ad hoc*-type forums in various areas. It would also mean an increase in the autonomy of these forums, which could lead to the disintegration of the process. It would be much more difficult to coordinate the process or to balance its various elements. But, on the other hand, institutionalization would increase the stability of cooperation and disengage it from the problems of the political-military dimension. This would probably favor collaboration in areas that are sufficiently far away from the hard core of national security interests.

The definition of *needs* is another problem area. In the original Mitranian concept, needs were associated with welfare. In the CSCE, welfare is not perhaps that important as a basis for cooperation. But functional cooperation is definitely needed in the protection of the environment, in organizing transportation, in encouraging trade in Europe and in strengthening the technological capacity of Europe. In fact the two economic systems of Europe face to a great extent similar problems, in particular *vis-à-vis* the rest of the world. The whole process of industrial restructuring serves as a platform for functional cooperation.

The third problematic issue is the *linkage* between the competitive and collaborative orders. Basically there are two possibilities. On the one hand, *the hierarchical approach* assumes that cooperation in non-security matters depends on whether progress is achieved in the security matters of the CSCE. Promoting cooperation is possible, but only if due respect is paid to the basic factors that shape the current political and economic order in Europe. In other words, enhancing cooperation is dependent on the security dilemma, i.e., on the dominant military-political structure in Europe.

Functionalism argues that the poor performance of the collaborative order of the CSCE is due to the practice of hierarchical linkage. Its solution to the linkage problem is *a two-tier model*, which rests on the assumption of the existence of parallelism between the two orders. The hard core of European security, i.e., matters of military security, follows a different logic from the less-sensitive areas. The two tiers can proceed at different speeds for as long as they have the same direction and the basic norms of the CSCE are respected.

A functionalist element in the two-tier model implies that there will emerge, at least in the long run, automatic spill-over to the security order. Spill-over means that functionalist collaboration in less sensitive areas of the CSCE will enhance collaborative elements also in matters in the political-military spheres.

Regional cooperation might prove that this linkage is possible to establish. If interactions, transcending block limits, on a regional basis, are regarded as valuable and made possible, could these pockets of collaboration develop into more comprehensive arrangements? On a regional basis, this is much easier to achieve, because the already existing historical as well as current structures of cooperation can be activated. Another reason for a regional approach is that there already are numerous proposals for regional arrangements.

4.3. The Problem of Change in the CSCE

The CSCE is first of all a *negotiated order* and as such contrasts with the notion of an *enforced order*. The two concepts point to the origins of international orders: they are either created by will and conquest, i.e., by force, or by consensus and legitimacy through negotiations. [These terms have been used by Henry Kissinger (1964) in his evaluation of the Congress of Vienna.] The dilemma of the CSCE is that the post-war European international order was created by force. It is a good example of an international system whose norms and rules are determined largely by the winners of a major war. Once the new order is created, stability is regarded as a virtue as such. Peace settlements do not provide specific methods or institutions for bringing about changes in such international systems (Gilpin, 1981).

Yet the CSCE has strong elements of change. Baskets 2 and 3 (economic cooperation and human contacts), if made effective, call for a profound transformation of Europe through collaboration. The CSCE philosophy implies necessarily that the changes in question must be peaceful, although the nature of change is very much different in the competitive order than what the collaborative approach implies. Narrow definitions of peaceful change, i.e., non-war changes, serve as the idea of change in the former interpretation. Changes are accepted within the limits of the existing international order, under the conditions of competition.

The possibilities for changes in the course of the process are very limited. Security matters are conditioned by so many external factors that the CSCE contributes to them only in a very limited way. Traditionally relevant methods would be, e.g., the revision of treaties or territorial changes. Both of these are extremely unlikely in the realm of the CSCE. In fact, even demands for such changes would run against the basic principles of the Final Act. Should such changes be initiated, the CSCE's role would be that of an executive body, not the role of initiator.

The term "peaceful" in its non-war definition implies that changes must note the existence of the status quo and must have some sort of regularity. Peaceful change must rely on regularized processes through which modifications are brought about and also made effective. Those processes must be so designed and established that they make changes possible, but do not threaten the power bases of the existing order. The status quo must be respected and the stability of international relations has to be maintained. And, most importantly, changes must be negotiated on a consensual basis, and national interests regarded as legitimate motives.

The collaborative view of change again would imply the establishment of an international order where institutions and common rules and laws give the central direction to international relations, i.e., the *restructuring of the international order.* This would require renouncing the use of force and war as methods of change. Instead, institutions and procedures would be created through which the contingent threat of war could be abolished and security established on a non-coercive basis. If this is to be realized, state sovereignty must somehow be limited.

The reconstruction of the European security system would imply a move toward the *functionalist idea.* Mitrany was basically hesitant about the possibility of creating a conventional collective security system. In his mind there were two possibilities: either to establish an autonomous internatonal authority with necessary powers and force to keep the peace, or to base the future international order on cooperation. His own proposal was a functional approach, which could best respond to the demands of international changes (Mitrany, 1944). In this flexible international order, the roles and functions of nation-states would also change in the long run.

In reality the CSCE sees peaceful change as a process whereby necessary corrections to the existing order and, in particular, to the existing status quo can be made in order to avoid the outbreak of war and to revise the rules and power relations of the international order for a better management of international society. This implies the *collective security approach* to peaceful change.

Basically the CSCE is bound to the concept of non-war change and shares much of the same philosophical background. Changes are needed essentially for avoiding war, but the possible areas of application can be seen in a broader perspective. The principal distinction between the non-war concept and the collective security concept is that the latter applies methods of peaceful change in modifying the status quo while the narrow definition accepts changes only within the status quo.

In the CSCE, transformation through collective security is close to the Axelrodian concept of producing collaboration. Peaceful change would mean that the experiences of the past and future expectations strengthen the subjective elements of security. Peaceful transformation in Europe is thus promoted by measures showing that cooperation pays and that expectations concerning the future of the European order could be more beneficial for the parties through collaboration. This can be done, theory implies, without touching the premises of the existing order.

One could also evaluate the CSCE by noting the distinction between the *individualistic and collective security concepts:* the former is based on the individual actions of each state for its own security, while the latter emphasizes that national security problems could best be settled on a collective basis. The individualistic security approach departs from the anarchy analogy and ends up with the insecurity of rivalry and competitition. The collective security approach again points to the ideas of common security interests and also to the interdependence of states in national security matters. In other words, instead of *objective* security measures (i.e., arms) *subjective* elements (i.e., the sense of security) are stressed. If taken as a totality, the CSCE strengthens the subjective elements.

4.4. How to Negotiate Change through Cooperation

The basic argument of this chapter has been that the CSCE is an extremely complicated and multidimensional process, which in many ways runs against conventional theoretical assumptions. I have argued that the most fundamental dimension is the tension between the security order and the aims to foster a collaborative order. In evaluating the CSCE from the point of view of cooperation, a similar tension emerges between the cooperation-under-anarchy approach and the functionalist approach. An additional problem is that the two orders should somehow be kept together.

A further argument was made, according to which cooperation is a matter of negotiation: one has to exclude a situation where collaboration would be enforced and where European states were ready to seek collaborative efforts from premises other than those of their free will. Conditions and needs actually push them toward cooperation, but basically for their national interests. This does not exclude the possibility that national interests and those of the whole group of 35 counries may coincide; in fact the Grotian doctrine supposes this to be the case.

The problem of applying bargaining theories to the CSCE seems to be, therefore, that individual preferences of states do not simply articulate themselves in the process. The CSCE is not a bargaining process in the normal meaning of the concept. I believe that the multidimensionality, the cross-cutting loyalties of the participants and the diversity of their interests shape the process in a way that does not easily fit into theories.

The CSCE belongs to the category of "nonconvergence" negotiations. This definition is given by Ronald Barston (1983). He argues that negotiations in the form of complex multilateral diplomacy are distinguished by innovative objectives and considerable structural uncertainty over the form that possible outcomes might take. He also refers to the flexibility in coping with structural complexities as well as to the innovative negotiating structures. Barston further argues that multilateral diplomacy is both disjointed and fragmented, but is also innovative and a learning process. All of these aspects of multilateral diplomacy describe the CSCE as a negotiation process.

Perhaps the most distinctive feature of the CSCE is that decisions are made on a consensual basis. Decision-making under the consensus rule is an essential factor shaping the negotiation procedures. J. Sizoor and R. Jurrjens (1984) argue that the consensus method helps to minimize the negative elements of other available decision-making procedures: the requirement of unanimity, the principle of majority rule and the special rights accorded the great powers in allowing them the right of veto. Maintaining the consensus rule is essential also for the future of the CSCE.

In analyzing the possibilities of collaboration in the framework of the cooperation-under-anarchy approach, one is naturally tempted to propose situation-specific theories (Jönsson, 1978). They would allow negotiating separately on a number of issues and would allow the formation of coalitions. In the CSCE the problem is, however, that the external conditions, such as great power relations or membership in military alliances, determine the framework of negotiations. No matter how specific the issue, in a game-related situation one cannot disengage it from the overall framework. Terrence Hopman (1978) has also pointed to the problem of asymmetrical power capabilities of the participants.

No matter how big the problems of the game theoretical approach to the CSCE negotiations are, it is obvious that the PD-type of framework will be in the forefront of studies of collaboration there. This is not only due to recent interest in the cooperation-under-anarchy approach, but also because the CSCE is basically understood as a game-related process. This image is strengthened by a number of studies of the early days of the process, in particular of the pre-Helsinki phase. Undoubtedly the phase of drafting the Final Act was a game to a great extent. But one is tempted to argue that its nature has changed since those days.

An important factor in shaping the CSCE process has been its institutionalization. It does not have permanent institutions as such, but it has become an institution in the relations between European states. Its establishment may have defied the theories, but it is after all a permanent aspect of European political reality. For some actors it has been of greatest value. The European Community, for instance, established and formalized its political cooperation procedure during the process. The Community spoke with one voice for the first time in the CSCE process. For smaller countries, the N+N in particular, the system has been valuable as well. The post-war alliance system in Europe offered very few possibilities for them to make their views known in Europe.

This all suggests that explaining negotiations for collaboration should take into account the institutionalization of the CSCE. When evaluating the dimensions of the institutionalized approach to negotiations, Knut Midgaard (1983) points in particular to the relevance of such an approach to cooperative negotiations. He argues that the content of institutionalized negotiations is characterized by four dimensions: agreement on purpose; on the set of parties; on the time, place, and context; and on different categories of rules.

Promoting collaboration in the CSCE through negotiations should rely on institutionalization. The CSCE actually meets most of the criteria that Midgaard proposes. The Final Act sets the purposes of negotiations quite accurately. Also the set of parties is accepted and so are most of the criteria concerning the time and place of negotiations. The problem of institutionalized negotiations is that the set of rules is not coherent enough. In other words, the CSCE needs more emphasis on the principles for the conduct of its work. Among these are principles on how the two basic dimensions of the process — the competitive and collaborative — can be interconnected.

References

Antola, E. (1985), Security and Cooperation in the CSCE, *Yearbook of Finnish Foreign Policy*. pp. 5-12.

Antola, E. (1986), Order and Change in the CSCE, *Österreichische Zeitschrift für Politikwissenschaft*, 4/86, pp. 271-282.

Axelrod, Robert (1984), *The Evolution of Cooperation*. New York, p. 3.

Axelrod, Robert and Keohane, Robert (1986), Achieving Cooperation under Anarchy: *Strategies and Institutions*, in: Oye, Kenneth A. (ed.), *Cooperation under Anarchy*. Princeton, p. 231.

Barston, Ronald P. (1983), International Negotiation: The Development of Central Concepts, *European Journal of Political Research*, vol. ll, p. 133.

Gilpin, Robert (1981), *War and Change in World Politics*, Cambridge, MA, pp. 20-33.

Hertz, John (1950), Idealist Internationalism and the Security Dilemma, *World Politics*, vol. 2, p. 157.

Holsti, K.J. (1982), Bargaining Theory and Diplomatic Reality: The CSCE Negotiations, *Review of International Studies*, vol. 8, p. 162.

Hopman, P. Terrence (1978), Asymmetrical Bargaining in the Conference on Security and Cooperation in Europe, *International Organization*, vol. 32, pp. 141-177.

Jervis, Robert (1982), Security Regimes, *International Organization*, 2, p. 357.

Jönsson, Christer (1978), Situation-Specific versus Actor-Specific Approaches to International Bargaining, *Political Research*, vol. 6, pp. 381-398.

Keohane, Robert (1986), Reciprocity in International Relations, *International Organization*, vol. 1, p. 6.

Kissinger, H. (1964), The Congress of Vienna, Stoessinger, John G. and Westin, Alan F. (eds.), in: *Power and Order: Six Cases in World Politics*, New York, p. 27.

Midgaard, Knut (1983), Rules and Strategy in Negotiations: Notes on an Institutionalist and Intentionalist Approach, *European Journal of Political Research*, vol. 11.

Mitrany, David A. (1944), *The Road to Security*, London, p. 14.

Mitrany, David A. (1946), *A Working Peace System: An Argument for the Functional Development of International Organizations*, London.

Sizoor, T. and Jurrjens, R. (1984), *CSCE Decision-making: The Madrid Experience*, The Hague, p. 42.

CHAPTER 5

Developing a Global Negotiating Machinery

Guennadi K. Yefimov

USSR Ministry of Foreign Affairs
Moscow
USSR

5.1. Introduction

The recent sharp increase in the number of international problems on which states have to negotiate and in the volume of the related paperwork has markedly enhanced the role of diplomacy and the importance of negotiations as an instrument of national foreign policy.

Stepped-up multilateral cooperation and more productive multilateral ties and contacts are especially required in such areas as maintaining and strengthening peace and security, curbing the arms race, developing economic relations, ensuring economic growth in developing countries, solving the energy and food problems, preserving the environment, and the use of oceans and outer space.

Connected with this is the question of whether the international community can build interstate relations on the basis of a new political thinking without relying on nuclear arms, and if nuclear disarmament is feasible.

These issues are being debated by public figures, politicians and diplomats who seek to establish facts, identify positions, find mutually acceptable solutions and reach agreements. The debate bears directly on whether the East and the West can define some common philosophical ground on which to build a safer and better world. Without clarifying further the issues and actors, without the search for common approaches or at least points of contact, there can be no mutual understanding or confidence, nor genuine agreements in vital areas.

Since the existence of different sovereign states is an objective reality of our age, mankind can collectively solve global problems only on the basis of the principle of peaceful coexistence, through joint and concerted actions and decisions. For example, to ensure a uniform approach of states that are so different in terms of their sociopolitical systems and the level of economic development, to the rational use of the economic potential of the oceans, the need was recognized for devising an international legal order that would govern the activities of all states without exception in the use of the world's marine environment and resources.

The Soviet Union has consistently and actively advocated international negotiations and consultations, on both a periodic and a permanent basis.

Along with the development of interstate bilateral cooperation, the increasing number and importance of multilateral relations and contacts have made it necessary for the world community to establish a global system of permanently functioning negotiating mechanisms. It is our view that international organizations — above all, the United Nations as well as UN-sponsored international conferences and other international fora — could serve as a foundation for such a global system of multilateral cooperation designed to govern interstate relations and to work out mutually acceptable solutions.

5.2. Types of International Fora

Depending on the composition of participants, international fora are generally divided into two categories: intergovernmental and non-governmental. In terms of their composition, they are subdivided into universal fora in which any state can participate; regional fora attended by states belonging to a specific geographic region, and fora comprising a given number of concerned or involved parties.

In terms of their status, there may be permanent international organizations, organizations that meet periodically within previously set dates to discuss a specific range of issues, and special or *ad hoc* fora convened to consider a particular topic.

Depending on their goals, international multilateral fora can be divided into peace negotiations or conferences, political conferences or organizations, and those dealing with economy, international law, and other special subjects. Also an international forum can simultaneously deal with several topics.

Even if they may differ in terms of their specific objectives, international multilateral fora are basically designed (a) to negotiate and adopt international agreements or charters of intergovernmental organizations — for instance, the 1945 San Francisco Conference, which adopted the UN Charter, and the 1968-1969 UN Conference on the Law of Treaties, which adopted the text of the Vienna Convention on the Law of Treaties; (b) to consider international problems and to draft resolutions, joint statements or other international documents — for instance, sessions of the UN General Assembly and other international organizations, the 1968 Teheran Conference and others; (c) to exchange views on specific issues — for instance, the 1963 UN Conference on the Application of Science and Technology for the Benefit of Less Developed Areas, held in Geneva.

5.3. Work of International Fora

Delegations representing at international fora the governments of their countries usually seek two objectives: reaching an agreement and taking the fullest possible account of their country's interests and foreign policy stance in such an agreement. It is not difficult to see that the two objectives are interdependent. Indeed, a state has no interest in drafting an international law or rule unless its provisions take into account that country's interests.

Early in the process of drafting an international forum's rules of procedure, the participating countries set out to work to achieve these twin objectives. Although the process may start prior to the commencement of an international forum, usually it takes place in the course of the forum's work. Since the participating states now attach an ever growing importance to matters of procedure, their discussion takes up all or most of the time in the work of preparatory organs (for instance, the 1973 organizational session of the Third Conference on the Law of the Sea and the 1973 multilateral consultations in Helsinki).

The drafting of the rules of procedure and work preceding the decision to convene an international forum comprise two stages: (1) reaching agreement among the participants on the provisions to be included in the rules of procedure and (2) their acceptance as binding on all the participants. The second stage may coincide with the completion of the first stage, which, as stated above, may commence prior to the official opening of negotiations or a conference.

Once the rules of procedure have been adopted, the participants begin drafting work based on those rules. The process of drafting may include consideration of several texts followed by putting together a draft that reflects in one way or another some of the wordings proposed earlier by individual participants. This new draft is taken as a basis for subsequent drafting work. In those cases when there is a single draft of an international legal document prepared by the International Law Commission (ILC) or by a legal body of another international intergovernmenral organization, the process of elaborating the final text on its basis consists in discussing various amendments and proposals. The final text of the document reflects in one degree or another the amendments and proposals adopted.

The essence of this process consists in confronting and conforming those aspects of the states' foreign policy positions that have a direct bearing on the text of the document — above all, the different legal positions of states that are relevant to the text of the document. It should be stressed that various states' positions regarding the text of what will become an international legal document and the content and mandatory character of the rules of procedure for that matter will require compromise and adjustment during the process of negotiation.

These negotiations include all the discussions and contacts aimed at bringing together the diverse and diverging positions of states and at achieving the common goals of an international forum. This broad interpretation of negotiations is deliberately given in order to cover all types of contacts among delegations. Discussion of just a single paragraph of a resolution also constitutes negotiations. In fact, at many intergovernmental fora the purely informative negotiations, private meetings and informal meetings between delegates that often take place outside the venue of the forum itself represent its most important part.

In the framework of contemporary international fora, decisions are made through procedures and negotiations that are, as a rule, open only at the opening and final stages.

At different intergovernmental fora, one can often witness processes that may first seem as running counter to the main goal of the negotiations, i.e., instead of working toward an agreement, the participants try to set up separate groups. The creation of such groups can, in its turn, lead to conflicts between different groupings with all the characteristics of a "win or lose" situation.

In view of the fact that, as a rule, the foreign policy positions of states differ in varying degrees, bridging the differences and elaborating a joint text become possible through mutual concessions. An agreement that is achievable through mutual concessions represents a compromise embodied in the text.

Thus, the process of conforming the positions of states at international negotiations and conferences means both confrontation and cooperation among states. In the course of such confrontation states, as is known, create groups. Group affiliation of states is based on similarities in their foreign policy positions and, consequently, in their international legal positions. However, states can achieve their goals and a conference can be successful only in those cases where, in the process of conforming states' positions, their cooperation outweighs confrontation, and not only in relations among states belonging to one and the same group, but also among states belonging to different groups.

It should be kept in mind that, in multilateral negotiation and conferences, agreements in most case are negotiated by states at two levels. One involves the alignment of positions between states that differ only marginally. The other involves the narrowing of differences between groups, which actually means elaborating decisions of negotiations or conferences. In other words, agreements among states participating in negotiation or conferences are not necessarily negotiated directly through their bilateral contacts. They can go by way of coordinating group positions, i.e., developing the collective will by groups of states in a given conference or negotiation.

Admittedly, given the largely different positions, aspirations and foreign policy objectives of states participating in international negotiations and the realities of international politics, a state's ability to conduct multilateral negotiations in a business-like manner and contribute to their success is now among the most powerful indicators of the maturity of its foreign policy and its dedication to the peaceful resolution of disputes and differences.

Analysis of multilateral conferences and negotiations also requires a comprehensive approach — they should be analyzed in close relationship to the practice of bilateral negotiations and conferences, for, in the final analysis, the success of multilateral fora hinges on bilateral agreements, on their status and level. It is basically incorrect to prioritize international fora and oppose multilateral diplomacy to "traditional" bilateral exchanges between states. If one were to compare multilateral intergovernmental negotiations and conferences with corresponding bilateral talks and meetings, one would not fail to see their basic commonality. In legal terms, multilateral negotiations and conferences are of the same nature as bilateral ones — cooperation and interaction of states. In political terms, they have in common the main objectives of communication. In diplomatic terms, many of their methods are similar. At the same time, one should also take into account the specific features of international negotiations, conferences and organizations, which constitute a relatively separate branch of international law and require appropriate classification and codification.

5.4. Rules of Procedure of International Fora

In context, the administrative and technical structure and functioning of multilateral fora merit special study. The use by participating states of various rules governing the organization, procedures and specific methods of diplomatic work, i.e., special instruments distinguishing multilateral negotiations from bilateral ones, affects in no small degree both the proceedings of international meetings and their results.

Knowledge of the practices of organizing and holding international fora is essential to acquire a better understanding of the essence of negotiations and to turn international fora into effective instruments of cooperation for enhancing peace and security of nations.

The rules of procedure of the United Nations General Assembly, influenced by the rules of procedure not only of the League of Nations but also of other intergovernmental organizations and conferences, are regarded as a major source of ideas and specific methods of settling problems in formulating the rules of procedure of intergovernmental conferences, organizations and other multilateral fora of today.

It would be incorrect, however, to assume that conferences held under the auspices of the United Nations use the same rules of procedure as the UN General Assembly. Such conferences adopt their own rules of procedure, elaborated as they are on the basis of the rules of procedure of the General Assembly.

It is true that the rules of procedure of the General Assembly are most widely used in developing procedural provisions for conferences convened by the United Nations, whereas other conferences normally use them only in cases where the rules of procedure of a conference do not provide for a particular situation but do provide for such a possibility. For example, the rules of procedure of the Paris Peace Conference of 1946 specified that on all procedural matters that were not provided for by those rules of procedure, the Conference and the Commissions would be guided, where appropriate, by the principles of the internal regulations of the UN General Assembly.

Despite the fact that rules of procedure and their numerous specific norms had been known long before the League of Nations was founded, it would be wrong not to take into account the existence of fundamental differences between the rules of procedure of intergovernmental organizations and the rules of procedure of intergovernmental conferences. Of no small importance here is the fact that major differences between the rules of procedure for international organizations and international conferences have existed and continue to exist, because some of them are predicated on differences in the very forms of international contacts while others either have just appeared or are on their way out.

Thus, in analyzing the major differences between them, it is necessary to proceed from the differences between intergovernmental conferences and intergovernmental organizations. Above all, account should be taken of the fact that while intergovernmental conferences have a relatively short duration, intergovernmental organizations operate on a standing and long-term basis. Virtually all intergovernmental organizations tend to expand their terms of reference, eventually dealing with questions which, while related to problems for whose solution they were specifically established and which are reflected in their charters, are nonetheless either different from them or of a kind not envisaged at the time the organizations were set up.

As noted above, the main reference point is the rules of procedure of the UN General Assembly. Even the original draft of its rules of procedure contained more than 100 rules. As of now, they contain 164 rules, divided into 18 sections and 5 annexes. The rules of procedure of the UN General Assembly not only regulate the activities of the most representative body of that universal organization but also, *mutatis mutandis*, have served and continue to serve as a basis for drafting rules of procedure for other intergovernmental organizations as well as rules of procedure for intergovernmental conferences.

As a single and coherent normative act, rules of procedure are usually designed to regulate the activities of an international forum, and to achieve its objectives of enhancing the efficiency of its proceedings. To achieve this dual purpose, rules of procedure fulfill both stabilizing and creative functions. On the one hand, they formalize the already existing international procedural relations while, on the other, they serve to change or restructure them in an orderly and agreed manner. These two functions are interdependent and parallel.

When states come to agreement to establish new procedural relations within the framework of an international forum, they incorporate such agreement into rules of procedure. For example, the Third UN Conference on the Law of the Sea approved a mixed system of making decisions by a majority of votes together with a principle of dealing with law of the sea questions "in a package", that is, as a single set.

The functions of rules of procedure are the decisive factor in determining their structure; since the structure of the rules of procedure for United Nations conferences is the most stable one, it would be useful to take them as an example. Rules of procedure for these conferences usually consist of ten chapters, which are in turn divided into 61–66 rules. Each of these rules contains one or several legal norms.

The legal norms contained in the rules of procedure basically regulate the following matters:

- Overall organization of the conference:
    • composition of delegations and credentials of representatives
    • establishment of committees
    • official languages
    • open or closed meetings
    • records of the meetings
    • duties of the secretary-general and the secretariat
- General and special rights of the chairman:
    • opening, conduct, suspension and adjournment of meetings
    • maintenance of order at the meetings
    • rulings on points of order and conduct of the proceedings
    • announcing and closing the list of speakers
- Special rights of delegates:
    • the right to make procedural motions
    • the right of reply
    • the right to raise a point of order
- Methods of making motions and decisions:
    • procedure for the consideration of proposals and amendments
    • the right to vote and the form or basis required for making decisions
    • methods of counting votes and conduct of voting
    • rules of voting

In spite of a great diversity of legal norms regulating these matters, all of them can be divided into four basic categories governing the legal status and activities of:

-   Delegations as representatives of their governments
-   Conference officers
-   Conference secretariat and its chief executive
-   Determination of a procedure for the adoption by the conference of decisions on the substance of the issues for which it was convened.

All other norms in one way or another are related (or even subordinated) to the norms falling under these four categories, which regulate the legal status of the three most important components of international fora and determine a mechanism for their functioning as a whole — i.e., the procedure for making substantive decisions. Experience, particularly that of the Conference on Security and Cooperation in Europe and the Third UN Conference on the Law of the Sea, clearly shows the special importance of the norms falling into last category. As for the norms related to those in the four categories, they regulate matters concerning the establishment and functioning of working bodies, types of meeting, working languages, etc.

The processes taking place in the framework of international fora on the basis of the rules of procedure are governed by actions and interactions, above all in the decision-making process, of the three components: delegations of states, top executives officers, and the secretariat and its chief executive.

5.5. Decision-Making Mechanism

To enhance the efficiency of decision-making processes, the provisions governing such processes in detail are included in their rules of procedure. The decision-making mechanism and the form of adopting decisions depend on the purpose of an international forum, relevant provisions of its rules of procedure, and on common practices established in the course of many years.

All specific decision-making procedures can be grouped within three systems — *traditional, consensus,* and *mixed.*

The commonly used *traditional* system of decision-making provides for voting as a basic method of establishing the will of participating states. The *consensus* system provides for the coordination of the participating states' positions without voting and, in the absence of formal objections, to the adoption of decisions as a whole. It means that only such decisions are worked out that could be accepted by all conference participants. However, in some cases conference participants, while accepting on the whole the substance of an agreed decision, specify in the records of the meeting or in a final document the reservations which they believe to be important. The *mixed* system of decision-making is a combination of the consensus and traditional systems. It is based on the desirability of reaching an agreed opinion by all participating states without voting until all possibilities for reaching such an agreed opinion are exhausted.

Within the *traditional* system used today at international fora, decisions are taken by majority vote (simple or qualified). Thus, for the General Assembly to make decisions on major issues, such as recommendations relating to the maintenance of international peace and security, a two-thirds majority of members of the General Assembly present and voting is required. The rules of procedure of the General Assembly stipulate that abstentions are not taken into account, which may result in a situation where the majority abstains while a decision is still taken. At the time of working out the rules of procedure, the Soviet Union objected. However, the majority preferred the traditional understanding that abstentions are not counted. Therefore, in the United Nations decisions are taken by the majority of members present and voting.

The need to elaborate new systems of decision-making was prompted by the changes which took place in the world after World War II and, most of all by those resulting from the unprecedented pace of scientific and technological progress and the emergence of numerous new and independent states — in other words, by the course of major trends in the evolution of modern society. Indeed, on the one hand, the scientific and technological revolution significantly complicated problems in the agenda of various fora of recent and present negotiations. On the other hand, the emergence of newly independent states increased by more than three times the number of states interested in discussing and resolving those problems on a multilateral basis. It is for these reasons that, along with the use of the traditional system, the consensus or mixed systems of decision-making have come into use — for example, at international fora with a large participation and with no basic text available in advance, although the issues on their agenda are highly complicated and important. The consensus or mixed systems of decision-making are also purpose-oriented processes involving the same three stages; however the structure and duration of each individual stage is different. The most time-consuming stage is the preparation of a text mainly within the framework of an international forum.

The consensus system has been successfully used at the Conference on Security and Cooperation in Europe (CSCE). The process of elaborating individual documents in the Final Act is a good example of this system's effective application by an intergovernmental conference, as well as a good indicator of its potential. Consensus also was the working method at the UN Special Sessions on Disarmament. This system is used at the Conference on Disarmament, and at the Vienna negotiations on the reduction on armed forces and armaments in Central Europe, Consensus is used rather widely in certain UN bodies, in particular in the General Assembly, the Security Council, in the Committee on the Peaceful Uses of Outer Space, the Special Committee on the Charter of the United Nations and on the Strengthening of the Role of the Organization, as well as in a number of other bodies.

The use of consensus in solving highly important issues has an overall positive effect. It is called upon to preclude imposing upon states the will of others through a mechanical majority. At the same time, the rule of consensus may lend itself to abuse on the part of those who seek to delay, hold up or block agreement. It is indicative that to thwart any unproductive use of consensus in the future, the participating states of the CSCE agreed that its rules of procedure should be applied in the course of subsequent CSCE meetings. Another negative aspect of the consensus method of adopting decisions is that it fails to take fully into account the positions of all major groups of participating states.

Although the term "consensus" has gained wide currency in the work of international organs and conferences, it is occasionally replaced by such terms as "without voting", "by acclamation", "without discussion", "unanimously", etc. While the meaning of the term "consensus" may frequently appear to be identical to the above notions, each of them has its own implication. For instance, the chairman, vice chairmen, rapporteurs and other officials presiding over international conferences or sessions of international organizations are generally elected by acclamation. Adopting a decision without discussion differs from consensus in that the latter may be preceded by a highly extensive general debate. Also, a consensus decision may be followed by vote-explaining statements.

"Unanimity" and "consensus" are often used interchangeably, although it would appear that while unanimity implies consensus, consensus does not always imply unanimity, as any party to a consensus may abstain, if it is put to a vote. Lawyers and diplomats differ on how to define consensus, and the formulations accepted by various international bodies also differ. An interesting definition of consensus was offered by the UN Economic and Social Council and by the

Population Commission in an annex to the draft rules of procedure of the 1974 World Population Conference. They recommended that the Conference should take decisions by consensus, adding that in accordance with the UN practice this would imply general agreement without voting rather than unanimity. The Special Committee on the Rationalization of the Procedures and Organization of the General Assembly defined consensus as a procedure for making decisions by way of reaching an agreed opinion, provided that such a procedure does not jeopardize the legitimate rights and interests of all sides.

At present, we can mention several provisions contained in the definition of consensus that enjoy some measure of general support — namely, that consensus is a decision, taken without a vote and in the absence of formally submitted objections, which does not cancel the right of any party to state fully its position. As a rule, consensus decisions are made after informal consultation and discussions at plenary sessions have taken place.

5.6. Conclusion

Analyzing the structure and functioning of multilateral fora, as well as their role and importance in international relations and negotiations, is an urgent task that should be addressed, given its theoretical implications and the practical requirements of interstate relations. We feel that, by formalizing and codifying the procedures and the functioning of the United Nations and other international fora, we can make an important contribution to the establishment of a global system of permanent negotiating mechanisms.

CHAPTER 6

International Negotiations: Mechanisms for the Management of Complex Systems

Frances Mautner-Markhof

International Institute for Applied Systems Analysis
Laxenburg
Austria
and
International Atomic Energy Agency
Vienna

Nothing is more important in life than finding the right standpoint for seeing and judging events, and then adhering to it. One point and *only one* yields an integrated view of all phenomena; and only by holding to that point of view can one avoid inconsistency [1].

6.1. Introduction

Negotiations are essential mechanisms of international cooperation to deal with risk, unpredictability, change and instabilities in the complex system of international order. To deal effectively with the international transboundary effects of technological and other risks, appropriate internationally negotiated instruments must generally be in place to provide a basis for further specific legal, technical and other actions to reduce, manage and compensate for the impacts of risk. Examples of international negotiations that lay the foundation for dealing with transboundary risk include the Conventions on Early Notification and Emergency Assistance in the Event of a Nuclear Accident, the Convention on the

Protection of the Ozone Layer, and the Helsinki Convention on the Protection of the Marine Environment of the Baltic Sea Area.

There are many potential and actual advantages in conducting international negotiations within the framework of international organizations or other multilateral mechanisms, provided they function effectively and within the terms of their mandates. In such cases, these organizations and mechanisms are important and unique fora that can contribute to achieving positive negotiations outcomes. One advantage is that they are in place — there is no need to negotiate on where to negotiate nor on the framework and functioning of the forum chosen.

An extremely important factor is the confidence that Member States have developed not only in the international organization or other multilateral mechanism (referred to hereafter simply as international organization), but also in each other's representatives to this international organization, through their frequent contacts within the context of working for and through the organization.

The international organization itself represents a kind of on-going or permanent international negotiation and forum for international cooperation. The positive experiences that its Member States have gained from their dealings with it constitute a formidable reservoir of goodwill that can be brought to bear both in international crises and negotiations.

The existence of an acknowledged professional and impartial international secretariat is the basis for the reputation and confidence that an international organization has and for the possible role it can play in the processes of international negotiations. An efficient, effective secretariat can, and can be asked to, provide impartial expertise and possibly to serve as a neutral third party in some cases. Further, in the implementation of and compliance with agreements, as well as in the maintenance of certain international systems or regimes, international organizations and their secretariats can and do play a unique role [e.g., the IAEA in the nuclear nonproliferation (NPT) regime and the international nuclear safety system, WMO in the international meteorological system, GATT in the international system of trade, IMF in the international finance system, etc.]. Inevitably, they will become important mechanisms in the maintenance and evolution of such systems/regimes and in proposing possible ways and means for dealing with actual or potential instabilities in the relevant international systems.

This leads to another important role or function of international organizations: their capability and potential to identify, develop and propose innovative uses of the processes of negotiations and of information and technology, to increase the flexibility and adaptability of the complex international system(s) of which they are a part. This can include initiatives by the head of the organization, requests by Member States for initiatives by the organization, or both.

There are many important and complex international issues, disputes and crises which cannot, or can no longer, be dealt with or managed on any but an international basis, often only within the framework of an international organization. The reasons for this can be found *inter alia* in the increasing interdependence and globalization affecting issues and national interests, more and more limiting the possibility of resolution or control by an individual country or small groups of countries. This is true for international trade and finance, environmental and health issues as well as for important areas of technology (nuclear energy, aviation) and security.

Owing to the increasing complexity of issues and disputes, and the fast pace of changes affecting both national and international interests, it has become essential for international agreements to contain sufficient flexibility in certain of their provisions to permit dealing with uncertainty and the needs of the parties to adapt to new and changing circumstances. In this sense, international negotiations, agreements and systems/regimes must be not only reactive but also anticipatory. All of this requires thorough information and effective fora for international negotiations.

The essence of achieving such aims, i.e., successful outcomes of international negotiations leading to increased (dynamic) stability in international regimes, is the ability to identify or create a new, optimal balance between (mutually agreed) options and constraints on both the state and systemic levels. This will require understanding *inter alia* how and why constraints/options at the state level can become options/constraints at the international, systemic level, and the effects that result from this. Not all constraints for a state are detrimental to its national interests, (a narrow definition of) sovereignty notwithstanding, nor are any and all options necessarily advantageous, especially when viewed from the broader perspective and higher level of the complex international system.

International organizations thus have a unique role to play and important functions to fill, provided they are, and are seen to be efficient, effective and capable of impartial and innovative support of and involvement in the increasingly complex and important processes of international negotiations.

The negotiations that resulted in the conventions on early notification and on emergency assistance in the event of a nuclear accident provide an effective example of how negotiations can serve to maintain and enhance the dynamic stability of a complex international system — in this case, the international nuclear safety regime — and of the role played by an international organization, the IAEA.

One of the main functions of a complex system of international order, and of the international negotiations through which it is developed and maintained, is to reduce risks, prevent accidents and avoid or manage crises. The impact of accidents such as Challenger, Bhopal, Seveso, Basel and especially Chernobyl and TMI knows no boundaries; they can be considered not only crises but also turning points. They present both unique challenges and opportunities for increasing technological safety and reliability, promoting technological development and application, and reducing and managing environmental impacts — through international cooperation.

The stability of the system also depends on the development, use and control of information and technology. This is because information and technology will provide the regulatory, communication, and adaptive mechanisms that a complex system requires to utilize effectively the input from its environment and to deal with potential perturbations that could lead to instabilities.

Such systems have the capability of dealing with instabilities through re-organization, via innovation, to states associated with higher levels of structural and functional complexity. The key task is, thus, how change in a system can be guided to innovation, which enables the system to evolve to new, dynamically stable states. In an increasingly interdependent world, the main sources of inno-vation that could provide the means for managing complex systems will depend on negotiations, information and technology.

6.2. Negotiation of the Conventions for Early Notification and Emergency Assistance in the Event of a Nuclear Accident

This study, undertaken within the framework of the IIASA Project on the Processes of International Negotiations, involves an analysis of the main processes and impacts of the negotiations to draft the conventions on early notification and emergency assistance in the event of a nuclear accident or radio-logical emergency — specifically, in the event of "a release of radioactive material which occurs or is likely to occur and has resulted or may result in an international transboundary release that could be of radiological safety significance".

The negotiations on the two conventions were held from 21 July to 15 August 1986, under the auspices of the International Atomic Energy Agency (referred to as the Agency or IAEA) in Vienna. Governmental experts from 62 Member States and 10 international organizations participated in these negotia-tions. The fact that these were government experts and not plenipotentiaries presented both a flexibility and a constraint in the negotiations. The final draft conventions were adopted by consensus. They were then forwarded, through the Agency's Board of Governors, to the Special Session of the IAEA General Conference held 24–26 September 1986 in Vienna. The two conventions were adopted by the Special Session on 26 September 1986 and opened for signature that day. The convention on early notification entered into force on 27 October 1986, and the convention on emergency assistance entered into force on 26 February 1987.

The negotiation of two major international conventions within four weeks represents a record in terms of both time and accomplishment. The importance and uniqueness of this exercise, which culminated in the Special Session of the IAEA General Conference, has become apparent and widely commended. Ambassador L.H.B. van Gorkom of the Netherlands, who served as Chairman of the meeting of the governmental experts who negotiated the conventions, called the Special Session "a remarkable and encouraging example of multilateral decision-making on vital urgent issues. It gave proof of the vitality of the system of international cooperation".

6.2.1. The role of the IAEA in the negotiations

Throughout, the role of the IAEA has been singled out as one of the key factors contributing to the success of these negotiations. US Secretary of Energy Herrington, in addressing the General Conference, said of the Agency: "There is no other organization to deal with nuclear safety issues that are global in significance. Had the IAEA not been involved, I doubt that we would have been able to negotiate the proposed new conventions on emergency assistance and early notification as smoothly and rapidly as we did". Other statements gave even more direct expression to this sentiment — stating that without the role played by the Agency, it is doubtful as to when and where these negotiations could have taken place and been completed, and what the outcome would have been.

Many of the governmental experts taking part in the negotiations had already known and worked with each other as part of the Vienna diplomatic community dealing with the Agency, or from previous negotiations or other professional interactions elsewhere. The reputation of these negotiators and a degree of knowledge of and confidence in their negotiating behavior had thus been established to some extent. This permitted the drawing up, informally and in advance, of the procedural arrangements for the meeting so that, when the meeting began, all mechanisms were in place for substantive work to begin on the first day, which it did.

The role of the Chairman, and the Bureau (consisting of the Chairman, three Vice Chairman and senior Agency staff) proved to be critical *inter alia* for monitoring and guiding the negotiations, problem resolution, making course corrections and breaking deadlocks.

The Chairman of the Meeting and the Director of the Agency's Legal Division were key players in dealing with what amounted to the main procedural issue of the negotiations — the conflicting interpretations of the operational meaning of consensus. In the last complex phases of the negotiations, much depended on the legal interpretation and the Chairman's implementation of consensus both as a procedure for drafting the two conventions and for transmitting them to the Board of Governors.

The draft texts of the two agreements were prepared by the Legal Division, an Interdepartmental Group and the Director General of the Agency within weeks and circulated by the Agency to all its Member States for consultations and instructions [2]. It organized and sponsored the meeting, and provided the administrative apparatus to ensure its smooth functioning and the services of its professional staff, which included highly qualified specialists in international law, nuclear safety, radiological protection and other key areas. Agency experts worked continuously to provide assistance and advice to the Chairman and Vice Chairmen and, upon request, to the delegates.

The Agency's role in dealing with information should be mentioned. The accurate and timely transmission of all proposals, drafts, etc., translated when needed, functioned smoothly. All background information needed for the negotiations was available, without information overload. Except in rare cases, no problems arose in the process of information collection, preparation and dissemination. This is not something to be taken for granted — such problems have disrupted the course of other international negotiations. The role of language itself should also be mentioned. The fact that the Chairman or Vice Chairmen could call open-ended or closed meetings on extremely short notice for impromptu off-the-record discussions was greatly facilitated by the knowledge that there would be one working language (English) and no need for translations and interpreters. The absence of this possibility can be and has been used as a bottleneck in other negotiations.

Another important factor contributing to the success of the negotiations was the history of US–Soviet collaboration within both the Agency framework and the nuclear nonproliferation regime. This provided the basis for the coordination and close cooperation that characterized their negotiating positions and even styles during the negotiation of the two conventions.

6.2.2. Negotiations processes and issues

The negotiation of the two conventions proceeded in parallel, and there was constant and important feedback between the two sets of negotiations. The work was intense. There was not only political will but also political pressure and necessity, as well as time urgency and world public opinion. And there were statements of world leaders — at the Tokyo Summit in May 1986, at the conclusion of the European Council in June 1986, and of General Secretary Gorbachev in May 1986 as well as in his letter of June 1986 to the Director General of the IAEA, Dr. Hans Blix [3]. The negotiators had constantly to take account of these factors. The usual groupings of countries were not so apparent as is often the case in large multilateral negotiations exercises. While the spirit of cooperation, and urgency, prevailed and many problems and disputed issues could be resolved, there were nevertheless critical problems and divergence of interests that threatened the success — i.e., the adoption by consensus of the final drafts of the two conventions — of the negotiations until nearly the end.

Throughout the negotiations there was constant interplay and sometimes conflict between national political, economic and security interests, on the one hand, and national and international public and political pressure to conclude the agreements, on the other. This was reflected in the key issues and disputes in the negotiations.

The key issue for the early notification convention was the scope — i.e., whether, in addition to all civilian nuclear facilities, military nuclear facilities, nuclear weapons and nuclear weapon tests should also be covered; also at issue — and still to be resolved — was an unambiguous and agreed definition of the term "radiological safety significance", and whether there should be dual or two separate triggers for early notification in case of a nuclear accident. For the emergency assistance convention, the key problems included emergency (pre-accident) planning, liability, reimbursement of assistance costs, and privileges and immunities. A definitive work on the legal and drafting history of these negotiations has been written by the Legal Advisor of the IAEA [4].

There was a constant tendency to expand the scope of the negotiations to include special issues and interests. In most cases, this increased the difficulties and introduced new obstacles to achieving consensus. In the end, it was generally accepted that the conventions should not be regarded as the end but rather as the beginning of a process to establish on a firmer and more predictable basis the enhanced international nuclear safety regime. Thus, these and other issues flowing from the two conventions have shaped the direction and agenda of subsequent bilateral and multilateral negotiations, as well as the Agency's future program and activities in nuclear safety, nuclear power and technical assistance.

An example that may have been in the minds of the negotiators of the conventions on early notification and emergency assistance is the negotiations that led to the nuclear nonproliferation treaty (NPT). There have been important achievements in nonproliferation through the NPT. However, in the case of this international instrument for the control of nuclear proliferation, what was left out of the nuclear nonproliferation regime (or system) — e.g., Argentina, Brazil, Cuba, India, Israel, Pakistan, South Africa and obligatory full-scope safeguards for nuclear weapons states (NWS) — has become in some key respects as or more important than what was put in. This experience brings out forcefully the need to include in a system those component parts which correspond to the reality of the system's purpose and survival. This placed an additional urgency on the need for the international nuclear safety system to comprise all important parts, and thus reinforced the political will and necessity to conclude meaningful, effective conventions with the widest possible adherence.

6.2.3. Outcomes and impacts

Negotiations, seen as a mechanism for dealing with uncertainty and potential instabilities in a complex system, must aim to be anticipatory rather than solely reactive exercises, for avoiding and reducing as well as for managing crises. This requires an innovative approach, which was certainly present in the negotiations for the two conventions.

The outcomes and impacts of the negotiations fall into two main categories that overlap in many cases: innovative development and use of information and technology; and innovative use of the negotiations process to increase the capability, flexibility and adaptability of the international nuclear safety system — all of which require international cooperation.

In the first category the need was identified for such measures as:

- Improving radiation monitoring systems, especially in developing countries, and the possible integration of such systems
- Establishing an effective international system of information communication and dissemination in the event of a nuclear accident
- A scientific and technical database upon which future nuclear safety improvements — and negotiations — can draw; in particular an international database of background radiation levels at agreed coordinated

geographical areas, for assessing transboundary releases of radiological
safety significance in case of a nuclear accident
- Improving the safety of present-generation reactors and developing safer
  reactors for the longer term
- Improved organizational and other measures for the management of
  nuclear power plants and nuclear accidents
- Harmonizing radiation protection measures, such as intervention levels, on
  the basis of existing international radiation protection standards [5].
- Establishing more objective criteria for early notification, including the
  definition of radiological safety significance
- Strengthening international guidelines for technical safety and personnel
  qualifications for nuclear power plants, which can be adopted by states as
  the basis for their national standards.

Under the second category, the use of international negotiations to introduce innovation that enhances the functioning and development of the system,
some of the most important outcomes and tasks were identified to be:

- The political will to conduct multilateral negotiations dealing with nuclear
  energy and nuclear weapons in a forum devoted to the peaceful uses of
  nuclear energy
- Bilateral and regional agreements for emergency preparedness and planning
  in the event of a nuclear accident
- A mechanism for rapid, effective emergency assistance
- Conventions on nuclear liability and compensation
- Agreements to prohibit attacks on nuclear installations and to deal with
  nuclear terrorism.

The Agency is playing and will play a key or lead role in many of these activities.
    Another main element of the nuclear safety regime is the Convention on
the Physical Protection of Nuclear Materials, which was opened for signature in
March 1980 and entered into force on 8 February 1987. The Agency also played
an important role in the drafting and negotiating of this convention.

6.3. Advantages and Implications of
International Negotiations
within the Agency Framework

The negotiation of these two conventions brought out clearly the advantages and
possibilities of international organizations in general and of the Agency in particular for international negotiations. It became clear almost immediately after the
crisis began that, if the Agency did not exist, it would almost have to be
invented. The fact that it was in place showed the potential of an international
organization to contribute to crisis management. No negotiating forum or

framework had to be negotiated, and states — and the Agency — were able to take advantage of this.

Some of the important questions preceding formal negotiations — prenegotiations — can consume a great deal of time. The fact that the states taking part in the negotiations were also Member States of the IAEA and had confidence in this organization was the basis for giving the Agency the tasks and responsibility for *inter alia* preparing the working documents, devising the informal rules of procedure, proposing the Chairman and his team and generally having the entire machinery for the negotiations in place. Prenegotiations on nonsubstantive issues were thus kept to a minimum.

Some of the other main advantages and consequences of the use of the Agency framework for these negotiations were:

- Inclusiveness as opposed to exclusiveness of the negotiations — that is, the broadest possible participation commensurate with meaningful negotiations and outcomes
- Operational awareness of interdependence and thus of the need for cooperation
- Previous successful experiences (results) in international negotiations (e.g., the NPT regime)
- Expectation of operative principles such as fairness, cooperation, positive sum (versus zero-sum) outcomes, etc.; "justice" could be seen to be done insofar as there was one state one vote, etc.
- Members of the Agency's governing bodies and participants in its program activities represent the real actors and decision-makers in the relevant nuclear-related issues
- Existence of a system of inter- and intragovernmental relations *vis-à-vis* the Agency
- Agency as a forum where negotiators, who had previous interactions with and some measure of confidence in each other, could explore unofficially what was and was not negotiable, define the scope of the negotiation, draw up procedural arrangements, etc.
- Role of an international secretariat in providing neutral or unbiased expertise for the development of working drafts and in serving as a potential bridging, monitoring and guidance mechanism during the negotiations process
- Follow-up by the Agency of the key parts of the agreements, e.g., through studies on international conventions for liability in the case of a nuclear accident, development of an international radiation monitoring system, enhanced international nuclear safety standards, etc.
- Agency itself representing an ongoing institutionalized international negotiation.

The fact that the Agency had a long history and acknowledged expertise and experience in nuclear matters also facilitated dealing with what may be called the *time* element of the negotiations, which consisted of:

- The political, legal and other *historical* aspects of the issues and factors impacting the negotiations
- The *urgency* of concluding these agreements, in light of public and political pressures for action
- The possibility of limiting the *duration* of the negotiations to what turned out to be an extraordinarily short time for concluding two major international conventions. Because of the knowledge that the Agency (and its Member States functioning through it) had of the issues, the parameters of what was acceptable on a given issue could be largely determined in advance of the formal negotiations
- An ability to monitor and assess important *changes* taking place in key factors in the negotiations, such as government positions, successful versus less successful procedures, etc.

6.4. International Negotiations as a Means of Risk Reduction and Crisis Management

The management and endurance of a complex system depends on its capability to deal with the implications and constraints of uncertainty, unpredictability and conflict — i.e., with risks, crises and instabilities.

Whether, how and what crises arise will depend not only on the specific technology involved, but also on the conditions prevailing within the system and on the environment in which the system is embedded. More specifically, there are not only technologically driven risks, but also systemic risks, which are associated with the system's organization, management, cultural environment and perceptions of risk. While the origin of a crisis is system-specific, the outcomes will have more general and widespread impact and relevance. Thus, the crucial importance of developing, through negotiations and other means, adequate mechanisms for maintaining systemic stability in the overall system and in its component parts (also systems).

Here it is necessary to point out a key difference between risks and crises. While risks can and do remain unrealized, crises are an actualization or realization of a specific set/sequence out of many possible sets or paths of risk. Technological and other risks have been identified and analyzed, technological and other measures have been devised, and implemented when feasible, to reduce some risks and their consequences. Risks may be inherent, static and confined to the technological impacts. A risk or risks made real by an event, which can lead to a crisis and instability in the system, is no longer so confined. It is then not only a technological risk, but also a dynamic technological, economic, political and social perturbation in the system. This makes the prevention and management of crises extraordinarily difficult.

So, while risks may be associated with a particular technology and environment, they can be dealt with abstractly, and the question of systemic survival and development also remains abstract. This is not the case for crises, as their development and management depend critically on the specific complex system and on the time in which they occur, and their impact may affect the survival of the system. Politicians, governments, industry and the public react by and large to impending or actual crises, rather than to abstractions concerning probabilities of risk (cf., for example, Chernobyl, TMI, Bhopal, Basel, oil shocks, etc.). However, after the TMI accident, the nuclear industries in a number of countries responded in a constructive and anticipatory (as opposed to reactive) manner to reduce the risks associated with nuclear power plants.

The two conventions and the emerging nuclear safety system are examples of how negotiations, agreements, and international cooperation generally, can be used to reduce risks and manage crises in the nuclear and other technological areas. Thus, negotiations and international organizations can be mechanisms for dealing with the rapidly increasing complexity, uncertainty and uncontrollability associated with technological change and risk, and in particular for

- Dealing with the diffusion and control of the positive/negative impacts of technology
- Devising innovative approaches (political, legal, institutional, technical) for the associated issues and problems.

This will be a continuous process, to keep pace with technological as well as social, political, and economic needs and developments, and will lead eventually to the emergence of complex interdependent systems for the utilization, management and control of technologically driven change.

6.5. Management of a Complex System

A complex system of international order is constantly experiencing perturbations that could lead to actual or potential instabilities or crises. To deal with these, the system will have to evolve to higher levels of organization and complexity, which requires new forms of — and a new balance between — systemic options and constraints.

For a complex system to be dynamically stable, options and constraints must be in some optimal balance with each other. Abrupt changes in either can cause the system to undergo a crisis or instability. These changes are exacerbated by a breakdown in cooperative and an increase in competitive modes of interaction between the system's main component parts and are accompanied by a decrease or loss of control. Cooperation can create possibilities for new options and needs for new constraints, to achieve systemic stability, control and development.

Identifying acceptable options and constraints in international negotiation must take into consideration each side's positions, interests, nonnegotiable areas (and the possibilities of change). Options and constraints are also a function of the negotiating environment, interactions, commitments, strategies, actions and goals — as well as of information, communication, perceptions, persuasion and expectations.

It became clear that the tendency toward instability in the international nuclear safety system, brought on by the Chernobyl accident and crisis, could be mitigated essentially by controlled and agreed changes in the possible options or states available to the system and to the entities (generally sovereign states) it comprises, and/or by changing (and usually increasing) constraints to achieve an appropriate balance with these options. This could only be accomplished through international cooperation and negotiation.

6.6. International Negotiations as Mechanisms for Innovation to Achieve Dynamic Stability in Complex Systems

The negotiations for the two conventions responded to the main threats to systemic stability and to the requirements for increasing the system's capability for development and for dealing with instabilities. They demonstrated and partially filled the need for international negotiations and conventions, and the international system they serve, to address and include preventive and anticipatory as well as reactive and emergency provisions and mechanisms. They basically sought to create, through international cooperation, mechanisms for increased adaptability, control, communication and constraints to guide change and innovation — for the reduction of risks and the prevention or management of crises. These were generally associated with increased constraints on the state level and increased options at the systemic level. Further, what appears to be an option or constraint at the state level may be the opposite at the international or systemic level.

For example, in the negotiations for the early notification convention, the obligation to notify (especially on a nonreciprocal basis) may be considered a constraint at the state level, but on the (higher) level of the international system this represents an increased option or possibility for dealing with crises and instabilities. Seen in this way, it is for a state both an option and a constraint, which ultimately serve its interests. Similarly, the requirement for enhanced, effective transmission of information to develop databases and communication systems for *inter alia* radiation monitoring and control also represents both an option and constraint.

Article 3 of the early notification convention, which enabled the achieving of consensus and certainly enhanced the broad acceptability and durability of the agreement, depended very much on an innovative solution that functions as both an option and a constraint. It increased the scope of events (possibilities) covered by the convention and met the minimum requirements of many countries desiring stricter, broader, full-scope coverage. At the systemic level it thus represents an increased possibility or option for dealing with actual or potential instabilities. For the NWS it represents an option insofar as they have the possibility or freedom, but not the legal obligation, to notify in the event of accidents involving nuclear weapons. Legally, it is an option. Morally and politically, it is closer to a constraint, especially in view of the statements made by the governments of the NWS on their intention to notify in the event of such accidents. Similar considerations apply to key aspects of the emergency assistance convention, especially in the rather hotly debated areas of emergency planning and the financial implications of nuclear liability and emergency assistance.

Thus, many provisions of these agreements represent, in a complex way, both options and constraints at the state or systemic levels, or both. But the main point is that on balance they serve the interests of these states, individually and collectively.

Sovereignty plays a major role in determining which options and constraints can and will be devised and accepted. It is thus one of the key factors determining what is and is not negotiable. Whether and on which issues a state has a static (rigid) or dynamic concept of sovereignty will determine the possibilities of cooperation, compromise and concessions in a negotiation. This concept reflects not only national interests and security, but also has cultural and ideological underpinnings. Sovereignty itself represents both an option and a constraint. Raymond Vernon has noted that, "one of the most important things a state can learn is how to negotiate away part of its sovereignty on favorable terms". And perhaps this sums up one of the main objectives of international negotiations.

A final word about negotiations. As waging war to resolve disputes and conflicts is now seldom a viable option for most states, waging peace requires introducing dynamic stability into a system of international order through the creation, by negotiations and other means, of a new balance between options and constraints that serve the interests of the system and the states it comprises. Thus, if war was once seen as a continuation of politics by other means, negotiations have now become, in many cases, a continuation (replacement) of war by other means. In this respect, international negotiations have become indispensable. The various agreements thereby negotiated not only serve the interests and objectives of the states and system involved, but also can become elements through which cumulative confidence and trust among states may evolve.

Notes

[1]   Von Clausewitz, Carl (1979), *On War*, Princeton University Press, Princeton, NJ, p. 606.

[2]   The draft texts provided the basis for the negotiations, drawing upon two documents, INFCIRCS 310 and 321, prepared by the Agency after the TMI accident and published in 1984 and 1985, respectively. These documents are nonbinding guidelines or recommendations on early notification and emergency assistance. The question may be and has been asked as to why TMI did not result in conventions rather than in guidelines. The answer lies *inter alia* in a lack of sufficient political necessity and will, which may have been associated with the absence of any serious radiological effects for the public and impacts outside of the plant.

[3]   Letter from M. Gorbachev, General Secretary of the Central Committee of the Communist Party of the Soviet Union, to H. Blix, Director General of the IAEA, INFCIRC/334, 20 June 1986.

[4]   Adede, Andronico O. (1987), *The IAEA Notification and Assistance Conventions in Case of a Nuclear Accident: Landmarks in the Multilateral Treaty-Making Process*, Graham and Trotman Ltd, London.
[5]   IAEA (1986), Safety Series No. 81: Derived Intervention Levels for Application in Controlling Radiation Doses to the Public in the Event of a Nuclear Accident or Radiological Emergency; and other NUSS documents.

CHAPTER 7

Experiences of a Negotiator at the Stockholm Conference

Klaus Citron

Ministry of Foreign Affairs
Bonn
Federal Republic of Germany

7.1. Introduction

On September 22, 1986, the 35 states from Europe and North America that had been participating in the Stockholm Conference [Conference on Confidence- and Security-Building Measures and Disarmament in Europe (CDE)] agreed on a substantial document that, for the first time in arms control negotiations, established *inter alia* on-site inspections as a matter of right.

This positive result of long negotiation was welcomed all over Europe and in North America as an important step in the process of the CSCE (Conference on Security and Cooperation in Europe) and as a contribution to the improvement of East–West relations.

7.2. Background of the CDE

The CDE was planned at the CSCE Follow-up Meeting in Madrid, 1980–1983. The 35 participants agreed, after long deliberations, on a precise mandate that set the negotiators the task of negotiating a set of mutually complementary confidence- and security-building measures designed to reduce the risk of military confrontation in Europe. All 35 Foreign Ministers participated at the opening of the Stockholm Conference in January 1984.

It was a welcome occasion for politicians from East and West and the neutral and nonaligned (N+N) countries to meet, in order to improve the cold climate that had developed in Europe after the implementation of the Western "double-track" decision. Ministers encouraged the negotiators to seek new ways to build confidence and security in Europe. It was the start of a long and patient negotiation of representatives of 35 sovereign states. We all knew that we could only succeed by achieving consensus of all of the 35 states, which meant that we had to gain the confidence and understanding of all participants, large and small.

7.3. Procedures and Processes of the Negotiations

Groupings

There were three groupings in Stockholm:

- The 16 countries of NATO, united on many military issues, but often divided on procedural matters and negotiation tactics.
- The seven countries of the Warsaw Pact, which most of the time followed Soviet suggestions, with a specific role for Romania; a group where the voice of the Europeans was sometimes heard in favor of compromise and moderation.
- The nine N+N countries, which do not belong to any alliance, but which have developed in the CSCE a kind of togetherness and a role of intermediary between East and West.

Starting positions

The negotiations opened with the presentation of the starting positions of the participants. It was the task of the negotiators to find out whether the positions were negotiable and whether there was a chance of compromise.

In the beginning the positions of East and West were far apart. The East put the emphasis on so-called political proposals apt to improve the international climate, e.g., a Treaty on the Non-Use of Force or an Agreement on Non-First-Use of Nuclear Weapons. The West stressed more concrete steps in the field of military information, notification and observation, to replace distrust by knowledge and understanding. The N + N were rather close to this Western approach but showed also some understanding for the Non-Use of Force proposal of the Warsaw Pact.

Procedures and tactics

Once the positions of all the participants were known, the task was clear: we had to try to overcome confrontational attitudes and to look for "common ground". This was done in Stockholm through multiple informal contacts among the many delegations. We tried to find out whether there was room for maneuver and flexibility. In the beginning we had to work through the N + N in order to get agreement even on procedural issues, e.g., the creation of working groups.

If the West would make a proposal, the East would say "no", simply because it came from the other side, and vice versa. As a consequence, both groups would try to channel their ideas through some of the N + N heads of delegations. These participants would combine Eastern and Western concepts with their own ideas and present the result to the plenary after having tested them with leading participants.

The Conference slowly moved along. It did so in the overall context of improving East–West relations. This helped, because less time was lost with propaganda speeches and harsh replies. Delegates were able to concentrate their energies on discovering common elements instead of aiming at the opponents' weak spots. Naturally, propaganda was not completely foregone, but it somehow was relegated to a secondary role. For example, tough speeches would be made by the number two or three member of a delegation, thereby indicating that it was a mere performance of duty.

Western delegates tried to convince their Eastern counterparts that it would be in the interest of all participants if the Conference could, first of all, concentrate on concrete measures of military significance. They indicated at the same time that they would be willing to consider as a compromise the reaffirming of the principle of Non-Use of Force as laid down in the Charter of the United Nations.

Stockholm, as other conferences in the field of arms control, proved to be a learning process for all the negotiators and their governments.

Concessions: what, when, how

Everybody slowly realized that results could only be achieved if starting positions were revised and adapted. Tactics played a major role in the consideration of the participants. It was the time for long internal deliberations, particularly in the Western camp.

- Should we adapt our positions?
- Was it too early to do so?
- Had we not learned in previous negotiations that the other side would just take our concessions without giving something in exchange?

-     How should compromises be achieved —
      through deals prepared by the N + N, or
      by unilateral steps to be followed by the other side?

The first outlines of possible adaptations of positions became visible when
the participants agreed at the end of 1984 on a new working structure. This new
structure indicated that the East was willing to pay less attention to those of its
proposals which the West considered "non-starters".

Evolution of working structures

The new working structure provided for five working group sessions per week,
each one being dedicated to one or more specific subjects. This opened the way
to a more sober debate on the real issues of the Conference — namely, the elaboration of CSBMs (Confidence- and Security-Building Measures) of military
relevance. Two additional meetings per week — one of them a plenary — permitted dealing with the subject matter as a whole or to making political statements of a general nature.

This formal conference structure was step by step complemented by informal bodies apt at serving the needs of the negotiators — for example, the so-
called "coffee-groups" where representatives of the various groups would meet
informally to search for solutions.

As the Conference progressed, it became more and more important for the
participants to steer the course of events. Heads of delegations had to keep track
of developments in the various subgroups to be able to discuss with their allies
the substance and the tactics to be used, This became particularly important
when the Conference in 1986 finally started to draft the first texts of a future
final document.

Role of the N + N countries

In accordance with CSCE tradition, the neutral and nonaligned representatives
were asked to act as coordinators of the various drafting groups. It was their
task to act as go-betweens, to encourage compromise, and to explore solutions to
difficult problems.

The progress of the various informal working groups depended partly on
the ability of the coordinator to convince the protagonists to settle on specific
formulas, which he then would register provisionally in his notebook. It was an
interesting experience to observe the negotiators and the coordinators at work.
It proved that, even at the time of superpower confrontation and East–West
conflict, human and intellectual qualities did play a considerable role in facilitating progress.

End game

The greatest part of the concluding document of Stockholm was negotiated during the last five weeks. Many of the elements of this document had been discussed before in the various working groups, but it was only under time pressure that governments were willing to adapt their positions and to accept some demands of other participants. It was indeed this concluding date of September 19, 1986, agreed upon early in 1986, which reminded all the participants that the time for negotiations was limited and the remaining time had to be used.

It is not my intention to describe the substance of the negotiations in detail, but it may be useful to give an example:

The most important element of the results of the Stockholm Conference was indeed negotiated entirely during the last four weeks of the Conference — namely, the agreement of all the participants to accept on-site inspections as a matter of right. The Western nations had asked for such inspections since the beginning of the negotiations, and the N + N had suggested almost the same provision under the term "observation upon request". But the East had considered such inspections unnecessary in the context of CSBMs. Only when this question became the decisive factor of the Conference did the Warsaw Pact countries accept a compromise proposal of the West — namely, the limitation of the number of inspections a country has to accept to three per year, instead of the original demand for an unlimited number of inspections.

There was another interesting experience in Stockholm: The closer we all came to an agreement, the more the negotiations took place among the most interested parties, i.e., the representatives of East and West whose countries would have to implement the bulk of the provisions of the accord. The N + N continued their role of coordinators, but much of the substance of the concluding document was prenegotiated between Western and Eastern representatives.

7.4. Some Conclusions and Lessons

Looking back at the negotiations and trying to draw some lessons for future negotiations, I come to the following conclusions, none of which is surprising:

- A negotiator in international negotiations needs patience. Obstacles that look gigantic at the beginning of a negotiation may become surmountable later.
- Problems cannot be solved simultaneously; they have to be approached one at a time.
- Not everything can be negotiated through "deals". From time to time, a unilateral move may encourage the other side to follow.
- Difficult knots that cannot be "opened" at the negotiating table can sometimes be solved by courageous politicians.

- Polemics do not really help a negotiation, but they cannot always be avoided.
- Public relations efforts can be useful to create public support for a negotiation. Pure propaganda, however, does not pay.
- Sincerity, openness, reliability — all these old-fashioned virtues — seem still to be useful tools in an international negotiation.
- New technologies and theories, though not yet sufficiently recognized by many diplomats, may become useful tools in the future to facilitate understanding and communication between negotiators.

CHAPTER 8

From Negotiations to Consultations

Rolf Kloepzig and Victor A. Richardson

*United Nations Industrial Development Organization**
Vienna

8.1. Introduction

This chapter describes and analyzes two aspects of international industrial cooperation. In the first part and starting with political mandates arising from
UNIDO's Conference in 1975, it traces the perception and implementation of
these mandates against a background of changing international economic relationships and positions taken by various decision-makers as well as the UNIDO
Secretariat. UNIDO's Second General Conference in Lima, 1975, has to be set
within the framework of international economic relationships at that time: the
Sixth and the Seventh Special Sessions of the General Assembly on Development
and International Economic Cooperation, the earlier dismantling of the Bretton
Woods arrangements for fixed exchange rates, the beginning of the turmoil in the
international finance and currency markets, the success of OPEC in increasing
the price of oil, the ongoing North–South dialogue and the concept of global
negotiations, and the aspiration of/request (demand) by the developing countries
for a New International Economic Order. All these factors undoubtedly
influenced the parties involved in UNIDO discussions, conferences, and decisions;
but it is beyond the scope of this chapter to attempt to link these diverse factors
to proceedings within UNIDO other than to note their relevance.

---

*The views and judgements expressed in this paper are those of the authors and do not neces-
sarily reflect those of the Secretariat. Messr. Kloepzig and Richardson are in UNIDO's Department for Industrial Promotion, Consultations and Technology.

In the second part of this chapter, provisions made to facilitate the negotiation process at the enterprise level are described, along with the means of assistance upon which participants can draw when engaged in such negotiations processes. These activities can be viewed as an innovative extension of traditional United Nations technical assistance activities. It should be noted, however, that particularly in 1975 technical assistance to the industrial sector in developing countries was hardly traditional — the UN Secretariat Department responsible for such activities, UNIDO, having been founded only seven years previously. Given the relative youth of assistance to industry in developing countries, whether in the form of technical assistance or industrial promotion, these activities should be regarded as still evolving.

8.2. UNIDO's System of Consultations and the New International Economic Order

UNIDO's System of Consultations received its initial definition and can be said to be the child of the Second General Conference of UNIDO, convened in Lima, Peru, 12–26 March 1975. This Conference adopted the "Lima Declaration and Plan of Action on Industrial Development and Cooperation" [1], which provided a special focus and industrial dimension to resolutions 3201 (S-VI) and 3202 (S-VI) of 1 May 1974 adopted at the Sixth Special Session of the General Assembly on the Declaration and Program of Action on the Establishment of a New International Economic Order. Moreover, the Lima Declaration adopted a number of policy guidelines and quantitative recommendations, including a target whereby the share of developing countries should be increased from the 1974 figure of less than 7% of total world production to at least 25% by the year 2000 [2].

Specifically, the Lima Declaration recommended that a System of Consultations be established between developed and developing countries in the United Nations Industrial Development Organization to facilitate the establishment of a new international economic order and the achievement of the Lima target of 25% [3]. The aims of the Consultations were to facilitate the redeployment of certain productive capacities in developed countries to developing countries, as well as to facilitate the creation of new industrial production facilities in developing countries. In the process of these Consultations, due account would have to be taken of information on the development of supply and demand, the cost and availability of technology and other production factors, the possibilities and conditions of investment, as well as the varied authority of different governments and the dynamics of industrialization [4]. It was on the basis of this mandate that the UNIDO Secretariat was requested to include among its activities a "system of continuing consultations at global, regional and sectoral levels". Moreover, UNIDO should be prepared to serve as a forum for the negotiation of agreements in the field of industry between developed and developing countries and among developing countries themselves at the request of the countries concerned [5]. Consultations should focus in particular on industries processing raw materials exported by developing countries or on industries that are energy-intensive, and should result in concrete proposals for inclusion in the development programs of participating developing countries [6].

The specific mandates related to Consultations and incorporated in the Lima Declaration and Plan of Action appear to have been supported by the international community as a whole. However, while no country voted against or abstained on any of the clauses related to Consultations and negotiations in the Declaration, a few countries expressed reservations or had particular interpretations of some clauses [7]. This was not the case with a number of other clauses contained in the Declaration and Plan of Action, nor with respect to the Declaration and Plan of Action as a whole. In view of the evolution of UNIDO's System of Consultations and indeed of UNIDO, this point requires further elaboration.

On the Declaration and Plan of Action as a whole, one country, the United States of America, voted against, while seven countries abstained [8]. More important perhaps were the individual clauses of the All other countries represented at the Conference voted in favor. Declaration where there were major differences of perception. These clauses could be placed, for the most part, into two categories: support for OPEC-type producer associations and support to a greater or lesser extent, using milder or stronger language, for the United Nations Charter of the Economic Rights and Duties of States involving nationalization and possible expropriation [9]. An example of a clause in the first category is found in the view that developing countries should change their traditional method of negotiation through joint action, strengthening producers' associations already established, encouraging the creation of new commodity associations, making arrangements for consultation and cooperation among various producers' associations, as well as making provision for mutual support as a precaution against any economic or other form of aggression. An example in the second category is the view that every state has the inalienable right to exercise freely its sovereignty and permanent control over its natural resources, both terrestrial and marine, and overall economic activity for the exploitation of these resources in the manner appropriate to its circumstances, including nationalization in accordance with its laws as an expression of this right, and that no state should be subjected to any form of economic, political or other coercion that impedes the full and free exercise of that inalienable right [10].

Perhaps of greater interest and certainly relevant to the North–South dialogue that accompanied the evolution of consultations and negotiations was the acceptance or acquiescence among the Western states of a number of other concepts that found expression in the Lima Declaration. Thus, there was the view that the unrestricted play of market forces was not the most suitable means of promoting industrialization and that the activities of transnational corporations should be subject to regulation and supervision [11]. In similar vein, the view that the policies of developing countries should emphasize the establishment and strengthening of mechanisms and institutions to regulate and supervise foreign investment and promote the transfer of technology was reflected. Moreover, developed countries should adopt policies progressively leading to structural adjustments within the developed countries and redeployment to developing countries. Developed countries should cooperate with the governments of the developing countries so as to ensure that the activities of transnational corporations were in conformity with the economic and social aims of the developing countries [12]. On the issue of cooperation among developing countries, developing countries should conclude long-term agreements on product specialization and correspondingly allocate production or product-sharing through industrial complementary agreements [13]. With respect to cooperation between developing and developed countries, financial resources available in some developing countries could be used for investment in other developing countries through bilateral arrangements, through the creation of a neutral international fund, or both. Urgent consideration should be given to the creation of such a fund, which could be financed by contributions from the developed countries and the developing countries with available resources [14].

8.3. Industrial Restructuring and Redeployment: Consultations and Negotiations

Subsequent to the Lima Conference, the UNIDO Secretariat and the Industrial Development Board implemented the Conference's decisions by instituting the System of Consultations managed by a Secretariat Unit significantly titled "Negotiations Branch" on an "experimental" basis. Between 1977 and 1979, this Negotiations Branch convened six Consultations at the industrial sector level, covering iron and steel, fertilizers, petrochemicals, leather and leather products, vegetable oils and fats, and agricultural machinery.

UNIDO's governing body, the Industrial Development Board, in requesting the Secretariat to convene these Consultations, also decided to monitor this Secretariat activity very closely, given the "experimental" and potentially sensitive status of the activity [15].

On the basis of the experience of these six sectoral Consultations, the Secretariat was able to conclude that the utility of the Consultation activity lay in the fact that it provided a global forum for the assessment of worldwide changes in various industrial sectors, for the identification of industrial sectors and programs in which investment could be promoted, for the consideration of alternative technologies, and for providing a context in which technical assistance could be requested and provided. Moreover, the results of these Consultations gave in 1979 a broad indication of such issues as:

(a)   The developing countries' share of sectoral world production by the year 2000.
(b)   The problems developing countries face in achieving the sectoral goals and a basis for negotiation and cooperation.
(c)   The need to develop improved and longer-term forms of international cooperation. for establishing the production facilities in developing countries in the specific industrial sectors.

(d) The need to improve the terms and conditions of financing required for the establishment of plants and associated infrastructure in developing countries.

(e) The scope for greater cooperation between developing countries themselves.

(f) The establishment of a mechanism to monitor progress in creating new industrial capacity in both developing and developed countries [16].

The Secretariat's conclusion also noted that some of the issues discussed at these Consultations could not be finalized without an element of negotiation between the interested parties [17].

Redeployment and restructuring can be seen to involve decision-making by (a) the entrepreneur (private/public) in the developed country; (b) the company or partner in the developing country; (c) the government of the developed country; and (d) the government of the developing country. The precise role of governments can be expected to vary according to the economic system of a particular developed or developing country and also often with the particular industrial subsector. Developing country governments generally assume a role in defining national development objectives and priorities, in establishing policies to direct and regulate foreign trade and the flow and allocation of domestic and external resources, as well as in defining the forms of international industrial cooperation — private foreign investment, joint ventures, licencing and other forms of agreements, etc. Similarly, governments of developed countries generally assume, at least, the minimum role of determining the framework for productive activity and for its external trade relations. Moreover, by 1987 all were aware that questions related to external trade policy are closely interrelated to government-determined budgetary policy and monetary and exchange rate policy.

By 1979 the UNIDO Secretariat had undertaken surveys and other activities at the enterprise level in a number of developed countries to ascertain entrepreneurs' interests in and motivations for participating in redeployment activities, and to identify various constraints in developed and developing countries that might impede redeployment of industry. One constraint identified was that the small- and medium-sized firms in developed countries frequently lack the staff, experience and international contacts needed for establishing and maintaining a cooperation arrangement with an enterprise in a developing country. There is often a lack of up-to-date information on country-specific and sector-specific facts required for an investment decision. Also, there is often a lack of well-conceived industrial projects and of defined areas of investment priorities in developing countries. Thus, there is an absence of a well-functioning mechanism or process by which priorities of the developing (host) country and the development potential of industry in developed countries can be matched.

Furthermore, companies in developed countries seem to be confronted with uncertainties as to government policies in both developed and developing countries affecting, *inter alia*, the importation of goods and components and the transfer of resources. Uncertainty with regard to regulation and economic policies in developed countries impede the realization of cooperating opportunities: there is fear that an envisaged reimport of the products of redeployed industries may be hindered by the application of tariff and other trade barriers in the developed country or regional grouping in question. Various administrative practices, regulations and policies in some developed and developing countries can impede capital transfers or planned relocation of some of a company's activities to a developing country [18].

At this point, we should consider a number of issues that in 1979 remained outstanding with regard to Consultations and negotiations. The first point relates to the role of governments of developed and developing countries. The second point relates to the issue of negotiations between developed and developing countries and among developing countries themselves. The third point relates to the implementation of conclusions and recommendations of the Consultation process so as to result in concrete proposals for inclusion in the development programs of participating developing countries. It should be emphasized that in the Lima Declaration and Plan of Action on Industrial Development and Cooperation, consultations and negotiations were regarded as instruments that would facilitate redeployment and assist developing countries in attaining a greater share in global industrial production, particularly in those sectors processing raw materials exported by developing countries [19]. However, documents are available that provide fairly clear perception of developed and developing country positions, as well as of the positions, i.e., suggestions, of the UNIDO Secretariat. These issues were considered at UNIDO's Third General Conference, 21 January to 9 February 1980, convened in New Delhi, India.

8.4. Consultations, Negotiations, Redeployment, and Restructuring at the Third General Conference in New Delhi

UNIDO's Third General Conference was a failure. It considered a large number of major issues of relevance to the industrial development of the Third World and international cooperation, but could come to consensus conclusions only on relatively minor matters related to an Industrial Development Decade for Africa, and to Women and Industrialization [20].

It should be noted here that matters related to the System of Consultations, though causing some difficulty among various delegations, did not comprise the major area of disagreement. Major disagreement was to be found on the issue of the external financing of development. Here, the Third World position was formulated in the rather extreme form as the Castro proposal for the transfer of US$300 billion to developing countries during the period 1980–1990 [21]. The OECD countries adopted a position emphasizing the role of foreign direct investment and stable investment conditions, including investment treaties and guarantee schemes [22]. The Secretariat put forward an analysis prophesying the debt crisis of 1982, and proposing a means of avoiding it based on globally applied quasi-Keynesian concepts, which had some similarity to the Brandt Commission's major proposals [23].

A draft text of a compromise overall resolution on industrialization and international cooperation proposed by the Chairman of the Conference was withdrawn because of a lack of a wide support, with the result that the original position paper of the Group of 77 (the developing countries) was put to the vote. The developing countries voted in favor, the OECD countries voted against, and the socialist countries of Eastern Europe voted in favor but with important reservations and interpretations. The report of the Conference also contains the original position papers of the OECD Group of developed countries, as well as that of the socialist countries of Eastern Europe [24]. The net result of this impasse, however, is that we have been provided with documents with a considerable degree of clarity for analysis.

On the question of the role of governments in the Consultation process, the Secretariat had convened Consultations, as a matter of practice, by addressing invitations to governments to nominate the persons who would comprise their representation/delegations. But were these persons "representatives" or "delegates" or merely "interested parties"? Moreover, these groups sat behind their country's flags or nameplates, as a matter of practice. The Secretariat had implicitly recognized the ambiguity with which these groups could be said to represent their countries. Equally, this ambiguity had been implicitly recognized by UNIDO's governing body, the Industrial Development Board, since the reports of Consultations, containing conclusions and recommendations arrived at by consensus, were subject to further review and decision by the Industrial Development Board. Additionally, the "temporary" rules of procedure used in the conduct of Consultations had been the extremely formal rules used by the Industrial Development Board, i.e., the rules of an intergovernmental body. Facilities had been provided by the Secretariat to allow for discussions to take place in plenary meetings with simultaneous interpretation in five languages. The most important documentation, as well as reports of meetings, were normally made available in all the official languages [25].

The position taken by the developing countries at New Delhi with regard to the role of governments was unambiguous. Representation at Consultations of developed countries should be at the official level so that definite commitments could be made. The System of Consultations was seen as a means of promoting redeployment of industry to developing countries and of assisting in the restructuring of world industry. Moreover, UNIDO through the System was called upon to serve as a forum for the negotiation of industrial agreements between developed and developing countries and among developing countries themselves, at the request of the countries concerned, so as to realize the potential of the System for redeployment of industry from developed to developing countries. All Member States are requested to cooperate in implementing the decisions and conclusions of Consultations [26].

The position of the OECD countries was rather different. Both with respect to the international redeployment of industry and to structural adjustment (the code word "restructuring" is not used), as much as possible reliance should be placed on market forces to encourage mobility of labor and capital. The role of governments was to influence indirectly market forces by providing incentives and removing impediments. The System of Consultations had proved to be useful, especially with respect to its information function. Both industry and government from industrialized and developing countries could be usefully served by the System, particularly by bringing together participants (at Consultations) from governments, industry, labor, consumer, and other groups as appropriate from both these groups of countries and providing opportunities for mutual exchanges and understanding. Future development of the System should take place on a pragmatic and voluntary basis, and it was important to preserve the consultative and open character of the System of Consultations. Direct interventionist or regulatory approaches by governments at an international level were not regarded as advisable [27]. With reference to the specific role of UNIDO in this activity, the OECD countries concluded that the promotional activities of UNIDO mainly serve the purpose of establishing contacts between partners in the industrialization process and have contributed to the effectiveness of UNIDO's technical assistance program. The System of Consultations should keep its consultative and nonobligatory character, and its value, as well as the value of its results, should be enhanced [28].

The position of the CMEA countries (the socialist countries of Eastern Europe) was also clearly stated. In this view, with respect to UNIDO activities related to the transfer of industries toward developing countries, UNIDO should act on the principle that this process should endeavor to provide developing countries with diversified industries and an independent national economy, and to strengthen the public sector. They share the expressed views of developing countries with respect to the inconsistency of theories on the economic and industrial growth of developing countries being automatically stimulated by economic progress in the advanced capitalist countries and transmitted through market mechanisms. They warn that if trends observed in 1979 continue, the System of Consultations would run the risk of becoming an advertising agency for private enterprises and of not fulfilling the tasks assigned to it in the Lima Declaration and Plan of Action on Industrial Development and Cooperation. The System must be subject to public control, with the participation of representatives of the State authorities of the participating countries, and not provide in developing countries a springboard for the economic activities of transnational corporations [29].

8.5. Resolution of Issues Relating to the Role of Governments, Negotiations, and Follow-up on Conclusions and Recommendations

One task undertaken by the Industrial Development Board after the failure to achieve a meaningful degree of consensus at the New Delhi Conference was to embark on drawing up formal guidelines to govern the operation of the System of Consultations. In this exercise, the Negotiations Branch, the Secretariat Unit of UNIDO that had been set up in 1976 to operate the System on an "experimental basis", had an operative role to play in facilitating the work of the open-ended working group of the Industrial Development Board. This working group was charged with proposing to the full Industrial Development Board a document that could be supported by consensus by Member States. Significantly, the Secretariat presented the working group with copies of the Lima Declaration and Plan of Action on Industrial Development and Cooperation where references to the System and to negotiations had received consensus, together with the rules of procedure of the Industrial Development Board itself, as well as that of the General Assembly. Some twenty or thirty meetings of this working group — some of which were very informal — were convened, at the end of which a text emerged. It has to be admitted that this text was not linguistically clear, but it was able to overcome the various difficulties to the extent of allowing Consultations to proceed within a generally acceptable framework rather than through an *ad hoc* arrangement with continual risks of disruption.

It must also be mentioned here that from the First Consultation Meeting in 1977, meetings had been characterized by the political caucus and "block positions", with plenary and committee meetings at times running in parallel with caucus meetings of the various political groups — the OECD countries, the CMEA countries, the Group of 77, sometimes indeed with separate African, Asian and Latin American–Caribbean caucuses. This situation tapered off in 1985. These considerations also found reflection in the agreed guidelines that were to emerge from the working group of the Industrial Development Board and that form the legislative basis on that the activities of UNIDO's System of Consultations operate. Selected clauses from these guidelines are quoted below in order to provide a clear reflection of a text that had been negotiated over a period of more than two years.

8.6. The System of Consultations [30]

Part I: Principles, objectives, and characteristics

1. The System of Consultations shall be an instrument through which the United Nations Industrial Development Organization (UNIDO) is to serve as a forum for developed and developing countries in their contacts and consultations directed toward the industrialization of developing countries.

2. The System of Consultations shall relate to cooperation between developed and developing countries and among developing countries themsevles.

3. The System of Consultations would also permit negotiations among interested parties at their request, at the same time as or after consultations.

4. The System of Consultations, as an important and established activity of UNIDO, is a valuable framework for identifying problems associated with the industrialization of developing countries, for considering ways and means to accelerate their industrialization, and for contributing to closer

industrial cooperation among member countries, in accordance with the
Lima Declaration and Plan of Action.

5.   The System of Consultations shall seek action-oriented measures toward
increasing the share of developing countries in world industrial production
and creating new industrial facilities in developing countries contributing to
the establishment of a New International Economic Order. To that end,
the problems associated with the industrialization of developing countries
shall be considered on a continuing basis from a policy, economic, financial,
social and technical point of view.

....

7.   The formulation of solutions to the problems addressed in the process of
consultations shall take account of the experience in industrial development
of countries with different social and economic systems.

8.   The Board shall consider the reports of the Consultation Meetings and the
conclusions and recommendations contained therein, as well as decide and
provide guidance on appropriate follow-up action.

....

10. All levels of Consultation Meetings shall be open to participants from all
member countries.

....

14. Consultations at the *sectoral level* may cover in particular:
(a) Changing patterns in the sector.
(b) The ways and means through which a substantial and effective contribution can be made to the industrialization of developing countries
and to the achievement of the objectives and targets set out in the
International Development Strategy for the Third United Nations
Development Decade as well as in the Lima Declaration and Plan of
Action.
(c) Elaboration of recommendations for action at national, regional,
interregional and worldwide levels.

....

20. The topics and sectors in respect of which Consultations are to be held, as
well as the level defined in paragraphs 11 to 14 at which they are to take
place, shall be determined by the Board. The Board shall decide every two
years on the program of Consultations, including preparatory meetings,
taking into account, *inter alia*, the financial implications, for the following
biennium corresponding to a financial period.

21. Each Consultation shall be prepared and the issues to be considered shall
be identified on the basis of:
(a) Studies by the secretariat of UNIDO, and where appropriate, by other
United Nations organs, internatinal organizations, or other relevant
bodies and institution.

(b) Discussions, individually or at appropriate meetings, of these studies and of other documents, among experts selected by the Executive Director, having due regard to equitable geographical distribution, and as appropriate in consultation with the member States concerned.

(c) Informal contacts with bodies and institutions that can effectively contribute to the preparation of the Consultations, and discussions where appropriate with permanent representatives of the member States of UNIDO.

....

23. Participants of each member country should include officials of governments as well as representatives of industry, labor, consumer groups, and others, as deemed appropriate by each Government.

24. International organizations and intergovernmental and nongovernmental organizations having consultative status with UNIDO shall be invited by the Executive Director to participate in the Consultations as observers.

Part II: Rules of procedure

28. Each Consultation Meeting shall elect a Chairman, a rapporteur and up to four Vice Chairmen. Due account shall be taken of the principle of equitable geographical distribution in the election of these officers who shall constitute the Bureau.

....

37. Interpretation shall be provided in all the official languages of the Board as are effectively required by participants in the Consultation. A speaker may use a language other than an official language of the Board, if he provides for interpretation into one of the languages used in the Consultation.

....

41. Substantive proposals and amendments thereto during the discussions may be introduced by any participant or observer, but a decision thereon shall only be taken by the participants.

....

44. During the discussion of any matter, a participant or observer may at any time raise a point of order, which shall be decided immediately by the Chairman and in accordance with these rules. A participant may appeal against the ruling of the Chairman. The appeal shall be immediately referred to the Bureau of the Consultation Meeting for decision. A participant or observer may not, in raising a point of order, speak on the substance of the matter under discussion.

45. All organs of Consultation Meetings shall operate on the basis of consensus
     among participants from each member country as defined by paragraph 23.
     If participants from a member country do not wish to join a consensus, this
     shall be made known through a spokesperson from among their number.
46. Each Consultation Meeting shall formulate a report, which shall include
     conclusions and recommendations agreed upon by consensus and also other
     significant views expressed during the discussions.

                                        ....

48. The adoption of the report shall be by consensus among participants.
49. The report of the Consultation Meeting, and the conclusions and recom-
     mendations contained therein, shall be submitted to the Board for decision
     and guidance on appropriate follow-up action.

     When the text of the guidelines was presented to the Industrial Develop-
ment Board for its adoption, various Member States felt it necessary to take formal positions or to give precision to their positions through the device of an
"explanation of vote" to be recorded verbatim. The CMEA countries were able
to acquiesce in the adoption of the guidelines by abstaining when the whole
document was put to the vote. Before this, the CMEA group forced a vote on
paragraphs 23, 41, 44 and 45 dealing primarily with the role of governments,
participants and observers. Thus, "all conferences and Consultations organized
by UNIDO as an intergovernmental organization should be held at the governmental level....Only representatives of the governments...can and should have
decisive voice in the formulation of orientations and recommendations on the
possibilities and prospects for industrial development in the developing countries..." [31]. Moreover, the spokesman for this group of countries proposed the
deletion from article 41 of the words "any participant" and from article 44 of the
words "or observer", since contradictions were to be found between UNIDO's
status as an intergovernmental international organization and the provision of
article 23 where representatives of private capital are placed on the same footing
as the representatives of the governments of participating states. In particular,
it was felt that the representatives of the transnational corporations should not
enjoy equal rights with representatives of governments in the formulation of
agreements and recommendations [32].
     A number of other spokesmen also recorded reservations without going as
far as taking the issue to a vote. Thus, the delegation of the United States of
America indicated precisely how this delegation interpreted certain articles of the
guidelines. The United States of America did not accept the Lima Declaration
and Plan of Action on Industrial Development and Cooperation as the mandate
for the Consultations and did not view the System as intergovernmental negotiations on redeployment of industry. Instead, there were successive decisions of
the Industrial Development Board, including the rules under discussion and
adopted, which formed the mandate for Consultations. The United States of
America viewed the New International Economic Order as a general, evolving
concept related to the desire of all nations to an expanding world economy. The
United States of America specifically did not accept the New International

Economic Order as defined by General Assembly resolutions 3201 and 3202 of the Sixth Special Session and by the Charter of Economic Rights and Duties of States. On the question of participation and article 23, participants need not include members from *all* the groups enumerated nor members from *any* particular group. It was hoped that Consultations would continue to be characterized by the free exchange of views and practical approach achieved previously [33].

The delegation of Iraq, speaking on behalf of the Group of 77, the developing countries, emphasized the "particular value in these rules to paragraph 3 which envisages the System serving as, *inter alia*, a forum of negotiations; paragraph 8 regarding the intergovernmental follow-up of Consultations, and the Board's role; and to paragraph 23 regarding the governmental nature of participation at Consultation meetings..." [34].

Despite the recorded reservations and specific interpretations of particular articles of the guidelines made by various countries or groups of countries, and which by their very nature remain unresolved, these guidelines have provided to date a workable legislative mandate for UNIDO's System of Consultations.

8.7. The Appraisal of the System in 1982 and Negotiations of Agreements

International secretariats often have to work on the basis of mandates or legislative objectives that are inconsistent, contradictory, or both. In May 1981, the Industrial Development Board decided to request the Secretariat to present an analysis of costs, results and achievements of each Consultation previously held. In fulfilling this request for what amounted to an appraisal, on quasi cost-benefit grounds, of the System of Consultations, and the work through which it was supported, the Secretariat had to define, as best it could, those outcomes of Consultations which could be held to constitute "results and achievements", and in so doing also to indicate those areas in which "results and achievements'" had not been possible [35]. Here the focus is on the issue of negotiations. It should also be recalled at this point that the Secretariat Unit responsible for the System of Consultations was in 1982 known as the "Negotiations Branch".

In meeting the request for an appraisal, the Secretariat noted that the System was designed to bring about a better understanding and closer industrial cooperation between developed and developing countries from which both groups stood to gain. The effectiveness of the System in attaining its objectives depended in part on its ability to identify problems in industrial cooperation that were of strategic importance for the industrialization of developing countries. In the last analysis, the effectiveness of the System depended on the active and constructive participation of the political, economic and social partners in working together on those problems and in elaborating broad, mutually beneficial agreements to facilitate their solution, thereby strengthening world industrial cooperation [36]. The ultimate benefit to be derived from this dialogue by both developed and developing countries depended on the systematic translation of

the opportunities revealed by the Consultation process into implemented industrial projects. In the view of the Secretariat, the Consultation process must be
followed by a negotiations phase, within or outside the System of Consultations,
so that Consultations would result in concrete proposals for inclusion in the
development programs of participating developing countries [37].

In a chapter subtitled "From Consultations toward Negotiations", the
Secretariat concluded, on the need for a negotiations phase to follow Consultations, that the basic conditions required for developing countries to achieve a
25% share in world industrial production appeared to be:

(a)   The recognition by all parties concerned, in both developed and developing
       countries, that there are mutual interests in negotiating indicative sectoral
       agreements so as to support the accelerated industrialization of developing
       countries and to overcome the current world economic crisis.
(b)   The promotion of new dimensions in international industrial cooperation
       corresponding to increasing world interdependence.
(c)   The utilization of the authority available to governments to negotiate
       agreements covering increased production in developing countries.

It was difficult to set sectoral indicative targets based on the aggregate target of 25% within an industrial framework that was continually changing.
Nevertheless, the fact that depressed economies within developed countries
needed to be revitalized might encourage policies that encouraged sales of plants
and equipment from developed countries and in so doing stimulated and
accelerated the industrialization of developing countries. It was recognized by
the Secretariat that sectoral indicative targets were dependent on input–output
relations for each industry, but the Secretariat stressed that such targets were
much more dependent on the political will to implement programs and projects
and in overcoming the obstacles caused by conflicting interests. These targets
would result from consensus, compromises, and from industrial cooperation
arrangements, and would have to move toward a future time horizon that had to
be selected and negotiated [38].

Under the subheading "The types of multilateral agreements that might be
negotiated", the Secretariat was clear with respect to this objective: "To avoid
any misunderstanding, it should be stated unambiguously that UNIDO does not
intend to provide a forum for negotiating industrial agreements at the enterprise
level nor for the negotiation of bilateral industrial agreements which lie purely
within the individual sovereign rights of governments" [39]. UNIDO could serve
as a forum for the discussion and perhaps negotiation of generalized or partial
multilateral agreements on an industrial sector in the following forms:

(a)   Generalized multilateral agreements might cover the distribution of pro-
       duction envisaged in the long term, together with an indication of the
       resulting trade envisaged between developed and developing countries and

of the transfer of resources and technical assistance required. Such a long-term development program for sectoral cooperation would be indicative, but would nevertheless serve as a general framework for the conclusion of bilateral agreements.

(b) Partial multilateral agreements might concern two groups of countries interested in taking concerted action regarding the future development of one or more sectors of industry. For example, it might be possible to envisage the establishment of mini-iron and steel plants in certain countries through such an agreement. The agreement might also take the form, at the request of a developing country, of an integrated program that would involve a group of developed countries interested in coordinating their efforts in order to develop in that developing country one (or a group of) industrial sector(s) or to undertake an important specific activity such as the accelerated training of industrial manpower [40].

In the ensuing debate of this issue in the Industrial Development Board, it was stated that greater emphasis should be given to the elaboration of action-oriented measures and programs designed to increase the share of developing countries in world industrial production. Most sectoral Consultations had reached agreement in principle on certain target levels for output of developing countries, and there was now an interest in negotiating indicative sector agreements which would include measures necessary to achieve these targets. Consultations should be followed by negotiations and the readiness of the Secretariat to provide such a forum at the same time as or after Consultations was appreciated. The process from Consultations to negotiations could not be separated, since one led to the other and should be encouraged.

Other countries, however, were of the view that the Lima target was an illustrative goal and therefore its disaggregation among industrial sectors could not be supported. Moving consultations toward negotiations was unacceptable and could destroy what was a useful program. Attention was drawn to the provision in the rules of procedure that "Consultations would also permit negotiations among interested parties at their request, at the same time...". Therefore, the subject need not be reopened [41].

In providing guidance to the Secretariat, the Industrial Development Board took note of the analysis of the System of Consultations contained in ID/B/284 as well as of consensus conclusions and recommendations of reports of Consultations convened in the previous year. With reference to chapter VI ("From Consultations toward Negotiations") of ID/B/284, the Board recalled the principles, objectives and characteristics of the System of Consultations as established in the rules of procedure under which the System would permit negotiations among interested parties at their request, at the same time as or after Consultations. The Board requested the Secretariat to take into account the views and concerns expressed during its discussions of this subject, particularly those relating to greater focus on practical and well-defined issues directly related to furthering progress in industrialization of developing countries [42].

8.8. From Negotiations to Consultations

On 1 October 1985, the United Nations Industrial Development Organization
acquired the status of a specialized agency of the United Nations family and
became fully responsible to its own Conference and Industrial Development
Board. Prior to that date it had been part of the United Nations Secretariat,
with a Chief Executive responsible to the Secretary-General of the United
Nations. In December 1985, the Secretariat published a leaflet designed to
attract participants to Consultations. In this leaflet "System of Consultations:
A Partnership for Progress through International Industrial Cooperation", the
System is described as an action-oriented forum designed to accelerate the industrialization of developing countries by encouraging the involvement of governments and industry. The System seeks measures to deal with industrialization
problems in a given sector from the policy, economic, financial, social and technical points of view. The objectives of the System are stated to be:

(a)   To assess worldwide changes in industrial sectors.
(b)   To identify industrial sectors and projects in which investment can be pro-
      moted.
(c)   To consider alternative technologies.
(d)   To recommend desirable policy changes at national and enterprise levels.
(e)   To promote direct negotiations among interested parties during, after and
      between Consultations.
(f)   To foster a better understanding of present and future industrial trends in
      terms of production, raw materials, finance, training and energy require-
      ments.
(g)   To create a context in which UNIDO's technical assistance can subse-
      quently be provided.

The reasons for participation are stated to be:

(a)   To obtain an overview of global supply and demand, with forecasts to the
      year 2000.
(b)   To learn of specific country needs in the developing world.
(c)   To appreciate the concrete, industry-specific concerns of developing coun-
      tries.
(d)   To negotiate directly ways to meet identified industrial needs, in a manner
      that is advantageous to all parties.
(e)   To gain an insight into suitable technologies, products and designs.
(f)   To ensure that the realities of the market place are fully considered.
(g)   To make sure that economic factors for investment and technology transfer
      are fully understood.
(h)   To facilitate international cooperation for mutual benefit — both
      North–South and South–South.

(i)   To identify and make initial contact with potential industrial partners.
(j)   To ensure that one is not part of the problem, but part of the solution.

In June 1986, as part of the restructuring of the Secretariat of "UNIDO as a specialized agency", the Organization Unit "Negotiations Branch" responsible for this activity was renamed and its bureaucratic status enhanced when it was officially designated "System of Consultations Division" in the newly created Department for Industrial Promotion, Consultations and Technology.

8.9. UNIDO's Activities in the Field of Technology Acquisition and Negotiation

Under its technology program UNIDO has developed extensive activities with the objective of assisting developing countries to create and to strengthen their capabilities for technology acquisition and negotiation. This has included three main elements: (a) institutional infrastructure and information, (b) training on transfer of technology negotiation, and (c) technological advisory services.

8.9.1. Institutional infrastructure and information

Many developing countries have established in the past regulatory agencies to evaluate and register transfer of technology agreements, and this has resulted in significant improvements in the overall process of technology acquisition and development. Such regulatory agencies provide their governments with information about the nature of technology inflows and supply conditions from different sources and for different sectors. Furthermore, these agencies identify various sectoral needs and coordinate actions with other policy-making institutions in order to stimulate flows of technology to preferred areas, according to the country's priorities. In addition, inputs are provided to national research and development institutions in order to ensure that the operations of such research and development facilities become more directly related to domestic technological needs. Local technological capabilities can be defended and provision made for fair negotiation conditions with directly beneficial effects on the balance of payments, on conditions for the assimilation of technology and on the competitiveness of local industry.

To date, UNIDO has successfully assisted many developing countries in setting up an appropriate legal and institutional infrastructure in relation to transfer of technology promotion and evaluation and has contributed continuously to upgrading the performance of national regulatory agencies. Training of staff on technology acquisition and contract negotiation has been provided, together with the promotion of exchange of experience and data among regulatory agencies on conditions of technology acquisition and policies and the conduct of surveys and studies on international trends in selected sectors.

8.9.2. Training on transfer of technology negotiation

Training activities aimed at improving negotiating skills for the acquisition of technology by public and private enterprises of developing countries were either implemented within training programs for technology transfer regulatory agencies or independently of such programs. The principal objective of these training activities has been to enable developing country enterprises to negotiate technology transfer contracts which, within the framework of a national technology transfer policy, will be fair and equitable. Such training activities have been organized in various forms. Seminars and workshops of an intersectoral nature have been designed to introduce the participants to the intricacies and major pitfalls in technology transfer contract negotiation and have been tailored to the requirements of the different clients.

In parallel with the organization and conduct of seminars and workshops, a substantial effort has been made to translate all the experiences and the materials amassed through the years by UNIDO into a training manual, which is intended to cover the whole range of subjects of which negotiators, decisionmakers and government officials dealing with technology acquisition and negotiation should be made aware. Such subjects include not only those directly related to the evaluation of the agreements, but also those which have an influence on technology options, the behavior of the parties and the results of the negotiation. To meet these objectives, new materials have been prepared on topics such as the role of intellectual property protection in technology transfer, sources of finance for technology transfer, project preparation, technology transfer through joint venture agreements, and the principles and strategies for negotiation. The overall objective is to ensure that training capabilities can be built upon by the countries themselves [43].

8.9.3. Technological advisory services

Together with its activities oriented to the creation and strengthening of institutional infrastructures and human resources in the field of technology acquisition, the technology program of UNIDO has been operating for several years a subprogram called Technology Advisory Services (TAS), aimed at providing rapid, objective, and impartial advice to governments and entrepreneurs of developing countries in negotiating technology acquisition. From its inception, assistance under TAS has included advice on the negotiation of joint ventures, turn-key deliveries, licensing agreements and technical assistance contracts in various fields such as pharmaceuticals, food processing, mining and minerals processing, and the automotive industry.

TAS is a program with proven capabilities in assisting developing countries when these countries face concrete problems related to contract negotiation. An increasing need for this kind of service has been identified not only in relation to major projects but also from small- and medium-scale entrepreneurs who have very limited access to local sources of information and specialized advice when faced with the necessity of dealing successfully with foreign suppliers. Major projects require missions to the field; but in order to expand the scope, flexibility and cost-effectiveness of TAS services, UNIDO provides a desk service to supply advice from the Secretariat based in Vienna on selected topics of negotiation, or to review technology contracts, or to supplement the analytical work carried out by the recipients or by the regulatory authorities for technology transfer in developing countries. These services are based on the work of specialized UNIDO staff as well as outside consultants, and this work is supported by the contributions of the different Units of the Secretariat. Thus, the work of experienced negotiators of technology agreements is combined with that of technical experts in various industrial fields.

A unique advantage of TAS is the possibility of easy access to an invaluable amount of information on the various conditions in contract agreements that can be collected through the Technological Information Exchange System. Governments of all developing countries may request UNIDO 's for TAS services. Public and private corporations in developing countries may also request such services on the condition that their governments endorse such requests. These requests can be presented through local UNDP offices or addressed directly to UNIDO [44]. In principle, all these services provided by the Secretariat should be reimbursed at actual costs.

8.9.4. Program on plant level cooperation for the transfer of technology

Creating mechansims for the transfer of industrial technology and know-how from developed to developing countries has been one of the approaches to upgrading technological capabilities in developing countries. One such approach can be found in the "Plant level cooperation for the transfer of technology to small- and medium-scale enterprises". The objective of this program is to match enterprises from developed and developing countries as cooperating partners and promote technology transfer agreements through the mobilization of the private and public sector (i.e., production enterprises) in the developed countries as sources of technology to partner enterprises in developing countries. This approach to technology transfer relies on treating technology as a marketable commodity and puts great emphasis on the knowledge, perceptions and decisions of individual entrepreneurs as the motive force.

At present the three ongoing projects in the program are all basically identical. Each is funded by an industrialized source country, covers three or four selected developing countries, and concentrates on a particular industrial subsector. One project is funded by Sweden in light engineering and metalworking industries, covering Egypt, Kenya and India; another project is funded by the Netherlands in food processing, covering China, Mexico, Sudan and Thailand; the third project is funded by Italy in engineering industries, covering Cameroon, Colombia, Peru, and Tunisia. The Swedish-funded project is at the most advanced stage and has allowed so far six enterprise-to-enterprise partnerships.

UNIDO's role in executing these projects includes ascertaining the technology requirements of selected enterprises in the participating developing countries; identifying potential partner enterprises in the source country with the requisite technological expertise and interest in engaging in an international transfer agreement; assisting matched potential partners in reaching final agreements based on mutual benefit (this involves drafting agreements, mediating negotiations, etc.); and providing follow-up assistance for adaptation or training to supplement the agreement between partners. In carrying out project activities, UNIDO cooperates with counterpart organizations in each participating country.

Notes

[1]   Lima Declaration and Plan of Action on Industrial Development and Cooperation, PI/38, UNIDO, Vienna, June 1975. Hereafter: Lima Declaration and Plan....
[2]   Ibid., para. 28.
[3]   Ibid., para. 26.
[4]   Ibid., para. 61(d).
[5]   Ibid., para. 66.
[6]   Ibid., para. 61(d).
[7]   United Kingdom of Great Britain and Northern Ireland, United States of America, Norway, Australia, see p. 71, Report of the Second General Conference, UD/CONF.3/31, UNIDO, Vienna, 1975.
[8]   Belgium, Canada, Federal Republic of Germany, Israel, Italy, Japan, United Kingdom of Great Britain and Northern Ireland, see p. 70, Report of the Second General Conference, ibid.
[9]   For voting pattern, see pp. 64–71, Report of the Second General Conference, ibid., where most Member States of the Organization for Econoic Development and Cooperation (the "Western" countries) either voted against or abstained.
[10] See paras. 32 and 47, Lima Declaration and Plan....
[11] See para. 43, Lima Declaration and Plan....
[12] See paras. 58(a), 59(c), 59(h), Lima Declaration and Plan....
[13] See para. 61(i), Lima Declaration and Plan....
[14] See para. 61(h), Lima Declaration and Plan....
[15] Strictly speaking, the Industrial Development Board in the pre-1985 years was an Advisory Board with certain functions delegated to it by the United Nations General Assembly.
[16] See pp. 100–101, Industry 2000 - New Perspectives, ID/237, UNIDO, Vienna, October 1979.
[17] See p. 100, ibid.
[18] See p. 98, Industry 2000 - New Perspectives, ibid.
[19] See para. 61(d), Lima Declaration and Plan....
[20] See pp. 55–56, Report of the Third General Conference of UNIDO, ID/CONF.4/22, UNIDO, Vienna, 11 April 1980.
[21] See pp. 76–77, ID/CONF.4/22, ibid.
[22] See pp. 110–111, ID/CONF.4/22, ibid.
[23] See pp. 22–23, ID/237, op. cit. and for details pp. 5–22, 42–58, Industry 2000 - New Perspectives, collected background papers, UNIDO/IOD/324, 19 December 1979.

[24] See pp. 105–128, statement and position paper by Group B, annex I, Report of the Third General Conference of UNIDO, *ibid.* and pp. 129–139, statement and position paper of Group D, annex II, Report of the Third General Conference of UNIDO, *ibid.*

[25] See the report of the First Consultation Meeting on the Fertilizer Industry, ID/WG.242/8/Rev.1; report of the First Consultation Meeting on the Iron and Steel Industry, ID/WG.243/6/Rev.1; report of the First Consultation Meeting on the Leather and Leather Products Industry, ID/WG.258/9; report of the First Consultation Meeting on the Vegetable Oils and Fats Industry, ID/WG.260/9; report of the Second Consultation Meeting on the Fertilizer Industry, ID/221; report of the Second Consultation Meeting on the Iron and Steel Industry, ID/224.

[26] See pp. 73–74, 85, Report of the Third General Conference of UNIDO, *op. cit.*

[27] See pp. 112–113, Report of the Third General Conference of UNIDO, *op. cit.*

[28] See pp. 119, 126, Report of the Third General Conference of UNIDO, *op. cit.*

[29] See pp. 132, 139, Report of the Third General Conference of UNIDO, *op. cit.*

[30] PI/84, UNIDO, Vienna, 1982.

[31] See p. 21, report of the Permanent Committee on the Work of its Sixteenth Session, ID/B/270, UNIDO, Vienna, 30 November 1981.

[32] See p. 22, ID/B/270, *ibid.*

[33] See pp. 23–24, ID/B/270, *ibid.*

[34] See p. 24, ID/B/270, *ibid.*

[35] See System of Consultations: An Analysis (1976–1981), ID/B/284, UNIDO, Vienna, 1 April 1982.

[36] See para. 5, ID/B/284, *ibid.*

[37] See para. 10, ID/B/284, *ibid.*

[38] See paras. 145–150, ID/B/284, *ibid.*

[39] See para. 154, ID/B/284, *ibid.*

[40] See para. 155, ID/B/284, *ibid.*

[41] See paras. 106–108, Report of the Industrial Development Board on the Work of its Sixteenth Session, ID/B/289, UNIDO, Vienna, 7 June 1982.

[42] See decisions, by consensus, of the Industrial Development Board, especially paras. 115–116, ID/B/289, *ibid.*

[43] UNIDO's training activities in transfer of technology negotiation.

[44] Technological Advisory Services.

PART II

International Trade
Negotiations

CHAPTER 9

Joint Ventures: Joint Interests in East–West Trade?

Urpo Kivikari

Institute of East–West Trade
Turku School of Economics
Finland

9.1. Introduction

Joint ventures located in European CMEA countries with a minority partnership of Western capital have become a particular focal point for discussion, after the Soviet Union in January 1987 adopted a decree allowing joint ventures on its territory.

The 15-year history of joint ventures in the CMEA region cannot exactly be summed up as an unmitigated success story. In a joint enterprise, all kinds of problems due to differences in the economic systems come onto the agenda. The gains for Western capital are often inadequate to overcome all the inconveniences anticipated. From the socialist countries' viewpoint, the joint venture serves a wide range of primary needs in East–West trade.

Only by developing the rules and incentives for joint ventures, in order to achieve a better balance of interests, will this form of cooperation gain ground. Moreover, essential changes in Eastern economic mechanisms are a precondition for developing the joint venture into a significant promoter of East–West trade.

9.2. A Slow Start in the Shadow of Economic System Differences

The adoption of special operational modes in the economic relations between socialist and capitalist countries is not as simple as in trade between capitalist countries. That is why operations of this kind in East–West trade provoke a lot more discussion than their actual significance might seem to warrant. In the last few months attention has especially been drawn to joint ventures, i.e., enterprises owned partly by Western capital although located in the CMEA region [1].

The joint venture is no newcomer to East–West trade. In 1971 Romania and in the following year Hungary were the first CMEA countries to adopt a joint venture law. Later, economic cooperation of this kind was made possible in Bulgaria (1981), Poland (1986) and Czechoslovakia (1986) [2]. The reason for the current increased interest in joint ventures is that the opportunities for such enterprises have been considerably extended in the CMEA region as of 1987. The most remarkable change has been the Soviet Union's adoption of this type of legislation in 1987 as a part of the country's economic and foreign trade reforms and in the wake of declining oil prices.

Fifteen years after the first emergence of such legislation in Hungary, the number of joint enterprises that have started up there is approaching 100. Yet by the end of 1986, the inflow of Western capital amounted to less than 3% of Hungarian imports from the West in that year. As far as other CMEA countries are concerned, a proper objective would actually be to get the first ten joint ventures working well. The explanation of the hitherto modest success of joint ventures lies partly in the sort of friction that has kept East–West trade at a low level on the whole. In addition, a certain asymmetry of interests has to be noted in this field.

Political rivalry and differences in economic systems are the two main factors that have exerted a negative influence on economic relations between the capitalist and socialist states. The impact of these factors has varied from time to time and depends much on which particular trading countries are involved. The form of the foreign trade operation is significant, too. Commodity exports and imports directly reflect prevailing political relations. Where there is political antagonism, commodity trade is easily disturbed by a variety of constraints, such as heavy tariffs and embargo measures. Of course, the removal of trade barriers is complicated by differences in economic systems, too. But these problems are not insurmountable, if political goodwill can produce an effect.

However, the fact undoubtedly is that in the adoption of more developed operations in East–West trade it is the friction caused by different economic systems that tends to grow, while the influence of political rivalry remains more in the background of business (see *Table 9.1*). A joint venture in which various kinds of economic activity are permanently entailed puts capitalist and socialist partners into very close and complicated contacts with each other. *Dissimilarities* in accounting practice, pricing, marketing, risk-taking — i.e., in economic thinking and in the economic mechanism as a whole — are much more real and disturbing in joint ventures than in commodity trade or in some simpler form of industrial cooperation [3]. These are the facts of the matter even though joint

ventures are released from the requirements of central planning and from many
of the regulations applied to domestic state enterprise in socialist countries.

Table 9.1. The impacts of political rivalry and differences in economic systems on various forms of East–West economic activity.

Economic Activity	Relative significance of negative impact of:	
	Political rivalry	Differences in economic systems
Commodity trade	strong	slight
Industrial cooperation	moderate	moderate
Joint ventures	slight	strong

9.3. The Incentives as Seen from the East

If in the past ideological grounds have served to impede the acceptance of
Western economic participation, today ideological principles appear to be of
small significance in comparison with the economic benefits the socialist governments find in joint ventures. The list of favorable features is growing long and
impressive. The order of preference might vary from country to country, but
some substantial motives are of general validity.

That East European countries have been getting deeper into debt since
1970s and that the Soviet Union has been faced with the declining price of oil
since 1985 are factors that have caused a more critical and restrictive policy
toward imports from the West. But these imports are of too great an importance to be diminished without the creation of a compensating mechanism. One
solution is to start producing inside a country's borders the good that were formerly imported. Production that utilizes domestic resources along with Western
resources provides an alternative to hard currency expenditure on the Western
market. When such a *substitution for imports from the West* is realized through
a joint venture, the socialist economy receives permanently, uninterruptedly, and
irrespective of hard currency reserves, high-quality products that might earlier
have been obtainable in smaller quantities, if at all.

The purpose of the joint venture is not only to improve supply on the
domestic market, but also *to develop exports.* Despite lengthy efforts, the value
and structure of exports to the West have not evolved as desired. Since the
bringing about of the necessary changes by one's own efforts takes more time
than is realized, the joint venture form is seen not only as a means of saving hard
currency, but also as a source of earning it.

The success of exports to the West depends not only on the kind of products but also on the ability to sell them. In *marketing* the channels and knowhow of the Western partner may constitute a significant contribution. Once a
common production process is in being, the transfer of Western influence will

take place in other spheres, too. It might promote *management*, since "managers" have not yet fully displaced the "directors" of the command economy in socialist enterprises. *Transfer of technology* will probably more successfully occur in the continuity of the common production, which characterizes a joint venture, than in a situation in which there is only occasional contact. With respect to total *capital inflow*, on the other hand, the direct role of joint ventures has not been very great.

Socialist cuntries, not least the Soviet Union (cf. Andreyev and Šenaev, 1986), have expressed repeatedly their intention of using more developed operations in trade with capitalist countries. In place of commodity trade, forms of industrial cooperation might be introduced, and such an operation could be a basis for joint ventures. This trend might be desirable for many reasons. Presumably one very significant point is that imported goods remain external to domestic production and are not really absorbed into it. After being used, the imported product has no lasting spill-over effects on the economy. In industrial cooperation, and even more in joint ventures, *Western input changes production from inside.* The impact is not restricted to material input, but expands through the production process. "Learning by working together" also has its effect on the whole environment of a joint enterprise.

The significance and influence of joint ventures are not strictly comparable with those of imports from the West. The increasing interest in this sort of operation, which so clearly intensifies growth, is easy to understand. It is highly likely that in many cases joint ventures appear to be a profitable use of socialist resources in the light of opportnity costs.

9.4. Grounds for Western Participation

In socialist countries the pros and cons of joint ventures are judged above all at the macrolevel, owing to the prevailing economic systems and to the great impact these operations have on the economy. In the West the decision to undertake the same joint venture is made on microeconomic grounds by a firm seeking profitability in its business,

Apparently, the main consideration of a Western firm in establishing a common project with a socialist partner is *market access.* A joint venture may be the relevant choice when the firm has to find the best way or at least a feasible one of acquiring, maintaining or increasing its market share in a socialist country. With time, the export of goods may turn out to be inadequate and has to be compensated for by forms of economic cooperation. The joint venture is a parameter of competition among Western companies insofar as it is the means preferred by the socialist country. In the long run it may better serve to establish stable sales in the host country than other forms of trade, and it may ensure third markets in other CMEA countries.

By locating certain activities in a socialist country, Western firms may seek *solutions to some problems of production.* Savings in the costs of the labor force, raw materials, transportation, etc., play a role. Moreover, restrictions and regulations concerning production (e.g., in relation to pollution) in the West also motivate direct investments.

As a permanent partner in joint production the Western firm gets a much better chance to *ensure the intended results* in regard to products, marketing, etc., than in the simpler forms of cooperation. A joint venture is a natural vehicle for the realization of *two-way technology transfer.* In general, techniques applied in production do not properly benefit from the results of expansive research pursued in the socialist countries. The joint venture provides a good vehicle for Western firms and Socialist countries interested in the commercialization of research.

The *status of "insider"* and familiarity with the socialist market also give the Western firm involved in a joint venture a relatively strong competitive position in traditional exports from the West to a socialist country.

9.5. Impediments to Success

The prerequisite for establishing a joint venture is a very simple one. As in any trading business, in this operation, too, mutual benefits have to be deemed adequate by both partners themselves. The advantages accruing to the partner will hardly disturb the realization of the joint venture, although the attempt to restrict and control the partner's gain has been widely harmful in East–West relations (cf. Kivikari and Nurmi, 1986). At the level of the individual enterprise, it is not relevant to counterbalance Eastern and Western gains. The decisive point for the Western partner is whether its expected benefits, usually somewhat difficult to foresee, are sufficient to outweigh the problems and risks arising in this kind of direct investment.

It is not unusual for the partners' *primary motives to contradict one another.* The Western firm may be interested in producing for socialist markets than in locating production in the East to reinforce the firm's competitiveness in the West. The socialist partner might be striving to earn hard currency by new exports rather than saving hard currency by new import-substituting production. When *profit transfer* is dependent on the hard currency earnings of a joint enterprise, there is a certain guarantee for the emergence of a joint interest in marketing to the West.

Because of strict *regulations,* the difficulties of anticipating *costs,* and a fear of *bureaucracy,* many Western firms hesitate to participate in a joint enterprise in a socialist country. The Western partner's equity may not usually exceed 49% of the founding capital. As well as being a significant restraint as such, it is also a symbol of the necessity to adapt to the rules of the alien environment. Apart from labor force costs, the level of cost is not too attractive for a foreign company, despite the domestically low level of costs in socialist countries. Problems of pricing are difficult to solve when putting together Eastern and Western inputs. How would an industrial lot and the infrastructure be evaluated in relation to Western equipment and know-how? Having to deal with unfamiliar institutions of a different economic system brings the Western partner extra expenses. Problems arising from differences in systems may be intensified by the rigid and bureaucratic stand of the authorities.

Participation in a joint venture often means to a Western firm involvement in a *complex pattern of activity*, the results of which may be of minor significance. The one firm alone has to take care of manifold tasks in acquiring equipment, know-how, financing, management, marketing, etc. This implies an immersion in a wide range of complicated problems compared to the modest role which participation in the joint venture might play in the firm's total business volume, and it raises the question of whether the effort is worthwhile.

The joint venture, when not located in a special "economic zone", has to adapt to the situation in the host country and integrate somehow into its economy. Of course, the socialist government creates for joint enterprises a set of rules and a framework primarily from the socialist partner's standpoint. So it is quite natural that, when problems arise, they show their darker side to the West.

Even from the socialist standpoint, all difficulties cannot be resolved in advance by appropriate rules and legislation. It is true that matters of principle induced by the introduction of Western ownership and motivation are to be dealt with by legislation (cf. Voznesenskaja 1986). But it is more a matter of practice to fit together in an operating business relationship the elements coming from a centrally planned economy and from a market economy. At any rate, a joint venture is a halfway arrangement which presents the socialist partner with new behavioral demands.

9.6. Lasting but Limited Support

The motives that speak for the adoption of the joint venture as an instrument for promoting East–West trade are not of a temporary nature. Joint enterprises serve the key interests of socialist countries in improving their ability to absorb Western input into the economy, in developing the structure of commodity exports and in aiding access to Western markets. Naturally, the significance of joint ventures depends on the role economic policy assigns on the whole to the division of labor with the West (cf. Köves, 1985).

From the Western point of view, the East is rarely as attractive an area for the establishment of a subsidiary as is the West or the South. The same holds for commodity exports from the Western countries to Eastern countries, which fluctuate below 5% of the total exports of the Western countries. When the joint venture is compared with other forms of operation in Eastern markets, it turns out to be a viable alternative provided that joint interests are sufficient to overcome diverging ones.

Recent reforms in socialist countries give evidence of an ever greater readiness to accommodate Western interests. Of course, such steps and the corresponding flexible attitudes will further the adoption of this quite new form of economic cooperation. But it can still be argued that long into the future the impediments to market integration will hinder the joint venture from developing into a really significant vanguard of internationalization. Nor is it to be expected that the joint venture alone can solve any of the basic problems that hamper East–West trade.

Notes

[1] Socialist countries own in part or in their entirety enterprises in capitalist countries, too. These firms are engaged mainly in commerce and service activities. They are excluded from review in this paper.

[2] Yugoslavia was the first socialist country to adopt such legislation in 1967. The number of projects started so far is about 250. The German Democratic Republic is at the moment the only European CMEA country that does not allow joint ventures with Western capital.

[3] It can be maintained that it is incorrect to name economic system differences as a source of friction. Actually, the main obstacle is the inability of the present socialist mechanism to get cooperation going between firms: this is true even in intra-CMEA relations (cf. Inotai, 1986).

References

Andreyev, Yu.V. and Šenaev, V.N. (otv. red.) (1986), *SSSR - Zapadnaja Evropa: problemy torgovo-ekonomičeskih otnošenij*, Meždunarodnye Otnošenija, Moskva.

Inotai, A. (ed.) (1986), *The Hungarian Enterprise in the Context of Intra-CMEA Relations*, Hungarian Scientific Council for world Economy, Budapest.

Kivikari, U. and Nurmi, H. (1986), A Game-Theoretic Approach to Political Characteristics of East-West Trade, *Cooperation and Conflict*, 21, 65–78.

Köves, A. (1985), *The CMEA Countries in the World Economy: Turning Inwards or Turning Outwards?* Akadémiai Kiadó, Budapest.

Voznesenskaja, N.N. (1986), *Smeššannye predprijatiija kak forma meždunarodnogo ekonomičeskogo sotrudničestva*, Nauka, Moskva.

CHAPTER 10

Interaction between the Theory and Practice of Trade Negotiations: Experiences and Proposals of a Practitioner

Charalambos Vlachoutsicos

Russian Research Center
Harvard University
Cambridge, Massachusetts
USA

10.1. Introduction

The main objective of the Project on the Processes of International Negotiations (PIN) is to improve the use of research results in international negotiations. Negotiators and policymakers have an increasing need for the theoretical knowledge that can be gained from analysis of negotiation results.

Recognizing that a real gap exists between negotiation theorists and practitioners, the PIN Project brings them together to share their insights. Attempting to understand the dynamics of their relationship is one way to decrease the gap.

10.1.1. Some definitions

Before proceeding, some definitions are needed. In this chapter, by "practitioner" I mean a person whose career lies in negotiating and concluding contracts or agreements of any kind in the international arena.

A "theorist" I define as any professional engaged in study, research, or teaching in the field of negotiation.

"Effective interaction" I define as the complementary working together of practitioners and theorists that results in communication and mutually satisfactory cooperation.

Obviously, there can be no black and white distinction between practitioners and theorists, as an increasing number of theorists are also involved in actual negotiation, and many practitioners find it increasingly helpful to adopt theoretical strategies.

10.1.2. Aims of this chapter

I have tried to organize some of the insights and thoughts gained from my experience in a way that might provide a suitable framework for the development of a logic necessary for both practitioners and theorists of negotiations, in order to conduct this interaction more effectively. It should be noted that the material presented should be considered as work in progress. Therefore, by design, this chapter is empirical and not exhaustive and permits only a general overview.

Drawing on my own experience as a negotiation practitioner interacting with theorists during the last two years at Harvard University, I will try to point out some of the problems we encountered and show how they affected our interaction. I will also try to formulate some rough guidelines for bringing theorists and practitioners of international negotiations closer together.

10.2. Experience

10.2.1. Background as a negotiator

For much of three decades I have been negotiating business in the international market. As manager of my family's company, I began dealing with both market and centrally planned economies. In the subsequent years there is hardly any form of international business transaction I have not negotiated. Since my experience lies mainly in negotiating business transactions, I will limit myself to the area of my specific expertise and leave it to others to decide whether my experiences and suggestions could also be applied to other fields of international negotiation.

10.2.2. Experience in interacting with theorists

In the two years I have spent as a midcareer fellow at Harvard University, I have had extensive opportunity to interact with negotiation theorists.

The genesis of this chapter was my experience with the Negotiation Roundtable, a working seminar of Harvard Business School faculty and students dedicated to learning more about negotiation. As time passed, I became increasingly aware of an attitude on the part of both the theorists and the practitioners that prevented them from seeing what each could gain from the other through their interaction. While they had the benevolent intention to come together, they did precious little to make the best use of all the time and intellectual effort devoted to the process. How often obscure terminology frustrated me, when I was unable to understand the notions and concepts during a discussion! How often mathematical abstractions confused rather than clarified an issue by adding chores instead of offering tools for solution! How often I saw tension build in the theorists from my own derailments of discussion from the track they needed to be on for their kind of thinking! One time at the Negotiation Roundtable this tension reached the point where I felt that the group would do better without my participation, when it thrashed out the theoretical concepts. This reaction is interesting, for during brainstorming and evaluating the results achieved, my contribution was greatly appreciated.

The more I got involved in this interactive process, the more I saw conflicting interests and potential gains in cooperation. The more I experienced these characteristics, the more similar they seemed to the key ingredients of the negotiation process itself! I came to the conclusion that, in order to try to understand and manage the interaction between practitioners and theorists, we must regard it as a negotiating process. Many of the conceptual tools that have been developed for the analysis of the negotiation process can be applied to this interaction.

10.2.3. Incentives for cooperation

Only a few years ago, the last time a practitioner would see his alma mater would be his graduation day. Academic institutions and scholarly works were out of bounds for practitioners, and vice versa. Each of the two sides was perfectly satisfied in doing its own thing in its own world, entirely independent of the other. They lacked no sense of fulfillment from not interacting with each other. During the last few years, however, things have changed.

I have seen an interesting trend develop. On the one hand, academic institutions increasingly take practitioners for certain periods of time and try to use their insights to give new dimensions to the academic environment and to improve the usefulness of their academic work. On the other hand, practitioners, haunted by fears of obsolescence, have begun enriching their midcareer experience by returning to academia. In this environment, both have benefited from sharing their interests.

I have found theorists in the field of negotiation to be increasingly frustrated by the immense discrepancies between the theory and practice of negotiation and especially by the vast complexity of the real negotiating process. I have seen this frustration of theorists grow, rather than diminish, as a result of the theoretical work done in recent years. This work has often been unhelpful in establishing meaningful links between negotiators and theorists. Theorists see the practitioners distancing themselves from a very large part of the theory, since they are unable to incorporate it into their daily routine of negotiation.

Practitioners have a similar frustration. They find that the mathematical expressions with which theorists represent the world of negotiating are too complicated to be of practical use. The complexity of all levels of economic and political life is increasing. High technology and the importance of internal as well as external negotiations between interdependent sides is growing. In a world where the importance of authority relations in organizations is declining and where consensus has to be achieved through negotiation, practitioners face narrower limits to what they can do without the input of theorists. These important changes are making the work of negotiators difficult and generating fears of obsolescence. The days are gone when practitioners could base their negotiations on little else than their own flair and intuition or could do their jobs by across-the-table "fencing".

Now there are incentives for cooperation:

Enhancing reputation with peers

Through my interaction with theorists, I feel that I have gained an edge on my competitors who remain isolated in their own worlds and that I have established a reputation with my peers for sophistication.

Recognition by the prestigious world of academia

My new exposure to academia not only satisfies my scholarly interests, but offers me the chance to gain recognition in the academic world — a status we practitioners so often envy.

Ambition for public service

This exposure gives me the opportunity to contribute the insights I have gained from my experience in negotiations to the advancement of the art and science of negotiation.

10.2.4. Obstacles and hurdles to effective interaction

As compelling as the need for it may be, I have often found interaction between theorists and practitioners obstructed. Both practitioner and theorist bring to their interaction a whole luggage of different understandings. Even if they wanted to reveal them, few can describe these understandings to themselves and still fewer can articulate them to others.

A practitioner's espoused theories are not necessarily equivalent to what he or she actually does. The experience of a practitioner may lie in areas quite different from those a theorist intends to examine. Very often, both people confuse what they absolutely need from the interaction with what they hope it will bring about. Many tend to feel adamant about their insights or their theories and thus become inflexible. Empirical evidence is often fragmented and anecdotal. Fears, suspicion, and hostility may lie barely below the surface, generating a litany of irrational behavior.

Though I have often sensed that a theorist was sincere in his effort to help me, lack of time on his part has not allowed this help to materialize. I have repeatedly experienced theorists becoming very excited about our interaction and getting many ideas from it and really wishing to pursue them in a continued interaction. Because they are so overburdened with their routines and absorbed in other undoubtedly equally exciting endeavors, however, little has resulted from our interaction other than "interesting" dinner and lunch conversations. More important, having focused their creative capacity on their own work, they seem unable to make the necessary intellectual investment in this interaction.

One of the effects of the very great workload of theorists is psychological saturation caused by their immersion in so many stimuli that a stage is reached where, for reasons of pure self-preservation, they cannot absorb anything more which does not fall into the very specific areas of their preoccupation. In any case, this might be one of the reasons they develop self-defenses which do into allow more stimuli to enter their field of perception and be processed. In other words, very often interaction of any depth with practitioners is simply too much for theorists to absorb.

The practitioner is used to a much shorter cycle of reward and punishment from his work. He has had a good or bad negotiating meeting and knows more clearly where he stands because he measures the reaction of the side he negotiates with, or he looks at the partial or total result much more directly.

Theorists, however, are used to waiting a much longer time for positive or negative feedback from their work, especially when it is research, writing a book, or developing a theory. A practitioner experiences considerable frustrations in academic situations from this far longer cycle of feedback. As Donald Schön says, "The process of communication, which is supposed to lead to a fuller grasp of one another's meanings, can only begin with nonunderstanding and nonacceptance".

I have often seen destructive elements spoil the atmosphere, obstruct communication, and make interaction so difficult and unpleasant that motivation dissipates and an impasse develops. In the usual unreflective, interactive setting, the elements of interdependence, on the one hand, and of conflict-producing factors, on the other, create an inescapable tension. Often there is lack of sufficient preparation by both theorist and practitioner. They have no clearly articulated guidelines, and both must feel their way along, buffeted by numerous pressures. The great complexity of this interaction has to be recognized. A few of these hurdles and the pressures that are brought to bear on those involved are rigidity, unrealistic expectations, conscious and unconscious resistance and resentment, suspicion, bias, and memory decay — all impede interaction. So do differences in work rhythm and decision processes, workloads, and priorities. Both practitioners and theorists feel a deterioration of status while they are on each other's turf, and the practitioner has difficulty articulating, absorbing, and generating academic material.

Practitioners often believe that theorists have all the knowledge and that they are in the position to conceptualize all problems or phenomena of the negotiation process clearly and give answers to the practitioners' anguish. Theorists may believe that practitioners have learned so much from experience that they know what is really going on in negotiations and therefore can answer the theorists' questions correctly. Little do they know how often practitioners blunder along or muddle through the problems of their work!

In my experience as a practitioner, I have found that theorists often waste a lot of time talking about things that cannot be put into effect and are completely removed from actual situations. I have sensed that theorists find practitioners much too subjective, narrowly identified with their own experience, and much too involved in the issues to be able to give the kind of objective overview theorists need to translate that experience into their own terms. Although what practitioners have to say may often make interesting dinner conversation, theorists may think very little of it can be of real use to guide their work or to save them from dead-end research.

Undoubtedly, a lot of myth on both sides stands in the way of either side perceiving the other clearly.

Coming from the front line of business negotiations to academia is a cultural shock that can place a great deal of strain on an individual. I went through stages of very intense anguish and insecurity about what value my experience could have for the theorists and about the tremendous lack of academic knowledge on my part. On the other hand, I have often sensed theorists to be insecure about their views on specific matters when compared with mine. Obviously, these feelings tend to build walls and to underline the differences between the two.

10.3. Modes of Interaction

10.3.1. The "give and take" mode

By familiarizing myself with some theoretical concepts, and by trying them out in my business negotiations, I slowly came to realize how great the contributions of academic research can be to the practitioner. It enables the negotiator to place his or her experience in perspective and to see the objectives, strategies, and gains involved in each negotiation. Each case that came to the Negotiation

Roundtable convinced me that the use of theoretical concepts can facilitate actual negotiations. Much of the negotiating process was clarified by concepts like "the sellers' surplus", the BATNA (Best Alternative to a Negotiated Agreement), "zones of agreement", the "negotiation dance", "symmetric strategic situations", "negotiation-efficient frontier", and "value-tree analysis", to mention but a few.

When I went back to Greece in the summer of 1986 and tried to introduce these concepts to some of the executives' negotiations routines, I encountered resistance from our managers. Nevertheless, the executives appreciated these concepts, and I have the impression that, slowly but surely, some of the concepts can become an integrated part of their negotiation planning and implementation.

At the same time, members of the Roundtable have repeatedly told me I have often made contributions by not letting the discussion get side-tracked and by stressing the necessity to narrow it down in order to come up with a concrete result — whether positive or negative.

A year ago in two of our sessions we were discussing the problems of the members of the General Agreement on Tariffs and Trade (GATT) who were organizing for the GATT talks. The issue was how the interests of GATT members influence their decisions about how to structure the talks. I remember that the discussion could not focus. The researchers involved suggested that to simplify the options for structuring the GATT negotiations, we assume only two options — namely, highly structured and highly unstructured GATT talks. Preference for structure or lack of structure, they said, reflected the complexity of internal negotiation in each member country.

As the discussion went on to other topics related to this issue, I became more and more conscious of our having missed a key element which I have so often experienced in my business career as explaining the negotiating behavior of a number of the members, and especially the smaller and weaker members of GATT. From my experience, I knew that the main effort some countries make, especially those which do not have the feeling that they can exert any influence on the direction international trade takes, is to find ways to continue as many tariffs on their imports as possible, while at the same time obtaining as many tariff exemptions for their exports as possible. Rarely have I witnessed more regulation-conscious bureaucrats than the alleged advocates of free trade of GATT. I believe that my intervention helped the theorists arrive at some useful ideas on how members could be helped to formulate their negotiating strategies and tactics in GATT. Then they could move away from the distributive bargaining attitude, so prevalent today, to trying to identify joint gains.

10.3.2. The "joint task" mode

I believe that open-ended interaction between practitioners and theorists on an issue can often become a waste of time for both. My most useful perceptions come from the instances when I felt *effective interaction with theorists took place as a result of joint reflection and action on a concrete common task.* I could give no better example than my experience in a seminar on international trade given at Harvard Law School by a professor of international business law.

As long as the general characteristics of trade law were discussed, my contributions were limited. As soon as we got into the concrete analysis of the implications of each condition of a rather long and involved business contract, however, my input became illuminating, applicable, and thus valuable. In this manner, as a number of the participating students told me, the whole course gained considerably in terms of the educational experience it offered. The key here, I believe, is that a setting had been created where not only was information exchanged, but also practitioner and theorist, drawing freely from their knowledge and experience, could create a far richer perspective than each one of them had before this interaction started,

Another good example for such a creative sharing of experience was the discussion at the Negotiation Roundtable, where members reacted to some of the thoughts I have expressed in this chapter and eventually integrated a number of my ideas into new constructs.

It is when theorists came to realize the importance of inductive rather than deductive reasoning, and when the interactionist approach was toward interpretive analysis based on the experience and perception of the interactors, that unknown aspects of the reality of negotiation evolved. It was during these instances when theory arose from the analysis of actual experiences and from the common emotional involvement rather than from preconceived postulates, that real progress was made. Nevertheless, tension between theorists and practitioners invariably exists. This situation is, however, not necessarily negative. Tension can be used creatively within the interactive process. After all, as happens in successful negotiations, tensions created by attitudes of confrontation are put to advantage by the different logic of the integrative process.

An example from my days as a negotiations practitioner may illustrate a way to use tension positively. One day, the director of a foreign trade enterprise, having unexpectedly interrupted the bargaining session, chose to make a number of totally unjustified derogatory comments about the volume of our company's purchases from his firm. His comments became so negative and insulting that if I had been in a less reflective mood, there would have been little else for me to do than to stop the negotiation and leave. With a very serious and hurt expression on my face, I put my papers in my briefcase and headed towards the door, I could feel the tension rising. Everyone was convinced that the director's brinkmanship had failed.

Instead of opening the door to leave the room, however, I passed it and walked around to the other side of the table, where I sat near the director, opened my briefcase, and put my papers on the table again. Then, in a quiet and relaxed voice, I indicated that this was a much more realistic place to sit when we negotiate. Considering the special problems of the product we were negotiating, our common opponent was actually the Greek market and not each other. In this manner, tension was diffused instantaneously and thus the impasse was broken. The demands of the Greek market were subsequently discussed in a much more constructive manner than even before the incident had occurred. The whole setting changed and negotiations went on successfully. Were it not for this mending of relations, they might very well have fallen through.

Let me come back to the issue of effective interaction between theorists and practitioners. It is mutual awareness of differing symbols and perspectives and their conveyance to each other in terms which are enlightening that creates the basis for genuine interaction, which in turn produces a collective and integrating understanding. It might be equally rewarding to consider what themes are absent from a specific interaction and to speculate together on the many possible interpretations of their absence. In this manner the questions of the reliability and validity of the practitioner's experience, which so often plague the theorist, take on a new dimension. The purpose of the interaction shifts from obtaining information from each other to working together on a real problem.

My exposure to the different rhythm of academia enabled me to adopt a more reflective stance in negotiating. This reflective stance not only helped me rid myself of much rigidity, but, by helping to diffuse tension, it facilitated communication. A gradual shifting of my sources of satisfaction from a constant urge to score points to concentrating on the main issues took place.

10.3.3. Interaction: A continuous process

Interaction between practitioners and theoreticians should be continuous. It is a dynamic process in which each can inform the other. For the reasons I have mentioned, both sides have to understand that as time goes on, they will become inextricably intertwined by the need for each other to do his work well. Therefore, each side should build interaction into its work routine.

As negotiation can be viewed as a process built of three phases — the pre-negotiation phase, the bargaining phase, and the post-agreement phase — so interaction between practitioners and theorists is a process with three phases — pre-interaction, interaction, and post-interaction. The benefits of interaction for both sides can be considerably enhanced if both sides are conscious of the phases of the process and spend the necessary time on each one of them.

For example, in the pre-interaction phase, the homework necessary for the interaction has to be done. Efforts to deal constructively with the interaction must begin with trying to establish a common definition of the problems to be tackled and must continue with creating the setting for a balanced amount of input from both sides.

Both sides' diagnosis of the purpose of the interaction and conscious effort to formulate what they expect from it are indispensable. Although each side should realize that its ideal solution is not attainable, its expectation should be formulated as well as an assessment of which interests are at stake and of which new interests could be created through the interaction. It should also be agreed that both sides are able and willing to try to satisfy this expectation. In this manner, practitioners with incentives and qualifications compatible with those of the theorists involved would be chosen, and a special effort to dovetail differences of interest would be made. Both sides should be given a stake in the outcome of the interaction.

In instances where this interaction requires some length of time, the ideal, I believe, would be the system of mentors. In other words, if practitioners are invited to academia to give and take, mentors should be provided with whom the practitioners can cooperate and discuss problems that arise in the process of interaction or any other part of their work in the academic setting. I believe that a mentor relationship would ensure that preparation for the interaction and its results would turn out best and would prevent much frustration on both sides.

For the actual interaction phase, more about the dynamics has to be understood. For the post-interaction phase, inputs from each side have to be recorded and evaluated so that the next interaction can be prepared.

An unpleasant interaction can dramatically affect future dealings. The practitioner who is berated may be unresponsive when his cooperation is later solicited. Indeed, building trust and confidence during the early stages of the interaction process is vital to maintaining the relationship.

The pre- and post-interaction phases may take much more time and effort than the interaction itself, and they must be conducted with a view to the new situation that will be created. From this description, it becomes clear that theorist–practitioner interaction represents a major financial and intellectual investment, if it is to be effective.

10.4. Tentative Conclusions: Prospects and Some Suggestions

If we look at the interaction between practitioners and theorists as a type of negotiating process, we suddenly have at our disposal the conceptual tools used in the analysis of negotiation processes. These tools can be used effectively to help understand and improve our interaction.

The most effective form of interaction for both practitioner and theorist is not debriefing or instructing, but working together on a tangible problem. This "joint task" mode of interaction is the best way a theorist can learn how a practitioner actually negotiates, and a practitioner can learn what he has to gain from theoretical concepts of negotiation.

Effective interaction between practitioners and theorists is far from easy. If this interaction is to be of some use for both sides, it has to be part of a longer, structured process. I would say that both practitioners and theorists have a lot to learn about how to interact effectively and how to benefit from their exchanges.

The purpose of this interaction is to complement the efforts made by both practitioners and theorists to increase their effectiveness in the fields of their particular endeavor. Dovetailing interactions with practitioners into areas of actual faculty research might address this problem. For this effectiveness to increase, each side has to help the other achieve a reasonable balance between scholarship and analytical skills, on the one hand, and a solid understanding of the realities that surround the negotiating process, on the other.

Practitioners and theorists should at all times of their interaction recognize that each has worked out and integrated into his subconscious numerous patterns, many of which differ considerably because of the nature of their work.

I fully agree with Professor Howard Raiffa that practitioners all too often act intuitively and in ways that are far more sophisticated than they can conceive of and articulate. The bridge between theory and practice is constructed less by each side trying to extract theoretical insight from experience than it is by cooperating with each other for mutual advantage. No debriefing can expose the principles that guide an effective negotiator better than working with the negotiator on a particular problem. It is through this cooperation that theorists and negotiators see which skills and personal traits could improve their performance and focus their thoughts. It is through cooperation that the abstract game links with the real case and that lessons from one field of negotiations suddenly seem useful in another.

Solving one problem in an actual situation with some theorists did more for my ability to think about the dynamics of negotiation than reading many academic papers or listening to many lectures. The theorists' analyses within this setting of joint problem-solving helped me to identify and define the issues and led me to consider the integrative as well as the distributive aspects of bargaining.

Only those who are open to integrating their ideas and who acknowledge the wisdom of both sides will make their interaction dynamic. Only then will insights be more than additive and emerge as new Gestalten [1]. Then the next stage becomes possible — mapping out the conception together and getting knowledgeable theorists to suggest an agenda for research.

I hope that some of my insights will be useful to both practitioners and theorists, not only in planning, structuring, conducting, and evaluating their interaction more effectively, but in developing an approach — if not a philosophy — to this interaction that will render it a satisfying and enriching experience.

As a step in that direction, I propose that IIASA–PIN initiate a theorist–practitioner forum in which practitioners from all fields of international negotiation would periodically meet with interested theorists to conduct effective interactions of the type I have described. This forum could advance PIN's objective to bridge the gap between the worlds of theory and practice in international negotiations.

Acknowledgments

I am indebted to may people for making this chapter possible. I am especially grateful for the inspiration and encouragement of Professor Howard Raiffa. Professors David Lax and Michael Wheeler and members of the Harvard Negotiation Roundtable and of the Harvard Program on Negotiation have made definitive contributions. I also owe great deal to the administrator of the Roundtable, Linda Lane, for making its meetings possible.

128   C. Vlachoutsicos

Although I have borrowed freely from the sources listed in the bibliography, this is
essentially a practitioner's account.

Note

[1] The *American Heritage Dictionary* of the English Language recognizes both "Gestalten" and "gestalts" as acceptable plurals. I prefer the original form, "Gestalten".

Bibliography

Argyris, Chris (1980), *The Inner Contradictions of Rigorous Research*, Academic Press,
New York.
Argyris, Chris and Schön, Donald A. (1974), *Theory in Practice*, Jossey-Bass, San Fran-
cisco.
Barber, Bernard (1963), Some Problems in the Sociology of the Professions, *Daedalus*
(Fall), 686.
Beveridge, W.I.B. (1957), *The Art of Scientific Investigation*, Random House, New York.
Bloor, David (1976), *Knowledge and Social Imagery*, Routledge & Kegan Paul, London.
Fisher, Roger, and Ury, William (1981), *Getting to Yes*, Houghton-Mifflin, Boston.
Goode, William, The Librarian: From Occupation to Profession, reprinted in Vollmer
and Mills, *Professionalization*.
Greenwood, Ernest, Attributes of a Profession, reprinted in Vollmer and Mills, *Profes-
sionalization*.
Hall, Edward T. (1959), *The Silent Language,* Doubleday, New York.
Haug, Marie, Deprofessionalization: An Alternate Hypothesis for the Future, in Hal-
mos, *Professionalism and Social Change*.
Havens, Leston (1976), *Participant Observation*, Jason Aronson, New York.
Illich, Ivan (1970), *A Celebration of Awareness: A Call for Institutional Revolution*,
Doubleday, Garden City, NY.
Jentz, Barry, and Wofford, Joan (1979), *Leadership and Learning*, McGraw-Hill, New
York.
Koufes, James M. (1987), Why Businessmen Fail in Government, *New York Times*
(March 8).
Laurence, Paul R., and Lorsch, Jay R. A New Management Job: The Integrator, *Har-
vard Business Review*, 45, 142–150.
Lax, David A., and Sebenius, James K. (1986), *The Manager as Negotiator*, Free Press,
New York.
Lynn, Kenneth (1963), Introduction to "The professions", *Daedalus*, (Fall), 649.
Mannheim, Karl (1936), *Ideology and Utopia*, Harvest Books, New York.
McIntosh, Peggy (1985), Feeling Like a Fraud, *Work in Progress Series*, Stone Center
for Developmental Services and Studies, Wellesley, MA.
Mintzberg, (1973), *The Nature of Managerial Work*, Harper & Row, New York.
Papert, Seymour (1981), *Mindstorms: Children, Computers, and Powerful Ideas*, Basic
Books, New York.
Polanyi, Michael (1958), *Personal Knowledge*, University of Chicago Press, Chicago.
Pressman, Jeffrey, and Wildsvsky, Aaron (1979), *Implementation*, University of Califor-
nia Press, Berkeley, CA.

Raiffa, Howard (1982), *The Art and Science of Negotiation,* Harvard University Press, Cambridge, MA.

Rein, Martin, and White, Sheldon (1980), Knowledge for Practice, DSRE Working Paper, October, MIT, Cambridge, MA.

Scheffler, Israel (1977), The Cognitive Emotions, *The Teachers College Record,* **79** (December), 171–186.

Schön, Donald A. (1983), *The Reflective Practitioner,* Temple Smith, London.

Singer, E.A. (1959), *Experience and Reflection,* University of Pennsylvania Press, Philadelphia.

Taylor, Frederick (1967), *Principles of Scientific Management,* (first published 1911), Norton, New York.

Warren, Catherine E. (1982), The Written Life History as a Prime Research Tools in Adult Education, *Adult Education,* **32** (Summer), 214–228.

Weber, Max (1940), Bureaucracy, in Oscar Grusky and George A. Miller (eds.), *The Sociology of Organizations,* Free Press, New York.

Wheeler, Michael (1967), *Organization and Environment: Managing Differentiation and Integration,* Harvard University Press, Cambridge, MA.

Wheeler, Michael (1985), Protocols for Debriefing Practitioners, Program of Negotiation, Working Paper 85–6, January.

CHAPTER 11

Conceptions of the Trade
Negotiation Process

Sven B. Lundstedt

Ohio State University
Columbus, Ohio
USA

11.1. Introduction

This chapter is about practitioner conceptions of international trade negotiation. Presented are the responses to a questionnaire by eleven individuals not randomly chosen and who do not constitute a representative sample. They serve as eleven case studies that provide some initial insights about underlying processes in international trade negotiation. Consequently, this is an exploratory effort, to be followed by a more extensive later phase.

This initial phase of this work does not pretend to offer definitive answers to basic questions about the underlying trade negotiation process. It only explores a range of possibilities and suggests how we might begin to think more critically and comprehensively about the process of trade negotiation by asking a variety of new questions.

A practitioner is defined as one who engages in trade negotiation. It is not uncommon to find that practitioners often cannot express in a self-analytical way their methods of negotiation beyond limited anecdotal description, a form of narrative story telling, because they are not trained or required by their work to do so. To avoid the difficulties of unstructured narratives, interesting though they may be, a questionnaire was created to explore systematically a number of central negotiation issues. But, even free association, anchored by leading questions, can be a useful way to conduct surveys if respondents can reflect systematically and analytically. Not all people can do this. Therefore, some guiding conceptual framework within which some free choices to respond are possible is needed to obtain meaningful responses.

My conclusions are tentative, subject to more extensive sampling. But, while suggestive and tentative, they imply that a greater appreciation is needed of the psychological complexity of international trade negotiation. Practitioners are no different from the rest of us who oversimplify complex processes. This is normal cognitive behavior adapted to performance efficiency and is something we all do routinely. One obviously cannot stop to think about all the subtle aspects of one's work or it would not get done. Whatever conscious, unconscious, or intuitive principles of negotiation and rules of thumb practitioners use, and no matter how competent they are, the technical principles they use usually do not describe fully the richness and the systemic complexity that underlie trade negotiation. As we will see, the issues that shape our understanding of international trade negotiation are numerous, reflect differing levels of analysis and are, for the most part, incompletely understood. As in most art forms, the performer only identifies the tip of the iceberg, as a rule especially when methods are used intuitively.

11.1.1. Criteria for a systemic view

General systems theory, which identifies the structure and dynamics of a system, is useful to understand a phenomenon as a whole. One cannot expect to form a useful, heuristic theory of trade negotiation that describes its overall complexity without a systems point of view. Following are some criteria for such a systemic view:

(1) A systems point of view assumes there is a context, or environment, with boundaries that mark off the system from others. That context is "ecological" in nature. That is, because negotiation is a human system, it follows the rule of succession (aging and change) as the key people and events involved in the system's environment act out their destinies. Given the assumption of constant but variable growth in some direction, one can usually find a life cycle pattern underlying a trade negotiation system as is found, analogously, in biological growth and decline. This means also that the underlying human conditions and attributes of trade negotiation are either in a state of evolution or devolution; they can be getting better or worse, as the case may be, but they never remain in a steady state.

(2) Resources needed for the survival of the system are introduced to the system according to some pattern and rate. They include not only money and budgets, but technological know-how, physical and environmental

attributes and, most important, people, who form the human biosocial system within which any negotiation takes place.

(3) With reference to the goals and objectives of trade negotiation, these resources are processed over time, which changes them. As we will see, the concepts discussed below reflect this on-going process and constitute aspects of a deeper element of social and procedural architecture formed by such processes and aided by social and technological inventions and innovation. But, since process and structure are always interrelated, quite different forms of, say, communication and trading behavior will result if a negotiation is structured bilaterally as opposed to multilaterally. For example, it stands to reason that if teams from two countries comprise the operational structure of a negotiation, one can expect much simpler patterns of communication, and thereby fewer problems, than if teams from several countries are involved. Usually the increase in communication complexity, as measured by an increase in the number of communication channels and messages, is exponential. So, in this case "more" is not always "merrier", but a source of increased complexity, higher risks of error and, in general, more problems for negotiators not only in communication and logistics, but in human relations and their management. As experience has shown, management of the negotiation system becomes a critical issue as sheer complexity of structure and functions increases.

(4) There are always products that result from any process, some useful and good, others not so useful and even bad. What may seem good at the moment may turn out to be bad later on, and vice versa. Time is also a critical variable in negotiation and plays an important part in reflecting the appropriate rhythm of events necessary for success of the negotiation system. The end results, or products, of negotiation are usually hierarchically ordered outcomes in the sense that one can always usually identify at least three levels: primary, secondary and tertiary. Occasionally, one might reach a fourth order. One of the paradoxes of any system's outcome is that successful primary outcomes may not lead to successful secondary and tertiary ones. Another way of saying this is that successful short-term outcomes may lead to unsuccessful longer-term secondary and tertiary outcomes. Paradoxically, unsuccessful short-term outcomes may result in successful secondary and tertiary ones. One example is that successful initial trading with a country that has high productivity, high quality and lower prices may in the longer run create the adverse secondary and tertiary outcomes of first capturing the trading partner's economy by price and product competition. This may affect the economic structure of the receiving country, creating lowered levels of productivity and higher unemployment — a case of an initial good leading to two bads. As far as the negotiation process is concerned, it would be very unwise not to reflect upon these

second- and third-order effects of the negotiation system at the very
moment one is counting one's profits and making acclamations about the
sweet taste of success.

(5)   The negotiation system always depends on good information for its success.
Feedback and feedforward about the system's behavior are needed to monitor its process behavior and outcomes and are essential for its control and
self-regulation. Since in a negotiation two or more parties usually comprise
the system, the communication network reflects a gradient of increasing
complexity as that number increases. And if the information and language
in the network is coded and encoded using different symbols and syntaxes,
the result can be highly confusing especially where the symbolism being
used means different things to people. Semantic paradoxes are commonplace, but can significantly affect trade negotiation outcomes.

In conclusion, a general system theory that identifies structure and functions in input, transformation and output relative to an environment in which
there are other competing systems is very necessary.

11.1.2. Characteristics of the sample

The background of the eleven respondents was predominately that of business,
although some came from other professions such as engineering. Some were
company presidents, some vice presidents, while one was a division manager.
One academic who had special knowledge of India was included. One was a corporation lawyer who has done much negotiating. There was one banker. Most
were from the USA, but there were one each from Greece, India, the Netherlands, and Iran. Five were from small firms, two from medium-sized firms, one
from a multinational corporation, one from a corporate law firm, one from a
government agency and the last from a university. One noted experiences of
over 100 negotiations, one between 50 and 100, one between 30 to 50, six
reported 5 to 50 and only one reported under 5.

Each was asked to identify some key negotiation experiences and then to
judge which of the several reasons given in the questionnaire explained success
and failure. The data showed that product fit and trust were most prominent.
In the failure category politics, poor objectives, high prices and trade barriers
stood out.

11.2. Results

11.2.1. Patterns

The respondents were asked which problems that led to failure seemed to come up over and over again. The answers given were as follows:

- "In most occasions sharp price diving by competitors".
- "Limits set by economic factors; overpricing; adverse competition; unclear goals and objectives".
- "Lack of reliability in supplies; bureaucratic problems with the Indian government ".
- "Limits created by domestic or foreign political conditions; foreign governments had unreasonably low maximum royalties which a foreign company could pay to a US company; problems with the foreign country's central bank in converting to dollars and permitting transfers to US; inflation (e.g., Chile); government ownership of real estate (e.g., Switzerland). Some of these fall under unreasonable trade barriers".
- "Lack of communication".
- "Lack of trust; little understanding of the other party's culture and history; domestic or foreign political factors".
- "Even with our (US) demonstrated willingness to negotiate and do business, we are not perceived as attractive partners owing to our size or the nature of the market".

11.2.2. Timing

When asked about the most important aspects of timing of the introduction of different agenda items, they said:

- "Critical: often in a first meeting no specific proposals are put forth; time is spent discussing the market situation, possible benefits of a business relationship and next steps; both sides try to answer the question: is this relationship worth building?".
- "Key to any negotiation is putting yourself in the shoes of your opposite number; best to find points where early agreement can be reached and where one can easily agree to get them on the table first".
- "Patience and the power of suggestion".
- "One must establish trust, confidence and mutual respect before getting to important aspects of the contract".

- "Exporter was seriously interested in developing products targeted to this market" (Demand pull).
- "Get objectives and goals outlined first. If you know what is needed then build trust and confidence that you can perform; assure that your product will work, is the best and up to the job".
- "Timing of introduction of new arguments or repeating of arguments is very important; listen to what the other party has to say!".
- "Lots of preparation, monitoring, follow-up; find the highest value for your counterpart; be conscious of any negative costs of doing business; readiness to reopen positive negotiations if one runs aground".

11.2.3. Duration

When asked if there is an optimal overall time period for successful negotiations, about an equal number said yes as did no. They made these comments about the length of successful negotiations:

- "As long as there is hope for progress".
- "Six to nine months".
- "A very brief period for an initial agreement then as long as it takes for the technical aspects".
- "Three to six months".
- "Two to three hours". (Respondent was probably thinking about each daily meeting.)
- "Depends on the relationship that can be created — how much sympathy and affinity".

There were some variations in responses, suggesting there are probably a wide number of norms. Perhaps there is a lot of pragmatic, contingent, behavior required because many negotiation systems are themselves highly differentiated. Consider also that time is interpreted differently in various cultures. For example, Americans are known to be impatient and want things done quickly. It is said that the Chinese and Japanese can wait much longer for the results of a negotiation. Asked how long an average negotiation should take, one would probably find much variation across cultures in the answers given.

Trade negotiations usually involve teams of people. There are always key leaders who stand out, but they are usually backed up by staff. Team behavior is critical and can result in success or failure depending upon the way a team is formed and managed, how well the people in it get along with one another and how well trained they are for their job. Teams always reflect the basic dynamics of human groups. A group's performance, for example, is determined by leadership behavior, and by how group members communicate, exercise social power, develop or fail to develop cohesiveness, form standards and norms and act upon them, develop motivation and levels of aspiration, and so on.

Group performance is also influenced by such important leader behavior as being supportive toward group members, team development, expecting high standards of work from everyone (group levels of aspiration), encouraging participation and *stakeholdership* and providing adequate technical support to enhance team learning and adaptation to new problems, or simply providing adequate tools to do the job. Lack of development of any of these five characteristics may cause problems of work satisfaction, team effectiveness and productivity achievement.

The following answers were given to the question concerning important criteria for successful performance of a negotiation team. Some of the responses are quite interesting, others somewhat naive or even technically incorrect:

- "Avoid any antagonism in one's own team". (Highly unlikely knowing how people work; but one should try to reduce it.)
- "The team must express capability". (We are not told what is meant by capability.)
- "Pay attention to the behavior of the team in dress, etc.; in this respect it is necessary to know who are the counter negotiators". (Evidently meaning those who are working against the negotiation goals, suggesting poor selection, coordination, commitment and even leadership.)
- "Form a small team with an obvious leader or with specific tasks associated with each member". (Again, an answer suggesting a need for an understanding of deeper group process.)
- "Establish trust, credibility, and a clear understanding of the goals".
- "Know the problems of your customer; pay attention and address all details".
- "Sound preparation, i.e., know as well as possible what the others side wants; build trust with the other side; be prepared to give in on certain points to get what you want; always have an outsider or superior with whom you must consult on key issues; this gives one time".

These rules of thumb would seem to have limited usefulness in team development, management or performance activity beyond the initial stages. They certainly provide only superficial diagnostic value and do not contribute to a method to create, or recreate, a new team to improve an old one.

11.2.4. Style and procedure

Trade negotiations usually involve procedural methods and personal style. Procedure is the routine by which daily administrative operations in trade talks are handled. Personal style is the unique way an individual one carries out such routines. Procedure and style are interrelated to the extent that both influence one another.

Some trade negotiators may be more informal than formal. Some may take risks, others few. Some are friendly, others unfriendly. Still others are tough, cold and calculating. It is hard to say which style works bests in all circumstances because there are paradoxes of stylistic conflict. Does one *hang tough* with tough cynical negotiators or respond with gentleness, tact, and courtesy? Perhaps there are some unusual negotiators who may be inclined to adopt an extreme contingency rationale requiring that their styles change often depending on the social and cultural environment in which they may be negotiating. Mercurial flexibility might appear to others that one is trying to be all things to all people. This style has obvious weaknesses in that it may lower trust because highly changeable behavior makes such a person hard to predict. Predictability is very important in a human relationship. At the opposite extreme, others may be too inflexible. A successful style is probably somewhere between these extremes.

The formal theory for stylistic differences comes in large part from the psychology of personality, especially the study of character. Character can be thought of as the structure of habits or traits that distinguishes uniquely one individual's personality from others and characterizes an individual's more or less permanent way of behaving. Whatever its ubiquitous cultural form, character structure pervades everything people do.

A stable character may seem to have a certain consistency over time; an unstable one, less. Particular character traits also suggest human qualities of strength and weakness that may be both desirable and undesirable in negotiation. The effect of character traits on other people can be profound. Traits that inflict pain will be disliked. If they provide comfort and pleasure, they will be liked. This is why good manners and etiquette are usually important in negotiation and help to avoid conflict. Because they increase expectation of further pleasure and reward, and reduce tension and anxiety, they encourage trust and openness, thus enhancing satisfaction of human needs.

The motivational consequences are clear. Traits that threaten others and inflict pain, psychic or other, invariably result either in fight or flight behavior. Such behavior encourages win–lose or zero-sum conflict, which then usually undermines negotiation and cooperation. Nasty, abrasive and obnoxious people are disliked primarily because they inflict pain. On the other hand, supportive and pleasant traits tend to reward others, creating attraction and anticipation of reward and increased cooperative behavior.

A negotiator, therefore, usually has a reasonably clear choice of strategy and tactics depending upon the outcomes desired. It is usually the paradoxes that arise in the mixed cases that are often difficult to manage. One side's choice may be to hold negotiations in such a way that they are supportive and pleasant. The other side may express painful and abrasive traits in a combative way. This has in the past characterized some East–West negotiations, which often have failed to resolve differences because there was too much conflict generated by such behavior. Mutual reward builds mutual cooperation, providing that memories of painful past encounters can be reduced in intensity by positive learning in the present.

Negotiation procedures reflect certain traits and suggest a range of methods. The words strategy and tactics could be used to describe the use of such methods. Recall, but only in a nonmanipulative sense, that in the past these terms were often associated with highly manipulative negotiation methods. When negotiators engage in mutual problem-solving in a reasonably open and trusting way, combative strategies and tactics are much less frequently needed as a basis for negotiation. These are sources of the paradoxes of the use of social power in negotiation.

The respondents were able to make distinctions between both rewarding and painful styles and procedures. *Rational* and *friendly* head the list of traits associated with success. Machiavellian and aloof behavior head the list associated with lack of success. Machiavellian behavior is commonly associated with being cunning, devious, untrusting and aloof, a deadly combination resulting in a personal assessment of such persons as sneaky and mysterious. Add to this bad image the traits of being ideological, tough and reticent and one has a recipe for potential conflict and failure in negotiation, if the other side is behaving differently. By contrast, appearing genuinely rational, friendly, participative, open-minded, sincere and supportive would seem to be a better basis for success because these traits reward and reassure others of one's good intentions and promise rewarding, successful outcomes.

Success in negotiation seems to be associated in the minds of these respondents with procedures that are flexible, creative, pragmatic; and lack of success, with procedures that are inflexible, highly controlled, rigidly formal and routine. But the high negative rating given to a high degree of delegation of functions seems unusual, yet is not hard to understand when one recalls that in negotiation a team's activity centers around a chief negotiator, who acts as a lead person, and not the staff. In another sense, if one wishes to encourage participation and involvement in a team, a team leader usually would try to increase the delegation of some functions. Perhaps trade negotiation is still seen in the light of a hierarchical command structure of management. If so, there are alternative forms of management that are not autocratically command-oriented and yet quite effective in reaching goals within an organized team social structure.

Other human characteristics associated with negotiation include learning, confidence and trust, interpersonal risk behavior, goodwill and benevolence, rank and status behavior, knowledge of culture, history and institutions, language ability and openness or *glasnost*.

11.2.5. Learning from past experience

A question was asked about the value of successes and mistakes as learning experiences which upon reflection help one to improve negotiation systems. The responses were that such learning was highly valued. They said:

- "Keep your mind open and flexible".
- "Very valuable, but should not be the only guiding principle".
- "History is always a good teacher".

- "Learning from mistakes better prepares one for future negotiations".
- "Once burned — twice learned".

Since most people of the kind represented in this sample place a high value on education and learning, one would not expect a different response. But these aphorisms are almost clichés, which is not what was asked for by the question. Yet, that level of response is in itself informative. It seems some practitioners cannot reflect thoughtfully on deeper aspects of their own learning process without some prompting and use of leading questions. We can speculate whether their responses would have been different if the respondents had been given a basic prompting framework within which to think about learning and a value checklist about what is worth learning as opposed to ignoring. It is also not uncommon to find that even educators cannot reflect critically on their own learning processes. "Know thyself", a phrase said to have been written on the Delphic Oracle, is a cybernetic process that probably still eludes most of us unless we are helped to search knowingly for it. Perhaps most people have difficulty in introspection.

Closely related to the issue of learning and how it should take place are evaluation and feedback. One critical aspect of any system's successful functioning is its ability to be a learning environment, encourage people in it to make corrections based on experiences and be self-regulating. The proper evaluation of actual experiences in trade negotiation requires that someone who is objective reflect systematically on the negotiation process, and then make available this diagnostic information, whether in staff meetings, seminars or some other form of briefing, in a way that promotes adaptive learning from experience. However, I suspect that this important adaptive way of judging how changes have to be made is already done intuitively in better negotiation systems, and perhaps not done at all systematically or even consistently in others.

11.2.6. Confidence and trust

Confidence and trust were rated high as very important in trade negotiation. The comments, which speak for themselves, were:

- "The counterpart negotiator must have the feeling that the final result is good for both parties".
- "With the distances involved in most international trade there can be no success without confidence and trust all around".
- "Without it [trust] no one wishes to invest".
- "The paper you sign is not worth anything if you do not agree in principle".
- "There is very little effective control or recourse that you can take, if the foreign company is untrustworthy. Trust is everything. If I do not like them as people and have a bad feeling about them, I would end the negotiations".

- "If you do not have confidence and trust, there will be no positive results".
- "If there is no trust in the other party, optimum negotiations are perhaps impossible".
- "Are you talking to the correct people? Can they deliver on their commitments? Do they perceive you as credible? Is there a history of business success in the past? [trust most important]".

11.2.7. Interpersonal risk-taking

In 1964 I developed the concept of *interpersonal risk behavior* to account for some underlying attributes of trust (Lundstedt, 1966). I argued that trust was a tautological concept (it does not explain causality in "trusting" behavior very well), although still a very important descriptive concept. Not only did trust require confidence in another, but more importantly it actually requires a willingness to share power and influence. Interpersonal risking is a willingness also to empower others; to share with them a part of one's influence and control, one's goodwill, information and knowledge and other intangible resources without too much suspicion and defensiveness. Trust always involves being a little vulnerable because one gives away some of one's perceived influence and control by sharing information and disclosing to others about one matter or another. Lack of trust has the opposite effect of lowering the rate of positive social exchange.

There is also a form of *subjective risk assessment* in use by everyone to judge events. Personal risk probability assessment is a probability assessment of the possible recurrence of either painful or rewarding events. It may not only be a function of the frequency of occurrence of the past event that determines its positive or negative weight in one's risk assessment, but its intensity plays an important part as well. This would help to explain why it is so hard to regain the trust of some people, because of the frequency and intensity of painful earlier experiences which can accumulate culturally and historically to affect an entire people so that it becomes a norm of routine behavior to be suspicious and on guard. The famous anthropologist Ruth Benedict reported evidence of just such differences in the Dobu culture and society in her well-known book, *Patterns of Culture*. Interpersonal risk behavior interprets an aspect of these complicated cultural responses and is an essential part of the process of negotiation across cultures and nationality groups. The respondents comments are given below:

- "Sharing information, if it is later found to be factual [true], builds *trust*. Openly discussing strengths and weaknesses". (In this example "expert power" in the form of information is given away.)
- "Builds the bridge of trust".
- "If you share your technology and trade secrets you must trust them" (assess the interpersonal risk to be low).
- "Helps to build strong relationships" (taking interpersonal risks).

11.2.8. Goodwill and benevolence

These attributes refer to being good-natured, considerate, amiable, solicitous, kind, compassionate, as contrasted with being unkind, malevolent, ruthless, heartless, cynical, cruel, and so on. The following are the responses given:

- "Probably not relevant during the negotiations, though useful in the social activities that usually accompany them".
- "In the long run goodwill increases your chances of success. People who are considerate of each other will give you the benefit of the doubt and be more willing to work with you when the going gets tough".
- "Helps to build necessary social relationships and openness".
- "Treat others as you would expect to be treated".
- "I would not do business with unkind, ruthless, cruel people. It is not conducive to long-term relations".
- "Negotiators should not be enemies".

11.2.9. Rank and status attributions

This category is concerned with deemphasizing invidious rank and status attributions toward others, and avoiding inadvertent, or conscious "put-downs" of others by approaching them as respected and valued persons and with preserving the negotiation relationship by deemphasizing personally cruel, chauvinistic, haughty, insolent, overbearingly arrogant or other prejudicial attributions. The responses were as follows:

- "Anyone who would act otherwise should not be negotiating".
- "Too much deemphasis in this area could result in loss of respect or face. Treat each situation as an individual case". (Where rank and status are very important, this is perhaps true. But there are qualitatively different forms of ranking behavior. Not all are demeaning of others.)
- "Highly unnecessary behavior. You rarely know who you are talking to or what they could mean to you in the future".
- "Highly unnecessary. Individual respect reflects upon one's company and on the country being negotiated with".
- "Alienating others in this way will damage relationships and begin on the wrong foot".
- "If the opposite number feels you have no respect for him/her as a person, forget successful negotiation".

11.2.10. Culture, history, and institutions

This category is about knowledge of culture, history and institutions in the other party's country. It involves an ability to talk knowledgeably about all three and to use such knowledge of domestic political and economic systems, philosophy, art and music, literature and great historical events.

The positive response was only moderate, indicating some uncertainty as to the value of this kind of knowledge in negotiation. This is somewhat unexpected, as the prevailing wisdom strongly suggests that such knowledge is essential to good relations. Perhaps this reflects a certain amount of ethnocentrism in the respondents. When a larger group is studied, we may find that such prevailing wisdom is indeed true. Suggestive respondent remarks are as follows:

- "Helps to build trust and understanding about how one's opposite thinks".
- "This has never been a factor; however, I have only worked with European countries".
- "Within Europe this is less important". (Perhaps because Americans share European culture and history.)
- "This builds confidence and trust with the other party and leads to a more relaxed atmosphere in negotiations".
- "Showing an interest by going to museums or art galleries is more important than knowing all the background. This assumes that encyclopedias and guidebooks have been read prior to discussions".
- "This knowledge shows interest and communicates to the other side that you are serious in your efforts".
- "Helps one to understand what motivates the other party and what turns them off. Gives a better understanding of marketing, personnel, and political problems".

11.2.11. Language ability

Language ability is the ability to speak and read some of the other party's language. It received a lower rating, and there seems to be some uncertainty about the universal importance of knowing a language, given the easy availability of interpreters. However, this is a very small sample, as was already pointed out, and we might find a quite different pattern of responses in a larger sample. Here are the written comments about language ability:

- "Most foreign negotiators that I have dealt with speak excellent English. In one case where I was dealing with Germans and spoke German, discussions became more relaxed as we continued in English".
- "[Language] helps build trust and most importantly, away from the negotiation table, helps one to understand what is in your opposite number's head".

- "[Knowledge of language] prevents misunderstanding through use of a translator".
- "Less room for misunderstanding; easier to explain one's position [with language knowledge]".
- "[Language is important.] It is like remembering a person's birthday or name — it is just a good show of earnestness and good faith".
- "Our motivation is monetary success. Language barriers are less important. However, almost everyone I have been involved with in trade negotiation speaks English or has someone on his staff that speaks English".
- "Avoid any barrier that can influence your own position in a negative way". (Language is important.)
- "A few words are important. A good translator who knows you and your goals and product can be the most important and most impressive help".

11.2.12. Openness

The final characteristic in this group is openness, which curiously enough received mixed reviews. Openness (glasnost) in the questionnaire is defined as candor and unsuspiciousness, but not naively unaware of realistic dangers. Some rated openness as most important, but not all.

It is easy to understand why in some negotiations guardedness, rather than openness, could be the rule rather than the exception. Initial suspicions are reduced only when one learns to trust, risk and have confidence in others; this usually comes later, only after one acquires them by experience rather than by verbal personal declarations of forthrightness and honorable behavior. Some forms of openness are also condemned as simply gullibility, and some may actually be forms of credulousness. But this has always been true. If openness leads to more information about the other party that improves the negotiation process and the relationships underlying it, then it is to be encouraged. The test of sincerity in others usually takes time unless they come highly recommended by reputable former contacts. But perhaps it is also better to have trusted and lost than not to have trusted at all, providing the stakes are not too high. The respondents said this:

- "Lots of things go wrong after the deal is signed and you must be able to work together on a flexible basis to solve future problems". (This is not quite an answer to the question, but certainly implies openness.)
- "This is the quickest way to build confidence and trust; may save time".
- "If you don't open up, chances are the other party will remain closed as well. Then how do you get into the other persons mind?" (to understand him or her).

11.2.13. Starting negotiations

The question was asked: given your own style and procedures, what is the best and proper way to open or reopen negotiations to make them successful? Are there special ceremonial things to do — customs, routines, timing, etc? This is a far from simple question and, as we know, first impressions are lasting. The respondents said this:

- "It is best to open with an informal event — e.g., a dinner away from the negotiation site where interpersonal rapport can commence".
- "No [special events]; it depends on convincing others that there is mutual benefit".
- "An open and friendly basis first. Get to know others on a somewhat person-to-person level. Never jump directly into negotiations".
- "The first meeting is normally to qualify for future business. Who are we? What is our philosophy of business? Who is the other party? What is their philosophy of business? Usually done at a lunch or dinner".
- "No [best way]. Each situation is different".
- "Develop a relationship which will create trust and warmth. Meeting and entertaining family members, I found, develops this trust".
- "Short informal talk that leads automatically to the subject. Some preparation necessary".
- "Get to know your counterparts; what their needs are; what motivates them. Spend social time with them".

11.2.14. Ending negotiations

The question was asked: Given your own style and procedures, how do you end trade negotiations to make them successful? Are there special ceremonial things to do, etc.? The respondents commented:

- "Let the other side know you value them, their business and that you appreciate their time and effort. Be sure to leave an indication that everyone came out a winner".
- "Nothing special other than to be sincere and to continue to develop a special relationship with the party and family as well as other members of the firm".
- "Give your counterpart the idea they have negotiated tough, but fair".
- "I usually celebrate with an expensive dinner".
- "Always have an informal dinner and do not discuss events of the negotiation".
- "Usually have no discrete end; relationships usually evolutionary, either gradually becoming more important and more complex or dissolving and terminating".

- "There are no special events or considerations".
- "There should be some written, signed document as tangible evidence of the work done; then an informal meal or other social event".

It is evident from this limited sample that there is no uniform technique of beginning or ending negotiations. But one cannot help wondering if there is not more to it than just this? The initial and final processes are probably not only complex, but very important, for future relations.

11.2.15. Negotiation etiquette

The question was asked: are there any basic rules of *negotiation etiquette*? That is, customs, social codes, norms, values, and right or wrong behavior which are necessary and upon which success is dependent? The answers were, for the most part, disappointing and clearly showed a lack of awareness of specific customs and norms except in one case where the respondent said: "In China one must eat what is prepared; failure to do so is considered an insult". The rest were much less specific. Again, this suggests an inability to come to grips with their own experiences in a reflective way. Yet, having researchers and educators put facts and concepts (often just their own prejudices) in the minds of practitioners by giving them lectures on comparative culture also does not always assure that negotiation will be better understood or, for that matter, cross-cultural under-standing improved. Somehow practitioners have to learn these things from their own experiences or perhaps aided skillfully by simulated learning experiences. Perhaps learning how to be observant and reflective in other cultures is a good place to start.

From the point of view of social anthropology, the study of social customs has always been of interest, especially those surrounding important instrumental social behavior such as the management of conflicts, resolution of disputes and, of course, the conduct of negotiation. From this perspective, international trade negotiation falls into the category of the study of comparative cultures, an approach from which much of value has already been learned. Research on prac-titioners is not unlike participant observation in ethnographic studies. Trade negotiation is part of the economic system, but goes beyond business transac-tions to include broader normative considerations such as other social customs, political behavior and a variety of other social system considerations.

One of these considerations is how normative behavior, such as ethical choice, actually occurs in negotiation. Ethical and legal practices in one culture often do not apply in another, or if they do are ignored based on reasoning using principles of situational ethical relativity of the form: "The cost of doing busi-ness in country A is to make side payments [even if it means breaking the law]". Yet if caught doing this, one may be liable for prosecution in one's home country if the law or other norm there forbids this behavior. This is an interesting para-dox of cross-cultural ethical and legal conflict management for which there are no simple answers. As the number of countries involved in a trade negotiation increases, the potential for legal and ethical conflict also increases. So if one chooses to respond in an ethically relativistic way, using situational ethical reasoning, one can often find oneself in an exquisite moral or legal dilemma, a sort of ethical and legal swamp from which there may be no escape. But there are equally disturbing paradoxes which arise from a very rigid use of ethical codes, which perhaps serve even as an abuse, or absolutist interpretation, of religious or other dogma. The solution often is to become the victim of the unresolvable conflict of ethical principles which this may entail and thus to cause some unhappy individuals to acquire as a defense against the pain of moral conflict a form of anomie, or normlessness, often leading to indifference and cynicism.

Living with such value contradictions for very long may be costly to the personality of an individual and may even destroy some integrity. Under these circumstances such protracted negotiations may become a way of inducing "burn-out", cynicism, or even more serious psychopathology. Such crucibles of moral conflict apparently are not for the faint of heart, or those unable to retreat from them strategically to rest, but who may eventually suffer a hardening of the heart, too. Perhaps, as a defense, this is how a person acquires that form of unfortunate alienation and detachment where one never can make any really meaningful moral choices, always standing apart as the real business of life goes on. This entire issue needs much critical study.

I explored this issue in a superficial way with this sample of respondents and found some interesting responses. When asked about dishonesty and subterfuge, or how one handles fraud, cheating, dishonesty, duplicity, and lying, the action most frequently cited as necessary was honest compromise, if that is even possible. This is also supported by a higher number of "no" answers to the question on whether to refuse to do business and break off negotiations. The two response sets are almost symmetrical. Does this, therefore, suggest that some are users of situational ethics, are pragmatic and single-mindedly problem-solving oriented to the neglect of ethical matters? Perhaps some are. But this is not the whole story. A number chose to correct fraudulent behavior and cheating and refuse further negotiations. Some chose to compromise, refuse to do business and call attention to cheating and fraudulent behavior and refuse further negotiations all at the same time — a tough job even for the most hardy pragmatists.

The other fundamental dilemma of international trade negotiation arises from cross-cultural norm conflicts. Often this is resolved for some by having subsidiaries run by foreign nationals handle these touchy normative conflicts by acting as a moral fiduciaries. To what extent does this way of approaching the ethical dimension affect the success or failure of actual negotiations? Quite probably in significant ways, including even culpability by remote association. Another side of this dilemma is the issue of whether or not a business person or government official is acting unethically when he or she does business with adversaries, a somewhat politically overdetermined and misunderstood issue of late in the United States. Or whether in so doing they are acting on behalf of a higher economic principle of some kind, such as comparative advantage and free trade, or the less elevated behavior of just ordinary greed.

11.2.16. Third-party neutral outside advisors and negotiators

The question was asked if one ever used third party negotiators, such as neutral personal or technical advisors, and how did they work out. Use of such adjunct personnel may often make the difference between success and failure in deadlocked situations. Yet how do practitioners view their usefulness?

It is not surprising that, when needed, they were seen as essential. But equally surprising were the judgements of best use, which placed language and cultural problems highest. Deadlocks, technical matters, communication and conflict resolution seemed to be less important. Perhaps this is a bias from the small sample size. But it is clear that the functional tasks which such intervenors are given more often than not are directed at restabilizing the negotiation system and bringing parties together. This role goes far beyond mere interpreter functions and is a highly critical one.

11.2.17. Special contacts within the other party's organization

The question was asked as to whether the practitioners knew of any very special individuals, or so-called insiders, in the other party's trade negotiation group or bureaucracy who were particularly helpful in making the negotiation successful. They may have done so by using creative ways to get around bureaucratic red tape or help one to reach key people who sped up procedures because they understood local customs. In a sense, these individuals were actually informal third-party helpers who had special local knowledge and skills.

As to their location in the social system, five respondents placed them at all levels — the top, middle, and bottom of the bureaucracy or other organization. Only one thought they existed, but had never met any. One heard others speak of them, but had no experience with them. Three concluded they should be used to facilitate negotiation, as an informal, unofficial source of help. Two thought they should not be used, as they would break protocol and undermine negotiations.

The concept that illustrates this widespread practice is a well-known sociological distinction between formal and informal social structure and social process. The formal organization, with its unrelenting "routinization of charisma", rationalization through rule-bound behavior, and other normative encumbrances, has only certain prescribed levels of functional efficiency. No matter how hard one tries one can never find a formal organization that works to its fullest efficiency and effectiveness, a result caused in part by the rather natural human tendency to fight against the deindividualization that comes from the controlling nature of much bureaucracy. To adapt to these painful rules and controls people usually just work around them and take informal shortcuts to reach their goals, or use the formal system in illegitimate ways to block productivity. Without an informal system to offer an alternative, the formal system would probably not work at all.

Moreover, in the informal system people can occupy certain functional roles such as guides, purveyors of information or combinations of them. In the United States there have in the past been some who have been referred to a bit sardonically as "inside dopesters" — the word dopester meaning someone who has special knowledge unattainable through the formal system and has it ready to give away for a price (not always a monetary one) before anyone else does. Earlier I made reference to the fact that negotiation takes place within a system. It is always a social system and has within itself both informal and formal subsystems. Successful, experienced negotiators seem to know intuitively how to use both.

Organizational theory and development, directed to improving organizational life, have since their inception tried to find ways to make the formal organization work more efficiently and effectively with fewer errors in work, less turnover, lateness, absenteeism and greater work satisfaction. Although this remedial process of learning is very complex, it can be characterized as an effort to make the formal organization more informal through increased participation, communication, freedom, supportiveness, and better team development. But even with these obvious improvements informal systems will still continue to exist to perform special human functions.

Trade negotiators would benefit by using informal systems, providing they do not have malevolent functions or do not undermine the true mission of trade negotiation by subverting its legitimate mission. Here are some comments by the respondents:

- "People with high political contacts can really speed things up and cut through the bureaucracy".
- "Lawyers and accountants from one side can often meet their counterparts from the other side on a professional basis apart from the negotiations". (Implying thereby a meeting to work informally.)
- "An export manager provided introductions to a financial director and to investment bankers to improve a relationship".
- "In one case a French manufacturer asked the French government to find a US distributor. This third party was helpful to both sides".
- "Sometimes they are helpful and speed up negotiations, but often there is confusion and delay in successful negotiations". (Apparently, here is an exception to the rule above.)

There are also principles which guide the proper use of informal contacts — a code on the appropriate use of the informal contact, if one wishes to call it that. An honest broker or go-between can be an enormous help. A negotiator or informal contact, however, who as inappropriate motives can undermine negotiations by his or her presence and actions in the system. Illegitimate informal practices, where they form a kind of "black market" of services, can be very costly to everyone. There is much to be said for keeping the trade negotiation process more or less pure.

11.2.18. Systemic concepts of negotiation

This category is based on the recognition that trade negotiations are also more than the sum of their parts. This simply means that all the parts of a trade negotiation (procedures, timing, style, etc.) have to be seen as a whole to be properly appreciated and understood. This is another argument for adopting a systems perspective of negotiation and one that recognizes the "ecological" determinants in negotiation which affect the life cycle of negotiations and their success and failure. The elements that comprise the "whole" of a negotiation system, however, seem to vary among these practitioners.

Below are listed some of the elements of the whole elicited by this question: "What are some of your ideas about how, in trade negotiation, one achieves this integration?".

- "Timing — beneficial need by both parties".
- "Economic conditions of countries involved".
- "Political attitude of countries involved".
- "Willingness to take risks" (both parties).
- "The qualification process — establishing credibility".
- "Background and history of other party".
- "Knowledge of competitors and other relationships".
- "Knowledge of the products under discussion".
- "Desire to establish long-term relationships".
- "Openness to serendipitous outcomes".
- "Team development and education".
- "Know one's goals and the other party's goals".
- "Set specific goals and procedures to deal with this party".
- "Do everything possible within normal guidelines to close deal" (exhaust all options).
- "Recognize and assure mutual gain" (emphasize mutual rewards).
- "Recognize that negotiation is expensive" (assess costs and benefits).
- "Be conscious of the limitations of top management's capacity to negotiate" (formal power is not all-efficient).
- "Delegate sufficiently to others in the team".
- "Recognize that negotiation is often a long-term evolving process".

Eventually, as the size of the sample of respondents is increased, we should begin to see a factor grouping in terms of central and peripheral factors in the negotiation process. There still remains, however, a determination of the configurational properties and functional patterns of these principles relative to different kinds of trade negotiation including one-on-one negotiations (dyadic negotiation), and what Howard Raiffa calls N-person negotiation systems which comprise groups of three or more negotiators representing different constituencies. The behavioral properties of such larger groups still remain to be explored and characterized more thoroughly.

At least two levels of analysis must be kept in mind as we attempt to find out how trade negotiation takes place successfully. The first level comprises the manifest processes of negotiation that are most immediately apparent to an observer. The second is the underlying latent process structure, or "deep structure", of the negotiation process. Since each influences the other, knowledge of both is needed to complete the picture. Practitioners seem to be less aware of the latent structure than the manifest one. Being concerned with practical problem-solving and getting results, their behavior is naturally more action-oriented without too much deep introspection about what they are doing. This may seems true of most practitioners. Surely negotiators would benefit by understanding the presence of latent processes both for diagnostic evaluation of the negotiation process and its eventual remediation if needed.

11.3. Concluding Remarks

This has been an exploratory analysis of a small sample of practitioner responses to a questionnaire about international trade negotiation. It is evident that the trade negotiation process today is not conceptualized well by those who are practitioners of this art. This conclusion alone suggests that some practitioners may benefit by learning about the trade negotiation process from others in new ways, and from researchers who bring more complex theories, so that the overall concept is widened and enriched by more theoretical variety and detail.

Practitioners also do not seem to reflect systematically upon what they do, as evidenced by the paucity of responses to some questions. This seems to be a function of an action orientation and perspective more than anything else, and not some lack of analytical capacity. Evidently this can be learned and, if suddenly valued by practitioners as being required for success in trade negotiation, would be learned. Much remains to be done also to understand the beneficial side effects of successful trade negotiation, for example, as in the indirect, positive but appropriate contributions it can make to cross-national diplomacy.

On the theoretical side it is evident that some form of general systems framework is an asset in practice, teaching and research about trade negotiation. Reference to such a theoretical framework was given in the introduction to this chapter. International trade negotiation is multidisciplinary in nature, requiring the conjoint appreciation and use of several disciplines including economics, psychology, sociology, anthropology, political science, history, and decision sciences, not to mention other technical and scientific disciplines necessary for an understanding of the product itself. This will place a burden for intellectual renewal upon those who want to study this kind of negotiation from the narrow perspective of a single discipline. Limited factor theories for subjects such as this one will never work nor lead to an understanding of the more complex forms of multilateral group negotiation. Our research theory and methods have to be integrative.

Reference

Lundstedt, Sven (1966), *Journal of Psychology*, 62, pp. 3–10.

CHAPTER 12

International Joint Venture Negotiations

Fritz F. Heimann

General Electric Company
Fairfield, Connecticut
USA

12.1. Introduction

This chapter addresses four main topics: first, the role of joint ventures in GE's business strategy; second, case studies of three GE international joint ventures; third, some lessons learned from GE's joint venture experience; and fourth, comments on the new Soviet decree covering joint ventures with foreign firms. As a lawyer for GE, a large US corporation, my focus will be pragmatic, rather than theoretical.

12.2. The GE Perspective

GE has long been the world's largest electrical manufacturer. From its traditional base in electrical products, GE has expanded into such fields as jet engines, medical equipment, plastics and financial services. GE's annual revenues are around $40 billion, of which $8 billion come from outside the USA. The non-US business is almost equally divided between export sales from the USA and sales from foreign-based operations. GE is the third largest US corporation, after IBM and EXXON.

Most of GE's markets are now international in scope. To survive and prosper, GE must be an effective world-class competitor. World leadership in terms of technology, market share and cost structure are the foundations on which GE's competitive strategy is based. These in turn shape GE's approach to joint ventures.

From GE's perspective there are four principal reasons for entering into joint ventures:

1. There are many national markets around the world where independent entry by an American corporation is difficult or impossible because of legal or political restrictions. Working with a local partner becomes a condition of entry.
2. To compete effectively may require some capabilities that GE does not possess. A partner can bring such additional resources into play.
3. An undertaking may be so large, or so risky, that joint venturing becomes a prudent way to limit our investment or our risk exposure.
4. Working with a partner may provide GE with a competitive edge, through costs savings, influential local contacts, foreign financing support or other advantages.

Generally more than one of these reasons for joint venturing will be present, as the following case studies demonstrate.

12.3. Three Case Studies

12.3.1. The gas turbine manufacturing associate program

One of GE's most successful joint venture programs has been in heavy duty gas turbines — that is, gas turbines used for electric power and industrial applications, as distinguished from aircraft engines. The program has been in existence for more than two decades and involves what we call "Manufacturing Associate (MA)" relationships with companies in the UK, Italy, Norway, Holland, Germany, Japan, and now China. The MA relationships consist of long-term contracts, generally for ten years; they do not involve the formation of joint venture corporations.

Under the MA program, GE makes available to the manufacturing associates the designs and technology to manufacture the stationary parts of the gas turbine. GE supplies the rotating components — roughly, a 50:50 split. The split makes sense because GE retains responsibility for the parts which require the most expensive machine tools, as well as the most critical quality control. The MAs make the components which have to be customized for the specific application. Both GE and the MAs sell complete units to customers all over the world.

The program has clear advantages for both GE and the MAs. The MAs are able to sell a broad line of the world's best gas turbines. For GE it provides increased market shares in areas where we have difficulty penetrating on our own. For example, the relationships with our MAs in Norway and Scotland have resulted in larger sales in the North Sea gas fields than GE could have achieved on its own. Similarly, when it comes to sales in countries where low-cost financing is a key factor, GE gains a competitive edge by working with joint venture partners whose governments provide more generous loans than the US Export–Import Bank.

On a project of the dimensions of the Soviet gas pipeline from Siberia to Central Europe, the MA program provided a vehicle for dividing the workload and the risk among GE and several MAs. That also made sense to the Soviet Gas Ministry, the purchaser of the gas turbines. During the current period of depressed market conditions, we have been able to continue development programs on larger and more efficient machines by drawing on the resources of the manufacturing associates.

12.3.2. GE Yokogawa Medical Company

GE has been a leader in medical diagnostic technology for many years, going back to the early development of X-ray equipment. In the last two decades GE has developed new diagnostic techniques including computed tomography scanners (CT), ultrasound and, most recently, magnetic resonance. Yokogawa became GE's distributor in Japan for CT scanners in 1976. Initially, Yokogawa was very successful, winning a large share of the Japanese market for CT scanners exported from the USA. However, our market share in Japan began to decline when other Japanese manufacturers developed lower-cost scanners.

In 1982, GE and Yokogawa formed a joint venture company in which GE held 51% of the stock and Yokogawa 49%. It had two objectives: first, to increase the market share in Japan for GE products, and second to manufacture products in Japan for worldwide distribution by GE. The program has been very successful in both CT scanners and ultrasound. The JV company is now also developing a lower-cost magnetic resonance machine. Our market share in Japan has been increasing rapidly, and the JV has also become a significant source of new products which GE sells around the world. Recently, GE's equity in the joint company was increased to 75%.

The joint venture uses the complementary strengths of GE and Yokogawa. GE provides worldwide product planning, distribution and technical support. Yokogawa provides a distribution network in Japan, and an excellent engineering staff capable of rapidly developing lower-priced models of equipment first developed by GE's US engineering organization.

12.3.3. GE–SNECMA's CFM-56 jet engine joint venture

The joint venture between GE and SNECMA, the French aircraft engine company, was initiated in 1972 to develop the CFM-56, a new jet engine in the 18,000–25,000 pound thrust class, a fairly small engine for short-range aircraft. (By comparison, the engines for trans-Atlantic aircraft are in the 50,000–60,000 pound thrust range). The objective was to develop an engine with significantly lower fuel consumption, less noise and reduced exhaust emission levels.

The joint program was attractive to SNECMA, and to the French government, because the technical, marketing and financial risks involved in the development of a new engine were considered too great for SNECMA to shoulder alone. GE was selected after a competition with Rolls Royce and Pratt & Whitney. The joint program made sense to GE for two reasons. We were in the midst of a costly program to develop a new family of large engines and were not ready to start another program on our own. GE also recognized that at least half of the market for the new engine was outside the USA and that a European partner could help win those orders.

The joint program got off to a very slow start. The US government was concerned about the transfer of advanced engine technology abroad. The issue was taken up at a summit meeting between Presidents Nixon and Pompidou in May 1973 at Reykjavik. That meeting led to a government-to-government agreement which defined the timing and scope of technology transfers.

The commercial negotiations began with a six-page memorandum of understanding, negotiated by the top executives from both sides. Thereafter, it took another year to develop a 200-page definitive agreement. One of our less appreciative clients remarked that it took the lawyers more time to do the paperwork than it took the engineers to design the engine. A 50:50 subsidiary corporation was formed under French law in September 1974. Airline orders were very slow in coming. The first order was not received until 1979. In recent years the program has grown into a great success. More than 3,000 engines have been ordered.

The joint venture operates under the direction of a twelve-man Board of Directors, six from each parent company. The directors include the head of GE's jet engine business and the President of SNECMA. The joint venture corporation has a French president. It has a small staff composed of people on loan from both parents. The bulk of the work is subcontracted to the parent.

Every effort has been made to split the work on a 50:50 basis. Because accounting systems and pay scales are so different, the work split is based on a manhours of work, not costs. Basically, GE makes the high-pressure portion of the engine and SNECMA the low-pressure portion, There are two assembly lines, one in France and one in the USA. Each portion of the engine is delivered to the joint venture company at an agreed price and each parent retains the profit on its portion of the work split. Because of differences in accounting systems, it is impractical to try to track costs and divide profits. Warranty obligations, insurance costs and other liabilities are split 50:50. Engine sales are made by the joint venture company with full backup guarantees from both parents.

12.4. Lessons Learned

GE's experience with joint ventures has been extensive. While these three case studies are success stories, we have also had our share of failures. A number of lessons have emerged from our experience.

Perhaps the most important is to be sure you know what your partner can do. That sound simplistic. However, GE's experience has shown that, while we are usually realistic in understanding our own limitations and recognizing the need for a partner, we can be too optimistic about the help the partner can provide. Let me illustrate.

During the mid-1960s, became popular in the USA to form joint ventures of electronic and publishing companies to enter the education market. The idea was that education could be improved by developing electronic learning equipment and software programs for classroom use. GE decided to participate. Because we did not know much about educational software, we formed a joint venture with Time Inc. GE had experience in electronics and Time was the most successful publishing company in the USA. The announcement of our joint venture received a good deal of publicity, and the stock market was duly impressed.

An elegant dinner was held to celebrate the signing of the agreement. After both sides has toasted each other with Chateau Margaux, one of the GE officers candidly admitted that we knew little about the education business and expressed his delight that we were working with a partner with the experience of Time Inc. One of the Time officers replied, with equal candor, that Time did not know much about education and had assumed that GE, with its outstanding reputation for strategic business planning, has figured out what the joint venture was going to do.

The discovery that neither one of us knew what we were doing was embarrassing, particularly after all the publicity. The solution decided upon was to hire an expert from the education field to be the chief executive. A search found just the right candidate, a former dean of the most prestigious school of education in America, who was then serving as the top education official in the US government.

Our education expert was successfully recruited and another dinner was held to celebrate his arrival. He gave an eloquent speech expressing his pleasure at joining two companies with the know-how of GE and Time. He was sure that they would make up for his lack of business experience and tell him what the joint venture was supposed to do. Needless to say, the joint venture never did develop into a real business, and was quietly buried after several years of losses.

The lesson from this experience is obvious. Neither GE nor Time had critically examined the capabilities of the other party. That mistake is easy to make because the negotiation of a joint venture is like a courtship. This tends to inhibit the critical faculties of otherwise astute businessmen. If two American companies can be as unrealistic about each other as GE and Time, the potential dangers are even greater when the prospective partners must overcome differences in language, in culture, and in economic systems.

Two variations on the same theme deserve comment. First, it is essential that joint venture partners must have compatible objectives. The objectives do not need to be the same. However, if they are not compatible. the joint venture will have constant friction. For example, GE's relationship with our gas turbine associate in Scotland involved different objectives. Their principal interest was to obtain manufacturing workload for their plant in Scotland. GE's interest was to obtain entry into new markets. While the two interests were different, they were compatible.

My second point is that both sides must have consistent views about the time element. If one party wants the joint venture to be successful quickly, while the other is prepared to wait for a decade, disagreements over how to manage the joint venture are inevitable. Even if the expectations of both parties are consistent, it is essential that the prospects be analyzed realistically in order to make sure that the expectations are achievable. Over-optimistic projections of how long it will take to achieve success will undermine the credibility of the management of the joint venture, and erode the support of the parent companies. The GE–SNECMA jet engine joint venture is unique in my experience in the length of time the parent companies were willing to wait before success was achieved. This unusual level of management patience was the result of the close involvement of top executives from both parents. Because they were directly involved, they had a realistic feel for the problems to be overcome. As a result, they did not become over-optimistic and avoided the danger of unpleasant surprises.

12.5. Soviet Joint Venture Decree

The new Soviet decree issued by the Council of Ministers of the USSR on January 13, 1987 provides for the establishment of joint ventures between Soviet organizations and firms from foreign countries. I would like to make a few comments on how the decree looks from the standpoint of a US lawyer.

There are some clear pluses. The very fact that the USSR is encouraging joint ventures with foreign firms is a dramatic step forward. In addition, the broad scope envisioned for such joint ventures is impressive. It includes industrial production, raw materials and foodstuffs; attracting advanced technology, know-how and managerial expertise; as well as development of exports and reduction of imports.

Other positive factors include the provisions giving joint ventures flexibility to develop their own plans, without having quotas assigned by government planning bodies, as well as flexibility to control their own import–export operations. Also helpful are provisions for some exemptions from taxes and from custom duties, and assurance of freedom from administrative requisitions.

The decree includes some features that appear negative from our perspective. These include the requirement that limits the foreign partner to a 49% interest, and the provision that both the chairman of the board and the managing director must be Soviet citizens. For a company such as GE, which considers itself an industrial leader, being confined to a junior partner role is a drawback. The issue is not one of pride, but of the ability to determine the success of the joint venture and to manage the risks.

Another area of concern is the provisions dealing with ruble convertibility. These appear to limit transfers out of the USSR to sums produced by the profits of the joint venture. Thus, if the joint venture is unsuccessful, the foreign party would apparently lose his entire investment. Similarly, the provision that all foreign currency expenses must be covered from sales of foreign markets would not be workable if the principal purpose of the joint venture is to serve the Soviet market. Differences between the official rate of exchange of the rubble and its market value represent another problem area.

The provision prohibiting joint ventures from divulging information to foreign governments would present serious problems for an American company. We must be in the position to make disclosures required by US tax laws, export control regulations and other US government requirements. Moreover, a joint venture involving a major US company and a Soviet organization would receive considerable publicity. Thus, it must be conducted so that both the US government and the Soviet government are kept informed and are satisfied that the joint venture meets the national interests of both countries.

In addition to these positive and negative factors, some areas of uncertainty will require further exploration. Perhaps most important is the issue of how a market-oriented joint venture would function in a state-controlled economy. While the decree provides that joint ventures will not be assigned quotas by government planning bodies, it is unclear how it will obtain supplies or how it will find a market within the USSR.

A second area of uncertainty relates to differences in accounting practices. In discussing GE's French joint venture, I commented on the differences between French and US accounting practices. The differences between Soviet and US accounting are undoubtedly much greater. These problems are not insuperable, but will require time and ingenuity to resolve.

A third issue is the subject of dispute resolution. It critically influences the confidence with which we approach international joint ventures. A businessman, going into a joint venture where his partner is an agency of a foreign government, will be concerned whether fair and objective methods for resolving disputes will be available. His level of confidence will be much higher if the dispute resolution mechanism is in a neutral country and involves a familiar mechanism, such as ICC arbitration.

Before concluding, let me comment briefly on how GE evaluates international joint venture opportunities. The issue for corporate management is always one of making the best choice among competing investment alternatives. GE's top management uses return on investment as a key measurement. Any investment opportunity must pass the test — whether it involves the construction of a new plastics plant, the purchase of a television station, or the establishment of an international joint venture. The financial analysis is based on a discounted rate of return. That means that profits more than five years out count much less than nearer-term profits.

GE also evaluates the risks. Here we differentiate between risks over which we have some control — risks that can be influenced through additional investment, more research spending, or by assigning more management talent — as distinguished from political and other risks that are essentially beyond our control. Any transactions involving substantial risks beyond our control must be carefully structured to minimize our risk exposure. A key objective in negotiating a properly structured joint venture should be that neither side suffers large losses if the joint venture has to be terminated for reasons beyond their control.

In conclusion, let me reemphasize that the issuance of the Soviet joint venture decree represents an exciting step forward. I suspect that the key to its success will lie in how flexibly it is administered. As my examples have illustrated, joint ventures can be structured in many different ways to meet the conditions of the particular project. The greater the flexibility permitted by the legal rules, the greater the ability of the parties to shape the joint venture to make it successful. Particularly at this stage, when participants on both sides have much to learn about each other, it is essential that the legal rules serve as a point of departure, and not as a set of stone tablets.

CHAPTER 13

Hungary's Accession to GATT

Janos Nyerges

Bureau of Systems Analysis of the
State Office for Technical Development
Budapest
Hungary

13.1. Introduction

The accession of Hungary to the General Agreement on Tariffs and Trade (GATT), and the negotiations leading to that result, should be seen in the first place in the context of Hungary's situation preceding, surrounding, and to a very large extent determining the process of the negotiation.

The internal situation can be summed up in the short statement that the extensive method of development, the economic policy based on the hitherto valid assumption of large reserves of manpower, became completely inadequate, even counterproductive. No rational allocation was possible; the constant and losing struggle with "bottlenecks" had a discouraging psychological and political effect not only on the working population, but also on the economists and planners as well. The most striking feature, especially as regards the external economy, was the persistent imbalance in trade and payments, due to the fact that the country was and remains very dependent on foreign trade.

As to the external situation, it was soon recognized that the easing of tensions between the East and West provided the opportunity to influence the trade policy situation of Hungary *vis-à-vis* the West. The slogan describing somewhat euphemistically that situation was that "trading is lagging behind politics". The interplay of these elements created an extraordinarily great impact on the thinking of economists, planners and the general public when looking for adequate solutions.

The main elements of the solution with respect to foreign trade policy, enabling Hungary to seek accession to GATT, were the change in the method of planning, the autonomy of enterprises involving broad possibilities for direct foreign trade activities, the profound changes in price formation, the establishment of organic links between external and internal prices, and — last but not least — the introduction of an effective customs tariff. The socialist character of the ownership of the means of production, the planning system and the monopoly on foreign trade have been maintained. It should be emphasized, moreover, that all these measures were designed to reform the economic mechanism and not in order to gain access to GATT. This accession should be regarded as a logical and welcome by-product of the reform.

Prior to the accession, Hungary's trade policy situation — the legal framework — was determined by a series of bilateral trade agreements (there was no such agreement with the USA) providing in most cases most favored nation (MFN) treatment and some specific clauses for pricing to avoid so-called "market disruption"; bilateral quotas, diminishing in number, were still present. Discriminatory treatment of the import of Hungarian goods was, while decreasing, still a characteristic feature. With the EC negotiating on behalf of its members, the member countries renounced their existing bilateral agreements.

Hungary, for its part, activated its participation in international trade policy fora, such as the Economic Commission for Europe and UNCTAD, with the aim of securing on a reciprocal basis most favored nation treatment and non-discrimination.

It was in this context that the possibility of acceding to the General Agreement on Tariffs and Trade was considered by the decision-making bodies.

Precedents with respect to socialist countries — long-standing Contracting Parties (Czechoslovakia and Cuba) and the conditions of accession of Yugoslavia, Poland and Romania — were taken into consideration.

The aim of such a move had to be defined in a realistic manner, avoiding illusions created by the friendly welcome of Hungary's new economic mechanism in the West, and by the precedents created by a number of socialist countries. While defining those aims, fears and misgivings of an economic, social, ideological and political nature had to be dealt with.

Specific interests of economic sectors, represented by government agencies, such as the Ministry of Finance, National Planning Office, National Board of Materials and Prices, to mention but the most important, had to be harmonized in complicated and cumbersome interagency negotiations. After the conclusion of these internal interagency negotiations, a government decision was adopted, with a mandate to begin the negotiations.

13.2. Phases of the Negotiation Process

13.2.1. Phase 1

The first phase was preparatory, informal and noncommittal in character. The type of contacts and talks varied from personal talks seeking information, points of possible agreements and disagreements, to semi-official but still informal meetings on the premises of GATT under the chairmanship of the Director General with the participation of the key Contracting Parties and Hungary.

In connection with the identification of specific problems it became clear that issues involving the procedural mechanisms of the negotiations, the legal framework and the functioning of GATT as an institution had to be dealt with. Extended talks, conducted during the whole process of negotiations, were held with the Secretariat of GATT. This was not a negotiation, but rather a learning process, which provided necessary knowledge that could be used as a valuable negotiating asset.

13.2.2. Phase 2

The second phase was the carrying out of the formal procedures, involving the:

- Presentation of the memorandum relating to Hungary's economic mechanism, laws and regulations; the status of the Hungarian enterprises; and trade policy aspects.
- Study of the questionnaire presented by the Contracting Parties to Hungary.
- Analysis of these written communications.
- Scrutiny of the existing Hungarian economic mechanism.

Behind the procedure lay the beginning of the substantive negotiations: all that was written or said had to be scrutinized and decided upon not only on the merit of each case and problem, but also as a part of the negotiating position. The aim of the Hungarian negotiator in this phase was to find out the intentions of the key Contracting Parties, before making any definite commitments.

Who were these key Contracting Parties? First of all, the members of the European Communities (EC), the main trading partners of Hungary. Their aim was clearly stated — they were interested in Hungary's accession for political and trade policy reasons. The political motives were, and are today, to loosen the ties of the small socialist countries to Comecon — and the Soviet Union; they were thus considering at the beginning making some differentiation between those countries whose trade policies are "inspired by the principles of GATT" (as a decision of the EC has put it) and those that are not. Specific encouragement was given to the Hungarian representatives by a number of EC member states. The trade policy aim was to consolidate the EC's discriminatory policy, consisting of applying quantitative restrictions against Hungary, by having it accepted in one form or an other through an eventual protocol of accession.

The United States had a similar aim as far as general policy was concerned, but opted for a more GATT-like solution — the accession of Hungary without any qualification. They were against the maintenance of discriminatory quantitative restrictions against Hungary, because they regarded these measures, not without reason, as being contrary to the main thrust of GATT — i.e., nondiscrimination. They had well-justified fears that the legalization of discriminatory measures, regardless of their impact on Hungary's exports, would mean the maintenance of bilateral trade, arrangements, thus excluding them from the totality of the prospective Hungarian market which, owing to the reform, was offering them some increased possibilities. Their position was legally weakened by the fact that new US legislation did not permit the establishment of relations with Hungary on the basis of the unconditional most favored nation clause, and they made it clear that they would have to invoke Art. XXXV of GATT. (In the case of the accession of Poland, they did not invoke this article, because the US legislation at the time of the Polish accession did not prevent their establishing MFN relations).

Other key Contracting Parties, such as Japan, Canada, Australia, etc., were equally interested to "have Hungary in", but opposed the maintenance of discriminatory quantitative restrictions against Hungarian exports for the same reasons as did the United States.

Having this in mind Hungary had two goals:

(1)   To accede to GATT without the political implications hoped for by the key Contracting Parties.
(2)   To accede to GATT on the basis of the observance of the unconditional most favored nation clause (Art. IV) and of the rule of nondiscrimination (Art. XIII).

Thus, the negotiations had a cooperative character insofar as the wish of the Contracting Parties and of Hungary coincided with the accession of Hungary to the General Agreement. On the basis of this concordance, the negotiations started. As to the conditions of accession, there were serious differences about which very heated discussions took place. The debated issues, especially the hitherto discriminatory treatment of Hungarian exports by the EC countries (and by some other, smaller countries of Western Europe), became essentially controversial and gave the negotiations a distinctly competitive character.

The main question for the Contracting Parties was to find out how firm the Hungarian position was. Their anticipation was that Hungary, after all, would "give in" in one way or another, as had some other countries in similar positions. They anticipated that the accession to GATT was for Hungary a "must", which had to be achieved by the Hungarian negotiator at any cost, preferably by working out loose and compromise solutions and texts.

This anticipation proved to be completely false. Hungary maintained its intial position during the whole negotiating process. This was a strategic surprise, which had its effect. As a matter of fact, the instructions to the Hungarian negotiator gave him liberty to abandon the negotiations, if the conditions specified in his instructions were not met.

This leads to some general observations as to the peculiarities of international negotiations. Countries, parties to such negotiations, are led in each case by a double aim. One is "political", establishing "good relations", or the inverse, to "demonstrate strength" and so on. These political aims are in most the cases linked with "higher considerations" such as the strengthening of one's own alliance or promoting some principles — all very respectable, but not always related to or determined by the countries' economic interests. In most cases, these interests are conflicting. This is especially true in the case of countries in a weak bargaining position — politically, economically, or both.

The dilemma facing the decision-maker, who has to instruct his negotiator, is to decide the priority of conflicting aims. The most frequent mistake is to try to avoid this dilemma while drafting the instructions. The moment of truth comes when the negotiating partner presents the negotiator with his own dilemma. One can witness in many cases a situation when the negotiator, having to pursue two or more strategic aims, had to abandon in a disorderly retreat essential economic interests, rights and claims for the sake of "higher considerations".

The problem is not whether these considerations are really "higher", but the fact that the decision-maker forgot to answer the question: "How high are these considerations?" or, more simply, "What price are we willing to pay for these considerations?". Hence, enigmatic texts emerge, interpreted by the partners having a better bargaining position in ways that in most cases are harmful to the economically weaker without being of any use in the noneconomic field.

As the above-mentioned example shows, a clear decision setting priorities permitted the Hungarian negotiator to avoid the trap so often encountered by many others involved in similar negotiations.

13.2.3. Phase 3

The third phase was bargaining in its purest form. Bargaining and negotiating situations had to be handled, such as one player against many, use and misuse of precedents, and so on. The result of the bargaining finally emerged in the form of presenting texts that contained specific provisions of an agreement between Hungary and the Contracting Parties of GATT. The context was highly legal and professional; the substance was political.

The precondition for an agreement was a balance of rights and obligations. Hungary, being in the relatively weaker position, strived to clarify these rights and obligations.

As a matter of fact, GATT is a perfect legal instrument, at least formally, as regards the balance of rights and obligations. An accession without qualification would have automatically given the benefit of this balance to the acceding party. This was, however, not the case. Specific situations and positions had to be resolved; here the balance of rights and obligations had to be considered very carefully.

Two such specific situations should be described here. The most important specific situation was Hungary's trading methods *vis-à-vis* a number of socialist countries not necessarily or exclusively member countries of Comecon. The Protocol of Accession to GATT gives Hungary the right to maintain its existing trading regulations with those countries (listed separately in Annex A of the Protocol of Accession). The actual situation was and still is that, as was pointed out in the Report of the Working Party on Hungary's Accession: Hungary does not apply customs tariffs to goods from countries listed in Annex A, because the method consisting in fixed quotas and prices does not permit tariffs to be applied. (It should be pointed out in this respect that on imports from socialist countries such as Yugoslavia, where no compulsory quotas and prices exist, tariffs are applied. Tariffs are also applied to goods imported from countries listed in Annex A in those cases where they are outside of fixed quotas and paid for in convertible currencies.)

This could be accepted by the Contracting Parties, under the condition that "these trading regulations or any change in them ... shall not impair her (Hungary's) commitments, discriminate against or otherwise operate to the detriment of Contracting Parties" (Protocol of Accession of Hungary to the General Agreement on Tariffs and Trade, Para. 3). A quasi-waiver has been granted to Hungary balanced by the above-mentioned Hungarian undertaking.

The other specific situation was linked with the wish of some Contracting Parties, mainly of the European Community, to depart from the general regulations dealing with market disruption, as provided for in Art. XIX of the General Agreement. The EC and other Contracting Parties sought and obtained a "selective safeguard" formula. This, however, was balanced by the confirmation of the commitment to liquidate the still-existing discriminatory quantitative restrictions. The deal appears in Para. 9 of the Report of the Working Party on the Accession of Hungary:

> Members of the Working Party considered it important to have in a protocol of accession a specific safeguard clause. Representatives of countries maintaining quantitative restrictions against Hungary's exports indicated in this connection that *the inclusion of such a safeguard clause would facilitate the removal of the restriction referred to in paragraph 8 above.* The representative of Hungary could agree to the inclusion of a safeguard clause, *provided it operates on a reciprocal basis. He also stated that his acceptance of such a safeguard clause was "in anticipation of early elimination of quantitative restrictions maintained against imports from Hungary inconsistently with Article XIII"* [emphasis added].

Two remarks should be made in this connection:

(1) The Hungarian representative made it clear that this important departure from the general rule is conditional.
(2) A similar disposition exists in the Protocols of Accession of Poland and Romania, but without the explicit condition of the early elimination of the discriminatory quantitative restrictions.

From the legal point of view, this disposition is not a perfect balance of rights and obligations. The Hungarian side paid an important extra price in order to enjoy its legal rights under the General Agreement. This could be considered as the expression of unequal positions of strength.

13.2.4. Phase 4

The fourth phase was to give form to the agreement. Here again the formal constraints came to the fore (Protocol of Accession, Report of the Working Party attached to the Protocol). The Hungarian schedule of concessions was a specific negotiating issue involving tariff concessions as a price of accession. Bargaining and real positions were to be reconciled between Hungary and its 21 negotiating partners. Tactics determined by the MFN-clause had to be found. Negotiations on the draft texts became the most important activity.

13.3. Texts and Language

Having studied carefully the Romanian and Polish Protocols of Accession, it was clear to the Hungarian representative that these texts were very poorly drafted, at least from the viewpoint of Hungary's interests. They lent themselves to various interpretations and were silent on substantial issues. Experience had taught him the simple truth expressed by a French author: "Rien n'est pire en diplomatie que le silence des textes, car il vaut accord au profit du plus fort ou du plus entreprenant" [Nothing is worse in diplomacy than the silence of texts, because it means an agreement to the benefit of the stronger or to the more daring party] (Alain Plantey, *La négociation internationale — principles et méthodes*, p. 179). Or to quote another expert in this matter: "The careful grammarian should precede the shrewd politician" (Frederic II of Prussia, *L'Antimachiavel*, XXVI).

One memorable incident of the negotiations on Hungary's accession should illustrate this point. After having agreed that the quantitative restrictions should be progressively eliminated at target dates, on the insistence of the EC the following additional text was adopted: "If for exceptional reasons, any such prohibitions or restrictions are in force as of January 1975 the Working Party ... will examine them with a view to their elimination".

Knowing the real intentions of the EC, in the face of its relentless attempts to seek loopholes for the maintenance of such restrictions, a very complicated debate took place to determine the relevant elements of such an examination. The EC offered an amazing variety of such elements, all implying that the mere existence of the specific price system prevailing at that time in Hungary should justify the maintenance of discriminatory quantitative restrictions. This was in clear contradiction to the dispositions of the General Agreement, so the EC was not in a position to declare its intentions openly. Hence, an array of subtle, unclear texts emerged.

While examining these texts, the Hungarian representative repeated his very simple question: "According to your text, will you be entitled to maintain quantitative restrictions inconsistent with Article XIII of the General Agreement?". The replies were evasive to put it mildly. The Hungarian question was repeated again and again: "Yes or no — will this text give you the right to discriminate against us?". Since the EC was unable to reply with "no", this final text was adopted: "The Working Party will take into account all relevant elements in order to evaluate the situation. ... *The mere existence of the price system in Hungary as distinct from its effects is not to be considered as the only relevant element*" (Report of the Working Party on Hungary's Accession Para. 8; emphasis added.)

Another example of the interpretation of texts by the strong could be given. The dispositions providing for the elimination of discriminatory quantitative restrictions stipulate that it should be implemented "progressively". The fact is that after the signature of the Protocol of Accession, no substantial progress was made and the bulk of the discriminatory quantitative restrictions remained. Conceptually, if one single quantitative restriction is eliminated in each decade, the process of elimination can be qualified as "progressive". The mistake of the Hungarian negotiator was that he failed to insist on the common determination of the meaning of the word "progressively".

There was another problem linked with the texts — the language, or rather, the terminology. The General Agreement has its own language, composed of notions of market or market-like situations, on legislative or judiciary texts prevailing in the signatory states at the time of the drafting of GATT, and on the texts of resolutions, decisions adopted later that became an integral part of the body of the dispositions. Some colloquial shortcuts, which refer to cases instead of quoting them, are widely used and correctly understood by the persons involved in the daily life of GATT, such as "grandfather clause", "escape clause", "enabling clause", "an Article XIX case", etc. This secret language is not understandable to the outsider, even if he is a business or chief executive of a huge multinational enterprise in a market economy. All this had to be translated into Hungarian for the information and use of the Hungarian authorities and of the members of the Hungarian negotiating team. A difficult task indeed, involving many misunderstandings and misrepresentations. Parallel difficulties arose when Hungarian legal texts were presented for scrutiny.

These differences in cultural background were sometimes visible, or better said, audible while listening to the argumentation of the different Contracting Parties. The representative of the EC spoke in French, while all the others spoke in English. This was, however, not the only difference. The argumentation of the EC was unmistakably based on the peculiar interpretation of the letter and spirit of the General Agreement, which implies that the Agreement is a rather loose set of principles, freely interpreted by each Contracting Party, thus creating considerable obstacles to finding out what was exactly the subject matter under consideration.

It became clear that the context of the negotiations made them a "rule-oriented" rather than a "power-oriented" negotiation. This was, from the Hungarian point of view, an asset rather than a liability. Discriminatory measures, which had been used hitherto toward Hungary, were clearly against the rules. No Contracting Party could therefore deny from the outset the benefit of these rules to a "newcomer". The heavy liability on the Hungarian side was that the Hungarian reform, the new economic mechanism, was completely new and unknown to the Contracting Parties. The burden of proof lay on the Hungarian side. The Contracting Parties' general interest in taking a hard look at the new Hungarian management system was a legitimate one. It was, however, clear to the Hungarian negotiator that the inquisitive attitudes of some Contracting Parties were motivated by the wish to find legal pretexts for the justification of their discriminatory policies.

The Hungarian experiences showed, however, that there is no such thing as a pure rule-oriented negotiation with no element of power diplomacy in it. But GATT as a negotiating framework strengthens the "rule" element, thus providing a valuable shield for a weaker participant.

As far as the role of the Secretariat is concerned, it was not limited to providing the necessary knowledge of the procedures, precedents and legal aspects to a newcomer, but was to some extent the role of a mediator and even an arbitrator. This can be illustrated by the following example.

Hungary, at the time of its accession, maintained a regulation according to which imports under cooperative contracts between Hungarian and foreign companies were eligible for individual tariff reductions or exemptions. Contracting Parties considered this as a case of conditional most favored nation status — not in conformity with Article I of the General Agreement.

The case was resolved against Hungary by the insertion of the following paragraph (Para. 12) into the Report of the Working Party on Hungary's Accession to the General Agreement:

> Members of the Working Party took note of the regulations submitted by the Hungarian delegation with respect to cooperation contracts, with particular reference to the question of tariff exemptions and reductions granted in this framework. Several delegations said that the implementation of such provisions would be inconsistent with Article I of the General Agreement. In response to a request for a legal opinion *the GATT Secretariat while emphasizing that questions of interpretation of the General Agreement were matters for the CONTRACTING PARTIES, and not for the Secretariat,* gave certain *comments,* inter alia that the prerequisite of having a cooperation contract in order to benefit from certain tariff treatment *appeared* to imply conditional Most Favored Nation treatment and would,

therefore, *not appear* to be compatible with the General Agreement. The Hungarian representative took note of these comments [emphasis added].

The cautious wording illustrates how rules have influenced the *de facto* arbitration of the Secretariat. In other cases, as mentioned before, the Secretariat provided its good offices toward finding compromise solutions on heavily debated, crucial parts of the texts.

The role of the Chairman of the Working Party was even more important. The Chairman's prerogatives were not limited to the legal and procedural aspects of the negotiations, but covered also the substance. He was active in seeking solutions acceptable to all concerned. These activities took place in the formal meetings of the Working Party, but more frequently informally, to the extent that, in the sauna of the Finnish Ambassador, negotiators were discussing and deciding important issues, presented later in official meetings as compromise solutions arrived at with due respect to the formal rules of procedure.

In this context it should be mentioned that informal contacts, talks and even negotiations were permanent features. These informal meetings took place mainly during the numerous meetings of the Working Party, which lasted more than four years. The Hungarian negotiator was very soon aware that the decision-making powers of the local representatives were limited, and that the central authorities in the capitals were not always given a clear picture or at least a picture that represented an authoritative description of the Hungarian positions, thus offering a better insights into these positions. Having this in mind, the Hungarian negotiator visited several capitals. He was aware, especially in the case of the EC, that the decision lies as always in the hands of the member countries. He knew that the so-called committee of Article 113 of the EC dealing with trade policy questions had a crucial role. He visited the chairman of the COREPER (Committee of the Permanent Representatives) in Brussels; members of this committee, however, refused to join such talks.

In all these meetings, the "power diplomacy" element unmistakably manifested itself.

In these talks in the capitals specific interests, problems, views and considerations were debated openly, observing the strictly confidential character of the communications given and received. The Hungarian negotiator and his partners observed strictly this confidentiality, which helped to arrive at an acceptable solution.

13.4. The Protagonists

During the years of negotiations it turned out that the main opposition to the Hungarian claim came from the EC, so the substantive discussions took place practically between these two sides. Other Contracting Parties, while actively participating, recognized that the EC had a stake, e.g., in maintaining a discriminatory policy against Hungary even if it became a Contracting Party. A very interesting description of this non-negligible specific factor in the negotiations over Hungary's accession appeared in the *Journal of World Trade Law*:

> For the EC in particular it is very important to maintain the right to accord less favorable treatment to the N.M.E.'s [non-market economy countries]. The cited reasons for this go beyond the perceived need for special means of dealing with market disruption. The reluctance of the N.M.E.'s to recognize the EC as a legal entity in such fora as the United Nations has created much ill will, and encouraged intransigent positions. They also maintain that the right to discriminate is an important element in maintaining a bilateral relationship in which the EC's bargaining power is enhanced. A frequent off-the-record cited factor is the animosity of some of the EC's chief negotiators toward all communist regimes (Patterson, 1986, p. 185).

There were formally, as well as substantively, only two delegations, each consisting of several members: one representing the Hungarian side, the other representing the European Communities.

Let us consider the Hungarian delegation. The task of conducting the negotiations with the Contracting Parties was assigned ex officio to the Ministry of Foreign Trade, the ministry responsible for the conduct of foreign trade policy. The head of the Hungarian delegation was thus the Director General of the Department of International Organizations and Tariff Policy. The administrative and substantive preparation fell under the competence of this Department. The preparation for the actual negotiations consisted in the drafting of position papers, the collection of relevant documentation, statistics, precedents, etc.

Tactics, fall-back positions, etc., were discussed by the delegation. This delegation consisted of representatives of the Department of Bilateral Trade Policy, Legal Affairs of the Ministry of Foreign Trade, the Ministry of Finance, the National Planning Office, the National Office of Prices and Materials, and the National Bank. The persons were chosen on the bases of their competence and their participation in the elaboration of the Hungarian customs tariffs.

Members of this delegation did not come from a homogeneous background: their specific concerns and interests were determined by the conceptions and approaches of the respective institutions which delegated them. At the beginning, these specific features came to the fore. The head of the delegation had to represent the general and, to some extent, the strategic policy considerations. On him, and on him only, rested the whole burden of responsibility. This gave him the necessary authority to make decisions. He reported regularly to the competent authorities. During the work of the delegation, a unity developed as to the perception and approaches, so the members of the delegation identified themselves with the actual tasks lying before them.

The EC delegation consisted of fewer members: the head of the delegation, a Director General of the EC from the Department of External Economic Relations, and a few civil servants of the EC. The representatives of the EC member countries were also present and took an active part in the negotiations. The EC decision-making process seemed more complicated, cumbersome and on some occasions more time-consuming than that of the Hungarian delegation. This illustrated that the EC was not as sovereign in its decision-making as it pretended to be. It was not clear, however, to what extent the method of reporting back and asking for instructions was used as a tactic.

13.5. Precedents

In negotiations, especially in multilateral negotiations, precedent even by implication plays a very important role: it is sometimes tacitly recognized as an almost binding rule. Article I of the General Agreement is a classical example of precedent codified as a rule. "Any advantage, favour, privilege or immunity granted by any Contracting Party to any product originating in or destined for any other country shall be accorded *immediately and unconditionally* to the like product originating in or destined for the territories of all other Contracting Parties" (GATT, Basic Instruments and Selected Documents, Volume IV, Geneva, March 1968, p. 2; emphasis added).

Having illustrated by this quotation the capital importance of precedent in international negotiations, especially of an economic character, it is important to recall that, prior to the Hungarian request for accession, the Contracting Parties considered the issue of an eventual accession of the centrally planned economy countries to the General Agreement and came to the conclusion that: "The CONTRACTING PARTIES' approach to the question of trade relations with centrally planned economies should continue to be on a pragmatic *country-by-country basis*" (conclusions adopted on 24 November 1967; emphasis added).

Precedents were, however, frequently and forcefully invoked by the Contracting Parties. Two centrally planned economy countries acceded to the General Agreement prior to the Hungarian accession: Poland and Romania. In both cases, in the absence of tariffs the respective countries have accepted quantitative import commitments. Poland undertook a 7% increase of its imports from the Contracting Parties, and Romania undertook that the same proportion of increase of its overall imports would be granted to the imports from the Contracting Parties. As to the elimination of the discriminatory quantitative restrictions, Poland agreed that their elimination will take place after a "transitional period" which, for reasons that never were clarified, was not determined by the relevant instrument of accession.

Romania, on the other hand, agreed to consider that the eventual increases of the discriminatory quotas have to be regarded as measures of elimination of the discriminatory quantitative restrictions. These cases were invoked by several Contracting Parties, mainly by those who wished to maintain discriminatory quantitative restrictions not consistent with Art. XIII of the General Agreement against Hungary.

The Hungarian delegation consistently and successfully refused to accept these cases as valid precedents. Formally, it referred to the above-mentioned conclusions of the Contracting Parties, providing for a country-by-country approach. As to the substance, it pointed out that the only tariff concessions could be Hungary's. As to the dispositions dealing with the elimination of the quantitative restrictions, the Hungarian delegation pointed out that while accepting the "progressive" elimination, a target date for their final liquidation was necessary; thus the loose-ended Polish formula was not acceptable. As to the "precedent" of Romania, the Hungarian delegation refused it on the grounds that it was nothing more nor less than the legalization of quantitative restrictions inconsistent with Art. XIII of the General Agreement.

The negotiating behavior of the main partner, the EC, was very peculiar. They insisted persistently: the case of Poland, for instance, was evoked no less than 149 times. This gave the Hungarian delegation a welcome opportunity to demonstrate on each occasion the inconsistency of the Polish text. The case was overdone by the EC and proved to be a tactical error. This was due to a miscalculation as to the final stand of the Hungarian delegation.

As to the negotiating behavior of the Hungarian delegation, it did not engage in lengthy discussions. It gave its reasons in a succinct form at the beginning and for years flatly refused any further considerations. "La mot sans phrases" was the vote of Abbé Sieyés during the long debate over Louis XVI's fate in the French Convention, thus ridiculing the weak character of those who felt the need for justification of their political will. A strong position is weakened by a surfeit of arguments.

The Hungarian delegation made use of some precedents, rather as an argument in discussion. Such was the case when the Contracting Parties tried to examine Hungarian actions according "to the books", whereas in identical cases they were transgressing the rules laid down in the books and "got away with it".

In one case, however, the precedent was embodied in the instruments of accession. In the part of the Report of the Working Party on the Accession of Hungary dealing with the notification of eventual subsidies, "the representative of Hungary stated that Hungary undertook in accordance with Article XIV: *1 and in accordance with the practice of CONTRACTING PARTIES* to notify regularly [of] its measures falling under Article XVI" (emphasis added).

13.6. Results

Seen from a purely legal, formal point of view, the results of the negotiations embodied in the Protocol of Accession, and the Report of the Working Party on Hungary's Accession to the General Agreement, are satisfactory for all parties concerned.

The rights and obligations contained in the instruments of accession, as well as those contained in the General Agreement to which Hungary became a full Contracting Party, are balanced.

The dispositions of these instruments required, however, a substantial change in the trade policy behavior of the signatories, especially of those whose trade policies were inconsistent with the dispositions of the General Agreement. These changes took place in a relatively short time in the case of smaller European market economy countries. The United States later disavowed Art. XXXV in all respects, except for the granting of most favored nation treatment in the tariff field, as stipulated in The bilateral trade agreement between Hungary and the United States.

The EC has failed so far to fulfill its obligations. It sought legal cover in the fact that the term "progressive", with respect to the elimination of quantitative restrictions inconsistent with Art. XIII of GATT, was not defined. They tried to give their own interpretation of the term "discrimination". They first advanced the thesis that only those quantitative restrictions should be regarded as discriminatory which are applied to Hungary alone; if a discriminatory measure is applied to one market economy country, this, according to the EC, is not to be regarded as "discrimination". Later they pretended that discriminatory measures applied to countries which they qualified as "state trading countries" are not discriminatory because of the differences in economic and social systems.

From a legal point of view, this does not hold. Paragraph 1 of Article XIII says:

> No prohibition or restriction shall be applied by any Contracting Party on the importation of any product of the territory of any other Contracting Party or on the exportation of any product destined for the territory of any other Contracting Party, unless the importation of the like product of *all* third countries or the exportation of the like product to *all* third countries is similarly prohibited or restricted (BISD, Volume IV, Geneva, 1969, p. 22; emphasis added).

The illegal character of any such restriction was explicitly confirmed by a legal opinion of the Secretariat of GATT during a subsequent meeting of the Working Party on Trade with Hungary.

Concerning the reference to the different nature of the Hungarian economic and social systems, it is worth mentioning that the Report of the Working Party on Hungary's Accession to the General Agreement "... considered that the Hungarian trading system had to be considered in the light of the existing system of economic management in Hungary, of which the adoption on 1 January 1968 of a customs tariff was an integral part". This text was adopted by the EC without reservation. The late emergence of the thesis about the "state trading countries" is a well-known "reservatio mentalis" with no legal force whatsoever, the more so as any interpretation of the dispositions of the General Agreement is a matter for the Contracting Parties and not for individual signatories.

The analysis of this situation is beyond the scope of this chapter. From a theoretical point of view only, one question could be examined: what if the more powerful party disregards the agreement arrived at after negotiations?

Hungary became a Contracting Party to GATT on 12 September 1973.

Reference

Patterson, Eliza R. (1986), Improving GATT Rules for Non-market Economies, *Journal of World Trade Law*, **2**.

CHAPTER 14

International Multiparty Negotiation: The Electrolux–Zanussi Case

Pietro Gennaro

Pronim Co. and Strategia e Oraganizzazione S.R.L.
Milan
Italy

14.1. The Problem and the Opportunity

Zanussi, a company employing originally about 18,000 people, with headquarters and major plants in Italy and Spain, had dominated the home appliance industry in Europe for a number of years. Mismanagement followed the death of its founder, Mr. Zanussi; in 1984 it was technically bankrupt. The company was considered a national problem, involving unions, banks and politicians.

The FIAT company nominated a new President, and an emergency plan was drawn up and agreed upon by the unions, reducing the work force and restructuring the business's portfolio. The plan called also for an injection of new capital, which the Zanussi family could not provide. The Electrolux company, which had developed quickly in several countries and wanted to become a world leader in home appliances, was approached by influential people; but they refused to consider a company in such a state in a country not familiar to them.

A meeting in Milan with Italian financiers failed also to gather the needed financial support. The new President resigned. A temporary President, a member of the family, was nominated to try again, while the Minister of Industry, prodded by politicians and unions, was trying to take care of the problem.

Zanussi had high market shares in the Federal Republic of Germany, Spain, the United Kingdom, France and, of course, in Italy. High operating losses and high indebtedness equaling sales were the major problems.

14.2. The Negotiation Parties

Actually, the case concerned a party, Electrolux, called to negotiate with several other parties. *Figure 14.1* describes the main links, both formal (solid lines) and informal (dashed lines).

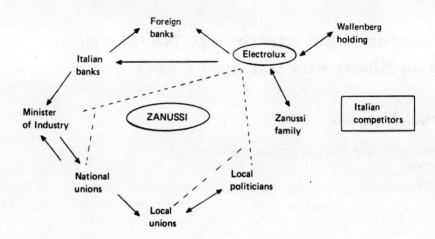

Figure 14.1. The Negotiation Parties.

14.3. The Negotiation Process

Mr. Rossignolo, President of the SKF Italian subsidiary — SKF being part of the same Swedish holding company that owns Electrolux and is controlled by the Wallenberg family — was asked by the influential FIAT Managing Director Cesare Romiti to try and convince Mr. Wallenberg to consider acquiring Zanussi, something they had refused a year before. Mr. Rossignolo pointed out to Mr. Wallenberg and the Electrolux top management that many Swedish companies, including SKF, had prospered in Italy for years; that Zanussi's high market share in the Federal Republic of Germany, France, the United Kingdom and Spain fit in well with the Electrolux global strategy; and that the Friuli local government had offered to refinance the company. He finally convinced them to explore the opportunity.

Mr. Werthen and Mr. Scharp, Electrolux President and Managing Director, respectively, agreed to come to Italy in May 1984. Mr. Rossignolo arranged meetings with the Minister of Industry and with the top management of Italian banks. Mr. Werthen and Mr. Scharp, on the basis of their first impressions, assigned to Mr. Rossignolo the role of negotiator for Electrolux.

In the meantime a team of Electrolux experts had come to the company and raised doubts about the feasibility of negotiating with so many diverse counterparts, but also confirmed Zanussi's market position and industrial capabilities. Electrolux promised to shift their orders for refrigerators and washing machines from independent suppliers to Zanussi; they also mentioned their interest in buying components (pumps, compressors, plastic and metal components, etc.) from Zanussi plants.

The Swedish and international press maintained that it would be very difficult for Electrolux to rescue Zanussi; whenever rumors about the impending deal emerged, Electrolux shares fell on the Stockholm Stock Exchange.

Mr. Rossignolo had to keep discussing and explaining not only with Electrolux, but with the local and national unions and politicians and the banks. In July 1984 the experts concluded that the work force cutback (about 30%), enacted the previous year, was now adequate; and Electrolux confirmed to the unions that they would guarantee the present level of employment.

In August 1984 after Electrolux agreed with the Zanussi family to buy their shares, an audit report about a foreign exchange contingent liability influenced them to reconsider; but in September they decided favorably. On the recommendation of Mr. Rossignolo, Electrolux persuaded Mr. Verri, then Managing Director at RIV-SKF in Turin, to accept the position of Managing Director. Mr. Rossignolo had already been designated as President.

Electrolux issued a "letter of confort" to the banks, and asked them to restructure the debt. Negotiations started.

From September to December 1984 other negotiations were conducted with the local politicians controlling Friuli Region, a development bank owned by the local government. Finally, in mid-December, after many hours of heated discussion, the Electrolux plan was accepted; the stock capital was canceled and new capital subscribed by Friuli Region (10%), Electrolux (49%) and a number of financial institutions. Electrolux had an option for a further increase in their capital investments, which would give them control.

Negotiations with banks were concluded a short time later, providing for a consolidation of debts at low rates and a medium-term repayment plan.

But Mr. Rossignolo and Mr. Verri, revising the Electrolux plan in January 1985, found that the employment agreement with the unions could not be kept: of 18,000 employed, taking into account the foreseen plant automation investment in three years, almost 4,500 people would have to be made redundant. They decided to present the facts and discuss them openly. In mid-February 1985 a meeting with delegates of the local and national unions was organized in Rome. The three national unions participated. The meeting, actually a long and heated negotiation session, lasted from Thursday to Saturday morning without interruptions, with breaks threatened more than once. At the end the Zanussi plan was accepted under the condition that its progress would be closely monitored by the unions.

14.4. Results

The first check in February 1986 was troublesome. Instead of dismissing 2,500 people in 1985, Zanussi laid off 2,800. On the other side the success of the new marketing effort, and higher than expected orders from Electrolux prompted the Zanussi management to ask for temporary overtime (which, according to Italian law, must be agreed upon by the unions). Discussions followed, and a strike was called. After three months, however, overtime was permitted.

Zanussi announced reduced losses in 1985, to about 30 billion lire (against 125 billion lire in 1984). At the beginning of 1987 they announced a profit for 1986 of more than 30 billion lire. A new advanced washing machine was introduced in 1986. The Zanussi top management stated that, since no new investment had been made, the results were due entirely to the new spirit that all Zanussi people had acquired, following meetings, seminars, job rotations, the launching of new projects, and a restructuring of the top management roles with a "management committee" headed by Verri — actions that had required a huge investment of time and attention by the top management.

14.5. Some Final Comments

This case could provide some valuable lessons on how to manage a complex negotiation process with many parties. First of all, it is necessary to define each party and their specific interests and motivations. Then one has to try to prioritize the agreements to be concluded, giving top priority to the agreements that can or should be made first, to influence the following ones. Agreement with the unions had to come first, in this case, because a strong argument could be made that no agreement with the present and future shareholders and the banks could be developed in the absence of an agreement with the unions. At the same time, such an agreement provided social pressure on the other parties, who could not easily appear to destroy a social settlement.

Another lesson is probably that being frank and honest, but firm, can overcome emotional positions of the counterparts, provided one has enough time and patience. And last but not least, social and political pressures can be directed to work for rather than against a negotiator; but, of course, this requires excellent negotiation skills.

CHAPTER 15

How to Negotiate for Joint Ventures

Gottfried A. Wolf-Laudon

Siemens AG Austria
Vienna
Austria

15.1. Introduction

Joint ventures, a form of partnership, are as old as commercial relationships. Precedents can be found in Roman law and in the English common law, but such customs also can be found in earlier societies.

We may define a joint venture as a *productive partnership–agreement* the result of which is uncertain because there is risk of loss or failure as well as the chance of gain or success.

Special problems have to be managed when a joint venture is negotiated and initiated, e.g., in a country which may have different laws, customs, commercial practices, and political and social institutions. The parties, while acknowledging the problems, must deem it worthwhile to solve them.

Negotiation is a process in which the parties (larger social systems, individuals, groups, organizations) with their own specific interests exchange and communicate knowledge, skills, motivation, resources and information in order to make and coordinate goal-oriented — e.g., joint venture — decisions. Decision making and negotiations are not identical, but there is a considerable overlap.

Negotiations for joint ventures are an elastic concept, where all elements of human behavior and of interpersonal and interorganizational contacts are in some way amalgamated according to patterns that differ from situation to situation. No elements should be neglected.

In his biography of Dr. Armand Hammer, Bob Considine (1975) documented the negotiations and joint venture strategies, tactics, operations and the life of one of the most fascinating and successful pioneers of East–West joint ventures. I recommend the book to anyone interested in the subject of negotiations in general or joint ventures in particular.

15.2. The Framework of a Joint Venture Negotiation

The framework in *Figure 15.1* may be of help in orienting themes to suitable levels, and in indicating negotiating and decision-making strategies, tactics, and operations for joint ventures.

Just now, the changing political climate favors development of East–West joint ventures. For example, the Conference on Security and Cooperation in Europe, held in Helsinki in 1975, and continuing in Vienna, recognized the value of such economic and technological cooperation as industrial joint ventures. The participating countries in that conference supported development of industrial cooperation, expressed determination to promote measures to create industrial cooperation and recognized that new forms of industrial cooperation and education can be applied to meet specific needs. Hungary, in the forefront of these agreements, had already in 1972 created legal preconditions to accredit, under Hungarian law, joint associations with enterprises from the West (see Conference on Security and Cooperation in Europe, 1975).

Substantive aspects and positions of the various negotiations for joint ventures attract most attention:

- Negotiating style (individual, group, organization, larger social system, national governments)
- Substantive long-term and short-term aspects (political, operational, strategic, tactical, methodological objectives)
- Complexity of negotiation situations (political, technological, economic, and social changes, problems, decisions, potential problems).

Investment in CMEA countries is now a very effective joint venture strategy. It has been possible to set up joint companies in Hungary since 1972 and in the Soviet Union since 1987. It is necessary for Western companies to learn on the spot what the CMEA markets need now and for the future, to exploit fully the unsaturated markets of the East.

This chapter is based on a case analysis of a successful East–West joint venture: a joint corporation between Intercooperation AG in Hungary and Siemens AG of Austria. I conclude that it is possible to have a successful commercial relationship in the form of a joint venture in another country, if certain conditions are met which include knowledge of that country's legal system, cultural

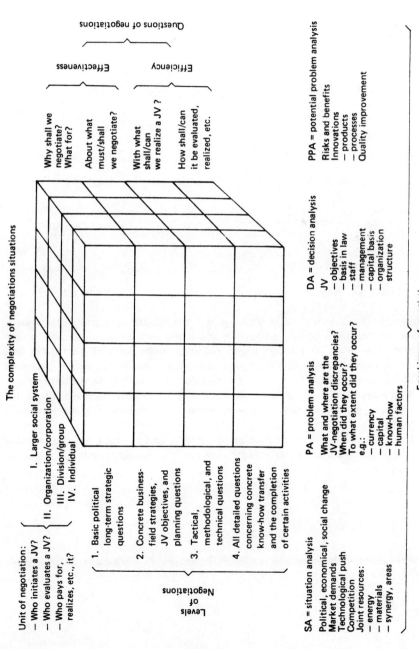

The complexity of negotiations situations

Unit of negotiation:
- Who initiates a JV?
- Who evaluates a JV?
- Who pays for, realizes, etc., it?

I. Larger social system
II. Organization/corporation
III. Division/group
IV. Individual

Levels of Negotiations

1. Basic political long-term strategic questions
2. Concrete business-field strategies, JV objectives, and planning questions
3. Tactical, methodological, and technical questions
4. All detailed questions concerning concrete know-how transfer and the completion of certain activities

Questions of negotiations

Effectiveness
- Why shall we negotiate? What for?
- About what must/shall we negotiate?

Efficiency
- With what shall/can we realize a JV?
- How shall/can it be evaluated, realized, etc.

SA = situation analysis
Political, economical, social change
Market demands
Technological push
Competition
Joint resources:
- energy
- materials
- synergy, areas

PA = problem analysis
What and where are the JV-negotiation discrepancies?
When did they occur?
To what extent did they occur?
e.g.:
- currency
- capital
- know-how
- human factors

DA = decision analysis
JV
- objectives
- basis in law
- staff
- management
- capital basis
- organization structure

PPA = potential problem analysis
Risks and benefits
Innovations
- products
- processes
Quality improvement

Focal issues of negotiations

Figure 15.1. **Framework for a joint venture negotiation.**

norms, political and social institutions and business practices. It is always much more than just a matter of understanding commercial practices alone.

First of all, success is based on excellent negotiators on both sides who are able and willing to analyze, to use synergy effects, to create a favorable *new* environment during managing in an unfavorable environment until the *joint venture* objectives are realized (see *Figure 15.2*).

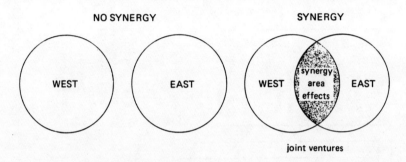

Figure 15.2. Creating a favorable negotiating environment through synergy effects.

15.3. How to Negotiate for (East–West) Joint Ventures

To understand a person from another group, organization, larger social system — especially one from a different culture and a different mentality — with whom discussions are being initiated, a negotiator must have the ability to listen and observe. An effective negotiating style is hardly possible unless one is prepared and able to listen and observe, as well as to motivate, participate and integrate.

These are the basic traits of the successful consensus-oriented negotiator. He should also have a marked readiness to learn and understand, and he should possess the gift of insight.

Under these conditions it may be possible to find common ground between thought processes often contradictory on the surface, thereby creating a negotiating symbiosis.

15.3.1. Integration style

Successful negotiations for joint ventures should be based on a consensus-oriented *integration style*, which demands the following:

The will and ability to cooperate

In general the joint venture philosophy demands that all those working on a joint project or within a joint corporation should cooperate intensively. An open interchange of ideas, which includes taking the trouble to appreciate the way the other side is thinking, is a basic requirement.

The balance between adaptation and innovation

One should strive to behave in a way appropriate to the situation while endeavoring to improve and use human capabilities. Joint *synergy*-improvement groups are an expression of a culture geared to adaptation and innovation through cooperation.

The ability to participate

Full participation in decision making and realization of decisions through working together characterize an effective joint venture management philosophy.

High motivation through target setting by consensus

The strategy, culture and structure of joint ventures have to be defined. This can be achieved in negotiations with the contributions of all partners using synergy effects. The discovery and development of attractive reciprocal services is equally important.

A capability to cooperate and integrate

Observing and harmonizing relevant demands and expectations through a cooperative way of thinking based on consensus is crucial to negotiating effectively for joint ventures.

Negotiations based on these five and other indicators not only increase the creative potential of all involved in the negotiation, but also mobilize the negotiation to everyone's advantage in an integrated fashion.

15.3.2. Contract negotiations

When negotiating for (East–West) joint ventures with a view to drawing up a contract, the following points should be observed:

Harmony

A favorable *new* joint venture environment (strategy, culture, structure) lays
great emphasis on compromise and consensus, avoiding unnecessary disputes.
The development and preservation of a harmonious business relationship, rather
than the achievement and maintenance of positions of advantage, is the essence
and purpose of negotiations. Differences of opinion between partners are therefore rarely fought out legally. A consensus is usually sought.

Information and preparation

It is important to collect and analyze information and data. Preparation for the
talks is therefore just as important as careful preparation for the decision.

Social hierarchy and courtesy

Effective negotiations for (East–West) joint ventures should have a highly
developed social hierarchy and system of courtesies in mind. They should not
only be outwardly polite at contract negotiations, but should also bear in mind
that the person leading the discussion is not necessarily the highest ranking
member of the group — his position as leader might be determined by relevant
specialized linguistic ability or technical knowledge.

Language

Negotiators on both sides should speak slowly and in short sentences, using simple words. Short, simple and slowly uttered sentences are important. All pic-
turesque expressions and idioms not in common use should be avoided. Effective
negotiators hear and think selectively. They are masters of not hearing and
ignoring what seems to be superficial.

Translation and interpretation

Negotiators for joint ventures should take an experienced interpreter with them.
It is not useful to rely on the other side's interpreter for the whole of the negotiations. Apart from the fact that interpreting is difficult and exhausting, one's
own interpreter should know and interpret one's position, which needs thorough
preparation. Negotiators for East–West joint ventures often do not let a
foreigner know if they have really understood a certain statement, let alone if
they agree with it. They are often artists in saying *No*.

Behavior

A calm and relaxed attitude indicates seriousness to the negotiating partners. Hyperactive, partly aggressive behavior and impatience can be interpreted as lack of discipline or untrustworthiness. Often negotiators do not make notes during a negotiation; and if one side does not, it is often better not to do so at all.

Body language

In the West people rely too much on verbal communication. Eastern negotiators are usually good observers, especially when it comes to a slight change of expression of gesture. When negotiating for joint ventures, one should also take note of nonverbal communication, i.e., body language and behavior.

The capacity to be silent

Silence, to experienced negotiators, does not mean that one does not agree, but that the partner is considering and thinking something over. One should not, therefore, become uncomfortable and try to bridge over or interrupt a negotiating partner's silence.

Addressing the negotiating partner

One should address the members of joint ventures negotiating team as a group and not as individuals. The highest in rank in the group may hold his position because of his length of service rather than because of great technical or other knowledge. Perhaps he is a very good negotiator. He must, however, in any case consult his colleagues before he can make a binding declaration. It is wrong to expect an answer from him immediately.

Moreover, pressure is usually seen as a means of concealing seriousness. Unsubstantiated personal assurances do not enjoy great credibility. Starting from a higher or lower price with the objective of reaching a compromise price, or attempting to reach a delivery date in the same way, is not effective for negotiating joint ventures.

15.3.3. Levels of negotiation

It is important to negotiate different themes for joint ventures only on the levels listed below (see also *Figure 15.1*).

Effectiveness questions

Why? What for? What? In negotiations with politicians or top management, basic political long-term strategic questions should be discussed. Details should be delegated as these are the business of middle management. **What? With what?** Concrete business field strategies, objectives, and planning questions should be discussed with the management division responsible and are passed on to top management as information.

Efficiency questions

With what? How? Tactical, methodological and technical questions should usually be discussed with those responsible, or with representatives of all departments affected by the decision. This is done after careful preparation. **How? When? Where? To what extent?** All detailed questions or questions concerning concrete know-how and the completion of certain activities should be discussed with those who will carry them out.

The framework in *Figure 15.1* may be of help in orienting themes to suitable levels, and in indicating negotiating and decision-making strategies.

15.4. Creating a Favorable "New" (Joint Venture) Environment while Managing in an Unfavorable Environment

The mobilization of human resources and their mental potential for the purpose of successful joint ventures should be given greater emphasis in the future than it enjoys today.

The driving forces in the structural change in the economies and societies of the industrial countries in the East and the West, but also in the developing nations, especially those of the Pacific, will be directed into new channels by increasing:

- Internationalization and globalization (market demand and technology push).
- Informatization and communication (know-how transfer).
- Humanization in the sense of tolerance of human nature and automation (office, network and factory of the future).
- Flexibility and mobility (synergy effects, creativity, innovation, etc.).
- Freedom in the sense of an ethic of responsibility (the ability to do more than we have to do).

At the same time there is a new way of thinking of the matter as a whole, which is developing and which can be observed worldwide. This holistic consciousness today characterizes the behavior of many politicians and managers, especially in internationally oriented institutions and enterprises. IIASA is a good example of this.

What characterizes effective *joint venture* and *human resources* management? It seeks to:

- Be effective — that is, to do the right things in the efficient, right, way.
- Be innovative — that is, to increase its ability for self-criticism and -renewal constantly, by knowing more, being capable of more, wanting more and having more courage of its own convictions.
- Awaken the mental abilities and talents hidden in the joint venture workers.
- Concentrate its own motivation and that of the workers on the strategic concerns of the joint venture and the specific demands of the new joint venture market and competition.

15.5. Common Joint Venture Practices

Joint ventures demand a cooperative, moral consciousness and behavior; i.e., putting a high ethical value on the undertaking. Experience shows that about 60% of the success of a joint venture depends on the relations between the personalities involved in the cooperation.

Joint ventures demand reciprocal understanding and recognition of the partner's logic in thinking as well as the development of a joint logic in thinking. This means a joint venture management must be capable of completing the set tasks cooperatively taking into account their specialist nature, character, and influence.

Managers in a joint East–West corporation need to learn, first of all, how to manage the *very new social system* of this cooperation and how to manage themselves in it. Joint management practices have to be focused on *joint effectiveness*.

Effectiveness is not a quality a manager from East or West brings to a joint situation. Effectiveness is best seen as something a joint management produces from a common task, goal or situation by managing it appropriately. *Effectiveness represents output, not input.* Effective common management practice must

First of all:	*Later:*
- do right things	- do things right
- produce creative alternatives	- solve problems
- optimize resource utilization	- safeguard resources
- obtain results	- follow duties
- increase profit	- lower costs
Strategic thinking:	Tactical thinking and operation:
KNOW WHY, KNOW WHAT	KNOW HOW

Joint venture managers must think in terms of performance, not personality. It is not so much what a joint venture manager does, but what he achieves together with his colleagues. Effectiveness should be measured as the extent to which the joint venture management achieves the output requirements — synergy effects — of their joint position. In practice, these are:

- The development of new areas of cooperation between those enterprises having a share in the joint company and the economic organizations and associated companies connected with those enterprises.
- The optimizing of research, development, production, distribution, assembly, maintenance and service capacities, as well as the joint development of raw material, intermediate products and software capacities.
- The concentration of joint forces on third-market projects which, without this breadth of synergy, could not be realized.
- The establishment and extension of lasting partnerships in scientific, technical, economic, organizational and legal spheres.

The above-mentioned bases of a joint enterprise afford joint venture management the chance to:

- Solve country-specific tasks and diverse problems more expeditiously, due to the common legal basis.
- Achieve continuous joint intent, target and strategic planning as well as a methodical employment of all resources.
- Appraise and calculate more realistically the possibilities and risks of new areas of cooperation.
- Achieve faster and more satisfactory solutions of large and complex technical and economic problems.
- Extend the application of cooperation to synergy areas of advanced technology.
- Choose, train and further educate suitable staff in a target-oriented way.
- Communicate continuously and hold coordination meetings, which will enable conflicts of interests to be discussed daily.

Joint ventures that are oriented toward their customers' needs and the future market demands require creativity, motivation and optimism and thereby also increase their ability to use joint *synergy effects*.

Productivity and effectiveness can be increased by improving performance with joint human resources. A mechanism for achieving strategic long-term increase in joint productivity and effectiveness is shown in *Figure 15.3*.

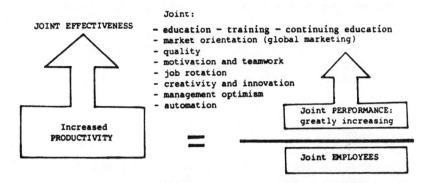

Figure 15.3. Strategic long-term increase of joint productivity and effectivess.

15.6. Key Elements for Effective (East–West) Joint Ventures

A joint venture is a special economic field and covers the new technical–economic possibilities that lie between the maintaining of independence in competition and the building of enterpises. It represents a synthesis between cooperation and competition, which is so difficult to imagine.

A joint venture is always closely connected to practice and leads to a cumulation of knowledge. As a part of an enterprise's strategy, its importance grows continually and is on the point of becoming a new basic dimension of the economy.

A joint venture is possible on three bases: horizontal, vertical, and complementary:

- **Horizontal joint venture:** when two or more enterprises with the same objective decide on joint venturing in one or more functions.
- **Vertical joint venture:** between the functions of companies, one subordinate to the other.
- **Complementary joint venture:** concerns the so-called cooperation between companies whose markets, products and services complement each other.

In addition to development, manufacturing, and marketing functions, the following are also preferred areas of joint ventures: data processing, automation, construction, project planning, consulting, engineering, education and training, maintenance and service, organization, and quality control.

Joint venturing as a rule develops increasing intensity in the following stages:
- Exchange of experiences and specialist symposia.
- Joint information-gathering and evaluating in the frame of market and system studies.
- Separating of an enterprise function.
- Separating of several enterprises' functions.
- Forming a joint venture management.
- Legal separation of a joint venture management.
- Founding a joint company.

The obligations and rights of the executive branch of a joint East–West enterprise are characterized by the following features:

- Joint basis in law.
- Joint staff.
- Joint management.
- Joint capital basis.
- Joint organization.
- Shared risks and benefits.

Bibliography

Considine, B. (1975), *The Remarkable Life of Dr. Armand Hammer*, Harper & Row, New York.
Von Czege, A. Wass, (1979), Ungarns Aussenwirtschaftsmodell, *Ökonomische Studien*, **28**, Gustav Fischer Verlag, Stuttgart, New York.
Conference on Security and Cooperation in Europe (1975), Final Act, Helsinki.
Ost-West-Zusammenarbeit in dritten Ländern, Bundesverband der Deutschen Industrie e.V. (1982), BDI Nr. 156.
West-Ost-Journal, Donaueuropäisches Institut Wien, Jupiter Verlag Gmb.
Wolf-Laudon, G. A. (1984), *Produktive Partnerschaft in der Wirtschaft*, Expert-Verlag, Grafenau, FRG.

PART III

Cultural, Psychological, and Political Factors in International Negotiations

CHAPTER 16

Cultural Predictors of National Negotiation Styles

Geert Hofstede

University of Limburg
Maastricht
and
Institute for Research of Intercultural Cooperation
Arnhem
The Netherlands

16.1. National, Professional, and Organizational Cultures in International Negotiations

Negotiators in international negotiations, by definition, have different national cultural backgrounds. "Cultural" is used here in the sense of "the collective programming of the mind which distinguishes the members of one category of people from another". National culture is that component of our mental programming which we share with more of our compatriots as opposed to most other world citizens. Besides our national component, our cultural programs contain components associated with our profession, regional background, sex, age group, and the organizations to which we belong. National cultural programming leads to patterns of thinking, feeling and acting that may differ from one party in an international negotiation to another.

The most fundamental component of our national culture consists of *values*. Values are broad preferences for one state of affairs over others. Values are acquired in the family during the first years of our lives, further developed and confirmed at school, and reinforced in work organizations and in daily life within a national cultural environment. Values determine what we consider as good and evil, beautiful and ugly, natural and unnatural, rational and irrational, normal and abnormal. Values are partly unconscious and because of their normative character, hardly discussable. We cannot convince someone else that his/her values are wrong. It is essential that negotiators share the national culture and values of the country they represent, because otherwise they will not be trusted by their own side.

Other components of national culture are more superficial — that is, visible, conscious, and easy to learn even by adults. They include *symbols*: words, gestures, and objects that carry a specific meaning in a given culture. The entire field of language consists of symbols; and a culture group's language can be learned by outsiders. Besides symbols, a culture has its *collective habits* or rituals, ways of behavior that serve to communicate feelings more than information; these, too, can be learned by outsiders, although not as easily.

Those involved in international negotiations will have developed a professional negotiation culture, which considerably facilitates the negotiation process. This professional culture, however, is more superficial than their national cultures: it consists of commonly understood symbols and commonly learned habits more than of shared values. Different types of negotiators will have their own kind of professional cultures: diplomats, bureaucrats, politicians, business people, lawyers, engineers, etc. Negotiations are easier with people from other countries sharing the same professional culture than with those who do not.

Finally, organizations, too, develop their own cultures. In the field of international negotiations, international bodies, such as IIASA, the IAEA, and the various other UN agencies, can play an important role because their internal culture facilitates communication. Again, and even more than in the case of professional cultures, these organizational cultures are superficial — that is, they reside on the level of the easily acquired common symbols and habits. Organizational cultures are not always an asset; they can develop into liabilities, too, by blocking communication instead of facilitating it.

The behavior of negotiators in international negotiations will thus be influenced by at least three levels of culture: national, professional, and organizational, besides the contribution of their own personal skills and character.

16.2. Dimensions of Differences in National Cultures

The remainder of this chapter will be devoted to national culture differences and their supposed impact on negotiation styles, because it is in this area that the author's research has been mostly focused. National culture differences, as we argued, reside to a large extent in values acquired in early life, and are therefore quite deep-seated, often unconscious and hardly discussable.

National cultural value systems are quite stable over time; elements of national culture can survive amazingly long, being carried forward from generation to generation. For example, countries that were once part of the Roman empire still today share some common value elements, as opposed to countries that did not inherit from Rome.

National cultural value systems have been measured in international comparative research projects. Such projects use samples of people from different countries as respondents on value questions. These samples should be carefully *matched* — that is, composed of similar people from one country to another, similar in all respects except nationality (same age, sex, profession, etc.). They need not be *representative* of the entire population of a country, although if this is possible, it makes the samples even more attractive. Two such international comparative value research projects were carried out by this author (Hofstede, 1980, 1983) and by Bond (1987), respectively.

16.2.1. The Hofstede–IBM study

The Hofstede research used a data bank containing 116,000 questionnaires of the values of employees of the multinational business organization IBM in 72 countries, and collected between 1967 and 1973. These employees represent extremely well-matched subjects of each country's population, because they do the same jobs with the same technology in the same kind of organization, have the same education levels, and can be matched by age and sex. Initially, data from 40 countries were analyzed; later on, this number was extended to 50, and data from 14 more countries were grouped into three geographic regions — East Africa, West Africa and Arab-speaking countries — bringing the total number of cultures covered up to 53. As the data were collected inside a capitalist enterprise, the socialist countries are not covered in this research project. However, matched data from a Yugoslav organization selling and servicing IBM equipment are included.

The IBM project revealed that the 53 countries covered differed mainly along four dimensions:

1. *Power Distance*, that is, the extent to which the less powerful members of organizations and institutions (like the family) accept and expect that power is distributed unequally. This represents inequality (more versus less), but defined from below, not from above. It suggests that a society's level of inequality is in the followers as much as in the leaders. Power and inequality, of course, are extremely fundamental facts of any society, and anybody with some international experience will be aware that "all societies are unequal, but some are more unequal than others".

2. *Individualism* on the one side versus its opposite, *Collectivism*. This describes the degree to which the individuals are integrated into groups. On the individualist side, we find societies in which the ties between individuals are loose: everyone is expected to look after him/herself and his/her immediate family. On the collectivist side, we find societies in which people from birth onward are integrated into strong, cohesive in-groups; often their extended families (with uncles, aunts and grandparents)

continue protecting them in exchange for unquestioning loyalty. The word "collectivism" in this sense has no political meaning: it refers to the group, not to the state. Again, the issue addressed by this dimension is an extremely fundamental one, relevant to all societies in the world.

3.   *Masculinity* versus its opposite, *Femininity*. The distribution of roles between the sexes is another fundamental issue for any society to which a range of solutions are found. The analysis of the IBM data revealed that (a) women's values differ less among societies than men's values; (b) if we restrict ourselves to men's values (which vary more from one country to another), we find that they contain a dimension from very assertive and competitive and maximally different from women's values on the one side, to modest and caring and similar to women's values on the other. We have called the assertive pole "masculine" and the modest, caring pole "feminine". The women in the feminine countries have the same modest, caring values as the men; in the masculine countries they are somewhat assertive and competitive, but not as much as the men, so that these countries show a gap between men's values and women's values.

The three dimensions described so far all refer to expected social behavior: toward people higher or lower in rank (Power Distance), toward the group (Individualism/Collectivism), and as a function of one's sex (Masculinity/Femininity). It is obvious, that the values corresponding to these cultural choices are bred in the family: Power Distance by the degree to which children are expected to have a will of their own, Individualism/Collectivism by the cohesion of the family versus other people, and Masculinity/Femininity by the role models that parents and older children present to the younger child.

4.   A fourth dimension found in the IBM studies does not refer to social behavior, but to man's search for truth. We called it "Uncertainty Avoidance": it indicates to what extent a culture programs its members to feel either uncomfortable or comfortable in unstructured situations. "Unstructured situations" are novel, unknown, surprising, different from usual. Uncertainty-avoiding cultures try to prevent such situations by strict laws and rules, safety and security, and on the philosophical and religious level by a belief in absolute truth: "There can only be one Truth and we have it". People in uncertainty-avoiding countries are also more emotional, and motivated by inner nervous energy. The opposite type, uncertainty-accepting cultures, are more tolerant of behavior and opinions different from what they are used to; they try to have as few rules as possible, and on the philosophical and religious level they are relativist and allow many currents to flow side by side. People within these cultures are more phlegmatic and contemplative, and not expected by their environment to express emotions.

Table 16.1 lists scores for the 53 cultures in the IBM research, which allow positioning them in each of the four dimensions (plus a fifth, which we will describe in the next section). These scores are *relative*: we have chosen our scales such that the distance between the lowest- and the highest-scoring country is about 100 points.

16.2.2. The Bond study

The other comparative value research project relevant to our topic was carried out by Michael Bond of the Chinese University of Hong Kong. He asked a number of Chinese social scientists to prepare in Chinese a list of basic values for Chinese people. After discussion and elimination of redundancies, this led to a 40-item Chinese questionnaire, which was subsequently translated into English. Through an international network of interested colleagues, this Chinese Value Survey was administered to 1000 students in a variety of disciplines (50 male, 50 female) in each of 22 countries from all five continents; the only socialist country covered was Poland. Wherever possible, translations into the local language were made directly from the Chinese. To a Western mind, some of the items such as, "filial piety" look exotic — so exotic that it was explained: "obedience to parents, respect for parents, honoring of ancestors, financial support of parents". Of course, to the Chinese mind, some of the items on the IBM questionnaire, designed by Western social scientists, may have looked equally exotic.

A statistical analysis of the 22-country Chinese Value Survey (CVS) results, based on the *relative* importance attached in a country to each value versus the other values, yielded again four dimensions. Twenty out of 22 countries were covered earlier in the IBM studies. Thus, we could compare the country scores on each CVS dimension to those of the IBM dimensions. One CVS dimension was very similar to Power Distance, one to Individualism–Collectivism (most of the Chinese values being associated with the collective pole), and one to Masculinity–Femininity. This in spite of the completely different questions, different populations, different moments in time, and different mix of countries. One dimension from the IBM studies, however, is missing in the CVS data. We did not find a CVS dimension related to Uncertainty Avoidance. We earlier associated this dimension with man's search for truth; it seems that to the Chinese mind, this is not an essential issue. However, we did find another quite clearly marked dimension. It is made up of the following values:

on the positive side

- persistance (perseverance)
- ordering relationships by
  status and observing this order
- thrift
- having a sense of shame

on the negative side

- personal steadiness and stablity
- protecting one's "face"
- respect for tradition
- reciprocation of greetings, favors
  and gifts

Table 16.1. Scores on five dimensions for 50 countries and 3 regions: rank number: 1 = lowest; 53 = highest (for CFD: 22 = highest)

Country	Power Distance Index (PDI)	Rank	Individualism Index (IDV)	Rank	Masculinity Index (MAS)	Rank	Uncertainty Avoidance Index (UAI)	Rank	Confucian Dynamism Index (CFD)	Rank
Argentina	49	18-19	46	31-32	56	33-34	86	39-44	–	–
Australia	36	13	90	52	61	38	51	17	31	9-10
Austria	11	1	55	36	79	52	70	29-30	–	–
Belgium	65	34	75	46	54	32	94	48-49	–	–
Brazil	69	40	38	27-28	49	27	76	32-33	65	18
Canada	39	15	80	49-50	52	30	48	12-13	23	4
Chile	63	29-30	23	16	28	8	86	39-44	–	–
Colombia	67	37	13	5	64	42-43	80	34	–	–
Costa Rica	35	10-12	15	8	21	5-6	86	39-44	–	–
Denmark	18	3	74	45	16	4	23	3	–	–
Equador	78	45-46	8	2	63	40-41	67	26	–	–
Finland	33	8	63	37	26	7	59	22-23	–	–
France	68	38-39	71	43-44	43	18-19	86	39-44	–	–
Germany, F.R.	35	10-12	67	39	66	44-45	65	25	31	9-10
Great Britain	35	10-12	89	51	66	44-45	35	6-7	25	5-6
Greece	60	26-27	35	24	57	35-36	112	53	–	–
Guatemala	95	51-52	6	1	37	11	101	51	–	–
Hong Kong	68	38-39	25	17	57	35-36	29	4-5	96	22
Indonesia	78	45-46	14	6-7	46	23-24	48	12-13	–	–
India	77	43-44	48	33	56	33-34	40	9	61	17
Iran	58	24-25	41	30	43	18-19	59	22-23	–	–
Ireland	28	5	70	42	68	46-47	35	6-7	–	–
Israel	13	2	54	35	47	25	81	35	–	–
Italy	50	20	76	47	70	49-50	75	31	–	–
Jamaica	45	17	39	29	68	46-47	13	2	–	–
Japan	54	21	46	31-32	95	53	92	47	80	20
Korea, Rep. of	60	26-27	18	11	39	13	85	37-38	75	19
Malaysia	104	53	26	18	50	28-29	36	8	–	–
Mexico	81	48-49	30	22	69	48	82	36	–	–
Netherlands	38	14	80	49-50	14	3	53	19	44	14
Norway	31	6-7	69	41	8	2	50	16	–	–
New Zealand	22	4	79	48	58	37	49	14-15	30	8
Pakistan	55	22	14	6-7	50	28-29	70	29-30	0	1
Panama	95	51-52	11	3	44	20	86	39-44	–	–
Peru	64	31-33	16	9	42	16-17	87	45	–	–
Philippines	94	50	32	23	64	42-43	44	10	19	3
Portugal	63	29-30	27	19-21	31	9	104	52	–	–
South Africa	49	18-19	65	38	63	40-41	49	14-15	–	–
Salvador	66	35-36	19	12	40	14	94	48-49	–	–
Singapore	74	41	20	13-15	48	26	8	1	48	15
Spain	57	23	51	34	42	16-17	86	39-44	–	–
Sweden	31	6-7	71	43-44	5	1	29	4-5	33	12
Switzerland	34	9	68	40	70	49-50	58	21	–	–
Taiwan	58	24-25	17	10	45	21-22	69	28	87	21
Thailand	64	31-33	20	13-15	34	10	64	24	56	16
Turkey	66	35-36	37	26	45	21-22	85	37-38	–	–
Uruguay	61	28	36	25	38	12	100	50	–	–
USA	40	16	91	53	62	39	46	11	29	7
Venezuela	81	48-49	12	4	73	51	76	32-33	–	–
Yugoslavia	76	42	27	19-21	21	5-6	88	46	–	–
Regions:										
East Africa	64	31-33	27	19-21	41	15	52	18	25	5-6
West Africa	77	43-44	20	13-15	46	23-24	54	20	16	2
Arab Countries	80	47	38	27-28	53	31	68	27	–	–
Bangladesh	–	–	–	–	–	–	–	–	40	13
Poland	–	–	–	–	–	–	–	–	32	11

For some countries, the values on the positive side are relatively more important; for others, those on the negative side. All of them are already found in the teachings of Confucius, dating from 500 B.C. However, the values on the positive side are more oriented toward the future (especially perseverance and thrift), those on the negative side toward the past and present. Bond has therefore called this dimension *Confucian Dynamism*. Country scores on Confucian Dynamism for the countries surveyed with the CVS are listed in the last column of Table 1, raising the total number of relevant dimensions to five. Interestingly, Individualism (both in the Hofstede and in the Bond study) is strongly correlated $(r = .84)$ with a country's wealth (per capita GNP), and we can prove with diachronic data that the causality goes *from* wealth *to* individualism. Confucian Dynamism is strongly correlated $(r = .70)$ with a country's economic growth over the past 25 years (increase in per capita GNP), with a likely causality *from* Confucian Dynamism *to* economic growth.

16.3. National Cultures and International Negotiations

Negotiations, whether international or not, share some universal characteristics:

- two or more parties with (partly) conflicting interests
- a common need for agreement because of an expected gain from such agreement
- an initially undefined outcome
- a means of communication between parties
- a control and decision-making structure on either side by which either side's negotiator(s) is/are linked to his/their superiors.

However, in international negotiations, the following characteristics vary according to the national negotiation styles of either side:

- the nature of the control and decision-making structure on either side
- reasons for trusting or distrusting the behavior of the other side (a certain amount of trust is an indispensable ingredient for successful negotiation)
- tolerance for ambiguity during the negotiation process
- emotional needs of negotiators, e.g., ego boosting or ego effacement.

If one knows the approximate position of a country's national cultural value system on the various cultural dimensions listed in *Table 16.1*, one can predict aspects of the negotiation style of its negotiators.

1. Larger Power Distance will lead to a more centralized control and decision-making structure (key negotiations have to be concluded by the top authority).

2. Collectivism will lead to a need for stable relationships, so that negotiations can be carried out among persons who have become familiar with each other over a long time (often, several years). Every replacement of one person by another is a serious disturbance of the relationship, which has to be reestablished from scratch.

In collectivist cultures, mediators or go-betweens have a more important role in negotiations than in individualist cultures. Formal harmony is very important in a collectivist setting; overt conflict is taboo. Mediators are able to raise sensitive issues with either party within an atmosphere of confidence and to avoid confrontation.

3. Masculinity leads to ego-boosting behaviors and sympathy for the strong on the part of negotiators and their superiors. Masculine cultures tend to resolve conflicts by fighting rather than compromising. Femininity leads to ego-effacing behaviors and sympathy for the weak. Negotiations between two masculine cultures are more difficult than if at least one of the cultures is more feminine. A historical comparison that can be cited in this respect is the difference between the solution of the Aland Island crisis between Finland and Sweden in 1921, and the Falkland Island crisis between Argentina and Great Britain in 1983; the first was resolved peacefully through a plebiscite, the second is still unresolved in spite of a bloody war. Both Finland and Sweden in our research are found on the feminine side of the scale; both Argentina and Britain on the masculine side.

4. Uncertainty Avoidance leads to a low tolerance for ambiguity and distrust in opponents who show unfamiliar behaviors; negotiators from uncertainty-avoiding cultures prefer highly structured, ritualistic procedures during negotiations.

5. Confucian Dynamism leads to perseverance for achieving desired ends even at the cost of sacrifices.

Obviously, such predictions should be checked in empirical research. Chapter 17, by Poortinga and Hendriks, in this volume is an example of how such research can be conducted.

16.4. Conclusion

For success in international negotiations, it is important that parties acquire an insight into the range of cultural values they are going to meet in the negotiations. This includes an insight into *their own* cultural values and the extent to which these deviate from those of the other side(s). Such insight will allow them to interpret more accurately the meaning of the behavior of the other side(s).

In addition to insight, cultural differences in international negotiations demand specific skills:

- For communicating the desired information *and* emotions to the other party by the spoken word, the written word, and nonverbal behavior.
- For preparing, planning, and arranging negotiations: making an appropriate use of go-betweens, choosing places and times for meeting, setting up the proper social gatherings, etc.

It is important that cultural differences in international negotiations be recognized as a legitimate phenomenon, worthy of study, and as a liability that skilled and well-trained negotiators can turn into an asset.

References

Bond, M.H. (1987), Chinese Values and the Search for Culture-Free Dimensions of Culture: The Chinese Culture Connection, *Journal of Cross-Cultural Psychology*.

Hofstede, G. (1980), *Culture's Consequences: International Differences in Work-Related Values*. Sage Publications, Beverly Hills, CA, and London.

Hofstede, G. (1983), Dimensions of National Cultures in Fifty Countries and Three Regions, in J. Deregowski, S. Dziurawiec, and R.C. Annis (eds.), *Expectations in Cross-Cultural Psychology*, Swets & Zeitlinger, pp. 335–355, Lisse, Netherlands.

CHAPTER 17

Culture as a Factor in International Negotiations: A Proposed Research Project from a Psychological Perspective

Ype H. Poortinga and Erwin C. Hendriks

Tilburg University
The Netherlands

As a medium of relationships between nations, negotiation can only gain from the quality of communication between states and between their emissaries. In other words, its success depends on often imponderable intellectual, psychological and social factors; and its failure is sometimes attributable simply to a misunderstanding based on the difference between value systems.

17.1. Introduction

This statement was made by Alain Plantey (1982, p. 536), a well-known and experienced French diplomat. It is an example of the widely held view that differences in cultural and psychological background between participating teams are an important reason why international negotiations often progress less smoothly than anticipated. It appears to us that most laymen as well as many experts agree with this viewpoint. Any experienced negotiator in international settings can relate some striking incidents where culture had a dramatic impact on the negotiation process, most often in a negative way. Like other expatriates, negotiators tend to have well-developed ideas about the personality and the characteristic mode of behavior of the typical member of a particular culture. Statements about how the Arab, the Indian, or the Japanese will act and react and also how you have to act in different cultural settings are easily obtained.

In such evaluative statements the term *culture* is used in a very broad and loose sense. It encompasses a wide range of phenomena, including norms and values, national character traits and aspects of language. Striking incidents can easily be interpreted retrospectively in terms of culture. This concept is so complex that one will find invariably some factor that can serve as a plausible explanation for whatever one wants to explain. Without denying the importance of cultural variables for international negotiations, we would like to emphasize that *ad hoc* use of culture as an explanatory concept resembles the *deus ex machina* in a bad stage play: when the plot has become too complex, the gods are called upon by the writer to provide the ultimate solution.

In the extensive research literature on the influence of sociocultural and psychocultural factors in the negotiations process, empirical evidence in which prevailing notions are critically examined is rarely found. In the present chapter, an approach is outlined which should permit making a more accurate assessment of the importance of culture in relation to other factors, notably the individual characteristics of negotiators and the substantive issues in a negotiations process.

It is widely believed that cultural factors influence the process and outcome of international negotiations, but scientific research is lacking on the manner in which these factors operate. The need for empirical evidence is substantiated by an analysis of the concepts of culture and personality, and an elaboration of the problem of attribution. A descriptive study is proposed, in which five groups of antecedents to success and failure in international negotiations are distinguished: cultural traits, cultural conventions, individual traits, specific reactions of individuals, and negotiation issues. Information on the (relative) influence of these factors is to be collected from three sources: participants in international negotiations, external observers, and social scientists.

17.2. Psychological Studies of Negotiations

A framework for research on international negotiations was outlined by Sawyer and Guetzkow (1965). The core of their article is a model, which in a slightly modified form is presented in *Figure 17.1*. This figure gives an overview of the various influences on the outcome of negotiations. From our point of view, the most interesting parts of the model are the aspects "goals" and "background factors". Here Sawyer and Guetzkow emphasize that impact of cultural-, individual- and issue-linked factors.

The appeal by Sawyer and Guetzkow (1965, p. 467) for more research was followed up only with respect to the individual- and issue-related factors. On cultural variables there have been only a handful of reported empirical studies, mostly following a single approach. The laboratory experiment is the research method; the subjects are mostly students; the bargaining situation is almost

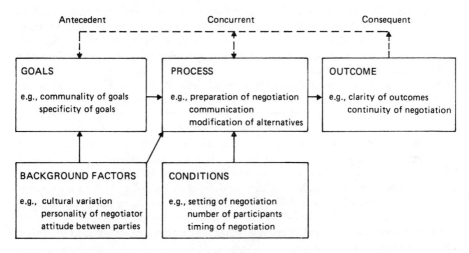

Figure 17.1. A model for negotiations (after Sawyer and Guetzkow, 1965).

always some sort of game (e.g., Prisoner's Dilemma) and the focus of research is the type of bargaining style displayed. The culture factor has been introduced by replicating this kind of study in different countries. Consequently, the differences found are *cross*-cultural differences in *intra*-cultural bargaining.

This kind of research does not give much insight into the effects of cultural variables on international negotiations, where *inter*-cultural interactions are important. In this respect, the plea by Sawyer and Guetzkow for more research still remains unanswered. Empirical evidence is needed in which the interactions of persons from different cultures is analyzed.

17.3. Culture as a Psychological Variable

The Dutch sociologist Bouman (1938) has given the following definition: "Culture is the lifestyle of a society. This lifestyle is the unity of mind and material form, the organic and impenetrable relation between belief and art expression, between intellect and technology, or between need and economic organization". He adds that any definition trying to achieve exhaustive description is bound to end up in vagueness. Bouman's definition is only one of many that can be found in the literature. They all have an essential aspect in common — namely, that culture permeates all aspects of the life of its members.

In further attempts to specify culture, social scientists have emphasized the observed coherence in behavior patterns. Often culture is conceived of as a system. Culture is then seen as an entity consisting of interrelated parts, each of which only can be understood with reference to the context in which it occurs. A related notion is that of the "Gestalt", where the total is more than the sum of the constituent parts. Culture in this sense is an integral aspect of the behavior of a person. For a recent analysis along these lines, we refer to Rohner (1984), who defines culture as a system of symbolic meanings. In this definition meanings imply beliefs, values and norms that, by and large, are shared by the members of a cultural group. Notions such as Gestalt or system only make sense if it is assumed that there are organizational principles inherent to culture. These principles can be defined at the level of the culture as a whole, or at lower levels of inclusiveness, such as the kinship system or value system.

In cross-cultural psychology there is a second orientation in which the importance of culture as a determinant of behavior is equally assumed. However, the analogy of a system or a Gestalt is missing. Culture is taken as a set of conditions analogous to the treatments or conditions in a laboratory experiment (Strodtbeck, 1964). From this perspective culture is reduced to a set of antecedent factors that can be analyzed and measured separately. An outspoken adherent of this viewpoint is Segall (1983, 1984). In his opinion, cross-cultural analysis starts with the observation of some important difference. The goal of empirical studies is the identification of variables in terms of which that observed difference can be explained.

In this second approach culture is conceived of as an array of distinguishable and rather unrelated antecedent variables. Their effects, which lead to differences in specific behaviors, can be traced without the need for a higher-order explanatory concept of culture. It has even been suggested that culture can be seen as a set of conventions, in the sense of more or less arbitrary agreements about what is right and what is proper, e.g., in social interactions, in the expression of art, or in traffic rules (Van de Koppel and Schoots, 1986; Poortinga 1986; Poortinga *et al.*, forthcoming). The arbitrariness of conventions is taken as evidence that they cannot be related to broader aspects of psychological functioning, such as the national character or value system.

Although we concur with the view that the study of a culture as a Gestalt or system can provide valuable insights, we disagree with the opinion that a culture can be studied only in that way. When the antecedent variables to a cultural difference have been identified, we assume that we have not missed some kind of essence that should be taken into account. For a proper representation of culture in an empirical research project, both the systems and the conventions orientation should be included. The results will have to show to what extent each of the two is valid.

Another major consideration in cross-cultural research has to do with the fact that anyone, be it researcher or negotiator, can only operate from the background of his or her own cultural experiences. Throughout any analysis of cross-cultural interaction, the difficulties in establishing effective communication between communicators should be realized. Three potential stumbling blocks on the road to effective communication can be distinguished (Kaufmann, 1968, p. 163): linguistic difficulties, intellectual short-circuits, and conceptual roadblocks (resulting from different cultures and value systems). This problem area has received considerable attention in the cross-cultural literature, (e.g., Bochner, 1982). We shall not deal with it here, but merely note its importance for the preparation of any cross-cultural research project.

17.4. Conceptions of Personality

Not only are people generally inclined to attribute broad psychological effects to culture, they tend to do something similar in the case of personality. Why does someone not perform his job properly? Because he is neurotic. Why does someone quarrel with his neighbors? Because he is aggressive.

In personality research stable structural psychological properties of individuals are referred to as "traits". Every person is assumed to possess each trait to a greater or lesser extent. We label a person by those traits that we see as predominant in his behavior pattern. If an individual's behavior can be described in terms of stable traits, it should be possible to predict his future behavior on the basis of this description. However, empirical research based on this approach has often shown disappointingly poor results. This has affected the theoretical status of the trait concept, (e.g., Mischel, 1968).

These research findings are quite in contrast with daily experience. The subjective evidence for stable characteristics in the behavior of a person is very convincing. There are plausible explanations for these suggestive but incorrect impressions. First, the constancy that we perceive is located not so much in the invariant behavior of the other person as in his invariant physical appearance. Somatic aspects, such as style of movements, are embedded in the image which we ourselves form of another person, (e.g., Argyle, 1975, p. 137). Second, there is so much information in the behavior of others that we cannot monitor and process it all. Traits are convenient categorizations that create a structure, even if this exists only in the eye of the beholder (e.g., Shweder, 1982). We organize our own reactions according to the traits we ascribe to someone. A mismatch between trait and actual behavior rarely creates problems., If a nasty fellow does something kind, we do not change our overall impression, but see it as an exception ("Who ever thought he would do that!"). Third, a striking difference has been noted between the interpretation of our own behavior and that of others. We tend to describe our own actions in terms of the demands of the situation or our goals and intentions. It is mainly the behavior of other that we label with trait-like consistent properties. We shall return to this attribution process later, as it has played an important role in the conception of the present study.

Simultaneously with the rejection of the trait concept, researchers began to attach more importance to external antecedents of behavior, i.e., determinants in the environment. In many respects, behavior is a reaction to the situation in which a person finds himself. Here a distinction is needed between the perception of a situation by a person (the subjective situation) and by others (the so-called objective situation). The subjective situation is colored by previous experiences and by personal expectations about the effects of one's own behavior. In the perception of situations there is undoubtedly regularity, especially if we study personality cross-culturally. A common cultural background leads to similarity within cultures in the reactions to specific situations. On this point there is no controversy, but the question is whether an observed difference can only be generalized to a set of situations that belong together in a particular culture on the basis of an (arbitrary) convention, or whether it reflects a trait-like difference that will manifest itself in many divergent situations.

Negotiators, as do all other people, interpret the behavior of others. In this chapter we try to trace these interpretations, both at the level of traits and at the level of more incidental events and reactions to a particular negotiation session.

17.5. The Problem of Attribution

In psychology, the process of seeking an explanation for an act of behavior in terms of antecedent factors is called attribution (e.g., Harvey, et al., 1976). Several research results have emerged, which all indicate that the human being is not capable of carrying out an attribution process accurately (Ross, 1978).

The most important principle observed in attribution research, at least in Western countries, is the so-called "actor–observer divergence" (Jones and Nisbett, 1971). It has been frequently found that actors and observers systematically differ in the attribution of an act of behavior. When an actor is asked to describe the cause of an event, he is likely to do so in situational terms. An observer, on the other hand, is more likely to do so in personal terms. A well-known example to illustrate this is the car crash. While investigating a car crash a policeman questions both the driver and a passing bystander. When asked for an explanation, the bystander will answer that the crash was caused by driving too fast. The driver himself, however, gives as an explanation that the road was slippery.

It will be obvious that the above-mentioned distinction between situation and trait explanations of personality can be conceived of as different attributions, i.e., attributions to situational factors and attributions to internal psychological factors.

The actor–observer divergence does not hold for every situation. It is dependent on the outcome valence of the event. When the outcome is negative, actors and observers are likely to react in the way just described. However, when the outcome is positive, attributions in more personal terms will be made by actors (Jaspars and Hewstone, 1982); see *Table 17.1*.

| | Outcome ||
	Positive	Negative
Actor	Personal	Situational
Observer	Personal	Personal

Table 17.1. Actor–observer differences in attribution.

A possible explanation can be found in the notions of "egocentric motivations" and "informational perspective". The first notion states that actors are egocentrically concerned with receiving credit for situations that have positive consequences and avoiding blame for situations that lead to negative outcomes.

For the actor in a negative situation, this leads to attributions to situational factors. In this way he is not responsible for the outcome. In a positive situation, however, situational attribution makes no sense; it would deny personal credit. Therefore, the attributions will more likely be to the person himself.

The notion of "informational perspective" accounts for the more personal attributions of the observers. The actor knows his own behavior in many situations, and is aware of its cross-situational variability. However, the observer may know nothing more about the actor than his behavior in a limited range of situations. He is likely to interpret incidental behavior as typical behavior, and make more personal attributions than the actor.

It is obvious that these findings can have important implications for the negotiation context. During negotiations, a negotiator is an actor. Therefore, when asked to describe the causes of the outcome of negotiations, he will respond as an actor. In the case of a negative outcome, this is likely to result in attributions to factors outside his own person and, by extension, his own side. In the case of success, the negotiator will be inclined to attribute cause in a more personal way. He is likely to refer to his own individual skills and to those of his delegation.

17.6. Negotiation Issues

It is clear that there is more to the outcome of international negotiations than cultural and individual factors. One can think of political relations between the parties, divergence of opinions, the need for a solution, and numerous other factors. But most important, the outcome of negotiations depends on the extent to which there is conflict or disagreement about the issues on the table.

It is frequently noted that the solution of a conflict on one or more issues is a *sine qua non* of negotiations (e.g., Rubin and Brown, 1975, p. 6). Therefore, it is hardly surprising that a large proportion of the scientific effort in negotiations research has been devoted to issues and issue-related factors. In their overview of the literature on bargaining effectiveness, Rubin and Brown (1975) suggest that a distinction should be made between tangible and intangible issues. By intangible issues, they refer to those factors that threaten bargainers with damage to their honor, self-esteem, face, reputation, status, or appearance of strength. These intangible issues can become superimposed on the tangibles, i.e., the problems and differences that are the actual reason for the negotiations.

It should be noted that issue-related intangibles as described can overlap with aspects of personality, as discussed earlier. It depends on the perspective of an observer whether the situation, or the person, or even his culture is considered as the explanatory factor. Despite the importance of the distinction between tangibles and intangibles, between strategies and tactics, or between abstract and concrete issues, negotiation issues are treated as a homologous category in our research. There are two reasons for doing so. First, the boundaries between the categories within each distinction are difficult to capture. To map them would require a considerable extension of this project. Second, the distinctions are not essential for our objectives — namely, to assess the contribution of cultural and individual factors to negotiation outcomes.

17.7. Method of the Proposed Project

Information on the influence of various factors on the outcome of international negotiations can be collected from three sources. The first source is ratings by the negotiators who participate in actual negotiation sessions and the preparations for these sessions. Negotiatiors can give an overall evaluation of the importance of the five categories. A more detailed and complete picture on the relative importance of the five factors will emerge when for each factor a set of questions is asked so that various aspects are covered more systematically. When this is done both for one's own party and the other party, it is possible to check the subject's ratings for various sources of attributions. In other words, *negotiator-as-actor* and *negotiator-as-observer* perspectives are incorporated in the design.

The second source of information consists of reports by others, i.e., *external observers* who had nothing to do with the negotiations. These persons differ from negotiators in the sense that they cannot be regarded as actors. Presumably they have little interest in the negotiation. Therefore, they are likely to be less susceptible to shifts in attributions.

The third source of information consists of ratings by social scientists (*experts*), who observe some specific aspect of the negotiation process on which they possess special competence. Experts can include psychologists, linguists and anthropologists. Their ratings are based on detailed objective analysis, as opposed to the overall impressions, which form the basis for the opinions of negotiators and external observers.

In the present phase of the project, the most important source of data is ratings by participants in real negotiation sessions. They will be asked to fill in a questionnaire. There are two kinds of questions: (1) on culture-, individual-, and issue-related factors; and (2) on the relative influence of each of these groups of factors on the negotiation process. The questions pertain to both one's own side and the other party in a two-party negotiation session.

Apart from standardized items, raters will also be asked to describe incidents that in their opinion had a critical impact on the progress of the negotiations. These case materials should prove to be valuable for training in cross-cultural communication. It may be noted that, contrary to prevailing practice, the incidents collected in the present project can be checked against the ratings of negotiators and experts.

Ideally, information on attributions should be collected from the negotiators not only after, but also before the negotiation process. Therefore, the negotiators will be asked, if possible, to fill in a questionnaire *before* a negotiation session and *after* the negotiation session has ended.

A slightly modified questionnaire will be completed by the external observers. They will do so on the basis of audiovisual recordings. Episodes with sensitive information can be deleted before the tapes are passed on to the external observers, if necessary.

In a later phase of the project, the audiotapes and videotapes will be used again, this time by experts. Psychologists, for instance, will direct their attention to nonverbal aspects, such as gesture. Linguists will focus on linguistic and paralinguistic aspects, such as the length of pauses between interventions by speakers from various cultures. Cultural communication experts will try to identify cultural antecedents of negotiations styles and strategies.

17.8. Conclusion

The outline of culture, personality, and negotiation issues in the previous sections forms the basis for the design of our project. Five categories of factors are distinguished, namely:

- **Cultural traits**, i.e., broad psychological characteristics common to the members of a culture, which "color" behavior in a wide range of situations (e.g., cultural values).
- **Cultural conventions**, i.e., the culture-bound aspects of behavior, language, communication, customs, etc., which are situation-specific.
- **Individual traits**, i.e., the psychological characteristics of an individual delegation member, by which he distinguishes himself from other members of his group in a wide range of situations.
- **Specific reactions of individuals**, i.e., reactions of an individual person that are not seen as typical of his behavior pattern.
- **Negotiation issues**, i.e., the problems and differences of opinion that are the actual reason for the negotiations, as well as the ways in which issues are handled to reach agreement, i.e., strategies and tactics.

The groups of factors are seen as important antecedents to which success and failure of international negotiations can be attributed. The central question we address is: What is the influence of each of the five categories on the outcome of international negotiations? To answer this question we shall make use of questionnaires as well as observations. Apart from participants in actual negotiations, relevant data will be gained from external observers and from social scientists who have expertise in the assessment of specific aspects of behavior.

References

Argyle, M. (1975), *Bodily Communication*, International Universities Press, New York.

Bochner, D. (ed.) (1982), *Cultures in Contact: Studies in Cross-Cultural Interaction*, Pergamon Press, Oxford.

Bouman, P.J. (1938), *Van Renaissance to Wereldoorlog*, H.J., Paris, Amsterdam.

Harvey, J.H., Ickes, W.J., and Kidd, R.F. (eds.) (1976), *New Directions in Attribution Research*. (Vol. I), Erlbaum, Hillsdale, NJ.

Jaspars, J. and Hewstone, M. (1982), Cross-Cultural Interaction, Social Attribution and Inter-group Relations, in S. Bochner (ed.), *Cultures in Contact: Studies in Cross-Cultural Interaction*, Pergamon Press, Oxford.

Jones, E.E. and Nisbett, R.E. (1971), *The Actor and the Observer: Divergent Perceptions of the Causes of Behavior*, General Learning Press, Morristown, NJ.

Kaufmann, J. (1968), *Conference Diplomacy*, Sijthoff, Leiden.

Mischel, W. (1968), *Personality and Assessment*, John Wiley, New York.

Plantey, A. (1982), A Cultural Approach to International Negotiations, *International Social Science Journal*, 34, pp. 535–544.

Poortinga, Y.H. (1986), *Psychic Unity versus Cultural Variation: An Exploratory Study of Some Basic Personality Variables in India and the Netherlands*, Report, Tilburg University, Tilburg.

Poortinga, Y.H., Van de Vijver, F.J.R., Joe, R.C., and Van de Koppel, J.M.H. (forthcoming), Peeling the Onion Called Culture: A Synopsis.

Rohner, P. (1984), Toward a Conception of Culture for Cross-Cultural Psychology, *Journal of Cross-Cultural Psychology*, 15, pp. 111–138.

Ross, L. (1978), The Intuitive Psychologist and His Shortcomings: Distortions in the Attribution Process, in L. Berkowitz (ed.), *Cognitive Theories in Social Psychology*, Academic Press, New York.

Rubin, J.Z. and Brown, B.R. (1975), *The Social Psychology of Bargaining and Negotiation: A Social-Psychological Analysis*, Academic Press, New York.

Sawyer, J. and Guetzkow, H. (1965), Bargaining and Negotiation in International Relations, in H.C. Kelman (ed.), *International Behavior: A Social-Psychological Analysis*, Holt, Rinehart and Winston, New York.

Segall, M.H. (1983), On the Search for the Independent Variable in Cross-Cultural Psychology, in S.H. Irvine and J.W. Berry (eds.), *Human Assessment and Cultural Factors*, Plenum, New York.

Segall, M.H. (1984), More than We Need to Know about Culture But are Afraid not to Ask, *Journal of Cross-Cultural Psychology*, 15, pp. 153–162.

Shweder, R.A. (1982), Fact and Artifact in Trait Perceptions: The Systematic Distortion Hypothesis, in B.A. Maher and W.B. Maher (eds.), *Progress in Experimental Personality Research* (vol. 11), Academic Press, New York.

Strodtbeck, F.L. (1964), Considerations of Meta-method in Cross-Cultural Studies, *American Anthropologist* (special publication), 66 (3-part 2), pp. 223–228.

Van de Koppel, J.M.H. and Schoots, A.H. (1986), Why Are All Trains in Holland Painted Yellow?, *Nederland Tijdschrift voor de Psychologie*, 41, pp. 189–196.

CHAPTER 18

New Political Thinking and International Negotiations

Sergey L. Kambalov

Diplomatic Academy
USSR Ministry of Foreign Affairs
Moscow
USSR

18.1. Introduction

The two central premises of the new political thinking are the concept of an integral, interdependent world, and the indivisibility of security. These ideas were recently developed into a practical policy with the formulation by the 27th Congress of the CPSU of the idea of a comprehensive system of international security.

Naturally, this is a concept yet to be introduced effectively into world politics. The idea of a comprehensive system is only at the very beginning of its difficult journey toward actual implementation in specific agreements and joint actions to create a safer and more stable world, and to build a system of mutually beneficial cooperation in many different fields. New political thinking is not an *ad hoc* adjustment, or correction of policy, but a new methodology for the conduct of international affairs.

International negotiations necessarily play a major, integral role in the implementation of the new political thinking on at least two counts. First, practically speaking, there is no other method to translate the idea of new political thinking into real practice of international politics. Certainly, unilateral actions can sometimes be really important. They could provide a decisive positive impetus necessary to make a radical breakthrough in seemingly deadlocked situations. But it is solely through an advanced system of international negotiations that a meaningful movement toward a universally acceptable solution of world problems can be assured and the results of this movement solidified in substantial and durable agreements.

Secondly, international negotiations are closely connected with the new political thinking because, to be effective in a changing world situation, international negotiations must proceed from new premises. Indeed, if the principles of interdependence of interests of the members of the international community and of the integral character of security are ignored, if there is an attempt to put pressure — be it political, economic, or military — on a party in a negotiation, an agreement secured in such a way is prone to create more problems than it solves.

Similarly, an attempt to "solve" a problem taken in isolation out of the context of its environment could be truly successful only if that solution is clearly understood to be merely a stage or an element in a larger process of dealing with the entire complex of related problems.

The process of implementation of the new political thinking in world politics is certain to influence the way international negotiations are conceived, prepared and conducted. Let us suggest just a few of probable consequences and demands.

18.2. Developing a Hierarchy of International Problems

The great number and variety of international negotiations undertaken in recent years (and their modest success so far) naturally create a desire to concentrate special efforts on vital problems that must be handled without delay. In other words, one is tempted to develop a hierarchy of problems to be solved through international negotiations.

Some experts doubt the wisdom of this approach and prefer to stress another feature of the emerging system of international negotiations — the interdependence or interrelatedness of subjects. Indeed, sometimes we come across unexpected, even paradoxical connections between seemingly independent processes. Therefore, the temptation to include any negotiation — even on a subject of "tertiary" importance — is quite strong for a scholar who dislikes leaving outside of the framework of his scheme even minor components of a process. But both common sense and the scholarly analysis of problems facing humanity demand that we develop a hierarchy of those problems. The criterion to be used is an assessment of the potential of a problem seriously to affect the interests of humanity on a global scale. By this criterion problems of security and survival — to which the new political thinking is specifically addressed — necessarily take the top place in the hierarchy.

The purpose of developing such an hierarchy is to create an environment in which a possible failure of a negotiation on a subject of "lower" importance is less likely to have an adverse effect on negotiations of a higher standing in this hierarchy. But a necessary precondition for such a safety mechanism is the acceptance by the negotiating sides of the proposed hierarchy of subjects of international negotiations. Otherwise a search for agreement on substantive issues could be burdened — or even displaced — by differences about the relative importance of this or that problem. Examples of trouble with exactly this kind of differences in the past are well known.

The task of developing a universally acceptable hierarchy is a very complicated one. Suffice it to say that the very notion of, for example, rational or irrational is intimately bound up with the specific cultural heritage of various people, different political cultures, traditions and many other things. To find a common denominator is quite a problem.

Nevertheless, it seems imperative that agreement be reached on determining a number of issues that are of overriding, global importance and that certain corrections in the approaches to these issues be made. National and group interests — not to mention demands of internal politics — should be unequivocally subordinated to the task of finding a solution to the grave problems facing humanity. We believe the USSR has provided a good example of such a reevaluation of its approach to international issues in the spirit of responsibility, realism and the supremacy of interests of mankind.

18.3. Cooperation and Interdependence

The priority given to problems of security and survival should not be construed as suggesting that other issues are not worthy of dedicated and urgent attention. On the contrary, the experience of the 1970s and 1980s shows quite clearly that, if major agreements are to be realized, they should be based on a solid foundation of contacts, cooperation and accords in many different spheres of international relations — trade, humanitarian issues, sports, information, and other areas. These positive processes create an environment where agreements on major issues are accepted as something natural, understandable and reasonable and therefore can be implemented comparatively easily. On the other hand, even a major breakthrough in negotiations on a vital issue is often viewed with suspicion, if it occurs against a background of disruption of contacts and curtailment of cooperation.

Cooperation in various spheres is immensely important by itself. Moreover, it should be the bedrock or material foundation of healthy political relations. Yet, it is quite clear that such a positive political effect will not materialize automatically. Experience shows that neither trade, however large the volume, nor cultural ties, nor extensive cooperation in other spheres can provide a solid guarantee of stability and positive development of political relations. We know that there were cases when problems of trade developed into a cause of worsening political relations. In other words, cooperation in many different fields is a necessary but not sufficient condition.

It seems that for cooperation to be politically effective it has to have certain qualitative characteristics. Among them are stability, a large number of participants, and actual and perceived mutual benefits. The whole process is of a cumulative character, and its real political effectiveness appears only at a certain stage of its maturity.

Interdependence, the interrelation of constituent elements of the system of international negotiations, should not in any way result in a situation where the failure or delay of a certain negotiation — however important its subject — affects negatively other negotiations. If we allow this to happen, the scale of a setback would seriously overshadow the initial problem, because it could a slow down (or even reverse) the process of building a general foundation, as mentioned above.

18.4. Confidentiality versus Openness

A problem we should examine thoroughly is the ratio of confidentiality and openness in international negotiations. On the one hand diplomacy in general and international negotiations in particular are simply impossible without reasonable confidentiality. Confidentiality is a certain insulation against the temptation to use negotiations for a side's own narrow political purposes. Unfortunately, this is exactly what often happens. The demands of internal politics dictate that negotiations and their results be publicly presented as a "victory" over the opponent. This naturally provokes the other side to issue publicly an indignant denial. The consequences for negotiations on the real substance can often be negative and unfortunate.

But the other extreme situation in a negotiation, when the positions of the sides or even the very fact of ongoing contacts is being kept secret, may be no less counterproductive. If negotiations do not result in an agreement, an unexpected announcement that negotiations took place — and brought no results — can only increase distrust, suspicion and skepticism.

Again, the unexpected announcement of successful negotiations is usually greeted at first by a chorus of congratulations and a general expression of satisfaction. But very soon critical, skeptical commentaries start to multiply. Doubts are expressed as to the effect of the agreement on national interests. Procedural violations (no adequate prior consultations with relevant bodies) are alleged, and so on. As a result, to strengthen the agreement (sometimes to save it) a hastily thrown together campaign of public education is introduced to explain the motives for agreement, its advantages over possible alternatives, etc. But it is always easier to educate than to re-educate.

Is there a way out of this contradiction? We believe we should clearly distinguish two things: negotiation contents and negotiation subjects. In the first case we have in mind such things as positions of the sides in a negotiation, their tactics, etc. Here a healthy amount of confidentiality is vital and unavoidable. In the second case it seems prudent and useful to have as wide a discussion of substantive issues as possible to develop various promising approaches and points of view in order to take into consideration everything meaningful and to weed out the rest.

18.5. Conclusion

The issues mentioned above are but a small fragment of a complex of problems facing negotiators today. We believe that many of these problems can only be dealt with on the premises of the new political thinking. That, in its turn, leads to the need for continuous and dedicated education — and re-education — of those engaged in the negotiations process directly or otherwise. Here the role of education and training establishments, such as diplomatic academies and institutes, is crucial.

CHAPTER 19

The Role of Forecasting International Relations in the Process of International Negotiations

Plamen Pantev

*Institute of International Relations
and Socialist Integration
Sofia
Bulgaria*

19.1. New Needs for Regulating the International System

A crucial problem faces more than 160 countries of the world: will the states at the end of the twentieth century be able to shape their own national interests in such a way that the traditional conflict of these interests is peacefully transformed into an interaction *manageable by all sovereign states in the common interest* and on the principle of *equal rights of states?*

The volume of international relations managed on a coordinated basis is rising and the mechanism for coordination of the positions of different subjects of international law and international relations is becoming more complex and varied. A typical example is the number and importance of international organizations and treaties. At the same time, any attempt or claim to neglect the sovereignty of a particular state bears grave risks for peace and security.

A very useful means of management in the international system is *contemporary international law*. It guarantees the most effective and peaceful functioning of the global system of international relations, preservation and respect for the sovereign rights of each state and the coordinated management of the system.

In the sphere of regulation of international relations *two tendencies dialectically counteract*: the objective increase in the need for regulating international relations through contemporary international law, on the one hand, and the intensification of the attempts to put international law aside and to legalize the threat or use of force as a dominant regulator, on the other hand.

Based on the common interests of mankind there arises the need for stable management of international relations and for *greater predictability* of the foreign policy behavior of states and of the international system. A better perspective is needed in all spheres of human and social activity to avoid any situation that endangers the existence of society, and to improve the conditions of its development.

International negotiations are no exception. On the contrary, they are a *specific instrument for solving or managing* different problems of international relations. They have an *increasing importance in the functioning and development of the international system.*

The *effectiveness* of this instrument for regulating the system of international relations greatly depends on the *hierarchy of national foreign policy priorities* embodied in the negotiating positions of states. The more that narrow national interests can be subordinated to common interests of mankind, the greater the possibility of effective negotiations. And vice versa: any declaration or claiming of "spheres of influence" or "spheres of vital interests" over territories, areas or space outside those of national jurisdiction of states do not bring about successful management of problems through international negotiations.

Every country involved in international negotiations tries to implement its own negotiating position as much as possible, thus realizing its foreign policy interests, purposes and principles. *The effectiveness* of any negotiation depends on the *compromising character of the attitudes of the partners,* i.e., each side must be sure that it is profiting, although it drops voluntarily some of its initial positions for the sake of common interests of mankind or of some legitimate interest of the partner.

International negotiations would be more effective if the necessity of *a common purpose of the global system of international relations* — the construction of a peaceful, demilitarized world — is realized and accepted. A more secure and predictable future for every state is an objective need of the international system nowadays. That need requires new political consciousness and behavior in international relations. "The new *political thinking* is called upon to raise civilization to a qualitatively new point. Even only for that it is not a single correction of the position but *a methodology of conducting international affairs*" (Gorbachev, 1987).

When the principles and norms of international law and common interests of mankind are considered as a main source of the negotiating position of state A, the uncertainty of the future foreign policy of that state is greatly diminished for the forecasting of state B. As Karl Deutsch (1971) noted, the main task of law is to make life more predictable. Therefore, the predictability of the foreign policy of a state and of its negotiating behavior increases if its guiding principles and purposes, its acts and results, are based on international law and the concept of peaceful coexistence of states. Thus, international negotiations themselves can reflect and enhance predictability in international relations.

19.2. National and International Forecasting of International Relations

The problems and tendencies discussed in the first section raise some questions concerning the necessity of new approaches and a new pace for international negotiations and the enrichment of the forms of national and international research to aid the international political process. The problems of national and international forecasting of international relations may provide a chance to analyze the process of international negotiations from a new viewpoint and to bring some new ideas to research on international negotiations.

19.2.1. National forecasting

The forecasting of international relations in a state has *many and different aims* with respect to its negotiating position. One of them may be to enrich the options for the negotiating position and to prepare a more flexible transition from one to another when conditions change. A second aim may be to study possible combinations of interactions of positions of the negotiating partners and the potential results. A third aim might be to anticipate the consequences of different possible outcomes of a negotiation. Discerning and studying the common interests of the negotiating states may also be an objective for the forecasters.

Another aim could be the study of the internal and external political conditions during the time of the negotiations. This aspect of national forecasting is important because it may throw light on the problem of the *ability of the states participating in the negotiations to manage the political processes inside their own countries* so that a consensus is reached for constructive outcome of the negotiations. Garthoff (1977) wrote about his experience as a SALT negotiator: "Nowhere more clearly or frequently than in SALT have internal governmental differences asserted and reasserted themselves and shaped and reshaped our negotiating approaches and objectives in a way which undercuts and greatly complicates pursuit of a consistent and effective negotiating strategy toward the Soviet Union".

National political forecasting, as already mentioned, plays an important role in the preparatory activity for international negotiations — forming the positions of the delegation, working on the final document, etc. In the process of the forecasting study, the possibilities and probabilities of realization of different political tendencies are revealed. In that context an important question is *the type of regulating factors of the forecast.*

Such a methodological position has a great practical value. Forecasts in the social sphere have a normative character and the so-called "effect of the forecast" or "self-fulfillment of the forecast" is that political decision-makers carry out their activity by fulfilling (or by preventing the fulfillment of) the forecast.

A question arises during the formation of the negotiating position of a state: *must the forecast of international relations comply with the requirements of international law* or not? There are at least two scientific arguments and one legal argument in favor of the obligatory compliance of any foreign policy forecast with the principles and norms of international law.

First, any human activity is an instrument in the process of acquiring knowledge of the world we live in. International law is no different and a forecasting study should take this into account. Furthermore, international law provides not only knowledge of the effectiveness of a managing instrument, but also of the readiness of a state to use peaceful means in settling its relations with other states. Second, international law has demonstrated in the last thirty-five centuries that it has a specific position and role in international relations and the tendency is that the importance of international law is growing. A forecast, intending to be scientific, should consider that fact, too.

The legal argument is that a forecasting procedure in the process of constructing the negotiating position of a state ends with a forecasting document having an official character. Its estimates are taken into consideration when planning the negotiating strategy and building the negotiating stance. All this activity is carried out by responsible state officials and agencies or by other people and institutions in the state. State activities and political forecasting should also serve the goal of implementing a state's international obligations according to international law.

19.2.2. International forecasting

More national and international research efforts are needed to help in coping with many important and complex problems, such as the global problems facing all countries, the identification of the common interests of mankind, the need for coordinated management of international affairs (international law having a special role), the reality of an interrelated and interdependent world, the generally increasing role of international institutions in the process of national political decision-making and the urgency for greater efficiency in international negotiations. Both international negotiations and international forecasting are tools in the process of managing of the global international system.

International forecasting of international relations should be *differentiated from* the international consultations and discussions of scientists and diplomats, organized by research institutes. It differs from the participation of experts in governmental delegations as members or advisers, including at the United Nations and other international organizations and conferences. It is different from the representation of a government in a specialized international organization or conference and from specific scientific and technical negotiations, whose objective is to carry out a technical study as a part of important political negotiations.

International forecasting of international relations may use the experience of all these forms of expert participation in assisting the international political process, as well as particular specialists who are needed for a specific forecasting research corresponding to the object of the negotiations. International forecasting for the purposes of international negotiations may be organized on a *permanent* or an *ad hoc* basis both within and outside the framework of an international organization.

Alexander Szalai (1978), a supporter of the idea of the necessity of forecasting of a systematic and methodical character in international organizations, especially in the United Nations, sees its major importance "in adding a new dimension to policy making, planning, and administration by enforcing a conscious and systematic consideration of a wide array of probabilities, alternatives, and prospectives", i.e., as a significant source of orientation of national planning.

The practical importance of international forecasting of international relations in the process of international negotiations lies also in the possibility for the negotiating sides to set coordinated objectives for the forecasting team, composed of representatives of the negotiating states as well as specialists from other countries, if the negotiating governments agree on that. Such tasks, which are significant for the constructive preparation of the negotiations, may include the study of the various aspects of the problems of the negotiations in relation to the potential common interests of the negotiating states and to common interests of mankind, as well as the possibility and variants of common purposes, objectives and positions in the process of negotiations.

There are certain *requirements* to which international forecasting for international negotiations should respond. Possible disagreements (about the topic and title of the forecast, its structure, methods, level of scientific expertise, etc.) should not turn into ideological and political polemics.

It is also necessary to follow the rules of scientific discourse, whose primary obligation is not to falsify facts. Governments should aim to give political instructions that do not contradict the interests of the political, economic, military, ecological and ethological security of mankind, the negotiating partners and other states. Further, no international forecasting forum should be used as a maneuver to divert the attention of public opinion from the core of the problems of the study, or to carry away the accent from the real negotiations to the forecasting research by the negotiating states.

Szalai (1978) expresses some doubts about the range of issues that member states of an international organization would agree to discuss in a forecast study, especially those in the spheres of peace, security and sovereignty, i.e., topics at the heart of international politics. At the same time, he provides arguments for the possibility and necessity of such forecasts, deriving these arguments from Articles I and XIV of the Charter of the United Nations.

Another very important argument in that direction can be added. In the agreement reached at the Stockholm Conference on Confidence- and Security-Building Measures and Disarmament in Europe, the member states of the Conference on Security and Cooperation in Europe obligate themselves to exchange annual plans of certain types of military activity as well as other information on security matters. Hence, taboos of discussing some delicate security issues might be lifted — in proportion to the political good will of building confidence among states with different political and social systems and to the real progress in arms limitation and reduction. The realization of the Stockholm Conference accords may serve as a test case, which, if successful, would lead to more radical measures in the confidence-building area of the CSCE countries.

19.3. Implications for the Education and Training of International Negotiators

Some ideas concerning the required skills of international negotiators arise from the problems discussed in Sections 19.1 and 19.2:

- To be able to view international negotiations as an instrument of managing the international system through managing its subsystems and concrete international relations.
- To try to realize the great responsibility of policymakers and international negotiators for the common interests of mankind, and to cultivate a common purpose for the global international system — namely, the construction of a peaceful world based on the principles of peaceful coexistence.
- To be able to evaluate all problems of negotiations in terms of the criteria of international law.
- To be able to place the common interests of mankind above narrow group or national interests.
- To be able to balance all regulating factors of international relations when forecasting international development, not overestimating the military–technical ones nor underestimating the political and legal ones. National forecasting activity as well as the forecast document should be in compliance with international law.
- To participate competently and constructively in international forecasting studies of international relations.

A preliminary discussion might be carried out to outline the objectives and content of a training program for international negotiators in connection with the development of these skills.

19.4. Conclusions

National and international forecasting of international relations may become a very useful instrument in the process of international negotiations, if carefully organized and subordinated to the constructive development and outcome of the negotiating process. Its major significance lies in the opportunity to use the results of the forecast study directly or indirectly in the process of international negotiations, thus combining the efforts of theory and practice in that field.

References

Deutsch, K. (1971), *The Probability of International Law*, New York, p. 89.

Garthoff, R. (1977), Negotiating with the Russians: Some Lessons from SALT, *International Security*, No. 1, Spring, p. 19.

Gorbachev, M.S. (1987), For a Non-nuclear World, For Humanism of International Relations. Speech at a meeting in the Kremlin with the participants in the international forum, "For a Non-nuclear World, For the Survival of Humanity", February 16, Moscow, *Izd. Politicheskoy literaturoy*, 1987, p. 15.

Szalai, A. (1978), Forecasting in the Context of International Organizations, in: Nazli Choucri and Thomas W. Robinson (eds.), *Forecasting in International Relations: Theory, Methods, Problems, Prospects*, W. H. Freeman and Company, San Francisco, p. 421, 422–423.

CHAPTER 20

Negotiations in Our Time

Institute of International Relations
Potsdam
German Democratic Republic

20.1. Introduction

In the past, states sought to protect or implement their political objectives abroad, i.e., their interests toward other states, chiefly in two ways: by using or threatening to use military force, or by means of diplomatic negotiations. In any case, diplomacy got the shorter end of the stick. It was needed, above all, whenever the point was

-    To gain the time needed for establishing military superiority
-    To frame coalitions that promised to be successful in a military conflict
-    To make maximum use of a military success through conquest of land, war indemnities, or any other increase in power, and to prevent the enemy as long as possible from regaining his strength
-    Or, in case of a defeat, to keep losses within tolerable limits and to set the stage for a new round in the trial of military strength.

At the present time, military force has ceased to be a means of achieving national interests abroad, owing to the destructive power of weapons, especially nuclear and chemical ones, and the resulting vulnerability of our planet and the danger of mankind's annihilation. Thus, war has ceased to be a way of continuing policy by other means, and there remains the difficult art of living together in peace, regardless of all differences in world outlook, social systems, race or religion. Relations of peaceful coexistence have become the only way possible for states to live together.

In these conditions international negotiations, i.e., the discussion of the modalities of interstate cooperation with all parties concerned, and the agreement on these modalities with the sovereignty of all states preserved, as well as the settlement of existing problems on a basis of mutual understanding, have become the most important or, what is more, the only applicable means of protecting the interests of states and of conducting their international relations. Disputes, too, can no longer be settled by power politics and unilateral actions of states but only by negotiations, which have become the only reasonable alternative to the use of power and to the policy of confrontation. If they are taken as a permanent, systematic process they will secure the peaceful functioning of international relations.

In view of the importance of international negotiations to the survival of mankind, it is necessary to develop the art of negotiating, to reach an understanding on the priorities of, and preconditions for, successful negotiating and to design a mechanism that helps promote cooperation, peaceful competition and the peaceful solution of controversial issues.

20.2. The Relationship between Interests and Readiness to Negotiate

The success of international negotiations is determined by the political will of the parties to reach a mutually acceptable result. Lack of will cannot be replaced or compensated for by any negotiating technique, neither by diplomatic cleverness, nor the use of negotiations support systems and computer aids. As all states first of all proceed from their own interests, governments will only agree to conduct negotiations if they

- Consider the solution of a certain question to be necessary in their own interest, and
- Recognize the principle that there is no possible solution except by coming to a mutual understanding, which can only be attained through negotiation.

A novel development in our time is that the interdependence of states has increased greatly. Mankind has begun to regard itself as one and to become aware of the regional and global interrelations not only between peoples and states, but also between man, society, and nature. The tendency is that this will lead to an increasing interest in negotiations and in substantial results. The common interest in mutually acceptable negotiation results includes issues relating to security, environmental protection, prevention of disasters and accidents, combating diseases and epidemics, and securing energy and food supplies. These and many more tasks confronting mankind cannot be solved on a unilateral basis any longer, but only jointly. The tendency will increase to reach solutions by mutual understanding, and this in turn will increase still further the importance of international negotiations.

20.3. The Relationship between a State's Self-Interest and Legitimate Interests of Its Negotiating Partners

For a state to conduct negotiations with an eye to reaching practical results means that it must not place its own interests above international law or above the common interest and that it must recognize that the other sides, too, have legitimate interests. The starting point for any search for a negotiated solution will be to define the legitimate interests of each side with mutual respect. On this basis alone it is possible to reach a positive negotiation result, i.e., to agree by mutual consent on either

-   The exchange of equal benefits in the political or any other field, observing the importance of the principle of reciprocity and mutual give and take, or
-   A settlement of interests on the basis of mutual concessions.

States with diverging interests can cooperate only if they are ready, on a reciprocal basis, to arrive at a balanced compromise, which should take into account the interests of all parties concerned in a fair and well-balanced way and lead to mutual advantage, and not be directed against the legitimate interests of any side. Negotiations must not be linked with demands in the form of an ultimatum. Making preconditions is as inadmissible as the presentation of accomplished facts. Negotiations must be conducted with the aim of reaching an understanding that preserves in the future the principle of sovereign equality and equality of rights between states, rather than with the aim of establishing a new winner–loser relationship.

20.4. The Relationship between a State's Security and the Security Interests of Other States

Because of the destructive nuclear potential that exists, all states have an objective interest in negotiations to preserve peace, prevent nuclear war and foster arms limitation that maintains and enhances international security. This common interest is a major basis for the chance of success.

To turn this objective interest into agreements under international law, it is necessary to recognize the fact that in our time there can be no unilateral security. It is impossible to base the security of one state on the lack of security of others. There must thus be a recognition of the legitimate security interests of others.

20.5. Creating an Atmosphere of Trust and Dialogue

Lack of mutual trust is one of the main obstacles to successful negotiations. Confidence cannot be created either by decree or by mutual agreement. Confidence can only develop in an atmosphere of cooperation, and this presupposes result-oriented negotiations in the interest of the peaceful functioning of the system of international relations. The most important method of promoting confidence, thus facilitating negotiations and making them a success, is political dialogue — indeed, this is a method acceptable to everyone. By a policy of dialogue the German Democratic Republic means the holding of meetings of high-ranking and top-ranking state representatives, which, leaving aside accidental and other short-term considerations, would be aimed at

- Stating one's own position, explaining one's aims in foreign policy and stating the reasons for it
- Conducting an exchange of views and information, thus clarifying the partner's aims and intentions
- Better understanding the partners' behavior and the motives for their actions
- Making the actions of both partners more predictable
- Clearing the way for an understanding or agreements on a compromise basis
- Preventing friction or tension, even if no mutually agreed solutions are arrived at.

This will be possible if the dialogue

- Succeeds in making clear and delineating the positions
- Leads to a reaffirmation of the principle of the peaceful settlement of disputes
- Promotes the continued search for promising starting points to reach a settlement on a compromise basis that is in the interests of each side
- Confirms the necessity of peaceful coexistence and of cooperation in terms of international norms.

PART IV

Theoretical Foundations and Methods of Analysis — 1

CHAPTER 21

International Negotiation:
A Process Worthy of Reexamination

Marcel Merle

Department of Political Science
Université de Paris-Sorbonne
Paris
France

21.1. Introduction

If one were to assign a rung on the scale of values to every concept of international vocabulary, negotiation would have a prominent position among the terms assigned a positive connotation. On the scale permanently fluctuating between war and peace, it would be located on the right side of the beam, at least at first glance as a substitute, if not an alternative, to the use of force. There is no doubt that better procedures exist to ensure understanding among nations. However, arbitration or international adjudication are more difficult to apply in that they require prior consent of the parties concerned, while the realm of negotiation knows no formal conditions of access, nor any limits in time or space. The preference for negotiation by all those concerned with preventing or settling conflicts is hence based on a long and solid experience. This also explains the concern with studying the mechanism of negotiation, to improve its use and increase its capabilities.

It is not surprising, then, that one turns to game theory. This allows one to formalize different case studies that actually occur and provides actors with a minimum of training necessary to exploit fully the techniques, which are usually sophisticated. Quantification introduces stringency in a field where intuition has often dominated. It also helps one to control accurately the results obtained.

234 M. Merle

Without underestimating the importance of such a procedure, the observer well acquainted with the empirical data is led to question the limits of this approach. To obtain significant findings, game theory assumes that the protagonists face each other in a duel. Throughout the process, which can be measured precisely from beginning to end, each party maintains control over all the elements that make up the problem to be solved: identification of the stakes; and cost and risk analyses inherent in all possible solutions. The ideal model for this confrontation is provided by a game of chess during which two players are engaged in a singular struggle under the eye of a watchful, though silent and inert public. Yet, every actual negotiation, including, of course, international negotiation, takes place in a context that tends to influence the behavior of the players (when it does not perturb the development of their strategy). All the parameters included in this environment must be reintegrated into the analysis, if one expects to understand the true mechanism of negotiation.

One comes to realize that the role of negotiation is less in clearing the way for compromise between two competing logics than in providing the place and time in which multiple contradictory claims of an undetermined number of actors compete with one another.

21.2. Nature of Negotiation

The first observation deals with the simplistic nature of the distinction between what De Martens (1831) called "amicable negotiation" and "assault", or to use the more figurative terms of Abbot de Pradt (1815), the opposition between "the sword" and "reason". Unfortunately, common sense reinforces the etymology that gives negotiation (as for commerce or business) the sense of a peaceful activity, based on the search for and advantageous compromise among honorable interests. Are not the terms of "bargaining" among those concerned, or of "brokers" for third parties, associated with that of negotiation? Common sense is unfortunately mistaken, just as is the *vox populi*, when it clamors for "negotiation" to resolve a diplomatic or social deadlock.

It is a mistake to think that negotiation can *always* be a substitute or an alternative to the use of force. In some cases, and unfortunately there are many, it can only sanction the existence of a power struggle in which one of the parties finds itself able to dictate its resolve over the other. When Chamberlain and Daladier signed the Munich Agreement in September 1938, they were merely bending before a force higher than their own. In this case, it would be preferable to speak of capitulation. Once one admits that "not everything is negotiable" (the principle beyond which no value's security can be saved), one is delimiting a space inside of which the conclusion of an agreement can do nothing more than ratify what has been or is being carried out.

Even when the power struggle is not simply masking a simple abdication, force or the threat of force is rarely absent from negotiation. Machiavelli mocked the "disarmed prophets". Abbot Mably (1757) acknowledged that "virtue, stripped of force, reveals its own weakness" and that "a state which only defends itself against its powerful neighbors with justice and moderation will be defeated sooner or later". Blackmail, implicit or explicit, is hence always capable of falsifying the development or end of a negotiation once the shadow of force spreads over it. In any case, the two protagonists hardly ever go to the negotiating table on an equal basis, in contrast to chess players who start out with the same pieces placed on the board in identical fashion.

To conclude on this first point, every analysis of a negotiation must take into consideration the state of the existing power struggle. All the means of pressure that both protagonists can use against each other must be considered: weapons, economic potential, geopolitical configuration, state of domestic public opinion, etc. Each means of pressure must be evaluated in light of the goal of the negotiation (military, political, economic, cultural, etc.) without, however, neglecting the possibilities of interaction among the different variables.

21.3. The Actor in Negotiations

The second observation seeks to clarify the position of the actor in negotiations. Classical terminology, in reflecting ancient and outdated practices, can contribute to putting people off the track. In diplomatic vocabulary, a negotiator can only commit the state authorities he represents if he is entrusted with "full powers" (plenipotentiary). Legal formality is necessary here as a guaranty *sine qua non* of respect for the will of the parties present. However, the legal status does not always cover the political reality. The granting or the exercise of "full power" (as when a negotiation is carried out "at the summit", e.g., between heads of state or governments) seems to suggest that the negotiator has every latitude to engage the battle with his protagonist. Clearly, every wise statesman or diplomat is well aware beforehand that his margin of maneuver is restricted by a series of constraints that are set by domestic conditions and by the amount and strength of the support that can be expected from his allies. He must use all his insight to detect the margin of maneuver of his protagonist in order to most accurately define the grounds for an understanding.

Nevertheless, the confrontation that culminates in negotiations cannot be reduced to a duel wherein each one moves as he pleases in relation to the assumed reactions of the adversary. This might have been the case under exceptional circumstances, whereby two men face to face had the capacity to determine the fate of nations (or at least that of their fellow countrymen), by virtue of their sole and unique free will. This level of effectiveness is uncertain even for an absolute monarchy. Cardinal Dubois, Foreign Affairs Minister under Louis XV noted in his memoirs: "I always found it harder to negotiate with my own Court than with foreign Courts".

Today it is widely accepted that the domestic political scene projects its shadow over areas that once were the province of diplomatic sparring. Henry Kissinger (1979) shed light on the fact that every negotiator must simultaneously struggle on two fronts, domestic and foreign. On the subject of the Paris negotiations over the conclusion of the Vietnam War, he wrote, "During this time,

Hanoi stayed out of the fray, coldly observing how the US negotiated, not with her adversary but with herself". This assertion can be verified by the naked eye in the case of democracies, where foreign policy is rarely carried out in secrecy and is thrice controlled: by parliament, public opinion and mass media. In the case of authoritarian countries, the existence of a domestic debate does not always appear as clearly. However, the split between "hawks" and "doves", the army and the party, and rival bureaucracies may nonetheless paralyze the negotiator who is active on the international scene.

When domestic pressures are clearly present *before* the start of a negotiation, the negotiator must attempt to insert them into his calculations. This will help facilitate his evaluation of his margin of maneuver. However, when the domestic pressures arise *during* the negotiations (as we have seen during the East–West disarmament talks or on the fixing of European farm prices), the negotiator must be careful to maintain a balance between the concessions that must be made to his foreign protagonists and the reactions these concessions can provoke within his own country. President Wilson had neglected this elementary precaution when he participated in the Treaty of Versailles and the League of Nations. The Senate's repudiation, which followed, set the United States back into an extended period of isolationism that unbalanced the international system between the two world wars. When a French agriculture minister agrees to a level of farm prices with his European counterparts, he knows (or should know) that he must offer compensation to the French farm sectors most affected by the revenue losses arising from the EEC tariffs.

The negotiator today is hence a Janus, a two-faced person, who must constantly maneuver with one eye on his foreign counterpart and the other on the domestic scene. The image of dialogue could still be considered an appropriate term for negotiations, provided that this dialogue takes place permanently on two levels: between states and within states. If one fails to keep this particular characteristic in mind, one can understand nothing about the "diplomatic" aspect of negotiation. Some negotiators refuse to take a reasonable risk in their discussions with their counterparts so as not to stir up problems on the domestic front, to avoid weakening their electoral position. Others are encouraged to multiply the number of spectacular concessions to stir up trouble in the ranks of the enemy camp over the heads of their partners at the negotiating table. The countless events of the disarmament negotiations (including the failure of the Reykjavik summit) are examples of both kinds of cases.

Contrary to the binary outline, induced by game theory, it is not two rationalities that confront each other in the framework of international negotiation, but two forces. Each one obeys a double rationality: maximize one's chances and minimize one's losses simultaneously, on two different checkerboards — that of the international power struggle and that of the domestic struggle [1]. In this difficult exercise, every error in calculation can be fatal for the one who makes it. When General De Gaulle negotiated Algeria's independence with the FLN, he knew that the major risk involved was to provoke the outbreak of a civil war in France. The maneuver that allowed him to achieve his double goal, after four years of efforts under particularly difficult circumstances, can be considered a model of "negotiation". In spite of noteworthy efforts to correct the mistakes of their predecessors, the Nixon–Kissinger team did not manage to find an honorable way out of the Vietnam quagmire (the loss of South Vietnam and the discrediting of the presidency). However, General De Gaulle, no doubt carried away by a striking series of diplomatic successes, neglected to cover the "domestic front" and to keep close enough watch on the management of domestic problems. In 1968 he was forced to face a protest movement, which greatly shook his international prestige, right up to the end of his mandate.

Under these conditions, is it possible to continue treating negotiation as a confrontation between two players free to play out their own hands and able to assume all the risks with full knowledge of all the facts? A positive reply would only be conceivable if one were dealing with perfectly homogeneous rival camps ("speaking in unison", to use the legal expression), or with exceptionally organized minds able to master all the facts of the game, as well as to anticipate all the reactions of both their multiple partners and their adversaries. These two possibilities seem all the more unlikely today in that the debate on two fronts puts the negotiator under pressure from the subnational actors whose random behavior grows with their number. International competition over the control of telecommunications, which has already been going on for several years and which has not yet been settled, is a good example of the inextricable confusion among national ambitions, cultural stakes, industrial interests, financial speculation and bureaucratic rivalries.

One arrives at the ultimate case where the traditional divisions (public/private, internal/external; technical/economic/political) become blurred to such an extent that they cloud the issue and block every attempt at a one-dimensional interpretation. There is no longer *one* negotiation in a linear fashion, but several negotiations developing simultaneously, which are linked. Their end result (should there be one) will not be the whole of all the partial results reached during the previous phases. Yet, a situation of this type is not, or is no longer, unusual in that the goal of negotiations is oriented more and more toward solving problems that integrate dimensions (technical, industrial, financial, cultural) which do not come under diplomacy in the traditional and narrow meaning of the term. Have not the methods of observation and analysis that served to decipher the behavior of past great statesmen (Talleyrand, Metternich, Bismark, Delcasse, etc.) become obsolete? Should the task of modern-day researchers not be to invent new methods of investigation adapted to a protean negotiation? (cf. Merle, 1980).

21.4. Changes in the Dimensions of Negotiations

The third observation tends to emphasize the importance of changes that have occurred in the dimensions of negotiation. Once again, we run the risk of becoming victims of a model that deals with forms which are disappearing. Tradition has given us two models: the face-to-face situation between two states and the multilateral conference. In both cases negotiation represented an episode that was specific and easy to define, because it was structured according to an unchangeable scenario: preparation, the actual talks and the conclusion (positive or negative). However, both procedures, bilateral and multilateral, usually remained separated in time and space. Of course, occasionally there were exceptions, e.g., when an international conference was used as a framework for a side settlement of a bilateral conflict. However, as a general rule, congresses or conferences had a collective mission to carry out, whereas bilateral negotiations were supposed to settle a specific problem between two concerned states.

Yet, these distinctions no longer relate to present-day practice. Even if the classical modalities of negotiation have survived (*ad hoc, tête-à-tête*), negotiation has become a permanent, continuous and universal instrument of international relations today.

From this moment on, limits in time no longer have significant meaning. Discussion of the leading international problems (disarmament, the North–South dialogue) are constantly on the agenda. Their development follows a continuous course, marked by ups and downs; yet no episode can be considered as decisive, not to say definitive. Within the framework of GATT, commercial negotiations have hardly ever been interrupted from one round to another. The continuity of negotiation has certainly been favored by the activity of international organizations, which has become permanent, and whose deliberations have led to results that effectively conclude a negotiation (i.e., the Conference of the Law of the Sea. whose final working stage spanned over nine years). In this instance, a bulky case study, full of information on the multilateral negotiating process, is available. However in many other cases, one can simply isolate arbitrarily and artificially a chronological sequence in a series that follows the law of perpetual motion. Because of our inability to limit an event in time, negotiation cannot be properly grasped.

To this difficulty one must add that of the limits of space. The isolation of negotiations in relation to each other is just a memory. Today the same problem is the object of simultaneous multiple negotiations in different milieu and places. A "trade" negotiation can take place at the same time in the framework of universal organizations (GATT, UNCTAD), within regional ones (EEC), among restricted partner groups (EEC/Third World for the multifiber agreement; EEC/USA for farm exports), and on a bilateral basis between two states linked by a trade agreement. The situation is similar for economic aid issues, which are the subject of bilateral bargaining, as well as of multilateral negotiations at the OECD, IMF and World Bank, to mention only the major partners present.

Henceforth, every fragmentary grasp of a piece of negotiation runs the risk of introducing some distortion into the analysis. A state can be willing to lose on one ground because it knows it can win on another; it can concede today what it expects to win back tomorrow. The simultaneity and ambiguity of negotiation activity paves the way for games of hidden compensation, which escape the observer who is concentrated upon a specific moment or place. Bargaining can even occur from one area of negotiation to another, although they appear to be unrelated. A good-will gesture in human rights can constitute a psychological advantage in a disarmament negotiation; direct or indirect financial aid can lay the groundwork for the conclusion of a military alliance, or reinforce it.

It is therefore becoming harder and harder to define an area of investigation within which a rigorous study of the mechanism of negotiation is possible. In a world in which actors and factors are more and more interdependent, situations are becoming so blurred that one cannot isolate one element without running the risk of changing its nature.

21.5. Conclusions

If these observations are correct, the lesson to be drawn would perhaps be to put aside the microscopic approach, or at least always to associate it with a macroscopic approach.

Rather than attempt to follow the details of a maneuver, which at best comes down to tactics, it appears preferable to start with the strategy of the actors present. This assumes in the beginning that the actors are not only identified, but that their characteristics can be determined and classified according to an adequate typology. Next, one should determine the hierarchy of the stakes for each political entity present. Thirdly, one should analyze the relationship between the objectives to be achieved and the means available in the different areas where a power has the ability to act. It is on the level of the intersection among the strategies used by the forces present that negotiation finds its place and uncovers its true face.

Reduced to a collection of recipes that the wisdom of nations has already codified, negotiation holds only a secondary interest. Only by situating it in its context, does it take on its full significance. It is a link in a chain that is interrupted by maneuvers. What distinguishes it from other links is that it offers the parties present an opportunity to resolve, at least temporarily, a part of their differences peacefully. However, this privileged moment cannot be understood or correctly interpreted, if one adopts the methods detaching it from what is happening upstream, from what is simultaneously occurring in the other theaters of operation, and from what will be happening downstream, No matter how perfect the techniques may be which improve its progress, negotiation is not an end in itself. It is merely an instrument to serve a policy — or, more precisely, to serve competing policies that temporarily find it convenient to seek accommodation. At the least, its study should not be used as an alibi to disguise the game of ambitions and the seriousness of the tensions that are becoming more tangled in a chaotic world.

Notes

[1] The same situation can be found in the area of labor negotiation. When unions negotiate with the government or with employers, it is always with the risk of being bypassed or repudiated by the rank and file afterwards (cf. the failure of the first Grenelle Agreements in 1968). However, since unions are often in a competitive situation among themselves, they are risking both their credibility and their audience in every difficult negotiation.

References

De Martens (1831), *Précis du droit des gens moderne de l'Europe*, Tome II, p. 19.

de Pradt (1815), *Du Congrés de Vienne*, p. 9.

Kissinger, Henry (1979), *White House Years* [French ed.], A. Fayard, p. 316.

Mably (1757), *Principles des négociations pour servir d'introduction au droit public de l'Europe fondé sur les traités*, p. 22.

Merle, M. (1980), The negotiations, in: *Pouvoirs*, P.U.F.

CHAPTER 22

In Search of Common Elements in the Analysis of the Negotiation Process

I. William Zartman

Johns Hopkins University
School of Advanced International Studies
Washington, DC
USA

22.1. Introduction

Like the famous blind men who confronted the elephant and brought back conflicting accounts of its salient characteristics, contemporary analysts of negotiation appear to be talking about different things under the name of the same phenomenon. Some have even called for a search for a common understanding of the subject so that analysis can proceed on the same epistemological track. This review, however, suggests that a common understanding of the negotiation process has already developed and analysts are using it. The diversity that can be found in a number of approaches — five of which are identified — merely displays different ways of talking about the same phenomenon, and in fact even involves the same questions and parameters presented from different angles and under different names. There is more unity than some have suspected and more complementarity, too, as different approaches reinforce and complement each other's analysis. However, many aspects of the process still remain to elude this common, but multifaceted, analysis. The common notion of the process has led analysts to confront these continuing problems, but there is, of course, no certainty that further answers to obdurate problems will not produce new terms of analysis and even new notions of the whole process.

22.2. Problem, Paradox, and Approaches

It is paradoxical and perhaps confusing that there is no single dominant analytical approach to negotiation. The confusion arises from the presence of many different attempts at analysis, sometimes inventing their own wheels to carry forward their insights and sometimes cross-referencing from a number of different analytical approaches. See cases in Zartman (1986, 1987a, 1987b). The fact that all of these are studies of great value only confirms the analytical confusion. The paradox arises because, behind this analytical diversity, there lies a single phenomenon to be analyzed. Although some authors have a hard time seeing the essential identity of the negotiation process [e.g., Young (1975)], most others, including those who then focus on different subtypes for analytical purposes, start with a common definition of the phenomenon [see, for example, Pruitt (1981), Raiffa (1982), Walton and McKersie (1965), and Iklé (1964)].

Negotiation is a process of combining conflicting positions into a common position, under a decision rule of unanimity, a phenomenon in which the outcome is determined by the process (Kissinger, 1969, p. 212). The essential element of process is important because it posits a determining dynamic, not just an assortment of scattered actions or tactics. The challenge then becomes one of finding the nature of that dynamic and its parameters. It is because this challenge has not been met to universal satisfaction that there are still a number of contending approaches to the study of the process. The same reason also explains, in part, why there is such resistance among practitioners of the process to adopting and applying the work of analysts to their own practice.

The question still remains: If there is a single recognized phenomenon, and if the various approaches that are employed to analyze that phenomenon are all insightful, why is there not greater consensus on how to explain negotiation? This study will propose some answers to that question, but in the process it will heighten — but also seek to remove — the paradox. The answer proposed is that each of the analytical approaches puts forward a deterministic analysis in its most rigorous form, but useful insights only when the unreal conditions of determinism are dropped; it is the clash between deterministic integrity and realistic looseness that keeps each of them separate from the others, trying to overcome its internal problems of analysis rather than facing external problems of coordination. The fact that many of the separate approaches are supported by a disciplinary basis also keeps them locked in their internal analytical problems. However, the underlying paradox is that the approaches are really more similar than has been recognized, not only in their study of the same phenomenon, but also in their answers to the same or similar questions in the same or similar ways, but under different disciplinary labels. Exorcising these differences may permit an economy of side movement and an increase of forward movement in the analysis of the negotiation process.

The basic analytical question for all approaches to answer is: How are negotiated outcomes explained? To find generalized answers and to get away from the idiosyncrasies of history, the analyst must find dominant operationalizable variables that provide terms in which the answer can be given. These in turn should be able to provide useful insights — indeed, even strategies or behavioral rules — for practitioners seeking to obtain the best possible outcomes for themselves. Thus, a practical form of the same question is: How can each party deploy efforts to obtain an outcome favorable enough to be acceptable to that party, but attractive enough to the other party to draw it away from its own attempts at a unilateral solution and win its acceptance of an agreement? Or, in the terms of the classical Toughness Dilemma, when should a party be tough and when should it be soft, knowing that conceding little will mean holding to its position but decrease the chances of an agreement; whereas conceding a lot will increase the chances of an agreement but move it away from the positions it values [Bartos (1987), Sebenius (1984), Zartman and Berman (1982)]? Five different "families" of analysis will be examined to see how these questions are handled and where the differences and similarities of the approaches lie [for attempts to show the differences in some or all these schools, see Walton and McKersie (1965), Young (1975), and Zartman (1978, 1987c)].

22.3. Structural Analysis

Structural analysis is based on a distribution of elements — in this case, of instrumental elements or power, defined either as parties' relative positions (resource possessions) or as their relative ability to make their options prevail (or to counter the other's efforts to make its options prevail). See Schelling (1960), Wriggins (1987), Bacharach and Lawler (1981), and Habeeb (1987). Structural analysis is the most commonplace, even journalistic, approach, and its deterministic statement that "the strongest side wins" is usually tautological and *post hoc*. To avoid the tautology, the definitional identity between power structure and winning has to be broken, by using an independent measure of power and by focusing on the way in which sides of different relative strengths achieve their outcomes. The latter has received some attention in the analysis of situations of asymmetry, where better performance by the weaker of the two sides presents an interesting challenge for explanation. While the general category of explanation given can be called "tactics", those tactics generally serve to restore the structural equality of power between the two parties [Snyder and Diesing (1977, pp. 118–244), Hopmann (1978), Deutsch (1973), Zartman (1985b), and Wriggins (1987)]. Various tactics provide various prescriptions for overcoming asymmetry.

Another body of literature associated with the same approach starts with a different structural assumption — of symmetry rather than asymmetry. Based on the finding that parties do best in negotiation when they are or feel equal (Rubin and Brown, 1975, pp. 199, 214–21) and that negotiation takes place when parties' unilateral achievement of their goals is blocked either by the other's veto or by their own incapabilities, some analysis has used structures of symmetry to identify situations most propitious for negotiation, using *when to negotiate* as a key to *how to negotiate* [Saunders (1985); Zartman (1985a)].

By these paths, by the time that structural analysis has moved away from its initial *post hoc* formulation that outcomes are determined by the power positions of the parties, it has shifted toward simply tactical analysis based on a different definition of power. Power no longer is a position or a possession — something a party "has" — but a way of exercising a causal relation — something one "does" to bring about an outcome, and not just the ability to do so [Habeeb (1987), cf. Lasswell and Kaplan (1950, p. 75), Simon (1957, p. 5)]. While such studies may also be termed structural because they deal with power, that element is treated as a responsive, incidental and situational characteristic rather than as an element in a theory or conceptualization of the negotiation process. This is a common problem with studies of power, and in the case of negotiations it has produced an array of insightful, if idiosyncratic, books of proverbs on how parties can be brought to agreement. Karass (1970), Nierenberg (1973), and Fisher and Ury (1981) emphasize various angles of insight into the negotiation process.

Yet despite a lack of theoretical focus or coherence, these studies do propose ways to induce one party to accept the other party's current offer or to induce it to improve its own offer. Whether stated or not, these tactics operate on either current offers, expectations, or alternative outcomes obtained without negotiation (security points). They do so in one of two ways — either by altering the value of current offers relative to the other two points of comparison (expectations and security points) or by identifying certain procedures ("fractionate" or "trade off") or atmospherics ("trust" or "confidence") that facilitate the basic process. All these tactics are acts of (attempted) power, and all of them are ways to bring about acceptance of a given offer. Furthermore, they all focus on a part of a common and general process of replacing unilateral and conflicting positions with a common position or outcome, whether that process is explicitly stated as such or not. Explicit statements about the nature of the process would be useful and would facilitate links between approaches, but even in their absence it is clear that the process is the same.

22.4. Strategic Analysis

Strategic analysis is also based on an array of elements, but its structure is one of ends, not of means. Strategic analysis, as portrayed in game theoretic matrices, begins with the assumption that outcomes are determined by the relative array of their values to the parties, under conditions of rational (i.e., preferred) choice. The standard strategic models — Prisoner's Dilemma Game (PDG) and Chicken Dilemma Game (CDG) — are symmetrical and therefore incorporate the same assumption of equality as that often found in structural analysis. It has frequently been noted that game theory excludes any use of power as a result of its rigorous analytical forms and its clear logic of determinism; it records values as given and shows the strategies that will be chosen and the consequences of doing so [Young (1975); Axelrod (1984)].

As a result, some have objected that strategic analysis is of real value only in comparing the decision to negotiate with the decision to hold out, again like the insights gained from an analysis of symmetrical structures. Since game theory values are given (and indeed, at worst, sometimes inferred from the strategies adopted), there is no way to fractionate or trade off, only to enter the value of any such external operations into the appropriate box in the matrix; and there is no way to change any of those values within the matrix, only to record any changes that may have occurred from one matrix to another.

Yet when the rigorous assumptions that provide the basis for its determinism are relaxed and game theory presentations are used heuristically as the starting point for analysis, a number of the associated limitations fall away and new possibilities appear. Strategic analysis shows that the only way to break out of deadlock is through asymmetry and that, therefore, instead of working to improve offers or cooperation (CC) (absolutely or in relation to expectations, which cannot be shown on a matrix), parties are best advised to alter the payoffs or perception of payoffs associated with nonnegotiated or unilateral outcomes (DD), i.e., the costs of defection or deadlock. This in turn brings in new understandings of power, seen as the use of security points to induce or resist changes in bargaining positions [Snyder and Diesing (1977), Zagare (1978), Brams (1985)].

Movement is the essence of the negotiation process, and movement cannot be shown on a matrix. But the conditions that produce movement — again, power — can be shown on a matrix and analyzed from it, just as movies result from a succession of stills. The result is the same process as indicated in the relaxation and refinement of structural analysis, in which parties move from their unilateral options to a common cooperative decision so shaped as to be more attractive than their security points.

The problem with strategic analysis at present is not its rigidity, but its limited scope. Many of the important and more detailed questions on how to move parties toward a common solution lie outside the analysis; even such important insights as the ways to reinforce commitment [Schelling (1960) and Baldwin (1987)] are triggered by a need to consider security points, but are outside game theory analysis. An effort to render more precise the importance of the security point (DD) in comparison to unilateral demands (CD, DC) and multilateral compromise (CC) is an important new advance of the strategic approach, but the actual calculation of Critical Risk depends on a difficult shift from ordinal to cardinal values in the matrix [Ellsberg (1975), Snyder and Diesing (1977)].

On the other hand, strategic categories of encounters can help answer some of the puzzling analytical questions of negotiations. For example, the Toughness Dilemma may be resolved by use of the two game theory dilemmas: Whereas parties who see their situation as a PDG may do best by playing soft to open and tough to punish [Axelrod (1984)], parties who see themselves in a CDG do better by playing tough to demand and soft to reward (see Chapter 13 by J. Nyerges in this volume). But this, in turn, confirms an answer from structural analysis to the Toughness Dilemma, based on appropriate tactics for strong and weak powers, respectively. Further examples could be produced where strategic

analysis, despite apparent limitations, ends up discussing elements of the same
process, and often the same process — power — as other approaches, but in
different terms. In so doing, it enriches the search for answers to the causal —
or power — question.

22.5. Process Analysis

Process analysis has the common feature of explaining outcomes through a series
of concessions determined by some element inherent in each party's position.
The particular element varies slightly according to the particular version of the
theory; most process analysis is based on a security point theory in some form,
although there are also a few other variations used. Process analysis indicates
that the party will concede on the basis of a comparative calculation of its own
versus its opponent's costs or of its own costs *versus* some acceptability level
[Zeuthen (1975), Cross (1969), Pen (1975), Hicks (1975), Snyder and Diesing
(1977)]. On this basis one can determine which party will concede how much
until the final point of convergence is reached. This, of course, provides a way of
diagramming a negotiation process that is the same as that discussed by other
approaches.

Other variations are end point theories and concession rate theories, the
first analyzing the parties' movement as a way to maintain a mutually fair and
maximizing outcome and the second analyzing the parties' movement on the
basis of reactions to each other's degree of concession, the two being parts of the
same process [Bartos (1978), Zeuthen (1975), Nash (1975), Cross (1969), cf.
Pruitt (1981)]. These latter variations (endpoint and concession-rate theories of
process) are prescriptively deterministic; that is, they indicate how parties will
act and where they will end up if they want to reach a mutually fair and maximizing outcome. But they also serve the useful function of providing a baseline
against which unfairness and power can be measured, and hence they are
relevant to some understanding of the process [Pillar (1983)].

But it can be seen that process theories, which originate in economics, are
in fact structural theories that indicate that the weaker party will concede until
the tables are turned, at which point the other party will concede in its turn, and
so on to agreement. Hence, they too are theories of power, with power measured
in terms of a comparison between offers and security points, or in terms of a
comparison between offers and security points, or in other words, in terms of
critical risk factors. Although they are constant-effect theories, to the extent
that parties can alter each other's or their own security points, they can exercise
power as well as simply possessing it; that variant reduces the deterministic possibilities of the theory but increases its reality. The similarity between process
and strategic theories has long been recognized [Harsanyi (1975), Wagner
(1975)], although their mechanisms are indeed different. The similarity with
structural theories should also be registered; although many structuralists would
probably not "read" game theory or "talk" bilateral monopoly, their analyses are
complementary, covering the same phenomena within the same process.

The neatness of process theory only works in idealized situations and then only with idiosyncrasies [Khury (1968), Bartos (1974, 1987), Hamermesch (1987)]. Concession behavior does not always match; often it mismatches or separates (tracks) [Pruitt (1981)], and parties do not even concede responsively but rather try to teach and learn, respond and elicit responses, at the same time, combining several types of behavior that makes theoretically neat patterns unrealistic [Cross (1969), Bartos (1987)]. But the point is that in the process, analysts are discerning both involuntary and voluntary, mechanical and manipulative, process and power elements that make up negotiation, all of them clustered about a similarly understood effort to combine conflicting positions into a common one.

As the references in this review are beginning to show, analysts do not even belong exclusively to one school or another but sometimes borrow naturally from different approaches. Yet the fact that the field is seen as pluralistic as it is, or that bibliographies remain largely in the author's discipline [Rubin and Brown (1975)], means that there is not enough natural borrowing and cross-referencing.

22.6. Behavioral Analysis

Behavioral analysis provides an obviously different explanation of negotiated outcomes by using the negotiators themselves as the focus of analysis [Jönsson (1978)]. The terms of analysis used are the personalities of the negotiators, either directly or in interaction. Personality in social psychology can be used to refer to personal predispositions that exist at a number of different levels, from biologically ingrained needs to more influenceable attitudes. At whatever level, this school of analysis responds to a common belief about negotiation — that "it all depends on the personalities of the negotiators". The challenge then becomes to translate that popular perception into identifiable and non-tautological variables that can be used for analysis.

A more literary and intuitive basis for behavioral analysis began with Nicolson's (1939) distinction between Shopkeepers and Warriors. It has been extended and developed through a number of forms into Snyder and Diesing's (1977) Softliners and Hardliners. There are many characterizations possible for these basic types, but some can be given in terms already used by other schools. The Hardline Warrior sees situations as a Prisoner's Dilemma Game and acts as a mismatcher, expecting toughness to lead to softness (and victory) and softness to lead to toughness, whereas the Softline Shopkeeper sees situations as a Chicken Dilemma Game and follows matching behavior, expecting toughness to lead to toughness (and deadlock) and softness to lead to softness. Thus, behavioral analyses take the same parameters as elements of the same process as other approaches, classifying them into typologies in terms of behavior.

A more developed approach involves categorizing personality types according to their Interpersonal Orientation (IO), an approach that is both more insightful and more complex because it is not merely dichotomous and because

its effects depend on interaction rather than on simple or direct taxonomic associations. Opposed to a Low IO type are two types of High IOs — Cooperators
and Competitors; either produces a positive result when negotiating with the
same type of personality; but when cross-paired, the match is unproductive
because the two types grate on each other. Rather than explaining an outcome
in its own terms, as the previous typologies tend to do, IO analysis operates on
the basis of a causal interaction [Rubin and Brown (1975)]. It also identifies
different types of outcomes, depending on joint or comparative maximization, a
point also developed in studies of Motivational Orientations (MO) [Rubin and
Brown (1975), Filley (1975)]. But this approach, too, deals with such elements
as the propensity to compromise, to construct positive-sum or divide zero-sum
outcomes, or to adopt a tough or soft line (i.e., a flatter or a steeper concession
rate) during the process of combining conflicting positions into a joint decision.

22.7. Integrative Analysis

Integrative analysis, like behavioral analysis, would seem to constitute an exception to the general understanding of a negotiation process. Although it, too, con-
ceives of negotiation as a process, its process runs through stages, in which the
outcome is explained by the performance of behaviors identified as specifically
appropriate to each successive stage [Gulliver (1979), Saunders (1985), Zartman
and Berman (1982), Zartman (1978), Druckman (1986)]. Rather than seeing a
process that works from fixed points of discord to a common point of convergence, integrative analysis emphasizes the disarray of parties' interests in their
own minds and the need to manipulate conceptualizations of the problem into
mutually satisfying positive-sum outcomes before proceeding to an elaboration of
a detailed division of the spoils. By extending its concept of the negotiation process back before the time when positions appear as fixed points, integrative
analysis not only allows for greater and more positive manipulation of those positions [Fisher and Ury (1981)], but also meets practitioners' understanding of
negotiation by drawing attention to the pre-negotiation part of the process [Ben-
dahmane and McDonald (1984, 1986), Zartman (1985b)].

But again, these positive aspects of the approach should not obscure the
fact that the subject is the same process as analyzed elsewhere. Its emphasis on
opening options is preliminary to a focus on closure, using expanded possibilities
of mutual benefit to buy agreement with an outcome that is less — or at least
different — than original demands: the same process can be described as giving
something to get something, a process of establishing terms of trade for an
exchange of items in the absence of fixed prices and even of fixed monetary units.
In previous terms, integrative analysis explores the mechanics of the Shopkeeper
but also, more realistically, of the Shopkeeper confronted with Warrior aspects of
the problem and with the need to get around them. Negotiators — at least
diplomatic negotiators, but probably most others — are not merely Shopkeepers,
who can make a deal on any issue; there are items better postponed and interests
that are properly nonnegotiable, and there are limits to acceptable deals that are

imposed by security points. If finding a common agreement through this maze is more than a matter of convergence, it is a matter of convergence as well.

A growing branch of this analysis focuses on precise mechanisms for identifying the best possible deal that can be gotten by both sides, given the differences in the nature of their interests. While this is a complex extension of the Nash (1975) solution that occupies a basic position in the strategic and process approaches, the complexity of stakes makes a simple positive-sum outcome too schematic to be useful [Valavanis (1958), Iklé and Leites (1962), Barclay and Peterson (1976), Raiffa (1982), Sebenius (1984)]. The process involves finding as many dimensions of components to the parties' interests as possible in order to provide the best trade-offs and thereby insure the greatest durability to the outcome. In addition to finding how much of a conflicting position a party must give up to gain assent, the process also involves finding how much of a non- (or less-) valued position a party can trade to gain a more valued position [Homans (1961), p. 62]. But the element of conflict is never absent, and the process of shaping a single multilateral decisions out of conflicting unilateral claims remains.

22.8. Negotiation as a Process

It should be clear that the study of negotiation has come a considerable way in the past two decades in building and expanding on a common concept of a process, sharpening the much looser characterization given in the *International Encyclopedia of the Social Sciences* [Iklé (1968)] as "A form of interaction through which [parties] ... try to arrange ... a new combination of some of their common and conflicting interests". The "form of interaction" has taken shape as a process of combining conflicting positions into a common outcome by joint decision, allowing more specific focus of attention on how this is done, whether by power, by patterns of movement, by restructuring stakes and values, by interacting personality types, or by a series of steps. Yet, just as clearly, there is much more to do to know the process, although many of those further directions are indicated by using the common concept of process as a starting point and the concept of power as the causal question.

22.9. Evaluation of Success

One problem raised by the notion of negotiation as a process is that of measuring success, an answer to which is necessary to an evaluation of behavior and prescriptions for its improvement. The question of success is more complex than it may appear [Zartman (1987a)]. The nature of negotiation is to arrive at the largest mutually satisfactory agreement, with any one (and therefore, each) side getting the best deal possible and the other (and therefore, each) getting at least enough to make it want to keep the agreement. By that very nature, negotiation is not a process of winning and losing, so that success must be evaluated against the problem, not against the adversary. There is, however, a subcategory of negotiations in which one party's aims are to deny the adversary a particular payoff rather than to get as much as possible for itself, making positive-sum evaluations more complex. Thus, a number of criteria are potentially relevant for the evaluation of success, but none of them gives a completely satisfactory answer.

First, *signature* of an agreement is a *prima facie* or nominal sign of success, because it indicates a judgment by the parties that they expect to be better off with the agreement than without and that they can do no better by either continuing negotiations or chosing an alternative outcome. Second, this perception can be verified empirically to see if the parties are indeed *better off*, either by comparing their condition before and after the agreement or by comparing their position afterward with their presumed position at the same time in the absence of an agreement (a more relevant comparison, but a counterfactual one that involves some judgment). While nothing says that the parties must be equally well off or even equally better off, further evaluations could also investigate how unequally better off the agreement made them and also whether they were Pareto-optimally better off — that is, whether or not they had missed opportunities to improve the condition of either of them without making the other less well off. Since some negotiations may be designed to redress power inequities while others may reflect power inequities, the criteria of success based on the relative improvement of the parties' positions will vary. Third, the results can be evaluated against the parties' *opening positions*, with all the caveats about the initial vagueness and inflation of demands that is inherent in the process. Nash solutions and Bartos solutions, discussed above under end-point determinism, are a function of opening positions and can serve as a baseline to evaluate actual outcomes. But all three of these criteria for evaluation have flaws and complexities that call for further work — there is currently very little — on systems of evaluation.

22.10. Division, Creation, and Exchange

Another topic of concern is the analysis of negotiations for three very different types of stakes: those solvable by division, those by creation and those by exchange. Although much of the earlier literature on negotiation focused on the more obvious topic of division [Schopenhauer (1896), Nicolson (1939), Schelling (1960)] with its notion of negotiation as winning or losing, much more attention lately has been drawn to the improvement of exchanges [Homans (1961), Axelrod (1970), Nash (1975), Sebenius (1984), Zartman (1987a)] with its notion of mutual satisfactions.

The importance of resolving problems by exchange bears much emphasis, for in their conflicts parties often forget that resolution by multilateral decisions means "buying" the other party's agreement by inducements through items that he values in order to make agreement attractive to him. At the same time, such emphasis carries a different image of negotiation from an encounter of conceding and winning, portraying instead a positive-sum process where "everyone wins (something)". Unfortunately, this is not the whole picture. Just as there must be a little Warrior in every successful Shopkeeper, so there is inevitably some zero-sum aspect to every positive sum. Once parties have created a greater good, there is some need to decide how to divide and share it. Furthermore, there are some stakes that are indivisible, and there are others that are unexchangeable and therefore necessarily divisible. These aspects of negotiation still await exhaustive or definitive treatment, and they are somewhat different from the earlier, insightful analysis of redistributive bargaining [Walton and McKersie (1965)].

To date, there are three ways of thinking about the problem of division. The first is to replace it in the context of exchange by means of *compensation*. By determining what the item is worth, the other party can counterbalance it through compensatory concessions. Unfortunately, some stakes have absolute or infinite worth, so that no compensation is possible. The second is to *restructure* perceptions of the stakes so that things are seen differently and the zero-sum nature of the outcomes is removed. Again, some stakes escape such creative reformulation, or even when the subject of an attractive formula they prove intractable in detail. The third is to manipulate notions of *justice,* which can then be translated to the specific — an idea akin to the previous notion of a creative formula. But that is merely to intellectualize the problem without solving it in many cases, since it is the conflicting notions of justice that make the problems of division so intractable. Obviously, practitioners need more help in ways of dealing with the zero-sum aspects of negotiations — the "Jerusalem Problems" — that lie beyond positive-sum creativity.

22.11. Toughness and Softness

A third topic of continuing inquiry highlighted by the generally accepted notion of the negotiation process is the Toughness Dilemma. The question of when to be tough and when to be soft, and the paradox on which it is based, has already been identified as the major tactical question for analysts and practitioners alike.

By now, it is plain that there is no way out of the dilemma as presented, and that correct and insightful answers depend on some intermediate variable, such as personality, timing, phase, power, etc. But there is still no sense of any hierarchy among these intermediate variables — other than the eternal debates among disciplines as to which gives the best analysis — and no notions as to which are trumps. Somewhere between the anecdotal proverbs and the unoperationalizable theory lies a not yet fully mined terrain of inquiry that may require new parameters.

22.12. Multilateral Bargaining

Finally, an area of negotiation that falls outside the current paradigm is multilateral bargaining. The current process notion has thus far worked to exclude effective consideration of multilateral negotiations, and those that have been treated well tend to be reduced to bilateral analysis. When not reduced to dyads, multilateral negotiation tends to be treated merely descriptively, even if insightfully, a problem that has posed particular challenges in regard to the successive GATT rounds [Preeg (1979), Evans (1971), Cline *et al.* (1978), Winham (1987)]. There have been a number of excellent attempts to devise an approach to multilateral negotiations [that is, large number of participants, not merely a few more than two, as in Raiffa (1982), Zagare (1978)], which indicate some promising directions [Zartman (1987c)].

One set of approaches treats multilateral negotiations as a problem in *coalition*-formation [Rubin and Brown (1975, pp. 64ff), Snyder and Diesing (1977, pp. 349ff), Raiffa (1982)]. However, coalition is a very different process from negotiation, and to the extent that it covers the shaping of outcomes to be decided up or down by some sort of weighted decision rule, it hides a separate negotiation process. There is something going on in the interstices of coalition that needs a separate analysis that is not yet available. Like the strategic approach to bilateral negotiations, to which it is related, coalition analyses study what happens between negotiations and impinges on them, but does not capture them. Two concepts, *preferences and scaling*, have been used in some different and imaginative ways by Sebenius (1984), Friedheim (1987), Nagel (1986), Hipel and Fraser (1984). But they, too, indicate ingredients to an agreement rather than the process by which it is obtained; as in coalition, negotiation becomes voting or at least approaches it. Other approaches are conceivable, but have not been used. For instance, small group dynamics might provide a new analytical context, as might a conceptual examination of the construction of an agreement out of individual pieces.

In multilateral negotiation as in the predominant bilateral mode, the two categories of ingredients are parties and stakes. Negotiated agreements are made of stakes by parties. Bilateral negotiation has its general process model as a basis for analysis, which permits many approaches to coexist and reinforce each other. Multilateral negotiations needs either to fit into that concept of process or invent its own basic model to enjoy the same benefits. In any case, in regard to bilateral negotiations, there are many blind men but only one elephant, and the two should not be confused with each other.

References

Axelrod, Robert (1970), *The Conflict of Interest*, Markham, Chicago.
Axelrod, Robert (1984), *The Evolution of Cooperation*, Basic Books, New York.
Bacharach, Samuel, B. and Lawler, Edward (1981), *Bargaining: Power, Tactics and Outcomes*, Jossey Bass, San Francisco.

Baldwin, David A. (1987), Bargaining with Airline Hijackers, in Zartman (1987b).

Barclay, Scott and Petterson, Cameron (1976), *Multi-Attribute Utility Models*, Designs and Decision, technical report 76-1, McLean, VA.

Bartos, Otomar (1974), *Process and Outcome of Negotiation*, Columbia University Press, New York.

Bartos, Otomar (1978), Simple Model of Negotiation, in Zartman (1978).

Bartos, Otomar (1987), How Predictable are Negotiations? in Zartman (1987b).

Bendahmane, Diane and McDonald, John (eds.) (1984), *International Negotiation*, State Department Foreign Service Institute, Washington, DC.

Bendahmane, Diane and McDonald, John, (eds.) (1986), *Perspectives on Negotiation*, State Department Foreign Service Institute, Washington, DC.

Brams, Steven (1985), *Superpower Games*, Yale University Press, New Haven, CT.

Cline, W.R. *et al.* (1978), *Trade Negotiations in the Tokyo Round*, Brookings Institution, Washington, DC.

Cross, John (1969), *The Economics of Bargaining*, Basic Books, New York.

Davidow, Jeffrey (1984), *A Piece in Southern Africa*, Westview, Boulder, CO.

Deutsch, Morton (1973), *Resolution of Conflict*, Yale University Press, New Haven, CT.

Druckman, D. (1986), Stages, Turning Points and Crises, *Journal of Conflict Resolution* 30: 327–360.

Ellsberg, Daniel (1975), Theory and Practice of Blackmail, in Young (1975).

Evans, J.W. (1971), *The Kennedy Round in American Trade Policy*, Harvard University Press, Cambridge, MA.

Filley, Alan C. (1975), *Interpersonal Conflict Resolution*, Scott Foresman, Glenview, IL.

Fisher, Roger and Ury, William (1981), *Getting to Yes*, Hougton Mifflin, Boston.

Friedheim, Robert (1987), The Third United Nations Conference on the Law of the Sea, in Zartman (1987a).

Gulliver, P.H. (1979), *Disputes and Negotiations*, Academic, New York.

Habeeb, W. Mark (1987), *Asymmetrical Negotiations: Panama, Spain, Iceland*, Johns Hopkins University Press, Baltimore, MD.

Hamermesch, Daniel (1987), Who "Wins" in Wage Bargaining? in Zartman (1987b).

Harsanyi, John (1975), Approaches to the Bargaining Problem Before and After the Theory of Games, in Young (1975).

Harsanyi, John (1977), *Rational Behavior and Bargaining Equilibrium in Games and Social Situations*, Cambridge University Press, New York.

Hicks, John (1975), *The Theory of Wages*, Macmillan, London.

Hipel, Keith and Fraser, Niall (1984), *Conflict Analysis*, Elsevier, New York.

Homans, George (1961), *Social Behavior*, Harcourt Brace, New York.

Hopmann, P. Terrence (1978), An Application of the Richardson Process Model, in Zartman (1978).

Iklé, Fred C. (1964), *How Nations Negotiate*, Harper and Row, New York.

Iklé, Fred C. (1968), Negotiation, in *International Encyclopedia of the Social Sciences*, Vol. 2, p. 117, Macmillan, New York.

Iklé, Fred C. and Leites, Nathan (1962), Political Negotiation as a Process of Modifying Utilities, *Journal of Conflict Resolution* 1: 19–28.

Jönsson, Christer (1978), Situation-Specific versus Actor-Specific Approaches to International Bargaining, *European Journal of Political Research* 6(4), pp. 381–398.

Karass, Chester (1970), *The Negotiation Game*, World, New York.

Khury, F. (1968), The Etiquette of Bargaining in the Middle East, *American Anthropologist* 70: 698–706.

Kissinger, H. (1969), The Vietnam Negotiations, *Foreign Affairs* 47: 211-234.

Lasswell, Harold and Kaplan, Abraham (1950), *Power and Society*, Yale University Press, New Haven, CT.

Lipson, Charles (1985), Bankers' Dilemma, *World Politics* 38 (October): 200-225.

Nagel, Stuart (1986), Microcomputers, P/G% and Dispute Resolution, *Proceedings of the Annual Meeting of the Society of Professionals in Dispute Resolution.*

Nash, John (1975), The Bargaining Problem, in Young (1975).

Nicolson, Harold (1939), *Diplomacy*, Oxford University Press, New York.

Nierenberg, Gerard (1973), *Fundamentals of Negotiating*, Hawthorn, New York.

Pen, Jan (1975), A General Theory of Bargaining, in Young (1975).

Pillar, Paul (1983), *Negotiating Peace*, Princeton University Press, Princeton, NJ.

Preeg, Ernest (1979), *Traders and Diplomats*, Brookings Institution, Washington, DC.

Pruitt, Dean (1981), *Negotiating Behavior*, Academic, New York.

Raiffa, Howard (1982), *The Art and Science of Negotiation*, Harvard University Press, Cambridge, MA.

Rubin, Jeffrey and Brown, Bert (1975), *The Social Psychology of Bargaining and Negotiation*, Academic, New York.

Saunders, Harold (1985), *The Other Walls*, American Enterprise Institute, Washington, DC.

Schelling, Thomas G. (1960), *The Strategy of Conflict*, Harvard University Press, Cambridge, MA.

Schopenhauer, Arthur (1896), *The Art of Controversy*, Allen and Unwin, London.

Sebenius, James (1984), *Negotiating the Law of the Sea*, Harvard University Press, Cambridge, MA.

Simon, Herbert (1957), *Models of Man*, John Wiley, New York.

Snyder, Glenn and Diesing, Paul (1977), *Conflict among Nations*, Princeton University Press, Princeton, NJ.

Valavanis, Stefan (1958), Resolution of Conflict when Utilities Interact, *Journal of Conflict Resolution* 2: 156-169.

Wagner, Harvey (1975), A Unified Treatment of Bargaining Theory, in Young (1975).

Walton, Robert and McKersie, Robert (1965), *A Behavioral Theory of Labor Negotiations*, McGraw-Hill, New York.

Winham, Gilbert (1987), *International Trade and the Tokyo Round Negotiation*, Princeton University Press, Princeton, NJ.

Wriggins, Howard (1987), Up for Auction, in Zartman (1987b).

Young, Oran (ed.) (1975), *Bargaining*, University of Illinois Press, Urbana, IL.

Zagare, Frank (1978), Game Theoretic Analysis of the Vietnam Negotiations, in Zartman (1978).

Zartman, I. William (ed.) (1978), *The Negotiation Process*, Sage, Newbury Park, CA.

Zartman, I. William (1985a), *Ripe for Resolution*, Oxford University Press, New York.

Zartman, I. William (1985b), Negotiating from Asymmetry, *Negotiation Journal I*, 2: 121-138.

Zartman, I. William (1986), Practitioners' Theories of International Negotiation, *Negotiation Journal II*, 3: 299-310.

Zartman, I. William (ed.) (1987a), *Positive Sum: Improving North-South Negotiations*, Transaction Books, New Brunswick, NJ.

Zartman, I. William (ed.) (1987b), *The 50% Solution*, 2nd ed., Yale University Press, New Haven, CT.

Zartman, I. William (1987c), *Many Are Called But Few Choose: Managing Complexity in Multilateral Negotiations*, paper presented to the American Political Science Association.

Zartman, I. William and Berman, Maureen (1982), *The Practical Negotiator*, Yale University Press, New Haven, CT.

Zeuthen, Frederik (1975), Economic Warfare, in Young (1975).

CHAPTER 23

International Negotiations and Cognitive Theory: A Research Project

Christer Jönsson

Department of Political Science
Lund University
Lund
Sweden

23.1. Introduction

This chapter outlines an ongoing research project at the Department of Political Science of the University of Lund, Sweden, the main purpose of which is to assess the role of cognitive factors in international negotiations. The project has branched out into three subprojects, which are described in turn.

First, concepts and insights from *semiotics* and *attribution theory* are combined to construct an analytical framework for the study of the communication aspects of international negotiations. The focus of this approach is the *signification* process: How do messages and signals acquire meaning in the course of negotiations? Diplomatic history is surveyed in an effort to confirm, disconfirm or modify hypotheses derived from semiotics and attribution theory. Second, an in-depth case study of the well-documented 1919 Paris Peace Conference is undertaken in an attempt to assess the significance of cognitive factors relative to situational factors in accounting for the process and outcome of negotiations. Third, in collaboration with Michael Shapiro of the University of Hawaii and Matthew Bonham of the American University, a modified version of the *cognitive mapping* technique is applied to international negotiations. In this new version, the emphasis is on discursive rather than psychological imagery, and the idea chain or "path" is privileged over the "actor". The cognitive map is thus conceived less as a psychological template than as a *discursive space*.

As this chapter reports on a research project in progress, it therefore deals primarily with research design rather than results. The project "International Negotiation and Cognitive Theory", which receives financial support from the Swedish Council for Research in the Humanities and Social Sciences, aims at assessing the role of communication and cognition in international negotiations.

This entails a focus on aspects neglected in the traditional game-theoretical approach to the study of negotiation. Game theory is essentially *static* in nature; it tends to *homogenize actors*; it "black boxes" the *information processing* aspects of negotiations; and it envisages *unitary* and perfectly *rational actors* (cf. Jönsson, 1983: 141). In our project, we are looking for a vantage point that permits *dynamic analysis*, takes *actor differences* into account, has *a realistic conception of the actor's information processing*, and *allows for the lack of cohesion and international bargaining within states*.

From the viewpoint of game theory, negotiation can be seen as communication superimposed on a game. The human capacity to acquire, reveal, and conceal information then becomes crucial, and creates the problem of interpretation associated with communication moves [Shubik (1967: 261), Rapoport (1964: 122-24), Goffman (1969: 4).

> Cognitive variables are needed to explain what images adversaries have of the game and of each other and what strategies each devises for play, for shaping opponents' perceptions of the game. Communication variables must be introduced to show how adversaries modify their initial images and strategies — or resist such modification — in the light of feedback from the other side (Sigal, 1979: 571).

Models focusing on information processing have indeed been suggested by students of negotiation. For instance, the economist Alan Coddington (1968) has suggested a skeletal model that has been adapted and developed by political scientists interested in international negotiation [Snyder and Diesing (1977: 282-339), Jönsson (1979: 15-16)].

Drawing on such conceptualizations, the present project attempts to integrate hypotheses and insights from contemporary approaches to communication and human cognition in a framework for the study of international negotiations. The project branches out into three partially overlapping subprojects, described in turn in the following subsections.

23.2. Communication in International Negotiation

> Perhaps the most neglected aspect of bargaining has been the role of various kinds of communications (Tedeschi and Rosenfeld, 1980: 225).

Bargaining and negotiation are subclasses of social communication. Fisher and Ury (1983: xi, 33), for instance, define negotiation as "back-and-forth communication designed to reach an agreement when you and the other side have some interests that are shared and others that are opposed", and argue that "without communication there is no negotiation".

Social communication involves the transmission of messages to which certain meanings are attached. These messages can be either verbal or nonverbal (cf. Johnson, 1974: 66). Thus, Schelling (1963: 21) introduced the term "tacit bargaining" for a communication process "in which adversaries watch and interpret each other's behavior, each aware that his own actions are being interpreted and anticipated, each acting with a view to the expectations that he creates". Just as the verbal components in a normal person-to-person conversation have been estimated to carry less than 35% of the social meaning (Johnson, 1974: 74), so nonverbal messages and "body language" constitute important aspects of bargaining between states.

In fact, both behavior and nonbehavior may constitute messages, especially in a negotiation setting. "Activity or inactivity, words or silence, all have message value: they influence others and these others, in turn, cannot *not* respond to these communications and are thus themselves communicating" (Simons, 1976: 50).

Consider, by way of analogy, the story about one psychoanalytically oriented school of social work where students were considered hostile if they came to class late, anxious if they came early, and compulsive if they came at the appointed hour (Simons, 1976: 42). By the same token, whatever a diplomatic negotiator does or does not do is willy-nilly scrutinized and interpreted by the adversaries. All of his behavior and nonbehavior, words and silences, assume message values. We can, for instance, recall Metternich's reputed reaction to the death of a Russian ambassador in the midst of sensitive negotiations: "I wonder what he meant by that".

In any negotiatory setting — either national of international — "saying is doing" and "doing is saying". As for the international environment, it has even been described as a "universal communications network" (Cohen, 1981: 29-30):

All acts, verbal or nonverbal, intentional or unintentional, are potential signals which feed into the network and are liable to reach all listeners and be read by them for the message which they convey. Moreover any message may be read together with, and understood in the light of, the collective body of evidence already communicated or later to be communicated by the actor about his expectations. The plea, therefore, that the meaning of a certain action has been misinterpreted is irrelevant. As in all systems of communications, the meaning of the information transmitted cannot be arbitrarily determined by the sender alone. It means what others understand it to mean in the light of the underlying grammar. Put another way, it is the reasonably foreseeable effect, not the announced intention, which defines the meaning and hence perceived purpose of an action. It is not what you intend to say that counts but what others take you to mean.

This applies, *a fortiori*, to international negotiations where a special kind of communication, *persuasion*, is predominant. Communication is designed to influence others by modifying their behavior and/or beliefs and attitudes [cf. Simons (1976: 21), Reardon (1981: 25)]. Negotiation, then, can be seen as mutual persuasion attempts. Successful negotiation "requires of each participant the ability not only to persuade but to be persuaded" (Keller, 1956: 181). In other words, persuasion may be seen as "a species of the genus commonly labeled *learning*" (Miller, 1980: 17). Consequently, negotiation entails a learning process of sorts: "Since negotiation involves value change and accommodation, it is a learning process in which each party is both teacher and student" (Zartman and Berman, 1982: 19).

It is my contention that in analyzing this multifaceted communication process we might draw on approaches to social communication that hitherto have not been applied systematically to the study of international bargaining: (1) semiotics and discourse analysis, which focus on signs and texts and the production of meaning; and (2) attribution theory and "judgment" research, those branches of cognitive theory whose main concern is the causal interpretation of information on the part of individuals.

These approaches adhere to that school in the study of communication which sees communication as the production and exchange of meanings. Their main concern is how messages interact with people in order to produce meaning (Fiske, 1982: 2-3). They see *signification* as an active process and use verbs such as "create", "generate", or "negotiate" to refer to this process (cf. Fiske, 1982: 49).

23.3. Semiotics and Discourse Analysis

Semiotics is the study of *signs* and the way they acquire meaning. Signs are "artifacts or acts that refer to something other than themselves, that is they are signifying constructs" (Fiske, 1982: 2). Semioticians emphasize the arbitrary nature of signs. The meaning of a sign rests on social convention. Signs are organized into systems of signification, or *codes*, which rely on a shared cultural background [cf. Fiske (1982: 68), Eco (1971: 13; 1985: 161)]. To uncover — or "dis-cover" (Blonsky, 1985: xxxix) — such codes is the task of semiotics.

Discourse analysis focuses primarily on *texts* and *discursive practices* rather than individual "signs", yet shares with semiotics the basic assumption that "the conditions surrounding the production of a system of meaning are none other than socio-historical and intersubjective" (Kristeva, 1985: 211).

> The flow of statments and meanings in any discursive practice, even the most austere, descriptively oriented ones are part of historically engendered, social practices which precede any speaker/author and, in addition, guide interpretive practices deployed on texts once they are produced (Shapiro, 1984: 2).

Codes and discourses depend upon a shared cultural background, upon "the unwritten, unstated expectations that derive from the shared experience of members of a culture" (Fiske, 1982: 82). Even within one society there may be several subcultures that produce different codes and discourses.

How, then, does this relate to international negotiations? Two sets of subcultures seem to condition communication in international negotiations: the national subcultures of the participating states, on the one hand, and a "negotiator subculture" on the other. The notion that national subcultures produce national "negotiating styles" has been developed by scholars and practitioners alike (cf. Jönsson, 1978). Less attention has been devoted to the shared norms, expectations, and discursive practices among diplomatic negotiators. Yet it seems reasonable to assume that there exists a distinct negotiator subculture and concomitant code.

Signs show varying degrees of *convention*, ranging from the purely idiosyncratic and private to the truly conventional and collective, and varying degrees of *constraints*, ranging from the arbitrary to the iconic (cf. Heradstveit and Bjorgo, 1986: 32-34). A piece of modern art is an idiosyncratic sign; a treatise on art history uses conventional signs (scientific language). The word "herrar" written on a door is an arbitrary sign (as any non-Swedish-speaking male in distress can verify); a drawing of a male silhouette is an iconic sign, ostensibly intelligible across language barriers.

Most signaling in a bargaining context, though not totally idiosyncratic and arbitrary, is less than conventional and iconic. This, in combination with the existence of multiple subcultures, makes the signification process problematic in international negotiations. When interpreted by members of different subcultures who bring different codes to them, signs may produce different meanings. Negotiators, therefore, have to be content with saying both less and more than they mean: less, because their verbal and nonverbal signaling will never immediately convey their meaning; more, because their signaling will always convey messages and involve them in consequences other than those intended (cf. Pocock, 1984: 32).

23.4. Attribution and "Judgment" Theories

Cognitive psychology explores the signification process from the viewpoint of the senders and receivers of messages. In recent decades various branches of cognitive psychology have converged into a common information-processing framework, inspired to a considerable degree by cybernetics. This has entailed important shifts in fundamental "model of man" assumptions. First, the conception of man as a passive agent who merely responds to environmental stimuli has given way to a conception of man as selectively responding to and actively shaping his environment. In addition, within the conceptualization of man as an active agent, there has been a shift away from cognitive balance theories viewing man as a "consistency seeker" to attribution theories viewing man as a "problem solver" or "naive scientist" (George, 1980: 56).

Whereas cognitive consistency theorists assume that people see what they expect to see by assimilating incoming information to pre-existing images and interpreting new information in such a way as to maintain or increase balance, attribution theorists are concerned with the individual's attempts to comprehend the causes of behavior and assume that spontaneous thought follows a systematic course that is roughly congruent with scientific inquiry.

No longer the stimulus–response (S–R) automaton of radical behaviorism, promoted beyond the rank of information processor and cognitive consistency seeker, psychological man has at last been awarded a status equal to that of the scientist who investigates him. For man, in the perspective of attribution theory, is an intuitive psychologist who seeks to explain behavior and to draw inferences about actors and their environments (Ross, 1977: 1974).

Attribution theory focuses on the perception of causation. Specifically, attribution theorists seek to discover the principles of "naive epistemology", the rules and heuristics laymen use in gathering and interpreting data. There are several competing models of the attribution process. For instance, theorists differ in their assessment of laymen's causal sophistication. Whereas Harold Kelley's influential work (1967, 1971) emphasizes the similarities with statistical rules of inference, the "judgment" school highlights biases in people's judgment (cf. Fischhoff, 1976). These differences do not seem to be as sharp today, when most attribution theorists tend to agree that people rely on certain "judgmental heuristics" or cognitive rules of thumb rather than analysis of covariance, but that this does not necessarily imply irrationality.

Perception researchers have shown that in spite of, and largely because of, people's exquisite perceptual capabilities, they are subject to certain perceptual illusions. No serious scientist, however, is led by such demonstrations to conclude that the perceptual system under study is inherently faulty. Similarly, we conclude from our own research that we are observing not an inherently faulty cognitive apparatus, but rather, one that manifests certain explicable flaws (Nisbett and Ross, 1980: 14).

Whereas semiotics and discourse analysis offer valuable concepts and classifications, attribution theory has yielded several hypotheses of obvious relevance to the study of communication processes in international negotiation. Let me briefly outline a few and suggest how they may apply to international negotiations.

23.4.1. "Representativeness" and "availability" heuristics

People tend to rely on "judgmental heuristics" that reduce complex inferential tasks to simple judgmental operations. The representativeness heuristics implies "the application of relatively simple resemblance or 'goodness of fit' criteria to problems of categorization" (Nisbett and Ross, 1980: 22). In the context of international negotiations, this points to the common tendency among statesmen to think in terms of historical analogies. In Ernest May's (1973: ix) apt summary:

> Framers of foreign policy are often influenced by beliefs about what history teaches or portends. Sometimes, they perceive problems in terms of analogies from the past. Sometimes, they envision the future either as foreshadowed by historical parallels or as following a straight line from what has recently gone before.

The availability heuristic means "objects or events are judged as frequent, probable, or causally efficacious to the extent that they are readily 'available' in memory" (Nisbett and Ross, 1980: 7). Psychological research indicates that vivid information is more likely to be stored and remembered than is pallid information (cf. Nisbett and Ross, 1980: 45). Translated to international negotiators, this implies that certain traumatic events are readily available and therefore tend to condition their interpretation of moves in the bargaining situation at hand.

> People are strongly influenced by events that are recent, that they or their country experienced first-hand, and events that occurred when they were first coming to political awareness. ... Many statesmen saw World War I as avoidable, and this fed appeasement. In turn, the obvious lesson of the 1930s was that aggressors could not be appeased and so post-World War II decision makers were predisposed to see ambiguous actions as indicating hostile intentions (Jervis, 1985: 22).

23.4.2. The fundamental error of attribution

Attribution theorists have pointed to a common tendency to overemphasize *dispositional* factors (stable personal traits) when explaining or interpreting the behavior of others, while stressing *situational* factors to account for one's own behavior. This hypothesis goes back to Fritz Heider's pioneering work in the 1950s in which he argued that people tend to attribute their own reactions to the object world and those of others, when they different from their own, to personal characteristics in others (cf. Kelley, 1967: 221). This idea was developed by Edward Jones and Richard Nisbett (1971: 80), who brought the difference between actors and observers to the fore, pointing to "a pervasive tendency for actors to attribute their actions to situational requirements, whereas observers tend to attribute the same action to stable personal dispositions".

Translated to international relations, Daniel Heradstveit's (1979) study of Arab and Israeli elite perceptions suggests that among adversaries the tendency is to explain one's own "good" behavior as well as the adversary's "bad" behavior in dispositional terms. Conversely, "bad" behavior of one's own side and "good" behavior by the other are attributed to situational factors. In brief, "I am essentially good, but am occasionally forced by circumstances to behave badly, whereas you are bad but are occasionally forced by circumstances to behave well".

The fundamental attribution error has been observable in US–Soviet negotiations over the years. The tendency to judge the adversary by who they are
rather than by what they do has frequently blinded the superpowers to important nuances and changes in the adversary's negotiating behavior.

23.4.3. Exaggerating the centralization, planning and coordination of others

The fundamental attribution error is often coupled with, and reinforced by, a
common tendency to see the behavior of the adversary as more centralized,
planned, and coordinated than it actually is (Jervis, 1976: 319–332). Henry
Kissinger's (1979: 52) observation on US–Soviet perceptions provides a good
illustration:

> The superpowers often behave like two heavily armed blind men feeling their way
> around in a room, each believing himself in mortal peril from the other whom he
> assumes to have perfect vision. Each side should know that frequently uncer-
> tainty, compromise, and incoherence are the essence of policy-making. Yet each
> tends to ascribe to the other a consistency, foresight, and coherence that its own
> experience belies.

23.4.4. The principle of non-common effects

When a perceiver observes an action and at least some of its effects, his basic
problem is to decide which of these effects, if any, were intended by the actor.
The "principle of non-common effects", formulated by Edward Jones and Keith
Davis (1965), holds that it is behavior that conflicts with expectations that tells
us most about an actor. Jones and Davis (1965: 228) argue that "the more distinctive reasons a person has for an action, and the more these reasons are
widely shared in the culture, the less informative that action is concerning the
identifying attributes of the person"; and also that "behavior which conforms to
clearly defined role requirements is seen as uninformative about the individual's
personal characteristics, whereas a considerable amount of information may be
extracted from out-of-role behavior" (Jones and Davis, 1965: 234). In the context of international negotiations this points to two sets of expectations derived
from the national and negotiator subcultures, respectively: national stereotypes,
on the one hand, and "normal" diplomatic bargaining behavior, on the other.
    Also of relevance to negotiations is the observation that "beneficial actions
tend to be much more ambiguous than harmful actions when it comes to deciding on the actor's true intention or his ultimate objectives in the situation. The
ambiguity of beneficial actions centers around the extent to which ulterior,

manipulative purposes may be served by them" (Jones and Davis, 1965: 259). Especially in negotiations between adversaries, concessions are frequently interpreted as tactical tricks, designed to lull one's vigilance.

23.4.5. The false consensus proposition

Related to the principle of non-common effects is the proposition that people tend to "see their own behavioral choices and judgments as relatively common and appropriate to existing circumstances while viewing alternative responses as uncommon, deviant, and inappropriate" (Ross, 1977: 188). One consequence of the propensity to assume that others generally share our reactions is "a tendency to attribute differing views to the personal characteristics of their holders" (Kelley and Michela, 1980: 464).

For example, to Western negotiators a pragmatic, "inductive" approach is normal: specific details are worked out before the general agreement is wrapped up, following Talleyrand's advice that "On s'arrange plus facilement sur un fait que sur un principle". Soviet negotiators, by contrast, prefer a "deductive" approach, insisting on an "agreement in principle" before negotiating the details of the agreement. This is considered the normal method — witness, for instance, the Soviet chief negotiator, Tsarapkin, in the nuclear test ban negotiations (quoted in Jönsson, 1979: 71):

> If we insist on first reaching agreement on the basic question this is not due to any personal considerations of ours, but is a natural requirement for conducting negotiations in a normal and businesslike manner.

Consequently, he described the Western approach as inappropriate:

> You are proposing to work on the details before agreeing on the foundation. This is tantamount to putting up a building without a foundation or a framework. Such a building will, however, collapse while it is still under construction (quoted in Jönsson, 1979: 72).

23.4.6. Misinterpreting the effect of one's own actions on others

Harold Kelley (1971: 8) has made an observation of direct relevance to negotiations:

> Interdependent persons often have occasion independently and simultaneously to plan and commit themselves to actions having mutual consequences. ... Failing to take account of these temporal patterns, persons may seriously misinterpret the effects their actions have on others.

In a negotiatory setting, this means that each party "tends to attribute to himself those actions of the other person that are consistent with the attributor's own interest" (Kelley, 1971: 19). The other side of the same coin is the common failure to realize that one's own behavior may be seen as threatening by the other side.

> You yourself may vividly feel the terrible fear that you have of the other party, but you cannot enter into the other man's counter-fear, or even understand why he should be particularly nervous. For you know that you yourself mean him no harm, and that you want nothing from him save guarantees for your own safety; and it is never possible for you to realize or remember properly that since he cannot see the inside of your mind, he can never have the same assurance of your intentions that you have (Herbert Butterfield, as quoted in Jervis, 1976: 69).

23.4.7. Exaggerated confidence in one's inferential capability

Robert Jervis (1986: 495) has argued that, "Since people often underestimate ambiguity and overestimate their cognitive abilities, it is likely that statesmen think that they can draw more accurate inferences from what the other state is doing than in fact they can". Others have commented on the tendency among decision makers to "perceive more order and certainty than exists in their uncertain, disorderly environments" (Kinder and Weiss, 1978: 723) and to make "unwarranted assumptions of certainty regarding opponents' intentions and the correctness of one's chosen policy" (Snyder, 1978: 353). Conversely, it has been argued that "the ideal negotiator should have a high tolerance for ambiguity and uncertainty as well as the open-mindedness to test his own assumptions and opponent's intentions" (Karrass, 1970: 37).

To summarize, international negotiators may be regarded as "intuitive semioticians". Attribution theory complements semiotics, insofar as it points to certain "judgmental heuristics" employed by "intuitive semioticians" when interpreting signaling in international negotiations. This brief outline of relevant hypotheses derived from attribution theory has been suggestive rather than exhaustive. In my continued research I shall elaborate these and other hypotheses in order, at the next stage of research, to survey diplomatic history for examples and counter-examples by which the hypotheses may be confirmed, disconfirmed, or modified.

23.5. The Paris Peace Conference of 1919

The second subproject consists of an in-depth case study of the extensive negotiations following World War I, carried out by research assistant Stefan Persson. In contrast to most contemporary diplomatic negotiations, the Paris Peace Conference is extremely well-documented. Not only are almost all central documents from the interstate negotiations published, but also the archives of the main actors have been opened to researchers. We are thus able to gain insights into the internal, within-nation bargaining process as well.

Briefly, the study is organized as follows (cf. Persson, 1986). First, agenda items where turning points can be identified in the negotiation process are selected for study (the Saar issue is one such agenda item). Second, extant theoretical works on negotiation are surveyed in search of explanations of change and adjustment on the part of the negotiating actors. Three distinguishable perspectives — the manipulative, cybernetic, and cognitive — suggest themselves.

The first perspective, which draws on yet departs from game theory, is what Oran Young (1975: 317) has labeled a "manipulative" conception of bargaining. This perspective focuses on the attempts by each player to outwit the other by means of "strategic moves" — such as commitments, threats, and promises — designed to modify the opponent's utilities and probabilities. Thomas Schelling (1963, 1966) is a prominent representative of this approach.

The "manipulative" conception is based on the assumption of *uncertainty* rather than complete information on the part of the negotiating actors, as in game theory. The choices of two or more actors engaged in strategic interaction are reciprocally contingent, which inevitably leads to an "outguessing" regress (Young, 1975: 14). Negotiation is thus seen as "the manipulation of the information of others in the interests of improving the outcome for one's self under conditions of strategic interaction" (Young, 1975: 304). In the game-theoretical vernacular, the manipulative perspective focuses on bargaining tactics designed to change the adversary's expected payoffs. Change in a negotiation is the result of successful manipulation of the opponent's calculation of utilities and probabilities.

The cybernetic perspective regards bargaining as a "self-stabilizing (i.e., outcome-reaching) process of output and feedback" and the bargaining actors as "a pair of linked servomechanisms" (Zartman, 1976: 37). Trial-and-error search, information processing, and uncertainty control are basic elements of the cybernetic understanding of bargaining. Uncertainty is assumed to be of even more fundamental importance than in the "manipulative" conception. Negotiators normally experience structural uncertainty; that is, "the nature of the possible outcomes and not just the probability associated with different outcomes is unknown" (Winham, 1977: 101). The cybernetic understanding of the bargaining process, in short, "is more akin to fitting the pieces into a puzzle than to convergence along a continuum" (Winham, 1977: 101).

In contrast to the game-theoretical rationality assumption, according to which each actor performs a comprehensive search and a detailed evaluation of all available alternatives, the cybernetic perspective suggests that "the central focus of the decision process is the business of eliminating the variety inherent in any significant decision problem" (Steinbrunner, 1974: 56). In a bargaining context, this implies searching for a *formula*, "a shared perception or definition of the conflict that establishes terms of trade" (Zartman and Berman, 1982: 95). One implication of viewing negotiation as a process for eliminating variety and reducing uncertainty is that "the development of common perceptions becomes more important than the exchange of concessions" (Winham, 1977: 97). Change

268   C. Jönsson

in negotiation, according to the cybernetic understanding, is produced by finding
a common formula rather than by successfully applying manipulative tactics.

The cognitive perspective, finally, focuses on the belief systems of the negotiating actors.

> It is often impossible to explain crucial decisions and policies without reference to
> the decision-makers' beliefs about the world and their images of others. That is to
> say, these cognitions are part of the proximate cause of the relevant behavior and
> other levels of analysis cannot immediately tell us what they will be (Jervis, 1976:
> 28).

Each actor comes to the negotiations with a set of beliefs and expectations
about himself, the adversary, and the bargaining issues, based on previous
experiences. As soon as negotiations begin, each actor is in a position to test and
either validate or adjust his initial expectations. To understand the ensuing
negotiation process, we need to explore the belief systems of the actor.

> Since each party to a conflict reacts not to the situation as perceived by the other
> but rather to the situation as seen from his own perspective, the nations are not
> reacting directly to each other. Under these conditions it is necessary to under-
> stand the perspectives guiding each national unit's activity, and thus how these
> perspectives differ, in order to grasp the actual flow of strategic interaction (Lock-
> hart, 1979: 38).

In comparison with the manipulative and cybernetic conceptions, the cognitive perspective emphasizes the obstacles to change in negotiations. First,
incompatible beliefs frequently complicate and aggravate international negotiations. Second, belief systems tend to be *resistant to change* (see Jervis, 1976:
291-296). Change is seen to occur when the negotiating actors modify "peripheral" beliefs; "central" beliefs are considered stable and unaffected by persuasion attempts in negotiations.

As this brief outline indicates, the three perspectives offer different explanations of change in international negotiations — successful manipulation of
expected payoffs according to the manipulative perspective, reduced uncertainty
through a common formula according to the cybernetic perspective, and modified
belief systems according to the cognitive perspective. The different perspectives
will be applied to the Paris Peace Conference in an attempt to assess their usefulness and degree of compatibility.

23.6. Cognitive Mapping

The cognitive mapping technique was developed in the early 1970s by a group of
researchers at Berkeley, including Robert Axelrod, Michael Shapiro, and
Matthew Bonham. It is a method of reconstructing the beliefs of actors on a
specific issue, coded in terms of concepts and causal links between concepts.

Drawing on graph theory, maps are constructed on which concepts are represented by points and causal links by arrows. An arrow with a plus sign indicates a positive causal link ("leads to", "contributes to", "increases", etc.), and an arrow with a minus sign a negative causal link ("prevents", "aggravates", "diminishes", etc.). All the causal chains, or "cognitive paths", of the studied actor are combined into maps. This map of the actor's belief structure allows us to assess the "centrality" of various concepts in terms of the number of arrows leading into it and out of it [for descriptions of the cognitive mapping technique, see Axelrod (1976), Bonham *et al.* (1979), Shapiro and Bonham (1982)].

Our research project includes a collaborative effort with Michael Shapiro and Matthew Bonham to modify the cognitive mapping technique to make it applicable to international negotiations (see Bonham *et al.*, 1987). This represents a continuation of work begun earlier on developing a cognitive mapping approach to collective decision-making. It is based on two shifts in the structure of previous theoretical thinking. First, the emphasis is on discursive rather than psychological imagery. Second, the idea chain or "path" is favored over the person or "actor" for purposes of elaborating the dynamics of the survival of alternative understandings of the bargaining issues. The cognitive map is thus conceived less as a psychological template than as a *discursive space* — an integrated set of categories, descriptions, explanations, and evaluations that direct not only identifiable settlements but, more generally, the "reality" perspective within which the possibilities and conditions of settlements emerge.

Rather than conceiving of persons having positions that they bring to decisions and then hold to them or alter them in confrontation with other positions, we conceive of positions as having persons. As a process of negotiation unfolds, its degree of success, within our conception, is to be related to the degree to which the parties can construct a shared discursive space, which amounts to their building of a shared "reality".

23.6.1. Example: Dissolution of the Swedish–Norwegian union

A preliminary study using cognitive mapping in its traditional actor-oriented variety may serve as an illustration of the direction of our recent thinking. The study concerned the negotiations on the dissolution of the Swedish–Norwegian union in 1905. Cognitive maps were constructed for the majority group in the internal Swedish deliberations (*Figure 23.1*) and for the General Staff of the Swedish military (*Figure 23.2*) as well as for the Swedish and Norwegian negotiators (*Figures 23.3* and *23.4*).

A first observation concerns the marked differences between the internal and external cognitive maps for the Swedish side. Whereas the military-security aspects of the Norwegian border fortifications were peripheral in the internal deliberations and were downgraded by the General Staff, they were centrally located in the argumentation of the Swedish negotiators. This illustrates, first of all, the need to take internal bargaining into account in studies of international

+ positive causal relationship, for instance increases
− negative causal relationship, for instance decreases
0 will not hurt, does not prevent, is not harmful to
θ will not help, does not promote, is of no benefit to
0 does not matter for, has no effect on, has nor relation to

Figure 23.1. Swedish majority group: internal bargaining.

Figure 23.2. The Swedish General Staff.

negotiations. But it also points to other strands of our recent concern with "discursive space".

It seems plausible to conclude that the external Swedish posture was tactically motivated. The Swedes did not consider it tactically sound to emphasize national honor or prestige concerns, which were central in the internal discussions, since that would make it impossible for Norway to accept the Swedish

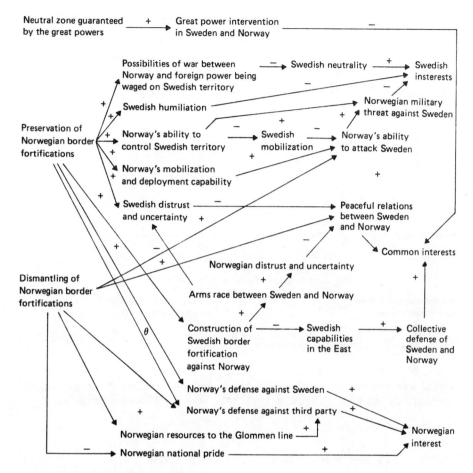

Figure 23.3. The Swedish negotiators.

demands without humiliation or loss of prestige. Moreover, there is reason to assume that similar considerations were behind the Norwegian posture in the Swedish–Norwegian negotiations. In other words, both sides chose a military-security discourse in their bilateral negotiations, while engaging in a prestige-status discourse at home (note the residue of "Swedish humiliation" and "Norwegian humiliation" in the maps of the negotiations). The similarities in the external discourse extended to individual concepts and paths. Witness, for instance, the prominence of the concept "peaceful relations between Sweden and Norway" in both cognitive maps. Also, concern about what effect dismantling or preservation of the border fortifications might have *vis-à-vis* third parties is reflected in both maps.

The discursive space of the Swedish–Norwegian negotiations of 1905 suggests that an agreement would require a formula that took into account the bilateral security concerns as well as defense against third parties, while avoiding

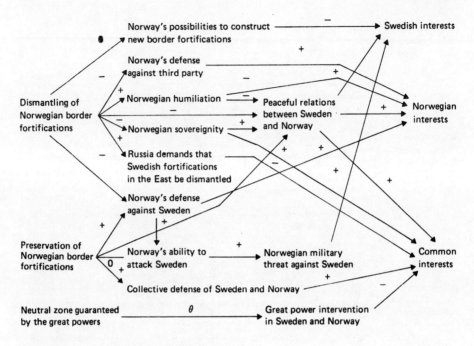

Figure 23.4. The Norwegian negotiators.

humiliation of either of the negotiating nations. The concept of a "neutral zone", which was introduced by the Norwegians and had figured marginally in the internal Swedish debate (Vedung, 1971: 332), constituted such a formula.

23.6.2. Example: Paris Peace Conference of 1919

Another example is taken from the 1919 Paris Peace Conference. In a meeting between President Wilson, Mr. Lloyd George, and M. Clemenceau in Paris on March 27, 1919 (Mantoux, 1964), Wilson's discursive chain begins with the category "excessive demands" and is linked to other categories by implication connections (which can be represented by signed arrows — see *Figure 23.5*).

According to Wilson's discursive chain, excessive demands create the impression of injustice, thus providing Germany with reasons for seeking revenge and creating discontent among the German people. Discontent leads to conflict and sows the seeds of future war. According to Wilson, these consequences can be avoided by "negotiations with moderation and equity", a category that reduces the impression of injustice.

M. Clemenceau's reply produces a reality that differs from that of Wilson's by using a national character discourse to explain the behavior of Germany (*Figure 23.6*). The "German spirit" creates the desire to impose force on others and

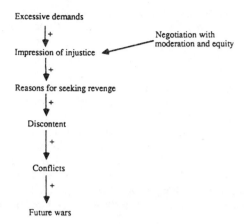

Figure 23.5. Cognitive map fragment for Wilson: March 27, 1919, 11:00 a.m.

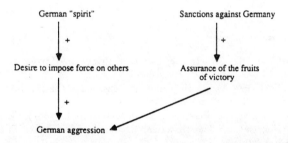

Figure 23.6. Cognitive map fragment for Clemenceau: March 27, 1919, 11:00 a.m.

leads to aggression. This can be avoided, according to Clemenceau, by imposing sanctions on Germany to assure the fruits of victory.

Clemenceau reminded the other negotiators quite explicitly that the interpretive practice of France differed from those of the United States and Great Britain.

> I beg you to understand my state of mind, just as I am trying to understand yours. America is far away, and protected by the ocean. England could not be reached by Napoleon himself. You are sheltered, both of you; we are not.

When Wilson proposed his idea of justice as the avoidance of "excessive demands" on Germany, Clemenceau proposed instead multiple interpretations of justice. He argued that "What we regard as just here in this room will not necessarily be accepted as such by the Germans", and he offered some evidence for differentiating the term: "Note that no one in Germany draws a distinction between just and unjust demands of the Allies". Later, in an attempt to build support for his position, he proposed another concept of justice:

There is a sense of justice as between allies which must be satisfied. If this feeling were violently thwarted, either in France or in England, grave danger might follow. Clemency toward the conquered is good; but let us not lose sight of the victors.

By introducing a new notion of justice and playing on the fears of "grave danger" (i.e., revolutionary movements), Clemenceau attempted to evoke a discursive space he shared with Lloyd George.

It should be evident from this example that much of what was at stake in the interaction between Wilson and Clemenceau involved not just differences in beliefs or other individual cognitive elements, but differences in the discursive spaces within which options were to be understood and valued. Hence, what we will attempt to recover, working within the bounds of our theoretical model, are the discursive spaces within which the Paris Peace Conference negotiations took place.

References

Axelrod, R. (ed.) (1976), *Structure of Decision*, Princeton University Press, Princeton, NJ.

Blonsky, M. (1985), The Agony of Semiotics: Reassessing the Discipline, in M. Blonsky (ed.), *On Signs*, Basil Blackwell, Oxford, UK.

Bonham, G.M., Jönsson, C., Persson, S., and Shapiro M.J. (1987), Cognition and International Negotiation: The Historical Recovery of Discursive Space. *Cooperation and Conflict*, 22(1).

Bonham, G.M., Shapiro, M.J., and Trumble, T.L. (1979), The October War: Changes in Cognitive Orientation Toward the Middle East Conflict. *International Studies Quarterly*, 23(1): 3–44.

Coddington, A. (1968), *Theories of the Bargaining Process*, George Allen and Unwin, London.

Cohen, R. (1981), *International Politics: The Rules of the Game*, Longman, London/New York.

Eco, U. (1971), *Den frånvarande strukturen: Introduktion till den semiotiska forskningen*, Cavefors, Lund.

Eco, U. (1985), Producing Signs, in M. Blonsky (ed.), *On Signs*, Basil Blackwell, Oxford, UK.

Fischhoff, B. (1976), Attribution Theory and Judgement under Uncertainty, in J.H. Harvey, W.J. Ickes, and R.F. Kidd (eds.), *New Directions in Attribution Research*, Vol. 1, Lawrence Erlbaum, Hillsdale, NJ.

Fisher, R. and Ury, W. (1983), *Getting to Yes: Negotiating Agreement Without Giving In*, Penguin, New York.

Fiske, J. (1982), *Introduction to Communication Studies*, Methuen, London/New York.

George, A.L. (1980), *Presidential Decision Making in Foreign Policy: The Effective Use of Information and Advice*, Westview, Boulder, CO.

Goffman, E. (1969), *Strategic Interaction*, University of Pennsylvania Press, Philadelphia, PA.

Heradstveit, D. (1979), *The Arab-Israeli Conflict: Psychological Obstacles to Peace*, Universitetsforlaget, Oslo.

Heradstveit, D. and Bjorgo, T. (1986), *Politisk kommunikasjon: Introduksjon til semiotikk og retorikk*, TANO, Oslo.

Jervis, R. (1976), *Perception and Misperception in International Politics*, Princeton University Press, Princeton, NJ.

Jervis, R. (1985), Perceiving and Coping with Threat, in R. Jervis, R.N. Lebow, and J.G. Stein (eds.), *Psychology and Deterrence*, Johns Hopkins University Press, Baltimore, MD.

Jervis, R. (1986), Representativeness in Foreign Policy Judgments, *Political Psychology*, 7(3): 483–505.

Johnson, D.W. (1974), Communication and the Inducement of Cooperative Behavior in Conflicts: A Critical Review, *Speech Monographs*, 41 (March): 64–78.

Jones, E.E. and Davis, K.E. (1965), From Acts to Dispositions: The Attribution Process in Person Perception, in L. Berkowitz (ed.), *Advances in Experimental Social Psychology*, Academic Press, New York/London.

Jones, E.E. and Nisbett, R.E. (1971), The Actor and the Observer: Divergent Perceptions of the Causes of Behavior, in E.R. Jones *et al.* (eds.), *Attribution: Perceiving the Causes of Behavior*, General Learning Press, Morristown, NJ.

Jönsson, C. (1978), Situation-Specific versus Actor-Specific Approaches to International Bargaining, *European Journal of Political Research*, 6(4): 381–398.

Jönsson, C. (1979), *Soviet Bargaining Behavior: The Nuclear Test Ban Case*, Columbia University Press, New York.

Jönsson C. (1983), A Cognitive Approach to International Negotiation, *European Journal of Political Research*, 11(2): 139–150.

Karrass, C.L. (1970), *The Negotiating Game*, World Publishing, New York and Cleveland.

Keller, S. (1956), Diplomacy and Communication, *Public Opinion Quarterly*, 20(1): 176–182.

Kelley, H.H. (1967), Attribution Theory in Social Psychology, in D. Levine (ed.), *Nebraska Symposium on Motivation*, Vol. 15, University of Nebraska Press, Lincoln, NE.

Kelley, H.H. (1971), Attribution in Social Interaction, in E.R. Jones *et al.* (eds.), *Attribution: Perceiving the Causes of Behavior*, General Learning Press, Morristown, NJ.

Kelley, H.H. and Michela, J.L. (1980), Attribution Theory and Research, *Annual Review of Psychology*, 31: 457–501.

Kinder, D.R. and Weiss, J.A. (1978), In Lieu of Rationality: Psychological Perspectives on Foreign Policy Decision Making, *Journal of Conflict Resolution*, 22(4): 707–735.

Kissinger, H. (1979), *White House Years*, Little, Brown, Boston, MA.

Kristeva, J. (1985), The Speaking Subject, in M. Blonsky (ed.), *On Signs*, Basil Blackwell, Oxford, UK.

Lockhart, C. (1979), *Bargaining in International Conflicts*, Columbia University Press, New York.

Mantoux, P. (1964), *Paris Peace Conference, 1919: Proceedings of the Council of Four, March 24th–April 18th*, Droz, Geneva.

May, E.R. (1973), *"Lessons" of the Past: The Use and Misuse of History in American Foreign Policy*, Oxford University Press, New York.

Miller, G.R. (1980), On Being Persuaded: Some Basic Distinctions, in M.E. Roloff and G.R. Miller (eds.), *Persuasion: New Directions in Theory and Research*, Sage, Beverly Hills/London.

Nisbett, R. and Ross, L. (1980), *Human Inference: Strategies and Shortcomings of Social Judgment*, Prentice-Hall, Englewood Cliffs, NJ.

Persson, S. (1986), Internationella förhandlingar och kognitiv teori. Paper prepared for annual convention of Swedish Political Science Association, Lund, Oct. 13–15.

Pocock, J.G.A. (1984), Verbalizing a Political Act: Toward a Politics of Speech, in M.J. Shapiro (ed.), *Language and Politics*, Basil Blackwell, Oxford, UK.

Rapoport, A. (1964), *Strategy and Conscience*. Harper and Row, New York.

Reardon, K.K. (1981), *Persuasion: Theory and Context*, Sage, Beverly Hills/London.

Ross, L. (1977), The Intuitive Psychologist and His Shortcomings: Distortions in the Attribution Process, in L. Berkowitz (ed.), *Advances in Experimental Social Psychology*, Academic Press, New York.

Schelling, T.C. (1963), *The Strategy of Conflict*, Oxford University Press, New York.

Schelling, T.C. (1966), *Arms and Influence*, Yale University Press, New Haven, CT.

Shapiro, M.J. (1984), Introduction, in M.J. Shapiro (ed.), *Language and Politics*, Basil Blackwell, Oxford, UK.

Shapiro, M.J. and Bonham, G.M. (1982), A Cognitive Process Approach to Collective Decision Making, in C. Jönsson (ed.), *Cognitive Dynamics and International Politics*, Frances Pinter, London.

Shubik, M. (1967), The Uses of Game Theory, in J.C. Charlesworth (ed.), *Contemporary Political Analysis*, Free Press, New York.

Sigal, L.V. (1979), The Logic of Deterrence in Theory and Practice, *International Organization*, 33: 567–579.

Simons, H.W. (1976), *Persuasion: Understanding, Practice and Analysis*, Addison-Wesley, Reading, MA.

Snyder, G.H. and Diesing, P. (1977), *Conflict among Nations: Bargaining, Decision Making, and System Structure in International Crises*, Princeton University Press, Princeton, NJ.

Snyder, J.L. (1978), Rationality at the Brink: The Role of Cognitive Processes in Failure of Deterrence, *World Politics*, 30(3): 345–365.

Steinbruner, J.D. (1974), *The Cybernetic Theory of Decision*, Princeton University Press, Princeton, NJ.

Tedeschi, J.T. and Rosenfeld, P. (1980), Communication in Bargaining and Negotiation, in M.E. Roloff and G.R. Miller (eds.), *Persuasion: New Directions in Theory and Research*, Sage, Beverly Hills/London.

Vedung, E. (1971), *Unionsdebatten 1905*, Almqvist and Wiksell, Stockholm.

Winham, G.R. (1977), Negotiation as a Management Process, *World Politics*, 30(1): 87–114.

Young, O.R. (1975), *Bargaining: Formal Theories of Negotiation*, University of Illinois Press, Urbana, IL.

Zartman, I.W. (1976), Introduction, in I.W. Zartman (ed.), *The 50% Solution*, Anchor, Garden City, NY.

Zartman, I.W. and Berman, M.R. (1982), *The Practical Negotiator*, Yale University Press, New Haven, CT.

CHAPTER 24

The System of International Negotiations and Its Impact on the Processes of Negotiation

Victor A. Kremenyuk

USA and Canada Studies Institute,
USSR Academy of Sciences
Moscow
USSR

24.1. Introduction

International negotiation is subject to many influences. As a situation in which sovereign partners meet to find a joint and mutual acceptable solution to a disputable problem, international negotiation attracts the attention of many interested parties both at home and abroad; and the more important the problem negotiated, the larger the scope of that attention, which is a significant factor in the conduct and outcome of international negotiations. This factor interacts with the dynamics of the process in a specific way; sometimes it works to achieve its stable and desirable outcome, but sometimes it interferes with and destabilizes the successful conduct of international negotiation.

   In assessing the role of this factor and its impact on the processes of international negotiations it is important to understand the nature of its influence and the different ways in which it can be brought to bear. There are purely domestic factors that may and indeed do have crucial impact on the processes of international negotiations, among which are: directives from the government that regards the international negotiation as a continuation of its foreign policy and tends to adjust it to the interests of that policy; and the concern of interested political groups, such as legislative bodies, political parties, major corporations, mass media, and the public. All of these sources of influence do not necessarily work in the same direction. More than that, in countries with multi- or bipartisan political systems these sources may produce so controversial an impact on international negotiation that it becomes a real challenge for the negotiators of those countries to convey a consistent and logical behavior, which, in turn, complicates the process and may cause its deadlock or failure.

There are purely international factors that also have a great impact on the international negotiation. Allies of the negotiating parties, third countries, international organizations, world press — all of them may interfere, both positively and negatively, in the normal sequence of events in the negotiating forum and contribute to its success or failure.

Those engaged in negotiations, practitioners, are fully aware of this impact. While they sometimes actively use it in their own interests, gradually a common understanding has emerged that, for the sake of the stability of the process, it is necessary to find ways to make international negotiations more independent of this impact and to reduce, to the extent possible, its interference in the way the sides in the negotiation handle their affairs. At least in some important cases, such as Soviet–US disarmament talks, the sides agreed from the very beginning to reduce as much as possible the interference of the external factors in the process of the negotiation.

Of course, it is absolutely impossible to reduce to nil the external influences on the process of international negotiations. In the contemporary world, every international negotiation is a part of a much broader network of negotiations and, explicitly or implicitly, it interacts with the network of which it is a part. Inherent ties among international negotiations have become a new phenomenon of the world of negotiations and, though many practitioners and researchers are aware of this, until recently it was not studied in depth, with all the possible conclusions that can be derived thereby.

24.2. The Problem

The problem here is as old as international negotiations. It is the problem of managing the negotiations to achieve two different though overlapping goals: to fulfill one's own purposes in the international negotiation and, at the same time, to contribute to the stability of the process and its successful outcomes (which is sometimes close to the former). The traditional way of achieving these goals and, hence, of managing the processes of international negotiations is to mobilize all possible factors to build up so-called "bargaining power" and to use it to elaborate an efficient negotiating strategy and appropriate tactics. Essentially, this way is still relevant in most cases. So, what then is the problem?

The problem is that international negotiations, as an object of management, has become much more complex and elaborate, and to cope with its growing complexity a successful negotiator has to take into account not only what was traditionally regarded as an essence of "bargaining power", but also the fact that his options and constraints are limited by the changing nature of contemporary international negotiations. In other words, the correlation of the management procedures and of the subject of management has to be reassessed to strike the desirable balance between what is managed and how it can be managed.

For this purpose it would be insufficient just to change the tactics or to find new ways to outwit the partner. The situation is much more sophisticated: the international negotiation is in the process of acquiring new and important functions and without a proper assessment of that it is impossible even to speak of a genuinely new approach to managing international negotiation. Sometimes these new functions are self-evident, as in the case of UN LOS Conference; sometimes they are not that visible, but this does not change much the necessity to treat the whole problem of international negotiations as a new and important feature of the international environment that demands the restructuring and rethinking of the traditional approach.

24.3. The Analytical Approach

International negotiations grow in number and diversity. Not only the traditional issues, such as national security, borders, trade, communications, etc., but various subjects from the sphere of scientific and cultural exchange, humanitarian problems, environment, outer space and oceans are being negotiated.

The growing number of international negotiations is an indicator of a much more significant process that is taking place underneath — the process of formation of *a certain system of international negotiations.* So far, this is not a comprehensive institutionalized system of international negotiations that incorporates talks between/among countries on all disputable and controversial issues. Many of these issues still are waiting to become the subject of talks. But, nevertheless, one can speak with full evidence of an emerging system, which has already become an integral part of international reality and thus far has not yet been assessed in all aspects, as it deserves.

First of all, it is not the mere number of separate international negotiations that makes one draw a conclusion that there is a system, although the rapidly and even dramatically growing number of international negotiations has already drawn the attention of many analysts. There are attempts to make inventories on a country-by-country basis [e.g., USSR–USA, as B. Blechman (1985) did in the area of prevention of the risk of nuclear war]. Others try to make such inventories for different problems: negotiations on arms control, trade, environment, etc.

It is the growing interaction among international negotiation fora that deserves attention and leads one to suggest that the growing number of international negotiations definitely is not developing sporadically (although sometimes it may seem so), but in some systematic way that reflects such crucial processes as the growing interdependence of nations and of disputable issues among them, the increasing impotence of traditional ways of resolving conflicts (such as military threats), and the increasing need to turn negotiation into the only possible institutionalized and codified way to resolve international disputes in the absence of a real alternative. In other words, the changing international environment has resulted in the emerging importance of international negotiations. International negotiations have been transformed from a forum of sporadic international interaction to the sometimes only thinkable way of conflict resolution under conditions of growing interdependence, which has contributed to the formation of a certain system (or subsystem, if it is regarded as a part of much broader system of international relations).

This means that any international negotiation now should be regarded not only within the framework of the foreign policy of the nations engaged in the negotiations, but also within the framework of a certain system of international negotiations to which it belongs. In this case some new factors of the negotiation appear which greatly affect the processes and the management of international negotiations.

24.4. The Conceptual Approach

This conclusion is based on a solid foundation of analysis made in different countries of the main features of the contemporary international system. Taken together, the major findings in this sphere are summarized in the following subsections.

24.4.1. Structural and functional features of the international system

The whole world system is in a transitional stage. Structurally, it is shifting from the bipolar world of the 1950s to a much more diversified (sometimes called multipolar, although this may not be correct, since it bears no accurate description) world structure. The process is far from being completed. Decolonization turned huge and rather loose political entities called colonial empires into an array of newly independent states. The different results of economic development brought into play new political forces and centers of power and influence. New alignments and groupings appeared both in the political and economic areas, such as the nonaligned movement, European Economic Community, OPEC, and so on.

On the functional side, this process is accompanied by the changing nature of the traditional means of interaction among states: the value of military power has diminished because of the impossibility of nuclear war and the constraints produced by the rough parity between the two major military blocks. The value of economic power has also changed, since the emphasis on it is shifting from the mere production of goods and commodities and finance, to technological innovation. The rising importance of humanitarian issues brings a new dimension to traditional power alignments and interactions.

24.4.2. Interdependence of states and issues

Those processes overlap and interact with another important element of the emerging international system — the growing interdependence of nations in all spheres. This notion is much broader than the one used in 1970s (especially after the oil crisis of 1973–1974). The interdependence of nations, which has become an objective reality of the 1980s, has several dimensions, the most important and prominent being interdependence in matters of security: the national security of any country in the present situation is inalienable from the security of others — there can be no security for one country if it threatens the others' security. The only possible solution of the security problem is common security, which can be attained only through a comprehensive and logical system of international negotiation. Another dimension is economic. The economic growth and development of nations has long ago ceased to be only their own concern. It is impossible to imagine now any country, large or small, which could cope with its development problems without cooperation with and from the outside world. The next dimension is the environment, which emphasizes to a large extent that all the nations of the world are interdependent and can only survive together.

The process of growing interdependence develops not only extensively (including new spheres in which nations become dependent on each other), but also intensively. This means that the spheres in which the countries find themselves dependent on each other also become interdependent. For example, the interdependence between security and economy, or the arms race and development, which is a subject for numerous discussions at international conferences, and the interdependence between the economy and environment (or to be more exact, industry and environment).

24.4.3. Complexity

A number of controversial issues have appeared at the cross-section of these two spheres of interdependence. Sometimes these issues have a very traditional character: controversies and conflicts in security, trade, finance, environment, etc. But if we look at them from the perspective of the environment in which they exist and of the complex network of interdependencies that produce them, it becomes clear that these controversial issues form some interconnected and mutually dependent network of conflicts. Such conflicts then have, as one of their main features, the ability to spill over to other spheres or to escalate, thus producing a "multi-layered" form of conflicts in which the issues of an ideological, confessional/ethnic, or other nature are interconnected. The growing complexity of the international system in this way produces no less complex types of controversies and conflicts, which should be adequately treated.

Now, what relation has all this to the processes of international negotiations? This is the subject of this chapter, with some suggestions that may be of interest to those engaged both in the theory and practice of negotiations.

24.5. Main Features of the System of International Negotiations

In the above-mentioned context international negotiation is regarded as the main means of conflict resolution, which, together with the unilateral actions of nations, can contribute in a significant manner to keeping the international system stable and predictable. *What are the main features that appear in international negotiations due to the process mentioned above?*

First, the emerging system of international negotiations tends to reflect both in its structure and essence the existing system of conflicts and disputes. Hence, it becomes more and more universal, incorporating the formal negotiations and consultations, informal talks and meetings of government officials, experts, public figures and others engaged in the activities of exchanging views and ideas on the possible ways to find a resolution to disputable problems. The mere existence of this huge international structure should be regarded as a kind of specific environment within which some specific "rules of conduct" exist: non-violence, adherence to joint problem-solving, cooperation, etc. This does not mean that even here there do not exist political and diplomatic struggle, coercion, threats and the like. But, nevertheless, this environment gives a maximum advantage to those who adhere to the "rules of conduct" and is rather unfriendly to those who try to break them.

Second, this system tends to become more and more autonomous. It is self-evident that a negotiation may be created, as a situation, only due to the sovereign will of the parties, but once in existence, it becomes to an extent estranged from that will, since it becomes *a part of the system* and is plugged into it through the information flows, interplay of interests, influence of the observing parties and so on. Within the system a negotiation acquires a second dimension (the first is that it is a continuation of a foreign policy) and becomes a part of an international network, which has its own rules and its own laws of dynamics.

Third, once it is a part of a system, a negotiation has to respond to the needs and elements of that system. The main demand is that it should contribute to the stability and growth (optimization) of the system. The entropy or disorder of the system can be prevented not through stagnation of an individual cell (part), but through its efficient operation, which means a successful and timely resolution of a conflict. Thus, the system and its basic parts have an interdependent relationship: the more efficient the functioning of each international negotiation, the more stable and durable is the whole system of international relations.

Fourth, the above factors place an additional burden on the process of international negotiation. Thus far, its main function was to serve the interests of the parties engaged. It was their interest and their will that primarily dictated the whole process, while the accepted rules served a secondary role in establishing the procedure. Now, with the emergence of the system of negotiations, parties to any international negotiation have to take into consideration not only their interests at the given negotiation, but also the whole array of their interests and positions at other negotiations and even the state of affairs at other negotiation fora. The decision-making process becomes magnified and complicated by several orders.

24.6. The Changing Structure of the Process

Since international negotiation acquires a dual capability — as a function of a foreign policy and a basic part of the stability of the international system — it cannot but experience some changes in its nature and process. As to changes in nature, partly they have already been. described: the burden of conflict resolution gradually shifts from unilateral actions and decisions to joint problem-solving and agreed solutions. At this particular moment this statement may sound premature, but the trend is evident. Even in the sphere of national security, there is no way to achieve durable solutions without taking into consideration the necessity to secure the legitimate interests of the other parties.

As to the process, the change is not that evident but gradually it is becoming more and more elucidated.

Professor R. Fisher (1986) of the Harvard Law School summarized the changes of the structure of negotiations in two models — Model "T" (for "traditional") and Model "A" (for "alternative"). This gist of his conclusions is that gradually the structure of the process of international negotiation has changed from strictly formal, diplomats-to-diplomats "one-shot" conferences to a combination of governmental and nongovernmental experts' talks, which become an indefinite, ongoing process working as a production line for producing a series of jointly agreed recommendations to governments on possible solutions of disputable problems.

To continue this trend, one can suggest that in time these international negotiations will become a kind of permanent, continuous diplomatic activity, which would then suggest to the appropriate governments either to sign an agreement with the other side or to take unilateral decisions within an agreed framework to solve a dispute without having an agreement. In any case, the role of international negotiations is changing from a mere form of government-to-government activity to a separate international function (thus institutionalizing its autonomy), producing a conceptual framework of possible agreements for governmental deliberation and decision.

But, meanwhile, recognition of the fact of the changing nature of the process poses several problems both for practice and research. In practice, this brings up several tasks:

1. To make an inventory of all contemporary negotiations with some definite and practicable classification along the following criteria:

   - Bilateral and multilateral (with some additional criteria, such as whether or not they are institutionalized, i.e., within the framework of existing international organizations, or noninstitutionalized).

- Formal (official) and informal (nongovernmental).
- By subject of negotiation (political, security, economic, environmental issues, etc.), which will permit developing an adequate database, which could be used both by the government agencies and researchers to have at least an idea of the scope and nature of the contemporary network of international negotiations.

2. To compare the existing network of international negotiations with the scope of the issues to be solved in international relations. It is understandable that this task will demand the introduction of stricter approaches to the evaluation of the issues. But each side concerned may unilaterally decide whether or not the existing network of international negotiations matches the scope of the issues and whether it forms an international joint problem-solving system. It is very possible that such a tremendous job will produce another problem — that of "negotiation on negotiation", how to rearrange the contemporary network of international negotiations to bring it close to the needs of the international problem-solving process.

3. The solution of these practical aspects of the problem will demand at least two types of research. One of them is relatively simple — a program for a computerized database on international negotiations, which would permit the collection of all the existing information on negotiations in some orderly manner, useable by negotiators of any country and international agency: when, where, who, what is negotiated, and what was the result (or absence of result). The only necessary condition for such a program is that it should be universal and distributed freely through the existing international information services. This would avoid some misunderstandings in assessing the number of negotiations and other parameters.

The other direction of research is much more complicated and will demand much more time. It includes:

- The assessment of the type and nature of systemic *changes* that have already happened and will happen in the conduct of negotiation, because of the existence of the system.
- The elaboration of the *necessary modifications* that should be introduced into the conduct of negotiations to bring it closer to the needs of the contemporary system.
- As a final aim, the elaboration of the *new code for negotiation*, which can be undertaken only on *genuinely international basis*.

One of the major consequences of the emergence of the system of international negotiations is that the negotiation process that is largely organized along traditional lines is becoming less and less effective. The process of negotiations, at least the most important among them, takes more and more time and is lagging behind the evolution of the international environment. The most evident examples are issues concerning security, trade and finance, and technology. The agreements achieved are very often regarded as inadequate and unjust, which makes them vulnerable to criticism and permits their opponents to insist on their abrogation.

In sum, the state of affairs in the area of international negotiation is not satisfactory, and needs substantive innovation. One of the most promising ways to do this on the international level is to treat international negotiations in terms of systems analysis and apply the systemic approach to devise the appropriate remedy.

References

Blechman, Barry M. (ed.) (1985), *Preventing Nuclear War: A Realistic Approach*, Midland Books.

Fisher, Roger (1986), *Negotiation Journal* 2(3).

CHAPTER 25

Paradigms in International Negotiation: The Example of "Good Faith"

Alain Plantey

Membre de l'Institut de France
Conseiller d' État
Paris
France

25.1. Introduction

First of all, I would not avoid one double question about paradigms in international negotiation: is such a study possible; if so, is such a study useful? My answers are definitely positive.

Using the word in its original, Greek and philosophical meaning, may I remind readers that *paradigma* is neither *deigma*, nor *dogma*. A paradigmatic approach implies a prudent quest for references, choice of models, selection of problems whose study governs the research, definition of methods suitable to the research and explanation of all the relations between these archetypes.

More precisely, debating, arguing and bargaining make large use of this kind of process, among nations even more than between individuals or firms.

States live in contact, and often are in rivalry with one another. None of them can be an exclusive model of civilization, of political, economic or cultural organization. In any state, power, interests and culture cannot be considered as abstract data; the environment into which their effects extend, and particularly the needs, ambitions and interests of other people must be taken into consideration.

International negotiation is an art of social relationship. Every diplomatic conference, every international organization, is a place where influences originate, where interactions operate between different models. If it is to succeed, every diplomatic dialogue must respect the pluralism of the participants, their cultural identities, their proper political views and wishes, the disparity of their strengths and weaknesses, the opposition of their ambitions and interests. In this sense, a good paradigmatic approach appears to be one of the basic conditions of international negotiations.

25.2. Paradigms in International Negotiations

In a changing world, seeking paradigms is a difficult task. Certainly, different approaches are possible and can be compared. Mine is a pragmatic one, as a result of personal meditations based upon years of diplomatic practice. Therefore, I would like to suggest three themes of discussion: the power of the state, national interest and cultural identity.

Power

Force, compulsion and violence are permanent and basic data of physical and social life. They unavoidably extend their effects in political relations among states: the perpetual recurrence of wars is sufficient to make this evident. Nevertheless, in the field of international negotiations, the paradigm of force requires a keener analysis.

Power is strength ordered by will, placed at the disposition of a strategic concept. The power of a state is not everlasting, neither is it absolute. It is relative, in accordance with the environment, depending on armaments, money, technology, culture and always limited by the power of other states. Alliances make it evident that strength is always relative and can be counterbalanced by other strength. International negotiation is the best means to moderate the effects of power and to create the beginning of security among nations.

National interest

It is generally admitted that national interest is one of the principal paradigms of international negotiation. Some authors and many politicians find in the doctrine of "Realpolitik" the basis of diplomacy. No doubt states are free when making their fundamental choices, and there is no international control of this sovereign capacity. However, national interest has no absolute character at all: its perception depends on personalities, periods, public opinion, environment and many other elements.

In every international negotiation, interest changes according to the needs, utilities, ambitions and tactics of each participant. The evolution of interest is the aim of a bargaining process. Good faith and trust are the conditions of its results and have a kind of policing effect in the international system. Therefore, the relativity of national interest adds to the relativity of power among the states.

Cultural identity

The same observation can be made about the third paradigm of international negotiation, even if in many cases cultural identity is a much stronger element than the two others. As the expression of the individuality of a people, cultural identity is a datum of civilization, a legacy of the past that marks off one state from the others and maintains its personality, its independence and its ability to negotiate. The strength of this paradigm is often subconscious, but often so active that it compels governments to initiatives, reactions, refusals or concessions. All cultural motives are not rational: ideologies and passions rarely give way to reason; their intransigence does not favor the process of bargaining. If international negotiation wants to remove these obstacles, it must use the pluralism of cultures to reconcile the dignity of all nations with mutual enrichment. Contacts help to influence this: as forms of communication between different cultures, international negotiations and organizations help to create new universal values that the world is looking for. The paradigm of cultural identity is also changing, but this evolution will be slow and deep.

International negotiation has to take into account, in its practical exercise, these three paradigms together. Each of them influences the other two: power is mobilized by national interests and cultures; interests are measured according to power; culture is an element of power. The study of diplomacy begins with the study of these concomitant paradigms, their evolution and their connections. But these problems must be approached with caution. Power, interests and culture cannot be precisely measured and their interactions or reactions are always contingent. This can explain one of the major difficulties of anticipating and forecasting in international relations.

25.3. A Systemic Concept of International Negotiations

Distances are today very different from what they were during many previous centuries. Science, technology and organization have transformed social communication, particularly in the field of international relations. There are no more impervious frontiers between states. In spite of strong national identities, the world is going forward in a growing movement of globalization.

As a result of progress in mathematics, electronics, telematics, methods and research in the fields of organizations and networks, great importance is now attached to the problems and the theory of systems. That means, in our field, the concept of an international society whose organized, integrated and dynamic totality is greater than the simple addition or juxtaposition of its elements — states, nations, and cultures.

This macroscopic approach of an integrated world gives a new strength to the systemic concept of international negotiation and to the hope of self-regulation in national politics by means of international negotiations or foreign policy. International organization can therefore be analyzed in the perspective of a whole set of networks.

Topics of scientific studies can be identified, to investigate and deepen the evaluation of the different paradigms in international negotiation and the relations between them: research on objective indicators for military, financial, economic, technological power; detailed and comparative approaches of national interests, with the analysis of their complex factors and of their interactions; regional or global studies in the field of connections, interdependences, solidarities and alliances among states.

Dynamic perspectives can also be displayed, thanks to the progress in gathering and handling data; for instance, the preparation and forecasting of the successive steps in commercial or military negotiation; the building of scenarios or models to make precise priorities, trends, threats, risks; and aiding development of alternatives or proposals before and during negotiation.

International organizations, nongovernmental institutions, transnational groups, financial networks, telecommunications, freedom of information, space observation and detection — all of these contribute to this global and systemic approach for our changing world, increasing the tasks of negotiators and adding to the number of elements to take into account in policy making.

It is clear than an increasing need for complete, exact and large amounts of information will stimulate the study of all the paradigms in international relations. Information is power, even in negotiation; it provides the ability to communicate, to bargain, to dominate. But it has to be organized information, classified with a method, according to a structural conception of reality and serving a strategic will.

Of course, the human world is not logical; passion often leads to action. Among nations, there is no regulating power; unexpected crises are always threatening peace and international harmony. But the analysis of international systems, with their proper paradigms, regulation mechanism and interactions, can be a useful approach to the knowledge and limitation of the risks in foreign policy. The search for and evaluation of information have always been one part of the diplomatic art. Today, negotiation for information has become a major part of international negotiations.

25.4. The Role of "Good Faith"

Empirical means for preparing and conducting international bargaining are moving progressively to elaborate methods of communication and mutual information exchange between states, taking into account the growing role of conferences and organizations. However, the need still remains for rules, discipline and confidence in international relations: in a changing world, good faith is, more than ever, a real paradigm in politics among nations.

Between states, fear and mistrust are natural, strong and lasting feelings, even if they are hidden and vague. Each state, in its external relations, is waiting for a certain, concrete and equivalent answer to proposals or concessions it offers. The diplomacy of immediate reciprocity appears among individuals or people who do not know each other, whose civilizations are different. It increases in its effects when doubt is possible concerning the sincerity, solvency or liability of partners in international negotiation.

No cooperation can be expected between nations without "credit" — a complex concept of trust, in which reciprocity is not required as soon as an agreement is concluded. If it means to be useful, the balance of interests must result from a process of action and reaction, with a view to a more or less distant future where each partner hopes to realize its purpose and to maximize its gains. Thus, international negotiation can be stimulated and contribute to a better world environment.

Credit has a double meaning: it is trust you convey and trust you obtain; it guarantees your offer and the assurances you receive as a counterpart. Diplomacy cannot create any stability, any process of stabilization, if states are not able and prepared to develop their relationships within a broad framework of fairness and mutual good faith. States have to increase confidence, to merit trust and to show their own trust. This is a difficult task in a large world, where ambitions and powers are in rivalry, where interests and needs are diverging, where cultures and ideologies are heterogeneous.

Despite these difficulties, no state that wishes to play its part in the international system can limit its hopes and actions by the consideration only of immediate profit. But work for the future compels the acceptance of risks. The role of international negotiation is also to reduce these risks through an intelligent approach to the issues, through a large amount of information on countries and leaders, and through good evaluation of what is desirable and what is possible. Diplomats work often without any shelter, in "terra incognita".

In such a difficult context, good faith is neither a legal principle, nor a purely moral rule. It is a discipline of behavior, with respect to a relational utility and even a political necessity. It is possible to engage in a negotiation without any trust in the partner, for instance, to lose time, to await better circumstances or to hide other intentions. But no negotiation can achieve a good and lasting conclusion if a general feeling of trust and satisfaction is not created.

In this sense, one can assert that good faith is a paradigm in international negotiation. But this paradigm is not an absolute one. It is not independent of the numerous and various facts and forms of civilization. The concept of good faith, in its international meaning, is complex and difficult to analyze for the basic reason that its content is relative to the culture, the history and the character of each nation. In every state, ethics have their own bases, rules and expressions. Good faith is a moral and social paradigm, not only in its meaning, but also in its expression. For instance, according to habits and traditions, "maybe" can be either a polite refusal or the way to an agreement. The real meaning has to be found through a good analysis of the context.

Thus, good faith must always be related and interpreted with respect to the cultural data of all the partners in the negotiation. And each partner has to develop an awareness and understanding on the part of the others — i.e., to create and to maintain the feeling, probability, or certitude — that its attitude is in accordance with the principles of good faith. International negotiations condemns expeditious processes, scornful superiority or arrogance and inattentive behavior that makes others anxious, suspicious or offended. This is not only a problem for implementing international agreements or treaties, but also for making them possible, desirable and credible.

It is the task and the privilege of the diplomat to make up for political misunderstanding, cultural ignorance, economic unequality in order to create the conditions of dignity, fairness, mutual understanding, sometimes even connivance, which are urgently needed between people of different cultures, races or continents. International good faith requires permanent information and reflection on others and also a patient and constant effort to give a good impression of one's own attitude, in order to be credible and to put others at ease.

In a world in which a growing economic, technical and cultural integration has to be developed, responsible leaders and public opinion will no longer accept negligence, delusion, disloyalty, irresponsibility and incoherence in diplomacy. Of course, fair play is not silliness or lack of foresight; transparency (glasnost) and sincerity are neither levity nor imprudence; treaties do not exempt states from precautions, guarantees and adaptation. Herein lies the art of diplomacy.

Good faith, a paradigm in international negotiation, must be studied and improved as a basic condition of peace.

CHAPTER 26

Synthesizing Themes of the US–PIN Program

Howard Raiffa[1] and James K. Sebenius[2]

[1] *Harvard University*
Cambridge, Massachusetts
[2] *The Blackstone Group*
  USA

26.1. The US–PIN Program

The International Institute for Applied Systems Analysis (IIASA), in coordination with its 15 National Member organizations (NMOs), initiated in 1986 a coordinated research and information collection and dissemination program on better understanding and improving the processes of international negotiations. The American Academy of Arts and Sciences, the NMO of the USA for IIASA, is coordinating the PIN program activities in the United States. Funding of the US–PIN Program has been provided by the Carnegie Corporation and the Burroughs (now UNISYS) Corporation.

   The US–PIN Program is one of several programs established to participate in the activities of the international PIN network. The international network is composed of the PIN project at IIASA and the PIN projects and programs in each of the national member organizations. The IIASA–PIN project has a central role in coordinating the activities of the national efforts and maintaining direct communication with each one, but there are also linkages being formed directly between individual national programs.

This chapter is, in part, a progress report of some of the activities of the US-PIN program. We very much welcome closer collaboration with the IIASA-PIN Project and with other NMO-PIN networks.

The US-PIN program has, from its inception, been guided by the "Proposal for an International Research Program on the Processes of International Negotiations", dated 25 July 1985, IIASA.

26.2. Organizational Structure of US-PIN

Under the American Academy Committee for IIASA a small Research Coordinating Committee (RCC) under the chairmanship of Harvey Brooks officially administers the program. Acting in coordination with the RCC for PIN is the Planning and Synthesis Panel, chaired by James K. Sebenius, which oversees the intellectual content of the program. The chairpersons of the five projects under the Planning and Synthesis Panel are represented in that Panel. An Advisory Panel interacts both with the RCC and with Planning and Synthesis Panel. The overall executive coordinator of the Program is Lance Antrim.

Funding is tight for such an ambitious program, and the question arises: why such an elaborate superstructure? Our funding enables us to invite researchers and practitioners to the American Academy to jointly devise and suggest research activities and directions. We do not have as yet adequate central funding for the execution of research, but we can approach and have approached various funding sources to finance specific research tasks. The present structure is designed to facilitate this necessary entrepreneurial activity. The US-PIN program collaborates closely with three other programs: the Program on Negotiation, centered at Harvard Law School, the Negotiation Roundtable, centered at Harvard Business School, and the Computer-Aided Negotiation (CAN) Project centered at MIT. Several doctoral students (both at Harvard and MIT) writing dissertations on topics of relevance to PIN are being jointly supported by US-PIN and its Harvard and MIT affiliates.

We, the authors of this chapter, both members of the Planning and Synthesis Panel, have participated and have perused the minutes of the meetings of the five working task forces, and have identified 13 recurrent themes that we hope will help to concentrate and integrate the loosely joined efforts of many researchers and practitioners with quite diverse disciplinary roots and contextual orientations. Perhaps some of these may be adopted by other NMO-PIN networks or by PIN-IIASA as synthesizing themes. We are still at a formative stage of development and we would welcome being influenced by others in redirecting our efforts: stressing some themes over others and adding or subtracting from our still-tentative list.

26.3. Synthesizing Themes

Theme 1:   Tension between creating and claiming: Need for a paradigmatic shift in approach from a win–lose to a win–win mentality.

Complex negotiations are rarely zero-sum. Hard positional bargaining may lead to poor agreements, impasses, and conflict spirals. All too often disputants fail to bake a large enough pie for all to share; they leave potential joint gains on the table because they fail to engage effectively in joint problem solving. Yet if one side is open, forthcoming, and inventive, that side may be exploited by a hard-bargaining opponent. Knowing this, sides may seek to protect themselves "by taking tough stances", to the detriment of all. This theme seeks to untangle the cooperative and competitive aspects of negotiation, looking for ways — whether individual, institutional, or procedural — to enhance outcomes for all disputants. The artful negotiator must balance a tension between two tactics: those employed to *create* positive gains for all to share and those employed to *claim* a favorable share of those gains.

Theme 2:   Linkage of issues

How flexible should we be in *linking* issues? Linkages can be used as carrots as well as sticks. In theory, and in the laboratory, it is often possible to join two intractable negotiations into one grand negotiation with an apparent zone of agreement. By combining separate negotiations a richer set of tradeoffs is thereby created that might lead to more maneuverability for compromise — especially if the disputants give differential weights to the importance of the separate components of the linked negotiation. But what are the limits? In the Camp David negotiations, it would not have made sense to link the powerfully divisive negotiations over the status of Jerusalem with the Sinai question. How far should we go before possible disadvantages of linkages (of divisiveness, increased complexity, etc.) override the benefits?

Theme 3:   Repetitive negotiations: Temporal linkages and the need to build better relationships

Our next theme looks at the effects of repetition on bargaining behavior and outcome. In repetitive negotiations the outcome of one set of negotiations sets the stage for the next round. It is often important for the disputants not only to bargain over substance, but to be mindful of building better relationships and trust that could help future negotiations. In this sense successive negotiations — even over different matters of substance — become linked. At first blush, repeated (rather than one-shot) negotiations might be thought to induce moderation. Yet, a bad experience, intentional or not, in an early encounter may impact through the interactive system and negatively affect later negotiations. Some bargainers may seek opportunistically to build trust in unimportant rounds and take advantage of counterparts in encounters with a great deal at stake. PIN researchers are trying to understand the conditions under which repetition improves outcomes over time, when it is harmful, and ways to foster or preclude it as appropriate.

Theme 4:   On cultural styles: Differences within and between cultures

How do various cultures respond to the expressed willingness to negotiate, to compromise, to the use of third-party intermediaries? What are the differences in cultural styles that impede fruitful negotiations? Why would country A want negotiators from country B to know about the sensitivities of country A? Could a primer for Soviet trade negotiators be written by Western businessmen that would help negotiations — and vice versa! Differences exist *between* cultures, but there may be a great deal of variation *within* a given culture across different contexts. For example, the Soviets, the Japanese and Western European countries may each resolve disputes about family issues, commercial contracts, and community matters in quite different ways. Are there important differences in the ways that countries negotiate about security matters versus international commercial enterprises versus environmental matters? When disagreements persist, it is all too easy to blame "cultural differences" rather than incompatible differences about substance or poor negotiating skills. PIN researchers are focusing on the role and effects of culture on negotiations among and within various societies.

Theme 5:   Synchronization of internal and external negotiations

Our next theme concerning the structure of most international negotiations has been pithily articulated by John Dunlop: not only are there negotiations across the table, but on each side of the table as well. In the simplest form we observe *agents* negotiating with each other on behalf of *principals* in their respective home countries, in a structure analogous to two lawyers negotiating for their clients. But this abstraction misses an important complexity: each agent-negotiator represents not a single principal, but a set of principals who often disagree among themselves. These principals, all from one country, represent factions with opposing internal interests. Indeed, we believe that one of the weakest links in international negotiations is our inability to synchronize internal and external negotiations. Discord about internal negotiations may inhibit the ability of our external negotiators to search for creative compromises. And the interaction between internal and external bargains can become extraordinarily complex. The agent often plays a dual role: as external negotiator and as internal mediator.

Theme 6:   Creative compensation of internal losers by internal winners

Our previous theme notes that negotiating "sides" are often nonmonolithic. Even with a superb compromise *across* the table, there will be losers as well as winners on each side of the table. For example, think what happens in trade talks that tear down tariff barriers. Many people (e.g., consumers, importers) are better off, but a few (e.g., domestic producers) suffer grievously. Economic theory says persuasively that internal winners should compensate internal losers — especially if the internal losers can be blocking minority — in order that broadly beneficial action (e.g., tariff reduction) be taken. But countries are rarely skilled in the art of this kind of internal compensation. Just reflect how badly we do on a purely internal manner of locating noxious facilities: waste-disposal sites, prisons, etc. "Yes it should be done; it would clearly be of immense general benefit; but *don't* put it in *my* backyard!" And the facilities go unbuilt. It is often not at all obvious how internal winners can compensate internal losers in a politically palatable manner. One often overlooked opportunity explores our second theme: use of linked internal negotiations to forge an acceptable internal compromise.

Theme 7:   Coalition dynamics

N-person game theory examines the behavior of players as they jockey for entry and for power within a set of shifting coalitions. The theory is not tidy even for the relatively simple case of rational players who use monetary payoffs. The normative theory has little predictive power nor does it provide prescriptive guidance. In complex negotiations with many issues (e.g., the Law of Sea) a given country might simultaneously belong to several different coalitions that focus on different sets of issues (e.g., economic, security, rights of passage). What is needed are insights, bolstered by a bit of theory and by empirical observations from real negotiations and laboratory experiments, about how players should negotiate, within and between coalitions, when several issues with incommensurate payoffs are at stake. Researchers are looking both at situations with a few players (e.g., 3 to 5) and with many players (on the order of 100). Surprisingly, the negotiations with many players often seem to exhibit simpler dynamics than those with many fewer participants.

Theme 8:   The roles of intermediaries or intervenors in international negotiations

For purely domestic disputes there is an array of helpful interventions by third-party "helpers": facilitators, counselors, fact-finders, ombudsmen, mediators, "Med-arbitrators", and arbitrators, to mention only the most prominent "helpers". Intermediaries play key roles in family disputes (in divorce, in settling estates), in labor management disputes, in community disputes, in environmental disputes and in other areas. There are a host of alternate dispute resolution interventions to help ease the burden on the courts and generate better outcomes for the participants. In the international arena, there are examples where intermediaries have played a helpful role (for example, President Carter at Camp David or the Pope in the Beagle Channel Dispute between Argentina and Chile). But there is a paucity of suitable institutions to play comparable roles. In international disputes questions arise such as: Should an intermediary be invited to join the negotiations? If so, *by whom?* To play what *role* (e.g., mediator or arbitrator)? At what *time* in the evolution of the dispute? And lastly, *who* should that intermediary be? We need to assess how useful third-party involvement can be stimulated; what institutional channels are available; how they operate; how they can be improved; what training would help; what new institutions and processes should be created.

Theme 9:   Role of "neutrals" for fact-finding and for modeling for analysis

One particularly important manifestation of the general problem addressed in the previous theme involves scientific disputes. How do we get good, fair, impartial analysis for international scientific disputes? Who should be building the models of atmospheric chemistry, of meteorology and of soil and water chemistry that could be used in negotiations about acid rain, about ozone depletion, about CO_2 accumulations, about radiation from Chernobyl? To facilitate the necessary learning in a negotiation setting, we need international counterparts of such US institutions as the Rand Corporation, Resources for the Future, Brookings Institution, the NRC/NAS committees. Of course, other countries have their own prestigious scientific institutions playing similar roles. But what international institutions can play such roles? Unfortunately UN agencies are often too politically charged to provide neutral analytical assistance to disputants, although there are notable exceptions (e.g., the IAEA, WHO, WMO). Can an intermediary to a dispute help provide analytical support or help to seek relatively "impartial or neutral" analytical support? Can intermediaries help the disputants to negotiate around a model (as was the case in the Law of the Sea negotiations)? Can IIASA play a role, or can IIASA spawn an institution that can play a role?

Theme 10:   Knowledge and negotiation: The value of information under conflict

The issues in many international negotiations are technically complex and the real interests of the participants unclear. Think of negotiations over fisheries conservation, transborder pollution such as acid rain, the CO_2 buildup, ozone depletion, renegotiation of foreign debt, arms control, and the like. There is a particularly acute need in such cases for the parties to *learn* about the nature of the problem and about their real interests as well as to *bargain* to advance their positions. Often these commingled adversarial and collaborative processes can become so entangled that neither is carried out very effectively.

In the eloquent words of our joint doctoral student, Arthur Appelbaum:

> Negotiators learn and negotiators bargain. Faced with ignorance, they learn with and from others about the choices that serve their purposes. Faced with conflict, they bargain over choices with others who pursue different purposes. But because a negotiator's partner-in-ignorance and adversaries-in-conflict commonly are one and the same, the two tasks of learning and bargaining tightly interweave. You often must learn what you want to do as you bargain to get something done.

The twin tasks of learning and bargaining usually are at odds. Players who hold information that can help you decide which choices serve your purposes may have reason to withhold, mislead, or exact a price for their knowledge. And when you engage in attempts to shape the beliefs of others, you often distort or deflect your own search for knowledge. But if you fail to learn when you bargain under conditions of uncertainty, you might find in the end that you don't really want what you bargained for. In this counterpoint of learning and bargaining lies a dilemma:

Horn 1.   To learn which outcomes serve your interests, you often must jeopardize the chances of attaining those outcomes.

Horn 2.   To bargain effectively for specific outcomes, you often must act before knowing how well those outcomes serve your interests.

The configurations of knowledge and interest that propel the learning and bargaining dilemma appear again and again in common and central managerial tasks. When they budget and invest, develop policies and shape institutional strategies, organizational players learn under conflict and bargain under uncertainty — and so, might gore or be gored with one of the dilemma's horns.

Theme 11:   Prenegotiations, or negotiating about processes before negotiating about substance

Before the bell "officially" sounds the start of the negotiations, an intense process has usually taken place that exerts enormous influence over the final negotiated results. This process involves working out a formal agenda, which issues will be joined in which working group, in what order, and by what processes (voting rules, interim and final deadlines, etc.). These initial choices must be negotiated and in this sense, prenegotiations are indeed bona fide negotiations. So too, are many postnegotiation procedures. US–PIN researchers are writing papers on pre- and post-negotiations, *qua* negotiations, and examining, in particular, two upcoming multilateral negotiations: the next round of GATT negotiations and the Antarctic Treaty.

Theme 12:   Negotiation analysis without negotiators: Use of surrogate disputants

Some disputes are "too hot" to negotiate. Some disputants believe they are better off not negotiating — not because the alternative to negotiation is so desirable, but because the outcome of negotiations may be even worse. There may be an asymmetry of power that negates, in the minds of one or more disputants, the advantages of negotiations. There may be a perceived weakness in starting negotiations. But perceptions may be wrong. Can an analyst help? How can recalcitrant disputants be lured to the formal negotiating table to deal constructively with their differences? One possibility is to do external analyses, sometimes with "surrogate disputants", which may vividly demonstrate the existence of an array of potential agreements that would be better than the no-agreement state for each party. Surrogates can be used to help the analyst (1) capture the essence of dispute, (2) articulate the interests of the disputants and assess their tradeoffs between conflicting objectives, (3) devise creative options, (4) formulate starting single-negotiating texts. And lastly, the analyst may be able to generate attractive alternatives that simultaneously beat the status quo for all disputants. Finally, real disputants could monitor the psuedo-negotiation and claim partial ownership of ideas if the process is productive.

Theme 13:   Securing insecure contracts through linkages

Our last theme examines the fragility or insecurity of international agreements. In purely domestic matters, we have a host of institutional arrangements backed by our judicial and penal systems for ensuring compliance with contracts and for securing negotiated agreements. There are also international mechanisms for "securing insecure contracts", but these tend to be weak. The problems of foreign debt renegotiation — in which past agreements no longer govern relations between debtors and banks — underscore the importance of an intricate network of past, ongoing, and future negotiations. Parenthetically, it might well be easier to get compliance in US–Soviet agreements if our societies were more intricately interwoven so that any given agreement would be implicitly linked to many other interactions.

PART V

Theoretical Foundations and Methods of Analysis – 2

CHAPTER 27

Effective Formation of International Concord for Conflict Solving: A Game Theoretic Approach with Risk Assessment

Fumiko Seo[1] and Masatoshi Sakawa[2]

[1] *Kyoto University*
   Kyoto
[2] *Department of Computer Science*
   Iwate University
   Morioka, Iwate
   Japan

27.1. Introduction

This chapter is concerned with effectiveness in formation of multilateral cooperation for international conflict solving. We present a game theoretic approach based on risk assessment.

In the present world, many complex problems involve conflicting national interests and, for solving them, the processes of international negotiation and formation of international agreements at some levels are required. These problems are international nuclear disarmament, international environmental protection, international opening of economic markets, etc., which include not only mutual conflicts among national interests, but also risk in a particular sense for people in every country. Thus, a hierarchical systems analysis in two levels is used: national and international. At the national level, a multidimensional risk function for each country is constructed, which independently reflects national interests in conflict with each other. At the international level, formation of an international concord for compromising the national interests is considered. An n-person cooperative game in the characteristic function form is used to examine the effectiveness of an alternative formation of international concord for solving conflict. Based on the multidimensional risk function, the characteristic function for the game is derived. The nucleolus as a solution concept is used in its alternative function forms.

In the following, Section 27.2 introduces the concept of the multidimensional risk function and presents a multidimensional risk analysis. In Sections 27.3 and 27.4, the nucleolus concept of the cooperative game and its extensions to the results of the risk analysis are discussed. In Section 27.5, a device to measure these incomparable solutions with the Pareto or quasi-Pareto optimal property in a comparable term is presented. In Section 27.6, a numerical example is discussed.

27.2. Construction of a Multiattribute Risk Function

27.2.1. Multiattribute risk function for a risky event

Multiattribute risk analysis involves a construction of a multidimensional (multiattribute) risk function (MRF) and its assessment. MRF is constructed as a result of evaluation with the probability for possible consequences of an event.

Consider an event A that has multiple impacts. Possible consequences of the event are uncertain and assessed in terms of multiple attributes that are selected as the measure for consideration of the multiple impacts and treated as uncertain quantities. Denote a set of m attributes as $X \triangleq \{X_1,...,X_m\}$ and a set of their quantities as $x \triangleq \{x_1,...,x_m\}$. A probability function $p_l(x_l)$, $l = 1,...,m$, is assessed subjectively for each attribute x_l. A set of probability functions $p \triangleq \{p_1,...,p_m\}$ defines a risk profile of an event A.

The multidimensional risk function (MRF) of the event A is defined on the risk profile p and represented as

$$R(p) = R(p_1,...,p_m). \tag{27.1}$$

Properties of MRF are as follows:

(i)   MRF represents a multidimensional adverse utility (aversion) function representing negative human preference. That is, a higher order of magnitude of the MRF-value indicates a higher degree of aversion for an event A.

(ii)   Assessment for MRF is subjectively performed on each element p_l in the risk profile p, whose value varies between 0 and 1, $p_{lj} > 0$, and $\sum_{j=1}^{n} p_{lj} = 1$.

(iii)   Assessment for MRF includes the value trade-offs between the attributes in terms of their probability.

Now we must consider representation theorems of MRF.

Assumptions:

(i)   Occurrences of attributes for possible consequences of an event A are independent of each other in the technological and political sense.

(ii)   Preference for (aversion to) an attribute is independent of preference for (aversion to) the other attributes.

(iii)   A trade-off between a pair of attributes is assessed independently of trade-offs of the other pairs of attributes.

Theorem 1 (Representation of MRF)

Under the three assumptions, the multidimensional (multiattribute) risk function for a state E_j is represented in additive form

$$R(p_1,...,p_m) = \sum_{l=1}^{m} k_l r_l(p_l), \quad \text{when } \sum_{l=1}^{m} k_l = 1, \tag{27.2}$$

or, in multiplicative form,

$$R(p_1,...,p_m) = \frac{1}{K} \left[\prod_{l=1}^{m} (Kk_l r_l(p_l)+1) - 1 \right], \quad \text{when } \sum_{l=1}^{m} k_l \neq 1, \tag{27.3}$$

where $0 < k_l < 1$. K is a solution of $1+K = \prod_{l=1}^{m} (1+Kk_l)$, where $K \neq 0$ and $K > -1$. $0 \leq r_l \leq 1$ and $0 \leq R \leq 1$.

$r_l(p_l)$ is a unidimensional risk function for a state E_j and assessed on the probability function $p_l(x_l)$, and $\partial r_l/\partial p_l > 0$.

Proof of Theorem 1 is straightforward on the same line as that for the multiattribute utility function (MUF) by Keeney and Raiffa (1976). Therefore it will be omitted here.

Assessment of scaling constants k_l, $l=1,...,m$, can be performed as the result of trade-off experiments between probabilities of attributes. The trade-off experiment is performed on the following questions.

Question I

Consider two probability functions, $p_r(x_r)$ and $p_s(x_s)$, for unwanted attributes, x_r and x_s, where x_s is the most important attribute to be taken into consideration. Suppose that a probability p_r for an occurrence of an unwanted attribute x_r will rise from 0 (the best situation) to 1 (the worst situation). Then, how much can the decision-maker (DM) admit degradation of the present situation for the most important attribute x_s in terms of its probability?

Question II

Consider a probability function p_s for the most important attribute x_s. On the one hand, consider a certain consequence in which the probability p_s takes the value 1 (the worst level), and all the other probabilities p_r, $r = 1,...,m, r \neq s$, take the value 0 (the best level). On the other hand, consider an uncertain consequence (lottery) in which all the probabilities p_l take the value 1 with a probability π or all the probabilities p_l take the value 0 with a probability $1- \pi$. How much is the π-value which makes those two consequences (certain and uncertain) indifferent for the DM?

These experiments correspond to the trade-off experiments for deriving k_r/k_s of MRF and basic k_s-value estimation, respectively.

27.2.2. Multiattribute risk analysis for national interest

The construction of MRF is performed at the national level in a hierarchical systems analysis for international affairs. A national action results in an event that has various international influences and over which national interests are in conflict with each other. Possible consequences of this event are first assessed in terms of MRF from the point of view of the national interest for each country.

In this process, diversification of risk assessment by collective choice should be taken into account and thus the degree of national consensus for the assessment of MRF should be examined. We have already presented a fuzzy multiattribute utility analysis for collective choice (Seo and Sakawa, 1985), where a fuzzification device for the multiattribute utility function (MUF) is introduced for treating diversification of evaluation by multiple decision-makers (MDM). For the time being, we will discuss an extension of this device to the assessment of MRF.

A device for fuzzy multiattribute risk analysis is as follows.

(i)   The unidimensional risk function $r_l(p_l)$ can be assessed as a fuzzy function that takes on a fuzzy number. The fuzzy number represents some dispersion of evaluation by MDM.

(ii) A fuzzy preference (aversion) order among the attributes is constructed as a result of collective choice. A non-fuzzy preference (aversion) order for the attributes, $X_s \succ X_r \succ ... \succ X_t$, is obtained, via the defuzzification process based on Zadeh's proposition (1971), from the fuzzy preferences (aversion) order. A degree of agreement for the derived preference order is calculated in a quantitative term. Corresponding to the derived non-fuzzy preference order of the attributes, a numerical order of the scaling constants k_l for r_l, $l = 1,..., m$, is determined. The trade-off experiment between probabilities, p_r and p_s, is performed on this numerical order of the scaling constants. This experiment derives relative values of the scaling constants k_r, $r = 1,..., m$, $r \neq s$, in terms of a scaling constant k_s that is placed for the most regarded attribute.

(iii) The value of the scaling constant k_s is also assessed as a fuzzy number such as the L-R type (Dubois and Prade, 1978), which represents a diversification of evaluation for k_s due to the collective choice.

(iv) The representation form for MRF, additive or multiplicative, is checked in terms of fuzzy comparison between the fuzzy numbers (Dubois and Prade, 1980). The question for the fuzzy comparison follows.

Question III

What is the truth value of the assertion

" $\sum_{l=1}^{m} \tilde{k}_l$ is greater (or smaller) than 1 "

The separation theorem with a threshold level Θ for two bounded and convex fuzzy sets (Zadeh, 1965) is used to answer this question.

(v) A fuzzy multidimensional risk function (FMRF) is derived via (i)–(iv).

(vi) By assigning alternative values to the attributes, alternative values of FMRF can be obtained.

Consider that a national event with some risky properties will occur in a country. Then risk assessment can be done with FMRF from the point of view of national interest. The alternative FMRF-values can be calculated for both the predicted or estimated values and the current values of risk assessment for political, economic, and technological consequences that possesses international multiple effects.

27.3. Nucleolus and Its Extensions for an N-person Cooperative Game for International Conflict Solving

The FMRF is evaluated for each country confronted with international conflicts of national interest. For solving international conflicts, international concords are constructed as the results of multilateral negotiations. We treat this process as a formation of a coalition and evaluate its efficiency in terms of an n-person cooperative game. Each Country i is treated as a player who is a member of a coalition S. A characteristic function $v(S)$ for a coalition S is defined on a total of decremental values of FMRF due to the formation of a coalition S:

$$v(S)=\sum_{i\in S}\frac{1}{s}R_i(p_i) - R_S(p_S) \qquad (27.4)$$

where $S\subseteq N$, $N \triangleq \{1,...,n\}$. R_i and R_S are FMRFs for Country i and coalition S, respectively; p_i and p_S are the risk profiles of a state in an event for them. The $v(S)$ in (27.4) is a coalition value, which indicates a decrease of the degree of international risk that occurs from a national event.

Define a payoff vector as $z \triangleq \{z_1,...z_n\}$, whose elements are decremental values of FMRF for a player (country) i, $i = 1,...,n$, due to the formation of a coalition.

In terms of an n-person cooperative game in the characteristic function form, the excess of a value of the game for a coalition S over the total payoff value is defined:

$$e(S, z) \triangleq v(S) - z(S), \quad S\subset N, \qquad (27.5)$$

where $N \triangleq \{1,...,n\}$ is a set of n-players (countries), and $z(S) \triangleq \sum_{i\in S} z_i$. The excess is regarded as a measure of dissatisfaction with an international coalition S at the payoff z. The core is defined as a set of all payoff vectors that cannot be improved by any coalition, and is shown by

$$e(S, z) \leq 0 \quad \text{(coalition rationality)} \qquad (27.6)$$

along with $z(N) - v(N) = 0$, where $z(N) \triangleq \sum_{i=1}^{n} z_i$.

The existence and uniqueness of the core are not necessarily assured in all cases. Thus, by relaxing the definition of the core (27.6), the concept that defines the quasi-core is introduced [Shapley and Shubik (1966), Schmeidler (1969), Maschler, Peleg, and Shapley (1979)].

Define the (strong) ϵ-core as a quasi-core concept relaxed with a parameter ϵ as

$$e(S,z) \triangleq v(S) - z(S) \leq \epsilon, \text{ for } all \ S \neq \phi, N, \qquad (27.7)$$

along with $v(N) = z(N)$. It means that the payoff vector cannot be improved by any coalition S, when a relaxing parameter ϵ is imposed on the payoff $z(S)$. The meaning of ϵ is interpreted as a tax transfer or a subsidy by an international mediator and represents an international adjustment factor. Based on this concept, the smallest ϵ-core that maximizes the excess is constructed, which is defined as

$$\epsilon_o(z) = \min_{z \in \chi} \ \max_{S \neq \phi, N} \ e(S,z) \qquad (27.8)$$

where χ is a set of preimputations that satisfies the collective rationality, $z(N) = v(N)$. $\epsilon_o(z)$ shows the payoff vector that minimizes the maximum dissatisfaction of the coalition S, and is called the least core, which provides the nucleolus $\mathcal{N}(z)$ of the game $\Gamma(N, v)$ via lexicographic ordering of the excess. The lexicographic ordering is defined as follows. Let

$$\Theta(z) \triangleq [\Theta_1(z), \Theta_2(z), ..., \Theta_{2^n}(z)]$$

be the 2^n-vector whose elements are the number $\Theta_k \triangleq e(S_k, z)$, $k = 1, ..., 2^n$, on $S \subset N$ arranged in a nonincreasing order. The lexicographic order is given by the relation $\Theta(z) \leq_L \Theta(y)$, which holds when $\Theta_i(z) = \Theta_i(y)$ for all $i < j$ and $\Theta_j(z) < \Theta_j(y)$. This means that, if there exists equality between the maximal values of the excess $\Theta_i(z)$ and $\Theta_i(y)$, $i = 1, 2, ...$, that are arranged in a nonincreasing order, then the next greatest values of the excess, $\Theta_j(z)$ and $\Theta_j(y)$, are compared with each other, and so on. The comparison is continued sequentially until the inequality is found. Then, the nucleolus of a game is defined as the set of payoff vectors such that

$$\mathcal{N}(z) \triangleq \{z \in \chi \mid \Theta(z) \leq_L \Theta(y) \text{ for all } y \in \chi\} \qquad (27.9)$$

Naturally, the payoff vector z is more acceptable than y. In other words, the nucleolus is defined as the payoff vector that minimizes the maximum excess.

The nucleolus as the solution concept for the quasi-core is obtained by solving at most $n-1$ liner programming problems [Kopelowitz (1967), Littlechild (1974), Owen (1974)].

As an extension of the nucleolus, define the concept of augmented ϵ-core that is enlarged with a parameter μ as

$$e_\mu(S,z) \triangleq v(S) - z(S) \leq \mu\epsilon \qquad (27.10)$$

along with $v(N) = z(N)$. The nucleolus $\mathcal{N}(\mu)$ is redefined on the augmented ϵ-core, and an augmented nucleolus is obtained as a solution by running repetitively a linear program. Consider the 0-normalization that is defined with $v(\{i\}) = 0$ for all $i \in N$. The augmented nucleolus $\mathcal{N}(\mu)$ is obtained by solving the following linear program, and the $\epsilon_o(z)$-value (27.8) is found.

(P)

       minimize ϵ
       z_i, ϵ

subject to

       $z_i \geq 0$ for $i \in N$

       $v(S) - (z(S) + \mu \, \epsilon) \leq 0$ for all $S \subset N$ (27.11)

       $v(N) - z(N) = 0$

The interpretation of the primal problem (27.11) with the augmenting parameter μ is clear. When $\mu = 1$, the solution to (P) provides the nucleolus. When $\mu = s$, the weak nucleolus is obtained, where s denotes the number of players in a coalition S (Shapley and Shubik, 1966). When $\mu = v(S)$, the proportional nucleolus is obtained (Young, Okada, and Hashimoto, 1982). Sakawa and others (1983) proposed the concession nucleolus when $\mu = \sum\limits_{i \in S} \Phi_i$, where Φ_i is the Shapley value. The Shapley value is defined as

$$\Phi_i(v) \triangleq \sum_{\substack{S \subset N \\ S \ni i}} \frac{(s-1)!(n-s)!}{n!} \, [v(S) - v(S - \{i\})]. \tag{27.12}$$

The second term of the Shapley value represents the marginal amount of contribution of a player i to the value of coalition S. The first term represents a total of the relative frequency for a player i to appear in every coalition S. Thus the value $\sum\limits_{i \in S} \Phi_i$ shows a total of the marginal contribution by each player to every coalition S weighted by the relative frequency of appearance of each player. The concept of the concession nucleolus defined in terms of (27.10) shows that the excess or the dissatisfaction of a coalition S should be divided by the sum of the marginal contributions of each player in the coalition S. In this concept, some kind of externality or "opportunity cost" for the participation of each player i is taken into account for every coalition S. Alternatively, when

$\mu = v(N) - v(N - S)$, the contribution nucleolus is found for a coalition S, as we call it here. These concepts enlarge the quasi-core concept in alternative ways.

27.4. Evaluation of an International Concord

At the international level in the hierarchical systems analysis, in which the game theoretic approach is used, the obtained FMRF-value for a country i is shown as

$$w_i^\dagger = R_i - z_i^\dagger, \quad i \in N \tag{27.13}$$

where w_i, $\sum_{i \in N} w_i = R_N$, represents an international allocation of total risk generated from a national policy with international effects among each country i after the construction of an international concord among n countries.

Alternative solutions $z^\dagger \triangleq \{z_1^\dagger, ..., z_n^\dagger\}$ of the augmented nucleolus provide alternative payoff values for each player (country). These solutions depend on alternative criteria and are not unique for the final decision.

For choosing the preferred solutions z^* from among the alternative solutions $z^\dagger$, we can examine the dual optimal solutions $y_S^\dagger$ and $y_N^\dagger$ generated from alternative programming formulations for the augmented nucleoli.

The interpretation of the dual variables is derived from the Lagrangian function of the primal problem (27.11):

$$L \triangleq \epsilon + \sum_{S \neq N} y_S \{v(S) - [z(S) + \mu\epsilon]\} + y_N[v(N) - z(N)] \tag{27.14}$$

Then, according to the sensitivity theorem of mathematical programming, considering that all variables ϵ, z_i, y_S and y_N are all functions of $v(S)$ and $v(N)$, from the Kuhn–Tucher conditions, one derives

$$\frac{\partial \epsilon}{\partial v(S)} = y_S \quad \text{for } y_S > 0, \ S \subset N, \tag{27.15}$$

$$\frac{\partial \epsilon}{\partial v(N)} = y_N \tag{27.16}$$

at optimum. It is known, from the first-order optimality conditions, that

$$-\sum_{\substack{S \subset N \\ S \ni i}} y_S = y_N \quad \text{and} \quad \sum_{S \subset N} y_S \mu = 1.$$

The dual variable y_S represents a trade-off between the "tax transfer" variable ϵ and the coalition value $v(S)$ for every coalition S. This property is also held for the grand coalition N. In other words, the evaluation prices y_S, $S \subset N$, for each coalition S and y_N for the grand coalition are imputed inversely corresponding to the marginal changes of the coalition values $v(S)$ and $v(N)$, that are made commensurable in terms of a marginal increment of the "tax transfer" variable ϵ. The y_S and y_N indicate inversely the shadow prices or opportunity costs of the coalition values measured commonly in marginal terms of the "tax transfer" variable ϵ. Larger values of y_S and y_N show relative inefficiency of $v(S)$ and $v(N)$, because a smaller value of maximum ϵ is more desirable in this case. These values y_S and y_N can be used as the measure of satisfaction with the coalitions (concords) S and N. The augmenting parameter μ denotes a discount factor that indicates a deviation from the balance game. When $\mu = 1$, the nucleolus implies that the game is balanced. *Figure 27.1* represents a summary of these results.

cases	y_S for $v(S)$	y_N for $v(N)$	equilibrium conditions
nucleolus	$\dfrac{\partial \epsilon}{\partial v(S)} = y_S$	$\dfrac{\partial \epsilon}{\partial v(N)} = y_N$	$-\sum\limits_{\substack{S \subset N \\ S \ni i}} y_S = y_N$
	$y_S > 0$		$\sum\limits_{S \subset N} y_S = 1,\ y_S \geq 0$
augmented nucleolus	$\dfrac{\partial \epsilon}{\partial v(S)} = y_S$	$\dfrac{\partial \epsilon}{\partial v(N)} y_N$	$-\sum\limits_{\substack{S \subset N \\ S \ni i}} y_S = y_N$
	$y_S > 0$		$\sum\limits_{S \subset N} y_S \mu = 1,\ y_S \geq 0$
disruption nucleolus	$\dfrac{\partial r}{\partial v(S)} = (1+r) y_S$	$\dfrac{\partial r}{\partial v(N)} = y_N$	$-(1+r)\sum\limits_{\substack{S \subset N \\ S \ni i}} y_S = y_N$
	$y_S > 0$		$-\sum\limits_{S \subset N} y_S(v(S) - z(S)) = 1,$ $y_S \geq 0$

Note. $\mu = 1$: nucleolus. $\mu = s$: weak nucleolus. $\mu = v(S)$: propertional nucleolus. $\mu = \sum\limits_{i \in S} \Phi_i$: concession nucleolus. $\mu = v(N) - v(N - S)$: contribution nucleolus.

Figure 27.1. Evaluation for nucleolus.

27.5. The Role of the Mediator in International Conflict Solving

The alternative solution concepts of the augmented nucleolus provide alternative payoff values and construct alternative risk allocation plans for each country.

National interests in these alternative plans are in conflict with each other. Generally, any selection rule among the alternatives has not so far existed. In this chapter, the dual optimal solutions of mathematical programming formulated for the game provide an analytical measure for comparative consideration of the alternative plans. However, in the next stage at the international level of the hierarchical systems analysis, the role of the mediator as an international coordinator should be introduced for resolving more complex problems of international politics.

In this stage, political decisions at a higher level should be made for reaching a more acceptable agreement among countries. The role of international organizations will be crucial at this stage. Although scientific and quantitative analysis for international conflict solving, which has been presented in the preceding sections, provides some reference material for decision support, there is still some room for international mediator to make a final decision.

27.6. Example

For simplicity, we will treat here an event A as a result of a national policy of a country B. Suppose that the country intends to promote an industrial development program on a coastal area of the upper stream of a large international river. This development program will have multiple adverse effects, which are economic, environmental and aesthetic, via emission and discharge of various pollutants in several countries. Thus, the national event A has a property of an international affair.

For coping with adverse effects for many countries, the two-level approach is used. First, at the national level, an MRF for each country is evaluated for multiple attributes such as decrease of income from fishing, forestry, agriculture and tourism, and damage to human health, etc. The degree of belief for the occurrence of these effects is still under uncertainty. Thus, these effects are evaluated in terms of MRF for each country independently of the others. The fuzzification due to collective choice in a country can lead to a constant FMRF for each country. Second, at the international level, affected countries will participate in negotiation with country B to mitigate the adverse effects. Alternative coalitions can be formed among these countries. Thus, game theory is applied.

Suppose that five countries are affected by B. Suppose that, at the national level, the evaluation of FMRF $R_i(p_i)$, $i = 1,...,5$, has already been done for each country i. For simplicity, we will use a "mean" value of the fuzzy number as the FMRF-value. These values are shown in *Figure 27.2*. Then, at the international level, the characteristic function $v(S)$ of the five-player cooperative game is defined as

$$v(S) = \sum_{i \in S} \frac{1}{s} R_i(p_i) - R_S(p_S) \tag{27.17}$$

$$v(S) \triangleq 100(\sum_{i \in S} \frac{1}{s} R_i(p_i) - R_S(p_s)) \; S \subseteq N$$

$$N \triangleq (1, 2, 3, 4, 5)$$

$v(\{1\}) = 0,$	$R_1 = 0.75$
$v(\{2\}) = 0,$	$R_2 = 0.65$
$v(\{3\}) = 0,$	$R_3 = 0.80$
$v(\{4\}) = 0,$	$R_4 = 0.90$
$v(\{5\}) = 0,$	$R_5 = 0.60$

$v(1, 2) = 70 - 60 = 10$	$v(1,3,4) = 82 - 50 = 32$
$v(1, 3) = 78 - 65 = 13$	$v(1,3,5) = 72 - 53 = 19$
$v(1, 4) = 83 - 68 = 15$	$v(1,4,5) = 75 - 50 = 25$
$v(1, 5) = 68 - 55 = 13$	$v(2,3,4) = 78 - 48 = 30$
$v(2, 3) = 73 - 59 = 14$	$v(2,3,5) = 68 - 50 = 18$
$v(2, 4) = 78 - 59 = 19$	$v(2,4,5) = 72 - 48 = 24$
$v(2, 5) = 63 - 55 = 8$	$v(3,4,5) = 77 - 45 = 32$
$v(3, 4) = 85 - 70 = 15$	$v(1,2,3,4) = 78 - 38 = 40$
$v(3, 5) = 70 - 58 = 12$	$v(1,2,3,5) = 70 - 37 = 33$
$v(4, 5) = 75 - 55 = 20$	$v(1,2,4,5) = 73 - 35 = 38$
$v(1, 2, 3) = 73 - 55 = 18$	$v(1,3,4,5) = 76 - 34 = 42$
$v(1, 2, 4) = 77 - 50 = 27$	$v(2,3,4,5) = 74 - 33 = 41$
$v(1, 2, 5) = 67 - 50 = 17$	$v(1,2,3,4,5) = 74 - 20 = 54$

Figure 27.2. Estimated values of the characteristic function.

where $S \subseteq N$, $N \triangleq \{1,...,5\}$, and evaluated as shown in *Figure 27.2*. In this evaluation (27.17), national equity is considered. The payoff values generated from alternative concepts of the nucleolus are shown in *Figure 27.3*. The obtained risk values (27.13) are also calculated there. As a result, the payoff values show that the most benefit will be brought to Player (Country) 4, the largest risk taker. However, among the alternative augmented nucleolus concepts, there are small conflicts of national interest. For Countries 3 and 4, the proportional nucleolus is most beneficial but, for the other countries, the nucleolus, weak nucleolus and contribution nucleolus are most beneficial. As a reference for choosing the preferred policy, the dual optimal vectors are generated and examined for the alternative nucleolus concepts. The results are shown in *Figure 27.4*. It is known that, for the grand coalition, the nucleolus is the most preferable and the weak nucleolus is second and so on. Efficiency is decreasing in order, toward the right. However, the final decision can be made by the international mediator based on these evaluations, but without any rigorous restraint by the above analytical results.

Player: i	1	2	3	4	5
Individual risk: R_i	0.75	0.65	0.80	0.90	0.60
Payoff vector: z_i (x 100)					
Nucleolus: $\mu = 1$	8.60	7.60	11.60	16.60	9.60
Weak nucleolus: $\mu = s$	8.60	7.60	11.60	16.60	9.60
Proportional nucleolus: $\mu = v(S)$	8.35	7.24	11.69	17.26	9.46
Concession nucleolus: $\mu = \sum_{i \in s} \Phi_i$	8.44	7.38	11.64	17.07	9.46
Contribution nucleolus: $\mu = v(N) - v(N-S)$	8.60	7.60	11.60	16.60	9.60
Obtained risk value: w_i (x 100)					
Nucleolus: $\mu = 1$	66.40	57.40	68.40	73.40	50.40
Weak nucleolus: $\mu = s$	66.40	57.40	68.40	73.40	50.40
Proportional nucleolus: $\mu = v(S)$	66.65	57.76	68.31	72.74	50.54
Concession nucleolus: $\mu = \sum_{i \in s} \Phi_i$	66.56	57.62	68.36	72.93	50.54
Contribution nucleolus: $\mu = v(N) - v(N-S)$	66.40	57.40	68.40	73.40	50.40

Figure 27.3. Numerical results for nucleolus.

	Nucleolus	Weak nucleolus	Proportional nucleolus	Concession nucleolus	Contribution nucleolus
y_S for $v(S)$: $v(1,2,3,4)$ $v(1,2,3,5)$ $v(1,2,4,5)$ $v(1,3,4,5)$ $v(2,3,4,5)$	0.20	0.05	0.00515	0.00463	0.0037
y_N for $v(N)$: $v(1,2,3,4,5)$	-0.80	-0.20	-0.02062	-0.01852	-0.01481
maximum ϵ-value	-4.4	-1.1	-0.1134	-0.10185	-0.08148

Figure 27.4. The dual vectors for coalitions and maximal ϵ-value.

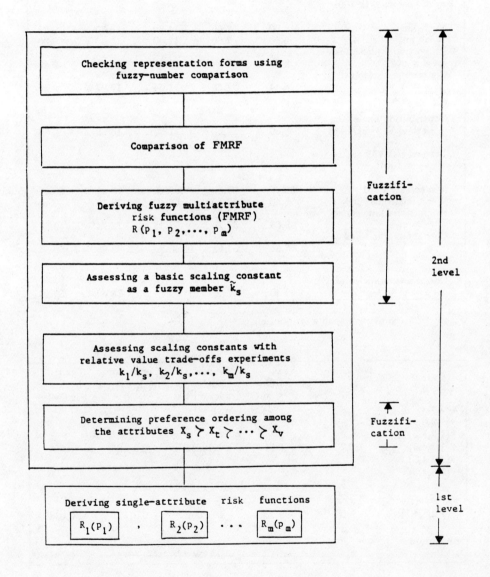

Figure 27.5. The operational method for deriving the FMRF.

References

Dubois, D. and Prade, H. (1978), Operations on Fuzzy Numbers, *International Journal of Systems Sciences*, 9, (6), pp. 613-626.

Dubois, D. and Prade, H. (1980), Systems of Linear Fuzzy Constraints, *Fuzzy Sets and Systems*, 3, pp. 37-48.

Keeney, R.L. and Raiffa, H. (1976), *Decisions with Multiple Objectives, Preferences and Value Tradeoffs*, John Wiley, New York.

Kopelowitz, A. (1967), Computation of the Kernels of Simple Games and the Nucleolus of N-Person Games, R.M. 31, Dept. of Mathematics, Hebrew University.

Littlechild, S.C. (1974), A Simple Expression for the Nucleolus in a Special Case, *International Journal of Game Theory*, 3, (1), pp. 21-29.

Maschler, M., Peleg, B., and Shapley, L.S. (1979), Geometric Properties of the Kernel, Nucleous, and Related Solution Concepts, *Mathematics of Operations Research*, 4, (4), pp. 303-338.

Owen, G. (1974), A Note on the Nucleolus, *International Journal of Game Theory*, 3, (2), pp. 101-103.

Sakawa, M., Tada, K., and Nishizaki, I. (1983), A New Solution Concept in a Cooperative N-Person Game and its Application, *Journal of Electronics and Communication Society*, J.66-A(12) [in Japanese].

Schmeidler, D. (1969), The Nucleolus of a Characteristic Function Game, *SIAM Journal of Applied Mathematics*, 17, (6), pp. 1163-1170.

Seo, F. and Sakawa, M. (1985), Fuzzy Multiattribute Utility Analysis for Collective Choice, *IEEE Transactions on Systems, Man and Cybernetics*, Vol. SMC-15, (1), pp. 45-53.

Shapley, L. S. and Shubik, M. (1966), Quasi-cores in a Monetary Economy with Nonconvex Preferences, *Econometrica*, 34, (4), pp. 805-827.

Young, H.P., Okada, N., and Hashimoto, T. (1982), Cost Allocation in Water Resources Development, *Water Resources Research*, 18, (3), 463-475.

Zadeh, L.A. (1965), Fuzzy Sets, *Information and Control*, 8, pp. 338-353.

Zadeh, L.A. (1971), Similarity Relations and Fuzzy Orderings, *Information Sciences*, 3, pp. 177-200.

CHAPTER 28

On the Time Aspect of International Negotiations and the Probability for Reaching an Agreement: An Incomplete Information Approach

Werner Güth[1] and Reinhard Selten[2]

[1] *Johann Wolfgang Goethe Universität*
  Frankfurt
[2] *Universität Bonn*
  Bonn
  Federal Republic of Germany

28.1. Introduction

There is a vast multiplicity of examples demonstrating that international negotiations often extend over rather long periods (e.g., several years) and end with no agreement at all, although an immediate agreement would be mutually beneficial. The most drastic and tragic examples are obviously international wars, where failing to reach an agreement usually implies heavy casualties and costly damages each day. But as we know from the theory of international trade, a delay in reaching an agreement on international trade or an international commitment to reduce the pollution of air and international rivers and lakes might also imply serious welfare losses. Thus it is an important task to explain why we observe long international negotiations and why they often fail to reach an agreement although international cooperation would be mutually beneficial. Only through understanding the causes of these phenomena can one hope to improve international cooperation, e.g., by changing the conditions and rules of international negotiations. Related to this is the problem that long processes of international negotiations often yield no agreement at all, although mutually profitable possibilities for cooperation exist.

Of course, it would be naive to expect that one can explain the time aspect of the results of all international negotiations by one theoretical approach. So the simple fact that many international negotiations take place at rather attractive places — for instance, Vienna in spring — naturally implies that the negotiators will want to stay at least for some days. Another reason for longer international negotiations might be that the negotiating individuals have to demonstrate to their own constituencies how important they are. The last phenomenon is more thoroughly discussed in the context of collective wage bargaining, where trade union leaders have to prove to their members how effective they are in improving working conditions.

Here we do not want to rely on such arguments referring to selfish motivations of the negotiators. A more important reason, in our view, for long and sometimes unsuccessful international negotiations is that national delegations are often not completely informed about the possible moves, the information conditions and the final goals of other countries. Thus, national delegations need time to find out the types of others and/or to demonstrate their own style and priorities. Usually this happens in the form of proving that certain proposals are by no means acceptable, i.e., one strictly refuses one possible agreement, although this can imply that one cannot reach an agreement at all. Thus our approach to explaining the time aspect of international negotiations as well as their results views long international negotiations as a process where bargainers try strategically to conceal or reveal their types depending on the perceived profitability of such measures. We show that a type-differentiating solution necessarily requires more than just one bargaining round and involves a positive risk of conflict in the case where no mutually profitable agreement is reached. Thus, there is a rational explanation for long international negotiations even if they do not always end with a mutually beneficial agreement.

Our analysis will assume that all negotiating parties know at least their own type. This means that they have a complete preference ordering over all possible negotiation results. In other words, we will assume rational negotiators, as is usually done in game theoretic studies. Of course, most of the phenomena discussed below (e.g., to prove their own type by risking conflict) will be present even in the case of negotiators with limited rationality. But if the negotiating parties are not completely rational, the negotiation process as such can serve other purposes than in the case of rational decision-makers. Most importantly, a limited rationality approach to international negotiations would view long international negotiations as a way by which the negotiating countries find out how the conceivable negotiation results should be evaluated. During long negotiation processes, limited rational negotiators will often try to learn why other parties argue for special results and whether these results will support or endanger their own positions. Our study, like any other game theoretic study, neglects the fact that international negotiations often have to last for longer time periods, since the negotiating parties do not know from the very beginning how the possible results should be evaluated.

In Section 28.2 we briefly introduce bargaining (games) with incomplete information. Section 28.3 provides some examples showing that international bargaining with incomplete information can extend over several negotiation rounds, and the probability of reaching no agreement at all is positive. Our final remarks discuss how our theoretical approach can be used to explain the results of ongoing international negotiations and how their prospects for yielding an agreement could be improved.

28.2. On Bargaining Games with Incomplete Information

To avoid the impression that our approach is restricted to bilateral negotiations, we assume n (> 1) countries trying to reach an international agreement. Information about other countries is incomplete if one does not know their possible moves, the information conditions at all possible stages of the negotiation process and how other countries evaluate the possible negotiation results. It can be shown (Harsanyi, 1967–1968) that all these information deficits can be reflected by not knowing the evaluation of the negotiation results by others.

Imagine, for instance, country i, which does not know whether another country j can really afford the cost of an international agreement reducing its pollution of air and water. This is remodeled by assuming that country j can reduce its pollution in any case, but that one possible "type of country j", would evaluate such a measure as extremely costly, making sure that in equilibrium this type will refrain from signing an agreement imposing such a measure on country j. Thus the expectations of country i concerning country j are adequately reflected by assuming that country i expects two types of country j, of which one will never sign the contract reducing pollution of air and water.

To define more precisely the possible types of the various negotiating countries $1,...,n$, assume that there is a given set $A (\neq \phi)$ of possible bargaining agreements including the status quo c when no agreement is reached. Here a potential agreement a in A with $a \neq c$ has to be seen as a complete description of all possible details of an international contract, e.g., an international customs agreement or the foundation of a common market such as the European Economic Community (EEC). A possible type t_j of country j can then be described as one possible evaluation of all agreements a in A by country j, i.e., t_j is mapping.

$$t_j : a \rightarrow t_j(a) \tag{28.1}$$

Here $t_j(a)$ is the utility/welfare which alternative a yields for type t_j of country j.

Let $T_j(\neq \phi)$ denote the set of possible types t_j of country j (including the true type) as expected by any other country. The main trick of modeling bargaining (games) with incomplete information (Harsanyi, 1967–1968) is to extend the bargaining analysis to all possible type constellations

$$t = (t_1,...,t_n) \in T := T_1 x...x T_n. \tag{28.2}$$

Thus, in analyzing the situation, country j not only considers what it will do given its true type, but also what it would do for any other possible evaluations t_j expected in other countries. In the terminology of game theory, this can be expressed by saying that we do not solve the game with players $1,...,n$, but with all possible types of all countries $1,...,n$ as players.

The game with types as players results by introducing a fictitious initial chance move determining the vector $t = (t_1,...,t_n)$ of types $t_j \in T_j$ of the negotiating countries $j = 1,...,n$. The result of this chance move is assumed to be only partially revealed to individual countries so as to capture the information deficits concerning other countries. So country i will be informed about its own type, but not necessarily about the types t_j of other countries $j(\neq i)$. By the conditional probabilities assigned to the different outcomes $t \in T$, given one's own type, one can, furthermore, reflect all subjective beliefs concerning the types of others [as shown by Selten (1982), one does not have to impose any restrictions on subjective beliefs; for an application of Selten's idea to international politics, see Güth (1985)]. Thus one solves an informationally closed game where incomplete information about types of others is transformed into strategically equivalent stochastic uncertainty resulting from unobservable chance moves.

In *Figure 28.1*, we have graphically visualized a bargaining game with incomplete information where $n = 2$, A contains two possible results — namely, the only possible agreement a and the conflict (no agreement) point c. Player 1 is of one possible type, which evaluates a by a_1 and c by c_1. Player 2 has two possible types t_2 and $\hat{t}_2$ evaluating a and c by $t_2(a)$, $t_2(c)$ and $\hat{t}_2(a)$, $\hat{t}_2(c)$, respectively. Player 1 expects type t_2 with probability p and $\hat{t}_2$ with probability $1 - p$ what is known by player 2. After the chance move determining player 2's type, player 1 has to choose between accepting the only possible agreement a (decision y_1) or not (decision n_1). Then depending on his type player 2 must decide between acceptance of a (decision y_2 and Y_2) or not (decision n_2 and N_2). The only possible agreement a is reached if both players have accepted it.

The obvious solution concept for bargaining games with incomplete information is the (perfect) equilibrium point [Cournot (1838), Nash (1951), Selten (1975)]. For our purposes we can define a (perfect) equilibrium point as a strategy vector for the game with types as players where every player loses by deviating unilaterally. To give an example, consider the game illustrated in *Figure 28.1* where

$$a_1 > c_1, \quad t_2(a) > t_2(c), \quad \hat{t}_2(a) < \hat{t}_2(c). \tag{28.3}$$

Since both player 1 and type t_2 of player 2 prefer a over c, they both will accept the only possible agreement a. Type $\hat{t}_2$ of player 2, however, prefers c to a and therefore chooses N_2. Thus the only (perfect) equilibrium point under the parameter restriction (28.3) is the strategy vector

$$s^* = (s_1^*, s_{t_2}^*, s_{\hat{t}_2}^*) = (y_1, y_2, N_2). \tag{28.4}$$

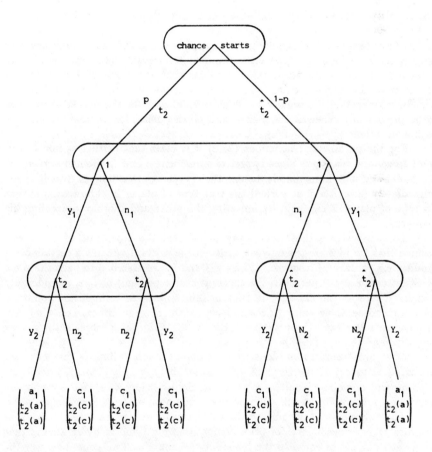

Figure 28.1. A two-person bargaining game with asymmetric incomplete information and one possible agreement a (first chance chooses the type t_2 or $\hat{t}_2$ of player 2 with probability p and $1 - p$, respectively; then player 1 decides between y_1 and n_1 without knowing player 2's type; finally, player 2 chooses between y_2 and n_2 or Y_2 and N_2 depending on his type; payoffs are given in the order 1, t_2, $\hat{t}_2$ at each endpoint)

If t_2 is present, agreement a is reached, whereas in the case of $\hat{t}_2$ conflict c results. It should be mentioned that the probability p of reaching the agreement a reflects only the expectations of player 1. Player 2 knows his own true type and can therefore conclude from the solution (28.4) whether bargaining will yield agreement a or conflict c.

28.3. Type-Revealing and -Concealing Negotiation Processes

Let us first discuss the extreme cases of type-revealing and -concealing negotiations processes where countries either immediately reveal their types or conceal them forever. To demonstrate this, consider that the game of *Figure 28.1* is played not once, but successively for infinitely many periods. Thus, to have an ongoing cooperation, agreement a, which is valid only for the period ahead, has to be periodically renewed [see Selten and Güth (1982), for another example of such a situation].

For the parameter restrictions (28.3) it is clear that neither t_2 nor $\hat{t}_2$ will want to conceal his type. Since t_2 prefers agreement a and $\hat{t}_2$ the non-agreement c, they both will immediately reveal their type so that player 1 will know immediately (after the first period) the true type of player 2. The reason is that no type of player 2 can gain by imitating the other and thereby concealing his own type.

To demonstrate that it can pay to conceal the true type of 2 forever, assume that 1 and 2 are the only countries in the world producing a certain commodity, e.g., a natural resource. Whereas 1 and t_2 are assumed to have the same constant cost c (≥ 0) per unit, the constant cost $\bar{c}$ per unit of $\hat{t}_2$ is considerably higher. There are no capacity restrictions and in case of competition countries have to choose their sales prices independently of each other, i.e., they are engaged in a Bertrand–duopoly game [Bertrand (1883); for a more recent survey see Allen and Hellwig (1986)].

Now, given our assumptions, competition of 1 and t_2 implies that both set prices equal to c and therefore earn 0 profits. If type $\hat{t}_2$ is present, price competition will obviously result in a price marginally below $\bar{c}$ or at the monopoly price, i.e., only country 1 will sell a positive amount and earn a positive profit.

The only possible periodic agreement a can be seen as an attempt to avoid the disastrous consequences of price competition for 1 and t_1 by arranging that both set their prices equal to the monopoly price and sell an equal share of the monopoly sales amount. Let us assume that the monopoly price is only slightly higher than $\bar{c}$ and that country 1 competes with $\hat{t}_2$. In this case country 1 will earn the monopoly profit even without the cooperative agreement a. Country 1 must therefore compare the expected gain from cooperating with t_2 with the expected loss from transferring part of its higher competitive profit to type $\hat{t}_2$.

Provided the market parameters are such that country 1 prefers agreement a to competition c, type $\hat{t}_2$ of country 2 will obviously never want to reveal himself. If country 1 learned that country 2 is of type $\hat{t}_2$, it would immediately stop renewing the agreement periodically and improve upon its result by setting its price marginally below $\bar{c}$. Knowing this, type $\hat{t}_2$ will always want to copy type t_2. Even if country 1 would not accept a for one period in order to learn about country 2's true type, type $\hat{t}_2$ would set his price equal to c in order to convince country 1 that he is not of type $\hat{t}_2$. Here it is, of course, implicitly assumed that $\hat{t}_2$'s discount rate is not too high. If in equilibrium country 1 knows this, it will not invest in such a costly experiment so that $\hat{t}_2$'s costly threat to set his price equal to c will never have to be executed. We therefore have an equilibrium of the infinitely often repeated game of *Figure 28.1* according to which all three players, country 1 and both types of country 2, will always renew the agreement a, and according to which country 1 will never learn whether type t_2 or type $\hat{t}_2$ of country 2 is present.

We now want to describe in a non-technical way how negotiation processes with type-differentiating results, i.e., how different types of the same players reach agreements with differing profitability, require a certain duration of the negotiation process and how more profitable results can be obtained only by facing a higher risk of conflict.

As a theoretical background, we could use the model of sequential bargaining under incomplete information theoretically analyzed by Rubinstein (1985). According to this model one of the two players makes a proposal a_t ($\in A$) in each round $t = 1,2,3,...$, which the other can either accept or reject. Whereas, in the case of acceptance, bargaining ends with the corresponding agreement a_t, rejection implies that now the other player can select a proposal $a_{t+1} (\in A)$ in the next round $t + 1$, etc. Rubinstein, who assumes positive time costs of bargaining, determines all relevant negotiation results by refining the concept of subgame perfect equilibrium points in an intuitive way. On the other hand, it is not straightforward how this analysis can be extended to cover bargaining with more than two players.

An interesting alternative of the model analyzed by Rubinstein is the model of Harsanyi and Selten (1972), who assume that all players $i = 1,...,n$ simultaneously can make a periodic proposal a_t^i and that all previous proposals are binding, i.e., an agreement a in A is reached if now or before all players have accepted it. That is, for all players $i=1,...,n$ there must exist some $\tau \leq t$ such that $a = a_\tau^i$. Bargaining ends with conflict c if in one period t no player i makes a proposal a_t^i which he has not made before, i.e., conflict results from the first negotiation round t without a concession. If A is finite, bargaining will therefore have to end after finitely many rounds of bargaining.

The disadvantage of the Harsanyi–Selten model is that it may have many (perfect) equilibria if the set A contains many agreements that are mutually profitable irrespective of type vector $t = (t_1,...,t_n)$. But as shown by Harsanyi and Selten (1972), one can select one of these equilibria as the solution by imposing some reasonable solution requirements. Here we will use the Harsanyi–Selten model. But instead of describing their solution concept in detail, we will simply rely on properties that any type differentiating equilibrium point has to satisfy.

Type-differentating equilibrium negotiation processes are time-consuming, since a type t_i of player i who reaches a better agreement than another type t_i' of player i must give a risk proof of his superior bargaining power. By a risk proof we mean that t_i is willing to fight for the better result, although this implies a higher risk of conflict. During the negotiation process a risk proof of t_i is typically of the form that, at a certain stage of the process, type t_i repeats an old proposal, i.e., makes no concession, whereas t_i' proposes some new agreement in order to avoid the possible deadlock where no player makes a concession and where conflict c therefore results.

Consider the situation where two bargaining parties 1 and 2 have to divide an amount of 100, i.e., the set A is the set of all possible allocations $a = (a_1, a_2)$ with $a_1 + a_2 = 100$ and $a_1 \geq 0$, $a_2 \geq 0$. Let all possible types $t_i \in T_i$ of party $i = 1,2$ evaluate all agreements a in A with $a \neq c$ by the amount allocated to party i, i.e.,

$$t(a) = (t_1(a), t_2(a)) = a = (a_1, a_2)$$

for all $a \in A$, $a \neq c$. Thus, types $t_i \in T_i$ of player i can only differ with respect to the evaluation $t_i(c)$ of conflict $c \in A$. An an obvious interpretation of such a situation is that one does not know the opportunity costs that an agreement $a(\neq c)$ implies for the others, i.e., how much others can earn in case of no agreement.

In *Figure 28.2* we have illustrated a type-differentiating solution for a situation with $n = 2$ where $t_i(c) = c_i$ is the amount which type t_i of player i receives in case of conflict c. The entries of the matrix are either the amount a_1 allocated to party 1 (if $a \neq c$) or conflict c. Since in the case of an agreement a in A with $a \neq c$ the payoffs a_1 and a_2 add up to 100, one can use a_1 to describe an agreement $a(\neq c)$. In *Figure 28.2* we have determined a_1 by distributing equally the surplus $100 - c_1 - c_2$, i.e.,

$$a_1 = c_1 + (100 - c_1 - c_2)/2.$$

Conflict c is imposed whenever it was impossible to give more than c to both parties.

The time-consuming aspect of type-differentiating solutions can now be illustrated very easily with the help of *Figure 28.2*. Assume that in the first round of bargaining for $i = 1,2$ all types $t_i \in T_i$ of player i propose the agreement a with $a_1 = 90$, i.e., both party 1 and party 2 demand 90 out of 100. Since no agreement a is reached, bargaining has to continue with the second round. If player i is of type t_i with $t_i(c) = 80$, he will repeat his proposal in the second round. Now, if both players $i = 1$ and $i = 2$ are of type $t_i(c) = 80$, this leads to conflict c in the second round of bargaining, since no party has made a concession. On the other hand, a type $t_i(c)$ with $t_i(c) < 80$ will concede by making a

c_2 / c_1	0	20	40	60	80
0	50	40	30	20	10
20	60	50	40	30	c
40	70	60	50	c	c
60	80	70	c	c	c
80	90	c	c	c	c

Figure 28.2. A type-differentiating solution for $n = 2$ in the special situation where for $i = 1,2$ types $t_i \in T_i$ differ only with respect to the evaluation $t_i(c) = c$ of conflict c; the entry of the matrix is either the agreement payoff a_1 of player 1 or c in the case of conflict.

new proposal, e.g., the one by which he demands only 80 for himself. Thus, bargaining can continue although no agreement has been reached in round 2.

Let us mention some possible negotiation processes yielding the results described by *Figure 28.2.* For $c_1 = 90$ and $c_2 = 0$, the bargaining process could be described as in *Table 28.1.*

Table 28.1. A negotiation process yielding the agreement $a = (90, 10)$ with a risk proof for type $t_1(c) = 90$ in round $t = 2$ to $t = 9$ where the agreement is reached.

Round	Proposal by $t_1(c) = 80$	Proposal by $t_2(c) = 0$
1	(90, 10)	(10, 90)
2	(90, 10)	(20, 80)
3	(90, 10)	(30, 70)
4	(90, 10)	(40, 60)
5	(90, 10)	(50, 50)
6	(90, 10)	(60, 40)
7	(90, 10)	(70, 30)
8	(90, 10)	(80, 20)
9	(90, 10)	(90, 10)

The assumption behind *Table 28.1* is that types $t_i(c)$ concede step by step by allocating 10 more to their opponent as long as their own agreement level a_i according to *Table 28.1* has not been reached. In the special case of *Table 28.1* this means that player 2 gives in step by step until the agreement $a = (90, 10)$ is reached.

In *Tables 28.2* and *28.3* we have described negotiating processes where first both players concede and where one player continues to concede until an agreement is reached (*Table 28.2*) or until he also stops to give in (*Table 28.3*).

Table 28.2. A negotiation process yielding the agreement $a = (60, 40)$ where first both players concede, then only player 2 until the agreement is reached.

Round	Proposal by $t_1(c) = 40$	Proposal by $t_2(c) = 20$
1	(90, 10)	(10, 90)
2	(80, 20)	(20, 80)
3	(70, 30)	(30, 70)
4	(60, 40)	(60, 40)
5	(60, 40)	(50, 50)
6	(60, 40)	(60, 40)

Table 28.3. A negotiation process yielding conflict c in the sixth round of bargaining where for the first time no player makes a concession.

Round	Proposal by $t_1(c) = 40$	Proposal by $t_2(c) = 60$
1	(90, 10)	(10, 90)
2	(80, 20)	(20, 80)
3	(70, 30)	(20, 80)
4	(60, 40)	(20, 80)
5	(50, 50)	(20, 80)
6	(50, 50)	(20, 80)

These examples should help to illustrate how time-consuming negotiation processes can yield type-differentiating results involving a considerable risk of facing conflict. What still has to be explained is why players do not reach an agreement immediately, e.g., by proposing immediately the agreement $a(c)$ prescribed by *Figure 28.2*. One reason is, of course, that players do not know their opponent's type. But even if he knew $t_2(c)$, player 1's type, $t_1(c) = 0$ would never get 90, according to *Figure 28.2*, although he first demands 90 for himself, then 80, etc. The reason for this is that the step-by-step concessions imply a risk proof of those players who do not make a concession.

As an example, consider the second round of bargaining in *Table 28.1*. Here player 1 does not concede, although this would imply c if player 2 were of type $t_2(c) = 80$. Similarly, player 1 does not concede in the third round, although c would result in the case of $t_2(c) = 60$, if $t_2(c) = 60$ would repeat his demand of 80. Here it is, of course, essential that the type t_i with bargaining power superior to that of t'_i in the sense of $t_i(c) > t'_i(c)$ is willing to accept the higher risk of conflict whereas the type t'_i will prefer to avoid it. In other words, the higher risk of conflict involved by the attempt to reach a more profitable agreement ensures that the superior type t_i will not be imitated by the weaker type t'_i of player i. That is why we say that a type-differentiating solution has to rely on risk proofs of superior bargaining strength.

Of course, for the examples of type-differentiating negotiation processes described in *Figure 28.2* and *Tables 28.1-3*, one would have to show that a superior type will actually prefer to face the higher risk of conflict c whereas a weaker type prefers to concede. Selten (1975) has analyzed a specific example with $n = 2$ and two possible types for each player in detail and shown that the solution can be a type-differentiating equilibrium point relying on a time-consuming negotiation process.

For an example where $t_1(c) = 80$ is willing to accept a risk proof that $t_1(c) = 60$ does not accept, consider again *Figure 28.2*. Since $t_1(c) = 80$ can either maintain his demand of 90 or decrease his demand to 80, he clearly will prefer not to concede. On the other hand, type $t_2(c) = 60$ can earn 90 only if he meets a player 2 of types $t_2(c) = 0$ whereas the next best result of 80 can be reached in the case of types $t_2(c) = 0$ and $t_2(c) = 20$.

Let $F_2(t_2(c) = c_2)$ denote the probability by which type $t_1(c) = 60$ of player 1 expects player 2 to be of type $t_2(c) = c_2$. Type $t_1(c) = 60$ has to compare the expected dividend $30\, F_2(t_2(c) = 0)$ for not conceding in the second round with the expected dividend $10\{F_2(t_2(c) = 0) + F_2(t_2(c) = 20)\}$ implied by maintaining a demand of 70 starting in the third round. One can easily see that for

$$F_2(t_2(c) = 20) > 2\, F_2(t_2(c) = 0)$$

type $t_1(c) = 60$ of player 1 will prefer to concede $a = (70, 30)$ instead of maintaining his demand for $a = (90, 10)$ by imitating the superior type $t_1(c) = 80$ of player 1. Since the type $t'_1(c)$ with $t'_1(c) < t_1(c)$ will lose more in the case of conflict than $t_1(c)$, he will be less eager than $t_1(c)$ to fight for more ambitious results. Owing to these different incentives of the different types, risk proofs of superior types can support a type-differentiating equilibrium negotiation process.

28.4. Final Remarks

The main conclusion of the above analysis is that often type-differentiating solutions have to rely on risk proofs of types and that such risk proofs require several negotiation rounds and a positive risk of conflict even in the case when mutually profitable agreements exist. In our view many international agreements reveal type-differentiating solutions, since countries that do not care about certain international problems (e.g., pollution of international waters) usually contribute little or nothing to overcome the problem.

Consider, for instance, an international agreement to stop the pollution of the Rhine. Obviously, the tremendous costs of such an endeavor can be covered only if those countries using the Rhine as a water reservoir have a strong interest in improving the quality of their drinking water. One can easily imagine situations where an agreement to stop the pollution of the Rhine can be achieved only if at least some of the countries reveal their strong interests in improving the quality of Rhine water and thereby their willingness to cover a considerable part of the necessary costs. If many countries are engaged, one country will often try to hide its own strong interests in order to make the other countries pay more. Such international negotiations will be a process during which countries strategically hide and reveal their types as illustrated by our analysis above.

Clearly, measures that improve the information about other countries' policies will reduce the need to prove one's type and thereby the risk of conflict, if a mutually profitable agreement exists. It is in this sense that intelligence services and international espionage can be useful, since they might build up trust that other countries keep their promises and do not misrepresent their interests.

Furthermore, if the same countries are engaged in several international negotiations, the possibilities to misrepresent strategically their own type are far more limited, since the *a posteriori* beliefs of earlier negotiations will become the *a priori* beliefs of later ones. This might explain why in reality we observe many international negotiations on rather specific projects instead of more comprehensive ones.

Naturally, incomplete information about other countries will be reduced if there is much international trade, cultural exchange, joint ventures, etc. This indicates that, when beginning international cooperation, negotiations will be more time-consuming and more likely to end in conflict. But after long-established forms of cooperation are in place, international negotiations should almost surely yield early agreements that take into account the true interests of the participating countries.

References

Allen, B. and Hellwig, M. (1986), Bertrand–Edgeworth oligopoly in large markets, *Review of Economic Studies*, 173, pp. 175-204.

Bertrand, J. (1883), Review of "Théorie mathématique de la richesse sociale" and "Recherches sur les principes mathématiques de la théorie des richesses", *Journal des Savants*, pp. 490-508.

Cournot, A. (1838), *Recherches sur les principes mathématiques de la théorie des richesses*, Paris.

Güth, W. (1985), An Extensive Game Approach to Modeling the Nuclear Deterrence Debate, *Journal of Institutional and Theoretical Economics*, 141, pp. 525-538.

Harsanyi, J.C. (1967–1968), Games with Incomplete Information Played by "Bayesian" Players, Parts I–III, *Management Science*, 14, pp. 159-182, 320-334, 486-502.

Harsanyi, J.C. and Selten, R. (1972), A Generalized Nash Solution for Two-Person Bargaining Games with Incomplete Information, *Management Science*, 18, pp. 80-106.

Nash, J.F. (1951), Non-Cooperative Games, *Annals of Mathematics*, 54, pp. 286-295.

Rubinstein, A. (1985), A Bargaining Model with Incomplete Information about Time Preferences, *Econometrica*, 53, pp. 1151-1172.

Selten, R. (1975), Bargaining under Incomplete Information: A Numerical Example, in: O. Becker and R. Richter (eds.), *Deutsche Wirtschaftsanalyse*, pp. 203-232.

Selten, R. (1975), Reexamination of the Perfectness Concept for Equilibrium Points in Extensive Games, *International Journal of Game Theory*, 4, pp. 25-55.

Selten, R. (1982), Einführung in die Theorie der Spiele mit unvollständiger Information, *Schriften des Vereins für Socialpolitik* N.F., 126, pp. 81-148.

Selten, R. and Güth, W. (1982), Game Theoretical Analysis of Wage Bargaining in a Simple Business Cycle Model, *Journal of Mathematical Economics*, 9 , pp. 177-195.

CHAPTER 29

Some Methodological Problems of Modeling International Negotiations

Mark A. Khroustalev

Center for the Systems Analysis of International Affairs
Moscow State Institute of International Relations
Moscow
USSR

29.1. Introduction

Investigations of international negotiations both by Soviet and Western research-ers are characterized by two main approaches: the historical-descriptive and the theoretical-methodological. The gap between these two approaches seems to be increasing. From our point of view the role of the latter is increasing steadily because it aims at reaching forecasting results, which is, in principle, not charac-teristic of the first approach. Within the framework of the second approach, modeling (using computers) has lately begun to play an important role, as it has unique qualifications for verifying hypotheses.

Modeling of social processes (including international negotiations) demands the solution of many theoretical and methodological problems, without which fruitful results will be hard to attain. The key methodological problem is to pro-vide a normative model that guarantees the fulfillment of general scientific requirements such as well-grounded necessity, completeness or sufficiency and, in the final account, the adequacy of any model. Strictly speaking, there can be no absolutely non-normative models, because the scientific consciousness of each researcher or practitioner is based on some sort of theoretical system that is reflected in his education. But when he uses a model intuitively, it may be classified as empirical (created on the basis of experience or "common sense"). It is impossible to prove scientifically the necessity, completeness or sufficiency of such a model.

Generally speaking, all historical-descriptive investigations may be classified as empirical models (very relatively, of course). In this respect their value is primarily factual, but can also be conceptual.

29.2. Levels and Stages of Analysis

Normativeness has three levels: the methodological, the specific-theoretical and the mathematical or technological. This division is based on the well-known philosophical triad: universal, specific and unique.

The methodological level provides normativeness on the basis of some *general laws* of the development and functioning of social systems. But being very abstract these laws cannot be applied directly to concrete processes and phenomena. The way from the *universal* to the particular extends across the *specific theory*, for only with its help can the transition be accomplished from general theoretical conceptions to operational ones suitable for quantitative measurement and experimental verification, the latter requirement being most important.

The modern period of the development of science is characterized by the obvious tendency of the creation of many intradisciplinary and interdisciplinary special theories (the so-called "middle-level" theories), which have now formed a rather complicated system of several dozens of scientific disciplines.

The abstract model is created on a special theoretical level, for its transformation into the concrete model it is necessary to introduce information about the modeled object. This information, as a rule, consists of some peculiarities about the unique features of the object, which play a very important role in modeling social processes. If they are not taken into account, it is difficult to guarantee a high degree of model adequacy.

The transformation of the abstract model into a concrete one by "filling" it with relevant information can be realized normatively (by scientific technology) or empirically (based on "common sense", experience, traditions, etc.). In practice the existing scientific methods (especially, the formalized ones) cannot substitute for the traditional logical-intuitional analysis.

Normativeness is involved not only in the above-mentioned levels, but also in the various stages of modeling. In general, there are three such stages: substantive, formalizing and quantifying, and consequently three types of models.

The starting point of modeling social processes is the creation of a substantive model, which, as stated above, may be empirical or normative and sometimes combined (empirical-normative). The transition from the substantive model to the formalized one is possible only if the former is normative. The formalization of the empirical and combined models has to overcome enormous difficulties. To avoid any misunderstanding, we wish to stress that under formalization we mean the formal-logical organization of the substantive model in its now-mathematical form. This requirement seems to be very important, as the application of mathematical methods often becomes some sort of end in itself.

By unifying the two groups of conceptions in one matrix and filling it with the corresponding information about the object under investigation — international negotiations — a methodological picture results as shown in *Table 29.1*.

Table 29.1. Stages and levels of analysis.

| Level | Stage | | |
	Substantive analysis	Formation	Quantification
Methodological	Philosophy	Social communication theory	Metamathematics
Specific-theoretical	Foreign policy theory	Systems analysis	?
Technological	Traditional information analysis	Content and event analysis, etc.	Factor and correlation analysis, etc.

Further, we shall focus our attention on the two upper levels, especially on the second stage (formalization), for it does not have sufficient definition. The effective use of computers as investigative instruments becomes possible only after the problem of adequate formalization has been solved. It is not by chance that we singled out the theory of social communication on the methodological level of the second stage, but this does not imply its universality. This only signifies that formalization will be conducted on this and on no other basis. However, on the strength of the multiple aspects of international negotiations, the formalized basis may change and, instead of social communication theory, social psychology or decision-making theory may be used. Correspondingly, a change will occur on the specific-theoretical level.

At the same time, the multiple-aspect nature of international negotiations (as with any social process) may be described with the help of a limited number of such scientific disciplines. Naturally, in creating a complete model of international negotiations the use of all these disciplines is necessary to various degrees, but it does not mean they are equivalent in providing model adequacy. Some of them, never having claim to completeness, can guarantee sufficiency; others cannot. It seems to us that social communications theory can guarantee the necessary sufficiency of the model, because it is based on the understanding of international negotiations as a method of finding compromise solutions for disputes among states with the help of social communication (direct, as a rule).

29.3. Key Elements of an International Negotiations Model

Within the framework of this definition, three key elements can be distinguished: contradiction, compromise, and communication.

Contradictions

In general the problems of social contradictions are investigated on the philosophical level, while foreign policy theory studies interstate contradictions, as a special type of social contradictions. If social contradictions are contradictions of social interests, interstate contradictions are contradictions of state interest, which, according to our understanding, constitute a synthesis of social, political and economic interests.

In this connection it must be stressed that the widespread English term "national interest", which has many meanings, is used here in its direct meaning. Its inconsistent use creates some logical confusions, which is absolutely impermissible in the process of formalization.

Social contradictions or disputes are qualified as relations between opposing interests. Depending on the character of these relations, contradictions are divided into antagonistic and non-antagonistic. This division is automatically applied to interstate contradictions. Since antagonistic contradictions cannot be solved by compromise, they naturally cannot be included in the scope of action of negotiations. Such a narrowed scope seems unfounded, as in this case antagonism is regarded as something undiversified and integral. This is not the case with interstate contradictions.

Formalization on the basis of systems analysis within the framework of the proposed matrix ("horizontal" formalization) permits a more correct solution for this problem, building upon and supplementing the substantive model in a certain sense.

Since the nature of the relations between opposed interests depends on their importance for each state or social entity, their systemic grouping will make possible different variants of those relations. The importance of any interest is determined by whether or not it leads to lowering the levels of the social entity's external and internal stability by hindering its functioning and development.

The above-mentioned considerations, may be summed up in terms of three groups or levels of interests: vital, basic and secondary. The proposed grouping is of a very generalized nature, determined by the subject matter of this work, and may easily be decomposed.

1. *Vital interests* are those that, if not realized, cause the social entity (system) to malfunction and/or hinder its development, which unavoidably leads to lesser (internal) stability and/or (external) security.

2. *Basic interests* are those that, if not realized, produce a malfunctioning and hindered development, which may (with greater or lesser probability) produce lesser stability and/or security.

3. *Secondary interests* are those that, if not satisfied, lead to malfunctioning and hindered development, which are not accompanied by lesser stability and/or security.

In short, viability is threatened with certainty, if vital interests are not satisfied; it is (with greater or lesser probability) threatened if basic interests are not satisfied; and it is not affected if secondary interests are not satisfied.

The above classification provides an opportunity to study a spectrum of probable pair-type conjunctions of interests of various levels that produce contradiction or conflict of interests. The matrix form of representation is given in *Figure 29.1.*

Among the nine elements of the matrix, three are identical by the rule of logic $(A_1/B_2 = A_2/B_1; A_1/B_3 = A_3/B_1; A_2/B_3 = A_3/B_2)$. Excluding logical redundancy, six pairs and therefore six types of contradictions or potential conflicts, remain:

1. Vital - vital
2. Vital - basic
3. Vital - secondary
4. Basic - basic
5 Basic - secondary
6. Secondary - secondary

B / A	B_1	B_2	B_3
A_1	A_1/B_1	A_1/B_2	A_1/B_3
A_2	A_2/B_1	A_2/B_2	A_2/B_3
A_3	A_3/B_1	A_3/B_2	A_3/B_3

Figure 29.1. A and B = social subjects (systems) that pose mutually incompatible interests: 1 - vital interests, 2 - basic interests, 3 - secondary interests.

These types of contradiction may be further classified into two groups depending upon whether or not a vital interest is present in a pair. The first three pairs represent antagonistic contradictions, the second three represent non-antagonistic ones. Within the first group, pair 1 (vital - vital) may be described as strictly antagonistic, while pairs 2 and 3 may be characterized as loosely antagonistic.

It is a matter of principle to specify the notion of loose antagonism because contradiction of that type may be solve on the basis of compromise, this possibility widening (at least, in theory) "the sphere" of negotiations.

Of considerable importance is the study of the second (vital - basic) and fourth (basic - basic) pairs, since the well-known psychological phenomenon of overstating one's interest and understating that of one's partner produces a situation in which one or both sides may find a strict antagonism where none exists.

Compromise

Having briefly considered the problems of contradiction, let us examine the second basic element of the above-mentioned definition, compromise, which implies a voluntary or forced exchange of concessions. Concession, in turn, is based upon consent by one of the sides having mutually incompatible interests to the settlement of a contradiction not in its favor — that is, with some interest not being satisfied. The parameter of a concession is determined by the significance of the unsatisfied interest. Vital interests are never subject to voluntary concessions and only in extreme cases may be ceded as a result of a forced concession. That is the case when the other party resorts to dictating a settlement, its extreme form being the ultimatum of unconditional surrender.

However, the compromise based on such a forced concession will always be entirely unstable, since the party that has been forced into the concession will continuously seek to depart from it — in other words, to render meaningless the agreement on which the compromise rests. Such is also the behavior of a party which is being forced to concede a great deal of its basic interests.

In general, any unequal and therefore forced compromise may be described as incapable in principle of resolving contradictions, but rather as postponing the solution, or at best, temporarily solving contradictions.

If an equal (voluntary) compromise is reached, both sides satisfy their vital interests. Their basic interests are satisfied either on an equal basis, or in favor of one of the sides. In the first case the compromise is mutually advantageous; in the second, it is one-sided.

Communication

As a rule, compromise is achieved in the process of negotiations, which are of form of social communication and can be subdivided into the representational and instrumental. Negotiations may further be divided into genuine ones (based upon representational communication) or pseudo- or mock negotiations (based upon instrumental communication).

Negotiations in the sense of representational social communication correspond to the idea of a voluntary compromise (mutually beneficial or one-sided), while the sense of instrumental communication is that they embrace the notion of a fictitious compromise (agreement), or "negotiations for the sake of negotiations". Employing the tactics of mock negotiations, one side or even both (taking the simplest case of a bilateral negotiating) aim at solving some problems other than those that are the subject of the negotiations. As a rule, these tactics are resorted to in order to save time, to start propaganda campaigns, to gain new allies, etc.

29.4. Summary and Discussion

Summing up the above: A probable variety of negotiations approaches and objectives is given by the representation in *Figure 29.2.*

A: Process of negotiation
B: Compromise approach
C: Simulation approach
1:    Mutually-beneficial compromise
2:    One-sided compromise
3:    Fictitious compromise
4:    Procrastination of negotiations

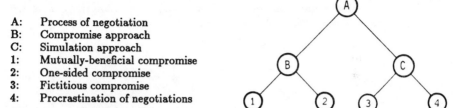

Figure 29.2. Negotiation approaches and objectives.

During the process of negotiations, particularly if they are prolonged owing to the character of the problems involved, either or both sides may change its approach. This may occur, e.g., because of some domestic developments, such as a cabinet change, forthcoming elections etc., or as a result of some changes on the international scene.

As a result, a situation may arise in which, while one side is prepared to offer a mutually beneficial compromise, the other seeks to prolong the negotiations. The various combinations of the sides' approaches in bilateral negotiations amount to six. It is also necessary to take into account the strategy aimed at dictating a settlement.

If the lifespan of an approach is to be taken into account, the number of combinations is even greater. For example, one side may just be starting the process of adopting an approach for a mutually beneficial compromise, while the other is already departing from it. In this case the first side's modified approach may have no impact on the position of the partner, i.e., the short duration of the favorable combination of approaches may render them useless.

Bilateral negotiations provide quite a number of probable combinations of various approaches by the two sides, and this number increases sharply in multilateral negotiations. A purely statistical study of a probable situation, where all the sides in multilateral negotiations adopt a mutually beneficial compromise approach, reveals that such a probability is much less than that of bilateral negotiations. Consequently, multilateral negotiations in general require more time than bilateral ones.

The above idea should not be perceived in a simplified way, because the laws of statistics by their very nature may not directly apply to any given negotiation. However, when CSCE negotiations are considered from this point of view, they provide sufficient grounds for the observation that, in practice, they have become tripartite negotiations. While two groups or "sides" — namely, the NATO and the Warsaw Pact countries — participated in the CSCE process as "already formed" entities from the very start, the third group or side (the neutral and non-aligned countries, or N+N) emerged during the negotiations. Thus, in this case the process of negotiations produced a new political reality, and this phenomenon is no doubt to be explained by some serious political considerations. We thus do not propose to account for it by rationalizing the negotiation process, but one possible manner in which to study such negotiations may be to try to deal with them minus these political components.

CHAPTER 30

Frameworks for Rational Decisions and Conflict Coefficients

Andrzej P. Wierzbicki

Institute of Automatic Control
Warsaw University of Technology
Warsaw
Poland

30.1. Introduction

A better understanding of the evolution of cooperative behavior [see, e.g., Axel-rod (1985)] as well as of the reasons and dynamics of processes that lead to conflict escalation [Wierzbicki (1983)] is today essential, for many known reasons. This understanding is typically hampered by the fact that the concept of rationality is not uniquely defined and is strongly culturally dependent. Thus, in cross-cultural relations, it is easy to misread the intentions of the opposite side and adopt strategies that lead to conflict escalation. The prerequisite for avoiding such traps is the readiness to learn about the other sides' concerns with open-minded tolerance and respect for cultural differences; such learning is one of principal aims of international negotiations.

Among many methods that can contribute to such learning, one group of methods is related to computerized games that simulate certain conflict situations — say, in economics or environmental problems — where playing these games by representatives of various cultures can contribute to a better understanding. Experiments with such games show, however, that mediation in conflicts is an indispensable tool, even in simulated games, if the outcome of such a game should be learning not only about a seeming inevitability of conflict

escalation but also about ways of overcoming conflicts. To support such mediation, methods for decision and mediation support must be extended for situations of plural rationality; the concept of quasisatisficing decisions and rationality is used for this purpose. As one of the positive extensions of the Raiffa concept of a fair compromise solution [see Raiffa (1953), Kalai and Smorodinsky
(1975), Thompson (1980)], the concept of conflict coefficients is adopted and proposed as a tool of supporting fair mediation in plural rationality situations.

  In previous chapters of the author related to this subject, it was shown
[Wierzbicki (1983)] that the nonuniqueness of noncooperative equilibria of games
is a frequent phenomenon that, together with the incompatibility of aspirations
of players, can result either in stabilizing disequilibria conflict outcomes or even
in conflict escalation processes in repetitive games, with outcomes much worse
for everybody than even noncooperative equilibria. Moreover, it was shown
[Wierzbicki (1984)] that the perceptions of the concept of rational behavior are
culturally dependent and thus pluralistic. Therefore, it is difficult to recognize
the incompatibility of aspirations of players and to distinguish a disequilibrium
conflict outcome from a noncooperative equilibrium outcome. As a way of overcoming these difficulties, the concept of quasisatisficing rationality and the use of
conflict coefficients were proposed. This chapter further develops these themes
by classifying more thoroughly various frameworks for rational decisions as well
as by analyzing the concept of conflict coefficients, their relation to cooperative
solutions of games and to order-consistent achievement functions used in
quasisatisficing decision analysis.

30.2. Plural Perceptions of Rationality

The impact of cultural background on the perception of what is rational might
be best illustrated by an episode (actually witnessed by the author) in which a
professor from a highly individualistic culture constructed a simulated game that
involved the social trap of the tragedy of common — the overutilization of a
common environment. A high degree of sophistication, displayed by certain specialists in game theory, was needed to avoid this trap; most representatives of
this culture could not avoid it. However, when played by representatives of a
quite different, collectivist culture, the game was soon made pointless: they proposed jointly to abandon the winning cards that corresponded to environment
overutilization and, when one disagreed, the remaining players abandoned the
privacy of their moves, which made the game trivial.

  The hierarchies of values that are historically established in different cultures do considerably influence the corresponding concept of rationality.
Another example [see Zsolnay and Kiss (1985)] is the differences between the
rationality of the industrialized, individualistic, environment-exploiting West
with moderate population congestion and that of the rural, Buddhist (which does
not mean collectivist but certainly is not individualistic), environment-immersed
East with large population congestion. Differences of basic hierarchies of values
cannot, moreover, be described as simple differences of tastes or preferences; if

we tried, for example, to follow utility theory when describing differences of hierarchies of values, we should have then to use discontinuous utility functions, which would make this theory inoperational.

A modern critical approach to decision theory proposes to replace the calculative or *analytic rationality* (of utility maximization or similar approaches) by deliberative or *holistic rationality*, the "hard" approach by the "soft" approach. The most logically consistent argument for the "soft" or holistic approach was given by Dreyfus (1985). Dreyfus argues — and supports this argument with experimental evidence — that a decision-maker is a learning individual whose way of making decisions depends on the level of expertise attained through learning. A novice needs calculative rationality; an experienced decision-maker uses calculative rationality in the background, while concentrating his attention on novel aspects of a decision situation. An expert does not need calculative rationality: in a known decision situation, he arrives at best decisions immediately, by absorbing (and intuitively processing, presumably in a parallel, still unknown way) all pertinent information. A master expert, while subconsciously making best decisions, continuously searches for "new angles" — for new aspects or perspectives, motivated by the disturbing feeling that not everything is understood, the feeling that culminates and ends in the "aha" or *"eureka" effect* of perceiving a new perspective. Thus, the holistic approach can be understood as the *rationality of the culture of experts*.

While accepting these arguments, we cannot use the holistic rationality prescriptions directly for dealing with cross-cultural conflicts; for who is a master expert on the hierarchies of values in various cultures? The history of diplomacy is full of blunders that resulted from insufficient cross-cultural experience. However, there is one element of paradigm shift that can be extracted from the holistic rationality perspective: the value of learning in decision-making is paramount, and *the main purpose of analytical approaches should not be to propose optimal decisions but to support learning*.

There are several frameworks for analytic rationality; most of these, after deeper analysis, turn out to be culturally dependent. The *utility maximization framework* has been long considered as expressing an universal rationality, as the basis of decision analysis; every other framework would be termed "not quite rational". The abstract aspects of this framework are the most developed and a monograph of several volumes would be needed to summarize them. Without attempting to do so, three points should be stressed here. First, the utility maximization framework is not universal, it is culturally dependent. Second, its descriptive powers are rather limited. Third, it is difficult to account for and to support learning within this framework.

As to the first point, consider the continuity assumptions made in the expected utility theory. A cornerstone assumption in this theory is that, given three ordered probability distributions of decision outcomes, no matter how disastrous the worst of them might be, there exist always probabilistic mixtures (lotteries) of the best and the worst outcomes such that these mixtures can dominate and be dominated by the middle alternative. Accordingly, the following question is admissible in this theory: "What should be a non-zero probability z such that you would bet 10 dollars on the lottery of $1-z$ chances of winning a billion dollars and z chances of nuclear war?" Many cultures would deny the validity of such a question on the grounds that this probability should be zero, that we cannot compare values that should be hierarchically ordered. Thus, *utility theory represents a cultural background* where everything, if not forbidden by law or ethics (which aspects are placed outside of the theory following the tradition of neopositivistic philosophy), can be measured on a common evaluating scale — say, by money. This is *the culture* of classical economics, *of an entrepreneur facing an infinite market* and supported by its "invisible hand" — provided he abides by law and religion and does not encounter disastrous alternatives that lead to new moral dilemmas. But what about political situations that might involve changing laws? What about cross-cultural situations where laws and religions are diverse?

As to the second point, there were many attempts by utility theorists to accommodate the paradox of Allois (1953). Consider four alternative lotteries: the first consisting of winning $1 million with probability 1.00; the second consisting of winning nothing with probability 0.01, winning $1 million with probability 0.89 and winning $5 million with probability 0.10; the third consisting of winning nothing with probability 0.90 and winning $5 million with probability 0.10; and the fourth of winning nothing with probability 0.89 and winning $1 million with probability 0.11. Consider two choices: one between the first and the second lottery and the second between the third and the fourth lottery. Most people asked about such choices would prefer the first to the second lottery and the third to the fourth lottery. But there does not exist any utility function consistent with both such choices.

Of many attempts to explain such a paradox, the most consistent with other experimental evidence is abandoning the basic assumption of independence. Let us assume, as supported by numerous empirical studies, that people do develop adaptively *aspiration levels* that might depend on the alternatives presented to them and that they use these aspiration levels when evaluating alternatives. Thus, their utility functions are nonstationary and change from case to case. Suppose, moreover, that people feel strong "regret" [see, e.g., Kahneman *et al.* (1982)] when the actual outcomes fall below their aspirations. Then a nonstationary, aspiration-dependent form of utility function might be as follows:

$$u(y, \bar{y}) = \begin{cases} (y - \bar{y})/\Delta y, & \text{if } y \geq \bar{y} \\ 100(y - \bar{y})/\Delta y, & \text{if } y < \bar{y} \end{cases} \qquad (30.1)$$

where $\bar{y}$ is the adaptable aspiration level, y the actual outcome, and Δy a range of outcomes (included in order to obtain an independence of affine transformations of variables in this function), say, $\Delta y = \$5$ million in this example. If we take reasonable aspiration levels to be determined by minimal expected values, that is, $\bar{y}' = \$1$ million for the first choice between the lotteries one and two and $\bar{y}'' = \$0.11$ million for the second choice between the lotteries three and four, the expected values of the nonclassical utility function (30.1) perfectly explain the typical preferences in these choices. If we assume that aspiration levels might depend on other experiences of the decision-maker — say, his accumulated wealth — we can explain also why a small number of people might actually prefer the second to the first lottery.

The third point is actually related to the above explanation of the Allois paradox: when trying to account for learning, we cannot assume utility function forms that are independent of available alternatives. The right of a decision-maker to change his mind when he has learned a new fact implies that his utility function might change from case to case and he might be inconsistent. Thus, the basic requirement of consistency of rational decisions, typical for utility theory, is inconsistent itself with the requirement that analytical frameworks for rational decisions should first support learning. A contemporary challenge for utility theory is to develop such modifications of this theory that would incorporate the processes and effects of learning. One of the ways of doing so might be a consistent study of the effects of aspiration levels on preferences.

This challenge is, actually, not quite new: it was raised over 20 years ago by the *satisficing rationality framework*, proposed by Simon (1958) and by many others that followed the *behavioral* criticism of the *normative* decision theory based on utility maximization [see also Simon (1958) for a review of the main points of this criticism]. This framework started with the empirical observation that people do form adaptive aspiration levels by learning and use these aspirations to guide their decisions. Very often, they cease to optimize upon reaching outcomes consistent with aspirations and thus make *satisficing decisions*. However, when building a rationale for such observed behavior, this framework postulated that people *cannot maximize* for three reasons: the cost of computing optimal solutions in complex situations; the uncertainty of decision outcomes that makes most complex optimizations too difficult; and the complexity of decision situations in large industrial and administrative organizations that induces the decision-makers to follow some well-established *decision rules* that can be behaviorally observed and often coincide with satisficing decision-making. This discussion on whether and in what circumstances people could optimize substantiated the term *bounded rationality* (which implies misleadingly that this is somewhat less than full rationality) applied to satisficing behavior and drew attention away from the essential points of learning and forming aspiration levels.

Meanwhile, two of the reasons for not optimizing quoted above have lost their relevance. The development of computers and computational methods of optimization, including stochastic optimization techniques, has considerably decreased the cost and increased the possibilities of calculative optimization. Moreover, the empirical results of holistic rationality indicate that expert decision-makers can easily determine best solutions in very complex situations even if they do not use calculative optimization. The third reason, supported by empirical observations, remains valid: *satisficing rationality is typical for the culture of big industrial and administrative organizations* (see also Galbraith, 1967). However, today it can be differently interpreted: the appropriate question seems to be *not whether people could, but whether they should maximize.*

Any intelligent man, after some quarrels with his wife, learns that maximization is not always the best norm of behavior; children learn best from conflicts among themselves that cooperative behavior is socially desirable and that they must restrict natural tendencies to maximization in certain situations. In any nontrivial game with the number of participants less than infinity, a cooperative outcome is typically much better for all participants than an outcome resulting from individual maximization. This situation is called a *social trap* and motivated much research that recently gave results of paradigm-shifting importance.

There are several basic types of social trap situation; among these, the most important seem to be the *tragedy of commons* and a similar, though more exacerbated *prisoner's dilemma*, in both of which an "individually rational" (read: resulting from individual maximization) solution gives much worse outcomes than a cooperative solution. Further exacerbation of these prototype situations leads to a qualitative change of their structure, typical for the *game of chicken* or *battle of the sexes* situation, where the individually maximizing solution ceases to be unique; this is the prototype of conflict escalation situations, discussed further in some detail. Rapoport (1985) gives a much more thorough classification of various social trap situations that have been studied both empirically and abstractly; however, he concentrates on strategies for playing games of the repetitive prisoner's dilemma type.

A finite number repetition of a prisoner's dilemma game does not change its properties; an infinite number of repetitions would change the qualitative character of the game. An essential change of the qualitative character, however, occurs when a repetitive prisoner's dilemma game is played in an evolutionary sense, that is, if various strategies for playing such a game, if successful, can multiply. This changes also the concept of an equilibrium of such a game; an equilibrium is not an assembly of individually maximizing strategies, but a strategy that remains successful in the evolutionary sense [see Maynard-Smith (1982)]. It turns out that evolutionary stable strategies include some strategies of a cooperative type. To analyze such strategies empirically, Axelrod (1985) organized several computer-simulated tournaments of evolutionary-type strategies for repetitive prisoner's dilemma games; a consistent winner in these tournaments was a cooperative-type strategy proposed by Rapoport and called tit-for-tat. This strategy assumes cooperation at the first encounter and, if the other side also cooperates, continuing cooperation; if the other side defects (cheats), it is punished in the tit-for-tat strategy by defection at the next encounter, but only once: the tit-for-tat strategy is forgiving and attempts to cooperate anew after punishment. This evolutionary stable strategy can be characterized as non-naive cooperativeness or altruism.

These remarkable results indicate a major paradigm shift. Neither short-term nor long-term maximization can rationally resolve the repetitive prisoner's dilemma. The introduction of a different type of *evolutionary rationality* gives a resolution to this dilemma. Moreover, evolutionary rationality is not based on maximization. In fact, it relaces maximization by some evolutionarily successful decision rule — a norm of cooperative behavior that is placed hierarchically higher than the tendency to maximize and plays a role of a moral principle. In the century of neopositivism, it is the first case when principles of an ethical type have been derived rationally by applying mathematical methods. By extrapolating these results, we arrive at the conclusion that in many more complex multi-actor decision situations, it might be rational — in the evolutionary sense — to forego maximization for the good reasons of avoiding a social trap or conflict escalation. Hence, the importance of the question of *whether we should maximize*, where "should" is understood in a normative evolutionary sense.

The importance of this question has been recognized by another analytical, culturally determined framework for rational decision making — that of *goal- and program-oriented planning* [see Glushkov (1972), Pospelov and Irikov (1976)], which represents the culture of collective economic or engineering planning. This framework is not restricted to planned economy countries; in fact, it had been independently developed — with some differences — as the *goals programming technique* [see Charnes and Cooper (1975), among many others], or later rediscovered in a different context [see Umpleby (1983)]. The goal- and program- oriented planning approach specifies two hierarchial levels of objectives: the upper-level objectives, called goals — for which desired values are specified, in a sense similar to aspiration levels, only less adaptable; and the lower-level objectives, called means — which are, in a sense, equivalent to decisions, but the actual decisions correspond typically to the allocation of means. Given means are then allocated — either holistically, by experts, or by using an optimization technique — to come as close as possibly to the given goals, which are typically not attainable. If the goals cannot be attained, modifications of means are considered until either the goals can be reached, or there are no further reserves in means. If the goals can be attained, no further optimization is performed; in this aspect, goal- and program-oriented planning is similar to satisficing decision-making. However, it differs from satisficing decision-making by the deliberate use of optimization techniques. There is no doubt in this approach that optimization techniques can be used; the question is whether they should be used upon attaining goals. This difference from the satisficing approach is particularly visible in the goal-programming technique, which has been sometimes classified as a type of satisficing decision-making. However, this technique is, in fact, an optimization method; thus, it contradicts one of the basic assumptions of satisficing.

When trying to incorporate the lessons from the perspective of evolutionary rationality, however, another question must be raised: why should we stop maximizing upon reaching goals? We should stop maximizing for good reasons, such as avoiding social traps or conflict escalation, but reaching given goals is not necessarily a good reason — perhaps the goals have been inadequately specified. When following the lessons from the perspective of holistic rationality — that the most important function of calculative rationality is as a support in learning — we should rather present to the learning decision-maker some alternative solutions, at least one efficient solution corresponding to a consistent maximization above given goals and another solution corresponding to just reaching goals. The decision-maker himself should decide whether there are good reasons for stopping maximization.

To support decisions that might be either maximizing or not, depending on a conscious choice by a decision-maker who might adhere to either a maximizing, or satisficing, or goal- and program-oriented perception of rationality, a generalized framework of analytical rationality has been proposed by the author [see, e.g., Wierzbicki (1984)] and called *quasisatisficing decision-making*. This framework also incorporates the conclusions derived from the holistic perspective: it assumes that the main purpose of analytical decision support is learning; hence, any approximations to utility functions must be nonstationary. From the satisficing framework, it takes the basic concept of aspiration levels and uses them in a similar way as in the goal programming technique — with the distinction that the maximization is not necessarily stopped when the aspiration levels are reached and, thus, efficient solutions can be always computed and proposed to the decision-maker.

We say that a decision-maker behaves in a quasisatisficing way if, aware of his objectives or decision attributes (with a possible distinction between primary and secondary objectives, such as in the goal- and program-oriented decision making), aware of scales of attainability of these objectives, aware of his aspirations (together with possible distinctions between various types of aspiration levels, such as reservation levels or goal levels), he tries to reach the aspiration levels by maximizing when the outcomes of admissible decisions fall below these levels; but, when the aspiration levels are attained, he can choose either to further maximize or to stop maximization for additional good reasons. Moreover, the quasisatisficing decision-maker is learning: he can change the specifications of his objectives, collect the information about their scales of attainability, and modify his aspiration levels. In this learning process, he might be supported by a computerized system that constructs simple nonstationary approximations to his changing utility function, based mostly on the information about his aspiration levels, and calculates either efficient decisions resulting from the maximization of these approximations, or just satisficing decisions.

Such approximations to changing utility functions are called *order-consistent achievement functions* [see, e.g., Wierzbicki (1986)]. Among many possible forms of achievement functions, a useful form is based on the information about four points on the scale of every objective or attribute: two of these points represent some (not necessarily tight) bounds on the range of attainability $y_{i,\min}$, $y_{i,\max}$, and two other points are a reservation level $\bar{y}_i'$ and an aspiration (goal) level $\bar{y}_i''$, where $y_{i,\min} < \bar{y}_i' < y_i'' < y_{i,\max}$ for each of p attributes, $i = 1,...p$. The achievement function is then constructed while accepting the following assumptions:

(a) The decision-maker prefers outcomes that satisfy all his reservation levels to any outcome that does not satisfy at least one of his reservation levels; similarly for aspiration levels.

(b) The satisfaction of the decision-maker at reaching (all, or the last of) his reservation levels can be measured by 0, while his satisfaction at reaching (all, or the last of) his aspiration levels can be measured by 1.

(c) The satisfaction of the decision-maker at reaching the maximum of the range of all outcomes can be measured by $1 +$, where $a > 0$ is a parameter (if $a = 0$, then the decision-maker behaves in a strict satisficing way); the dissatisfaction of the decision-maker at reaching the minimum of the range of at least one of the outcomes can be measured by $-b$, where $b > 0$ is another parameter.

(d) If an attribute shows underachievement when compared to its reservation (or aspiration) level, and other attributes show overachievements, the decision-maker is willing to accept a compensation of the underachievement by the average overachievement in other attributes (all measured relative to the scales implied by points $(y_{i,min}, \bar{y}_i{}', \bar{y}'',y_{i,max})$ with a weighting coefficient c, where $0 < c < p$.

(e) Since all available information for the construction of this special utility function has been already used, the simplest form of this function that would satisfy (a), (b), (c), (d), obtained through linear interpolation, is postulated. Such a function has the following form:

$$u_i(y_i) = \begin{cases} b((y_i - y_{i,min})/(\bar{y}_i{}' - y_{i,min}) - 1), & \text{if } y_{i,min} \leq y_i \leq \bar{y}_i{}' \\ (y_i - \bar{y}_i{}')/(\bar{y}_i{}'' - \bar{y}_i{}'), & \text{if } \bar{y}_i{}' < y_i < \bar{y}_i{}'' \\ a(y_i - \bar{y}_i{}'')/(y_{i,max} - \bar{y}_i{}'') + 1, & \text{if } \bar{y}_i{}'' \leq y_i \leq y_{i,max} \end{cases} \tag{30.2}$$

while the aggregation is defined by:

$$s(y, \bar{y}'\, \bar{y}') = u(y) = \left(\min_{1 \leq i \leq p} u_i(y_i) + (c/p) \sum_{i=1}^{p} u_i(y_i)\right) / (1 + c) \tag{30.3}$$

This achievement function can be interpreted as a cardinal utility function, since it is independent of affine transformations of the scales of attributes. Its maxima are not only efficient, but also properly efficient [with trade-off coefficients bounded *a priori* by c and $1/c$; see Wierzbicki (1986)]. Its level sets approximate from outside the shifted positive cone R_+^p. Functions of similar types have been extensively used in so-called DIDAS, decision support systems, [see, e.g., Grauer, Lewandowski, and Wierzbicki (1982)], as well as in the SCDAS decision support system [see, Lewandowski, Johnson, and Wierzbicki (1986)].

30.3. Conflict Coefficients for Mediation Support

In simulated games used for illustration of social traps and related phenomena, it occurs quite often that Nash equilibria resulting from unilateral maximizations of utility of all players are not unique (as in the prototype cases of "the game of chicken" or "battle of the sexes", where there is a small, finite number of equilibria; in more complicated examples, there might even be infinite numbers of equilibria). Each player can then select a strategy corresponding to an equilibrium that appears rational to him.

Typically, however, these selections do not correspond to one equilibrium (for example, because of incompatibility of aspirations of players) and the resulting multistrategy does not result in an equilibrium. Typically, its results are much worse than expected by all players. In a repetitive game. this can lead to a process of *conflict escalation*, that is, going away from equilibrium outcomes with worsening of results [see Wierzbicki (1984)]. Playing such a game is quite instructive for the players; but we must also show them ways of overcoming this trap of conflict escalation. For this purpose, a negotiating or mediating procedure must be introduced. To support such a procedure, the concept of conflict coefficients [see Wierzbicki (1986)] is useful. These conflict coefficients generalize — for the case of nonconvex sets of attainable objectives, for the case of multiple objectives of each player, as well for the case of various decision situations, including noncooperative equilibria and conflict escalation cases — the concept of the Raiffa cooperative solution [see Raiffa (1953), Kalai and Smorodinsky (1975), Thompson (1980)].

Consider an assembly of p objectives of m players, and suppose all objectives are maximized. We shall first analyze the case when $m = p$ and each player has just one objective that can be interpreted as his utility function; later, we will analyze a more general case. Let $Y \subset \mathbf{R}^p$ denote the set of attainable objectives under admissible multidecisions, that is, the assemblies of decisions of all players. Typically, this set is given implicitly by a set of admissible multidecisions X and an outcome mapping $f: X \rightarrow \mathbf{R}^p$ where $Y = f(X)$, but we need for this discussion only the relations in the objective or outcome space. Let $\bar{y} \in Y$ denote a *status quo* outcome — called also disagreement outcome [see Roth (1979)]. For each $y \in Y$ and $\bar{y} \in Y$, define the following coefficient of deviation from ideal (or utopia) outcomes:

$$d(y,\bar{y}) = \max_{1 \leq i \leq p} \; (y_{i,\max}(\bar{y}) - y_i) \, / \, (y_{i,\max}(\bar{y}) - \bar{y}_i) \qquad (30.4)$$

where:

$$y_{i,\max}(\bar{y}) = \max_{y \in Y(\bar{y})} y_i; \quad Y(\bar{y}) = \{y \in Y : y_i \geq \bar{y}_i, \, i = 1,...p\} \qquad (30.5)$$

are the components of the ideal or utopia point $y_{\max}(\bar{y}) = (y_{1,\max}(\bar{y}),...y_{i,\max}(\bar{y}),...y_{p,\max}(\bar{y}))$ relative to the *status quo* point $\bar{y}$. If these components would be jointly attainable, $y_{\max}(\bar{y}) \in Y(\bar{y})$, then by choosing $y = y_{\max}(\bar{y})$ we could make the deviation coefficient $d(y,\bar{y}) = 0$ and there would be no conflict between the objectives of the players. Typically, however, $y_{\max}(\bar{y}) \notin Y(\bar{y})$, the utopia point is not attainable. The drawback of the deviation coefficient $d(y,\bar{y})$ is that it depends on the dimension p of the space of objectives. To correct for this dependence, we can follow the suggestion of Kreglewski (1984) and use the following transformation to define the *current conflict coefficient* (more precisely, the conflict coefficient measured at the current outcome y relative to the status quo outcome $\bar{y}$):

$$c(y,\bar{y}) = 2d(y,\bar{y}) + (p(p-2)/(p-1))d(y,\bar{y})(d(y,\bar{y}) - 1) \qquad (30.6)$$

This transformation is needed because we would like to have $c(y,\bar{y}) = 1$ if

$$y_i - \bar{y}_i = (1/p) \sum_{i=1}^{p} (y_{i,\max}(\bar{y}) - y_i) \quad \text{for all} \quad i = 1,...p \tag{30.7}$$

which corresponds to a good intuitive interpretation of measuring the conflict by 1 if the players have to accept the simplest compromise between objectives; whereas $d(y, \bar{y}) = (p-1)/p$ in this case; by postulating $c(y, \bar{y}) = 0$ if $y = y_{\max}(\bar{y})$ and $d(y, \bar{y}) = 0$, $c(y, \bar{y}) = 2$ if $y = \bar{y}$ and $d(y, \bar{y}) = 1$, and by assuming the simplest quadratic transformation that meets all these three requirements, we obtain the formula (30.6).

The interpretation of the current conflict coefficient is as follows. The components $y_{i,\max}(\bar{y})$ of the utopia point relative to status quo point measure the maximal attainable improvement for the ith player, provided all players cooperatively concentrate on this improvement, but all other players do not accept results worse than their status quo components. The current conflict coefficient measures, in relative units, the distance of a current outcome y from this particular utopia point. Values such that $0 \leq c(y, \bar{y}) \leq 1$ indicate that the current point y gives to every player improvements at least as good as the simplest compromise (30.7); values $1 < c(y, \bar{y}) < 2$ indicate that there is some improvement over the current status quo point, but worse than the simplest compromise (30.7); finally, values $c(y, \bar{y}) > 2$ indicate that y is worse than the status quo point, possibly as a result of conflict escalation. Thus, the current conflict coefficient can be used when simulating games to indicate to all players the intensity of the current conflict situation.

For further applications in mediation and negotiation processes, we can define the minimal cooperative conflict coefficient (more precisely, the minimum of the conflict coefficient, which in this case is always attained at a cooperative, weakly efficient solution):

$$c_c(\bar{y}) = \min_{y \in Y(\bar{y})} c(y, \bar{y}) \tag{30.8}$$

which can be interpreted as an indicator of the cooperative decision and outcome that minimizes conflict, given the status quo outcome $\bar{y}$. The minimal cooperative conflict coefficient has the following properties [see Wierzbicki (1984), Bronisz and Krus (1986), Bronisz, Krus, Wierzbicki (1987)]:

Theorem 1

If Y is convex compact and $m = p$, then the minimum in (30.8) is attained at the Raiffa cooperative solution and is thus (at least weakly) efficient. If Y is compact, then $0 \leq c_c(\bar{y}) \leq 1$; if Y convex, $c_c(\bar{y}) = 1$, if the part of the efficient boundary of Y dominating $\bar{y}$ is a linear manifold, and $c_c(\bar{y}) \leq 2$ for nonconvex Y.

Recall that the Raiffa cooperative solution can be also characterized by the axioms of invariance under positive affine transformations of utility, of symmetry, of weak Pareto optimality (weak efficiency), and of individual monotonicity — see Thompson (1980) and Bronisz, Krus, Wierzbicki (1987). The use of conflict coefficients generalizes the Raiffa solution for nonconvex Y. The weak efficiency property can be considered a drawback of the Raiffa solution; when using the concept of conflict coefficients, we can propose two specifications of the Raiffa solution that are always efficient (Pareto optimal, not weakly Pareto optimal). The first specification consists in supplementing the max term in (30.4) by a linear term with a small coefficient, such as in (30.3); observe that the deviation coefficient (30.4) can be interpreted as a special case (with changed sign) of the achievement function (30.3). After such modification, all minima of the corresponding conflict coefficient $c(y, \bar{y})$ are not only efficient, but also properly efficient (with bounded trade-off coefficients). The second specification consists in using the conflict coefficient without modifications as defined by (30.4) and (30.6), but supplementing its minimization over $Y(\bar{y})$ by a lexicographic maximin principle — see Rawls (1971); Bronisz, Krus, Lopuch, (1987).

Another possible generalization is the use of the conflict coefficients in preventing conflict escalation even if there is no possibility of cooperative action and only noncooperative Nash equilibria must be considered as possible final outcomes. Suppose there are many such equilibria; thus, conflict escalation can occur. Let $Y_N \subset Y$ denote the set of all outcomes corresponding to nonunique Nash noncooperative equilibria in the game. Since a conflict escalation process can lead to a status quo outcome $\bar{y}$ that is dominated by points in Y_N, a relevant question might be how to support negotiation and mediation that would lead even to jointly acceptable noncooperative equilibrium. We can use then a suitable modification of the definition of the conflict coefficient: Y should be replaced by Y_N in the formulae (30.5) to (30.8) to define the *minimal noncooperative conflict coefficient* $c_n(\bar{y})$. Most of the properties of $c_c(\bar{y})$ can be suitably modified for this case.

30.4. Conflict Coefficient for Multi-Objective Games Situations and Interactive Mediation Processes

We consider here a case when each player has p_i objectives, that is, $p = \sum_{i=1}^{m} p_i > m$, and assume — say, because of cultural differences between players — that the objectives of a player cannot be consistently aggregated into a utility function. If the players have multiple objectives, they could try to manipulate the outcomes of a mediation process by aggregating or disaggregating their objectives — that is, by changing the number of them. The results of Bronisz and Krus (1986) on the generalizations of the Raiffa solution for this case indicate that a manipulation-free mediation process can be organized by asking each player to define an aspiration point in the space of their objectives and defining a *conflict coefficient relative to aspirations*, in the following way.

Let $y = (y_i, ... y_i, ... y_m) \in \mathbf{R}^p$ denote the joint outcome for all players, $y_i \in \mathbf{R}^{p_i}$ denoting the outcome vectors and $y_{i,j}$ single outcomes for individual players. Let the attainable outcome set $Y \subset \mathbf{R}^p$ and a status quo point $\bar{y} \in Y$ be given. Suppose a player defines his aspiration point $\tilde{y}_i \in \mathbf{R}^{p_i}$. By maximizing — over $y \in Y(\bar{y})$ defined similarly as in (30.5) — the following achievement function:

$$s_i(y_i, \tilde{y}_i, \bar{y}_i) = \min_{1 \leq j \leq p_i} s_{i,j}(y_i, \tilde{y}_i, \bar{y}_i) + (\epsilon/p_i) \sum_{j=1}^{p_i} s_{i,j}(y_i, \tilde{y}_i, \bar{y}_i) \qquad (30.9)$$

where

$$s_{i,j}(y_i, \tilde{y}_i, \bar{y}_i) = (y_{i,j} - \tilde{y}_{i,j})/(\tilde{y}_{i,j} - \bar{y}_{i,j}) \qquad (30.10)$$

with some small $\epsilon > 0$, a decision support system can compute an attainable and efficient outcome:

$$y_{i,\max}(\tilde{y}, \bar{y}) \in Arg \max_{y_i: y \in Y(\bar{y})} s_i(y_i, \tilde{y}_i, \bar{y}_i) \qquad (30.11)$$

This outcome is, in a sense [see Wierzbicki (1986)] the best attainable response to the aspirations of the player (if the player does not like this response, he can modify it by changing his aspirations — although he clearly cannot obtain unattainable outcomes just by increasing aspirations) under the assumption, however, that the moves of all other players contribute to attaining this outcome as long as other players' outcomes are not worse than the corresponding components of the status quo point $\bar{y}$. Therefore, the outcome $y_{i,\max}(\tilde{y}, \bar{y})$ is not a reasonable outcome of the bargaining process; a vector $y_{\max}(\tilde{y}, \bar{y}) = (y_{1,\max}(\tilde{y}, \bar{y}), ... y_{i,\max}(\tilde{y}, \bar{y}), ... y_{m,\max}(\tilde{y}, \bar{y}))$ composed of these outcomes is typically not attainable and thus will be called an *utopia point relative to aspirations;* the subvectors $y_{i,\max}(\tilde{y}, \bar{y})$ are called here *individual utopia point components.*

Observe that the differences $y_{i,\max}(\tilde{y}, \bar{y}) - \bar{y}_i$ between the individual utopia point components and the corresponding status quo components constitute directions of improvement desirable for the ith player. Observe also that, if the set Y is convex, the simple compromise point:

$$y = \bar{y} + (1/m)[y_{\max}(\tilde{y}, \bar{y}) - \bar{y}] \qquad (30.12)$$

belongs to this set and is attainable.

Thus, we can assume that each player can agree to a joint outcome moving in the direction $y_{\max}(\tilde{y}, \bar{y}) - \bar{y}$ if the stepsize coefficient in this direction does not exceed a scalar value $\alpha = \min(\alpha_1, .. \alpha_i, .. \alpha_m)$ where α_i are *confidence coefficients* specified by players. This *principle of limited confidence* [see Fandel and Wierzbicki (1985), Bronisz, Krus, Wierzbicki (1987)] can be interpreted as the fact that, in many practical applications, the players do not have full confidence in their ability to describe and predict precisely the consequences of their decisions and possible outcomes; thus they prefer to proceed cautiously in negotiations and try to limit the improvements of outcomes of other players. The use of the minimal confidence coefficient follows from the fact that a unanimous agreement is needed for any cooperative improvement of the status quo point. Reasonable values of the confidence coefficient for this multicriteria game in the convex case are at best between 0 and y_m; while admitting a more general case and a technical adjustment of the confidence coefficients, however, we can consider all confidence coefficient values between 0 and 1.

For this purpose, we define first the coefficient of deviation from the utopia point relative to aspirations:

$$d(y, \tilde{y}, \bar{y}) = \max_{1 \leq i \leq m} \max_{1 \leq j \leq p_i} (y_{i,j,\max}(\tilde{y}, \bar{y}) - y_i)/(y_{i,j,\max}(\tilde{y}, \bar{y}) - \bar{y}_i) \qquad (30.13)$$

and observe that, if we move along the direction $y_{\max}(\tilde{y}, \bar{y}) - \bar{y}$, the minimal value of this deviation coefficient and the maximal step-size for attainable outcomes in this direction sum up to 1. Thus, we can define:

$$\alpha_{\max} = 1 - \min_{y \in Y(\bar{y})} d(y, \tilde{y}, \bar{y}) \qquad (30.14)$$

and admit any confidence coefficients that are not larger than $\alpha_{\max}$. Moreover, we can as well generalize the concept of the conflict coefficient to the multiobjective case, relative to the aspiration levels of the players:

$$c(y, \tilde{y}, \bar{y}) = 2d(y, \tilde{y}, \bar{y}) + (m(m-2))/(m-1)d(y, \tilde{y}, \bar{y})(d(y, \tilde{y}, \bar{y}) - 1) \qquad (30.15)$$

This conflict coefficient has properties similar to those specified in Theorem 1; its minimal value can be determined together with $\alpha_{\max}$:

$$c_c(\tilde{y}, \bar{y}) = \min_{y \in Y(\bar{y})} c(y, \tilde{y}, \bar{y}) \qquad (30.16)$$

$$= 2(1 - \alpha_{\max}) - (m(m-2)/(m-1))\alpha_{\max}(1 - \alpha_{\max})$$

and the following theorem holds:

Theorem 2

If $Y(\bar{y})$ is compact, then the minimum in (30.15) is attained at a weakly efficient solution, generalizing the Raiffa cooperative solution. Moreover, $0 \leq c_c(\hat{y}, \bar{y}) \leq 1$ if Y is convex, $c_c(\hat{y}, \bar{y}) = 1$ if the part of the efficient boundary of Y dominating $\bar{y}$ is a linear manifold, and $c_c(\hat{y}, \bar{y}) \leq 2$ for nonconvex Y.

While using the principle of limited confidence supplemented by the concept of the minimal conflict coefficient or the maximal confidence coefficient, we can construct an interactive process of negotiations (supported by a mediator or a mediating decision support system). Each round of negotiations, t, starts from the current status quo point $\bar{y}^t$. Each negotiator (player) specifies, in confidence to the mediator, his current aspiration point in the space of his objectives, $\tilde{y}_i^t$, and his current confidence coefficient, α_i^t. The mediator — either by holistic, deliberating reasoning, or using a decision support system with the model of the game — determines the individual utopia components relative to aspirations (which he communicates confidentially to individual negotiators). The maximal confidence coefficient α_{max}^t, the resulting confidence coefficient $\alpha^t = \min$ $(\alpha_1, ... \alpha_i, ... \alpha_m, \alpha_{max}^t)$ as well as the minimal conflict coefficient $c_c(\tilde{y}^t, \bar{y}^t)$ and the increase of the conflict coefficient corresponding to the resulting decrease of the confidence — these coefficients he can communicate to all negotiators. Along with these coefficients, he can compute and communicate to all negotiators the proposed result of this round of negotiations, $y^t = \bar{y}^t + \alpha^t(y_{max}^t - \bar{y}^t)$; if all negotiators agree to this result, it is accepted as the status quo point $\bar{y}^t+1$ for the next round. Axiomatic properties of such a process have been investigated by Bronisz, Krus, Wierzbicki (1987).

30.5. Conclusions

Most analytical frameworks of rational behavior, even when aimed at universality, are culturally dependent. The lessons from the holistic framework of deliberative rationality show that the main purpose of using an analytical framework is that of learning. Thus, even when starting from the utility maximization framework, we should not assume consistency of a decision-maker and must admit nonstationary approximations to his utility function.

This leads to the quasisatisficing framework of rational behavior that takes into account the learning and changing aspirations of a decision-maker. This framework incorporates most of the properties of other analytical frameworks, based on other culturally dependent perceptions of rationality. Therefore, it can be used for supporting decisions in cross-cultural contexts. For multi-actor decision situations of this type, including the cases of social traps or conflict escalation in simulated games, the concept of a conflict coefficient generalizes the Raiffa cooperative solution and helps to measure conflict intensity as well as to support mediation and negotiation.

References

Allois, M. (1953), Le Comportment de l'Homme Rationnel devant le Risque: Critique des Postulates et Axiommes de l'Ecole Americaine, *Econometrica*, 21, pp. 503-546.

Axelrod, R. (1985), *The Evolution of Cooperation*, Basic Books, New York.

Bronisz, P. and Krus, L. (1986), Supporting of Negotiation in Bargaining Problem with Multiple Payoffs, mimeograph, Institute of Systems Research, P.A.Sc.

Bronisz, P., Krus, L., and Lopuch, B. (1987), Experimental System Supporting Multiobjective Bargaining Problem, a Methodological Guide, in: A. Lewandowski and A. Wierzbicki (eds.), *Theory, Software and Testing Examples for Decision Support Systems II*, International Institute for Applied Systems Analysis, Laxenburg, Austria,

Bronisz, P., Krus, L., and Wierzbicki, A.P. (1987), Towards Interactive Solutions in Bargaining Problems, submitted for publication in *Operations Research*.

Charnes, A. and Cooper, W.W. (1975), Goal Programming and Multiple Objective Optimization, *Journal of the Operations Research Society*, 1, pp. 39-54.

Dreyfus, S.E. (1985), Beyond Rationality, in: M. Grauer, M. Thompson, and A.P. Wierzbicki (eds.), *Plural Rationality and Interactive Decision Processes*, Proceedings, Sopron 1984, Springer-Verlag, Berlin.

Fandel, G. and Wierzbicki, A.P. (1985), A Procedural Selection of Equilibria for Supergames (mimeograph).

Galbraith, J.K. (1967), *The New Industrial State*, Houghton-Mifflin, Boston.

Glushkov, V.M. (1972), Basic Principles of Automation in Organizational Management Systems [in Russian], *Upravlayushcheye Sistemy i Mashiny*, 1.

Grauer, M., Lewandowski, A. and Wierzbicki, A.P. (1982), DIDAS - Theory, Implementation and Experience, in: M. Grauer and A.P. Wierzbicki (eds.), *Interactive Decision Analysis*, Springer-Verlag, Berlin.

Kahneman, D. *et al.* (1982), *Judgment under Uncertainty: Heuristics and Biases*, Cambridge University Press, Cambridge, UK.

Kalai, E. and M. Smorodinsky (1975), Other Solutions to Nash's Bargaining Problem, *Econometrica*, 43, pp. 513-518.

Kreglewski, T. (1984), private communication.

Lewandowski, A., Johnson, S., and Wierzbicki, A.P. (1985), A Selection Committee Decision Support System: Implementation, Tutorial Example and Users Manual, mimeograph, presented at the MCDM Conference in Kyoto, Japan, August 1986.

Maynard-Smith, J. (1982), *Evolution and the Theory of Games*, Cambridge University Press, Cambridge, UK,

Pospelov, G.S. and Irikov, V.A. (1976), Program- and Goal-Oriented Planning and Management [in Russian], Sovietskoye Radio, Moscow.

Raiffa, H. (1953), Arbitration Schemes for Generalized Two-Person Games, *Ann. Math. Stud.*, 28, pp. 361-387.

Raiffa, H. (1982), *The Art and Science of Negotiations*, Harvard University Press, Cambridge, MA.

Rapoport, A. (1985), Uses of Experimental Games, in: M. Grauer and A.P. Wierzbicki (eds.), *Interactive Decision Analysis*, Springer-Verlag, Berlin.

Rawls, J. (1971), *A Theory of Justice*, Harvard University Press, Cambridge, MA.

Roth, A.E. (1979), Axiomatic Models of Bargaining, *Lecture Notes in Economic and Mathematical Systems*, 170, Springer-Verlag, Berlin.

Simon, H.A. (1957), *Models of Man*, Macmillan, New York.

Simon, H.A. (1958), *Administrative Behavior*, Macmillan, New York.

Thompson, W. (1980), Two Characterizations of the Raiffa Solution, *Economic Letters*, 6, pp. 225-231.

Umpleby, S.A. (1983), A Group Process Approach to Organizational Change, in U. Wedde (ed.), *Adequate Modeling of Systems*, Springer-Verlag, Berlin.

Wierzbicki, A.P. (1983), Negotiations and Mediation in Conflicts, I: The Role of Mathematical Approaches and Methods, in: H. Chestnut *et al.* (eds.), *Supplemental Ways of Improving International Stability*, Pergamon Press, Oxford.

Wierzbicki, A.P. (1984), Negotiation and Mediation in Conflicts, II: Plural Rationality and Interactive Decision Processes, in: M. Grauer, M. Thompson, and A.P. Wierzbicki (eds.), *Plural Rationality and Interactive Decision Processes*, Proceedings, Sopron 1984, Springer-Verlag, Berlin.

Wierzbicki, A.P. (1986), On the Completeness and Constructiveness of Parametric Characterizations to Vector Optimization Problems, *OR-Spektrum*, 8, pp. 73-87.

Zsolnay, L. and Kiss, I. (1985), Different Dissolutions of the Man and World Problem, in: M. Grauer, M. Thompson, and A.P. Wierzbicki (eds.), *Plural Rationality and Interactive Decision Processes*, Proceedings, Sopron 1984, Springer-Verlag, Berlin.

CHAPTER 31

Aspirations and Aspiration Adjustment in Location Games

Wulf Albers

Universität Bielefeld
Bielefeld
Federal Republic of Germany

31.1. Introduction

This chapter gives a first outline of some central ideas of aspiration approaches for location games. The theories have been developed by observing more than 400 experimental location games, mainly involving free face-to-face communication.

Section 31.2 introduces the *paradigm of location games*, which are a generalization of the situation of n players with ideal points $x_1,...,x_n$ in $\mathbf{R}^n$ having to agree on a solution point $x \in \mathbf{R}^n$ by simple majority rule, where each player tries to obtain a result that is as near as possible to his ideal position. It seems that — for instance, by using factor analysis methods — the paradigm can be applied to a wide class of political decision problems.

In Section 31.3 aspirations and the *aspiration equilibrium* are introduced as a *rational solution concept*. Aspirations are assumed to develop parallel to the bargaining process; they are supposed to be such that within a coalition a player only agrees to an alternative if its utility fulfills his aspiration. In the aspiration approach the aspirations of all players are considered simultaneously. Equilibrium conditions for such aspiration profiles $(a_1,...,a_n)$ are introduced. The result can be interpreted as an extension of the quota concept or of the generalized quota concept [Albers (1974)] to location games.

In Section 31.4 *aspiration adjustment processes* are modeled from a rational point of view. Aspiration adjustment paths are introduced as limits of stepwise aspiration adjustment. The end points of maximal paths have in some respect the character of ϵ-equilibria. Related to the observed behavior, a path section rule is given, which, under reasonable conditions, seems to reduce the number of paths in a way such that all paths have the same end points. So, by applying some principles of observed behavior, the rational theory could be refined in a way such that a unique aspiration profile can be predicted.

However, these predictions essentially differ from observed bargaining results. The reason for that seems to be the *difference between bargaining processes and aspiration adjustment processes.* Aspiration adjustment processes, as modeled here, are based on the assumption that each player maximizes his aspiration. In bargaining processes this aim is confounded with a necessity to stop the bargaining process at a point, when one is himself in the formed coalition. From this point of view, it can become reasonable to reduce one's demands essentially below one's adequate aspiration.

Section 31.5 gives a more *behavioral approach.* It is assumed that players can deviate from their aspiration as long as the condition "a stronger player should not get more than a weaker player" is fulfilled (where the strength is given by the theoretical value of the aspiration of Section 31.4). This principle selects a certain set of alternatives for each coalition. In addition, two conditions are introduced, namely: (a) within a coalition a player i has to justify high outcomes by outcomes in other coalitions, including i, with at least the same utility to himself, and (b) the others have to justify low outcomes of i by outcomes with at most the same utility for i in other coalitions, including i. Applying this principle repeatedly, one obtains for each coalition a set of alternatives as predicted outcomes. This approach can be interpreted as a consequent extension of the equal share analysis of Selten (1972). At present, the predictions of Section 31.5 seem to give the best descriptive solution concepts for location games.

Section 31.6 introduces the *formation of blocs.* Blocs are not-winning coalitions of similar players, who bargain with one vote and with a joint utility function (which is obtained from the utility functions of the bloc members by a rule of fairness). Blocs are formed only if thereby the aspirations of all players of the bloc increase. So the formation of blocs does not make sense by its immediate outcome, but through the related transformation of the game.

31.2. Basic Tools

31.2.1. The space of alternatives

The task of economic, social, or political decision-making is to select one out of many alternatives. Here the space of alternatives is denoted by X. It is modeled as an m-dimensional Euclidean space. The coordinates of the space can be, for instance, amounts of different budgets or outlays within parts of budgets, depending on the degree of aggregation of the decision or the analysis.

The coordinates can also be obtained by factor analysis. Empirical experiences with factor analysis indicate that for most applied problems the extension to a space with more than six or seven dimensions does not give significant additional insights. In fact, in many cases only the three or four most significant factors really have explanatory character.

In the examples below the space is restricted to two dimensions to allow the situation to be presented graphically.

31.2.2. Utility functions

It is assumed that the preferences of the players can be modeled as quasiconcave utility functions, i.e., the utility functions induce iso-utility contours that are borders of convex sets (cf. *Figure 31.1*).

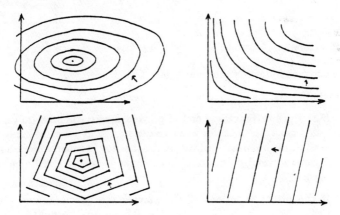

Figure 31.1. Examples of utility functions illustrated by the corresponding iso-utility contours.

31.2.3. Pareto-optimality

In n-person decision making it is rational to select Pareto-optimal alternatives:

> DEFINITION: An alternative $x \in X$ is *Pareto-optimal* for a set S of decision-makers, if there is no other alternative $y \in X$ that is strictly preferred to x by all decision-makers in S (i.e., $u_i(y) > u_i(x)$ for no $y \in X, i \in S$).

By this condition the set of reasonable outcomes is essentially restricted, as the examples of *Figure 31.2* show. *Figure 31.2(a)* shows the Pareto-line between two individuals connecting the ideal points of the players. *Figure 31.2(b)* shows the "triangle" of ideal points for three players. The boundary of the triangle consists of the Pareto-lines corresponding to the two-person subcoalitions.

(a)   (b)

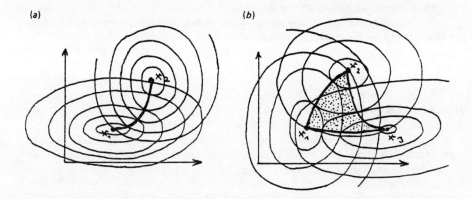

Figure 31.2. Examples of sets of Pareto-optimal points.

Generally the following theorem holds.

THEOREM: Given a space of alternatives $X = \mathbf{R}^m$:

(1)   If the utility functions of the players are continuous (not necessarily quasiconcave), then for each coalition $S \subseteq N$, the mapping from the set U of possible utility functions to the corresponding sets of Pareto-optimal points of S is continuous (using the Hausdorff topology).

(2)   If the utility functions of the players are quasiconcave, then for all utility levels $u^* = (u_1^*, \ldots, u_n^*) \in \mathbf{R}^n$ for each coalition $S \subseteq N$ the corresponding sets

$$X(S, u) : \{x \in X \mid u_i(x) \geq u_i^* \text{ for all } i \in s\}$$

are convex.

(3)   If the utility functions of the players are strictly quasiconcave and their maxima are obtained on X, and $|S|$ denotes the number of players in S, then there is a continuous mapping of an $(|N|-1)$-dimensional simplex (with vertices $s_i, \ldots, s_n$) to X such that:

(a)   The set of Pareto-optimal points of N is the image of the simplex.

(b)   For each subcoalition S of N the set of Pareto-optimal points is the image of the facet spanned by the vertices $(s_i | i \in S)$.

(c)   For each player $i \in N$ the ideal point x_i (which maximizes his utility) is the image of s_i.

(d)   For each two-person coalition $\{i, j\}$ the set of Pareto-optimal points is a path connecting their ideal points x_i, x_j. [Note that (a), (c), (d) follow from (b).]

Difficulties that may arise when the utility functions are only continuous and not quasiconcave are shown by the example of *Figure 31.3*. The Pareto-sets of two-person coalitions need no longer define paths between the ideal points of the players.

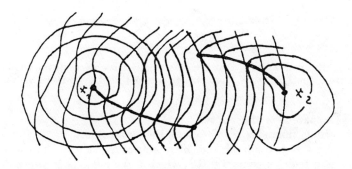

Figure 31.3. Example showing that for utility functions which are not quasiconcave the set of Pareto-optimal points of two players need not define a path between their ideal positions x_1, x_2.

The example of *Figure 31.4* shows that the set of Pareto-optimal points of three players does not generally need to be isomorphic to a two-dimensional simplex.

The example of *Figure 31.3* indicates that the quasiconcavity of the utility functions avoids discontinuities and thereby simplifies the bargaining problem.

31.2.4. Location games

DEFINITION: A *location game* $\Gamma = (N, X, u, W, d)$ is given by

-   A set of n players, $N = \{1, 2, ..., n\}$, the subsets of N being called coalitions

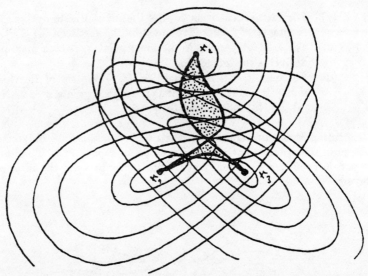

Figure 31.4. Example showing that even for strictly quasiconcave utility functions, the set of Pareto-optimal points of three players does not need to be isomorphic to a triangle.

- A space X of alternatives
- Utility functions $u_i : X \to \mathbf{R}$ of the players on X
- A set W of coalitions (i.e., of subsets of N), called winning coalitions
- A default outcome $d \in \mathbf{R}^N$, which is the outcome if no winning coalition is formed.

The idea of the game is that the players of a winning coalition can determine an alternative $x \in X$ as the outcome of the game. So that the problem of the location game is: which winning coalition is formed and which alternative is selected by the coalition. [A more general approach is given in Laing *et al.* (1983).]

It is assumed that the space X of alternatives is an m-dimensional Euclidean space $\mathbf{R}^m$, that the utility functions of the players are quasiconcave and obtain their maxima on X, and that there are no two winning coalitions with empty intersection. [Complements of winning coalitions — coalitions which are neither winning nor losing — are called blocking. In the following, the outcome of blocking coalitions (the default outcome) is supposed to be sufficiently unattractive that blocking coalitions can be ignored.]

The examples given in this chapter and the experiments performed only involve three-, four-, and five-person games with $X = \mathbf{R}^2$. The utility functions are given via ideal points $x_1, \ldots, x_n$ (or via ideal lines $l_1, \ldots, l_n$) by the respective (negative) Euclidean distances from the ideal points (or lines). The winning coalitions are given by simple majority rule.

In this framework it is the aim of a player to arrange a coalition and thereby verify an alternative x that is as near as possible to his ideal position x_i (or his ideal line l_i). Of course, the interests of the players are usually contrary, so that it is a matter of bargaining as to which coalition is formed and which alternative is selected.

31.2.5. Interpersonal comparison of utility

In Section 31.5 we assume that there is a strength ordering on the players with the consequence that, if possible, a stronger player should not get less than a weaker player. This implies a common agreement on the interpersonal comparison of outcomes, or, more precisely, a common agreement on scales $\bar{u}_1, \ldots, \bar{u}_n$ by which the outcomes of the players $1, \ldots, n$ can be measured, where each scale u_i is a mapping from X to $\mathbf{R}$. These scales have the character of utility functions, and it seems reasonable to assume that they can be obtained from the individual utility functions u_i of the players by stricly monotonic transformations.

Under this assumption we can replace the individual utility functions $u_1, \ldots, u_n$ by the scales $\bar{u}_1, \ldots, \bar{u}_n$ as long as the analysis only refers to the ordinal character of the utility functions. Moreover, $\bar{u}_1, \ldots, \bar{u}_n$ give the additional property that interpersonal comparisons of outcomes are possible.

In this chapter the results of Section 31.4 make sense for utility functions of both types u_i and $\bar{u}_i$. However, from a behavioral point of view, the path selection rule in Subsection 31.4.5 implicitly requires the interpersonal comparison, since otherwise a behavioral selection of "most symmetric aspiration profiles" is difficult to motivate. Section 31.5 should be based on functions of type $\bar{u}_i$.

In our experiments the monetary incentives $\tilde{u}(x) := c_i - \alpha \, |x - x_i|$ were multiples of the (negative) Euclidean distances of X from the respective ideal positions $x^i \in \mathbf{R}^n$, with additive constants c_i, which were different for different players and not known in advance. (The constants depended on the success of other players in the same position as player i.) In this setup the distances from the ideal positions suggest themselves as evaluation functions $\bar{u}_i$. It seems reasonable to assume that also in other situations the Euclidean distances from the ideal positions can be spontaneously selected as scales to perform the comparison of outcomes.

This means that the outcomes of the players are implicitly compared with their *maximal possible* outcomes. It is interesting to remark that in characteristic function games (with payoff 0 in all one-player coalitions) the players directly compare their numerical outcomes. So in this situation each player compares his outcome with the *worst* outcome he can get. In both cases canonical reference points have been selected to obtain interpersonal comparability, but in wholly different ways.

31.3. Aspirations

31.3.1. Aspiration profiles

In this approach aspirations are modeled as minimal demands of utility, so that a player i with an aspiration a_i will agree to an alternative $x \in X$, only if $u_i(x) \geq a_i$.

It is assumed that in each state of the bargaining process each player has an aspiration a_i, which may be adjusted at the next stage. The aspirations of the players define an aspiration profile $a = (a_i,...,a_n) \in \mathbf{R}^n$.

NOTATIONS: For an aspiration profile $a \in \mathbf{R}^n$ let

$X(S,a) := \{x \in X \mid x \text{ Pareto-optimal for } S \text{ and } u_i(x) \geq a_i(x) \text{ for all } i \in S\}$

$coa\ (a) := \{S \in W \mid X(S,a) \neq 0\}$

$coa_i(a) := \{S \in W \mid X(S,a) \neq 0, i \in S\}$

$X(S,a)$ is the set of those Pareto-optimal alternatives of S that fulfill the aspirations of all players of S. $coa(a)$ are those winning coalitions that can fulfill the aspirations of all of their members by an adequate alternative. So the coalitions of $coa(a)$ may be denoted as "feasible coalitions"; $coa_i\ (a)$ are the feasible coalitions containing player i. Correspondingly, we introduce feasibility of players:

NOTATION: A player is called feasible (with respect to a) if $coa_i(a) \neq 0$.

31.3.2. Aspiration adjustment process and bargaining process

Analyzing people who are bargaining in a location game, one has to distinguish the development of aspirations in an *aspiration adjustment process,* (which can be modeled by the aspiration profiles a^t at different points of time $t \in T$), and the *bargaining process,* which may be given by a sequence of proposals (at different points of time) and by the information as to which player agreed to which proposal (at which point of time), where a *proposal* (x,S) is a pair $x \in X$, $S \in W$. The idea behind a proposal (x,S) is that the players of S might, should (or already have) agree(d) to the alternative x. If the players of S have agreed to x, then (x,S) can have the character of an interim agreement or a final agreement.

The problem of empirical observation is that the bargaining process can be observed directly, while the aspiration adjustment process can only be observed indirectly by its influences on the bargaining process.

Relations between these two processes can be formulated by introducing revealed aspirations, which have to fulfill assumptions such as:

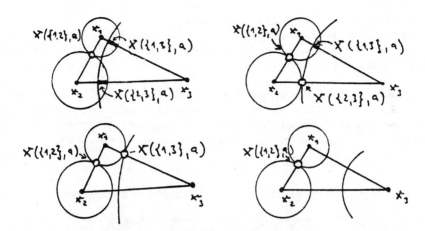

Figure 31.5. Examples of feasible points X(S,a) and feasible coalitions for different aspirations in a three-person location game.

(1)   A player i will agree to a proposal (x,S) only if it fulfills his revealed aspiration (i.e., if $u_i(x) \geq a_i$).

(2)   A player $i \in S$ who agrees to a proposal (x,S) thereby indicates that his revealed aspiration a_i is not higher than $u_i(x)$, which follows from (1).

(3)   A player who actively changes from (x,S) to (y,T) (with $i \in T \cap S$) has a revealed aspiration $a_i > u_i(x)$.

In Albers (1986) the relations of the aspiration adjustment process and the bargaining process are worked out in detail for apex games. In that paper the bargaining process is analyzed and the aspiration adjustment process behind the bargaining process is modeled implicitly. Here the aspiration adjustment process is modeled directly, and the bargaining process is not modeled. (It should be remarked that the approach here can be easily transferred to one-step characteristic function games.)

31.3.3. Dependence of players

Let $a = (a_1, a_2, \cdots, a_n)$ be an aspiration profile. Then we say that a player i depends on player j if every feasible coalition of i contains player j, while player j has a feasible coalition without player i:

DEFINITION: i *depends on* j at a if $coa_i(a) \underset{\neq}{\subseteq} coa_j(a)$.

In such a situation it can be reasonable that player j asks player i to reduce his aspiration and j himself increases his aspiration in such a way that afterward still $coa_i(a) \subseteq coa_j(a)$. In fact, if i gets less than his aspiration in an alternative coalition of player j without player i, then player j can even force i to reduce his aspiration by threatening to form a coalition without i.

If, on the other hand, for all coalitions in $coa_j(a) \setminus coa_i(a)$, the corresponding proposals (x, S) fulfill the aspirations of player i, then the proposals $(x, (S \cup \{j\}) \cup \{i\})$ are also feasible under simple majority rule, and $coa_i(a)$ cannot be a subset of $coa_j(a)$. So, under simple majority rule, the argument that a dependent player can be forced to reduce his aspiration always holds.

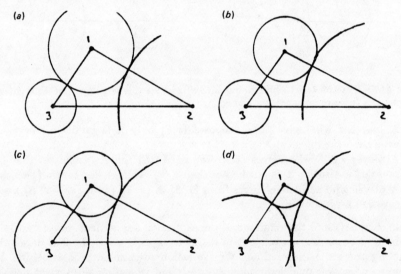

Figure 31.6. Aspiration adjustment in a three-person game.

The definition of dependence may be explained by the example of *Figure 31.6.* Consider the situation with aspirations as given in (a). Here players 2 and 3 depend on 1. Player 1 can force player 2 to reduce his aspiration and 1 can increase his aspiration by the same amount [see (b)]. Now player 3 has to reduce his aspiration, if he wants to find a coalition partner [see (c)]. Steps (b) and (c) can be repeated unless players 2 and 3 form an alternative coalition and thereby lose their dependence on 1. The corresponding result, where all players are independent, is given in [d].

In the following we shall use the

NOTATION: $dep_i(a) := \{j \in N \mid i \text{ depends on } j \text{ (with respect to } a)\}$

31.3.4. Aspiration equilibrium

Figure 31.6 (d) gives a very acceptable solution for this specific game. In order to generalize this to arbitrary location games we give three properties that are met by the example:

	- Each player is feasible, i.e.,
(A1)	$coa_i(a) \neq 0$ for all $i \in N$

- If all players of a set $S \subseteq N$ increase their aspirations, then at least one of them is infeasible or dependent afterward, i.e.,

$(\bar{A}\bar{2})$ $\bar{a}_i > a_i$(all $i \in S$), $\bar{a}_k = a_k$ (all $k \in N \setminus S$),
$\Rightarrow$ either $coa(\bar{a}) = 0$, or there are $i \in S$, $j \in N$ such that $coa_i(\bar{a}) \subsetneq coa_j(\bar{a})$.

- No player depends on another, i.e.,

(A3) $coa_i(a) \subsetneq coa_j(a)$ for no pair $i, j \in N$

Property (A1) is obvious; (A3) has been discussed above. $(\bar{A}\bar{2})$ can be explained by *Figure 31.7*, which shows situations where players can increase their aspirations (see the dotted lines) and can afterward still verify their aspirations without becoming dependent.

Using these axioms we define

DEFINITION: The *aspiration equilibrium* is the set of aspiration profiles that meet (A1), $(\bar{A}\bar{2})$, and (A3).

In the following we shall replace $(\bar{A}\bar{2})$ by the condition

- If all players of a set $S \subseteq N$ increase their aspirations, then afterwards either there is no feasible coalition, or for one player of S the set of players on whom he depends increases, i.e.,

(A2) $a_i > a_i$ (all $i \in S$), $\bar{a}_k = a_k$ (all $k \in N \setminus S$)
$\Rightarrow$ either $coa(\bar{a}) = 0$, or there is $i \in S$, such that $dep_i(\bar{a}) \supsetneq dep_i(a)$.

It is easy to prove that condition (A2) can replace $(\bar{A}\bar{2})$ if (A1) and (A3) hold:

REMARK: The aspiration equilibrium is the set of aspiration profiles that meet (A1), (A2), (A3).

The advantage of formulation (A2) is, however, that it makes sense to apply it, even if (A3) does not hold. Since (A2) is a condition that reduces the slack (cf. the examples of *Figure 31.7*), condition (A2) will enable us to consider aspiration profiles that meet (A1) and (A2) when condition (A3) is not yet met, and we can define a movement of such profiles in a way that attempts to fulfill condition (A3) in the end.

According to conditions (A1)–(A3), the following behavioral rules can be introduced:

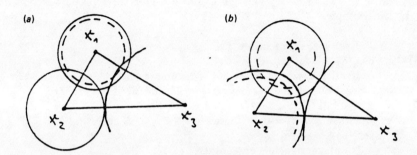

Figure 31.7. Aspirations in a three-person game with ideal points that do not meet condition (A2).

(i)   A player reduces a_i if $coa_i(a) = 0$
(ii)   All players i of a set $S \subseteq N$ increase their aspirations from a_i to $\bar{a}_i$ if $coa_i(\bar{a}) \neq 0$ and $dep_i(\bar{a}) \subseteq dep_i(a)$ for all $i \in S$
(iii) A player reduces a_i if he depends on another player.

LEMMA: An aspiration profile is an aspiration equilibrium if it is stable with respect to (i)–(iii).

Figure 31.8 gives some examples of aspiration equilibria in different location games.

31.3.5. Predictions related to the aspiration equilibrium

The prediction of the aspiration equilibrium theory is that the aspiration adjustment process stops in an aspiration equilibrium profile a and that the corresponding bargaining results are all proposals (x, S) with $S \in coa(a)$ and $x \in X(S,a)$.

EXAMPLE: For the three-person game with ideal points of *Figure 31.9*, there is only one aspiration equilibrium. The corresponding feasible coalitions are $\{1,2\}$, $\{1,3\}$, and $\{2,3\}$; and the corresponding alternatives are $x_{1,2}$, and $x_{1,3}$, and $x_{2,3}$, respectively.

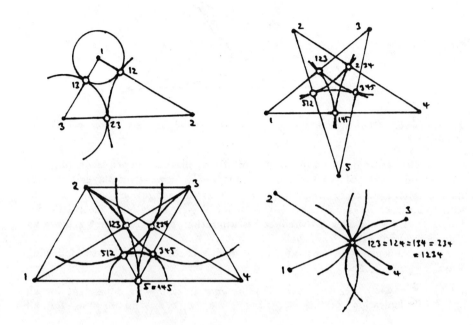

Figure 31.8. Aspiration equilibria of different location games.

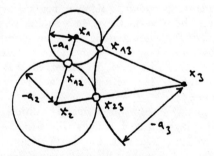

Figure 31.9. Predicted results of a three-person game.

31.3.6. Modification of the aspiration equilibrium

The definition of Subsection 31.3.3 is a first approach to a reasonable definition of an aspiration equilibrium. One problem of the definition may be illustrated by an example (see *Figure 31.10*).

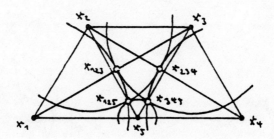

Figure 31.10. Example motivating a modification of the aspiration equilibrium definition.

In this example, for the given aspirations, player 1 depends on player 2 (and symmetrically player 4 depends on player 3). However, if player 1 reduces his aspiration, player 2 cannot in return increase his aspiration (neither in coalition $\{1,2,5\}$ nor in $\{1,2,3\}$). From this point of view there is no motivation for player 2 to press player 1 to reduce his aspiration, since he cannot achieve an (immediate) advantage from that.

This consideration motivates us to modify condition (A2) in the following way:

$(\bar{A}\bar{2}')$ $coa_i(a) \subsetneq coa_j(a)$ only if j becomes infeasible or dependent for all aspiration profiles $\bar{a}$ with $\bar{a}_i < a_i$, $\bar{a}_j > a_j$ and $\bar{a}_k = a_k$ for all $k \neq i, k \neq j$.

This means that it is impossible for player i to reduce his aspiration and player j to increase his in a way that permits a feasible coalition to j.

This modification, so to speak, restricts the pressure of player j on player i to such cases where something similar to side payments from i to j are possible. In this context it should be remarked that, in a similar way as here, aspiration equilibria can be defined for characteristic function games (where side payments are always possible). For these games, however, conditions $(\bar{A}\bar{2})$ and $(\bar{A}\bar{2}')$ are equivalent. It must, however, be remarked that the new definition does not solve all problems. In fact, it does not even solve all problems imposed by the example.

Assume players $\{3,4,5\}$ form a preliminary coalition and agree upon the point x_{345}. What will players 1,2 do? They will propose a coalition $\{1,2,3\}$ with an outcome $\bar{x}_{123}$, which is nearer to the ideal position of player 3 than x_{123} (and therefore also nearer than x_{345}). Player 3 can, of course, accept this offer, since the new proposal cannot be dominated by any coalition that does not include player 3 (except in the case that one of the players essentially reduces his aspirations). So, implicitly, player 3 can force player 1 (or 1 and 5) to reduce their aspirations.

The dependence of player 1 on player 2 therefore works against player 1, because player 2 clearly prefers x_{123} to x_{125}, so that, under certain pre-histories of the bargaining process, player 1 cannot use x_{125} as a counter-argument. Thereby he becomes dependent (on player 3).

The threat described here works differently from that given when we introduced the definition of dependence. There we argued that, if i depends on j, then j can threaten player i *to reduce his aspiration* and otherwise form a coalition with somebody else. Here he threatens player i to form a *specific coalition* with player j. Restricting player i to this alternative, he may become dependent on somebody else, and thereby he can be forced to reduce his aspiration.

This argument again results in the conclusion that the dependent player must reduce his aspiration. However, we are not sure whether in every situation where one player depends on another, there are forces working in such a way that the dependent player has to reduce his demands.

31.4. Modeling the Aspiration Adjustment Process

The aim of this section is to model the aspiration adjustment process in a normative way with continuous time as an aspiration adjustment path. Such a path is defined as a limit of aspiration adjustment sequences with discrete points of time. Maximal paths are selected, paths are normalized by assuming "a constant speed of change" and, by applying the observations of experiments, a path selection condition is introduced.

31.4.1. Aspiration adjustment chains

DEFINITION: An *aspiration adjustment chain* is a sequence $\bar{a} = (a^1, a^2, ...,)$ of aspiration profiles such that for all $r \in N$, $i \in N$ one of the following conditions holds:

(1) $a_i^{r+1} < a_i^r$ and $coa_i(a^r) = 0$

(2) $a_i^{r+1} > a_i^r$ and $coa_i(a^r) \cap coa_i(a^{r+1}) \neq 0$ and $dep_i(a^{r+1}) \subseteq dep_i(a^r)$

(3) $a_i^{r+1} < a_i^r$ and i depends on some player j in $coa(a^r)$, and there is no player k who depends on i in $coa(a^r)$

(4) $a_i^{r+1} = a_i^r$

(*) Moreover, it is assumed that for a given r
  - case (2) is not applied, if there are $i \in N$, $\bar{a}^{r+1} \in \mathbf{R}^N$ fulfilling condition (1)
  - case (3) is not applied, if there are $i \in N$, $\bar{a}^{r+1} \in \mathbf{R}^N$ fulfilling condition (1) or (2).

EXPLANATION: Conditions (1)–(3) refer to the corresponding conditions of the aspiration equilibrium and to conditions (i)–(iii). These conditions are ordered by (*) in a hierarchical way, i.e., (1) is applied before (2) and (2) is applied before (3). Examples are given in *Figures 31.11* and *31.12*.

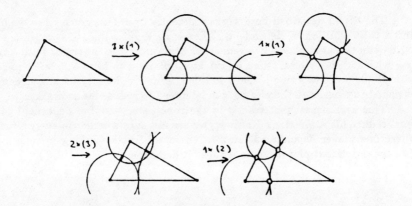

Figure 31.11. An aspiration adjustment sequence in a three-person game.

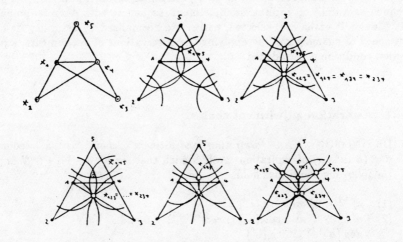

Figure 31.12. An aspiration adjustment sequence in a five-person game.

In these examples the single steps of aspiration adjustment have been performed in a special way so that players in symmetric positions have been treated equally, and that all players who reduced their aspirations from one step to the next reduced them by the same amount.

Of course, it would have been possible to subdivide the processes into finer processes with finer steps of aspiration adjustment. In the limit, paths of aspiration adjustment are obtained. The definition of paths requires us to define the fineness of aspiration adjustment sequences:

DEFINITION: An aspiration adjustment sequence $\bar{a}$ has fineness $\epsilon \in \mathbf{R}, \epsilon > 0$, if $|a_i^{r+1} - a_i^r| < \epsilon$ for all $i \in N, r \in \mathbf{N}$.

31.4.2. Aspiration adjustment paths

Let $T : [0, t]$ or $[0, t]$ (i.e., the set of real numbers between 0 and t including 0, but not necessarily including t).

DEFINITION: $\alpha: T \to \mathbf{R}^N$ is an *aspiration adjustment path*, if

(1) There is a sequence of aspiration adjustment sequences $^1\bar{a}, ^2\bar{a}, ^3\bar{a}, ...$, and
(2) There are monotonically increasing mappings $^i\tau : \mathbf{N} \to T$ $(i = 1, 2, ...)$ such that
   (a) $\{(^i\tau(r), {^i\bar{a}^r}) \mid r \in \mathbf{N}\}$ converges to $\{(t, \alpha(t)) \mid t \in T\}$ (Hausdorff topology)
   (b) the fineness of the sequence $^i\bar{a}$ converges to 0 (for all i)
   (c) $\max_{r \in \mathbf{N}} ({^i\tau(r+1)} - {^i\tau(r)})$ converges to 0 (for all i).

From this definition follows

LEMMA: Every aspiration adjustment path α: $T \to \mathbf{R}^N$ is continuous.

Moreover, I presume that every aspiration adjustment path is piecewise differentiable.

For the examples of *Figures 31.11* and *31.12* aspiration adjustment paths can be obtained by refining the drawn process. Then each figure just shows the vertices of the path, and the path is obtained by connecting these vertices by straight lines of aspiration adjustment in $\mathbf{R}^N$.

31.4.3. Maximal aspiration adjustment paths

DEFINITION: An aspiration adjustment path α: $T \to \mathbf{R}^N$ is *maximal* if there is no aspiration adjustment path β: $U \to \mathbf{R}^N$ such that $T \subsetneq U$ and $\alpha(t) = \beta(t)$ for all $t \in T$.

This maximality condition refers to the tails of the paths:

LEMMA: For each aspiration path $\alpha : T \to \mathbf{R}^N$ there is a maximal aspiration path $\beta : U \to \mathbf{R}^N$ with the same initial point (i.e., $\alpha(0) = \beta(0)$) which extends α (i.e., $\alpha(T) \subseteq \beta(U)$).

Maximal aspiration adjustment paths can lead to aspiration equilibria and, obviously, each aspiration equilibrium can be presented as the end point of a maximal aspiration adjustment path.

An aspiration adjustment path can be interpreted as a permanent effort to fulfill conditions (A1)–(A3) of the aspiration equilibrium. From the hierarchy of the aspiration modification conditions for aspiration adjustment chains, it follows that aspiration adjustment chains permanently have to reach aspirations that meet (A1) and (A2) before a new effort can be made to fulfill (A3). From this follows

THEOREM: For each aspiration adjustment path $\alpha : T \rightarrow \mathbf{R}$ there are points $t^1 < t^2$ in T such that
(1) $\alpha(t)$ meets (A1) if $t \geq t^1$
(2) $\alpha(t)$ meets (A1) and (A2) if $t \geq t^2$.

Of course, the only point t^3 for which $\alpha(t^3)$ meets (A3) can be the end point of the interval T. However, it need not be that the path really meets an aspiration equilibrium. To characterize properties of the end point we introduce

DEFINITION: An aspiration profile $a \in \mathbf{R}_N$ is an *aspiration ϵ-equilibrium* if
(1) a meets (A1) and (A2), and
(2)   For no pair $i,j \in N$ with $coa_i(a) \subsetneq coa_j(a)$ is there an aspiration profile $\bar{a}$ such that $\bar{a} < a_i - \epsilon$. $\bar{a}_j > a_j + \epsilon$, $\bar{a}_k = a_k$ for $k \neq i,j$, and $coa_i(\bar{a}) \subsetneq coa_j(\bar{a})$.

So an aspiration ϵ-equilibrium can be interpreted as a point in which condition (A3) is insofar fulfilled that the dependence of player i on j cannot justify a change of the aspirations by more than ϵ. Now we can formulate

THEOREM: The end point $\alpha(t^*)$ of a maximal aspiration adjustment path is a limit point of aspiration ϵ-equilibria (i.e., for each $\epsilon > 0$ there is an aspiration ϵ-equilibrium a^ϵ such that $|a^\epsilon - \alpha(t^*)| < \epsilon$).

31.4.4. The speed normalization

The following remark says that a monotonic transformation of the time scale T of a path defines a new path:

REMARK: If $\alpha : T \rightarrow \mathbf{R}^N$ is an aspiration adjustment path and $f: \mathbf{R} \rightarrow \mathbf{R}$ is a continuous strictly monotonic increasing function with $f(0) = 0$, then $\gamma := \alpha \circ f^{-1} : f(T) \rightarrow \mathbf{R}^N$ is an aspiration adjustment path.

The only difference of the two paths α and β are the "speeds" $d\alpha/dt$ and $d\gamma/dt$ at different points of the path. Since we are not interested in the speed of the aspiration adjustment, we normalize it:

SPEED NORMALIZATION: An aspiration adjustment path $\alpha: T \to X$ is speed normalized, if for all $t \in T$:

$$\Sigma_{\{i \in N | d\alpha_i(t)/dt < 0\}} \left| \frac{d\alpha_i(t)}{dt} \right| = 1$$

The following theorem says that "every aspiration adjustment path can be speed normalized":

THEOREM: For every aspiration adjustment path $\alpha: T \to X$ there is a strictly monotonically increasing function $f: \mathbf{R} \to \mathbf{R}$ such that $\gamma := \alpha \circ f^{-1}: f(T) \to \mathbf{R}^N$ is speed normalized.

So we can restrict our considerations to speed normalized aspiration adjustment paths without loss of generality. In the following we shall only consider speed normalized aspiration adjustment paths.

31.4.5. Path selection rule and open start condition

Experimental observations indicate that subjects select paths that are, so to say, "most egalitarian". To define this we introduce the

NOTATION: For each aspiration profile $a \in \mathbf{R}^N$ let $lex(a)$ be the vector obtained from a by reordering the components of a decreasingly.

Now we can formulate the

PATH SELECTION RULE (PSR): Let $\alpha: T \to \mathbf{R}^N$, $\beta: U \to \mathbf{R}^N$ be two speed normalized aspiration adjustment paths, and let $t^* \in T$ be maximal subject to $\alpha(t) = \beta(t)$ for all $t < t^*$. Then β *is preferred to* α, if there is an $\epsilon^* > 0$ so that for all ϵ with $0 < \epsilon < \epsilon^*$ $lex\beta(t^* + \epsilon)$ is lexicographically smaller than $lex\,\alpha(t^* + \epsilon)$. A speed normalized *path α fulfills PSR*, if there is no speed normalized path β which is preferred to α.

In addition, we define the

OPEN START CONDITION (OSC): A speed normalized path $\alpha: T \to \mathbf{R}^N$, which meets the path selection rule, meets the open start condition if $\beta(U) \supseteq \alpha(U)$ for every path $\beta: U \to \mathbf{R}^N$ with $\beta_i(0) \leq \alpha_i(0)$ for all $i \in N$ (i.e., a path that meets the path selection rule meets the open start condition, if it can be continued at the starting side to arbitrary aspiration profiles below the initial aspiration profile $\alpha(0)$ of the path).

In the following we will restrict our considerations to "regular" paths:

DEFINITION: An aspiration adjustment *path is regular*, if it is maximal, speed normalized, and it fulfills PSR and OSC.

Now we can formulate the

CONJECTURE: For each location game, there is at least one regular aspiration adjustment path.

The idea is that for a given game Γ all regular aspiration adjustment paths should lead to the same end point. One step in this direction is made by

LEMMA: For every location game Γ there is a unique aspiration profile $a^2(\Gamma)$ such that for every regular aspiration path $\alpha\colon T \to X$ *either* there is $t^2 \in T$ such that $\alpha(t^2) = a^2(\Gamma)$, and $[\alpha(t)$ meets $(A1)$ and $(A2)] \Leftrightarrow [t \geq t^2]$; *or* there is a regular aspiration path $\beta\colon U \to X$ such that $\alpha(T) \subseteq \beta(U)$ and $a^2(\Gamma \in \beta(U))$.

More generally we define

DEFINITION: A location game is regular, if all of its regular aspiration adjustment paths end in the same aspiration profile. We denote this profile by $a^*(\Gamma)$, and call it the *regular aspiration profile* of Γ.

Of course, if a location game Γ has a unique aspiration equilibrium, then this is the regular aspiration profile of the game. However, for more complicated games, the regularity principle can serve to select a specific aspiration profile.

It seems that "almost all" location games are regular:

CONJECTURE: let $\Gamma = (N, X, u\ W, d)$, and for any $(x^1, x^2, \ldots, x^n) \in X^N$ let $u^x\colon X \to \mathbf{R}^N$, $d^x \in \mathbf{R}^N$ such that

$$u^x(z)\colon = u(z-x) \text{ for all } z \in X$$
$$d_i^x\colon = d_i + \max_{i,j \,\in\, N}|x^i - x^j|, \text{ and let}$$
$$\Gamma^x\colon (N, X, u^x, W, d^x)$$

then for any $z \in X$ and any ϵ-ball $U_\epsilon(x)$ round z the set $\{x \in U_\epsilon(x)\,|\,\Gamma^x$ not regular$\}$ has Borel measure zero.

The idea is that by the (suggested) theorem a unique solution profile can be assigned to almost all location games. But even if the theorem is wrong, the set of possible end points of aspiration adjustment paths that meets the aspiration adjustment rule and the open start condition essentially restricts the set of predicted results of the aspiration adjustment process.

EXAMPLES: The aspirations shown in *Figures 31.11* and *31.12* give the vertices of the respective regular aspiration adjustment paths. In both examples the end points $a^*(\Gamma)$ are unique. Both paths are started with aspirations given by the ideal positions of the players.

31.4.6. Strategic behavior

The preceding subsection describes in which way aspiration adjustment processes develop. It seems reasonable that rational players can foresee the further development of the process and the question arises if this might cause them to change their behavior

For instance, if a player i depends on another player j, then player j can refuse to ask player i to reduce his aspiration and to increase his own aspiration. Thereby the aspiration adjustment process can stop at an early point of the aspiration adjustment procedure. The consequence of this is that in many three-person games only the coalition $\{1,2\}$ is formed.

The main difference between the aspiration adjustment process and the bargaining process is that the aspiration adjustment process is modeled in a way that assumes that it is in the interest of every player to maximize his aspiration value. However, the aspiration has to be verified as an outcome! And since usually a player is not contained in all feasible coalitions, he cannot be sure to verify his aspiration.

From this point of view it may even be reasonable to demand essentially less than one's adequate aspiration. It might perhaps even happen that all players are willing to reduce their aspirations below the aspirations reached in the aspiration adjustment path. But there is a limit to such aspiration reductions. Aspirations are not at the free disposal of the players; they must be regarded by the others as adequate demands. The question arises: which deviations of aspirations from those of the aspiration adjustment process are accepted by the players? Experimental results suggest that players *accept deviations from reasonable aspiration profiles as long as players with higher aspiration values get higher outcomes than players with lower aspiration values*. These conditions reduce the purpose of the aspiration adjustment process to finding an order of strength on the set of players, with the implication that — if possible — a stronger player should get more than a weaker player. This idea will be modeled in Section 31.5.

31.4.7. Relation to the competitive solution

Although defined in a very different way, the concept here is closely related to the "competitive solution" of McKelvey, Ordeshook, and Winer (1978); the following definition is given according to Forman, Laing (1982):

DEFINITION: A set C of proposals is called a *competitive solution* if

- (0) (finiteness) for each coalition $S \subseteq N$ there is at most one alternative $x \in X$ such that $(x, S) \in C$
- (1) (internal stability) $(x, S), (y, T) \in C \Rightarrow (y, T)$ does not dominate (x, S)

(2)   (external stability) for each $(x,S) \ni C$ which dominates a proposal in
       C there is a proposal $(y, T) \in C$ such that (y, T) dominates (x, S)
       where: (y, T) dominates (x, S) if T is winning and $u_i(y) > u_i(x)$ for all
       $i \in T \cap S$

For many games the competitive solutions are given by the sets
$U\{X(a,S) \mid S \subseteq N\} = U\{X(a,S) \mid S \in coa(a)\}$ of the aspiration equilibria
a.

Figure 31.13 (a) gives an example of a location game that has a unique
aspiration equilibrium (given by the radii drawn in the figure). But the sets
related to the aspiration equilibrium do not form a competitive solution, since
$(x_{235}, \{2,3,5\})$ is dominated by $(x_{145}, \{1,4,5\})$. However, $\{(x_{123}, \{1,2,3\}),$
$(x_{145}, \{1,4,5\}),\ (x_{234}, \{2,3,4\})\}$ form a competitive solution.

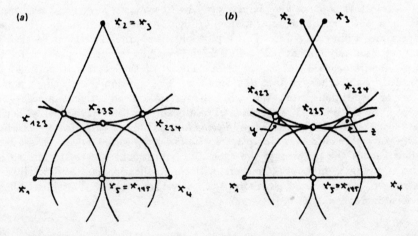

Figure 31.13. Two examples of location games and corresponding aspiration equilibria
given by the drawn radii. Game (b) has no competitive solution.

The situation in this game can be characterized as one where player 5 has
the only function to support the proposal $\{x_{145}, \{1,4,5\}\}$ if coalition $\{1,4\}$ is
formed. This consideration reduces the essential part of the game to the active
interest groups $\{1\}$, $\{4\}$, and $\{2,3\}$, where the coalitions $\{1,2,3\}$, $\{4,2,3\}$, and
$\{1,4\}$ are possible, of which $\{1,4\}$ is necessarily supported by player 5.

A slight modification of the example [see *Figure 31.13* (b)], generates the
game for which for each aspiration equilibrium the corresponding set of proposals neither fulfills the internal nor the external stability condition. In this example omitting the dominated proposal $(x_{235}, \{2,3,5\})$ still leaves the external

stability violated. I strongly suggest that this game *has no competitive solution.*
The role of player 5 is similar to that in example (a); however, the idea of the
aspiration equilibrium can no longer be presented in the framework of the competitive solution approach.

31.5. Order of Strength and Generalized Equal Share Analysis

31.5.1. The order of strength

The following concept is based on a strength ordering on the set of players:

DEFINITION: $\succsim$ is a strength ordering on N, if it is
transitive (i.e., $i \succsim j, j \succsim k \Rightarrow i \succsim k$)
reflexive (i.e., $i \succsim i$ for all $i \in N$)
complete (i.e., $i \succsim j$ or $j \succsim i$ for all $i,j \in N$).

We write $i > j$ if $i \succsim j$ and not $j \succsim i$.

Within this section it is not important where the strength ordering comes
from. Observing experimental games, it seems that it is one of the subjects'
questions in the game to find out their bargaining strengths, i.e., to find out who
is stronger and who is weaker than oneself. It seems that the answer is obtained
during the bargaining process, sometimes by hypothetical bargaining.

According to the aspiration approach, it may be suggested that the
strength ordering is induced by the aspiration values of the unique joint final
aspiration profile of all maximal aspiration adjustment paths that follow ASR
and OSC. And, in fact, this seems to be the most reasonable candidate to induce
a strength ordering.

But it may also happen that players follow the aspiration adjustment path
only in the beginning of their considerations and then switch to another criterion, which explains the strength ordering obtained at that state. Albers and
Brunwinkel (1987) consider such a criterion, which says that a player i is
stronger than another, if there are more players whose ideal positions are
nearer to the ideal position of i than players whose ideal positions are nearer
to that of the other. Another criterion may be the distance from the gravicenter
of the set of ideal points: a player is stronger, if he is nearer to the gravicenter.
However, it now seems to the author that these alternatives are only pseudo-
criteria, which are used to confirm the players' feelings of strength that they
developed during the bargaining process.

31.5.2. Predictions related to the order of strength

The idea related to the strength ordering is that within a coalition a stronger player must not agree to get "less" than a weaker player. This is made precise by the following definition of dominance:

DEFINITION: Let $\succsim$ be a strength ordering on N,S a winning coalition, and x,y two alternatives. Then y *dominates* x *with respect to* S *and* $\succsim$, if for each $i \in S$ one of the following conditions holds true:

(1) $u_i(y) > u_i(x)$
(2) $u_i(y) \leq u_i(x)$ and there is a player $j \succsim i$ with $u_j(x) < u_i(x)$ and $u_j(y) > u_j(x)$.

It is reasonable that a player will agree to a change from x to y if his utility increases (condition (1)). Moreover, we assume that a player can be forced to accept a point y with a lower utility than x if there is a player j who is not weaker than i $(j \succsim i)$ so that j has the right not to accept the alternative x (in which he gets less than j), and to suggest an alternative proposal instead, which increases his utility $(u_j(y) > u_j(x))$.

The arguments that are stable with respect to this dominance for a given coalition S are:

DEFINITION: If S is a winning coalition, then $X(S, \succsim)$ is the set of all alternatives that are not dominated with respect to S and $\succsim$. If S is not winning, then $X(S,\succsim)$ is defined to be empty. $X(S,\succsim)$ is denoted as the *set of stable alternatives of S with respect to* $\succsim$.

From the definition of dominance follows immediately

REMARK: For all $S \subseteq N$ and all strength orderings on N, all alternatives $X(S,\succsim)$ are Pareto-optimal for S.

Examples for sets $X(S,\succsim)$ are given in *Figures 31.14* and *31.15*. The examples show that a player can get more than another player, although he is not stronger than the other.

31.6. The Adjustment Process of Solution Sets $X(S, \succsim)$

It seems reasonable to assume that the solution sets $X(S, \succsim)$ induce strategic considerations of the players by arguing with possible outcomes in other coalitions. Specifically, if a coalition S is formed, a player i can argue that he should not get less than in his worst alternative proposal that does not involve the other players of S, and partners of i can argue that he should not get more than his maximal outcome in an alternative coalition that does not involve them. Of course, in this context it is important to know the outcomes of which coalitions

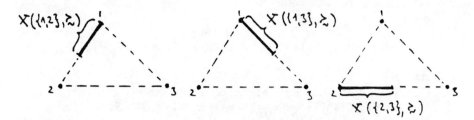

Figure 31.14. The sets $X(S,\succsim)$ of the two-person coalitions in a three-person game with $1 \succ 2 \succ 3$.

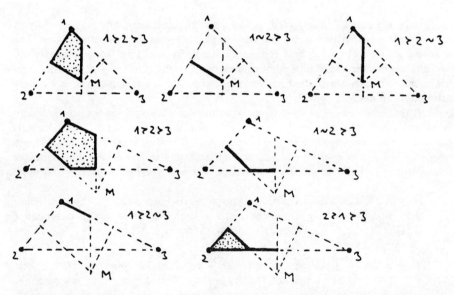

Figure 31.15. Examples of sets $X(S,\succsim)$ of three-person coalitions with different orders of strength.

can serve as arguments; here we assume that the set ϱ of these coalitions is given. The argument of player i will be extended to arguments of subsets of S. Moreover, the alternatives involved in the arguments of a player i must be restricted to such proposals (y, T) that involve player i as an essential decision-maker, i.e., those that are not Pareto-optimal for $T \backslash \{i\}$.

Applying this idea induces a reduction of the solution sets $X(S,\succsim)$ to $X'(S,\succsim)$. Then the same procedure can be applied to the new sets, etc., so that a stepwise adjustment process is obtained.

Correspondingly we define the following set adjustment procedure:

SET ADJUSTMENT PROCEDURE:
Let $\varrho \subseteq W$. We define the sets $X_\varrho^r(S) \subseteq X$ by induction over r for all $S \in \varrho$, $r \in \mathbb{N}$:

   step 1: $X_\varrho^1(S) := X(S, \succsim)$ for all $S \in \varrho$
   step r: let $X_\varrho^r(S)$ be given for all $S \in \varrho$. Then $x \in X_\varrho^{r+1}(S)$ if

(1) $x \in X_\varrho^r(S)$
(2)   There is no $I \subseteq S$ such that for all $T \in \varrho$ with $I \subseteq T$ and
      for all $y \in X_\varrho^r(T)$ and $u_i(y) > u_i(x)$ for all $i \in T \cap S$
(3)   There is a subset $S^* \subseteq S$ such that
      (a)   x is Pareto-optimal for S^*, and
      (b)   For every $i \in S^*$ there is $T \in \varrho$ with $i \in T$, $T \neq S$ and
            $y \in X_\varrho(T)$ such that $u_j(y) \geq u_j(x)$ for all $j \in T \cap S$

Here (2) can be interpreted in the sense that no subcoalition I of S must accept a proposal when it can be sure to get more in any other coalition that contains I. Condition (3) first reduces S^* to S by omitting some players who are not needed to make the compromise on X tight; for the set of remaining players, S^*, it is assumed that each of them should not get more than in his best alternative in another coalition.

It must be remarked that from experimental observations we are not sure whether to include condition (3) in the reduction procedure or not. And, in fact, there are good reasons not to apply condition (3), if one assumes that players only check if a proposal gives high enough amounts to the others, since danger comes from players who get too low amounts and therefore change the coalition.

REMARK and DEFINITION: Applying the procedure of the preceding definition repeatedly, one obtains for each coalition $S \in \varrho$ a sequence $X_\varrho^1(S), X_\varrho^2(S), \cdots$ which, in finitely many steps, leads to a set $X_\varrho^\infty(S) := \bigcap_{r \in \mathbb{N}} X_\varrho^r(S)$.

Figure 31.16 gives an example showing the development of the sets $X(S, \succsim)$. It should be mentioned that strength ordering $\succsim$ and the set ϱ cannot be arbitrarily selected. For a given strength ordering the set ϱ of "reasonable coalitions" should be at least such that $X_\varrho^\infty(S, \succsim) \neq 0$ for all $S \in \varrho$ (since otherwise coalitions serve as arguments during the set adjustment procedure, which in the end are not entered because they do not give stable results). On the other hand, the strength ordering should be such that it permits at least one set ϱ.

DEFINITION: Let Γ be a location game, $\varrho \subseteq W$ and $\succsim$ a strength ordering on N.

   ϱ is consistent for $\succsim$, if $X_\varrho^\infty(S) \neq 0$ for all $S \in \varrho$

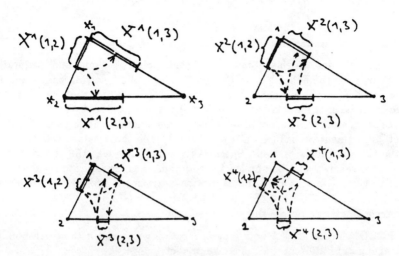

Figure 31.16. An example explaining the set adjustment process: location game with ideal points and strength $1 \succ 2 \succ 3$, according to $a^*(\Gamma)$, $\varrho = \{\{1,2\}, \{1,3\}, \{2,3\}\} = coa(a^*)$.

$\underset{\sim}{\succeq}$ is consistent for Γ, if there is $\varrho \subseteq W$ which is consistent for $\underset{\sim}{\succeq}$.

Moreover, one should require that within the sets ϱ each player is feasible (i.e., $\varrho_i \neq 0$) and no player is dependent (i.e., $\varrho_i \subsetneq \varrho_j$ for no pair $i, j \in N$). [Note that $\varrho_i := \{S \in \varrho \,|\, i \in S\}$.]

In the following section we show that aspiration profiles that are end points of aspiration adjustment paths induce strength orderings (by $i \underset{\sim}{\succeq} j \leftrightarrow a_i \geq a_j$) and sets of coalitions $\varrho := coa(a)$, which are consistent.

31.6.1. The set adjustment process starting with $X(S, \underset{\sim}{\succeq})$, $S \subseteq N$

Now we assume that the strength ordering is obtained by an aspiration profile, which is the end point of a maximal aspiration adjustment path:

THEOREM: Let a be the end point of a maximal aspiration adjustment path, let $\underset{\sim}{\succeq}^a$ be the strength ordering induced by a (i.e., $i \underset{\sim}{\succeq}^a j \leftrightarrow a_i \geq a_j$), let $\varrho := coa(a)$, and let $X_\varrho^1(S) := X(S, \underset{\sim}{\succeq}^a)$ for all $S \in \varrho$. Then for all $S \in \varrho$

(1) $X(a, S) \cap X(S, \underset{\sim}{\succeq}^a) \subseteq X_\varrho^r(S, \underset{\sim}{\succeq}^a)$ for all $r \in N$, and therefore

(2) $X(a, S) \cap X(S, \succsim^a) \subseteq X_\varrho^\infty(S, \succsim^a)$

(3) $X_\varrho^\infty(S, \succsim^a) \neq 0$

So $\succsim^a$ is consistent for the game, and ϱ is consistent for $\succsim^a$.

Generally, one can say that for an end point of a maximal aspiration adjustment path the definitions of this section have the following character: the solution sets $X(S, \succsim^a)$ are extensions of the sets $X(a, S)$ and the set adjustment procedure reduces these sets back into the direction of the sets $X(a, S)$.

As we remarked, it is not clear whether one should exclude condition (3) of the set adjustment procedure. If it is excluded, then the obtained sets are larger and the theorem holds as well. Specifically — and this was the aim of Section 31.5 — this theorem can be applied to the unique regular aspiraton profile a^* of a regular game. In this case the aspiration adjustment procedure extends the predicted areas $X(S, a^*)$ to $X_\varrho^\infty(S, \succsim^{a^*})$ (with $\varrho = coa(a^*)$).

Accordingly, we obtain the

PREDICTION: Let Γ be a regular location game and a the corresponding regular aspiration profile. Then we predict

(1)   A coalition $S \in coa(a)$ will be formed, and

(2)   The corresponding outcome in S will be in $X(S, \succsim)$, where $\succsim$ is the strength ordering induced by a.

It must be remarked that, from the present state of experimental observation, it cannot be definitely decided if the sets $X^1(S, \succsim^a)$, $X^2(S, \succsim^a)$ or $X^\infty(S, \succsim^a)$ are the best predictors of experimental outcomes. This may also depend on knowing to what extent social phenomena can influence the result and thereby on the experimental presentation of the game.

The examples of *Figures 31.17* and *31.18* show that this extension of the predicted areas is essential and necessary to explain experimental results. Moreover, the pure aspiration adjustment path concept (with maximality, PSR, and OSC) leads to point predictions, which are usually not met by experimental results. Overall, the procedures of Section 31.5 extend the predicted regions in a way that fits the experimental results quite well.

31.6.2. Links to equal share analysis and equal division bounds

The procedure described here is related to the equal share analysis [Selten (1978, 1972)] and the equal division bounds concept [Selten (1982, 1985)]. Both concepts have been developed for characteristic function games. The latter concept is only defined for three-person games; however, Selten only considers sets similar to $X^2(S, \succsim^a)$ in the equal share analysis and similar to $X^3(S, \succsim^a)$ in the equal division bounds concept.

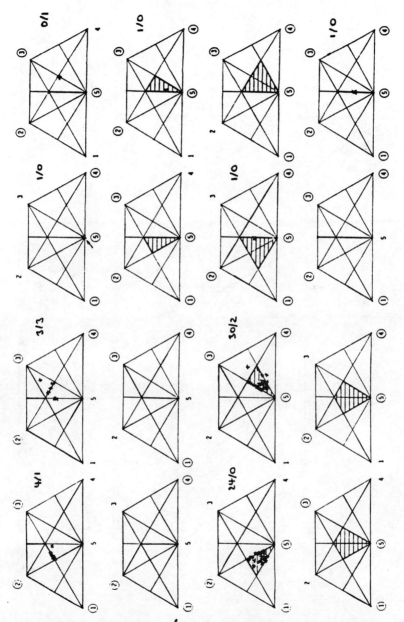

Figure 31.17. Solution sets $X^1(S, m^{a^*})$ and experimental results of a location game with ideal points. Players within a coalition are marked by a circle. The numbers x/y refer to correct/incorrect predictions (including ε-neighborhoods).

388

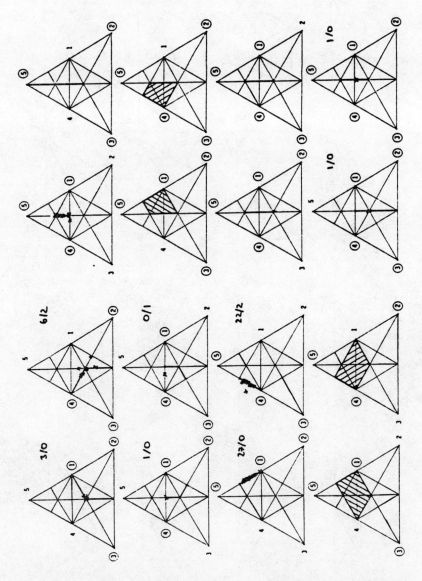

Figure 31.18. Solution sets $X^1(S, succap^{a^*})$ and experimental results of a location game with ideal points. Players within a coalition are marked by a circle. The numbers x/y refer to correct/incorrect predictions (including ϵ-neighborhoods).

31.7. Formation of Blocs

Albers (1978) described phenomena in characteristic function games that can also be detected in location games — namely, the formation of blocs. We introduce this idea with an example (see *Figure 31.19*).

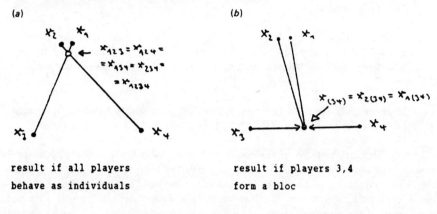

(a)

result if all players
behave as individuals

(b)

result if players 3,4
form a bloc

(c)

result if ⟨1,2⟩ and ⟨3,4⟩
form a bloc, respectively

Figure 31.19. Example describing the formation of blocs in a four-person location game with ideal points.

In the original game the aspiration equilibrium is given by the intersection point of the diagonals $\overline{2}\,\overline{4}$ and $\overline{1}\,\overline{3}$; all aspirations are fulfilled within points (the point is the core point of the game) [see *Figure 31.19 (a)*].

Now, players 3 and 4 might have the idea to form a subcoalition. Although this does not not give them an additional outcome immediately (since 3,4 is not winning), this improves their bargaining situation, if they form then replace their different ideal points x_3 and x_4 by a joint ideal point — for instance, the mid-point x_{34} of x_3 and x_4 — and if they from then on try to verify a result that is as near as possible to x_{34}. In this case the result of the modified game is x_{34} [cf. *Figure 31.19 (b)*].

Of course, players 1 and 2 will answer by forming a subcoalition $\{1,2\}$ with a joint proposal x_{12}, which may be the mid-point of x_1 and x_2. Then the result of the aspiration adjustment process will be the mid-point of x_{12} and x_{34} [see *Figure 31.19 (c)*]. This result shows that the formation of the subcoalition $\{3,4\}$ improves the overall result of players 3 and 4.

Generally we define

DEFINITION: A *bloc* is the formation of a non-winning coalition S, which replaces the utility function of its members by a joint utility function and from then on behaves as one player (with the aggregated number of votes).

Here we only consider the case where the joint utility function is obtained by subsuming the individual utility functions in selecting a new ideal point.

Now we cannot generally say by which principle this new ideal point is selected. One might think of the center of the smallest circle containing all positions of the bloc members, or of the gravicenter of their ideal points, or of a proportional reduction (or an equal-amount reduction) of the aspirations of the original game until a point in the Pareto-surface of the bloc coalition is obtained. At present it seems reasonable to predict the convex closure of these alternatives as reasonable agreement points of the bloc players for a joint ideal position.

The question arises: under which circumstances will players form a bloc? One point is that the conditions of communication must permit them to agree on a joint utility function. The central idea, however, is the

BLOC FORMING PRINCIPLE: A bloc $S \subseteq N$ is formed if thereby the aspirations given by the end points $a^*(\Gamma)$ of the aspiration paths increase for all players of the bloc.

In our example this principle leads to bloc $\{3,4\}$ in a first step and to bloc $\{1,2\}$ in a second step.

However, we also observed formations of blocs that did not increase the aspirations of its members. These did not refer to the aspirations or the aspiration adjustment process, but to specific proposals of the bargaining process:

If a certain proposal (S,x) is regarded as the final state of the bargaining process by all members of S, then the players outside S will definitely not consider their aspirations as possible outcomes but (usually) less than that. It can then be that these players (or a part of them) by forming a bloc (i.e., a subcoalition with a new joint utility function) change the game in such a way that the new aspiration values permit new coalitions including the bloc, and that all bloc members afterward have adequate aspirations that are higher than their outcomes in (S,x).

The central question of such a situation is whether the bloc will hold afterward or if this coalition is only used as a tool to extend the bargaining process beyond a point that is unfavorable for the players of the bloc.

Albers (1978) could show that there are situations where blocs do hold, even if breaking the bloc would increase the aspirations of all of its members; however, these aspirations could not be verified in a coalition including the whole bloc. It seems that the reason that such blocs do not break up can be modeled by loyalty potentials [see Albers (1986a and 1986b)], which are built up among "similar" players in "similar" positions, and which influence the decision behavior in a similar way as additional outcomes of the bloc players. The corresponding examples are characteristic function games.

Acknowledgment

I thank Jim Laing for helpful comments, especially in the area of bloc formation. Readers are referred to Laing and Olmstead (1978) and Laing *et al.* (1983).

References

Albers, W. (1974), Zwei Lösungskonzepte für kooperative Mehrpersonenspiele, die auf Anspruchsniveaus der Spieler basieren, in: *Operations Research Verfahren XXI*, Meisenheim.

Albers, W. (1978), Bloc Forming Tendencies as Characteristics of the Bargaining Behavior in Different Versions of Apex Games, in: H. Sauermann, (ed.), *Coalition Forming Behavior*, Tübingen, pp. 172-200.

Albers, W. (1979), Grundzüge einiger Lösungskonzepte, die auf Forderungsniveaus der Spieler basieren, in: W. Albers, G. Bamberg, and R. Selten (eds.), *Entscheidungen in kleinen Gruppen*, Mathematical Systems in Economics, No. 45, Tübingen, pp. 11-39.

Albers, W. (1986a), Reciprocal Potentials in Apex Games, in: R.W. Scholz (ed.), *Current Issues in West German Decision Research*, Frankfurt, pp. 157-172.

Albers, W. (1986b), *Ergebnisse experimenteller Standortspiele I*, Working Papers No. 151, Institute of Mathematical Economics, University of Bielefeld, July.

Albers, W. (1986c), *Ergebnisse experimenteller Standortspiele II*, Working Papers No. 152, Institute of Mathematical Economics, University of Bielefeld, July.

Albers, W. and Albers, G. (1983), Prominence and Aspiration Adjustment in Location Games, in: R. Tietz (ed.), *Aspiration Levels in Bargaining and Economic Decision Making*, Berlin.

Albers, W. and Brunwinkel, A. (1987), Equal Share Analysis for Location Games, in: R. Tietz, W. Albers, and R. Selten (eds.), *Bounded Rational Behavior in Experimental Games and Markets*, Berlin.

Forman, R. and Laing, J.D. (1982), Metastability and Solid Solutions of Collective Decisions, *Mathematical Social Sciences* 2, pp. 397-420.

Laing, J.D. and Olmsted, S. (1978), An Experimental and Game-Theoretic Study of Committees, in: P.C. Ordeshook (ed.), *Game Theory and Political Science*, New York University Press.

Laing, J.D., Nakabayashi, S., and Slotznick, B. (1983), Winners, Blockers, and the Status Quo: Simple Collective Decision Games and the Core, *Public Choice*, 40, pp. 263-279.

McKelvey, R.D., Ordershook, P.C., and Winer, M. (1978), The Competitive Solution for N-Person Games without Transferable Utility, *American Political Science Review*, pp. 599-615.

Selten, R. (1972), Equal Share Analysis of Characteristic Function Experiments, in: H. Sauermann (ed.), *Contributions to Experimental Economics*, Vol. III, Tübingen, pp. 130-165.

Selten, R. (1978), The Equity Principle in Economic Behavior, in: H.W. Gottinger and W. Leinfellner (eds.), *Decision Theory and Social Ethics, Issues in Social Choice*, Dordrecht, pp. 289-301.

Selten, R. (1982), Equal Decision Payoff Bounds for 3-Person Characteristic Function Experiments, in: R. Tietz (ed.), *Aspiration Levels in Bargaining and Economic Decision Making*, Berlin, pp. 265-275.

Selten, R. (1985), *Equity and Coalition Bargaining in Experimental 3-Person Games*, Working Paper No. 154, Sonderforschungsbereich 303, University of Bonn.

Selten, R. and Krischker, W. (1982), Comparison of Two Theories for Characteristic Function Experiments, in: R. Tietz (ed.), *Aspiration Levels in Bargaining and Economic Decision Making*, Berlin, pp. 259-264.

CHAPTER 32

Tools for Cooperative Negotiation between Two Departments of a Large Corporation: Cultural and Strategic Aspects

Albert David

*Laboratoire d'Analyse et Modélisation de Systémes
pour l'Aide á la Décision (LAMSADE)
Université de Paris-Dauphine
Paris
France*

32.1. Introduction

Introducing negotiation support systems inside a large organization raises specific problems that result not only from modeling difficulties. When several actors or groups of actors decide to work together, they go beyond the traditional sequential procedures. New problems arise that were previously not clearly formulated. The decision frontiers widen; different — and potentially conflicting — strategies and cultures appear. Cooperative, nonsequential decision-making may involve organizational changes: the evolutionary design of appropriate tools can help build a common representation of the problem and lead to more effective decisions.

This discussion will be based on the example of new product design in the automobile industry, at the level of negotiations between the Marketing Department and the Engineering Department.

32.2. Joint Decision-Making within the Organization: A Complex Cooperative Negotiation

32.2.1. General formulation of the problem: The meeting of three actors

The term "negotiation" can be understood in many different ways. When we try to support negotiations inside an organization, it is important to define well which type of situation is referred to.

Imagine a large industrial corporation, composed of various departments (Finance, Marketing, Production, etc.), each subdivided into a certain number of teams. Our discussion may be represented by the following general formulation: two divisions X and Y, belonging to distinct departments, coexist within the organization. Both are involved in the decision processes, but have no direct contacts. Now suppose they wish to cooperate, to improve the quality and the effectiveness of their decisions.

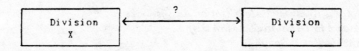

Figure 32.1. What does "cooperation" mean?

As *Figure 32.1* suggests, what occurs when two groups of actors decide to work together can be analyzed from various points of view. We will put the stress on the two main factors that structure this interaction: the culture and the strategies of each group.

Moreover, if a "mediator" (from outside the organization) is called by division X to design and to introduce tools (computer-aided or not) to support the cooperation, a complex relation is created between three actors (*Figure 32.2*) — divisions X and Y and the mediator with his negotiations support system — each of them representing a culture, a rationality, a strategy.

32.2.2. Consequences of traditional sequential procedures for conflict solving

The organization chart in *Figure 32.3* — taken from the automobile industry — does not pretend to describe the complexity of real decision processes: it only illustrates our discussion.

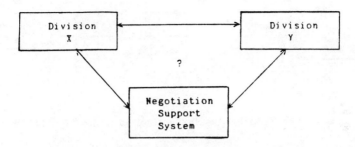

Figure 32.2. X, Y, and the negotiation support system: a complex interaction.

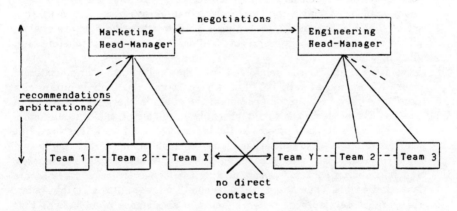

Figure 32.3. A traditional organization chart.

This simplified organization chart shows a traditional Taylorian type of organization: each department — the Marketing Department and the Engineering Department — is composed of several subdivisions, each subdivision or team being in charge of a particular aspect of product design or management (marketing design, style, doors, engine, etc.). At the upper level, the head managers meet and negotiate, supported by recommendations from their respective staffs. From the upper level to the lower level: arbitrations; from the lower level to the upper level: recommendations that will "rationally" support intuitions and orientations. But at the lower level, discussion remain within a department. There are generally no direct contacts between teams from distinct departments: each division has its reserved field of competence, and the project (the future product) circulates sequentially from one department to another (*Figure 32.4*).

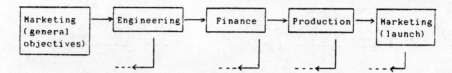

Figure 32.4. A sequential decision process.

In this type of organization, conflicts are solved in three different ways:

(1) Arbitrations and competitive negotiation (upper level: formal, planned meetings).

(2) Sequential problem-solving and functional division of work. To face complexity, it is often easier to treat the various aspects of a problem separately or sequentially. This corresponds to the traditional, still widespread belief that a complex problem can always be subdivided into a set of simple subproblems, each giving birth to a specific partial decision, all decisions being easily aggregated afterward to form a coherent and efficient whole

(3) "Avoidance" strategies, reinforced by the well-known "organizational slack" [Cyert and March (1963)] of large corporations. The definition of a problem depends on the composition of the group in charge of managing it. The quality of decisions would probably be higher if the various actors involved in the decision process at the lower level could work together. But the individual and organizational cost of such changes may be heavy. Different and potentially conflicting cultures, strategies, work, analyses, and information sources appear, making the former situation more secure and comfortable. The "organizational slack" allows, up to a certain point, the parallel development of work and the coexistence of objectives that would turn out to be competitive in a more "transparent" system.

32.2.3. A cooperative negotiation

When two groups of actors (in our example, division X of the Marketing Department and division Y of the Engineering Department) decide to work together, they go beyond the traditional procedures and hierarchical relations: they create a very particular type of cooperative negotiation. New problems arise that were previously not clearly formulated. A common language and a common problem representation must be found to ensure both a correct translation of Marketing objectives into their technical meaning and an effective synergy between technical research and its marketing consequences.

32.3. Building a Common Problem Representation: Cultures and Strategies

The design of a new car results from a very long and complex decision process that involves several hundreds of persons. In our example, even a relatively "small" problem (fixing objectives in terms of comfort or noise level of the future car) is complex enough to make impossible any global modeling: no "optimal" or "true" solution can be found. Moreover, the various tools that can be used and the procedures that can be introduced represent a certain culture and reveal — sometimes in a very subtle manner — a certain conception of management [Pascale and Athos (1981)]. They constitute a "new deal" with respect to the strategies and the culture of the actors concerned; they may even give birth to conflicts and incompatibilities, eventually leading to a return to the former traditional procedures. A few examples will illustrate these ideas.

32.3.1. Strategies

When the various tools and models that could help describe or analyze a problem are implemented, the necessary data are too often supposed to be "given" ("data" is the Latin word for "given") or already collected. When the data collection difficulties (cost, time, low precision, nonmeasurability, etc.) are taken into account, a second aspect is generally neglected: information has a strategic dimension. This dimension, well known to professional negotiators or in more competitive contexts, is surprisingly ignored in the type of situation we are describing. Cooperation supposes information exchange. Building a common problem representation requires that each division communicates at least a part of the information that supports its point of view. The strategic consequences of the cooperation must be carefully analyzed as the negotiation procedures are elaborated, because the strategies involved may constitute a major obstacle to reaching the minimum level of "transparency" and "honesty" required for an effective negotiation.

Let us give a short example, Engineers of the Engineering Department are judged, among other criteria, on their creativity, which leads them to develop systematically new solutions. A few months ago, one of the engineers elaborated a very elegant and original — but expensive — technical solution. Of course, he hoped that his solution would be selected for the future product. Consequently, he was logically led to under-evaluate intentionally the other products of the brand on that particular criterion so that his hierarchy, alarmed by such a bad score, would adopt his project. Though this example is a bit caricatured, it clearly appears that a database including this type of information does not have the reliability required for a real negotiation support system.

32.3.2. Cultures

When people from different continents meet — for instance, North Americans with Japanese or Koreans with French — they may discover cultural differences that go far beyond the way to say "Good morning!" or to shake hands. Perceptions of time and space, definitions of what are "a good compromise" or "a fair negotiation" are different [Hall (1969 and 1973), Hofstede (1984)].

A negotiation between two departments within a corporation raises the same kind of problems. Of course, national values are not involved here: more specific variables appear, mainly professional values, which can explain a part of each department's point of view, behavior and strategy within the organization. Three examples will illustrate the importance of cultural variables.

First, engineers are experts. Their behavior is therefore different from the behavior of a nonspecialist. The expert will, for instance, notice very detailed imperfections and under-evaluate a product whose global characteristics are quite acceptable or to over-appreciate a car if its designers have solved a certain technical problem in a particularly elegant or original way. What is for the average consumer — therefore for the Marketing Department — an almost invisible imperfection could not be ignored by the engineer: in that case, he would appear, in his colleagues' opinion, as a bad expert.

A second cultural variable is linked to how each department sees the truth. For the Marketing Department, the "truth" is mainly statistical: it comes from the analysis of large surveys of representative samples of the population. Moreover, the analysis of consumer behavior includes psychological, highly subjective considerations: we are close to social sciences, where imprecision, ambiguity and subjectivity play an important part. The technical culture of the Engineering Department is closer to the traditional epistemology of experimental sciences: "truth" exists and can be measured; the first attitude of the engineer to explain a phenomenon will be to determine and measure its various components. This explains, for instance, our difficulties in introducing some elements of multiattribute utility theory [Keeney and Raiffa (1976)] or the multicriteria decision-aid methodology [Roy (1985)]: "Our measures are objective: why associate a utility function to a variable or build a criterion?" was the first response. Conflicts between the Marketing Department and the Engineering Department can therefore come from the way the experts, because of the instruments they use to collect and manage information, will treat problems — according to their scientific attractiveness and their measurability, and not with regard to the average consumer's opinion.

The third example is slightly different. It shows how a very simple graphic representation can lead to very important changes in the way a problem is identified and solved. In the Marketing Department, the statisticians traditionally represented a variable by a scaled vertical axis, on which the various cars were placed according to their score on that variable. Several criteria were represented with as many vertical scales (*Figure 33.5*).

    Suppose that the statistician now uses the graphic possibilities of a spread sheet to plot this type of graph. The standard graph of Lotus 123, for instance, is not a monodimensional vertical graph: it is a two-dimensional X Y plot (*Figure 32.6*).

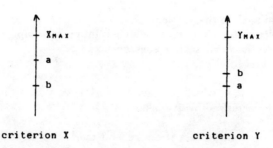

Figure 32.5. A traditional sequential representation.

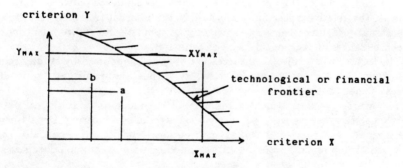

Figure 32.6. Widening the problem: a two-dimensional XY plot.

    This new graphic representation is not only different graphically, it leads the decision-maker to consider the interaction between X and Y. The ideal point (XY_{max}) is probably infeasible (for instance, a car with a very high maximum speed and a very low fuel consumption) or strongly depends on a technological or financial frontier. This is a good example of how the logic of a very simple model can generate important changes in the way problems are analyzed — toward less sequential, more global decision processes.

32.4. A Decision Support System for Cooperative Negotiation

32.4.1. Modeling: A complex environment

The traditional normative description of problem-solving consists of four successive steps:

(1)   Identify and analyze the problem.
(2)   If the problem is too complex, subdivide it into more simple subproblems.
(3)   Generate solutions and analyze consequences.
(4)   Choose the best solution.

The environment in which we have to work is very far from this idealized view; it can be characterized by five points:

-   The whole decision process (from general marketing objectives to product launch on the market) lasts about five years. This means that the set of possible actions is only partially defined as the project grows.
-   The various subproblems are not mutually independent. For instance, no decision concerning the maximum speed level should be made without considering the fuel consumption level. Even the design of the seats can have indirect but important consequences on another part of the car.
-   The complexity of the product, the high interdependence between subproblems, the relative uncertainty concerning the internal (research results) or external (consumer behavior or strategy of competitors) environment make consequences of decisions difficult to estimate.
-   The history of a project is a succession of fights, supported by studies reinforcing the various points of view; it is not the result of "rational" cost–benefit analysis.
-   The Marketing Department manipulates large amounts of statistical data, but at a rather aggregated level, whereas the Engineering Department manages very precise technical information, but not systematically collected, which makes more difficult the building up of a common database.

In such a context, how can we introduce a negotiation support system and of what could it be made?

32.4.2. Methodology: An evolutionary design

It is now widely accepted that decision support systems — and this is even more accurate for negotiation support systems — should be designed in an evolutionary way. Their implementation requires a careful methodology to ensure a successful interaction between an "ethnographic" analysis of decision and negotiation processes (in terms of cultures, strategies, learning possibilities of the various actors) and the design of relevant tools.

At least three different aspects should be taken into account:

- Relevance concerning the complexity of the problem (the model must neither be too simplistic nor constitute an uncontrollable black box).
- Relevance concerning modes of cooperation desired by the two groups of actors.
- Relevance concerning the way each division or department has to justify its orientations, recommendations or decisions within the organization, and particularly toward its own hierarchy.

32.4.3. Which tools to support the cooperation?

Many tools exist, simple or sophisticated, that could help the two groups to work together. The more important needs were expressed at three levels:

- Quick data management (sorting, listing, and simple mathematical operations such as means, standard deviations or medians).
- Quick and easy data graphic representations (profiles, two-dimensional XY plots, etc.), for immediate use during work sessions.
- More sophisticated tools for interactive preference modeling and multivariate data analysis and description.

This explains our intensive use of:

- A spreadsheet with graphic possibilities for data management and visualization.
- Regression analysis to bring out relations between the consumer's satisfaction and the technical characteristics of the product (which is a way to build an analytical bridge between the Marketing Department and the Engineering Department).
- PREFCALC [Jacquet-Lagréze (1982)] for interactive preference modeling, this preference being either the consumer's opinion or the individual perception of an expert who wants to "understand" better his own point of view.

32.5. Concluding Remarks

As they tried to build a common representation, to define a common language, to ban meaningless words (i.e., to create a common culture), the two groups of actors started a fruitful process of thinking over their own way of working, past and present. If this cooperation lasts, the decision frontiers will have to be made precise: what would the problem become if the Financial Department or the Quality Department (which also make recommendations concerning future products) were progressively included? Which kind of culture and which conflicting strategies would appear? And what would this "horizontal" cooperation become if members of the hierarchy participated? Experience seems to show that the expert in charge of the design and implementation of negotiation support tools (let us call him a mediator) should mention this dimension, but let the actors concerned decide whether or not to enlarge the group to members of other parts of the organization.

References

Cyert, R.M. and March, J.G. (1963), *A Behavioral Theory of the Firm*, Prentice-Hall, Englewood Cliffs, NJ.

Hall, E.T. (1969), *The Hidden Dimension*, New York.

Hall, E.T. (1973), *The Silent Language*, New York.

Hofstede, G. (1984), *Culture's Consequences: International Differences in Work-Related Values*, Sage Publications, Beverly Hills, CA.

Jacquet-Lagréze, E. (1982), *Logical PREFCALC*, Euro Décision.

Keeney, R.L. and Raiffa H. (1976), *Decisions with Multiple Objectives: Preferences and Value Trade-offs*, John Wiley, New York.

Pascale, R.T. and Athos, A.G. (1981), *The Japanese Art of Management*, Simon and Schuster, New York.

Roy, R. (1985), *Méthodologie Multicritére d'Aide á la Décision*, Economica.

CHAPTER 33

A Computer Network-Based Teleconferencing System to Enhance the Effectiveness of Multilateral Negotiations Fora

Vladimir F. Pryakhin

USSR Ministry of Foreign Affairs
Moscow
USSR

33.1. Introduction

Normally both multilateral and bilateral disarmament negotiations, with rare exceptions, come under the category of political negotiations. Hence, their specific features such as

- Dependence on the overall world political situation.
- Special, stricter rules of procedure (consensus).
- Extreme irregularity in attaining practical results.

The complexity of disarmament negotiations and the particular importance that the problems discussed there have for the national security of states determine these talks' special status and specific rules of procedure. At no other negotiations is the rule of consensus so strictly observed.

The extreme irregularity of such negotiations brought about the use of the term "breakthrough", which vividly describes progress reached at the talks after many months or sometimes years of seemingly fruitless exchanges. It is not the purpose of this chapter to review the process of forming political will for concluding treaties in the field of disarmament. Political will is undoubtedly a major precondition for the success of disarmament negotiations. It is shaped by a number of factors inherent in the international situation.

This chapter, instead, will study the possibility of enhancing the effectiveness of negotiations, given that all participants without exception display political will for their successful completion.

We believe that such an approach, although *a priori* and somewhat one-sided, is quite valid, *since an effective negotiating mechanism is in itself an important factor that helps to shape political will for the success of the negotiations.*

The negotiating mechanism cannot of itself dismantle the political barriers that divide the participants, but it can help to identify and distinguish between obstacles to agreements. Expert analysis and discussion may well reveal that many problems dividing the participants in the negotiations are technical rather than political, while technical problems previously thought to be insurmountable may prove to lend themselves to solution.

Moreover, it should be kept in mind that international negotiations are becoming increasingly complicated, technical and loaded with important scientific, technical and legal details.

All this makes it quite relevant to examine the problem of enhancing the effectiveness of international negotiations, including disarmament talks, assuming the existence of political will. In our view the negotiations to ban chemical weapons held within the Conference on Disarmament (CD) are significant in this respect. Technically and legally, the subject matter of these negotiations is so complex that, even when an overwhelming majority of participants seek to achieve practical results, there are quite a few technical difficulties that objectively impede an early elaboration of agreements.

What then are the ways to enhance the effectiveness of such multilateral negotiations? Some traditional ways to enhance the effectiveness of multilateral negotiating fora long employed by the international community have probably not yet been exhausted. These include, in particular, increasing participation, extending the negotiating time frame, increasing the number of experts on various subjects in some delegations, improving the quality of interpretation at negotiations, as well as providing negotiators with skilled interpretation for longer hours, increasing the number of auxiliary working bodies and making it possible for negotiators to go, if necessary, on extended official missions away from the venue of the talks, thus making them more mobile.

The Geneva negotiating fora serve as a concrete example illustrating the application of all these methods to enhance their effectiveness. In the framework of this Conference it seems to be appropriate to raise the question of reviewing a broad application of technical facilities and aids for conducting negotiations on political issues, including disarmament negotiations.

We believe that a certain technological basis to that end already exists. Organizational and scientific information systems for automated dialogue, which are in fact sophisticated teleconferencing systems based on computer networks, are particularly promising aids for multilateral negotiating fora.

The application of such systems fully corresponds to the intensified life style of contemporary society at large, with the role of communications being constantly on the rise. It is well known that the costs involved in providing people with information during the process of their activities are continuously rising. Soviet experts estimate that communications costs including cable, telex and telephone expenses are several times higher than those involved in the technical processing of information. Losses resulting from inadequate or untimely decisions because of incomplete information are high.

33.2. Potential Benefits of ADOSIS (automated dialogue organizational and scientific information systems)

Network-based computers, which exchange information upon the users' request, produce a new, effective communication environment both for political negotiators and technical experts. Such a communication environment is characterized by low cost and easier accessibility, user-friendliness and developed "intellect", high speed of information transmission, a powerful means of information display and the potential for documenting textual and graphic information.

Automated dialogue information systems used within the structure of negotiations could make it possible, by means of automated information exchanges with major data banks available to the international community, to provide negotiators with more modern and effective means of communication between groups of people whose traditional forms include conferences, meetings, etc. It is for this reason that such systems are called computer network-based teleconferencing systems, thus distinguishing them from fundamentally simpler electronic mail systems.

The following example can be cited by way of illustration. The joint Soviet–US document on the prohibition of radiological weapons took 49 meetings to be finalized, including meetings of the drafting group that worked hard during several rounds a year. Only 34 meetings were held to discuss that issue during the initial two years at the Geneva disarmament negotiating forum, while there was an actual need for a continuous examination of that particular question with a view to finalizing numerous technical details. *Organizational and scientific information systems for automated dialogue are capable of making the negotiating process a continuous one* and could enable a qualitative breakthrough in expanding chronological frameworks for conducting negotiations. Thus, the negotiators are actually provided with continuous contact, regardless of whether they are physically present at the venue of negotiations — for instance, in Geneva — or remain at their permanent place of work.

In this context a substantive remark seems to be in order. Participation *per se* in international negotiations held in major world centers designed for that purpose is becoming a symbol of the modern way of life, and participating in such negotiations is regarded as a matter of prestige. In this connection, the wide application of computer network-based teleconferencing systems to the process of international negotiations has been opposed because of fears that such systems could phase out negotiations as a form of international communication.

Such fears are totally groundless. Direct communication between political negotiators can never be supplanted. The introduction of ADOSIS has a different purpose — namely, to set the stage for political negotiations as such, relieve them from technical details, reconcile to the utmost those issues and details on which agreement can be reached at the expert level, and ensure a higher level of expertise in technical and political matters.

At one point there was a legitimate question raised in the framework of the Geneva disarmament negotiating forum to the effect that work at this forum did not take place more than 12 weeks a year, the balance of time being spent on vacations, leaves and discussions of procedural matters. The introduction of automated dialogue systems could make it possible to expand considerably these time limitations on negotiations.

As for the fears that contacts between computers will replace contacts between people, we believe that with the application of ADOSIS the international community will be able to enlarge quantitatively the agenda of negotiations, incorporate more issues and technical categories, and increase the number of negotiating fora and eventually the number of political contacts between negotiators.

One of the functions of ADOSIS, which can be easily applied within the framework of a multilateral negotiating forum, is to make available to negotiators advanced means of electronic mail which include:

- Printing out newly arrived or as yet unread personal messages addressed to a given user or groups that include a given user.
- Reviewing newly arrived messages.
- Retrieving messages from key fields, contexts or associative relationships.
- Readdressing messages.
- Generating new messages.
- Interrelating messages to generate strings of messages.
- Forwarding messages to individual users, groups of users or to all users.
- Automatically acknowledging message receipt by the addressee.
- Storing messages in the system's archives or user's personal archives.

It is easy to see that the above functions of electronic mail encompass most of the functional machinery of multilateral negotiations.

Besides performing the electronic mail functions, ADOSIS can provide negotiators with a capability to engage in simultaneous exchanges of information at both the political and expert levels. To that end, the following functions may be envisaged:

- Compilation of the list of currently active system users.
- Establishment of bilateral interactive links between two users or a multilateral link among a group of users.

- Exchange of information among those users who have established the interactive link.

It should be noted in passing that the simultaneous address subsystem could include the possibility of an active involvement in negotiations of non-governmental organizations, as well as of organizations representing various segments of public opinion and the scientific community, whose recommendations to the negotiators could then be more competent. Therefore, the computerization of negotiations would promote their globalization both in terms of the number of issues discussed and the number of participants. In our view, this is fully consistent with the scope of the political goals of negotiations, which is to ensure international peace and security.

33.3. Possible Roles of ADOSIS in the Various Stages of Negotiations

It is not difficult to see that each subsystem of ADOSIS has its analogue in a time- and space-related structure of bilateral and multilateral negotiations, including political negotiations. The stages leading to multilateral negotiations can include the following:

(1) At the beginning of a negotiation one or several future participants formulates the subject matter of the negotiations. Teleconferencing systems could enable any state to formulate an initiative in accurate and well-defined terms or to sponsor international negotiations on any technically complex subject, if its political interests so require.

(2) At the second, preparatory stage, the sponsoring state seeks to enlist support for the subject of negotiations among other members of the international community and form an action group for the purpose of, e.g., adopting relevant documents of the international community, such as United Nations General Assembly resolutions, joint statements by the groups at the Geneva Conference on Disarmament, etc.

An example of such a document is the joint document CD/200 submitted by the group of Socialist countries at the Geneva Conference on Disarmament and issued in 1981; it contained proposals to enhance the effectiveness of the machinery of the Conference (then called the Committee on Disarmament).

As a rule, documents of that kind are drafted, negotiated and issued by the negotiators whose political positions are close. All the more significant is the indisputable fact that in this case, too, computer network-based teleconferencing equipment can help provide a better rationale for the proposals made by cosponsors to initiate negotiations. In principle, no one can rule out the possibility that like-minded cosponsors, after careful discussion through the teleconferencing system, will come to the conclusion that it is objectively impossible to propose the initiative in question. In that case, the participants of the action group (cosponsors) would take a well-founded decision to refrain from proposing a joint initiative. This must also be seen as a useful result of the application of teleconferencing.

(3) As soon as the display of the chairman of the multilateral negotiating body has reproduced the specific proposal by the sponsor or the cosponsors to initiate negotiations on the subject, the third, and politically most important, stage of the preparation of negotiations will start — namely, drawing up the agenda for the negotiating body's session.

There have been periods in the history of the Conference on Disarmament where negotiation of the agenda for a current session took four, five or even more months out of the year's total of four to five months of work. This was due, of course, to political differences in the positions of the negotiating states. Computer systems alone will not eliminate such differences; however, they may be used to take account of all the proposals available, which may facilitate the search for possible solutions and accelerate negotiation of the agenda.

(4) The next negotiating stage is no longer preparatory, but rather substantive. That is, after the *agenda* and the *work program* have been adopted, the multilateral negotiating forum enters the stage where delegations of the participating countries present their political positions on the individual agenda items.

Records show that this stage in the negotiations requires computerization least of all. By this time, political positions will already have been prepared and agreed upon among the groups of like-minded states. Oftentimes, the main task before the delegations at this stage is to present those positions with maximum effect not so much for the benefit of their negotiating partners as for the press. At this stage, the negotiations usually serve as the platform from which political statements are made by the Secretary General of the United Nations, heads of state, foreign ministers and other political leaders.

In substantive terms, the main point at this stage in the negotiations will usually be whether or not there is a consensus on the establishment of subsidiary bodies to conduct specific negotiations on a particular issue on the basis of an agreed mandate.

(5) This stage of the negotiations consists in negotiating the mandate of any subsidiary working body that has been formed. A political comparison of the positions is also essential at this stage. The teleconferencing techniques might be used here on a somewhat larger scale, because work proceeds on the texts of draft mandates in open-ended subsidiary groups of all kinds. The discussions within the framework of the Geneva Conference on Disarmament on the mandate of the subsidiary working body on the agenda item

entitled "Prevention of an Arms Race in Outer Space" during its 1984 session demonstrated that, along with three formal draft mandates, up to a dozen or even more papers can be discussed informally. It is much easier and more efficient to compare and negotiate such drafts on a teleconferencing display than on paper.

(6)   The use of computers by subsidiary working bodies:

(a)   As soon as negotiations start in a subsidiary working body on the basis of an agreed mandate, which usually provides for the preparation of legally binding papers in a particular area, a new stage begins where the use of computers is in our view highly desirable today and absolutely imperative in the future. As a rule, negotiations in a subsidiary working body start with a review of all the existing agreements and documents in this area. The computer memory is an excellent working instrument for such a review.

(b)   The work on a text of a document on the basis of submitted proposals and drafts, as well as the discussion and negotiation of provisions of a future agreement (or convention) in a subsidiary working body, constitute the most important stage of negotiations. At this stage, we perceive the possible use of computer network-based teleconferencing techniques as involving some of the data that characterize results of the work of specially formed groups, e.g., the Ad Hoc Committee on Chemical Weapons of the Conference on Disarmament (CD), set up by the CD for the period of the 1985 session [1]. This example, in our view, is a most appropriate illustration for improving the effectiveness of international negotiations, because there is an increasingly clear-cut consensus emerging in the world community on the question of banning chemical weapons — a development that is propitious for the success of the negotiations.

Nevertheless, even in these relatively favorable circumstances, the efficiency of the work of the Ad Hoc Committee on Chemical Weapons and its subsidiary working bodies was rather low as far as the technical aspects are concerned. Between February 27 and August 19, 1985, there were 12 meetings of the Ad Hoc Committee [2], i.e., one meeting every week and a half of the session's work. At the same time, there were 17 meetings held by working group A [3], 12 by working group B [4], and 14 by working group C [5] of the Ad Hoc Committee. In addition, there were numerous open-ended consultations held by the Chairman.

These seemingly humble figures look quite different if seen by the negotiators themselves, i.e., members of the delegations and experts. In fact, out of 286 persons on the consolidated list of participants in the 1985 session, only two or three dozen experts could fully concentrate on the extremely difficult matter of the negotiations. A number of delegations — namely, half of those represented at the Conference — did not even have any experts on some of the priority items of the agenda.

For that matter, it should be noted that in spite of the heavy schedule, experts spend much time on problems such as checking and comparing documents, searching for necessary documentation and moving about Geneva and the Palais des Nations. To this should be added the large translation workload done by both the Conference secretariat and national delegations.

A rough analysis of the work performed by the Ad Hoc Committee on Chemical Weapons of the Conference on Disarmament during the 1985 session shows that in our opinion, it could have been done at least twice as fast and at a significantly higher level of expertise, if effective computer-based systems to aid negotiations had been available.

33.4. Potential Benefits of Problem Information Subsystems of ADOSIS

In this connection, the future introduction into the negotiating practice of a problem information subsystem is promising. This subsystem is an integral part of the automated dialogue organizational and scientific information systems that are being currently developed by specialists in a number of countries [6, 7].

This subsystem offers the following possibilities, which are directly consonant with operations carried out during the meetings of subsidiary working bodies of a multilateral negotiating forum or conference (e.g., the CD):

- Printing out a list of conferences available to a given user, hooking up to a selected conference, and obtaining the list of its participants.
- Retrieving conference-related data (reports, documents, materials, decisions, opinions, resolutions, etc.) from key fields, contexts or associative links.
- Reviewing titles of sections of working documents, and, if necessary, reviewing the content of the sections selected.
- Formulating a new section (with no specific format or patterned after one of the formats used for a given problem), identifying key fields of a newly formulated section, establishing a fixed link between the newly formulated section and one of the previous sections (fixed association or continuation of a previous section), establishing a substantive link between the new section and one or several previous sections (substantive association for organizing section "strings" on a given problem).
- Submitting a problem under discussion as a whole, its section, a block of sections or an associated string of sections for coordination or for a vote, as well as taking note of the fact and results of such coordination (unconditional with an associated "dissenting opinion", "objection", etc.) or voting.
- Obtaining information on the results of such a coordination or vote on a given problem.

- Storing in a participant's personal archives the sections of the conference documents sponsored by him; arranging a new section out of several old ones in any sequence; documenting the section, a sequence of sections or strings of associated sections; and removing sections.

As a reflection of the negotiating experience accumulated in international practice, the conference subsystem practically replicates the (model of) negotiations. One of the participants in the teleconferencing may be appointed as presiding officer (chairman) and in such a case he alone can perform a number of functions. Of the functions listed above, this may include submitting sections for coordination or for the vote, removing sections, and establishing document formats that have been adopted for the subject at hand. The presiding officer may also admit or dismiss participants, or determine a participant's status out of one of the following:

- Observer without the right to vote or coordinate, or the right to codify old sections and introduce new ones.
- Nonvoting technical officer without the right to vote or coordinate.
- Participant without the right to coordinate.
- Full-fledged participant enjoying all possible rights of a delegate.
- Senior participant partially endowed with a leader's rights.

In addition to its other merits, this kind of system enables new participants, at both the expert and political levels, to join the negotiating process promptly.

A number of the subsystem's functions is performed automatically. Upon joining the conference, a new user is automatically provided with information on the total number of sections, the number of new sections (with which the user is not yet familiar) and the number of sections to be coordinated or voted upon. When drawing up a new section within one of the document formats adopted by a given conference, the formating is carried out automatically. If a deadline or a phased schedule is set for solving a problem, the message subsystem is then used to issue regular reminders to all delegates involved about the approaching deadlines.

A major advantage of computer network-based teleconferencing systems is that they make it possible to overcome language barriers between negotiators. By and large, the existing mechanism of multilateral negotiations already permits dealing with the language problem both through the use of highly skilled interpretation and translation and through the continuous upgrading by the negotiators of their proficiency in foreign languages. The requirements for the emerging "globalization" of negotiations, however, present the language problem in a new light, because of a sharp increase in the number of "topics" (specific subjects) of international negotiations as well as in the number of direct and indirect negotiators, especially at the expert level. To overcome the language barrier, computer teleconferencing systems may be employed to help the users independently to formulate (unless an adequate standard version is available) the texts of all inquiries and messages within the system. This is achieved by arranging all textual information contained in the external interface in special files (one per each version of the interface). With this structural pattern, the teleconferencing mechanism can be changed to a "new" language simply by preparing yet another version of the text stored in the service file of the external interface. In a similar fashion, the system can be adapted to the terminal equipment employed by the user.

33.5. Concluding Remarks

A large-scale introduction of teleconferencing may raise a possible problem: that the "globalization" of negotiations will result in a loss of their structure or usual hierarchy. We feel that this would not be the case, since the teleconferencing system itself provides for a certain hierarchy among the negotiators as well as selecting out information known in advance to be useless to a given negotiator or expert.

At the same time, the introduction of teleconferencing systems makes it possible to achieve its main objective, namely a possibility of taking into account and of incorporating in the final documents of negotiations any constructive opinion, conclusion or judgment, wherever and at whatever level they may be expressed.

As noted above, teleconferencing and computerizing the multilateral or international negotiating process cannot substitute or make up for a lack of political will to conclude the agreements under negotiation. We are strongly convinced that political will to achieve agreements is a specific state of political thinking of negotiators and others involved in the processes of negotiations, which evolves as a result of a number of factors in international affairs. Computerized aids for the negotiating process and the use of the most advanced information technology are intended to promote political will for productive negotiations.

Listed below are some of the possible effects of computerization on the political will of negotiators:

- Computerization can provide an opportunity to separate political and technical issues in the course of negotiations.
- It can raise the level of expertise.
- As a result of using the computer network-based teleconferencing mechanism, the negotiating process can acquire a global dimension, viz:
  • The number of negotiators can become larger.
  • The number of problems under discussion can increase.
  • A longer period of time can be allocated for dealing with problems.
- In the long run, the introduction of computer network-based teleconferencing into the negotiating mechanism could aid in the development of approximate computer models of international negotiations, which could enhance the effectiveness of negotiations to promote international cooperation and security.

Notes

[1] Document of the Conference on Disarmament, CD/551.
[2] UN document A/40/27, p. 42.
[3] *Ibid.*, p. 91.
[4] *Ibid.*, p. 103.
[5] *Ibid.*, p. 127.
[6] Hittz, S.R. (1978), *The Network Nation: Human Communication via Computer*, Massachusetts.
[7] Hittz, S.R. (1985), *Online Communities: A Case Study of the Office of the Future*, Ablex.

CHAPTER 34

The Mediator as a Third Negotiator

Guy-Olivier Faure

Université de Paris-Sorbonne
Paris
France

From the strategic analysis of a mediator's actions one can construct a model that portrays the relations between the different parties involved in a mediated negotiation. Identifying and studying the motivations of all the actors enables one to develop new concepts. These concepts will explain, first, the position of the mediator in relation to the parties and, second, his contribution that modifies the entire negotiating framework. Both of these conditions govern the process and the outcome of the negotiation. The various strategic positions that may be adopted by the mediator, combining partiality and non-neutrality, are analyzed in this chapter.

The methodology applied to this work consists of an integration of real-world observations made from the perspective of different fields: sociology, anthropology, social psychology. It aims at proposing a conceptual framework able to give an accurate account of the rationale at work in a mediation intervention.

34.1. Introduction

Mediation is a social process that occurs in the case of very particular situations, for the most part highly conflictual negotiations that result in a deadlock. None of the parties involved in the conflict wishes to make any or any more concessions, but the stalemate is in itself very costly for both sides. This is the case in an open conflict, such as a war, or in a mere refusal of any economic cooperation between two neighboring countries.

Mediation is defined by Touval and Zartman (1985) as a "form of third-party intervention in conflict for the purpose of abating or resolving that conflict through negotiations".

It can be radically distinguished from other forms of third-party interventions, such as arbitration, because a mediator never takes a decision instead of the parties, as an arbitrator would. He interferes in a complex process in order to direct this process toward a potential agreement between the parties. the ultimate decision belonging to these parties. However, the mediator is not powerless, contrary to well-accepted theories.

Although such an activity has not yet been thoroughly studied nor adequately conceptualized, mediation has a broad field of application including family disputes, labor relations conflicts and international disputes.

Mediation has traditionally been part of international conflicts. There is a very old and on-going tradition of mediation in international conflicts. A quite exhaustive study [Holsti (1983)] takes a census of 94 conflicts since 1919 and shows that 42 among them have been mediated. In most of the cases, the conflict stemmed from a territorial dispute. The USA, the UN, the Pope, the Organization of African Unity, the Organization of American States, the International Red Cross, and Algeria have been among the most active mediators in the last two decades.

34.2. The Rationale of Mediation

In the first theoretical works on negotiation, mediation appears to be either just ignored, as in the case of Walton and McKersie (1965), or portrayed in a quite idealistic conception that becomes totally unrealistic as soon as applied to international situations. Such an approach has been illustrated by Peters (1952) and Simkin (1971). Being themselves professional mediators, they offer a strongly idealized self-reconstruction of their own experiences. Their research tends to represent the mediator as a powerless judge. To be efficient, the mediator must have a high status and must not have or show personal preferences. His only purpose is to implement justice and work for the common good.

From a Lewinian approach, McGrath (1966) suggests a broader model able to integrate more dimensions and forces operating during the mediation process. Meanwhile, his concept of a mediator still belongs to the former category, because he postulates that the mediator represents the whole social system in which both conflicting parties interact. By experimenting with the McGrath model, Touzard (1977) points out that such a model is more suited to formal than to informal negotiation. As most international negotiations are of an informal nature, this model is difficult to apply.

Looking at mediation in international conflicts, one may emphasize several points. The mediator's intervention has a structural influence on the negotiation system itself. It changes a dyadic relation into a triadic system, thus changing the logic of equilibrium. The mediator introduces new values into the game. He has his own representations, goals, strategies and tactics. By intervening in the interaction, he increases the number of issues at stake. A mediator involved in an international dispute has his own conception of what international order should be and what an acceptable attitude within a relationship should be.

A triadic interaction may elicit complex strategies. Each party strives to create a favorable unbalanced situation. Such an attitude has rather narrow limits because, for instance, if the intervention of a mediator leads to an obvious loss for one party, the victim may merely break the triadic relation. However, the efficiency of a mediation is not necessarily related to a strictly balanced intervention with regard to the two parties. The efficiency depends more on the expectations of the parties, it being understood that they can get more than what they would get without the intervention of a mediator. The usefulness of the mediation must not be evaluated based on what each party obtains compared to the other, but regarding what each party estimates he would have received within the dyadic relationship.

34.3. The General Model

As sketched in *Figure 34.1*, the general model includes a number of actors far beyond the basic triadic relationship: the negotiator's and mediator's constituencies and environments.

The negotiator's constituencies, such as governments, may sometimes bring enough weight by themselves into the general system to cause the mediator to adopt specific strategies toward them. For instance, if a negotiator sticks to an excessively rigid attitude, the mediator may threaten to bring this excessive rigidity to the attention of his constituency.

Environments are of different types: public opinion; the system of international relations; and other states. They may have a strong influence on the negotiator's strategies and may be viewed as levers that could be used by the mediator. For instance, in case of a protracted deadlock he could make both parties understand that he is going to inform the media concerning his recommendations. Environmental influences may concern the mediator as well because he may care about his reputation. If he considers that he will be in some ways evaluated according to his capability to get both disputants to reach an agreement, he may take this as a strong incentive. By the same token, his constituents may strongly influence his behavior, if they have power to affect his career. These constituents may be a government or an international organization.

The mediator is involved in a complex network within which operate conflicting rationales. He has to determine his action, define strategies, and modify equilibria in order to achieve his own goals as well as to help the parties in reaching some kind of agreement.

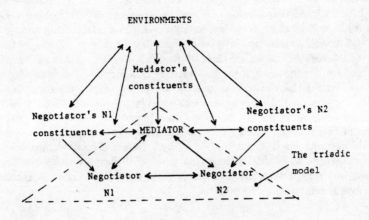

Figure 34.1. The mediation model.

34.4. The Mediator: His Position and His Contribution

34.4.1. Impartiality

The mediator is usually described as impartial and neutral in his intervention [Peters (1952), Simkin (1971), Muench (1963), Young (1967), Northedge and Donelan (1971)].

To be impartial can be defined as being careful not to favor any side, not to show any preference for one disputant or the other. Recent international mediations however, show a different reality. Partial mediators may be able to carry on their project and manage an agreement between strongly opposed positions. For instance, this was the case of the Algerian mediation between the USA and Iran on the US hostages.

The most important thing for the two parties concerning the mediator is that each will have a more positive outcome through his intervention. The fact that the mediator is impartial or partial is less important for them. On the contrary, partiality may be advantageous for the party in disfavor if the mediator wields some power over the other party.

Partiality exercised within certain limits may be the initial device that leads a negotiation process to some agreement. In such a case, impartiality appears more as an openly stated value than as an operating variable.

If negotiators are strongly committed to conflicting ideologies, it is very unlikely for a mediator to adopt a position half way between the two sets of values. There is no way to establish a kind of arithmetical mean of the different values at stake. The mediator, then, will just favor the solution closer to his own values.

The mediator, by manipulating the information, by influencing the parties, by putting pressure on them on occasion, directs the process of mediated negotiation toward a new equilibrium that does not correspond to what could have been reached if the negotiation had been left to its own dynamics.

34.4.2. Neutrality

There is a general confusion between the concepts of impartiality and neutrality. Researchers tend to use them as synonyms, but they refer to different types of action. Impartiality means not favoring either party. To be neutral means not intervening in the situation, not influencing the result of the negotiation.

It is rather an exception for a mediator dealing with international matters not to express any judgment, not to suggest any solution, but to work only as a facilitator or a go-between. In most cases, the mediator introduces into the process elements such as pressure, arguments, threats or rewards that will affect the outcome in some way. For instance, concerning the Camp David agreements, the US mediator involved himself in modifying the issues at stake and the global value of the game by offering economic aid to Egypt and the construction of a strategic air base to Israel.

The very principle of an intervention goes against the idea of neutrality because, by getting involved in the initial dyadic relationship, the mediator modifies the structure of the conflict. Moreover, non-neutrality increases the likelihood of reaching an agreement, because it provides new means of action and incentives in the shape of rewards or threats of punishment such as a withdrawing of support.

34.5. The Mediator's Intervention: The Model

If one considers that a fair solution should be the settlement point that could be reached through the dynamics of the dyadic relationship without any intervention of a third party, partiality could be defined as the modification of the outcomes introduced with the action of the mediator (*Figure 34.2*). The position of the mediator is described by axis (N1 N2). The two ends correspond to the positions of the negotiators. Axis (N1 N2) concerns only the distribution of the existing resources.

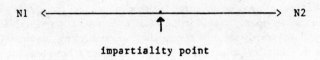

impartiality point

Figure 34.2. The position of the mediator regarding partiality.

Non-neutrality is shown in *Figure 34.3* by an orthogonal axis (G1 G2), whose length and orientation correspond to the intervention of the mediator on the joint outcome. Non-neutrality may directly affect the system as a whole or just one party.

If the mediator brings into the system a personal contribution, it will be shown by a certain length of the two vertical vectors (G1 G2). If he brings some reward only for the benefit of one party, it will be shown through one vector. If he does not bring anything into the mediation system (G1 G2) will not appear. This will correspond to the neutral position.

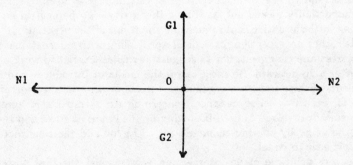

Figure 34.3. The position of the mediator in regard to partiality and non-neutrality.

34.5.1. The mediator's position

The different positions that may be taken by the mediator during his intervention can be shown with respect to the two variables partiality and non-neutrality.

The top left and bottom right quarters of *Figure 34.4* correspond to areas where partiality and non-neutrality are both involved. The mediator manages in such a way that the party he favors gets a larger part of the outcome than he would without the mediator's intervention. In this case, the mediator also gives an additional gain to his favored party.

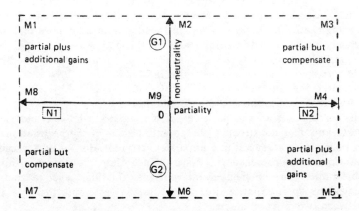

Figure 34.4. Two-dimensional plot of the mediator's positions with respect to partiality and non-neutrality.

The top right and bottom left quarters correspond to situations in which the mediator behaves in a partial way and as a consequence gives some advantage to one of the parties, but compensates the other party by adding to his gains:

- M1 corresponds to the position of a mediator who is totally partial toward negotiator N1 and who, moreover, gives to N1 a supplementary contribution in comparison with the product of the system. The US mediation during the negotiation of Nankin (1945–1947) between the Kuomintang and the Chinese Communists is an example of such an attitude, N1 being in that case the Kuomintang.
- M2 shows the position of an impartial mediator who would evenly split the gains resulting from the initial negotiation. This mediator would, however, give any additional gains to N1.
- Segment M2 M6 represents the new resources brought by the mediator or made available from the negotiation system through the action of optimization by the mediator. The US mediation of Camp David is an illustration of such a practice. President Carter maintained a fair impartiality toward

both parties, but raised their gains by bringing more benefits into the deal: economic aid for Egypt and a new air base for Israel.

- M3 corresponds to a mediator who strongly favors one party in the share of the existing resources within the system and who adds, as a counterpart, a personal compensation for the other party. This was the case in the Trieste conflict. The US helped Italy to get the town of Trieste, but compensated by giving Yugoslavia financial aid.
- M4 indicates a mediator who does not enlarge the scope of the possible benefits, but who gives an advantage to negotiator N2 in the share of the gains. Algeria used such a strategy during the US–Iran negotiations concerning the US hostages in Teheran by adding nothing more than what was already available and favoring Iran over the USA.
- M5 strictly corresponds to a situation similar to the one described in M1.
- M6 corresponds to the one described in M2.
- M7 corresponds to the one described in M3.
- M8 corresponds to the one described in M4.
- M9 corresponds to the positions of a mediator who does not favor any party and does not broaden the potential gains of the negotiation. He has in such a case a neutral and impartial attitude. He can be a passive facilitator or a mere presence who keeps the negotiators' behavior within acceptable limits. In the field of international relations, such a role may be played by an international organization that attempts to solve a conflict between two of its members.

One can see that there are many positions the mediator may take. M9 is the case corresponding to the first conception of mediation, built up from observations made in the field of industrial relations.

The nine positions analyzed here are extreme cases. In fact, there is an infinite number of positioning possibilities for the mediator. All of them can be situated into the area illustrated by *Figure 34.4*.

34.5.2. The outcome of a mediation

The different positioning possibilities of the mediator can also be shown on the area of possible agreements. The type of area chosen corresponds to the hypothesis of a highly conflicting negotiation, as presented in Luce and Raiffa (1957, p. 93).

The concave curve in *Figure 34.5* refers to a situation in which mediation is a real necessity. The shaded area shows the set of possible agreements between the two negotiators with reference to their respective utilities. The area within the dotted line corresponds to the new set of possible agreements resulting from the intervention of the mediator. Furthermore,

- M1 represents the maximization of N1's utility. The maximum that could be previously reached before the intervention of the mediator is M8.

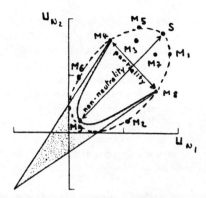

Figure 34.5. The mediator's positioning within the area of possible agreements.

- M2 corresponds to a payoff for N2 that could be one possible equity point (M9) to which a personal contribution from the mediator is added.
- M3 represents a maximization of N2's utility. The corresponding utility for N1 is raised with the contribution of the mediator.
- M4 corresponds to the maximized utility obtainable by N2 without any specific contribution from the mediator.
- M5, M6, M7, M8 correspond symmetrically to the positions M1, M2, M3, M4.
- M9 represents an equilibrium showing the "fair" solution with an impartial and neutral mediator careful not to bring into the game any personal resources to increase the global outcome.
- S should be the Nash solution, corresponding to the strategy of an impartial mediator who brings into the game a bilateral contribution. It describes an equivalent situation to the one shown before with the segment M2 and M6.

34.6. The Mediator's Motivations

The concept of a partial and non-neutral mediator is quite adapted to real-world situations and particularly to relations between states. The mediator is a negotiator who introduces new goals and extra resources into a deadlocked game and is able to start it up again. *Figure 34.5* shows that the strategy of a neutral and impartial negotiator is one strategy among many, but, moreover, that such a strategy does not lead to the best outcome for either party.

The intervention of the mediator can be justified by several types of reasons, which fall into two main categories: external and internal. Reasons that are external to the will of the mediator are institutional. International organizations, such as the Organization of African Unity or the Arab League, foresee generally a possibility of mediation in case of a conflict between two of their members.

The mediator in such cases does not intervene on his own, but because he has been appointed by his institution. Such a situation does not exclude other personal motivations on the part of the mediator: reputation, career, power, etc.

If there are several possible solutions for settling the dispute, the mediator will be inclined to favor the one that is the most advantageous for himself or for his organization. The mediator may also intervene for personal reasons. His motivation may be to gain something or to avoid a loss. During the two years the French hostages have been kept by the Moslem Shiites in Lebanon, seven different mediators have attempted to enter into the negotiating process. What is at stake for the mediator in such a negotiation is that in the case of a successful intervention the two parties will be indebted to him. He is in a position to ask for something in return.

The case of the border conflict between Algeria and Morocco in 1963 also shows the potential gains (political prestige, power) that are expected by the mediator if he leads the parties to an agreement. Tunisia, the Arab League, Ghana, Iraq, Ethiopia and eventually Mali tried within two weeks to bring the disputants to a compromise. The mediator may act in order to prevent a loss for himself. This was the purpose of the USA at the time of its mediation in the Greek–Turkish conflict over Cyprus in 1964. Both countries are members of NATO and any conflict between them would have weakened the position of the alliance and, consequently, of the USA. The USA acted in order to minimize its losses.

The mediator may act in order to prevent one of his allies from losing face. This was the case of the US mediation between the Netherlands and Indonesia concerning the future of West Iran. The Netherlands could no longer counter the guerrilla movement initiated by Indonesia. It was necessary for the USA to find a solution that would make the inevitable withdrawal of the Netherlands, its ally, not appear to be a defeat. The mediation of Ellsworth Bunker led both parties to agree on a formula that included a temporary administration of the contested territory by a third party, the UN, then the transfer of the administration to Indonesia, which would organize a referendum on self-determination. In this way, the change of sovereignty did not appear as a surrender of the Netherlands to the conditions put forward by Indonesia, but as compliance with the suggestions of an ally.

Another motivation of a mediator may be avoiding a possible loss in influence resulting from the successful intervention of another country. In that case, those competing for the role of mediator see their own prestige highly raised. This is a reason why the superpowers for years vied to help India and Pakistan settle their chronic dispute. This was especially true of the Soviet intervention of Tashkent, which followed the 1965 war.

A mediator, whether it be an individual, an organization or a country, may also act for ethical reasons, aiming to fulfill moral obligations. The Quakers' international action is quite relevant, if referred to such goals.

Negotiators themselves may be highly motivated to reach an agreement. Thus, managing a compromise may become an essential value for them to carry out. Such a motivation incites them to internalize the goals or the constraints of the other side and to develop a personal concept of a fair solution. The negotiator changes his role and becomes a mediator, as Iklé (1964) underlines, while analyzing the behavior of some Western negotiators in front of Soviet diplomats. In fact, performing the functions of a mediator, the negotiator acting in a dyadic relation remains a negotiator and only modifies his goals and constraints. The changing variable throughout the whole process of negotiating is the propensity to reach an agreement.

34.7. Concluding Remarks

Mediation is an activity that does not require impartiality and neutrality as conditions for success. The mediator has the characteristics of a negotiator. He intervenes in the dyadic relation with his own set of goals and constraints and may only use a limited number of strategies and tactics.

Through his intervention the whole structure of the game is modified and becomes a triadic interaction. But if the mediator can be defined as a negotiator involved in a relationship with two parties, this three-player game cannot be analyzed as a mere coalition game. Such an approach would bring the mediator beyond the limit of what could be accepted and would result in the very negation of the mediation process.

A mediator who appears to connect his interests exclusively with those of one party would lead the whole system to collapse.

It is within these two limits — i.e., no longer a dyadic relation, but not yet a coalition game — that the particular rationale of the mediator may be specified.

References

Holsti, K. (1983), *International Politics: A Framework for Analysis*, Prentice Hall (4th ed.), Englewood Cliffs, NJ.

Iklé, R. (1964), *How Nations Negotiate*, Harper & Row, New York,.

Luce, R. D. and Raiffa, H. (1957), *Games and Decisions*, John Wiley, New York.

McGrath, J.E. (1966), A Social Psychological Approach to the Study of Negotiation, in: R.V. Bowers (ed.), *Studies on Behavior in Organizations*, University of Georgia Press, Athens, GA.

Muench, G.A.A. (1963), A Clinical Psychologist's Treatment of Labor–Management Disputes, *Journal of Humanistic Psychology*, 3: 92-97.

Northedge, F. and Donelan, M. (1971), *International Disputes: The Political Aspects*, Europa Publications, London.

Peters, E. (1952), *Conciliation in Action*, National Foreman Institute, New London, CT.

Simkin, W.E. (1971), *Mediation and the Dynamics of Collective Bargaining*, Bureau of National Affairs, Washington, DC.

Touval, S. and Zartman, I.W. (ed.) (1985), *International Mediation in Theory and Practice*, Westview Press, Boulder, CO.

Touzard, H. (1977), *La médiation et la résolution des conflits*, PUF, Paris.

Walton, R.E. and McKersie, R.B. (1965), *A Behavioral Theory of Labor Negotiations*, McGraw-Hill, New York.

Young, O. (1967), *The Intermediaries: Third Parties in International Crisis*, Princeton University Press, Princeton, NJ.

CHAPTER 35

On Getting Simulation Models Used in International Negotiations: A Debriefing Exercise

Laurent Mermet and Leen Hordijk

International Institute for Applied Systems Analysis (IIASA)
Laxenburg
Austria

35.1. Introduction

Problems approached through international negotiation — especially multilateral negotiation — tend to be large-scale and long-term. They involve complex phenomena and issues that can only be grasped with the help of scientific research. Furthermore, since their complexity and rather global nature usually makes these problems cross the boundaries of single scientific disciplines, results from various fields have to be synthesized in a way that:

- Represents adequately the global functioning of the phenomena involved at the biophysical level.
- Adapt to the way members of the international community formulate the problem when engaging in negotiation.

428 L. Mermet and L. Hordijk

Such synthesis of existing data and understanding to assist decision-making is one of the main objectives of systems analysis in general, and of simulation modeling in particular.

The matter is notoriously difficult to grasp in the abstract, and involves skill and experience. Therefore, to formulate an answer to the question of how to get a model used, we have chosen an approach where one of us (L.M., who is a management science researcher) "debriefed" the other (L.H., who is an experienced practitioner in building models and getting them used).

The material presented here is based mainly on the current experience of Leen Hordijk as leader of the Acid Rain project at IIASA. This project's RAINS model can be used to simulate the emission of acidic pollutants in Europe, their transport and deposition, and their effects on the environment. The purpose of the simulation work is to provide a technical reference basis for current negotiations to curb acid rain in Europe, especially in the framework of the Convention on Long-range Transboundary Air Pollution, located in the United Nations' Economic Commission for Europe, Geneva. In the course of building the model, much effort has been devoted to try and ensure its actual use. The skill in these efforts stemmed from L. Hordijk's previous experience with similar "modeling-for-use" projects, especially in the Netherlands. In the course of the exercise, we also discussed these cases when necessary to complement the example of the RAINS model [1]. Although mainly based on experience with RAINS, this chapter is by no means an account about getting that particular model used in international negotiations.

The aim of debriefing is to tap expertise acquired "on the job". It consists of making explicit, through systematic questioning, the more or less implicit understanding of a certain problem that a practitioner has acquired over time. It is an attempt to put skill acquired through experience into a form more accessible to analysis and teaching.

But debriefing raises methodological problems: how should the information "extracted" be structured, and how should the questioning be organized accordingly?

We approached this question in a novel way, so that the study presented here really had two goals:

- To contribute to a better understanding of the skills involved in getting models used in international negotiations.
- To experiment with a relatively new method for debriefing practitioners in matters of strategies and negotiations.

We first briefly present the methodological guidelines we adopted for the exercise. We then present in more detail that part of the material produced by the debriefing results which is relevant to the issue of the use of models.

35.2. Debriefing "in Terms of Games": The Methodological Framework

Even a bulky piece of analysis can include only a limited amount of information. By comparison with any article or a book, the amount of understanding involved in a practitioner's skill is overwhelming. To capture such extensive understanding in the narrow limits of analysis causes serious problems, be it in terms of the total amount of information involved, of the variety of themes or fields to be covered, or of the number of details that are unconnected in practical thinking, but cannot be left that way in analysis. The debriefing concept is intuitively appealing, but raises challenging methodological problems [2].

The most traditional solutions are akin to surveys and memoirs. In a debriefing conducted like a survey, one will ask the practitioner a predetermined set of questions, very much like what is familiar from magazine polls. This approach provides precise and comparable answers covering the questions considered to be important by the interviewer. But knowing what questions to ask is half of the issue. The approach requires in particular that a good understanding of the problem's structures be available beforehand.

Memoirs, or totally free-wheeling interviews, represent the opposite extreme. The choice of issues and the structuring of the problem are chosen entirely by the practitioner. The result is usually lively and informative, but loosely structured. Typically, a practitioner will not structure the problems he has faced and solved in a systematic manner; he will rather underline, and comment on, those aspects of the matter which to him are novel, interesting, challenging, or which he thinks are usually overlooked. The core of his know-how, the basics and reflexes on which his skill is based, will thus often escape formulation because he is unaware of some, considers others to be too trivial or lacks proper formulation.

Our objective in this exercise was mainly to identify the most basic, most general structures and dynamics of the strategies and tactics involved in building a model for use by policy-makers in a negotiation context. We considered that only on this basis could details, refinements, and the advanced understanding of good practitioners be integrated into a coherent, transferable whole. We had to find a debriefing formula focusing on the structuring of the problem, rather than on the solutions to all the various difficulties associated with it, and which vary so much from one particular case to the next. A survey-type formula could not be retained because it produces much content, but is not very effective in exploring the structure of problems.

To unravel the particular structures of the subject of the debriefing — getting models used in our case — can only be left to the "debriefed" practitioner, as the exercise goes along. But the practitioner cannot formulate the way he implicitly structures his approach of situations unless he receives help, especially questions and hints on what kind of structures can be looked for. This help, and the tools allowing it, have to be the contribution of the "debriefer".

In parallel with the present study, extensive work is under development on the potential of various analytical frameworks and methodological tools to help bridge the gap between practitioners and researchers in strategies and negotiations in natural resources management. Our methodological thinking relied largely on results of this work [3].

Analytical frameworks used to help to structure a problem, or to make the structuring of a problem explicit (as in the present debriefing) have to pursue several objectives at the same time. They must be consistent with the way people spontaneously structure their understanding of problems in practical thinking. They must be suitable for use and in particular allow simultaneous description of a problem, and prescriptive and normative approaches to it. They must have a clear connection and consistency with the analytical theories in the area involved.

This last condition suggests that the structures that can be proposed for practical problems should inevitably rely on one or several of the few paradigms that are used to structure thinking in research.

In view of the complexity involved in institutional tactics and strategies, the system paradigm would currently be most likely considered to underlie debriefing. One could, in effect, conduct a debriefing in terms of systems, involving, for instance, the mapping of systems boundaries, its elements and their interactions, the identification of feedback loops, of internal and external factors influencing the emerging evolution of the state of the system, and so on [4].

However, the system paradigm poses serious problems hindering its use in the preparation of strategic action, such as intervention in a negotiation, or institutional tactics associated with scientific work. Suffice it to mention one major impasse associated with analysis of practice in terms of systems. Either the decision-maker or negotiator is considered as part of the system, or he is viewed as being outside of the system. In the first case, the following dilemma occurs:

- If the system is well understood, the actor's choices are determined and predictable, this places him in a very bad situation for action, and makes analysis of the problem a futile attempt on his part.
- If the actor exercises some degree of freedom in action and is strategically astute, he will try to remain as unpredictable as he can. Then the possible understanding of the system will remain very limited.

In the second case, if the actor is considered as being outside of the system, no understanding of the latter can give indications on the rationales for his actions.

It follows that the system paradigm is suitable to understand complex problems on which actors are negotiating or deciding, but cannot at the same time integrate the subjective logic of action in the analysis and be of practical use to prepare action.

The research effort mentioned above suggests that the game paradigm provides a sound analytical framework to bridge the practice–research gap [4]. In particular, it structures situations in a way that supports both an analysis by the observer and the preparation of action by the player in the game, as the example of any familiar game will show. This choice of the game paradigm seems to find support:

- In the extensive use that practitioners in all fields make of game metaphors, such as rules of the game, winner, loser, move, points, to be put in check, and so on.
- In the empirically acknowledged usefulness of simulation games to promote understanding of complex issues involving tactical and strategical interaction.
- In the use in theoretical research of approaches that are based on analysis of some aspects of games, for instance, in game theory and decision analysis.

Since the game paradigm fulfills the conditions we have mentioned earlier in a way the other currently used analytical frameworks do not, we have selected an analysis in terms of games as the guideline for the exercise. To avoid misunderstandings, it should be made clear that the game concept used here is quite different from the one found in game theory. What we have in mind is a much broader framework suggested by the more complex forms of games, in particular simulation games, which involve not only scores, choices and strategies, but also many other aspects, including such intangibles as role-playing, excitement or reluctance, and intuition [5].

On this basis, the guideline for the whole exercise, which covered seven two-hour interviews over a period of one year, was a two-part question, constantly repeated in various forms: If "Building Models for actual Use in an international negotiation" is the name of a game (we will call it the BMU game); and if you are a player in this game whose assigned objective is to get the model built and used:

- What best description can you give of the most important features and structures in the game?
- What should a beginner in the game learn first as he starts playing the same role you presently have?

We started without any further detailed conception of what the general elements and structures of a game are. Exploring these was also one of the aims of the exercise. We just let ourselves be guided by the manifold "natural concepts" associated in everyday thinking with the word game, and by constant analogies with various popular games. Gradually, a fairly clear image of the real-life game of "Building a Model for actual Use in international negotiation" emerged.

35.3. Getting a Simulation Model Used in an International Negotiation

35.3.1. General framework of the game

When confronted for the first time with a new game, one will first see the board or game space, the other players and the various elements of the paraphernalia: dice, fake (or real) money, chips, and so on. One will also very soon learn the principles and the crux of the game: "Monopoly", for instance, is about real estate speculation, and the crux of the game is to put everyone else out of business. What are the equivalent basic structures in our BMU game?

The basic structure of the game is presented in *Figure 35.1*, which shows that playing BMU is actually playing simultaneously four quite distinct games:

(1) Each member of the research team is involved as an active participant in one or another scientific field, the results of which are to be synthesized in the model. Each scientific field is more or less clearly bounded, with a relatively stable set of players, whose interactions follow the rules of the scientific game. In BMU, there are as many such games as required by the scope of the model and the composition of the team; we have called them Scientific Field Games (FG).

(2) A modeling effort is often pursued within a certain institutional framework. It can be, for example, a project of a consultancy firm, or a program of an institute. This framework is a distinct game with its specific bureaucratic or economic rules, stakes and tricks: we refer to it as the Parent Institution Game (PG). Part of the effort of any modeling team is spent on surviving or prospering in this element. How the players do it and how they succeed has a strong bearing on whether and how the model gets completed, and eventually used.

(3) Use of the model occurs in a specific decision-making environment, such as an international conference or an international organization. This constitutes yet another distinct game, with its players, its own rules and outcomes: we call this the Use Game (UG).

(4) Finally, building the model is a distinct game in its own right, obviously of central importance here. We will call it the Modeling Game (MG). Its players are the members of the research team, and its desired outcome is the completion of the model.

The crucial principle in BMU is active creation and successful maintenance of a kind of constructive coherence between such disparate semi-closed scenes as a set of scientific fields, an international policy debate, a research bureaucracy and its financial supporters: an easy statement, but a difficult achievement!

In the following analysis, we will be primarily concerned with the Use Game, and with those aspects of the Modeling Game that are relevant for getting

433

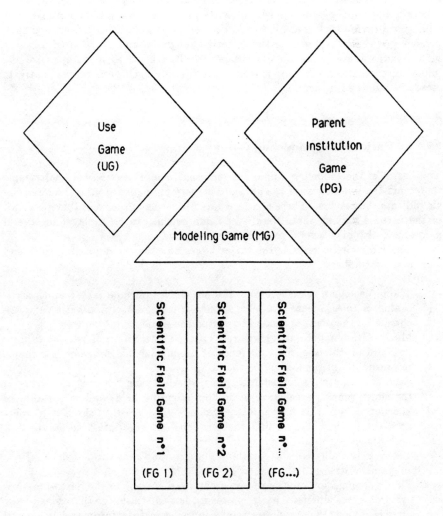

Figure 35.1. General structure of the BMU Game.

the model used. The general description of these games as provided here is meant to help model practitioners, their financial supporters and their evaluators, in organizing their thinking about the issue of getting the model used. They can use this material to identify and structure relevant information when preparing a model for use.

However, it is not enough to identify what information is needed, and to structure it once it is obtained: obtaining it is a challenge in itself. Our first recommendation will be that one needs to identify in each country — and more generally in each subgame one will have to enter — an experienced person who is willing to provide such information as deemed necessary. We have named such persons grey-haired experts in the scientific subgames and grey-haired advisors in the bureaucratic and political subgames. It is hard to overemphasize the importance of taking the time and effort to identify such persons and cultivate steady relations with them.

35.3.2. Basics of the Modeling Game

The basics of the Modeling Game are represented in *Figure 35.2*. The triangle represents the boundaries of the game. The various shapes around the large circle indicate the players. These are designated in terms of the roles they play, not of the persons playing these roles: the same person can be a player in several games, and also play several roles in the same game.

The large circle contains the major issues and the corresponding rules and interaction structures:

- The project plan sets the basic rules on which the game relies: aims, attribution of roles, means available, time available, etc.; these basic rules are changed if the plans are modified during the game.
- Much of the model quality will rely on good integration of various submodels and on the scientific coherence of the whole; this subgame is a major responsibility of the leader.
- Each participating scientist is a specialist; he is thus "chasing two hares at the same time": excellence within his scientific field, and integration of knowledge from this field into the model. It is rare that these two objectives totally coincide, so that there is constant negotiation to assure that both concerns get addressed satisfactorily.
- The use and allocation of available logistics and secretarial help is also a subgame of its own right.
- Finally, simulation models run on computers. Access to the hardware, programming the different parts of the model, and assuring that, when they are assembled, the composite model functions satisfactorily and is reasonably user-friendly, is a complex and absorbing game, the results of which have a crucial bearing on the quality of the model for users.

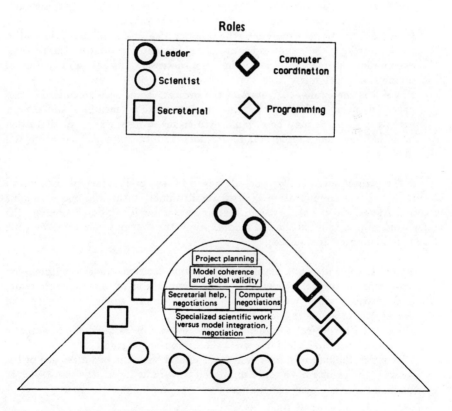

Figure 35.2. The Modeling Game.

35.3.3. Phases in the Modeling Game

Many games, if not most, go through successive stages, setting different contexts for the interactions of the players. They can be procedural stages written into the rules — for example, when a deadline is set in the research contract for the various steps in the completion of the project. They can also be more informal phases appearing when the progression of the effort modifies its environment and its agenda. The evolution of BMU can be represented by seven successive periods, which are represented in *Figure 35.3*.

The first three phases correspond to a stage in which the project can be considered as preliminary:

-   Phase 1 is the original idea of starting such a project: "it would be interesting — and maybe useful — to build a model of this or that phenomenon"; this is a short, totally informal, often overlooked phase.
-   Phase 2 is the transformation of the original idea into an actual proposal to start the effort; the main issues are clarifying and formulating the project, overcoming skepticism, identifying the necessary means and potential financial supporters.
-   Phase 3 is the exploratory start of the project: some seed money has been gathered, small-scale work is done to demonstrate feasibility and usefulness, a conference may be organized to secure a network of collaborators; in brief, financial supporters, researchers and the parent institution are "giving it a try".

If the project successfully proceeds beyond these preliminary phases, it will acquire a full-size configuration, a firm institutional status and more reliable funding. Appetizers are history, and the time has come for the main course: the major work now is to build the full model. As in the previous one, this stage can also be divided into three phases:

-   Phase 4 is the project's development: major decisions have to be made on computer hardware, model structure, composition of the research team, and relations with potential users. The promises made are bigger and bigger, the products to show remain meager.
-   Phase 5 is the project's implementation: everything is available to actually do the work, gather the data, write the computer programs, etc.
-   Phase 6 is the end of model construction and the time of fullest use of the model: the results have to be published in various forms, the model has to be finalized, debugged and documented.

Basically, the work is done. The team can dissolve and its members seek other scientific adventures. But the model is still there. Especially if it is used, it will need maintenance, upgrading, instructions to users, etc. This is phase 7: follow-up and clearinghouse.

Stage	Issue	Phase	Dominant Issues
1	Planning the model	1	Is use the central issue of the planned model, an interesting application, or a protective facade?
		2	Is the idea of use precise and realistic? Is it defined in an operational fashion?
		3	Have potential users been contacted? What is their level of interest?
2	Building the model	4	Enter the use fora, overcome opposition, get users involved, integrate potential for use in the model design.
		5	Keep users informed and involved, make sure model building stays in line with potential use.
		6	Ensure timely editing of results, documentation of programs. Start actual use.
3	Follow-up	7	Provide relevant service (maintenance, adaptation,...). Obtain evaluation from users.

Figure 35.3. Ensuring potential for use in model building.

35.3.4. Model-building with use in sight: Issues and phases

Of the various subgames in the Modeling Game, project planning, model coherence and computer negotiations are directly relevant for the ultimate use of the model. Usability should be a major concern in these activities, starting right at the onset of the model-building effort. How, specifically, can this goal be met?

A second look at the phases we just described will help answer the question. The issue of use presents itself quite differently at the various stages of the game as we just described them. We have sketched this in *Figure 35.3*.

During the three phases of the preliminary or planning stage, the issue is to evaluate the chances that the model will be used. From the use point of view, is it worth pursuing, funding, institutionalizing? This question presents itself differently in each phase of the planning:

- In phase 1, the issue is to clarify the place of use in the original idea. Is it central, so that use is the main aim of engaging in the exercise; is it planned as the natural outcome of producing new and useful information; or is it a facade prompted by the financial or institutional pressures toward immediately usable products of research?
- In phase 2, one should be able to ascertain whether the idea of use is precise and realistic. At this stage, an operational definition of use should be provided, and not only a definition in principle. For the latter, it would suffice to state that the model is for use by practitioners in negotiations about the topics covered by the model. For an operational definition of use, it will be necessary to specify the particular practitioners, the negotiation forum, and how precisely the model would be used.
- In phase 3, one can start finding out if the envisaged users are really interested in the idea. At this stage potential users should be contacted, at least at an informal level. Their reaction will be important: are potential users politely skeptical, interested in principle, or already giving signs of an operational intention of use?

At the second stage, when research is done at a full-scale level, the priority for the partners in the modeling effort is to get the model build and used. This involves the following issues:

- In phase 4, the model should be made known to the users' forum or fora, so that the involved parties can start considering it as a resource for negotiation or decision making This involves surmounting inevitable opposition, and receiving or creating opportunities to present the effort to all parties concerned. In this phase, it is also important to provide the users with an opportunity to get involved in the project — for instance, by participating in review meetings, by providing data, etc. Finally, it is at this time that rather irreversible decisions are made about the structure of the model. Needless to say, the envisaged use has to be one of the bases for this design; for this, user feedback is essential.

- In phase 5, the project should maintain users' attention and keep the users involved. In this phase, everyone in the modeling team is very absorbed in getting the model done and running. At the same time, the users have many subjects of interest other than a model that has not yet delivered anything. Also, competition is likely to emerge. One may be tempted to feel that what has been acquired in the previous phases may be taken for granted, but one should not. Especially since the technical task of building the model becomes so absorbing at this stage, it will take a special effort to keep users informed and involved, and to make sure that the model itself does not, for technical reasons, stray away from its potential intended use.

- In phase 6, one must ensure that the products will be available on time, in a form suitable for use. This winding-up phase of projects is delicate, because it puts the team in a paradoxical situation: if the research work is nearly finished, all resources will tend to be attracted to other projects that are in more challenging phases. If the team continues to work, it will always be tempted to go a little farther in research, rather than just documenting what has been achieved. In this phase, actual use of the model should also start: there should be intense activity of the modelers in the Use Game.

If the model has not made its way to actual use in phase 6, it is unlikely to make it later on, because the indispensable resources, energy and momentum will no longer be available. If the model does start to get used, then it is important to provide users with good service, because most of the use will happen after the core research is over. This follow-up phase is largely a matter of logistics for maintenance and adaptation of the model. It is also at this stage that the effort should be evaluated by the users, not by the proponents of the model!

35.4. Basics of the Use Game

35.4.1. Board and players

We just discussed what "use" looks like from the point of view of those financing, supervising and building the model. We sketched an image of this as a specific environment, which we have called the Modeling Game. Seen from there, the "users" have a strong tendency to be viewed, even if only implicitly, as a rather abstract, mistakenly unified entity. But the term "users" covers a whole set of people and organizations with different interests, who operate in a specific and diverse environment, which we have called the Use Game. To get users involved, to obtain their support, it is necessary to understand to a certain extent the games they are playing. In fact, a certain amount of involvement in the Use Game will usually be necessary to remove barriers and build enough support for actual use.

As above, let us start with an overview of the board of the Use Game, as sketched in *Figure 35.4*. In international negotiation, model use will, more often than not, be conducted in the framework of some organization, convention, or other set of procedural mechanics. This is a game in its own right. Main players are the delegates, chairperson, and other negotiators. In the game set, there will usually be a secretariat to facilitate the procedure and assist with technical matters. Secretariat members are also players; they will play their own marbles in the game, somewhat like the banker in a casino game. Also, *ad hoc* technical working groups are likely to be formed to face those issues that are both complex in content, and politically sensitive. Each one is a subgame of a sort.

Furthermore, no delegation is a transparent and monolithic reflection of a country. In each country that is a party to the negotiations, there are likely to be debates about the interests to promote at the international forum, and about the best strategy for doing so. The latter can include the use of a simulation model. This is yet another game in which national administrative organizations (agencies, ministries, etc.) are the parties, and in which individual players are leading scientists (collaborators, competitors, friends, or supporters of the model we are trying to get used) and officials (each of whom also has a certain potential as ally or opponent). In each country, the interplay between science, policies and politics seems to follow specific patterns and rules with which experienced nationals in the field have learned to play.

35.4.2. Getting it used: Targets and moves

Given this general background, which strategies should the model-builder follow to get his product used? To answer this question, it is necessary first to get an idea of the possible winning or losing outcomes — that is, of the possible types and levels of use.

The notion of the use of models in international negotiation oscillates between two extreme concepts of the role of complex applied studies and decision-support systems in controversial decision-making. A somewhat caricatured account will help to describe the debate.

At one extreme is a vision that is part of the current folklore of decision-support systems. Underlying many proposals and — mostly preliminary — developments, is a fantasy of negotiators gathered around a colorful screen displaying a "negotiator-friendly" computer program. It answers their questions swiftly, thanks to a large database and to simulation models based on the result of state-of-the-art, impartial scientific studies. At last confronted with objective and understandable information, following long stages of groping in the dark, the negotiators can play with the program and explore the many facets of the issue. Before they are even aware of it, they have abandoned their entrenched positions, hammered out joint gains, and they all wind up as winners. If this utopia were true, international negotiations could be considered just another type of video-game [6].

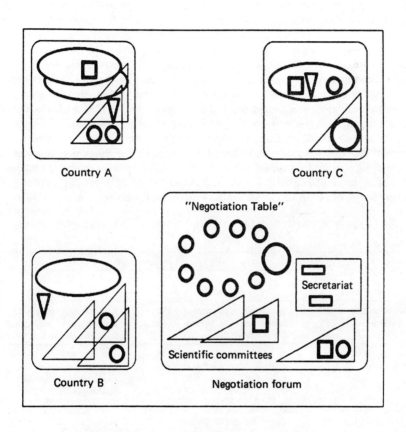

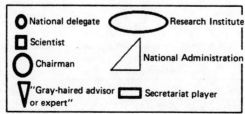

Figure 35.4. The Use Game.

At the other extreme is a more acid concept of simulation models — and of any applied studies — as just another play in the tactics of decision-making processes. In this view, negotiation is so dominated by politics that, if a model is used at all, it will be by a party that finds its position supported by its results. If another party holds a different position, it will always find an alternative model to support it, or interpret the existing data differently. If it does not find such an alternative model, it will fund its development. In the end, the negotiators, armed with competing models, will shoot divergent results at each other [7].

There is some truth in both of these concepts, and a lot of room for intermediate positions. We propose to organize this range of potential use situations in the following two dimensions. The first rests on the distinction between use by all negotiators collectively, or by only one or some of the negotiating parties. The second dimension is based on a distinction between the simulation model seen as the active ingredient pushing the negotiation process along, and a model seen as a more neutral scientific reference for discussions in a negotiation process that itself remains fundamentally based on politics. To these situations of use, we would like to add situations of nonuse, by one (or a few) or by all participants, at a level of indifference to the model, or of actively fighting it. The resulting scope of possible use or nonuse situations is sketched in *Table 35.1.*

Table 35.1. Types and levels of use of a simulation model in the negotiation process.

	User level	
Role of model	*Individual*	*Collective (joint use by all parties)*
Model as a motor of the process	A party promotes the model as an active basis for its position	All parties agree to use the model as reference framework for the process
Model as source of information	A party uses the model to complement the argumentation of its position	The model is considered by all parties as one source of information used in the process
Model indifferent because marginal or useless	A party is reluctant to move from the political to a more technical ground	The negotiation is so adversarial that "rational" analysis of the problem plays little role
Model undesirable	A party disagrees on the science or fights the model as a tactic in the negotiations politics	Prospects for the use of the models are terrible

At the most ambitious level of use, the model is a moving force in the process. It can be used as such by one or a few delegations. This is particularly the case when a party wants something done about a problem, but faces strong reluctance supported by scientific uncertainty on the exact nature, extent, or origin of the problem. A model is a powerful way for such parties to mobilize what scientific evidence there is, and if possible, force consideration of the issue. A model can also be used as a key activating factor of the process by all parties jointly. This is in particular the case when there is agreement to use the model as a common framework allowing proposed solutions to be tested, possible joint benefits to be explored, etc. This concept of the model as a mediator seems to dominate, so to speak, the emerging efforts in computer-aided negotiations.

This is, however, a very ambitious concept of the use of models, one which seldom comes true. But the use of models should not be seen as an "all or nothing" situation. It can be conceived, like the use of any applied science, in a more traditional fashion. In this way, research results provide a source of information and reference for the rationality of envisaged solutions, which is mobilized as necessary in the course of the negotiation process, itself moved and dominated by procedures and politics. Again, the model can be used individually as a rationale to defend a politically established position, and to work out its technical details. It can also be used collectively as a yardstick to foster better articulation of positions, and as a reference for discussion of details.

Nonuse can stem first from indifference to the model. This is likely to be based on the view that the predominance of politics makes complex and still uncertain scientific results irrelevant. Most of the time, this will be because one party — or the whole negotiation — is highly politicized. It can also happen because negotiators are weary of complex models. They can perceive these as providing results, which, since the negotiations cannot understand their basis, could as well be arbitrary, and will reduce their degree of control on the outcome of the negotiation.

Finally, it can happen that one, a few, or many of the parties will fight the use of the model in the negotiation. If too many of the parties fight the use of the model, one might want either to reconsider the value of the model, or to consider another decision-making forum for its use. If the opposition just comes from one or a few parties, it is quite natural. It can stem from a disagreement about facts or concept of the model, which then has to be dealt with at the scientific level. This can be the case, for instance, if one country has quite specific, if marginal, technical problems, and these do not receive adequate attention in the model because it is based on the general case. But opposition also often stems from tactics: it can be a way to maintain a level of high uncertainty about the issue if this is favorable to one's position; it can be a way to delay the procedures and discussion; it can be a way to deny the existence, the significance, the cause of a problem, or the possibility of remedying it. In that case, the difficulty has to be dealt with at the political level.

To this point, what we have done is basically to associate precise and structured — although very general — descriptions with the notions of "users" and "use". How do they combine when it comes to action — that is, to getting the users to use the model?

35.4.3. Getting it used: The process

It must first be realized that the modeler is only a quite marginal player in the Use Game. His possibilities for direct intervention are very limited: an occasional presentation of the modeling work and results, or participation in a technical working group. We have also seen that the use of the model necessitates action at the political level to put it on the agenda, to overcome opposition, etc. Action at this level is necessary, but it can only be indirect, through the intervention of players with influence in the Use Game: active delegates, chairpersons, influential secretariat members.

Furthermore, we have seen that the initial attitudes of delegates and other players with regard to the model could be actively supportive (usually on political grounds), mildly supportive (usually on technical grounds), reticent or hostile (on political or technical grounds, or due to ignorance). The crux of action here is to find ways to make these attitudes evolve favorably. Those changes in players' positions that are connected to the credibility and relevance of the model do not require tactics beyond good modeling work and sound presentations when the opportunity is given (of course, making sure the opportunity is given is an important point of strategy). But when it comes to influencing positions at the political level, one will have to leave the initiative to active allies: those who tend to support the model on political grounds.

These intrinsic limits to the intervention in the Use Game finally make the strategic concerns of the modeler much simpler than they might have looked at first sight. These concerns are threefold:

(1) Building a model that is fit for use, i.e., scientifically state-of-the-art and adapted to users' needs.
(2) Acquiring a clear enough picture of the Use Game to know what one is facing, and identify what strategic and tactical help will be necessary, and its potential sources.
(3) Making active allies in the Use Game — those who will be the actual promoters of the model, and will be able to overcome opposition.

At first sight, these conclusions seem to pertain entirely to a concept of the use of the model by one party or coalition in the negotiation, as opposed to its collective use by all parties to help with the process (in other terms, it would correspond only to the left column in *Table 35.1*). This is not so, however. The following discussion of this issue should permit an integration of these two extreme concepts of the use of models in negotiation, as well as give a better idea of the Use Game. What has to be considered here is the dynamic process of getting the model used.

Indeed, the use of a simulation model is still too often seen as a static issue — as if, at the end of its building, the model would or would not be used, as a product is or is not sold after production. But one look at the Game Use board and at *Table 35.1* makes it clear that it should rather be understood as a dynamic process. Many of the players in the Use Game will have to be approached separately. They will have varied attitudes toward the model, and use it — or not — in different ways. It will be a long-lasting effort to neutralize the hostile and turn the potentially interested into actual users.

In this gradual development, we have seen that the action is basically in the hands of a limited number of active supporters of the model. If they succeed in getting the model adopted, it will be through a process of diffusion, gradually rallying parties to its cause. This diffusion process is narrowly linked with the negotiation process. The latter consists of each active party trying to rally the others around a position that it finds acceptable. The model is a means to that end: it helps rallying positions first around a framework one finds acceptable, thus laying the table for solutions one finds acceptable. Both processes are parallel, each one reinforcing the other: progress in the negotiation makes the model easier to adopt, and vice versa.

This, we hope, gives a clearer view of how the Use Game works in addition to its basic static structures, as we have proposed. However, it still does not seem to apply to the concept of collective use of the model, which is strikingly put forward by the motto: "the computer as mediator". A key to that issue can be found in the concept of the mediator as a third negotiator, proposed by Faure in Chapter 34 of this volume. Following his argument, it is rather mistakenly assumed that the mediator or the chairman is considered to bring into the process a type of intervention totally different from that of the negotiators themselves — a difference often captured by the term neutrality. Faure shows examples of non-neutral but very effective mediation interventions, and proposes a consideration of the mediator as just another negotiator in the process, egoistically pursuing his own agenda. The difference is that, for a variety of reasons, the mediator's agenda involves among other things trying to make the other parties reconcile their differences. So it can be that a mediating negotiator actively promotes a simulation model, leading to a process of diffusion exactly similar to what we just described when one party promotes the model for its bargaining ends.

Actually, the most convincing existing example of the "computer as negotiator" confirms this point of view. In his description of the use of an MIT model of the economics of deep-sea mining in the Law of the Sea (LOS) convention negotiations, Sibenius shows the chairman of the convention skillfully using the model to promote his agenda of helping parties reconcile extreme initial positions. He shows how the model, because it was relevant and scientifically credible, was instrumental in salvaging a negotiation process that was close to total deadlock [8].

So the two concepts of the role of a model in negotiation, respectively, as a support for partial positions and as a means to foster cooperative problem-solving, are not essentially different. One role can even lead to the other. In all cases, the actual use of a model results from its promotion by one or a few players with influence in the negotiation. When successful, this promotion results in a gradual spreading of the acceptance of the model, in close connection with the negotiation process.

35.5. Conclusion

We started the exercise described in this chapter moved by the following motives and orientations:

- We regarded the practical use of simulation models as important both to help reach better outcomes in negotiations about complex issues, and to justify the big investments made in building simulation models.
- We considered that such practical use of models rests above all on their scientific credibility, but also depends to a considerable degree on relevant strategic initiatives on the part of the proponents of the model. The success of such initiatives, we thought, relied largely on specific skills acquired through experience.
- To improve the use of models, we were interested in the possibility of facilitating the acquisition of such skills by modelers. This could be done, we thought, by providing them with a relevant analysis of the main issues and possibilities for action involved in the situation of trying to get a simulation model used.
- In our view, this analysis had to be based mostly on debriefing: an explication of the practical understanding acquired by a practitioner with several successful experiences in the process of building models that actually got used.
- Finally, we regarded the prospects of success of such a debriefing as scant if it were based on a traditional survey-type questionnaire or on free-wheeling interviews, so we decided to try a new approach of debriefing "in terms of games".

In the course of the exercise, we have obtained significant results in three directions: a clarification of the issue of the use of a model in international negotiation, the tentative development of practical methodological tools to improve effectiveness in getting a model used, and the fruitful testing of a new debriefing method. We will briefly review each of these three results.

First, the exercise has provided a clarification of the issues involved in model use. It has helped dispel a rampant vision that somehow, magically, models will make their way into the negotiation process and do what negotiators have hitherto been unable to do themselves. The use of a model should not be viewed as a "yes or no" issue: it has varied modes and degrees. The user(s) of the model cannot be considered as a monolithic entity or a homogeneous lot, but as people with various interests and positions with regard to the model and operating in institutional environments of their own. Use should not be postponed to the end of the modeling effort, because it can only be the result of a gradual dynamic process, in which building the model and getting it used are closely connected.

Secondly, this clarification of the issue of use has produced tools that can facilitate the diagnosis of problems associated with the use of a particular model. These tools provide guidelines on how to identify the relevant elements in a use situation, how to take into account the issue of use at various stages of model-building, how to define what kind of use is a realistic aim, how to identify practical initiatives that can be taken. We hope that these guidelines have some degree of general value, so that they can be used both as a practical guide to getting models used, and as a support to facilitate discussions, planning, and evaluation of the use of a model. Its potential users cover the whole range of actors involved in the construction of a model: the model builders themselves, their financial supporters, their collaborators, the supervisors of the effort, etc.

Thirdly, we consider the exercise and those of its results presented here as one successful test of the method of debriefing in terms of games, which we had set out to define and test. Some concepts for such use of the game analytical framework have emerged in the course of the debriefing. They appear in this presentation of the results; however, it is too early to present them in a systematic fashion. Going farther in that direction will require further experimenting with debriefing in terms of games, integrating in this practice the results of the more theoretical work on the game concept (which is being pursued in parallel [9]) and articulating the use of the game approach for debriefing with its use for training and education on which work is also being developed in parallel with the effort presented here [10].

Notes

[1] It is important to note that the present chapter does not address specifically the use of this particular model, but problems of use and debriefing methodology in general. For a introduction to the RAINS model and its use, see: J. Alcamo *et al.* (1985), Integrated Analysis of Acidification in Europe, *Journal of Environmental Management*, 21; L. Hordijk (1986), Acid Rain Abatement Strategies in Europe, in T. Schneider (ed.), *Acidification and its Policy Implications*, Elsevier.

[2] Confronted with the same problem, M. Wheeler has selected a different approach from the one proposed here. He writes: "Presenting a comprehensive view of everything that a practitioner does would be too formidable a task; instead, we have searched for issues or themes of special importance. In one instance, for example, we explored with an environmental advocate how he balances negotiation and litigation strategies; interviewing a mediator, we looked at the opportunities and obstacles to early intervention" (Michael Wheeler (1985), *Protocols for Debriefing Practitioners*, Program on Negotiation Working Paper 85-2, January). By contrast, the approach we have retained here aims at forming a global image of the innumerable things a practitioner does and of the way they are related to each other.

[3] L. Mermet (1987), *Game Analysis: An Analytical Framework to Bridge the Practitioner–Researcher Gap in Negotiation Research*, IIASA Working Paper WP-87-084, September.

[4] One will find an example of a methodology to interview practitioners which rests on a combination of survey techniques and systems perspective in chapter 11, by Sven B. Lundstedt, in this volume.

[5] For a discussion of simulation games, see Ingolf Stahl (1983), *Operational Gaming — An International Approach*, Pergamon Press.

[6] On the perspectives and limits of computer models to support social decisions, see: D.H. Meadows and J.M. Robinson (1985), *The Electronic Oracle*, John Wiley.

[7] This view is defended in a nuanced and informed way in: GRETU (1980), *Une étude économique a montré... Mythes et réalités des études de transport*, Paris, Cujas, 1980.

[8] James K. Sebenius (1981), The Computer as Mediator: Law of the Sea and Beyond, *Journal of Policy Analysis and Management*, 1, (1), pp. 77-95.

[9] See note [3].

[10] L. Mermet (1986), *Aims in Nature, Means in Society: Negotiation and Strategy Analysis for Environmental Management*, IIASA PIN Project, May.

CHAPTER 36

Dynamic Solution of a Two-Person Bargaining Problem

Piotr Bronisz and Lech Krus

Systems Research Institute
Polish Academy of Sciences
Warsaw
Poland

36.1. Introduction

This chapter deals with a two-person bargaining problem given by a set of the payoff vectors attainable by the players through some joint actions and by a disagreement point reached if the players fail to agree. Bargaining problems have been studied by, among others, Nash (1950), Raiffa (1953), Kalai and Smorodinsky (1975), Kalai (1977), Meyerson (1977), who propose some solutions; but they are confined to one-shot solution concepts that describe only possible final agreements for the bargaining problem.

The dynamic bargaining process presented here starts from the disagreement point and, through successive agreements of the players, leads to the final payoffs. The successive agreement points reflect the progress in the bargaining process. In the chapter, we consider the continuous case of the process, presented in Bronisz, Krus, and Wierzbicki (1987), in which the successive agreement points form a continuous trajectory. To assure "fairness" in bargaining, the equal concession axiom is imposed, which says that the Lebesgue measures of payoffs refused during the process in the regions favorable to particular players are the same.

We show that there exists one and only one dynamic solution of the bargaining problem satisfying the axiom. This solution is described by an initial-value problem, which was also considered in the Raiffa (1953) continuous solution concept. Therefore, the obtained result can be treated as axiomatization of the Raiffa continuous solution of two-person bargaining problem. The properties of the Raiffa continuous solution are shown. Moreover, we compare the solution to the Nash and the Kalai-Smorodinsky solutions.

36.2. Problem Formulation and Definitions

A two-person bargaining game is defined by a pair (S,d), where S (called an agreement set) is a subset of two-dimensional Euclidean space $\mathbf{R}^2$ and d (called a disagreement point) is a point in S. The pair (S,d) has the following intuitive interpretation: every point $x = (x_1, x_2) \in S$ represents the von Neumann-Morgenstern utility levels for players 1 and 2 that can be reached when they act jointly. If the players fail to agree on an outcome in S then they receive $d = (d_1, d_2)$ utility levels.

We employ a convention that for $x,y \in \mathbf{R}^2$, $x > y$ implies $x_i > y_i$, and $x \geq y$ implies $x_i \geq y_i$ for $i = 1,2$. For (S,d), we say that $x \in S$ is a strongly Pareto-optimal point if there is no $y \in S$ such that $y \geq x$ and $y \neq x$. The boundary ∂S of S is defined by $\partial S = (x \in S$: there is no $y \in S$ with $y > x)$. For convenience, let $\mathbf{R}_y^2 = (x \in \mathbf{R}^2: x \geq y)$ and $S_y = (x \in S: x \geq y)$.

We confine our consideration to the class $\mathbf{B}$ of bargaining games (S,d) satisfying the following conditions:

B1. $S \subset \mathbf{R}_d^2$
B2. S is compact, convex, and there exists $x \in S$ such that $x > d$.
B3. S is comprehensive, i.e., if $x \in S$ and $d \leq y \leq x$ then $y \in S$.

We assume implicitly $(S \subset \mathbf{R}_d^2)$ that the outcomes that are less favorable to one of the players than the noncooperative outcome d can be disregarded. The convexity assumption is made because we assume that randomization on different outcomes is possible; the comprehensiveness assumption is made because we assume that the players can freely dispose of utility.

For any game $(S,d) \in \mathbf{B}$, a dynamic bargaining process can be described by a function $\lambda : [t_o, t_f] \to S$. We assume that the process satisfies the following conditions:

C1. Continuous, i.e., λ is a continous function.
C2. Progressive, i.e., $\lambda(t') \geq \lambda(t)$ for any $t_o \leq t \leq t' \leq t_f$.
C3. Starts at the disagreement point and leads to the boundary of S, i.e., $\lambda(t_o) = d$, $\lambda(t_f) \in \partial S$.

As was mentioned, we confine our consideration to continuous processes starting from the disagreement point and leading to an efficient payoff vector. Axiom C2 states that no player will accept an improvement of the payoff of the other player at the cost of diminishing his own payoff.

In this chapter, a dynamic bargaining process is identified with the course of the process in the payoff space (independently of possible parameterization ways). From condition C2, it follows that a trajectory $\Lambda = \{\lambda(t): t_o \leq t \leq t_f\}$, called an *agreement trajectory*, describes completely the process in the payoff space; it starts at the point $\min \leq \Lambda = \lambda(t_o)$, the successive points on the trajectory $x \in \Lambda$ reflecting the progress in the process, and it leads to the final payoffs $\max \geq \Lambda = \lambda(t_f)$.

Let C denote the class of all trajectories in $\mathbf{R}^2$. By a dynamic solution of the bargaining problem, we mean a map $F : \mathbf{B} \to \mathbf{C}$ such that for any game $(S, d) \in \mathbf{B}$ the agreement trajectory $F(S, d)$ is generated by a function satisfying conditions C1–C3.

Observe that the dynamic solution concept differs from the solution concept proposed in the classical literature on the bargaining problem. For any game $(S, d) \in \mathbf{B}$, a dynamic solution gives not only the final payoffs for the players, but also pictures how they reach them.

We impose on a dynamic solution the following two axioms:

A1. For any game $(S, d) \in \mathbf{B}$, if $x \in F(S, d)$ and $(S_x, x) \in \mathbf{B}$ then $F(S_x, x) = F(S, d) \cap S x$.

A2. For any game $(S, d) \in \mathbf{B}$, let $R_i(S, d) = \{x \in S$: there exists $y \in F(S, d)$ such that $x_i > y_i$, $x_j = y_j$ for $j \neq i\}$ for $i = 1,2$. Then $\mu[R_1(S, d)] = \mu[R_2(S, d)]$, where $\mu[\ ]$ denotes the Lebesgue measure.

Axiom A1 states that if the players reach payoffs x during the bargaining process, then the payoffs belonging to $S \backslash \mathbf{R}_x^2$ play no role in the further part of the process. For any game $(S, d) \in \mathbf{B}$, the agreement trajectory $F(S, d)$ cuts the agreement set S on two sets $R_1(S, d)$ and $R_2(S, d)$ (see *Figure 36.1*). The set $R_i(s, d)$, $i = 1,2$ is the region favorable to the ith player with respect to the trajectory $F(S, d)$ in the sense that the payoffs belonging to $R_i(S, d)$ are, roughly speaking, "better" for the ith player and "worse" for the counter player than the points belonging to the trajectory $F(S, d)$. We require that the Lebesgue measure of each region $R_i(S, d)$, $i = 1,2$ be the same.

It is easy to verify that axioms A1 and A2 involve the following axiom:

A3. *Equal concession axiom*: For any game $(S, d) \in \mathbf{B}$, if $x,y \in F(S, d)$ and $x \leq y$ then $\mu[R_1(S_x, x) \backslash R_1(S_y, y)] = \mu[R_2(S_x, x) \backslash R_2(S_y, y)]$.

The dynamic bargaining process can also be considered as a give-and-take policy in which each player makes concessions from the payoffs in his favorable region. Axiom A3 says that in passing from x to y, the measure of payoffs excluded from consideration in each region favorable to a particular player is the same (see *Figure 36.2*).

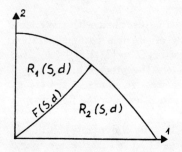

Figure 36.1.   Figure 36.2.

36.3. Results

To present the main result of this chapter, let us consider for a game $(S,d) \in \mathbf{B}$ the initial-value problem:

$$dx_2/dx_1 = (f_2(x_1) - x_2)/(f_1(x_2) - x_1) \tag{36.1}$$

$$x_2(d_1) = d_2 ,$$

where $f_1(x_2) = \max\{x_1 : (x_1, x_2) \in S\}$, $f_2(x_1) = \max\{x_2 : (x_1, x_2) \in S\}$.

Intuitively for any $(x_1, x_2) \in S$, $f_1(x_2)$ and $f_2(x_1)$ are the maximal payoffs that players 1 and 2, respectively, might hope to receive in the game (S_x, x).

From Peano's Existence Theorem and from the Extension Theorem [Hartman (1964)] for any game $(S, d) \in \mathbf{B}$, there exists one and only one maximal solution $f : (d_1, x_1^*) \to (d_2, x_2^*)$ of the initial-value problem (36.1) (the maximal solution means the solution defined on a right maximal interval). The point $x^* = (x_1^*, x_2^*)$ defined by $x_2^* = \lim_{x_1 \to x_1^*} f(x_1)$ belongs to the boundary of S. Moreover, from the continuity of functions f_1 and f_2, it follows that function f is continuously differentiable.

This initial-value problem was suggested by Raiffa (1953) as a reasonable and plausible description of the bargaining process.

Now we can prove the following theorem and corollary [see Bronisz and Krus (1986)].

Theorem

There is a unique dynamic solution $F^* : \mathbf{B} \to \mathbf{C}$ satisfying the equal concession axiom. For any game $(S, d) \in \mathbf{B}$, the agreement trajectory $F^*(S, d)$ is generated by the maximal solution $f : (d_1, x_1^*) \to (d_2, x_2^*)$ of the initial-value problem (36.1), i.e., $F^*(S, d) = \{(x_1, x_2) \in S : \quad x_2 = f(x_1) \quad \text{for} \quad d_1 \leq x_1 < x_1^*, \quad \text{or} \quad x = (x_1^*, x_2^*) \text{ where } x_2^* = \lim_{x_1 \to x_1^*} f(x_1)\}.$

Corollary

$F^* : \mathbf{B} \to \mathbf{C}$ is a unique dynamic solution satisfying axioms A1 and A2.

36.4. Raiffa's Continuous Solution and Its Properties

The Raiffa continuous solution is defined as the result of the dynamic solution satisfying the equal concession axiom, i.e, the Raiffa continuous solution is the function $\Psi : \mathbf{B} \to \mathbf{R}^2$ such that for a game $(S, d) \in \mathbf{B}$, $\Psi(S, d) = (x_1^*, x_2^*)$ ($= \max \geq F^*(S, d)$) where (x_1^*, x_2^*) is the final payoff vector of the dynamic solution satisfying the equal concession axiom (see Theorem).

We can prove the following properties of the Raiffa continuous solution [see Bronisz and Krus (1986)]:

P1. Feasibility: $\Psi(S, d) \in S$.

P2. Uniqueness: $\Psi(S, d)$ is a unique point in S.

P3. Continuity: Let $(S_j, d) \in \mathbf{B}$ be bargaining problems defined for a sequence of sets S_j such that $\lim_{j \to \infty} S_j = S$ (in the Hausdorf topology) and let $(S, d) \in \mathbf{B}$. Then $\lim_{j \to \infty} \Psi(S_j, d) = \Psi(S, d)$.

P4. Strong individual rationality: $\Psi(S, d) > d$.

P5. Strong Pareto optimality: $\Psi(S, d)$ is a strongly Pareto-optimal point in S.

P6. No dictatorship: If $I(S, d)$ denotes the ideal point of (S, d), i.e., $I_i(S, d) = \max \{x_i : x \in S, x \geq d\}$ for $i = 1, 2$, then either $\Psi(S, d) = I(S, d)$ or $\Psi(S, d) < I(S, d)$. We say that (S, d) is a symmetric problem if $d_1 = d_2$ and if for each $x = (x_1, x_2)$ in S, the point $y = (x_2, x_1)$ belongs also to S.

P7. Symmetry: For a symmetric game, $\Psi_1(S, d) = \Psi_2(S, d)$.

P8. Invariance under positive affine transformations of utility: Let $\mathbf{A} : \mathbf{R}^2 \to \mathbf{R}^2$ be a positive affine transformation defined by $Ax = (a_1 x_1 + b_1, a_2 x_2 + b_2)$, where $a_1, a_2 > 0$. Then $A\Psi(S, d) = \Psi(AS, Ad)$.

P9. Strict risk sensitivity: If a game $(S, d) \in \mathbf{B}$ is transferred into a game $(T, d) \in \mathbf{B}$ by replacing player j with a strictly more risk-averse player, then $\Psi_i(T, d) > \Psi_i(S, d)$ for $i \neq j$.

The next three properties describe the relation between two games (S, d) and (T, d) belonging to **B**, which are connected in geometric ways. Quoting Thomson and Meyerson (1980):

> If T is obtained from S by the addition (or the elimination) of points that are all located in a region favorable to a particular agent, one might want the solution to move in his favor (or against him). Such requirements may be seen from a normative viewpoint, as fairness conditions, or from a descriptive viewpoint, since no player could reasonably be expected to accept a solution that would fail to satisfy them.

The presented properties strengthen those proposed by Thomson and Meyerson (1980). Let $(S, d) \in$ **B**, $(T, d) \in$ **B** be such that $S \neq T$ and let j denote the counter player to player i.

P10. **Strict adding:** If $\{x: x_i \leq \Psi_i (S, d)\} \cap S = \{x: x_i \leq \Psi_i (S, d)\} \cap T, S \subset T$, and $\Psi(S, d) \in \partial T$, then $\Psi_i(T, d) > \Psi_i(S, d)$.

P11. **Strict cutting:** If $\{x: x_i \leq \Psi_i(S, d)\} \cap S = \{x : x_i \leq \Psi_i(S, d)\} \cap T$ and $T \subset S$, then $\Psi_j(T, d) > \Psi_j(S, d)$.

P12. **Strict twisting:** If:
    (i) $\Psi(S, d) \in \partial T$,
    (ii) $x \in T \backslash S$ implies $x_j \leq \Psi_j(S, d)$,
    (iii) $x \in S$, $x_j \leq \Psi_j(S, d)$ implies $x \in T$, then $\Psi_i(T, d) > \Psi_i(S, d)$.

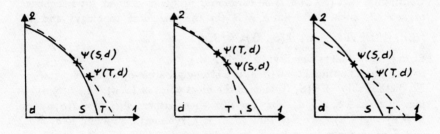

Figure 36.3.   Figure 36.4.   Figure 36.5.

Figures 36.3, 36.4, and *36.5* illustrate properties P10–P12 for $i = 1$. In each figure, two bargaining games (S, d) and (T, d) are presented (the first game is drawn with a continuous line and the second one with a broken line). In *Figure 36.3,* adding alternatives favoring the first player, by going from S to T, leads to an improvement of his payoff according to P10. In *Figure 36.4,* eliminating alternatives favorable to the first player, by going from S to T, results in a deterioration of his payoff according to P11. In *Figure 36.5*, twisting S to T around $\Psi(S, d)$ in favor of the first player leads to an improvement of his payoff according to P12.

36.5. Comparison of Raiffa's Continuous Solution to Nash's and Kalai-Smorodinsky Solution Concepts

The Raiffa continuous solution can be compared to the classical solution concepts: the Nash solution $N : \mathbf{B} \to \mathbf{R}^2$ [Nash (1950)] and the Kalai-Smorodinsky solution $K : \mathbf{B} \to \mathbf{R}^2$ [Kalai and Smorodinsky (1975)]. Each of them satisfies the properties of strong Pareto optimality, symmetry and invariance with respect to affine transformations of utility. These three properties treated as the axioms and the axiom of independence of irrelevant alternatives define the Nash solution; while these three properties and the axiom of individual monotonicity define the Kalai-Smorodinsky solution. Moreover, each solution has the properties of continuity, strong, individual rationality and risk sensitivity [see Roth (1979)]. However, the two last-mentioned axioms are not fulfilled by the Raiffa continuous solution. In contradistinction, the Nash and the Kalai-Smorodinsky solutions do not satisfy the properties P10–P12.

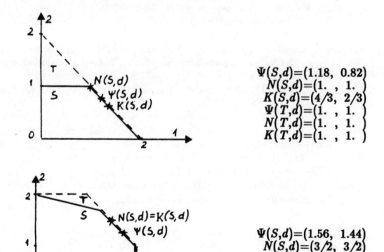

$$\Psi(S,d)=(1.18,\ 0.82)$$
$$N(S,d)=(1.\ ,\ 1.\ )$$
$$K(S,d)=(4/3,\ 2/3)$$
$$\Psi(T,d)=(1.\ ,\ 1.\ )$$
$$N(T,d)=(1.\ ,\ 1.\ )$$
$$K(T,d)=(1.\ ,\ 1.\ )$$

Figure 36.6.

$$\Psi(S,d)=(1.56,\ 1.44)$$
$$N(S,d)=(3/2,\ 3/2)$$
$$K(S,d)=(3/2,\ 3/2)$$
$$\Psi(T,d)=(3/2,\ 3/2)$$
$$N(T,d)=(3/2,\ 3/2)$$
$$K(T,d)=(3/2,\ 3/2)$$

Figure 36.7.

To illustrate these solutions, let us consider examples in *Figure 36.6* and *36.7*. In each figure, two bargaining games (S, d) and (T, d) are presented (the first game is drawn with a continuous line and the second one with a broken line). On the right-hand side of the figures, the values of the solutions for games (S, d) and (T, d) are given [the values $\Psi(S, d)$ are calculated approximately].

Acknowledgment

The authors are indebted to Professor A.P. Wierzbicki for inspiration on this subject.

References

Bronisz, P. and Krus, L. (1986), A Dynamic Solution of Two-Person Bargaining Problem, Report ZTSW-17-3/86, Systems Research Institute, Polish Academy of Sciences.

Bronisz, P., Krus, L., and Wierzbicki, A.P. (1987), Towards Interactive Solutions in Bargaining Problems, (forthcoming).

Hartman, P. (1964), *Ordinary Differential Equations*, John Wiley, New York.

Kalai, E. (1977), Proportional Solutions to Bargaining Situations: Interpersonal Utility Comparisons, *Econometrica*, 45, pp. 1623-1630.

Kalai, E. and Smorodinsky, M. (1975), Other Solutions to Nash's Bargaining Problem, *Econometrica*, 43, pp. 513-518.

Kihlstrom, R., Roth, A.E., and Schmeidler, D. (1981), Risk Aversion and Nash's Solution to the Bargaining Problem, in: *Game Theory and Mathematical Economics*, D. Moeschlin and D. Pallaschke, (eds.), North-Holland.

Myerson, R.B. (1977), Two-Person Bargaining Problems and Comparable Utility, *Econometrica*, 45, pp. 1631-1637.

Nash, J.F. (1950), The Bargaining Problem, *Econometrica*, 18, pp. 155-162.

Raiffa, H. (1953), Arbitration Schemes for Generalized Two-Person Games, *Annals of Mathematics Studies*, 28, pp. 361-387.

Roth, A.E. (1979), Axiomatic Model of Bargaining, *Lecture Notes in Economics and Mathematical Systems*, 170, Springer-Verlag, Berlin.

Thomson, W. and Myerson, R.B. (1980), Monotonicity and Independence Axioms, *International Journal of Game Theory*, 9, pp. 37-49.

PART VI

Training for International Negotiations

CHAPTER 37

Negotiations for Results: How to Develop Related Executive Skills

Pier Luigi Bontadini

IFAP
IRI Institute for Management Research and Development
Rome
Italy

37.1. Introduction

Negotiation, in organizational terms, is a process in which persons or groups with their own specific interests exchange knowledge, resources, and information in order to make and coordinate decisions. It is a process wherein the parties involved exercise a mutually conditioning influence as they seek positive results through a critical consideration of differing expectations in order to assume and redistribute opportunities, requests, and proposals for suitable organizational behavior patterns. In the final analysis, we can define it as an evolutionary adaptation process whereby organizations grow by dominating their own internal and external relations. It is a transverse way of "becoming organized".

Pursuant to this assumption, IFAP has conducted empirical research in select Italian management circles. On the basis of the experience acquired by 30 successful managers, a training model on negotiations was drawn up for medium- and high-level management staff with multimedia aids, which, in addition to the ordinary teaching tools, also includes a database with 2,000 entries available for use during actual negotiations. This training model is very flexible and takes into consideration the participant's level of acquired knowledge, the client's needs, and the actual time available.

A fundamental assumption is that *there is no universally valid model of negotiation.* Such an exercise involves internal and external factors, which make the situation very different from case to case. The external factors include the relative cultural environment or the presence of parties not directly represented in the negotiations; the internal factors include elements such as the relationship between the negotiator and his own targets in time, the relationship between negotiators, the influence of earlier relations and respective future expectations. These are just a few of the elements that make it difficult to fit negotiations into an ordinary model structure. In the organizational realm there are also intrinsic factors rendering negotiations all the more peculiar, owing to the forces at work within an organization.

However, this complexity should not lead to the pessimistic conclusion that the situation is impossible to understand. Despite the inherent diversities, it is possible to identify and analyze the negotiation process as a succession of logical steps where, in a more or less purposeful way, a series of elements are used and whose effectiveness depends on a certain number of factors both internal and external to the process as such.

The researcher's task entails:

- Highlighting the structure of the logical steps involved in the negotiation exercise as it takes place.
- Identifying the elements most frequently used in negotiations.
- Studying the possible relations between negotiation situations and effectiveness in the use of the negotiations elements.

37.2. Organizational Dimensions for Negotiation

First of all, however, one should consider the intrinsic reasons behind the special nature of negotiation in an organization. We can identify three organizational dimensions where negotiations are required. The "trigger" in all three of them is a change that is deemed necessary to achieve greater coherence and that involves the organization to a greater or lesser degree, according to the dimension in question.

The cultural dimension

The cultural dimension is the area where a series of reference or guideline values are advanced, defined, and assimilated. These values are destined to condition at length the environment in which the organization is situated and, at the same time, represent a sort of justification with respect to the inner workings of the organizational system itself. This "cultural" dimension coincides with the birth of the organization, whether in terms of the whole company or an independent part thereof. This is a process that sets the borders separating the "inside" from the "outside" and the criteria for "belonging" to the organization.

The structural-operational dimension

This is the area where operational targets are set, resources are allocated, and responsibilities are assigned or claimed among the various people within a more limited time frame, compared with the time element in the cultural sphere. In this time frame as well we encounter the handling of daily activities in target pursual.

The regenerative dimension

The regenerative dimension is where efforts are deployed to change a culture or a well-established organizational structure to realign them with the relative reference environment and move toward an evolutionary organizational process whose management determines the company's survival. This process cannot be left to chance and calls for the full assumption of direct and innovative responsibility on the part of management.

These three dimensions overlap in temporal terms and influence one another, to differing degrees. While, in the past, interaction took place over longer periods of time and under rather stable conditions (to the extent of enabling individuals and organizations to "digest" each and every innovation at a natural pace), nowadays this phenomenon is much faster and often involves unpredictable changes in direction. This means that evolutionary adaptation is difficult unless properly managed. The phenomenon is so difficult that only the more "dynamic" organizations grasp the occasions for change and transform them into opportunities to alter the relationship with the external environment to their own advantage and thereby force others to succumb or try to catch up.

It is clear that the negotiation issue assumes a fundamental importance in each of the three dimensions mentioned above. In all three, in fact, the essential point is to reconcile interests as well as the ways of looking upon contrasting and "necessarily" conflicting objectives. Since situations and objectives differ as to the actors in their mutual relations as well as in their approach to the organization and the global environment, the characteristics of the negotiations and the talents required to manage them in an effective way also differ.

In each of the three dimensions the process of change may be perceived completely or in part by the actors involved and, in that sense, may receive an additional thrust. Or else it may not be noticed at all, in which case the actors continue their work and more or less consciously ignore the innovative stimulus elements.

37.3. Organizational Strategies

A manager involved in situations such as those just described has very serious responsibilities, since his behavior can sanction an existing situation (change or the status quo according to what is happening at a given time in an organization). Then again, direct action on his part may be considered indispensable either to block or channel a change, because it may assume negative features, or else to diffuse an uneasy situation.

There would seem to be two categories of skills necessary for a manager:

(1) The diagnostic skills for interpreting reality and defining the targets that will serve as the basis for his action.
(2) The ability to lead the organization toward the set targets. With respect to the organizational dimensions indicated earlier (cultural and strategic–operational) and by facing a noticed or unnoticed change in the system, a manager has three options:
   - Direct action.
   - Mere adaptation of the present opportunities.
   - Acceptance of events without guiding the system to change, i.e., a passive stance.

By crisscrossing the organizational dimensions and the process of change in the organization with the options, we have a picture of the organizational strategies open to a manager. The outcome matrix in *Table 37.1* indicates 12 action possibilities a manager can employ to pursue the targets as defined above in (1).

Table 37.1. A manager's options in the face of change.

	Organizational dimension			
	Cultural		Strategic–operational	
Options	*Change noticed*	*Change not noticed*	*Change noticed*	*Change not noticed*
1. Direct action	Enhance the spontaneous change phenomena	Create diversity/ inequalities; foster subsystem confrontation	Formalize targets and behavior patterns	Push different targets
2. Opportunistic stance	System facelifting	Sit back and wait	Maintain course without touching targets	Rebalance/review targets and functions
3. Passive stance	Repress/isolate the emerging situation	Eliminate diversity/ inequalities sharpen control measures	Remove roles/functions from certain targets and vice versa	Make the present targets coercive

The negotiation exercise plays an essential yet not exclusive role, but demands ways and means gauged to each of the possibilities in terms of the specific target pursued by a manager with his options, with regard to his counterparts' stance in relationship to the specific options, and with respect to the objective reasons behind each option.

37.4. The Research Project

In line with the assumptions made, the actual research was conducted in Italy and involved a series of interviews with 30 "successful" managers (e.g., managers who had reached the top of the career ladder and stayed there over a long time) on the basis of the consideration that negotiation abilities in one's own market or environment constitute one of the factors in success. Also part of the initial postulate was the conviction that each "environment" is defined by rules of behavior that a "good negotiator" respects in order to emerge.

The purpose of the research project was to bring out the underlying structures, if they actually existed.

The managers interviewed came from areas as different as industry, business, labor unions, public administration, and sport federations. These interviews were followed by others with sociologists, psychologists, and experts in international negotiations.

The actual interview was conducted with reference to a standard geared to bringing out for each manager the ways and means ordinarily employed in negotiations, the elements used according to the various situation, and a judgement on their effectiveness according to the situation. The interview ended with one or more examples of significant negotiations in which the manager had been involved.

Each interview lasted between 45 minutes and 2 hours and was videotaped. This provided a substantial amount of material available for repeated review and analysis. The study of the literature in this area and the material collected made it possible to identify a large number of variables which, in due modular arrangement, are used in the various negotiation situations.

It is possible to make an hypothesis on the succession of the logical steps making up the vast majority of negotiations, but the experience of these successful managers confirmed the initial assumption: there are so many negotiation models that the possibility of reducing them to a few fundamental schemes is most doubtful. What is most important, however, is that good negotiations differ from bad ones according to the way in which the constitutent elements are used: actors, targets, time, pressure, processes, etc.

The research project disclosed in rather clear terms the way in which successful negotiators achieve coherence in the use of the elements in each negotiation exercise according to the circumstances.

37.5. Teaching Target

The lesson learned from the research project has become the main teaching target: to help people to understand that negotiation is a process of evolutionary adaptation whereby the actors involved dominate the objective complexity of the issue tackled, the related environment, and the contrasting interests at stake by using the negotiaton elements in a coherent way.

To develop the skills necessary for negotiating, the transfer of the knowledge acquired through this research takes place through two channels:

(1) A clear idea of the negotiation process, its logical phases, and inherent elements.
(2) The manager's progressive immersion into the complex nature of negotiaton in order to train him in the use of the elements according to the objective nature of the negotiation situation.

The ultimate target is to make the managers able to dominate the negotiation process, to know how to gear the use of the elements according to the various situations, and especially to know how to develop their own range of negotiation models in harmony with their own personality and with the situations they ordinarily experience.

37.6. Teaching Strategy

To achieve the teaching targets it seemed advisable to have the participants follow the same process used in the research project, and this was made possible by the way the information was collected. This information is summarized in *Figure 37.1.*

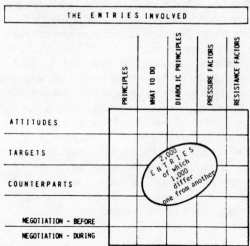

Figure 37.1. Entries.

37.7. Teaching Method and Tools

The peculiar feature of the methods adopted is that the participant is introduced into a "cognitive itinerary" where he himself becomes an *explorer* into the possibilities offered by the information collected during the research phase. With the instructor's assistance he can go over alternative negotiation models, explore the usable elements (2,000 entries), mentally position them in his own preexistent model, and come up with others suited to the situations typical of his daily life. The material collected was organized for presentation in the form of the following multi-media teaching tools and methods:

- **Films:** prepared from the videotapes of the interviews with the successful managers that contained the most discordant replies; these short films (3-12 minutes) were prepared taking fully into account each logical step in the negotiation process.
- **Lectures:** traditional, with the use of transparencies.
- **Examples:** geared to each logical step in the process.
- **Questionnaires:** to stimulate the participant's analysis of each logical step in the process.
- **Tests:** to check on the progress made by the participants.
- **Simulation exercise:** to stimulate the participants to relive special negotiation situations; these simulations were usually videotaped.
- **Database:** this includes all of the microvariables related to the various moments in the negotiation process and can be accessed directly by participants on a personal computer.
  The use of the data base is necessary because of the high number of entries involved. They are expressed in qualitative form, entail a series of instructions or suggestions, and can be located by using the matrix crisscross parameters (*Figure 37.1*) with the definition of a set of conditions freely selected by the participants by using a very simple personal computer access program.
- **Working session:** the typical format of a working session is as follows:

(1) Introduction (by the instructor).
(2) Projection of the film as a stimulus.
(3) Filling in of the questionnaire (around 10 items) where each participant judges the stimulus effect of the film.
(4) Discussion, in small groups, with summary input by the instructor.
(5) Support exercises.
(6) General discussion.

Each working session is dedicated to one logical step in the negotiation process.
The teaching activity ends with the simulation of a complex negotiation exercise. Ordinarily, it aims at reproducing a full-involvement situation by using a subject of common interest to all the participants, who rotate in the roles of negotiator and observer.

- **Negotation session:** a typical negotiation session includes:

  (1) An introduction by the instructor and the assignment of tasks in small groups.
  (2) Group work to define the negotiation strategy: the database is available for the determination of strategies to be employed.
  (3) Report by the group to the instructor on the strategies selected.
  (4) Videotaped negotiation simulation.
  (5) Review of the taped simulation and discussion.
  (6) Evaluation of negotiation effectiveness through a comparative analysis of the strategies reported by the groups before the negotiation simulation, and of the actual situation during the exercise.

  The instructor can always liven up step (4) by introducing incidents that compel the participants to reformulate their strategies while the negotiation process is under way.

- **Flexibility:** the program has been designed with the following flexibility factors:

  (1) *Adaptation to the participants' level of knowledge:* During the course it is always possible to adapt the learning process to the needs of the group of participants. By using performance tests, the instructor can check the actual level of knowledge and then either concentrate on elements yet to be grasped in full or leave aside familiar material.
  (2) *Adaptation to the amount of time available:* In practice the optimal length of the program is 3–5 days for middle-level managers. However, the program can be shortened or extended without introducing any substantial changes.
  (3) *Adaptation to the client's needs:* When focusing directly on management problems, the program can be adapted to the typical situations summarized in *Table 37.1.* In this way exercises and simulations can be introduced for each of the hypothetical situations a manager may face when tackling a change in a situation more or less shared by the organization and according to the options he may wish to pursue.

37.8. Conclusions

To have a better understanding of this training project, the following aspect must be considered. Once the problem has been identified and before outlining a training program, training personnel ordinarily have to draw up a working hypothesis according to their own model, collect all of the information required, and then, on this basis, check whether the model is valid or has to be adapted to the specific situation. Only after this preliminary research work can the training activity be designed and delivered in such a way as to respond fully to the relative requirements.

Therefore, research and training represent two phases of the same job, but ordinarily they remain distinct, the former handled by the instructors, and the latter with the participants called upon to interact via a model not designed by them.

The special feature of this model resides in using research as part of the training process. If the participants, and not only the instructors, check the validity of the initial model, they are provided with a unique opportunity to practice the aggregation and input of their own concrete experience. However, this does not suffice. With this method the participants are stimulated to compare their own negotiation conduct with behavior patterns adopted by others, although in sometimes different circumstances, which have been studied by the instructors in drawing up the initial model. In the case in question, the negotiation behavior patterns considered were those of the successful managers in quite different sectors.

In this way the initial model can be adapted and improved upon at any time by the participants themselves, according to their own concrete situations. This means that the structure of the training process is *open* in the sense that it can be traveled in any direction desired and used by anyone who wants to delve into current problems.

All of this takes place in a completely transparent way. From the very outset, the work to be done is explained to the participants who thereby understand the meaning and usefulness of the training process. In the final analysis, this training model embodies three special features which are more consonant with scientific work than with a traditional training model. The features are as follows:

(1) *Interactive:* it gives each participant an opportunity to contend with behavior patterns and variables taken into consideration by others and compare them with his own reference reality.
(2) *Simulative:* it offers the possibility to simulate all types of operational situations.
(3) *Experimental:* it provides for a constant verification of individual behavior models at each moment of the training process.

Alternative negotiation possibilities emerge if enough time is set aside for brainstorming between men with company experience along with the counsel of the instructors. These possibilities can always be checked by the learning group from the viewpoint of coherence. The instructors involved in the project have stated that:

A series of learning tests we conducted during the course immediately after the most important steps in the teaching process confirmed the progressive convergence of the participants on the suggested cognitive itinerary more so than on the negotiation model presented. This made it possible for them to introduce order into past experience and reflect on what was being offered in class.

The method adopted goes beyond the sphere of negotiations to which it was applied. In more general terms we can say that when a person advances in his career, he is not always able to adapt rapidly to the new position of responsibility. With the cognitive itinerary adopted for negotiations, this person is trained to tackle a problem, define that problem to the degree of constructing an interpretative model (moving from information collection to the ordering thereof), defining action in the context of the model, and checking the results. In effect, this becomes a concrete simulation of a management activity, not conducted explicitly, but actually *during* an activity used to acquire a management skill.

This is why, if the training experience is well conducted, it can be most effective in the development of the participant's capabilities.

CHAPTER 38

Training in International Negotiating:
A Learning Instrument

Willem F. G. Mastenbroek

Holland Consulting Group
Amsterdam
The Netherlands

38.1. Introduction

For ten years workshops on international negotiating have been organized by the Governmental Training and Conference Institute in the Netherlands. The program of the workshops was developed by this author, who devised a learning instrument with the objective of facilitating effective feedback on negotiating styles [1].

This chapter describes that learning instrument in the form of four scales, which express different kinds of negotiating activities: obtaining substantial results; influencing the balance of power; promoting a constructive climate; and procedural flexibility.

The scales were developed in close interaction with practitioners. They are used to provide participants of workshops on international negotiating with specific feedback on their negotiating styles and tactics. They also proved to be a good basis for discussing the negotiating process.

The purpose of this chapter is twofold:

(1) To share my experiences in developing these learning tools.
(2) To communicate with consultants and educators in other countries, who are engaged in developing instruments and workshops aiming at more

effective international negotiations, with the ultimate goal of developing a plan for future exchange and collaboration.

38.2. Learning Tools

An important part of the workshop on international negotiating is devoted to the simulation of real negotiations. For instance, participants negotiate on a treaty concerning the chemical pollution of the Rhine or international transport problems. These simulations are videotaped.

The participants are supplied with information on the effects of their negotiating behavior. In the first conferences 12 scales were used to systemize behavioral feedback. Over the years it became evident that improvements and adaptations of these scales were necessary. All scales were reformulated and gradually only six remained as the most relevant. The efforts here described were broadened to other negotiating areas as well. Now the scales are used in workshops on a wide variety of negotiations.

Four of these scales are described in this chapter. They express different kinds of negotiating activities:

- Obtaining substantial results.
- Influencing the balance of power.
- Promoting a constructive climate.
- Procedural flexibility.

These activities, each of which is dealt with in the following subsections, contain some dilemmas that sometimes make it difficult for negotiators to make the right choices. The other two scales, which are still in the stage of development, deal with empathy toward other cultures and the handling of constituencies.

The development of these learning tools started ten years ago with the selection of three perspectives:

(1) Negotiation as a skill based on handling a number of dilemmas. Material on this is scattered throughout the literature; see, for example, Karras (1970).
(2) Negotiation as a process with a structure in time; see Douglas (1962), Himmelman (1971), Zartman (1978).
(3) Negotiation as a complex of various types of activities. A classic work by Walton and McKersie (1965) is based on this perspective.

The first perspective was worked out in more detail and combined with the other two [Mastenbroek (1987)]. Gradually, important and specific negotiating techniques, which also have found recognition elsewhere [Fisher and Ury (1981), Dupont (1982)], were integrated. While profiting from the knowledge and experience of competent negotiators, and challenged by questions and critical remarks, it became evident that improvements and adaptations were desirable and possible. Thus, only four negotiating dilemmas have remained from the original list of twelve, two have been added and all have been drastically reformulated.

38.2.1. Obtaining substantial results

An important category of negotiating activity concentrates on influencing the *content* of the outcome. This involves such matters as information, arguments, facts, agenda, concessions and positions. These activities directly focus on obtaining *tangible results*. They proceed from the intention of reaching a solution by dividing *costs and benefits* in a favorable way.

The most important activities in this category are:

- Exchanging information about aims, expectations and acceptable solutions.
- Influencing one another's perceptions of what is attainable.
- Working step by step toward compromise with mutual concessions.

These activities are common ground to negotiators. Most negotiators pay a lot of attention to them (but the experienced negotiator also shows a keen awareness of the other three dimensions).

The tactical choices a negotiator has to make in this area can be understood as the balancing of conceding versus more tenacious or even stubborn behavior. This dilemma is clarified in *Figure 38.1* with some examples.

1	2	3	4	5
lenient, indulgent ←		*tenacious, testing* →	*hard, stubborn*	
Information and arguments are presented as open for discussion		Firm presentation of facts and arguments but margins are taken for granted	Information and arguments are presented as self-evident and unassailable	
The interests of the other side are accepted as they are described		The interests of the other party are tested in order to discover his priorities	The interests of the opponent are challenged or ignored	
Generous concessions facilitate the working out of compromises		Impasses are part of the game, relatively small concessions are possible	Tendency to set ultimatums, provoke crises and "final offer, first bid"	

Figure 38.1. Conceding versus stubborn behavior along a scale.

38.2.2. Influencing the balance of power

Negotiators show a keen interest in the balance of power among them. They may find it tempting to establish a more favorable balance of power or to test the power and resistance of the opponent. There are different ways of *strengthening one's own power position at the negotiating table*. Important tactics in this respect are:

Fighting. Such tactics are directly aimed at subjugating the opponent. Examples include ignoring the other party's information and arguments; feigning emotions such as anger and impatience.

Manipulating. This is a more indirect attempt to strengthen one's position at the negotiating table. The most subtle are the manipulations that affect a person's feeling of self-esteem — for instance, insisting on having one's way as if it were the only logical thing to do, or displaying a dynamic attitude so that people who do not go along get the feeling they are "retarding" progress.

Facts and expertise. Knowledge of the history; background about the negotiating partners; having facts and material at hand that are favorable to one's own position and being able to present them clearly are all essential for this tactic.

Exploring. This technique, which we will treat in more detail, can strengthen a person's position for several reasons. Exploring means taking a certain power of initiative: posing questions, giving information, making proposals, creating a possible package deal. Exploring also means trying to consider the interests of the opponent in a sense that a person's attitude is characterized by "How do *we* find a solution to this *together!*" This legitimates a person's performance; it lends a person authority.

Intensifying the relation. The relationship with the opponent can be strengthened by developing acceptance and trust. This strengthens the *mutual* dependency.

Power of persuasion. Elements of persuasion are:

-   A clear, well-structured manner of explaining one's own opinion.
-   A reasonably relaxed, but not nonchalant, attitude. Manipulating and fighting can provide a temporary advantage, but risk escalation and irritated personal relations. The other tactics are more constructive.

Strengthening the starting position. There are several ways to strengthen and consolidate one's position before the negotiations really get started. Some important means are:

-   Having *alternatives*. Not only alternative solutions for the items on the agenda, but also different ways of reaching one's own goals, perhaps with others.
-   *Political access* and political intuition. Easy access to the relevant centers of power is of special importance.
-   *Status.* Tangible success, informal authority, hierarchical position, personal

trustworthiness, and credibility are all matters that contribute to status.
- *Support of others.* Having allies during the meeting, being able to obtain support from other countries not present. Not operating in isolation.

These are *"facts"* that will show their effectiveness at the negotiating table. All activities between parties are colored and modeled by the balance of power. No wonder negotiators are very sensitive to changes in the power and dependency balance. The dilemma here is that power games increase the risk of escalation. At the same time, it is sometimes necessary to test the balance of power. Not being able to do this or not recognizing that one is being tested or perhaps even somewhat provoked makes one appear weak and encourages exploitative behavior. The challenge is to preserve that factual dependence on a firm, unaggressive footing. The ways people cope with this dilemma are shown in *Figure 38.2.*

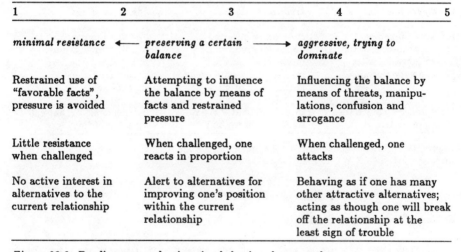

1	2	3	4	5

minimal resistance ⟵	*preserving a certain balance* ⟶	*aggressive, trying to dominate*
Restrained use of "favorable facts", pressure is avoided	Attempting to influence the balance by means of facts and restrained pressure	Influencing the balance by means of threats, manipulations, confusion and arrogance
Little resistance when challenged	When challenged, one reacts in proportion	When challenged, one attacks
No active interest in alternatives to the current relationship	Alert to alternatives for improving one's position within the current relationship	Behaving as if one has many other attractive alternatives; acting as though one will break off the relationship at the least sign of trouble

Figure 38.2. Bending versus domineering behavior along a scale.

38.2.3. Promoting a constructive climate

Negotiators consider it important to promote a constructive *climate* and respectful personal *relationships*. An irritated or very formal atmosphere hampers effective negotiating. So they try to develop *trust, acceptance, and credibility.* In this way they give evidence of their mutual dependence and foster a relationship based on this dependence.

Examples of tactics in this area are:

- **Paying attention to each other's opinions.**
- **Promoting informal and open contacts.**
- **Avoiding loss of face.**

-   Behaving predictably and seriously, not using ploys and stratagems or "pulling a fast one".
-   Distinguishing role behavior (e.g., a firm demand) from personal goodwill and mutual respect.

The dilemma one has to face is that trusting the other without reservation means running the risk of seriously weakening one's own position and of over-compromising. So one must develop a kind of calculated trust, while remaining fully aware of the exploitative possibilities of a very personal and confidential relationship. Trust and credibility are important. But at the same time, investing heavily in trust and personal relations may readily be seen as overbearing, or as weak and silly. This dilemma is illustrated in *Figure 38.3.*

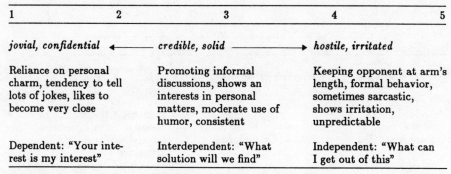

| 1 | 2 | 3 | 4 | 5 |

jovial, confidential ←——— *credible, solid* ————→ *hostile, irritated*

Reliance on personal charm, tendency to tell lots of jokes, likes to become very close	Promoting informal discussions, shows an interests in personal matters, moderate use of humor, consistent	Keeping opponent at arm's length, formal behavior, sometimes sarcastic, shows irritation, unpredictable
Dependent: "Your interest is my interest"	Interdependent: "What solution will we find"	Independent: "What can I get out of this"

Figure 38.3. Jovial versus hostile behavior along a scale.

38.2.4. Procedural flexibility

How explorative is a negotiator? Some negotiators search persistently for solutions that are relatively satisfying for both parties. This can be done without falling into the trap of making concessions. For this purpose people need ideas on how to proceed and they need to be able to use these procedures flexibly. Examples of such behavior include extensive exchange of information, trying out a variety of tentative solutions, thinking aloud, and informal questioning. The integrative potential of the situation will then be fully utilized. Exploring occurs by searching for common interests: Do the parties share some basic assumptions? Are relatively small concessions possible that might mean a lot to the opposite party and vice versa? Can a combination of mutual advantages be created in a package deal?

The basic idea behind all this is *interdependency*. Parties are negotiating because they are interdependent. Interdependency means common interests. So try first to make the common good as tangible as possible. The two poles of this behavior are indicated in *Figure 38.4.* This also can turn out to be a dilemma.

Repetitive rigid behavior has to be avoided; on the other hand, too much flexibility can appear as opportunistic and impulsive behavior.

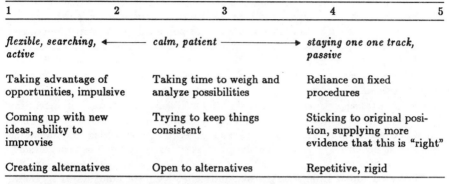

1	2	3	4	5

flexible, searching, ← calm, patient → staying one one track,
active   *passive*

Taking advantage of opportunities, impulsive	Taking time to weigh and analyze possibilities	Reliance on fixed procedures
Coming up with new ideas, ability to improvise	Trying to keep things consistent	Sticking to original position, supplying more evidence that this is "right"
Creating alternatives	Open to alternatives	Repetitive, rigid

Figure 38.4. Exploring versus avoiding behavior along a scale.

Practitioners as well as researchers stress over and over the *great importance of an active strategic attitude for skillful negotiating.*

Negotiations go through a number of phases. The notion of phases as an approach to the study of negotiations is well established [Douglas (1962), Gulliver (1979), Himmelman (1971), Zartman and Berman (1982)], but relatively unexplored. Here we use a model with three phases as a procedural technique to improve flexibility.

(1) Start with a *diagnosis* of mutual premises and interests; investigate where interests overlap and keep an eye on the priorities on both sides. Scanning other options and *alternatives* is also part of this.
(2) Introducing a very broad *"platform proposal"* is often an effective next step: the proposal can serve as an outline for
(3) *Amendment and alteration* until a compromise is reached.

Using these phases can help to prevent the situation from developing into hostile arguments about positions.

38.3. Conclusion

Providing specific feedback on negotiation styles is the most important purpose of the four scales. Other learning connected with their scores on the scales proved important to the participants. Some examples:

-    Firmly going after your interests does not mean showing the other party disrespect, irritation and distrust. *Separate the relationship from the content.*

- Do not confuse a power struggle with obtaining favorable material results. *Firm negotiating has little to do with scoring points, dominating the discussion, threats and manipulations.*
- Try to have formal or informal "preliminary talks", where parties can survey each other's interests and ideas before taking pronounced positions.
- Attempt to devise alternatives. Do not respond too quickly with judgments or counterarguments. Instead look for alternative proposals and solutions.
- Enlarge the negotiating field. More issues over a longer period of time sometimes increase the chance of a package deal that is relatively favorable to both sides.
- Work with "platform proposals". If one disagrees, instead of defending one's own proposal at all costs, a party simply inquires under what conditions one's proposal would become acceptable, or which modifications would be needed. Next, one does not start arguing but proposes amendments of one's own. Especially on complicated issues with several parties involved, this strategy may prove quite effective. Someone states a general outline of possible agreement. This outline is then specified and amended in a number of sessions.
- Movement when a deadlock is imminent:

  - Seek more and different information instead of correcting and negatively judging information.
  - Search for the problems that lie at the root of the impasse instead of convincing and threatening.
  - Emphasize equality and mutual dependence (for example, by exploring the negative consequences of a continuing impasse) instead of acting superior or withdrawing.
  - Adjourn and create informal contacts instead of going on and on with meetings.

Most of these examples are effective tactics on the procedural flexibility scale. They can be summarized in the maxim *"Be flexible but firm"*. In evaluations of the workshops, participants often rated highly their learning in this respect.

Note

[1]   The part of the workshop devoted to the handling of cultural differences was developed in cooperation with Dr. C. Dupont (Professor, University Lille and CRC/Paris).

References

Douglas, A. (1962), *Industrial Peacemaking,* Columbia University Press, New York.

Dupont, C. (1982), *La négociation: Conduite, théorie applications,* Dalloz, Paris.

Fisher, R. and Ury, W. (1981), *Getting to Yes,* Houghton-Mifflin, Boston.

Gulliver, P.H. (1979), *Disputes and Negotiations: A Cross Cultural Perspective,* Academic Press, New York.

Himmelman, G. (1971), *Lohnbildungen durch Kollektivverhandlungen,* Dunker & Humblot, Berlin.

Karras, C.L. (1970), *The Negotiating Game,* Thomas Crowell, New York.

Mastenbroek, W.F.G. (1987), *Conflict Management and Organization Development,* John Wiley, Chichester, UK.

Walton, R.E. and McKersie, R.B. (1965), *A Behavioral Theory of Labor Negotiations,* McGraw-Hill, New York.

Zartman, I. William (ed.) (1978), *The Negotiation Process,* Sage, Newbury Park, CA.

Zartman, I. William and Berman, Maureen (1982), *The Practical Negotiator,* Yale University Press, New Haven, CT.

PART VII

International Negotiations on Development and Environmental Issues

Negotiating a Research Project on Negotiation: The Fixed Link (Transchannel) Prenegotiations

Christophe Dupont

Lille-I University (IPA-IAE) and
Research Center for Management (CRC)
Jouy-en-Josas
France

39.1. Preliminary Observations

On November 30, 1984, the President of the Republic of France, Mr. Mitterand, and the Prime Minister of the British Government, Mrs. Thatcher, held a joint summit meeting. The agenda included a possible revival of the recurring project of providing a fixed link between the United Kingdom and the Continent.

This transchannel project had been envisaged for almost two centuries; and agreement to build a tunnel, which led to some preliminary work, had even been signed in the early 1970s and then cancelled by British request. But November 1984 seemed to mark a new turning point.

Mrs. Thatcher's official statement after meeting the French President made it clear that the political will was — this time — real. That statement was the beginning of a long, complex and very particular set of negotiations. On January 20, 1986, the two governments announced at Lille the choice of the design selected from among rival projects: it would be a tunnel rather than a bridge or some other alternative (such as a bridge or a combined bridge and tube connected by two artificial small islands). One month later, on February 12, 1986, a treaty was signed at Canterbury by the two governments and on March 14, 1986, a quadripartite concession agreement was signed by France, the United Kingdom, and two private organizations — France Manche (a French consortium) and CTG (Channel Tunnel Group, a British consortium) — which together became the *concessionaires* of the project and from that date on merged into an original unique organization: *Eurotunnel* (see *Figure 39.1*).

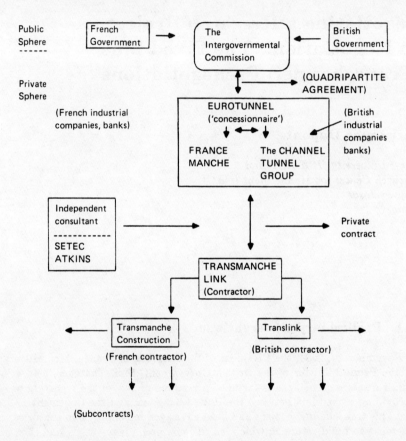

Figure 39.1. A simplified representation of the institutional set-up of the channel tunnel project.

As of April 1987, these treaties are in the process of ratification; Eurotunnel has established headquarters and offices in the United Kingdom and France; contractors have been awarded a construction contract; work is in progress on both sides of the Channel and some preliminary private financing has been arranged. Yet the project will be final only after ratification and the exchange of instruments [1]. In the meantime, some uncertainties still remain and complex negotiations continue unabated, since some issues are not fully resolved and some others continually crop up as the project gradually takes life and leads to daily operational problems.

This chapter centers on the prenegotiations, a period here defined as extending from November 30, 1984 to Jananuary 20, 1986. The chapter is the result of a research that will cover principally the negotiations from January 20, 1986 to the end of 1986. Therefore, it may be viewed as preliminary background for that research.

The chapter is mainly descriptive, but an effort has been made to refer various facts and events to relevant aspects of the theory or practice of international negotiations. The title points to a major difficulty facing researchers on negotiation, that of having access to true and viable sources of information, including interviews with real actors and sometimes discussing confidential data. Obviously, the researcher is bound by some *rules of the game,* and the following analysis scrupulously abides by such rules as relating to *off-the-record* comments of the persons interviewed. Another recognized limitation is that the work is only beginning, which explains its descriptive orientation without reliance on a sophisticated methodology.

39.2. Scope and Organization of the Research: A Brief Overview

The research project was launched as an essentially academic venture as regards context, structure and orientation. Yet some possible practical applications might be obtained as a welcome by-product.

The theme of the research was discussed by a university professor in charge of a graduate class on project management and by the author, whose interests — academic and practical — include negotiating, especially international negotiation [2]. As usual, time allocation and finance proved, at that juncture, to be obstacles to be surmounted. Yet this was in the end only secondary to what proved to be the major problems encountered: delineating the scope and purpose of the study, selecting the most promising angles of attack and — perhaps the most robust of all the obstacles — seeing to it that a minimal number of appropriate persons — knowledgeable, open-minded, and having themselves lived through the negotiating process — could be approached and, subject to not violating in any way the inevitable confidentiality attached to certain aspects, interviewed both in the United Kingdom and in France. Such interviews had to be conducted both in public and in private circles, both at national and regional levels, not to mention the variety of statuses and professions involved (government officials, administrators, high-level managers, legal advisers, bankers, construction professionals, etc.).

It was decided that the research should in a first (and possibly only) stage be characterized by the two following major constraints:

(1) Time and resource limitations would make it necessary to concentrate on some selected issues of particular relevance to the initiators of the project. Among these were:

(a) To clarify the decision-making process and what place the negotiating mode had in it.

(b) To look into the prenegotiations and the formal negotiations thereafter, examining to what extent existing *theories* of negotiation help explain the process actually observed.

(c) To clarify transcultural aspects and provide some recommendations in that respect.

(d) To examine the problems faced by peripheral actors in the decision-making or negotiation network (this refers notably to small firms negotiating some form of participation in the carrying out of the project).

Time and budget were severe given constraints. Whereas part of the job could be considered as a normal academic assignment and would not require special allocations, the extra resources were defined and limited to about 30 man-days. Needless to say, this would not permit in-depth research; however, it was deemed adequate (combined with a *normal* assignment) to lay the foundation for a future more elaborate work.

(2) From a methodological viewpoint, the approach should be based on the study of published documentation and literature and on interviews both in France and in the United Kingdom. Strict observance of confidentiality should be adhered to. Additionally, regarding more recent developments and unresolved issues, no attempt should be made to decode strategies pursued by the actors.

The present chapter may be considered as part of item 1(b). Although, with regard to the research project as a whole, the author will cover the four points mentioned, contributions were made by other researchers for points 1(c) and 1(d)[3].

39.3. Prenegotiations and Background Factors

Most models or studies of negotiations [e.g., Sawyer and Guetzkow (1965) or, more recently, Zartman and Berman (1982) and Touval and Zartman (1985)] insist on the importance of background factors and their emergence in the prenegotiation phase, i.e., the rather loosely defined period up to some marked turning point setting the stage for the initialization of the formal process.

In the case of the Fixed Link negotiations, prenegotiations may be dated from the early 1980s to the joint meeting of November 30, 1984.

A simplified chronology of events is instructive. After a standstill of a few years following the cancellation of an agreement to build a tunnel in the mid-1970s, some interest in reviving the idea began to develop in several quarters. In France, the Region Nord-Pas-de-Calais — a local authority recently created as part of the the effort to *decentralize* the historically heavily centralized administrative decision process — launched a number of initiatives under the impetus of two prominent (socialist) political leaders [4] in order to revive the issue [5]. In the late 1970s, on the other hand, contacts had been established between officials of the Nord-Pas-de-Calais Authority with their counterparts of the county of Kent [6]. In the private sphere, banks and a few industrial companies, especially in engineering and public works, continued to study certain aspects of an eventual project. In the United Kingdom, in 1981, the Select Committee for Transport of the House of Commons presented a report comparing the ten solutions that could then be envisaged for a privately financed link [7]. Interestingly, some form of joint cooperation in the two countries continued, as was evidenced by the publication of two official reports: one by an Anglo-French Study Group and one by an Anglo-French Financing Group. In France, the Region Nord-Pas-de-Calais launched yet another study with the help of the Bechtel consultant group.

As regards prospective private promoters, two loosely structured organizations comprising bankers and industrial companies were engaged in some form of activity (e.g., drawing up details of projects; making studies on and searching for financing; lobbying). One such group was CTG, entirely British, formed in 1984 by seven members; the other was Euroroute, composed of nine banks and companies, both British and French.

Two other events of interest should be noted. First, the purchase in July 1984 of the Sealink ferry company by J. Sherwood (a later prospective candidate for the project). Second, the development of contacts in the summer and fall of 1984, on the one hand, between officials of the two governments and, on the other, between prospective promoters and national government officials.

From a methodological viewpoint several elements are of interest. They include:

- Identification of parties and their characterization.
- Early emergence of key issues and the different values placed on their associated stakes by the parties involved.
- Factors entering into bargaining power.

This regrouping falls within the framework of simplified models of negotiation, which postulate that the negotiation process is strongly influenced from the start — relative to the object of negotiation (the issues) — by three main driving interacting forces: parties, stakes (value of interests; preoccupations; constraints; the risk factor), and the relative balance of power. The combination of these forces not only determines to a large extent the type of negotiation (integrative, distributive, etc.), but also structures the dynamics of the process (as evidenced *a posteriori* by the analysis of strategies and tactics).

39.3.1. Parties

One of the most important features of the Fixed Link prenegotiations is the development of an intricate network of actors. The structure of the network — which emerged early in the prenegotiation stage and was later (after January 20, 1986) simplified, but simultaneously complexified — could be represented graphically by a series of poles connected in a multidimensional way. A brief description of this network is summarized as follows.

Several different dimensions have to be considered: some of these acted as preconditions or constraints for the other, some were closely linked, others not, and some overlapping was also present.

Dimension 1 concerns the actors and the corresponding activities relating to the two national governments. In the prenegotiation stage, bilateral contacts were organized and conducted by various members of government, essentially the Office of the President, the Prime Minister, and ministers in charge of transport, but also the Foreign Office and the Ministry of Finance (for France); and the Prime Minister, the Ministry of Foreign Affairs, the Secretary for Transport and the Treasury among others in the case of the United Kingdom. Obviously, key aides as well as the embassies had their part in this process. This dimension is typically in the realm of classical diplomacy. This group of actors belonging to the public sphere must be extended to include senior officials of the two (nationalized) rail transportation systems (BR and SNCF). These organizations, whose interests were at stake in the project, played a key role in the whole negotiation process (prenegotiations and later).

In a sense, each government tried to assess the political will of the counterpart in that part of the search process. Some events or discussions were also determinant in framing the future scope of the negotiations. For example, a consensus was reached that the problem was bilateral, not multilateral (as would have been the case through the intervention of the EC [8]; and there was the clear indication from the very beginning that, on the British side, the project — whatever its physical design — would not involve public money [9].

Dimension 2 of the network of parties is closely related to the preceding one: it can be defined as the involvement of parliamentarians, especially in the United Kingdom. Members of the parliaments were not only lobbied by their constituencies (for or against the project) but also by various associations some of which were national in character, while others — such as the Conseil francobritannique — were in fact binational.

One of the specificities of the Fixed Link prenegotiations was network dimension 3, made up of factors belonging to government bodies and to the people forming the initial private promoters. In the United Kingdom, both CTG and Euroroute were active in order to obtain appropriate information on the chances of the project really being supported by the government and under what conditions, while also undertaking initiatives of many sorts to influence the decision-making process at the political level. That such prenegotiations were particularly intricate derives from the fact that the promoters had to fight on many fronts. Both promoters were allied in so far as the first priority was simply to influence positively the decision to go ahead; but they had clearly opposite interests insofar as they were rivals to obtain the contract award. Strategies had therefore to be extremely subtle since, to make matters still more complicated, the eventuality of facing pressure by the governments to join forces had also to be considered.

Dimension 4 represents the process through which the promoters had to secure a binational basis, that is, comprising both British and French partners. Euroute did not have to face that problem but, as Nicholas Henderson (1987) later wrote in a very detailed account of the maneuvering that took place, much energy and time had to be devoted by CTG to finding an appropriate French partner (which became France-Manche). Many parties, both private and public, were involved in this organizational problem. Sub-networks of relationships were formed and developed negotiating activities. At this stage a key factor — important for the theory of negotiation — was the role played by a few key individuals, their drive, their motivations and their qualities as negotiators as well as their ambiguities.

Dimension 5 of the network relates to national versus *regional* actors. The problem was that key decisions (to go ahead or not, major guidelines) would be made by the central governments and the promoter(s), while major impacts would affect local territories: principally, the County of Kent and the Region Nord-Pas-de-Calais. In the prenegotiation phase officials and private parties in both regions were therefore very active in attempting to be included into the decision-making process. Their negotiating task was also very delicate, as they not only had to deal with their central governments (not overlooking the prospective attitude of the other government), but also had to consider their own bilateral regional relationships.

A sixth and final dimension represents the group of private operators intent on participating in varying degrees and in multiform ways in the prospective works and services. Some of these operators were national in scope, but many were small, specialized, potential subcontractors. Obviously, they faced a very difficult negotiating task, which in the prenegotiation stage consisted mainly in trying to obtain information and perhaps get ready to act in due time. The negotiator at the periphery of a network is no doubt in a weak position.

The description of the actor network should also mention public opinion, evidently not a party as such, yet ever-present through the media and the lobbies. This often forgotten and diffuse factor may not be a party; it should however be included as an *invisible* actor in the negotiation process.

39.3.2. Issues and Associated Stakes

During the prenegotiations the issues that were debated were relatively straight-forward and *global* (as opposed to *detailed*).

For the governments and associated bodies and officials the problem could be formulated in a twofold proposition:

(1)   Should a fixed link project be revived?
(2)   If so, under what preconditions and constraints?

For promoters and the other parties involved the prenegotiation stage consisted mainly in prenegotiating their expected participation and influence in the undertaking and the design of the project.

Issue analysis at this stage illustrates several basic elements of the theory and practice of negotiation. As regards governments, an influential factor was the clear awareness that the two parties had both joint and divergent interests and priorities (i.e., different stakes), but that an overriding element was their interdependency: there simply could not be in this matter a unilateral decision. Joint interests included political and economic aspects, especially as the United Kingdom was now an active member of the European Community [10]. But priorities (stakes) were valued quite differently on each side of the Channel. In the United Kingdom the key priority was — apart from the politically symbolic gesture of a link to the Continent — the economic benefits that would derive from a more efficient way to transport goods and passengers. The approach was that of an overall cost–benefit analysis embracing many aspects, including transport cost savings, impact on employment, travelers' convenience, security and preservation of environment. Among these the latter, viewed as constraints, had a high psychological value.

In France the global picture was not at all ignored, but it would seem that a high priority, compared with Britain, was the long-term need and the present opportunity to extend across the Channel a unified efficient rail transport system, including high-speed, high-tech trains. Another important stake for France was the revitalization of the Region Nord-Pas-de-Calais, which had suffered from the partial destruction of its industrial structure composed of such declining industries (under European conditions) as coal-mining, textiles and steel. In contrast, the problem for Kent was more to preserve the "garden of England" than to restructure the existing industrial base. Finally, a difference in priorities and constraints was the demand by the United Kingdom for exclusively private financing whereas this issue was more open in France, where some form of government financing was not excluded.

Among the recent advances in negotiation theories are the analysis of joint benefits and the search for linkages between different priorities by parties. As applied to the Channel prenegotiations, one can sense simultaneously the opportunities and the difficulties of attempting to link priorities. This is because at this *formula* stage [cf. Zartman and Berman (1982)] issues were to a large extent qualitative and represented *principles* rather than items tradeable through some common system of value.

Another factor that was likely to impede the exchanging of priorities was the power balance at this stage (see below). Historically, the pressure to build a fixed link had come from France, and especially from its North region. By letting it be known that the United Kingdom was now in favor of the project, their negotiators were in a position to structure some of the initial rules of the game: no new rail system from the coast to London, no public financing, a high priority on security and health issues ("from terrorism to rabies") and on the environment. In exchange for these preconditions some commentators have stated privately that the British negotiators were much more ready to compromise on technology, especially as French technology enjoys an enviable reputation in this field [11].

Issue identification and analysis is, in a way, simpler with regard to the nongovernmental actors. Their problem was desperately clear: influencing the decision-making process to the best of their abilities (and interests). This meant negotiating for information (i.e., getting qualitatively relevant rather than quantitatively abundant data and opinion), locating the right level of decision-makers, persuading again and again, and, last but not least, positioning in advance for the next stage of the process.

Again referring to negotiation theory and practice, the importance of good preparation for the negotiators becomes obvious. Preparing for the future (as uncertain as it looked) meant a lot of high-level as well as meticulous paperwork. For if in this prenegotiation stage CTG and Euroroute were allies in the sense that both had an interest to force the decision, both were also rivals who had to build their future bargaining power by adjusting their initial plans, sharpening their arguments and "sowing now to harvest later". These strategies required much technical competence (preparation) and skill (negotiator's experience and qualities) [12].

As will be shown briefly in the next section, issues were manifold in number and complexity: the architecture and design of the project (with such complicated questions as the comparison between rival technical solutions: tunnel versus bridge? A combination of both? A tube? etc.), the financial and economic aspects, the necessity to take account of government preoccupations, expectations, preconditions, constraints and unveiled preferences. Difficulties were compounded by the fact that each party had to deal with its national authorities while not ignoring the negotiating positions of the other government.

39.3.3. Power

It is difficult at this time to proceed to a detailed analysis of the power balance, as not enough is known of the true motivations, strategies and role-playing of the main negotiators.

On a global scale, concerning government positions, the scanning of published information and the analysis of the first series of interviews would make it appear that the United Kingdom had the edge in the initial prenegotiation power balance for the reasons already mentioned. This is also in conformity with recent research on power in negotiations in which the emphasis is put on the degree of mutual dependency of parties.

Some commentators suggest that the British team of negotiators was able to get themselves organized in a more rapid and cohesive way than their French counterparts. The latter apparently had to face a slower, more intricate decision-making machinery. It may also be that the French, especially the private sector and banks, were hampered by doubts regarding the real intentions of the British, because of events in the early 1970s.

Another point of interest is the rivalry between the two British groups vying for the future award of the contract. This may have had the effect of stimulating initiatives and imagination, which in turn strengthened the British position in the first prenegotiation encounters. Also, contrary to what is generally taken as a characteristic of British negotiators in general — who are often seen as purposely indecisive and pragmatic in the early sequences of negotiations, while keen and able to move swiftly and play surprise tactics later on — it would seem, at least from the comments of some interviewees, that the British negotiators came from the start with a tight package of arguments and positions that helped them structure the dynamics of the process [13]. A third additional point to consider, although its relevance rather pertains to the subsequent stages, was the financing issue: as the British made it clear that "not a public penny" would be available for the project, whatever it might be, the role of the City in future financing was an element that gave inherent strength.

The time factor has also to be analyzed. The key element in this respect was the scheduling of elections in both countries. France was the first on the list as May 1986 was a crucial dateline; whereas for the United Kingdom, barring advanced elections, the government had more time at its disposal [14].

39.4. The Core of the Process: November 30, 1984 — January 20, 1986

The 14-month period between the "green light" signal of the two governments (November 30, 1984) and the announcement of the decision to go ahead with the tunnel project (CTG and France-Manche merged henceforth into the joint organization: Eurotunnel on January 20, 1986 constitutes the core sequence of the negotiations. A turning point was the *Invitation to Promoters* in April 1985 to submit proposals within certain guidelines "to develop, finance, construct and operate a fixed link across the Channel".

As final decision-makers, both governments had now to negotiate a wide array of issues ranging from the crucial choice of the type of design (selection among the rival schemes) to writing down binding provisions on manifold issues: institutional, technical, legal, financial and the like. This represented an enormous task, as documents produced during this period clearly show: dozens of volumes and thousands of pages. Negotiating activity was practically continuous throughout the period, involving in one form or another the large number of actors identified in the preceding section.

As this chapter is centered on the prenegotiation stage, the analysis of the core of the process is deferred pending the completion of the research. However, a few preliminary remarks are made below.

First, the shift from prenegotiations to negotiations proper involved the gradual institutionalization of the process. As soon as the statement of intention was made in November 1984, bilateral meetings between British and French officials were held. Appointments were made of the principal negotiators (Messrs. Lyall and Rudeau), whose first task was to write down *guidelines* framing the terms and conditions that proposals by the interested promoters would have to meet.

Meanwhile, and in less formalized procedures, promoters had to prepare their cases for later screening. The negotiating component of this exercise was to obtain rapid and accurate information while persuading officials in each government of the validity of one's own proposal. This task involved drawing up detailed studies and comparative assessments, initiating contacts and analyzing expectations, constraints, criteria and intentions of all those involved in the decision-making process. This meant working through a complex network, as the decision at the top would result from a combination of personal preferences and arguments and recommendations from a number of decision-influencing people or bodies.

A point of interest for the theory and practice of negotiations (apart from adequate and relevant preparation) is the need for *flexibility*. A good illustration is the early comprehension by the CTG group (which was later to win the award) that the drive-through issues might tip the balance in favor of the Euroroute scheme. The response was twofold. The first part was defensive (demonstrating that the bridge, spiral and tube system raised considerable problems, technically and financially). Another part was offensive, showing that the tunnel scheme could be made flexible by inserting provisions to the effect that at some later stage an addition could be made to the present design which would permit the drive-through requirements.

Another development deserving careful study is the inevitability of the *coalition issue* in multilateral negotiations. Should parties seek alliances, enter coalitions or play it alone? What is the best strategy in a given situation? Again the Channel tunnel history provides some material relating to that issue (in the given circumstances). The problem arose particularly as the deadline for submissions came closer: the CTG–France-Manche group had to decide whether to join other promoters (particularly a late-comer, the James Sherwood group), given the fact that some government pressure was exerted to combine schemes and resources, a move that was also favored by some potential contractors.

One of the key moments in the negotiation process was the appointment and the meeting of an Evaluation Committee designed to recommend the favored scheme. Groups had to submit their proposals before October 31, 1985. The proposals were examined by a committee of six experts, half British and half French. This group had to assess the comparative merits of the four proposals and make a recommendation. Unfortunately, little has filtered out so far from the work of this committee, but clearly any research on the Channel tunnel project will have to probe into this matter [15].

At the end of this process the decision was taken, on January 20, 1986, awarding the *concession* to the future Eurotunnel group. Now the negotiations became quadripartite: the two governments and the British and French groups constituting together Eurotunnel. A treaty was signed on February 12, 1986 and a *concession agreement* on March 14, 1986. Negotiation of these agreements involved a great number of institutional, legal and technical matters that are of a great interest to those studying the process of negotiation. Some of the issues raised by these agreements are still being negotiated.

Some of the issues raised in the negotiations were, for instance, the way to combine two very different legal systems; to ensure that parity would be respected in decision making and in financial matters (a very original solution was found in this respect with the concept of the *unit* made up of two parts — half British, half French); to create a machinery for coordination at the government level (an intergovernmental committee), etc. Some of the more intricate or unsolved issues were studied in some depth at a British–French Colloquium, organized in April 1987, by the University of Kent at Canterbury, the proceedings of which are to be published.

Notes

[1]   As of mid-April 1987, the matter was put on the agenda of the spring session of the French National Assembly. Senate ratification would follow the finalization of the British procedures. As regards the United Kingdom, the second reading of the Bill was completed at the House of Commons; it still requires approval by the Lords and would then come back at the House of Commons for a third and final reading. Amendments could be possible under these various procedures. In France as in the United Kingdom, ratification implies the assent of the President and the Queen, respectively. Then instruments have to be exchanged. It is only then that the treaties become effective in national as well as international law.

[2]   Professor Debourse of Lille-University, who is also the Director of the *Regional Development Agency*, a local authority in charge of research and various activities at the *regional* (local) level.

[3]   For the former, a small consultant organization specializing in transcultural problems: I.C.M. (Paris), and for the latter, an academic and consultant: P. Audebert of Lille University and CRC.

[4]   The mayor of Lille, P. Mauroy (later Prime Minister from 1981 to 1983), and one of his key aides, M. Delebarre, later a minister in the socialist government (until 1986).

[5]   The socialists won the elections in May 1981.

[6]   Such contacts mainly took the form of joint seminars and colloquia; e.g., in 1977 and 1978.

[7]   The reference to private financing was particularly important because one of the reasons for the cancellation of the project in 1974 was the United Kingdom's financial difficulties facing the Labour government at that time.

[8]   European Community envisaged here in its institutional structure.

[9]   These two points are partly interconnected as EC intervention would have presented a budgetary problem.

[10] From a strategic viewpoint, it may well be that the United Kingdom's favorable attitude toward a fixed link (in spite of the historical record and the reluctance of a part of public opinion) was a calculated move to impress on other Community members its attachment to *Europe*, at a moment when the United Kingdom position was rigid on certain major problems such as the EC budget and the agricultural policy.

[11] As Sir Nicholas Henderson humorously comments in *Channels and Tunnels* (1987, p. 46), [the French] "had after all, pioneered both the Suez and Panama Canals". He adds that "They had by the 1970s become the world expert in transportation systems".

[12] See, for instance, the 1987 contribution by Nicholas Henderson (the then chairman of CTG). His contribution is now one of the sources of public information on many details and anecdotes in the prenegotiation and (early) negotiation stages.

[13] However, on one important point — the so-called *drive-through* issue, i.e., direct passage without cross-boarding via a shuttle system — the British position was left undetermined, as there were both proponents (Euroroute) and adversaries (CTG) of that alternative.

[14] It is interesting to note that the time factor may now tend to redress the power balance as the tunnel issue has become a commitment of the Conservative Party and as ratification has proved a more difficult process in the United Kingdom than in France. The French government has now taken the position that finalization of ratification (which is certain in the French Parliament) would be scheduled only after the British process is itself finalized.

[15] Many other aspects are worth studying. An example is the *sub-negotiation* which officials of the Nord-Pas-de-Calais Region were able to conduct with the Government, on the one hand, and the four contenders, one the other, to obtain certain guarantees as to the benefits for the *Region* of the carrying out of the Project.

References and Bibliography

Assemblee Nationale (1987), No. 611. Projet de loi portant approbation, en tant que besoin, de la concession concernant la conception, le financement, la construction et l'exploitation d'une liaison fixe à travers la Manche, signée le 14 Mars 1986, Paris, France.

Eurotunnel (1986, 1987), *Briefing Papers and News*, issued intermittently by Eurotunnel, Portland House, Stag Place, London and Tour Franklin, Paris-la-Defense.

Henderson, N. (1987), *Channels and Tunnels*, Weidenfeld and Nicolson, London.

H.M.S.O. (1982), Report of the Anglo-French study group, Cmd 8561, June.

H.M.S.O. (1973), *The Channel Tunnel: A U.K. Transport Cost-benefit Study.*

Liaison Fixe Transmanche (1986), France et Royaume-Uni/France Manche/Channel Tunnel group (Concession Agreement of 14.03.86).

Region Nord-Pas-de-Calais - Conseil Regional (1986), Le Tunnel sous la Manche. Actes du Forum du 10.10.86. Lille, France.

Sawyer, J. and Guetzkow, H. (1985), *Bargaining and Negotiation*, in: H. Kelman (ed.), *International Behavior*, Holt, Rinehart and Winston, New York.

Touval, S., and Zartman, I.W. (1985), *International Mediation in Theory and Practice*, SAIS Papers, No. 6, School of Advanced International Studies, Johns Hopkins University, Westview Press, Boulder, CO, and London.

Zartman, I.W. and Berman, M.R. (1982), *The Practical Negotiator*, Yale University Press, New Haven, CT, and London.

CHAPTER 40

Report of the US Environment and Natural Resources Task Group*

Program on the Processes of International Negotiations

American Academy of Arts and Sciences
Cambridge, Massachusetts
USA

40.1. Special Characteristics of Environmental Disputes

International environmental and natural resource issues raise many questions that are common to other topics of negotiation. Examples include such questions as the uses of scientific and technical information, the perception of national interests, the relationships between internal and external conflicts, and

---

*Co-Chairs:
  Gail Bingham, Conservation Foundation, Washington, DC
  Lawrence Susskind, MIT/Harvard, Cambridge, Massachusetts
Members:
  Richard Andrews, University of North Carolina, Chapel Hill, North Carolina
  Susan Carpenter, ACCORD, Inc., Denver, Colorado
  Robert Hollister, Tufts University, Medford, Massachusetts
  Christopher Joyner, Woods Hole Oceanographic Institution, Woods Hole, Massachusetts
  Peter Loucks, Cornell University, Ithaca, New York
  Kem Lowry, University of Hawaii, Honolulu, Hawaii
  Dorothy Nelkin, Cornell University, Ithaca, New York
  Joanne Nichols, Tufts University, Medford, Massachusetts
  Robert Stein, Environmental Mediation International, Washington, DC
  Konrad von Moltke, Dartmouth College, Hanover, New Hampshire
  Michael Wheeler, MIT, Cambridge, Massachusetts
The Environment and Natural Resources (ENR) Task Group began meeting in October 1986. The group agreed to focus on international (or what we prefer to call transboundary) disputes involving the management of natural resources or problems of environmental quality control.

others. At the same time, however, they also raise additional issues that are distinctly different from other topics of negotiation, many of which are growing in importance to practitioners as well as interesting to theorists. Examples of these differences follow.

Nature of the Issue

Several of the most important international environmental issues involve a global public interest in the outcome that should transcend the more limited national interests of the negotiating parties. Examples include effects on the global climate and the uses of oceans and outer space. In such cases, the legitimate interests of large numbers of potential victims may not be adequately represented in the negotiations unless new forms of surrogate representation are instituted.

A second special characteristic of some environmental issues is the possibility that irreversible adverse changes may result from some outcomes. Examples include the effects of chlorofluorocarbon emissions (CFCs) on stratospheric ozone, other climate-related issues such as CO_2 and the greenhouse effect, and extinctions of species (whales, for instance).

Third, a large class of natural resource and environmental issues involves the over-exploitation of open access resources, such as ocean fisheries and pollution of common seas and airsheds. These issues are often too simplistically identified as "tragedies of the commons"; there are in fact many examples of regimes by which they can be managed, protected, and allocated, but such regimes require international negotiations to convert them in one way or another from open access to common property resources. One existing example is the International Whaling Commission.

Finally, similar problems are evident in many natural resource and environmental issues on less than a global scale, in cases involving resources that are regionally shared across international boundaries. Examples include large international rivers, acid rain, and exports of hazardous chemicals and wastes — all issues, incidentally, which are already subjects of study at IIASA. All these issues involve situations in which the existence of national boundaries blocks or complicates the creation of management regimes that are necessary to protect beneficial natural systems and processes.

Note that in some cases, such boundaries may even frustrate the implementation of effective measures within national boundaries: if it is cheaper to send hazardous wastes to an unsafe dump in a nearby country, costlier but safer technologies in the country of origin will not be used without either public subsidies, export restrictions, or international negotiations to assure uniform minimum safety standards and close such "pollution havens".

Special questions for negotiators that arise in many of these types of issues include:

- Imbalances in power between upstream and downstream nations. Such issues may require identification of negotiable linkages to other issues in which the power relationships are reversed.
- Resources that move: for example, migratory fish that may breed in one nation's jurisdiction, grow to fishable but prebreeding size in another, and be safely fishable from a conservation perspective (mature and postbreeding) only in a third. Such resources may require international management regimes including compensation to the first two types of nation for their conservation efforts.
- Finally, localized issues that happen to involve international borders present particular problems in that local interests on both sides must be filtered through national bureaucracies and policies that are often subject to different priorities and extraneous linkages as well as slower and often insensitive local needs and concerns.

Scientific and Technical Questions

In addition to the different nature of many natural resource and environmental issues, such problems often have several other special characteristics. One is the central role of scientific and technical questions, and perhaps even more, of scientific and technical uncertainties. Unlike trade and military security negotiations, moreover, these complexities and uncertainties are often in fields new and unfamiliar to traditional government and business negotiators.

This is stressful, and typically results either in the disbelief or discounting of the new information, in redefining the issue back into more familiar terms (such as trade or national interest terms), or in an enlargement of the role and power of technical experts in the negotiation process — for example, the creation of negotiation processes among technical representatives that parallel or precede those of plenipotentiaries, often shaping key assumptions and other terms of debate. Such expert negotiations deserve careful study in their own right.

Nontraditional Participants

International environmental issues have also been associated with significantly expanded roles for nontraditional participants other that scientists, as sources both of information and of influence in the negotiations. This, too, is stressful, since such groups frequently represent points of view different from those of traditional government and business elites and even in conflict with traditional views of the national interest. One result is to complicate greatly both internal and external aspects of the negotiation process.

40.2. New Issues

Simply by virtue of being new issues on the agenda for international negotiation, many natural resource and environmental issues pose both new problems and new opportunities. On the one hand, they often have low status with traditional participants, and may accordingly be poorly understood or poorly handled; and bottlenecks in negotiation may arise because of the small number of individuals either interested, qualified, or allocated to negotiate them.

On the other hand, they do sometimes present situations where all parties can be made better off through negotiated solutions; they sometimes do offer opportunities to focus on questions of mutual and global concern when other issues are stalemated by more divisive national interests; and the small number of individuals involved is itself an opportunity to develop new common understandings, precedents, and ways of approaching such issues for the future.

For all these reasons, we believe that international resource and environmental issues present important and interesting topics for investigation in their own right, as well as for the insights they may produce concerning more generic issues of international negotiation processes. We also hope that such a research agenda would both complement and add strength to the excellent program of environmental research already under way at IIASA.

40.3. Formulating a Research Agenda

All of these differences helped to shape the group's attempt to outline priority issues for further comparative or collaborative (international as well as interdisciplinary) research. The group specified ten important research themes:

(1) What new international institutions (or what adaptations of existing institutions) do we need to handle international environmental disputes more efficiently?

(2) What roles should there be for nontraditional participants (citizens, nongovernmental organizations, subnational units, etc.) in international environmental dispute resolution?

(3) What role does technical–scientific data (and technical support systems) play in international environmental dispute resolution? How are data verified? How are they transformed into policy or agreements?

(4) What sorts of educational efforts and skill-building are needed to help resolve transboundary environmental disputes more effectively?

(5) How are national interests perceived and defined in international environmental disputes?

(6) How can linkages across and within issues be exploited in transboundary environmental dispute resolution?

(7) How should the parties involved determine what is negotiable and what is not in international environmental disputes?

(8)   What role do the media play in shaping perceptions, stimulating public concern, and in regulating the participation of various stakeholders in transboundary environmental disputes?

(9)   How does internal group or national conflict affect negotiations in transboundary environmental disputes?

(10) What are the processes by which informally negotiated settlements of transboundary environmental disputes are ratified?

Having compiled this list, our next objective was to select three or four of these themes that might be the focus of preliminary study by members of the group. Once these themes were selected, we hoped to prepare a series of Working Papers that we could discuss prior to the IIASA meeting in May 1987. We also hoped to commission follow-up research efforts jointly with teams in other PIN-sponsoring countries and to encourage doctoral students in the United States to focus their dissertation research on the themes outlined and developed by the group. Finally, several members of the group expressed interest in developing an extensive prospectus for a book on international transboundary environmental disputes that might encourage and direct further experimentation and theory-building.

40.4. Four Themes

The group requested and received proposals from individual members. Four were selected.:

(1)   Dorothy Nelkin, Professor of Science, Technology, and Society at Cornell University, Ithaca, New York, agreed to prepare a Working Paper on *The Role of the Media in International Environmental Negotiations.*

(2)   Konrad von Moltke, Senior Fellow at the Conservation Foundation in Washington, D.C. and Adjunct Professor of Environmental Studies at Dartmouth College, agreed to prepare a Working Paper on *Scientists, Environmentalists, Local and Regional Officials: Nontraditional Participants in International Environmental Negotiations.*

(3)   Christopher Joyner, Senior Research Fellow at the Marine Policy Center, Woods Hole Oceanographic Institution and Associate Professor of Political Science at the George Washington University, agreed to prepare a Working Paper on *US National Interests and The Antarctic Mineral Negotiations Process.*

(4)   Francisco Szekely, Assistant Director for International Environmental Studies, Energy and Environmental Policy Center, Kennedy School of Government at Harvard University, in conjunction with Scott McCreary, a doctoral student in the Department of Urban Studies and Planning at MIT, agreed to prepare a Working Paper on *Applying the Principles of Environmental Dispute Resolution to International Transboundary Resource Conflicts: The Case of the US–Mexico Border.*

Drafts of these four papers were reviewed by the group at a meeting in March 1987. Revisions have been made and the completed versions of the Working Papers will be available through the Working Paper series of the Program on the Processes of International Negotiation at the American Academy of Arts and Sciences, 136 Irving Street, Cambridge, Massachusetts 02138.

While the views contained in the papers do not necessarily represent the views of all the Task Group members, the group as a whole has endorsed their publication in the shared belief that they frame very important questions. In addition, the ENR Task Group is eager to broker collaborative research efforts with PIN-sponsored groups in other countries that share our interests.

40.4.1. The influence of the media

Was Three Mile Island an "accident" or an "incident"? Was Chernobyl a "disaster" or an "event"? Is dioxin a "doomsday chemical" or a "potential risk"? Are accidents "normal" or are they "aberrant" events? Dorothy Nelkin points out that "selective use of adjectives can trivialize an event or render it important; marginalize some groups, empower others, define an issue as a problem or reduce it to a routine". She points out that "the actual influence of these judgments on environmental negotiations depends in part on the media's effect on public attitudes and on policy decisions".

Professor Nelkin has reviewed most of the post-World War II research on the media's impact. She points out that

> the common thread running through most of this research is that the effect of the media messages depends on the social and cultural context in which they are received and on the selective interest and experience of the reader or television viewer. In the case of esoteric environmental problems, people have little direct information or pre-existing knowledge to guide an independent evaluation. Then the media, as the major source of information, define the reality of the situation for them.

Professor Nelkin believes that "the media ... establish a framework of expectations that can help to set the goals and the agenda of negotiations. Once covered in the press, isolated events soon take on meaning as public issues". In addition,

> journalists identify pressing issues for negotiation through their selection of newsworthy events. They help create the judgmental biases that underlie the positions of negotiators and the relationships that develop during the negotiations process. They can set up the potential for negotiated agreements, influencing patterns of legitimacy, creating demands for regulation and control, and putting political pressures on those involved in international disputes. They stimulate demands for accountability, forcing negotiators to justify themselves to their constituencies.

In addition to analyzing the factors that account for media coverage of environmental problems in developed Western nations, Professor Nelkin goes on to sketch a full-fledged study that would examine media coverage of similar transboundary environmental disputes in different countries and its effect on international negotiations. She focuses particularly on the ways in which the media affect the agenda of negotiations, the process of negotiation and the relationships among the parties; the ways in which the media obtain information about ongoing negotiations; and the effect the media can have on implementation of negotiated agreements.

In discussing Professor Nelkin's paper, the members of the Task Group explored possible models that have been used to portray the mechanisms by which media messages shape the public's agenda and perceptions and the ways that these in turn are translated into standards and terms of agreement for upcoming or on-going negotiations. There was general agreement that the operations of these mechanisms are terribly unclear at present.

40.4.2. The role of nontraditional participants

Professor von Moltke points out that "the underlying fiction of international negotiations is that sovereign states can speak for all interests within their jurisdiction". He also asserts that "the need for international measures to protect the environment has created a new problem in terms of participation in international affairs by groups which have not traditionally had a role in them". Indeed, he goes so far as to claim that "sovereign states can probably not speak for the needs of environmental protection".

Professor von Moltke admits that it is "extremely unlikely that environmental resources will be assigned rights by international law in the foreseeable future". But he believes that there will be a "further enlargement of the circle of persons and institutions which are recognized as having legitimate interests, and consequently a right of participation in international negotiations". Such a right will require the adoption of appropriate measures to ensure that it can be fully and effectively exercised. "Among the groups most likely to receive such recognition are scientists, environmental organizations, and decentralized levels of government, none of which have a recognized independent role in traditional diplomacy".

Professor von Moltke provides a detailed review of the ways in which scientists and scholars participate in environmental policy debates within various countries. His conclusion is that appropriate environmental decision-making requires that some means be devised by which independent scientific analysis can find its way into the resolution of ideological or political disputes. He does not, however, have a specific suggestion as to how the involvement of independent scientists in transboundary environmental dispute resolution might be accomplished.

Along somewhat similar lines, Professor von Moltke explores the increasing role for environmental advocacy groups in policy and site-specific disputes in a number of Western nations and suggests that environmental interests exist at the international (and perhaps global) level and that these need to be "articulated effectively for purposes of negotiation".

International negotiating processes have adjusted slowly to the existence of nongovernmental organizations (NGOs). In fact, as Professor von Moltke reports, "the 1972 Stockholm Conference is widely viewed as a watershed event for NGO participation in general, since this was the first instance in which the United Nations made a systematic effort to include NGO input in an intergovernmental conference". Under United Nations rules of procedure "a wide range of organizations by now has ready access to the plenary negotiating sessions, but the ability to actually influence decisions rests heavily on the ability to obtain access to national delegations".

"More than many other issues of international policy, environmental affairs involve all levels of government: frequently the resources which require protection are controlled by local or regional authorities". Yet, as Professor von Moltke indicates, "the issue of ensuring adequate participation of local and regional authorities in international negotiations is not an issue which can be solved internationally: it is largely a domestic issue for each country, particularly for countries with federal structures".

In reviewing Professor von Moltke's paper, the Task Group noted that the problem of involving nontraditional interests in transboundary dispute resolution was primarily a problem of structuring simultaneous and interlocking processes of negotiation. Scientists from many countries might meet before or in parallel with national delegations, but the dilemma is how to mesh what the two groups deem to be important. Similarly, environmental or other NGOs might meet before or during formal negotiations between countries; the question is how the results of the separate meetings will be merged. While the Task Group did not have specific recommendations regarding experiments that might be tried to explore new process options, the members did feel strongly that international collaboration on this question in the form of joint research efforts might be especially useful.

40.4.3. Defining national interests

As Professor Joyner defines it, the "national interest may be considered the general, persistent, and long-term purpose the people and government of a state see themselves serving". Thus, "a state's national interest is rooted in the social consciousness and cultural identity of its people". Through a close look at the multilateral negotiations that have taken place since 1982 among a select group of states — the Antarctic Treaty Consultative Parties — Professor Joyner has attempted to probe the mechanisms by which national interests have been formulated and integrated into transboundary negotiations.

Professor Joyner has categorized various subparts of a national interest. He defines "primary national interests" as "those deemed essential to preserving a state's physical, cultural and political identity. These can never be compromised or traded off". Then he goes on to define "secondary", "permanent", "variable", "general", and "specific" national interests. The importance of each is examined in the context of the Antarctic minerals negotiations.

The parties to this negotiation are

> striving to create an institutional mechanism with a structure capable of efectively managing mineral activities, promoting scientific cooperation, ensuring economic priorities and protecting the circumpolar environment — all to be accomplished without disturbing the geopolitical stability afforded by the pre-existing Antarctic Treaty System.

The procedures that each country uses to determine its policy preferences (in line with its national interests) are important. Professor Joyner looks particularly at the internal negotiations process within the United States.

"The process of determining whether some Antarctic minerals policy squares with the national interest begins with the basic formulation of the US in an interagency task force". Then a basic formulation is set on paper. This is followed by several rounds of internal and external review.

The Task Group spent a great deal of time discussing the points raised in Professor Joyner's paper. In particular, the group explored the importance of "unofficial" or "informal diplomacy" in defining the national interest. It also examined the disproportionate impact that the chairman of the interagency task force has in such a process. The group asked about the importance of the "decision rules" by which a final definition of national interests is made prior to entering into negotiations with other countries. Should "consensus" to be the goal?

The group tried to model the chain of events by which grassroots groups might express their views to the individuals or party in power and how these individuals in turn formulate instructions to the country's negotiating team. It was intrigued with the problem of how best to redefine national interests in light of the offers and information that arise during the international negotiations. This was an area that the Task Group felt would lend itself to further (comparative) research.

40.4.4. Potential uses of mediation

Dr. Szekely and Mr. McCreary focused on the prospects for using mediation to resolve transboundary environmental disputes. They concentrated on sewage and air quality disagreements between the United States and Mexico. They concluded that the full process of mediation currently being used to resolve domestic environmental disputes is not likely to work in an international context. They also believe, though, that some elements of environmental mediation —

particularly the assistance that a nonpartisan facilitator can provide in generating new options — are applicable in international situations.

Dr. Szekeley and Mr. McCreary summarize the key attributes of conventional bilateral negotiations and compare them with the features of environmental mediation as practiced within the United States. Conventional negotiations are handled by formal delegations and constrained by national legislation, bilateral treaties, and the rules of international law. Each delegation usually arrives with predetermined statements of its position, from which it cannot depart substantially. Information is generated separately by the parties and often withheld. Each side has its position and perhaps a fallback. Very few options are generated jointly. Much of this process would have to be changed if the model of environmental mediation were adopted.

The negotiations would be conducted informally, almost in a joint problem-solving style. The interactions would be managed by a "neutral" acceptable to both (or all) parties. The separate groups would work to develop information jointly and to invent as many options for mutual gain as they could. The ground rules for their interaction would be invented on an *ad hoc* basis by the parties themselves. The result of the negotiations would be a consensus document that the countries would then have to transform into a binding agreement through the more traditional treaty-implementing machinery.

Szekely and McCreary explore why such a process might well have been of value in the case of the US–Mexican negotiation over sewage problems between San Diego and Tijuana, and conclude that the negotiations were less productive than they might have been because the parties quickly locked themselves into stringent negotiating positions that left little room for creative problem-solving that would have served both sides interests more effectively.

Szekely and McCreary propose a research agenda that they hope will interest scholars in other countries for exploring the possible uses of mediation in bilateral environmental negotiations. They suggest that the United States and Canada as well as Switzerland and Germany explore the prospects for mediating acid rain disputes. Secondly, they propose collaborative case studies on the export of hazardous waste involving Belgium, France, and Austria. Finally, they propose case studies of "transfrontier fisheries exploitation" involving Canadian, Japanese, and Australian counterparts.

40.5. Future Directions

The Environment and Natural Resources Task Group has only scratched the surface. There is a great deal more to be done in just defining the issues that ought to be the focus of future research. We believe that we have identified ten useful themes. We are also pleased that the first four papers we commissioned have helped us to develop a clearer sense of how these themes might be explored further.

All four themes that became the subjects of the papers we commissioned could well be looked at by counterpart groups in other countries. We are well aware that our bias toward the American experience may be leading us in directions that are not especially interesting or appropriate when looked at from other vantage points. That is why we feel so strongly that the next step ought to be to put together, with IIASA's help, international teams of PIN-sponsored researchers who can take a truly cross-cultural perspective on the important environmental and natural resource questions that are the focus of our inquiry.

CHAPTER 41

The Politics of Ozone:
What Determines National Policies
Toward the Protection of the
Ozone Layer?

Tapani Vaahtoranta

University of Turku
Turku
Finland

41.1. Introduction

Man may be changing the distribution and the quantity of the stratospheric ozone layer to an extent that will have adverse global consequences. Since no part of the earth is likely to escape the biological and climatic effects of ozone depletion, protection of stratospheric ozone should be in the interest of all governments. However, no binding international regulations on potentially harmful activities have been implemented. Why are sovereign states not acting, although they are facing a potential global threat? What explains national policies? Both system-level and domestic factors seem to influence national preferences.

41.2. The Global Commons

International pollution is a phenomenon where polluting agents emitted by a source state are transmitted through a medium bringing about detrimental effects in the territory of another state. The international commons are those parts of the biosphere that are beyond the national jurisdiction of any country. They are the property of no state. The atmosphere and the ozone layer are examples of the global commons. No state can avoid the global consequences of ozone depletion, nor can it be prevented from emitting pollutants into the atmosphere. If ozone is depleted, all states will be victims, including those emitting pollutants.

It is sometimes pointed out that, although no state can escape the harmful effects of pollution of the global commons, every state gains by polluting them. This is due to the fact that each state gets all the benefits from national polluting activity, but its harmful effects are shared among all states. Besides, without international cooperation unilateral measures to reduce emissions would not stop international pollution. Consequently, no rational state should be willing voluntarily to reduce pollution. This pessimistic assumption of the politics of international pollution has led to the conclusion that the policy of sovereign states will end up in the global "tragedy of the commons" [Hardin (1977), Ophuls (1977)].

The tragedy may, however, be avoided, since in the long run pollution of the global commons is likely to have adverse impacts on all states. The commons can be polluted freely as long as clean air or water is abundant. Restrictions become necessary when pollution is about to produce catastrophic effects. Since the enclosure of the global commons is impossible, international cooperation is the only peaceful way of avoiding the tragedy [Brown *et al.* (1977), Wijkman (1982)]. It is currently debated whether rational states are willing and able to accept behavioral constraints to maximize their own long-term gains, i.e., to avoid the tragedy by forming international regimes [1].

41.3. Ozone Depletion

The ozone depletion theory was first presented in 1974 (Molina and Rowland). It was claimed that chlorofluorocarbon (CFC) chemicals would be transported to high altitudes, destroying ozone. Less stratospheric ozone means that more harmful solar ultraviolet-B (UV-B) radiation is reaching the earth's surface. UV-B is known to cause human skin cancer. Ozone depletion is also likely to cause other harmful biological and climatic effects. Despite intense research, many uncertainties still remain concerning the theory. The amount of likely ozone depletion and its causes and effects are not known without doubt. Since the publication of the Molina–Rowland theory, the magnitude of the predicted ozone depletion has varied between 3% and 20%. And no general agreement exists on the cause of the observed thinning of ozone over the Antarctic.

There are four major CFCs that are produced in commercial quantities: CFC-11, CFC-12, CFC-22 and CFC-113. CFC-11 and CFC-12 are used as aerosol propellants. CFC-11 is also used extensively in manufacturing plastic foams. CFC-12 and CFC-22 are used as coolants in refrigeration and in air conditioning applications. The use of CFC-113 as a solvent in the electronic industry is growing rapidly. In assessing the significance of each CFC as a potential ozone depleter, both the amount of production and the lifetime in the stratosphere must be considered. The major CFCs in this regard are CFC-11 and CFC-12. Both have high production levels and relative depletion potency. CFC-113 is produced in smaller quantities, but it is thought to be almost as effective a potential ozone depleter as CFC-11 and CFC-12 [Hammit *et al.* (1986), Gibbs (1986)].

CFCs were first developed in the 1930s [Gibbs (1986)]. During the 1950s and 1960s CFC-11 and CFC-12 production grew rapidly, more than 10% per year. The rapid growth came to an end in the 1970s. Because of concern about the potential effects of CFCs on the ozone layer, several nations unilaterally restricted their use as aerosol propellants. As a result of these national regulations, production of CFC-11 and CFC-12 declined in the 1970s, although their nonaerosol applications continued to grow into the 1980s. By now the full effects of the unilateral restrictions have been seen and aerosol use in countries without regulations is growing. Production has returned to nearly the same level achieved before the implementation of national restrictions. Current production of CFC-11 and CFC-12 accounts for about 80% of all CFC production in the world. Use of CFC-22 and CFC-113 has steadily grown since the 1960s. Consequently, the overall trend in CFC use is upward, both for aerosol and nonaerosol applications.

41.4. International Negotiations

The United Nations Environment Programme (UNEP) established in 1981 an Ad Hoc Working Group consisting of legal and technical experts appointed by governments to elaborate a global framework convention for the protection of the ozone layer. The Working Group met for the first time in January 1982. It held a total of four sessions [2]. The Vienna Convention for the Protection of the Ozone Layer was signed in 1985 by 20 states and the EC. The emphasis of the convention is on scientific research and information exchange, since governments could not agree upon specific regulatory measures to protect the ozone layer. The Vienna conference, however, adopted a resolution requesting UNEP to convene a working group to continue work on a protocol on regulatory measures. This protocol was signed on 16 September 1987 by 24 states including the EC. The protocol must be ratified by states representing two-thirds of the world's consumption of these chemicals, in order to enter into force.

The emphasis of this chapter is on the national preferences expressed during the negotiations leading to the Vienna Convention. The following states sent experts or observers to attend all four sessions of the Ad Hoc Working Group: Argentina, Australia, Belgium, Canada, Denmark, Finland, France, the Federal Republic of Germany, Italy, Japan, the Netherlands, Norway, Sweden, Switzerland, the Union of Soviet Socialist Republics, the United Kingdom and the United States of America. The major western industrial nations strongly influenced the progress and the outcome of the negotiations. They also produce most of the world's chlorofluorocarbons.

The Nordic countries worked actively from the beginning for internationally binding regulations on CFC emissions. Sweden, Norway and Denmark also implemented unilateral restrictions on aerosol uses of chlorofluorocarbons [3]. Finland, Norway and Sweden submitted a draft text of the convention at the first session of the Working Group. The text served as a basis for the work. Denmark had also participated in preparing the draft text. In the view of the Nordic governments, despite existing uncertainties, the essential part of the evidence clearly pointed towards worldwide reduction of CFC emissions [4]. Article 1 of the draft contained the basic obligation: "The contracting parties shall limit, reduce and prevent activities under their jurisdiction or control which have or are likely to have adverse effects upon the stratospheric ozone-layer". Finland, Norway and Sweden hoped that concrete measures of regulation could be specified in an annex to be attached to the convention [5].

The Netherlands clearly supported the general obligation of the Nordic draft. Others considered that the evidence did not point to the need for such action, and that international cooperation should therefore mainly relate to improving scientific knowledge of the problem. This view was expressed particularly by Japan, which considered regulatory measures "premature" [6]. The need for an annex that would be an integral part of the convention was also questioned. It was considered more appropriate to adopt protocols that would enable each state to decide whether it wished to join only the convention or also the regulatory protocol.

Later four alternative texts were proposed for Article 2, now containing the general obligations. They ranged from urgently imposing specific obligations to protect the ozone layer to merely exchanging scientific information. Three groups of countries could be recognized at the second sessions [7]. The Nordic countries aimed at bringing about an internationally binding instrument to protect the ozone layer. The Netherlands, Switzerland and, with reservations, Australia, Canada and the Federal Republic of Germany shared their view. Canada and the Federal Republic of Germany also had unilaterally reduced use of CFCs in aerosols, and the Netherlands had introduced warning labels on aerosol containers stating that CFCs were decreasing the ozone in the stratosphere.

The United States, the United Kingdom, France, and Japan formed the group clearly opposing the Nordic initiative. The United States, however, was the first country to impose unilateral restrictions on chlorofluorocarbons. The manufacture and distribution of fluorocarbons for nonessential aerosol uses were banned in 1978 [8]. The United States was agreeable to a protocol concerning nonessential aerosol uses, but maintained that more research was needed before other regulations could be implemented [9].

France, Japan, and the United Kingdom were among the most reluctant western industrialized nations to agree on fluorocarbon regulations. None had implemented unilateral restrictions on CFC emissions. France and the United Kingdom, however, adopted the recommendations made by the European Community. In 1980, the Council of the European Community required member states to take appropriate measures not to increase the CFC-11 and CFC-12 production capacity and to reduce by at least 30% the aerosol use of these CFCs by the end of 1981 compared with 1976 levels.

The third group consisted of the developing countries that were mainly concerned about the costs of the convention. They were particularly interested in avoiding any stipulations that would endanger the building up of industries in their countries.

In 1983 Finland, Norway, and Sweden submitted a new draft text of a regulatory annex where the fluorocarbons and their uses were considered in two parts. Article 1 contained the measures for ending the used of CFC-11 and CFC-12 in aerosol cans, except for essential uses. Article 2 referred to measures to control, limit and reduce emissions of CFCs in the sectors of plastic foam, refrigeration, solvents and others. The authors later agreed to regard the text as a proposed protocol [10].

The new Nordic approach had important results. The United States, Canada and New Zealand supported the general objective of Article 1, although they considered Article 2 inappropriate at that time. Australia, Denmark, the Netherlands and Switzerland accepted, with few reservations, the Nordic draft. In other words, the United States and the Nordic nations together demanded internationally binding regulations on nonessential aerosol use of CFCs. Belgium and the United Kingdom took a more negative stand by arguing that Article 1 went too far. No protocol should, according to them, go further than the limitations accepted by the European Community. Italy did not want to discuss any regulations before the signing of the convention, and Japan totally rejected the Nordic proposal [11]. Chile, France, the Federal Republic of Germany, Greece and the United Kingdom eventually submitted an alternative to the Nordic draft protocol on binding emission regulations, recommending only more research [12].

A newly formed coalition, consisting of Canada, Finland, Norway, Sweden, and the United States (the Toronto Group), submitted in 1982 a new draft protocol, which became the basis of the discussion. Three other states, Austria, Denmark and Switzerland, supported the draft. The concrete goal of the draft protocol was a reduction of the use of CFCs in aerosol spray cans [13]. Critics of the draft saw no need for a protocol dealing with the limitation and reduction of CFCs emissions. Specifically, the United Kingdom, Italy, and France supported the implementation of a production capacity cap [14].

The disputes could not be settled before the signing of the Vienna Convention, and the conference adopted a resolution requesting UNEP to set up a working group to continue to strive to arrive at a protocol. Japan was the only country arguing that it was too early to decide on continuing the work [15]. Although the main difference between the approaches has remained since the conference, states seem to be reaching a compromise. The Toronto Group aimed at gradually reducing use and production of CFC and eventually banning all use. The EC countries first tentatively agreed to implement a production freeze on some CFCs and later to reduce production by 20%.

Upon entry into force of the protocol to limit and reduce consumption of CFCs, production of CFCs would be capped at the 1986 level, reduced by 20% after three years and then by another 30% after eight years. The protocol is expected to enter into force by 1991 [16].

41.5. Explaining National Policies

It is commonly assumed in the study of international relations that states are rationally behaving actors pursuing self-interest. In system-level explanations it is further assumed that each state calculates the costs and benefits of alternative courses of action, depending on its position in the structure of the international system. The system is supposed to determine the behavior of all states, and domestic characteristics rarely influence the outcomes of national policies at the system level. This view is well argued in Waltz (1979, pp. 79–101).

If one applies these assumptions to the politics of international pollution, the primary goal of each state should be to keep its own area free from adverse effects of pollution. Every state should aim at exporting its own pollutants into the territories of other states or into the international commons and at reducing that part of international pollution it is importing. The position of a state in the import–export structure of international pollution makes it either a net exporter or net importer of pollutants and their adverse effects. Net importers should support international regulations on pollution and net exporters should oppose them.

In the case of the ozone layer, each government would presumably have all others eliminate their ozone-depleting emissions and make its own contribution only to the extent that it is a net benefit for its own country. Since each state gets all the benefits from emitting CFCs and the harmful effects of emissions are divided among all states, it should not be in the short-term interest of any state to regulate chlorofluorocarbon emissions. This is the fear of Garett Hardin (1977): the tragedy of the commons may result, since all states are likely to be free riders when the pollution of the international commons should be regulated.

But states are not placed in the same way in the structure of CFC pollution. The positions differ depending on the amount of chlorofluorocarbons states are emitting, and they may not be equally vulnerable to adverse effects of ozone depletion. The structural propositions concerning state behavior in the politics of ozone can be stated as follows:

(1) The more CFCs the state emits into the atmosphere in relation to the amount of adverse effects likely to be caused in its territory by all

chlorofluorocarbon emissions, the less likely a state is to engage in international cooperation to reduce the emissions.

(2)   The more adverse effects the CFCs emissions are likely to cause in the territory of a state in relation to the amount of chlorofluorocarbons emitted by it, the more likely a state is to favor international controls on CFC emissions.

The effects of ozone depletion are not likely to be equally distributed. Light-skinned populations in the Northern Hemisphere are known to be more vulnerable to ultraviolet radiation than are darker-skinned populations. It is assumed that, owing to the low rates of skin cancer in Japan, the Japanese would be less concerned about potential ozone depletion. Some Britons are said to believe that they would actually benefit from increased ultraviolet radiation despite their less-pigmented skin. But it seems unreasonable to explain national policy on the basis of these assumptions. Too many uncertainties are related to the potential consequences of ozone depletion. Besides, it is assumed that the mild temperature increases causes by ozone depletion would aid agriculture in the Northern Hemisphere, but would have seriously adverse effects in the rest of the world [17]. No part of the world is likely to avoid all harmful effects of ozone depletion, nor are consequences known without doubt. It seems more reasonable to see how much each state is depleting ozone in order to determine its position in the pollution structure.

Production of CFC-11 and CFC-12 are here used to determine the CFC pollution structure (*Table 41.1*), since they are the most important potential ozone depleters. The table illustrates the situation in 1974, when the Molina–Rowland theory was published. The US share of total production has dropped since the middle of the 1970s to about 30% because of its unilateral ban on aerosol uses of CFCs. A state benefits from CFC production by selling a part of it and consuming the rest. In either case the CFCs are eventually transported into the stratosphere. Major producers of fluorocarbons also are their main consumers. Those states producing most CFCs should, according to the structural proposition, be the most reluctant to accept regulations on this industry.

The pollution structure seems to determine the extreme approaches to the ozone issue. First, the Nordic countries, Austria and Switzerland produce no CFC-11 or CFC-12, and all strongly support binding regulations on fluorocarbon emissions. Second, France, Italy, Japan, and the United Kingdom are main producers and have opposed the Nordic initiatives. The Soviet position is more ambiguous. The Soviet Union neither supported the Nordic initiatives, nor openly joined France, Italy, Japan and the United Kingdom. Although the Soviet Union produced relatively little CFCs in 1974, by the end of this century its production of CFC-11 and CFC-12 may grow faster than production in any other country [Quinn *et al.* (1986), pp. 41–42].

The preferences of the United States, Canada, the Netherlands and, to a lesser extent, the Federal Republic of Germany are more problematic. According to the pollution structure, they should have a more negative attitude toward regulations. Domestic determinants must be considered to explain their policy.

Table 41.1. Production of CFC-11 and CFC-12 in 1974 (thousand tons) [18].

Country	Production
USA	376.0
Federal Republic of Germany	88.3
France	72.0
United Kingdom	72.0
Japan[a]	40.3
Italy	38.0
USSR	32.1
Netherlands	29.0
Canada	23.5
Australia	16.0

[a]Production in 1973.

As cited in Enloe (1975, p. 132): "The wealthy worry about car fumes. We worry about starvation". It is is often assumed that rich nations want environmental protection, since they can afford it. This seems to conform rather well to the politics of ozone (*Table 41.2*).

Table 41.2. Gross domestic product per capita in 1974 (US dollars) (Statistical Yearbook).

Country	GDP per capita
United States	6,640
Canada	6,080
Federal Republic of Germany	5,890
France	5,190
Netherlands	4,880
Australia	4,760
Japan	3,800
United Kingdom	3,360
Italy	2,770
Soviet Union	2,300

The United States, Canada, and the Federal Republic of Germany are wealthier than those major CFC producers opposing international regulations on emissions. The low level of economic development of developing countries explains why they are worried that international protection of the ozone layer may become too costly by preventing them from developing new industries.

According to a common political explanation of environmental policy, important bureaucracies in all countries favor economic growth. Only public pressure can make governments spend on environmental protection. Effective public pressure has two preconditions. First, concrete incidents of environmental degradation must take place. Second, the political system must allow raising environmental issues and pressuring decision-makers. The United Kingdom, Japan, and the USSR are mentioned as countries where the political system dampens citizen mobilization [Enloe (1975), Kelley *et al.* (1976)]. In Canada, the

Federal Republic of Germany, the Netherlands, and the United States environmental protection has been a highly salient issue. This seems to conform to their policy toward the protection of the ozone layer. But in another case of air pollution — acid rain — their preferences differ. The Federal Republic of Germany, Canada and the Netherlands favor restrictions on sulfur emissions causing acid rain, but the United States did not join the agreement calling for a 30% reduction of sulfur emissions. Why? Pollution structure may also explain this difference.

There are concrete incidents of environmental degradation in the Federal Republic of Germany, the Netherlands and Canada, since all are net importers of international pollution. The Federal Republic of Germany and Canada suffer from acid rain caused beyond their borders. As a downstream country the Netherlands imports the pollutants emitted into the Rhine by the upstream states. The governments are under strong public pressure to reduce pollution. This pressure and the position of their countries as net importers of some international pollution may explain why they also have a positive attitude toward the protection of the ozone layer. They may hope that policy in the ozone negotiations could enhance leverage with their main polluters.

In the United States, however, the "high environmental consciousness" does not seem to determine policy toward all international pollution. Public pressure does not seem to be enough, if a country is a net exporter of international pollution and strong domestic interest groups are against regulations. The United States exports three times as much acid pollutants to Canada as it imports from it; and the electric utility industry, high-sulfur coal producers and the United Mine Workers oppose proposals calling for reduction in sulfur emissions [Wilcher (1986)]. The chlorofluorocarbon issues is different. The costs of regulating aerosol uses of CFCs were low in the United States. An economic impact assessment completed in 1977 estimated that restrictions would impose only modest, short-term costs and that consumers would actually save in the long run by relying on cheaper substitutes. The 1978 ban of nonessential aerosol uses of CFCs conformed to this estimate [Stoel *et al.* (1983), p. 58, Cumberland *et al.* (1982), pp. 79–81, 88–92]. Recently, the US CFC industry has had success in developing new forms of fluorocarbons that do not threaten the ozone layer. Not surprisingly, the environmentally conscious public got an influential ally when Du Pont, the largest producer of CFCs in the world, called in 1986 for a worldwide limit on emissions of the harmful chemicals [19].

41.6. Conclusions

Garret Hardin is afraid of the global tragedy. If all states find it rational to pollute the global commons, ecocatastrophe will occur. Only a radical change in state behavior could avoid the tragedy. But the experience of the ozone negotiations implies that all states do not behave according to the Hardin's pessimistic assumption.

States producing no chlorofluorocarbons want to protect the ozone layer. Controlling CFC emissions would not cost them much, and the potential damage to their population and environment caused by ozone depletion would be reduced. Since these countries have very few means of pressuring the main producers, their policy alone is not likely to save the ozone layer.

The group of CFC producers favoring international regulations is more important in avoiding the tragedy. Also, the policy of these countries seems to be determined by pollution structure. They all are net importers of other types of international pollution. In other words, local or regional ecocatastrophes seem to be needed before main polluters join the international environmental effort.

Domestic economic factors also seem to affect national environmental policy. The more economic resources a country has and the less costly reducing pollution is, the more likely a country is to support international regulations on pollution.

The analysis of the ozone negotiations suggests that the tragedy of the global commons may not be inevitable. A protocol specifying regulatory measures to reduce CFC emissions was signed in September 1987. States seem to be able to form regimes to maximize their long-term ecological interests. But one must remain cautious. The ozone depletion theory was already established in 1974. The protocol was a compromise, and only a first step towards the original Nordic goal. Since the phenomenon of ozone depletion is not completely understood, we do not know if the regulations go far enough.

Notes

[1]   For the literature on international regimes, see particularly Axelrod and Keohane (1985); Brown *et al.* (1977); Keohane (1983 and 1984); Krasner (1983); Stein (1983); and Young (1986).
[2]   The final report of the Ad Hoc Working Group is UNEP/IG.53/4.
[3]   For unilateral regulations on chlorofluorocarbons, see, e.g., Bevington (1986); *Environmental Policy and Law* (1983); Stoel *et al.* (1983); and Gladwin *et al.* (1982).
[4]   Statements of 20 January 1982 by Erik Lykke, Director General, Ministry of Environment, Norway; and by Dr. Antti Kulmala, Representative of Finland.
[5]   UNEP/WG.69/3, p. 1 and UNEP/WG.69/CRP.2, p. 2.
[6]   UNEP/WG.69/CRP.1.
[7]   *Environmental Policy and Law* (1983); UNEP/WG.78/8, pp. 2-3, 5; and UNEP/WG.78/CRP.10.
[8]   Exempted essential uses include some drugs, pesticides, lubricants, and cleaners for electronic equipment, and articles necessary for safe aircraft operation. These uses constituted in 1979 only 4.3% of the total use of CFCs in the United States.
[9]   UNEP/WG.94/5, p. 3.
[10]   *Environmental Policy and Law* (1983) and UNEP/WG.94/r, p. 3.
[11]   UNEP/WG.94/4/Add.1, 2, and 3.
[12]   UNEP/WG.94/CRP 34.

[13] Introduction of Draft Protocol, Geneva, 22 October 1984. Address delivered by Canadian delegate, Dr. A.J. Chisholm, on behalf of Canada, Finland, Sweden, Norway, and the United States.

[14] UNEP/WG.110/4, pp. 9-10.

[15] UNEP/IG.53/5, p. 2.

[16] See *World Environment Report*, 25.6.1986, pp. 99; *International Herald Tribune*, 18.12.1986; Helsingin Sanomat 28.2.1987; and *International Herald Tribune*, 2-3.5.1987, p. 6.

[17] For the likely impacts of ozone depletion on different parts of the world, see, e.g., Cumberland *et al.* (1982, pp. 32-33, 57) and Stoel *et al.* (1983, p. 69).

[18] The production of the OECD countries is published in Organization for Economic Cooperation and Development (1982, p. 39). The Soviet figure is from Fluorocarbon Program Panel (1985, p. 14). The countries included in *Table 41.1* produce almost all the world's CFC-11 and CFC-12. Small quantities of these chlorofluorocarbons are also produced in Argentina, China, Brazil, India, Spain, and Eastern Europe.

[19] *International Herald Tribune*, 18.12.1986 and 14.4.1987.

References

Axelrod, R. and Keohane, R.O. (1985), Achieving Cooperation under Anarchy: Strategies and Institutions, *World Politics*, 38 (October), pp. 226-254.

Bevington, C.F.P. (1986), Chlorofluorocarbons: Production, Use, Trade, and Current Regulations in the European Economic Community. UNEP Chlorofluorocarbon Workshop, paper submitted for Topic 1, Metra Consulting Group Ltd., March.

Brown, S., Cornel, N.W., Fabian, L.L., and Weiss, E.B. (1977), *Regimes for the Ocean, Outer Space, and Weather*, Brookings Institution, Washington, DC.

Cumberland, J., Hibbs, J.R., and Hoch, I. (eds.) (1982), *The Economics of Managing Chlorofluorocarbons*, Resources for the Future, Washington, DC.

Enloe, C. (1975), *The Politics of Pollution in a Comparative Perspective*, David McKay, New York.

Environmental Policy and Law (1983), Vol. 10, No. 2, pp. 35-35, 71; Vol. 11, No. 3, pp. 58-59.

Fluorocarbon Program Panel (1985), *1984 Production and Sales of Chlorofluorocarbons CFC-11 and CFC-12*, Chemical Manufacturers Association, p. 14.

Gibbs, M.J. (1986), *Summary of Historical Chlorofluorocarbon Production*, ICF Incorporated, pp. 3-6, Washington, DC.

Gladwin, T.N., Ungelow, J.L., Walter, I. (1982), A Global View of CFC Sources and Policies to Reduce Emissions, in: J. Cumberland *et al.* (eds.), *The Economis of Managing Chlorofluorocarbons*, Resources for the Future, Washington, DC.

Hammit, J.K., Wolf, K.A., Camm, F., Mooz, W.E., Bamezai, A., and Quinn, T.H. (1986), *Product Uses and Market Trends for Potential Ozone-Depleting Substances, 1985-2000*, Rand Corporation, RAND/R-3386-EPA, May, Santa Monica, CA.

Hardin, G. (1977), The Tragedy of the Commons, in: G. Hardin and J. Baden (eds.), *Managing the Commons*, pp. 16-30, W.H. Freeman, San Francisco, CA.

Kelley, D.R., Stunkel, K.R., Wescott, R.R. (1976), *The Economic Superpowers and the Environment*, W.H. Freeman, San Francisco, CA.

Keohane, R.O. (1983), The Demand for International Regimes, in: S.D. Krasner (ed.), *International Regimes*, pp. 141-171, Cornell University Press, Ithaca, NY.

Keohane, R.O. (1984), *After Hegemony*, Princeton University Press, Princeton, NJ.

Krasner, S.D. (1983), Structural Causes and Regime Consequences: Regimes as Intervening Variables, in: S.D. Krasner (ed.), *International Regimes*, pp. 1-21, Cornell University Press, Ithaca, NY.

Molina, M. and Rowland, F. (1974), Stratospheric Sink Chlorofluoromethanes: Chlorine Atom Catalyzed Destruction of Ozone, *Nature*, 249, pp. 810-812.

Organization for Economic Cooperation and Development (1982), *Report on Chlorofluorocarbons*, OECD, Paris.

Ophuls, W. (1977), *Ecology and the Politics of Scarcity*, pp. 143-151, 214-215, W.H. Freeman, San Francisco, CA.

Quinn, T.H., Wolf, K.A., Mooz, W.E., Hammit, J.K. Chestnut, T.W., and Sarma, S. (1986), *Projected Use, Emissions, and Banks of Potential Ozone-Depleting Substances*, Rand Corporation, N-2282-EPA, pp. 41-42, Santa Monica, CA.

Statistical Yearbook of Finland (1976), Helsinki, Central Statistical Office of Finland, p. 440.

Stein, A.S. (1983), Coordination and Collaboration: Regimes in an Anarchic World, in: S.D. krasner (ed.), *International Regimes*, pp. 115-140, Cornell University Press, Ithaca, NY.

Stoel, T.B., Jr., Miller, A.S., and Milroy, B. (1983), *Fluorocarbon Regulation*, Lexington Books, Lexington, MA.

Waltz, K.N. (1979), *Theory of International Politics*, Addison-Wesley, Reading, MA.

Wijkman, P.M. (1982), Managing the Global Commons, *International Organization*, 36, 3 (Summer).

Wilcher, M.E. (1986), The Acid Rain Debate in North America, *Environmentalist*, 6, 4, pp. 292-293.

Young, O.R. (1986), International Regimes: Towards a New Theory of Institutions, *World Politics*, 39, 1 (October), pp. 104-122.

CHAPTER 42

An Experimental System Supporting Negotiation on a Joint Development Program

Piotr Bronisz and Lech Krus

Systems Research Institute
Polish Academy of Sciences
Warsaw
Poland

42.1. Introduction

International cooperation presents many examples of bargaining problems. Let us consider several countries interested in the development of production of some kind of goods. Each country can decide to realize its own independent development program or they can create a joint program. Undertaking a joint development program can result in benefits (due to scale effects) in comparison to programs developed independently. Thus there is an incentive for cooperation and negotiation on benefit allocation among countries.

A development program is characterized by volumes of produced goods and required resources. It is typically considered as a unicriterion problem in which the cost of resources is minimized under the assumed volumes of developed production, or the production is maximized under the constraints resulting from the given limited resources. Such unicriterion models are not suitable for real decision-making problems. Decision-makers, especially in non-market economy countries, have various preferences related to the particular kind of resources and the volume of developed production. Let us observe that prices in nonmarket economies are not necessarily a good way for aggregating resources into a joint cost. Therefore, we might also consider a multicriteria model in which particular resources are considered as independent criteria to be minimized and amounts of the produced goods to be maximized. An experimental system illustrates a new algorithm of interactive search for a cooperative, efficient solution in a multicriteria bargaining problem.

42.2. Problem Formulation

Let $N = \{1,2,...,n\}$ be the finite set of players (decision-makers), each player having m objectives. A multicriteria bargaining problem can be described in the form $(S, S_1, S_2, \cdots, S_n)$, where $S_i \in \mathbf{R}^m$ is a disagreement set of the ith player, $i \in N$, $S \in \mathbf{R}^{n*m}$ is an agreement set of all the players.

The bargaining problem has the following intuitive interpretation: every point x, $x = (x_1,x_2,...,x_n)$, $x_i = (x_{i1},x_{i2},..., x_{im}) \in \mathbf{R}^m$, in the agreement set S represents payoffs for all the players that can be reached when they cooperate with each other (x_{ij} denotes the payoff of the jth objective for the ith player). If the players do not cooperate, each player $i \in N$ can reach the payoffs from his disagreement set S_i. The players are interested in finding an outcome in S that will be agreeable to all of them

We say that $x \in \mathbf{R}^k$ is a Pareto-optimal point in X if there is no $y \in X$ such that $y \neq x, y \geq x$.

For simplicity, we assume that each player tries to maximize each of his objectives. The proposed interactive process consists of two phases. In the first phase, each player $i \in N$ acts independently of the others on his disagreement set S_i to select the most preferable Pareto-optimal point d_i. In the second phase, the players bargain over the agreement set S, assuming that $d = (d_1, d_2,..., d_n)$ is the status quo of the players.

42.3. First Phase: Multiobjective Decision Problem

To select a Pareto-optimal outcome in S_i, $i \in N$, we utilize the Rawlsian lex-min principle [see Rawls (1971); Imai (1983)]. The proposed approach is very close to the achievement function concept [Wierzbicki (1982)] from the point of view of the user. Analogously, a special parametric scalarization of the multiobjective problem is utilized to influence the selection of Pareto-optimal outcomes by changing reference points. Under some nonrestrictive assumptions about the sets S_i, $i \in N$, they can be determined in a simple way (even in a case of complicated nonconvex sets where the problem of maximizing the Tchebyshev norm can be ill-conditioned). The corresponding algorithm is based on several (at most m) directional maximizations using, for example, a bisection method that works very quickly and effectively. [For a more detailed description, see Bronisz, Krus, and Lopuch (1987)].

42.4. Second Phase: Cooperation

Let $d_i \in S_i$ be the Pareto-optimal outcome in S_i determined in the first phase by the ith player, $i \in N$, and let $d = (d_1, d_2, \ldots, d_n)$ be the resulting status quo point. Now we reduce the problem to the pair (S,d), where S is the agreement set. If there is a point $x \in S$ such that $x > d$, then the cooperation of the players is profitable.

We are interested in a constructive procedure that is acceptable to all players, starts at the status quo point and leads to a Pareto-optimal point in S. The procedure can be described as a sequence, $\{d^t\}_{t=0}^k$, of agreement points d^t such that

$$d^0 = d, \; d^t \in S, \; d^t \geq d^{t-1}, \text{ for } t = 1,2,\cdots, \; d^k$$

is a Pareto-optimal point in S. (The assumption $d^t \geq d^{t-1}$ follows from the fact that no player will accept improvement of payoffs for other players at the cost of his concession). At every round t, each player $i \in N$ specifies his improvement direction $\lambda_i^t \in \mathbf{R}^m, \lambda_i^t > 0$ and his confidence coefficient $\alpha_i^t \in \mathbf{R}, 0 < \alpha_i^t \leq 1$. The improvement direction λ_i^t indicates the ith player's preferences over his objectives at round t. The confidence coefficient α_i^t is introduced because any player has limited ability to describe precisely his performances and to predict all possible outcomes in S.

We propose an interactive negotiation process defined by a sequence [for justification, see Bronisz, Krus, and Wierzbicki (1987)]:

$$\{d^t\}_{t=0}^\infty \text{ such that } d^0 = d, \tag{42.1}$$
$$d^t = d^{t-1} + \epsilon^t * [u(S, d^{t-1}, \lambda^t) - d^{t-1}] \quad \text{for } t = 1,2,\ldots$$

where $\lambda^t \in \mathbf{R}^{n*m}$, $\lambda^t = (\lambda_1^t, \lambda_2^t, \ldots, \lambda_n^t)$ is the improvement direction specified jointly by all players, $u(S, d^{t-1}, \lambda^t) \in \mathbf{R}^{n*m}$ is the utopia point relative to the direction λ^t at round t defined by

$$u(S, d^{t-1}, \lambda^t) = \tag{42.2}$$
$$(u_1(S, d^{t-1}, \lambda_1^t)), u_2(S, d^{t-1}, \lambda_2^t), \ldots, u_n(S, d^{t-1}, \lambda_n^t)).$$

$$u_i(S, d^{t-1}, \lambda_i^t) = \tag{42.3}$$
$$\max_{\geq} \{x_i \in \mathbf{R}^m : x \in S, x \geq d^{t-1}, x_i = d_i^{t-1} + a\lambda_i^t \text{ for some } a \in \mathbf{R} \}.$$

Moreover, $\epsilon^t = min(\alpha_1^t, \ \alpha_2^t, \dots, \ \alpha_n^t, \alpha_{max}^t) \in \mathbf{R}$, where α_{max}^t is the maximal number α such that $d^{t-1} + \alpha[u(S, d^{t-1}, \lambda^t) - d^{t-1}]$ belongs to S.

Intuitively, the utopia point $u(S, d^{t-1}, \lambda_i^t)$ relative to the direction λ^t reflects the "aspiration levels" of the particular players when the improvement direction λ^t is specified at round t . The individual outcome $u_i(S, d^{t-1}, \lambda_i^t)$ is the maximal payoff in S for the ith player from d^{t-1} according to improvement direction λ_i^t, while ϵ^t is the minimal confidence coefficient of the players at round t (we assume that no player can agree on a coefficient greater than his) such that a new calculated agreement point belongs to S . It can be shown [Bronisz, Krus, and Lopuch (1987)] that such a procedure is finite and converges to a Pareto-optimal point in S under a relatively weak assumption.

42.5. Simplified Model of a Joint Development Program

The model relates to two countries (treated as players) that consider implementation of development programs. A program requires some amount of resources of various kinds and gives as a result some volume of production. Each country can realize the project independently, or they can decide on a joint development program. A joint program, owing to scale effects, can allow for a decrease of required resources at a given production volume or an increase of the production under given resources in comparison to two independent programs.

In the model, two kinds of resources are considered: labor and capital. Each player is assumed to maximize the obtained production volume and to minimize the resources put in the joint program. The problem consists in a choice of the production scale of the joint program and the sharing of the required resources and of the production volume — which should be agreeable and possibly close to the preferences of the players.

To deal with the case of maximization of objectives only, we assume that each player has given a disposable fund of capital assets $C_i \in \mathbf{R}_+$, and disposable labor resources $L_i \in \mathbf{R}_+$ $i = 1,2$, and tries to maximize slack variables $sc_i = C_i - c_i$, and $sl_i = L_i - l_i$, where c_i, l_i are the capital and labor resources, respectively, which should be put into the joint project by the ith player.

The development program, which can be realized on various scales, is described by two functions:

$$c(p) : \mathbf{R}_+ \to \mathbf{R}_+, \text{ and } l(p) : \mathbf{R}_+ \to \mathbf{R}_+$$

where $c(p)$ are capital assets required in the program ofthe scale or production volume p, and $l(p)$ are labor resources required in the program. Assumed shapes of the functions are presented in *Figure 42.1*. A similar shape has been obtained by Bronisz and Krus (1986) in an example of a joint water resources project. In the model, the same forms of the functions are assumed for independently and jointly realized programs, but even in this case the problem is not trivial.

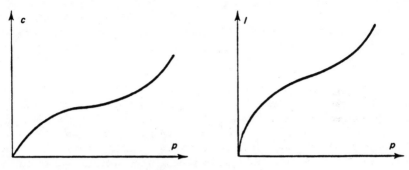

Figure 42.1. The functions $c(p)$ and $l(p)$.

Each player $i = 1,2$ maximizes three objectives: p_i, sc_i, sl_i. The disagreement sets are described by: $S_i \subset \mathbf{R}^3_+$

$$S_i = \{ (p_i, sc_i, sl_i) \in \mathbf{R}^3 : c(p_i) \le C_i - sc_i, \tag{42.4}$$
$$l(p_i) \le L_i - sl_i\}, \qquad i = 1,2.$$

The agreement set has the form : $S \subset \mathbf{R}^{2 \times 3}_+$

$$S = \{(p_1, sc_1, sl_1, p_2, sc_2, sl_2) \in \mathbf{R}^6 : c(p_1 + p_2) \le C_1 + C_2 - sc_1 - sc_2, \tag{42.5}$$
$$l(p_1 + p_2) \le L_1 + L_2 - sl_1 - sl_2\}.$$

In this example, the negotiation process proposed above has been incorporated into an experimental system of bargaining support.

42.6. Short Program Description

The experimental system of bargaining support with multiple objectives has been built for a simplified model outlined in the previous section. It can be considered as an illustration of the theoretical results related to the interactive process in a multicriteria bargaining problem and its application in support of negotiations. The program description is illustrated by *Figures 42.2* through *42.10* from an example session.

The system aids two players, each maximizing three objectives, to find an acceptable, cooperative, Pareto-optimal solution in an interactive procedure. This is done in two phases:

(1)   A status quo is derived.

(2)   A cooperative solution is found.

The status quo is defined as being a composition of the outcomes preferable to players in the noncooperative case. The cooperative solution is found in an iterative process starting from the status quo point.

The main menu is presented in *Figure 42.2*. By selecting F2 and F3, respectively, players 1 and 2 can activate the first phase.

The first phase deals with the noncooperative case, in which the players look for preferable outcomes assuming independent realizations of the development programs. Each player determines Pareto-optimal outcomes and selects the preferable one. This is done in two steps. In the first step, the player defines reference points in his objective space according to his preferences. The system calculates related Pareto-optimal outcomes using the approach described in Section 42.3. In the second step, the player selects the preferable outcome among the obtained outcomes. *Figure 42.3* shows the status quo (first phase) menu, and *Figure 42.4* illustrates an example of results obtained by player 1. Having seven points characterizing the Pareto set in numerical and in graphic forms, the player has selected the seventh one as the preferable outcome. Player 2 acts in the first phase in an analogous way. After that, by selecting F4 in the main menu, the players go to the second phase.

The second phase deals with the cooperative case. It proceeds in a number of iterations. Each iteration consists of two stages (see *Figure 42.5*, the negotiate menu):

(1)   Both players define their desired, preferable directions for outcomes improvements.

(2)   The system calculates the cooperative outcome on the basis of the status quo point and the directions of improvement specified by the players according to the solution concept presented in Section 42.4.

In the first stage, each player tests directions improving his outcome and selects a preferable one. This is done in three steps (see *Figure 42.6* the find player direction menu). In the first step, the player defines a step coefficient. In the second step, the player defines improvement directions according to his preferences. Then the system calculates related improved outcomes, assuming that the improvement direction of the counter player does not change (i.e., the direction of the counter player is assumed to be the same as in the previous iteration). In the third step, the player selects the preferable direction among the tested directions. *Figure 42.7* gives an example of the results obtained by player 1. The player has selected the fourth direction as the preferred one.

The cooperative outcome is calculated in the second stage (activated by F4 of the negotiate menu). The cooperative outcome can be pictured by F2–F3 of the calculate agreement point menu (see *Figure 42.8*).

The process is repeated until a Pareto-optimal outcome is reached. In the example presented, the session consists of four iterations. The results obtained are shown in the players report, *Figures 42.9* and *42.10*.

```
        The System aids two players to  find
an acceptable cooperative solution. This is
done in two phases:
first  - a status quo is derived,
second - a cooperative nondominated
               solution is found.
The status quo is defined as being
a composition of the preferable players
outcomes in a noncooperative case.
The cooperative solution is found in an
process starting from the status quo.



MAIN MENU
-> F1 - Information
-> F2 - Find Player 1 Status Quo
-> F3 - Find Player 2 Status Quo
   F4 - Negotiate Cooperative Solution
   F9 - Quit
```

Select option :

Figure 42.2. Main menu of the experimental system of bargaining support.

```
This phase deals with the noncooperative
case .The player tests Pareto outcomes  and
selects the preferable one. This is done in
two steps:
first - the player defines his preferences
        as references points in his objective
        space. The System calculates   related
        Pareto outcomes,
second - the player selects among obtained
        Pareto outcomes the preferable one.




PLAYER STATUS QUO MENU
-> F1 - Information
-> F2 - Test Pareto Outcomes
   F3 - Select Preferable Outcome
   F9 - Return to Main Menu
```

Select option :

Figure 42.3. Status quo menu.

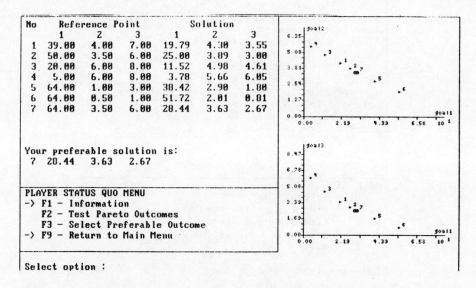

```
No    Reference Point        Solution
      1      2      3      1      2      3
1   39.00   4.00   7.00  19.79   4.30   3.55
2   50.00   3.50   6.00  25.00   3.09   3.00
3   20.00   6.00   8.00  11.52   4.98   4.61
4    5.00   6.00   8.00   3.78   5.66   6.05
5   64.00   1.00   3.00  38.42   2.90   1.80
6   64.00   0.50   1.00  51.72   2.01   0.81
7   64.00   3.50   6.00  20.44   3.63   2.67


Your preferable solution is:
7  20.44   3.63   2.67


PLAYER STATUS QUO MENU
-> F1 - Information
   F2 - Test Pareto Outcomes
   F3 - Select Preferable Outcome
-> F9 - Return to Main Menu

Select option :
```

Figure 42.4. Example of results obtained by player 1 after selecting F2 from the main menu.

```
This phase deals with the cooperative case.
At each iteration of this phase :
first - both players define their desired
        directions for outcomes improvements,
second - a new agreement point is calculated
         from previous one according to
         players directions.




NEGOTIATE MENU
-> F1 - Information
-> F2 - Find Player 1 Direction
-> F3 - Find Player 2 Direction
   F4 - Calculate New Agreement Point
   F9 - Return to Main Menu

Select option :
```

Figure 42.5. Negotiate menu.

This is the first stage of the Negotiate
Phase. The player tests directions improving
his outcome and selects the preferable one.
This is done in three steps:
first - the player defines step coefficient
second - the player defines directions
          according to his preferences.
          The System calculates related
          improved outcomes (a counterplayer
          action is assumed)
three - the player selects among the tested
          directions the preferable one.

FIND PLAYER DIRECTION MENU
-> F1 - Information
-> F2 - Define Step
   F3 - Test Improvement Directions
   F4 - Select Preferable Direction
   F9 - Return to Negotiate Menu

Select option :

Figure 42.6. Direction menu.

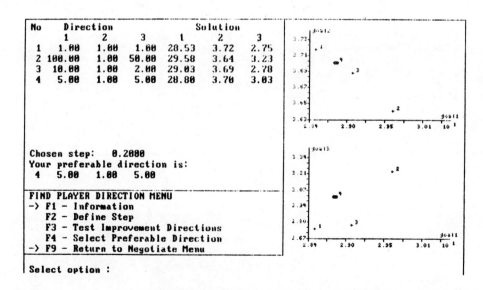

Figure 42.7. Results obtained by player 1 after selecting F4 from the direction menu.

```
┌─────────────────────────────────────────────────┐
│ This is the second stage od the Negotiate        │
│ Phase. The System has calculated the new         │
│ agreement point for both players.                 │
│                                                   │
│                                                   │
│                                                   │
│                                                   │
│                                                   │
│ ─────────────────────────────────────────────── │
│ CALCULATE AGREEMENT POINT MENU                    │
│ ─> F1 - Information                               │
│ ─> F2 - Player 1 Report                           │
│ ─> F3 - Player 2 Report                           │
│ ─> F9 - Return to Negotiate Menu                  │
└─────────────────────────────────────────────────┘
 Select option :
```

Figure 42.8. Calculate agreement point menu.

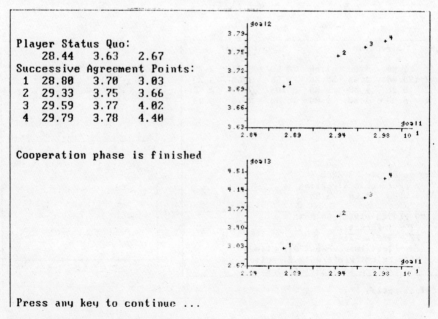

Figure 42.9. Player's report for player 1.

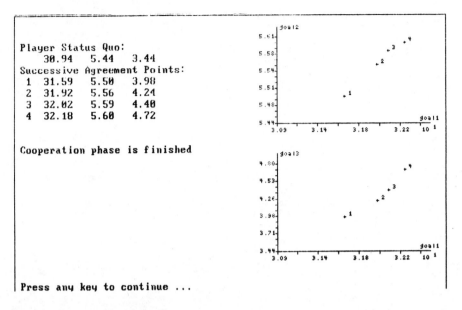

```
Player Status Quo:
    30.94    5.44    3.44
Successive Agreement Points:
  1  31.59    5.50    3.98
  2  31.92    5.56    4.24
  3  32.02    5.59    4.40
  4  32.18    5.60    4.72


Cooperation phase is finished
```

```
Press any key to continue ...
```

Figure 42.10. Player's report for player 2.

References

Bronisz, P. and Krus L. (1986), Resource Allocation and Cost Sharing in Common Enterprise. Game Approach, Proceedings of the Polish–DDR Symposium on Nonconventional Optimization, Prace IBS PAN, Warsaw.

Bronisz, P., Krus L., and Lopuch B. (1987), An Experimental System Supporting Multiobjective Bargaining Problem. A Methodological Guide, in: A. Lewandowski and A.P.Wierzbicki (eds.), *Theory, Software and Testing Examples for Decision Support Systems*, International Institute for Applied Systems Analysis, Laxenburg, Austria.

Bronisz, P., Krus L., and Wierzbicki A.P. (1987), Towards Interactive Solutions in Bargaining Problem, manuscript.

Imai, H. (1983), Individual Monotonicity and Lexicographical Maxmin Solution, *Econometrica*, 51, pp. 389-401.

Rawls, J. (1971), *A Theory of Justice*, Harvard University Press, Cambridge, MA.

Wierzbicki, A.P. (1982), A Mathematical Basis for Satisficing Decision Making, *Mathematical Modelling*, 3, pp. 391-405.

Wierzbicki, A.P. (1983), *Negotiation and Mediation in Conflicts I: The Role of Mathematical Approaches and Methods*, Working Paper WP-83-106, International Institue for Applied Systems Analysis, Laxenburg, Austria. Also published in: H. Chestmat *et al.* (eds.) (1983), *Supplemental Ways to Increase International Stability*, Pergamon Press, Oxford, UK.

IIASA Conference on the
Processes of International Negotiations

List of Participants

18–22 May 1987

European Community (EC)

Mr. Michael Goppel
Head of the Delegation of the EC
to the International Organizations
in Vienna
Hoyosgasse 5
A-1040 Vienna

**International Atomic Energy
Agency (IAEA)**

Dr. Hans Blix
Director General
Wagramerstrasse 5
P.O. Box 100
A-1400 Vienna

United Nations Industrial Development Organization (UNIDO)

Ms. Irene Lorenzo
Head
Industrial Training Branch
Department of Industrial Operations

Dr. Victor Richardson
Senior Industrial Development Officer
Systems of Consultation Division
Department for Industrial Promotion,
Consultations and Technology

Mr. Anatoli A. Vassiliev
Deputy Director General
Department of Industrial Operations
Wagramerstrasse 5
P.O. Box 300
A-1400 Vienna

Austria

Ambassador Franz Ceska
Ambassador to Belgium
Rue d'Abbaye 47
B-1050 Brussels

Dr. Winfried Lang
Ministry of Foreign Affairs
Ballhausplatz 2
A-1014 Vienna

Dr. Alfons Kloss
Ministry of Foreign Affairs

Dr. Gottfried Wolf-Laudon
Director
Siemens AG Austria
Siemensstrasse 90
A-1211 Vienna

Bulgaria

Dr. Plamen Pantev
Institute of International
Relations and Socialist
Integration
Boulevard Pentcho
Slaveikov 15-a
Sofia

Canada

Ambassador Jacques Gignac
Permanent Representative of
Canada to the International
Organizations in Vienna
Dr. Karl Lueger-Ring 10/IV
A-1010 Vienna

China

Mr. Lu Feiqian
Alternate to the Resident
Representative of the People's
Republic of China to the IAEA
Steinfeldgasse 1
A-1190 Vienna

Ms. Shen Xing Fen
Ministry of Foreign Trade
and Economic Relations with
Foreign Countries and
UNIDO

Egypt

Ambassador
Mohammed Ibrahim Shaker
Ambassador to Austria
Gellmeyergasse 5
A-1190 Vienna

Dr. Mohammed Ezzeldin Abdelmoneim
Councillor of Embassy
Embassy of Egypt

Finland

Professor Esko Antola
Department of Political Science
University of Turku
SF-20500 Turku

Professor Urpo Kivikari
Department of Economics
University of Turku

Ms. Paula Repo
Finnish Institute of
International Affairs
Pursiniehenkatu 8
Helsinki

Mr. Tapio Saarela
Minister-Counsellor
Embassy of Finland
Untere Donaustrasse 13-15
A-1020 Vienna

Mr. Tapani Vaahtoranta
Department of Political Science
University of Turku

France

Mr. Albert David
Université de Paris-Dauphine
LAMSADE
Place du Marechal De Lattre de
Tassigny
F-75775 Paris Cedex 16

Professor Christophe Dupont
Université de Lille I and
Centre de Recherches et
d'Etudes des Chefs d'Entreprises(CRC)
5, Rue de la Liberation
F-78350 Jouy-en-Josas

Dr. Guy-Olivier Faure
Université de Paris-Sorbonne
202, Boulevard Saint-Germain
F-75007 Paris

Professor Marcel Merle
Department de Science Politique
Université de Paris-Sorbonne
23, Rue du Laos
F-75015 Paris

Ambassador Alain Plantey
Membre de l'Institut de France
Conseiller d'Etat
6, Avenue Sully Prudhomme
F-75007 Paris

Ambassador B. Vernier Palliez
25, Grande Rue
F-78170 La Celle St. Cloud

German Democratic Republic

Professor Horst Grunert
Institut für Internationale
Beziehungen an der Akademie
für Staats- und Rechts-
wissenschaften der DDR
August Bebel Strasse 89
DDR-1502 Potsdam-Babelsberg 2

Germany, Federal Republic of

Professor Wulf Albers
Institut für Mathematische
Wirtschaftsforschung (IMW)
Universität Bielefeld
Universitätstrasse 25
D-4800 Bielefeld

Professor Rudolf Avenhaus
Universität der Bundeswehr München
Fakultät Informatik
Werner-Heisenberg-Weg 39
D-8014 Neubiberg

Ambassador Klaus Citron
Auswärtiges Amt
Adenauerallee 72
D-5300 Bonn
and
Embassy of the Federal
Republic of Germany
Metternichgasse 3
A-1030 Vienna

Professor Wolf Häfele
Vorsitzender des Vorstands der
Kernforschungsanlage Jülich
Postfach 1913
D-5170 Jülich

Professor Fritz Krückeberg
Director
Gesellschaft für Mathematik
und Datenverarbeitung mbH
Postfach 1240
Schloss Birlinghoven
D-5205 St. Augustin

Dr. Alexander Mühlen
Bundesakademie für
Öffentliche Verwaltung
Auswärtiges Amt
Simrockstrasse 1
D-5300 Bonn-1

Mr. Reinhard Überhorst
Beratungsbüro: Diskursive
Projektarbeiten und Planungsstudien
Marktstrasse 18
D-2200 Elmshorn

Hungary

Ambassador Janos Nagy
Ambassador to Austria and
Permanent Representative of
Hungary to the International
Organizations in Vienna
Bankgasse 4-6
A-1010 Vienna

Professor Janos Nyerges
Bureau of Systems Analysis of the
State Office for Technical
Development
P.O. Box 565
H-1374 Budapest

Dr. Laszlo Zatyko
Deputy Commercial Director
Transelektro Foreign Trading Co.
Muennich F. u. 13
H-1394 Budapest

Iceland
Ms. Sigridur Snaevarr
Counsellor
Ministry for Foreign Affairs
Reykjavik

Italy

Dr. Toni Cucciniello
IFAP
IRI Institute for Management
Research and Development
Rome

Professor Pietro Gennaro
President, Pronim Co. and
Strategia e Organizzazione
S.R.L
Via Larga, 23
I-20122 Milan

Ing. Giancarlo Venturini
Foreign Affairs Division
IRI
Via Veneto, 89
I-00187 Rome

Japan

Professor Fumiko Seo
Kyoto Institute of Economic
Research
Kyoto University
Yoshida-Honamachi, Sakyo-ku
Kyoto 606

Netherlands

Ambassador
Lodewijk H.L.B. van Gorkom
Ambassador to Austria and Resident
Representative of the Netherlands
to the International Organizations
in Vienna
Untere Donaustrasse 13-15
A-1020 Vienna

Professor Geert Hofstede
Director
Institute for Research of
Intercultural Cooperation (IRIC)
Jansbuitensingel 7
NL-6811 AA Arnhem

Dr. Johan Kaufmann
Institute for Advanced Study in the
Humanities and Social Sciences
Wassenaar
A. Gogelweg 25
NL-2517 JE The Hague

Dr. Willem F.G. Mastenbroek
Director
Holland Consulting Group
Sophialaan 19
NL-1975 BL Amsterdam

Dr. Paul W. Meerts
Netherlands Institute for
International Relations
Clingendael 7
NL-2597 VH The Hague

Dr. Ype H. Poortinga
Subfaculteit Psychologie
Tilburg University
Postbus 90153
NL-5000 LE Tilburg

Poland

Dr. Piotr Bronisz
Systems Research Institute
Polish Academy of Sciences
6 Newelska St.
PL-01-447 Warsaw

Dr. Lech Krus
Systems Research Institute
Polish Academy of Sciences

Ambassador Tadeusz Strulak
Permanent Representative of
Poland to the International
Organizations in Vienna
Hietzinger Haupstrasse 42c
A-1130 Vienna

Professor Andrzej P. Wierzbicki
Institute of Automatic Control
Technical University of Warsaw
Ul. Nowowiejska 15/19
PL-00665 Warsaw

Sweden

Mr. Carl-Johan Gunnarson
First Secretary
Embassy of Sweden
Obere Donaustrasse 49-51
A-1020 Vienna

Professor Christer Jönsson
Department of Political Sciences
Lund University
Box 52
S-22100 Lund

Mr. Jan Kronholm
Minister
Embassy of Sweden

Ambassador Dag Malm
Ambassador to Austria and
Resident Representative of Sweden
to the International Organizations
in Vienna

Switzerland

Mr. Robert Weibel
Center for Applied Studies in
International Negotiations
11a, Avenue de la Paix
CH-1202 Geneva

Union of Soviet Socialist Republics

Dr. Sergey L. Kambalov
Senior Researcher
Diplomatic Academy
USSR Ministry of Foreign Affairs
Moscow

Ambassador Oleg N. Khlestov
Resident Representative of the USSR
to the International Organizations
in Vienna
Wohllebengasse 4
A-1040 Vienna

Dr. Mark A. Khroustalev
Deputy Head
Center for the Systems Analysis of
International Affairs
The Moscow State Institute of
International Relations
Moscow

Dr. Vladimir F. Pryakhin
USSR Ministry of Foreign Affairs
Moscow

Professor Artem V. Serguiev
USSR Ministry of Foreign Affairs
Moscow

Dr. Guennadi K. Yefimov
USSR Ministry of Foreign Affairs
Moscow

United States of America

Professor Richard N.L. Andrews
Institute for Environmental Studies
University of North Carolina
311 Pittsboro Street
Chapelhill, NC 27514

Mr. Lance Antrim
American Academy of Arts and
Sciences
Norton's Woods
136 Irving Street
Cambridge, MA 02138

Mr. Felix Bloch
Minister-Counsellor
Embassy of the United States
of America
Boltzmanngasse 16
A-1090 Vienna

Professor Tom R. Burns
Center for Conflict Resolution
George Mason University
4400 University Drive
Fairfax, VA 22030

Dr. Fritz Heimann
Associate General Counsel
General Electric Co.
3135 Easton Turnpike
Fairfield, CT 06431

Mr. Maurice J. Katz
Counsellor for Nuclear Technology
US Mission to the IAEA
Obersteinergasse 11-15
A-1190 Vienna

Mr. Paul Kimmel
Creative Associates International, Inc.
3201 N. Mexico Ave., N.W.
Washington, DC 20016
USA

Professor Sven Lundstedt
Ohio State University
1775 College Road
Columbus, OH 43210-1399

Professor Howard Raiffa
Harvard University
Graduate School of Business
Administration
Soldiers Field Road
Boston, MA 02139

Mr. Michael Sternberg
Counsellor for Political Affairs
Embassy of the United States
of America

Mr. Carlton R. Stoiber
Counsellor for Nuclear Policy
US Mission to the IAEA

Mr. Charalambos A. Vlachoutsicos
Russian Research Center
Harvard University
1737 Cambridge Street
Cambridge, MA 02138
and
East/West Committee
International Chamber of
Commerce, Paris

Professor H. Peyton Young
School of Public Affairs
University of Maryland
Suite 1218
Social Sciences Building
College Park, MD 20742

Professor I. William Zartman
Johns Hopkins School of
Advanced International Studies
Johns Hopkins University
1740 Massachusetts Ave., N.W.
Washington, DC 200036

Ambassador Warren Zimmermann
Chairman of the United States
Delegation to the CSCE

IIASA

Dr. Thomas H. Lee,
Director

Professor Boris Segerstahl,
Deputy Director

Mr. Jean-Pierre Ayrault,
Secretary to IIASA

Dr. Frances Mautner-Markhof,
Principal Investigator, PIN Project

Mr. Laurent Mermet,
PIN Project

APPENDIX B

Summary of the IIASA Conference on the Processes of International Negotiations

The IIASA Conference on the Processes of International Negotiations, held on 18-22 May 1987 at IIASA, Laxenburg, brought together high-level researchers and practitioners with experience in international negotiations from international organizations, the diplomatic community, and multinational enterprises. The Conference was organized by the IIASA PIN Project, which is funded by a grant from the Carnegie Corporation (USA).

The Conference succeeded in bringing together researchers and practitioners — in total over 80 participants from 19 countries and three international organizations — in an interactive and quite unique manner, and was a step on the road to bridging the gap between these two groups involved in the processes of international negotiations. This was accomplished through the panels, the discussions on the papers presented, and informal exchanges.

The Conference also provided a vehicle for increasing understanding and communication between various research disciplines and approaches, e.g., between those working on quantitative or mathematical analyses and on the qualitative or institutional analyses of international negotiations. Researchers from various countries were able to learn about work going on elsewhere and to discuss what their approaches have in common and where they differ.

The Conference not only brought out differences between researchers and practitioners, as well as among various branches of research, but also modalities to bridge these gaps. Specifically, it provided a basis for forward-looking proposals and for approaching the problem in a comprehensive manner to meet the interests and requirements of all those concerned with the processes of international negotiations. The interaction between these groups highlighted the importance of further research and of enhanced communication between researchers and practitioners and among researchers, at a level commensurate with effective action and measures to improve the processes of international negotiations.

This Conference dealt with many of the most importance aspects of international negotiations including the role of international organizations and other multilateral mechanisms; cultural, political and linguistic factors; international trade negotiations; theory and methodology; and education and training. An area that seems to be of growing interest, and of specific relevance to IIASA, is the use of decision support systems, knowledge and data bases, and computer-aided negotiations tools to assist negotiators and the negotiating process, perhaps as a neutral third party. This is inevitable, at a time when both information and information technology and its applications are experiencing explosive growth.

The Conference brought out the need for an infrastructure to facilitate such research and communication, among countries and researchers, and between theorists and negotiators. The IIASA-PIN Project and its PIN networks within IIASA's National Member Organizations (NMOs) can provide such an international, multidisciplinary infrastructure. In this way the impact of national considerations and of different economic, political and social systems can also better be taken into account in international negotiations. The PIN infrastructure and mechanism is conducive to the elucidation of the these factors and could thus provide unique advantages and possibilities for advancing the understanding and improving the processes of international negotiations.

Thus, the Conference was an important learning experience for the processes of international negotiations, and a forum for acquiring a unique focus on this increasingly important topic.

This summary of the Conference on the Processes of International Negotiations cannot and will not be exhaustive. It covers some of the main issues addressed, results of discussions and proposals for possible future activities to be undertaken by the IIASA-PIN Project and its NMO-PIN networks. These will constitute some of the many inputs to IIASA's planning process.

The key points and ideas that emerged may be summarized as follows.

Negotiations can and should contribute to predictability, equity and security among states. In achieving such goals, negotiations also become important confidence-building measures. Thus, negotiations will have an increasing role to play in maintaining a dynamic stability in the relations among states.

It became clear that an agreed common framework or representation of the processes of international negotiations does not exist now. But the differences are not so large as they may appear, since all are looking at the same process. It is important to try to move toward a common understanding at least of what the similarities and differences are, and to try to approach, to the extent possible, a more unified agreed representation or paradigm of the processes of international negotiations. In so doing, one must bear in mind that any theory or representation will of necessity shed light on some facts and be silent about others, since theorizing means simplifying. The mark of a good theory or paradigm is to be able to encompass and explain, as well and as simply as possible, the largest number of facts and phenomena.

In this sense it was felt useful to study problems in as comprehensive a manner as possible, taking into account the inherent complexities and interconnectedness of the various functions and processes of international negotiations, and the need for more coherence between increasingly interdependent international negotiations issues and activities.

International organizations play a key and growing role in international negotiations. As instruments established by governments, they respond to their needs. The use of international organizations cannot be pushed by their secretariats, but the efficient functioning, initiatives and innovative proposals of these international secretariats are important factors determining whether or not governments will choose to use a particular international organization or other multilateral mechanism as a negotiating framework.

Negotiations are important mechanisms for dealing with the international transboundary effects of technological risk, and the impacts of technological development in general.

There are many basic similarities and differences between commercial and other types of international negotiations, in terms of parties involved, issues and goals. Increasingly important are negotiations for joint ventures involving developed and developing countries, and countries with different economic systems.

The processes of international negotiations do not come to an abrupt halt with the signing of an agreement. A need exists for pre- and post-agreement (or contract) negotiations. While the provisions and mechanisms to ensure compliance must be clearly delineated in an agreement, it was felt useful to look at the advantages of agreements having a defined degree of flexibility to permit jointly agreed adaptation to changing circumstances and requirements.

Education and training are important for improving both the processes of international negotiations, and communication among those involved. The input and involvement of practitioners is considered essential for the most effective and relevant research, education and training (design, implementation and evaluation). Research should be used as part of the training process. Mechanisms should be devised for the collaboration of practitioners and researchers on specific tasks in both research and training activities.

An area of growing interest and importance is the use of decision support systems and computer-aided negotiations tools to enhance the efficiency and effectiveness of the processes and outcomes of international negotiations. In this connection it was emphasized that expert systems and knowledge bases cannot and will not replace experts, or their knowledge and experience.

Much was learned about the work and interests of the NMO-PIN networks. Their activities often have a wide area of overlap and complement each other usefully. This diversity of activities can increase the chances for generating innovative ideas. The PIN Project can serve an important function in coordinating and enhancing collaboration and coherence between the networks' research and other activities.

Many fruitful possibilities emerged from this Conference which could be pursued by IIASA and its NMO-PIN networks. Possible modalities for implementation of these research and other activities include: the IIASA-PIN Project; the NMO-PIN networks, coordinated by IIASA-PIN; and external collaborative projects with periodic meetings both in the NMO country and at IIASA to assess results and discuss future directions for work. Since the PIN Project is based on networking activities, IIASA will continue to rely on the support and input of the NMO-PIN networks.

Proposals for further PIN activities and research included the following:

(1) It was agreed that it would be very useful to study how the role and effectiveness of international organizations and other multilateral mechanisms in international negotiations could be enhanced. In connection with this, it is important to identify the characteristics of a good international organization and international secretariat. For example, to what extent are the real actors in a given issue area represented and committed to participating in the organization? How can the capabilities of an international organization be strengthened in order to take anticipatory as well as reactive measures to deal with disputes and issues through international negotiation?

(2) Also important is a study of the existing network or system of international negotiations, and the list and scope of issues to be dealt with by international negotiations. Specifically, it was proposed to make an inventory of potential future issues (regional and global) requiring international negotiations — i.e., to identify opportunity areas for future international negotiations.

(3) Another essential task is to identify the common patterns and denominators of international negotiations, and the reasons for their success or failure. It would thus be useful to study the institutionalization of international negotiations and their characteristics in terms of specific agreed criteria.

(4) It would be important to understand evolution of procedures, especially decision-making procedures such as consensus, in international negotiations (in the context of the UN, CSCE, etc), and the role of presiding officers.

(5) The role of mediators and other third parties is another worthwhile study area.

(6) How does public opinion affect the processes of international negotiations?

(7) An important input into the processes of international negotiations for joint ventures would be the development of case studies that address such key factors as the legal, financial and organizational implications and impacts both at the country and enterprise levels.

(8) Another key task for research is to look at ways and means — including computer-aided training tools — to enhance the capabilities and results of education and training in the field of international negotiations. Important training goals include how to help negotiators to develop further their capabilities for adaptation to and innovation in negotiations processes; and to master the art of "catching the ball in the air" — i.e., recognizing and responding to unexpected signals, moves, etc., that could prove important for advancing the negotiations process.

(9) An area of widespread interest for research and increasing importance for international negotiations is the application of computer systems to facilitate the processes of international negotiations. This includes the development of agreed international, and internationally accessible, databases, and

studying which computer-aided negotiations tools (such as interactive models and computerized conference systems) could be developed. (It should be noted that some international organizations already have such international databases). Supporting this could be a joint investigation of whether and how common understandings or agreed definitions of key terms and concepts in international negotiations could be developed.

(10) It is an important aim of research to increase the applicability of decision science methodologies and analytical techniques to real-life problems by, for example: integrating the contributions of various analytical methods; developing existing techniques of decision sciences for application in the framework of contradictory or conflicting interests; encouraging practitioners and researchers to work together on specific tasks; associating the user in analytical work; testing via simulations how analyses translate into reality; and using an intermediary between researchers and practitioners (for formulation of real problems, interpretation of results, etc.)

(11) An interesting and potentially useful study, which could improve knowledge of both the processes of international negotiations and the strengths and characteristics of various theories and methodological approaches, would involve taking one or two carefully selected international negotiations and using various theories or methodologies to analyze them. Then the results of the various approaches could be compared.

The results and proposals of the Conference taken together indicate that this approach to the study of international negotiations could become a vehicle and spearhead for reconciling the quantitative and qualitative methods of analysis, as well as the abstract *versus* practical- or user-oriented studies and approaches. This could be accomplished through the "operationalization" of theoretical approaches, taking into account the complexity and interconnectedness of international negotiations.